D0983295

The History of
American Foreign Policy

The History of American Foreign Policy

Jerald A. Combs
San Francisco State University

ALFRED A. KNOPF   NEW YORK

First Edition

9 8 7 6 5 4 3 2 1

Library of Congress Cataloging in Publication Data

Combs, Jerald A.
　　The history of American foreign policy.

　　Bibliography: p.
　　Includes index.
　　1. United States—Foreign relations.　I. Title.
E183.7.C656　1986　　　327.73'009　　　85-12644
ISBN 0-394-34146-5
ISBN 0-394-35689-6 (v.1 pbk.)
ISBN 0-394-35690-X (v.2 pbk.)

327.73009
C731h
1986

Manufactured in the United States of America

For Art and Meg Combs

PREFACE

Anyone who has experienced the bitter debates over United States policy toward Iran, El Salvador, or Vietnam understands that American foreign policy inevitably generates controversy. Yet most people expect a history of American foreign policy to be a simple narrative of the "truth" about the past. They seem unaware that events of the distant past created just as much controversy as those of the present day. They also seem to assume that historians will be unaffected by past controversies, let alone by present ones.

Unfortunately, historical study cannot provide a final truth about the past. Historians can approach the truth by close study of the documents surrounding critical events in America's diplomatic history, but their accounts are still affected by their own experiences, judgments, and predilections. These differences have given rise to several opposing views of the history of American foreign policy.

Some historians see American diplomacy as having been a fairly successful blend of democratic idealism and realistic concern for American national interests. They generally assume that American values of liberty, democracy, and free enterprise are worthy goals which, if encouraged throughout the world by American diplomacy, will benefit all the people of the earth as well as the United States. They portray most of America's wars as justified resistance to foreign aggression. For instance, they see the American Revolution and the War of 1812 as necessary battles against British tyranny. They look upon westward expansion as the spread of liberty and civilization against reactionary colonial regimes and tragic but doomed Indians. They emphasize the aggressiveness of the Mexicans leading to the Mexican War and the tyranny of Spain in Cuba and the Philippines prior to the Spanish American War of 1898. They regard the two world wars as gallant crusades to save Europe from the tyranny of Kaiser Wilhelm's Germany and then of Hitler's Nazis. Finally, they tend to see the events of the Cold War, including Korea and Vietnam, as part of a noble if occasionally inept resistance to the expansion of Soviet and Communist plans for world domination.

This view, which I will call the nationalist interpretation of American foreign policy, represents the outlook of many secondary school texts, politicians, newspapers, and television commentaries. It also continues to have strong support in the academic world. It can lead to blatant superpatriotic flag waving, as in the speeches of some politicians, but it also can be the sophisticated conviction of scholars who have examined the realistic alternatives available to American statesmen at various times and concluded that in most circumstances America's leaders chose properly.

For the most part, those who hold the nationalist view are politically conservative. Among politicians, Ronald Reagan in his more ideological and less pragmatic moods would be a good example. An extraordinarily informed scholarly account of American foreign policy from this point of view is the classic text, *A Diplomatic History of the United States* (4th ed., 1955) by the dean of American diplomatic historians, Samuel Flagg Bemis. Some liberals, however, also hold to the nationalist view. Liberal journalists, for instance, often write exposés of American blundering or cruelty in a particular instance such as the Vietnam war, but contrast that with the rest of America's supposedly decent and successful history. Good examples of such journalistic liberal nationalism are David Halberstam's account of the Vietnam war, *The Best and the Brightest* (1972), and Seymour Hersh's biography of Henry Kissinger, *The Price of Power* (1983).

A second and more critical interpretation of the history of American foreign policy is the so-called realist view. This has probably been the dominant interpretation among diplomatic historians since World War II. Realists insist that American foreign policy generally has been too naive, idealistic, and moralistic. They believe that Americans, regarding their own nation as more peaceful and moral than others because of America's democratic form of government, have oscillated foolishly between a policy of isolation designed to insulate themselves from evil foreigners and their meaningless wars, and a policy of crusading internationalism designed to eliminate foreign evils by making nations over in America's image. For instance, realists argue that America's devotion to total victory over Nazi Germany and unconditional surrender destroyed Central Europe and left a vacuum of power that naturally tempted the Soviets to expand. Instead of meeting that expansion with a realistic negotiating stance, the United States first hoped to deter it by peaceful intentions and goodwill, then overreacted to the failure of this naive approach by embarking on an excessive military buildup and an anti-Communist crusade. Realists believe the United States must follow a steadier policy based on national interests rather than grandiose democratic ideals, and seek peace through a balance of power rather than some utopian vision of a world without conflict.

Although many American diplomatic historians share this realist outlook, they often divide over its application to particular events. Hard realists emphasize the need for the United States to protect its national interests and the world balance of power by dealing with adversaries from a position of unassailable strength. America must be willing to take significant risks, including major military action, to prevent the expansion of its adversaries even in morally ambiguous situations or in areas others might see as unimportant to America's most vital interests. Thus, they favor a very activist American foreign policy. Henry Kissinger is a good example of a contemporary politician and historian who operates from this perspective. For a good history of American foreign policy written from this point of view, see Thomas A. Bailey's popular *A Diplomatic History of the American People*, now in its tenth edition (1980).

There are a number of soft realists, however, who argue that a proper analysis of America's national interest, the balance of power, and the limited ability of military action to accomplish worthwhile policy goals should have led the United States to greater restraint in its relations abroad. Soft or restrained realists generally think that greater patience and more expert diplomacy might have saved the United States from some of its wars and crusades and avoided its present overextension. The most prominent advocates of this view among diplomats and publicists have been George Kennan, Walter Lippmann, and Hans Morgenthau. In general, it is the view to which I subscribe and from which I have written this account.

While realists have chastised American foreign policy for excessive idealism and moralism, another group of critics known as revisionists argue that American diplomacy instead has been realistic and self-interested to the point of rapaciousness. Revisionists regard the primary theme of American diplomatic history not as an oscillation between isolationism and interventionism, but as continuous aggressive expansion. They see American imperialism beginning with the westward movement, extending through America's attempts to protect its markets and capitalist economy in the first and second world wars, and culminating in recent efforts to preserve American economic interests in Vietnam, the Middle East, and Central America.

The most radical of these revisionists believe that American imperialist foreign policy will not change unless the United States becomes a socialist nation. They agree with Lenin's theory that imperialism is the product of capitalism's intrinsic need to expand its markets and sources of raw materials. Capitalist nations must continually expand their economies by acquiring either formal or informal colonies, because only in this way can the elite that monopolizes the internal wealth of the nation find new resources to buy off the masses, whose exclusion from the benefits of their labor would otherwise lead to a revolutionary redistribution of the nation's goods. Radicals believe that this redistribution of goods would enhance the purchasing power of the vast majority of the people, augment economic demand, and thus increase production and jobs. America's prosperity would no longer depend on overseas expansion and aggression, and the major motive behind imperialism and war would be gone. Failing this, the United States and the other capitalist nations would continue to expand, inevitably clash in their competition for markets and resources, and bring war and destruction on the earth. You will not find many American politicians who hold this point of view; they have difficulty being elected in the present American political climate. But you will find a strong statement of this perspective in Gabriel Kolko, *The Roots of American Foreign Policy* (1969), and Sidney Lens, *The Forging of the American Empire* (1971). An excellent scholarly survey written with similar assumptions but with a much more restrained tone is Lloyd C. Gardner, Walter F. LaFeber, and Thomas J. McCormick, *Creation of the American Empire* (1976).

Moderate revisionists also criticize America's rapacious expansionism and imperialism, but they tend to stress the economic factor in foreign policy somewhat less than the radicals. They see American diplomacy as the product of bureaucratic as well as economic elites, of ideological and psychological factors like racism and fear of communism as well as capitalist expansion, and of well-intentioned error as well as malevolence. They also find some leaders and episodes in American history with which they sympathize, especially Franklin Roosevelt's attempts to accommodate the Soviet Union during World War II. An excellent survey of American diplomacy from this moderate revisionist point of view is Thomas G. Paterson, J. Garry Clifford, and Kenneth J. Hagan, *American Foreign Policy: A History* (2d ed., 1983).

In the following work, I, like the authors of all the other texts mentioned above, have tried to write a balanced account of the history of American foreign policy. But like them, I cannot help but be affected by my own experiences and point of view. I have tried to compensate for this by ensuring that even when the narrative expresses strong opinions about an episode, it presents other interpretations as well. The reader will also find detailed discussions of conflicting interpretations in the historiographical essays that follow each chapter. These essays trace the development of the major schools of historical thought outlined in this introduction, schools I think affect not only histories of past American diplomacy, but the making of present policy as well.

ACKNOWLEDGMENTS

I have incurred many debts in writing this book. I had a chance to compose several of the Cold War chapters in a National Endowment of the Humanities Seminar with Robert A. Divine at the University of Texas in the summer of 1982. Professor Divine and the members of the seminar have been extremely helpful. One member, Professor Wayne Knight of C. Sergeant Reynolds College, read the entire manuscript and made many useful suggestions. He also did much of the work researching and obtaining the illustrations. Professor Richard H. Immerman of the University of Hawaii gave an excellent critique of the chapters on later American diplomacy. Others who generously donated their time and knowledge to the project include Professors John Tricamo of San Francisco State University, Herbert Margulies of the University of Hawaii, Lou Gomolak of the University of Texas, and Kathy Scott of the Iowa State Historical Society. Readers for the press at various stages of the manuscript include Professors Walter LaFeber, Kinley J. Brauer, Mark Lytle, Robert C. Hildebrand, and Franklin W. Abbot. My wife, Sara P. Combs, helped edit the manuscript and locate the maps. With all the help I have received, any errors of fact or interpretation that remain are my own fault.

All Chinese names are Romanized according to the more familiar Wade-Giles system because this was the system in use for most of the period covered in this book and the system used in all the reference materials.

CONTENTS

MAPS

The History of
American Foreign Policy

CHAPTER 1

The American Revolution and the Origins of American Diplomacy

EARLY AMERICAN FOREIGN POLICY: NEUTRALITY AND EXPANSION

One of America's leading diplomatic historians, Ernest May, has characterized early American foreign policy as "pacifist and isolationist." There is much truth in this label. Americans did try to avoid entanglement in the wars and alliances of the great powers of Europe, just as George Washington had advised them to do in his famous Farewell Address. President Martin Van Buren said in the 1840s that Americans still regarded nonintervention and neutrality "with a degree of reverence and submission but little, if anything, short of that entertained for the Constitution itself." With its neutralist stance and its tiny army and navy, the United States seemed a peaceful haven to many Europeans who immigrated to escape the continuous wars and burdensome military obligations of their homelands.

Yet the image of early America as "pacifist and isolationist" is misleading. Americans did not want total isolation from Europe: They avoided political entanglements as best they could, and some even sought cultural isolation to prevent contamination by Europe's supposedly corrupt antirepublican society. But Americans did not want commercial isolation. Trade with Europe was vital to the American economy, and if Americans designed their neutrality to avoid entanglements in Europe's wars, they also designed it to increase their foreign trade. Under international law, neutral nations could trade unmolested with nations at war, and the United States intended to benefit from this protection. Americans also hoped to reinforce the protection of international law by making their trade so valuable that no nation would risk interfering with it. So, early American policy toward Europe is far better characterized as neutralist rather than isolationist.

Nor was early American diplomacy truly pacifist. Even though Americans wanted neutrality to keep them out of European wars, they were ready to fight for their neutral rights, as they proved in 1812. In addition, despite the reverence Martin Van Buren insisted Americans held for noninterven-

1

tion, the United States joined the major powers of Europe in claiming and exercising the right to intervene in other nations to protect the lives and property of its citizens abroad. The United States considered this to be "nonpolitical" intervention and therefore a legitimate function of diplomacy. America conducted over one hundred such interventions prior to 1900, ranging from forced debt collection to the bombardment of towns that had imprisoned American sailors.

It was not only the belligerent pursuit of neutral rights and "nonpolitical" interventions that belied the image of early American foreign policy as pacifist and isolationist; on the North American continent and in the Caribbean, the United States was aggressively expansionist. It conquered the Indians, purchased Louisiana from France, extorted Florida from Spain, and took the Far West from Mexico. There were even profound expansionist aspects to episodes that were essentially defensive efforts to secure independence and neutrality, such as the American Revolution and the War of 1812.

The twin themes that dominated American foreign policy prior to the twentieth century were neutrality and expansion, rather than pacifism and isolationism. Of the two themes, neutrality was at first the more important. Until after the War of 1812, the nation's diplomacy was essentially defensive rather than offensive. The desire to expand American trade and territory always hovered in the background, but it remained secondary to the desire of the United States simply to survive and preserve what it already had. After the War of 1812, however, Americans felt secure from destruction at the hands of hostile European powers for the first time in their history and could turn their attention with confidence to westward expansion. Neutrality toward Europe remained a cornerstone of American diplomacy for the rest of the nineteenth century and occasionally, as during the Civil War, it reemerged as the dominant concern. But for the most part territorial expansion became the primary theme.

THE ORIGINS OF EARLY AMERICAN FOREIGN POLICY

"These United Colonies are, and of a right ought to be free and independent States," and as such should seek "foreign alliances." So proclaimed Richard Henry Lee of Virginia to the Continental Congress in June 1776. After vigorous debate, the Congress agreed. This famous resolution embodied the contradictory impulses that would compete for dominance in America's foreign policy during much of the new nation's early existence—the desire for independence from Europe and the need for foreign connections. Nonentanglement was the eventual victor. Washington's Farewell Address, warning against foreign influences and permanent alliances, became almost an eleventh commandment for Americans of the nineteenth century. But it was neither an easy nor a permanent victory.

The American Revolution probably did more than anything to turn Americans against European entanglements. Behind the primary grievance of the colonists against England, taxation without representation, was the conviction of many Americans that the connection with Great Britain had impeded expansion of their trade and territory. The British mercantile system had monopolized American commerce and limited the growth of manufactures. Parliament had frustrated the territorial ambitions of the Americans. Acting on the assumption that they would gain access to vast tracts of land, the colonists had cooperated with the British to eliminate French control of Canada and Louisiana during the French and Indian War. Yet with the Proclamation of 1763, the British had temporarily halted settlements beyond the Appalachians. Then the Quebec Act had given administration over much of the Ohio Valley to Canada rather than to claimants in the original thirteen colonies. In their disappointment, many Americans recalled still another instance of British betrayal. In the 1740s, during the War of the Austrian Succession, New Englanders had captured the strategic French fortress of Louisbourg, guardian of the mouth of the St. Lawrence River. In the final peace treaty, however, the British had returned it to the French in exchange for concessions in Asia of no value to the colonists. Such incidents convinced many Americans that their ties to Europe through Great Britain had involved them in wars so little related to American interests that the United States would be well advised to avoid such bonds in the future.

American attitudes toward Britain's European rivals reinforced this disposition to shun alliances. Most potential allies had long been enemies of the colonists. Spain had made the initial claim to the Western Hemisphere and viewed the British as trespassers. A long period of desultory warfare on America's southern frontier resulted, stimulating hatred between the Spanish and the settlers. The French in Canada and Louisiana also had been bitter antagonists of the Americans, and these colonists murdered one another enthusiastically during the century of warfare between their mother countries. Americans regarded France and Spain as corrupt and effete Catholic regimes whose superstitious subjects were willing victims of perpetual inquisition and enslavement. The American image of the French was summed up in a line from a popular song of the time—"When Gallick hosts, ungrateful men, our race meant to extermine. . . ." To most Americans, an alliance with such powers was no improvement on their old colonial relationship with Great Britain.

America's geographical situation reinforced the colonists' inclination to keep the Europeans at arm's length. All the great powers were three thousand miles across the Atlantic. The United States was surrounded by the colonies of these nations, but such thinly populated neighbors posed no threat without the long-distance backing of the mother countries. As America's population grew, military invasion from any source would become even more difficult. Benjamin Franklin calculated that the nation's population was doubling every twenty-three years. John Adams figured that this growth guaranteed the addition of twenty thousand fighting men each year. He thought the physical size of America might protect against invasion as well. Only a "multitude of posts" and an army a hundred thousand strong, Adams argued, could hope to conquer and garrison even a few of the states. Intellectual tradition also supported separation of the two hemispheres. More than two centuries before the revolution, the pope had drawn a line of demarcation down the Atlantic to separate the colonial spheres of Portugal to the east and Spain to the west. The British and French disregarded the papal proclamation to plant their own colonies, but the line still had some influence. European leaders came to disregard many conflicts "beyond the line" as somehow outside the realm of civilization and not necessarily cause for war between the mother countries.

British Whig reform tradition, the same philosophy that so influenced American resistance to taxation without representation, confirmed the revolutionaries' inclination for nonentanglement. The British Whigs had long sought to avoid excessive entanglements with European powers. They urged concentration on overseas trade and empire rather than on continental politics. Such trade would promote a strong navy that could defend the moat of the British Isles, the English Channel, and thus prevent an invasion of the homeland. This would make a large standing army, the traditional enemy of internal liberty, unnecessary.

The Americans, already disposed to agree with the Whig outlook on domestic affairs, readily adopted much of Whig foreign policy as well. Like the British Whigs, Americans would avoid foreign entanglements. They would rely on an even larger moat than the English Channel, the Atlantic Ocean, to protect the homeland. They too would avoid the large standing army that might threaten internal liberty. Even for the frontier, no large army would be necessary, because Americans were certain that the country's rapid population growth, the local militias, and a few regular troops at strategic frontier forts would be adequate for the purpose of westward expansion.

The British Whig emphasis on a navy, however, was more debatable in America. Many Americans thought a navy essential to defend their ships and coastline, and they echoed the British Whigs in pointing out that a navy did not threaten internal liberty in the same manner as an army. Ships could not be used so easily to disrupt legislatures or coerce farmers. Opponents, however, warned that naval building and maintenance would require heavy taxation which would strengthen a potentially despotic central government. They argued that the Atlantic moat supplemented by coastal defenses would suffice to protect America against a major invasion from the sea, and that America's neutral policy toward Europe combined with Europe's need for American commerce would deter interference with American shipping.

The belief that Europe desperately needed American trade undergirded much of America's early attitudes toward foreign affairs. It allowed Americans to rationalize their desire for nonentanglement and peace with their equal desire for the profits of overseas commerce. Like the eminent French *philosophes* who wrote at the time of the American Revolution, many Americans hoped that free and extensive commerce would render balance of power politics and warfare obsolete. If each nation's prosperity depended upon a network of international trade, no country would risk attacking another. Militarism, "a dangerous prejudice, a carry-over from barbarism, a remnant of former chaos," would be replaced by free commerce that pacified and unified the peoples of the world. So Americans urged that colonialism be ended and other artificial barriers to world trade abandoned. Free governments responsive to the will of their people should be established. These governments would be more peaceful than monarchies, many Americans believed, since only monarchs stood to gain by war while their people supplied the deaths and taxes.

Free trade and anticolonialism gratified America's interests as well as its ideological proclivities. America could afford to support free trade because it needed access to foreign markets. In the absence of large-scale domestic manufactures, it had little need to protect its home markets against foreign competition. America could oppose colonialism because it had no colonies of its own and was surrounded by the colonies of European powers, which severely restricted foreign commerce. Foreigners were expected to trade with colonies only through the mother countries. This worked little hardship on European nations, since they were neighbors. But these mother countries were thousands of miles away from the United States.

In its desire for freer trade, America naturally championed such doctrines as neutral rights and freedom of the seas. The United States saw these doctrines as both morally correct and helpful to American interests. Since the United States expected to be a neutral and to have a navy inferior to those of the major powers, it was to America's interest to promote an international law that protected the trade and shipping of neutrals against the desire of powerful warring nations to interfere with them.

While all Americans hoped that extensive commerce might help the United States protect its neutrality, a good many recognized that this neat package of ideals and interests might not always hold together. Thomas Jefferson, for instance, warned that America's determination to share in the world's commerce and shipping meant "Frequent wars without a doubt," as America's ships, property, and seamen might be insulted or captured. Occasionally Jefferson saw this danger as a reason to abandon commerce and navigation entirely, but most of the time he was confident that America's trade itself could be a powerful enough weapon to deter war. Jefferson and other Americans had had considerable experience in wielding trade as a weapon. Before the revolution, their boycotts of British goods helped to force repeal of the Stamp Act of 1765 and the Townshend Duties of 1767. Most Americans were quite prepared to follow the same policy again if it became necessary. They would use commerce to manipulate the balance of power system if the Europeans refused to accept free trade as a substitute for outmoded military competition.

THE FRANCO-AMERICAN ALLIANCE: CHALLENGE TO NONENTANGLEMENT

In the revolutionary tract *Common Sense*, which circulated in America almost as widely as the Bible and crystallized opinion in favor of independence, Thomas Paine spelled out America's developing attitude toward foreign policy. He denounced the British connection because it tended "directly to involve this continent in European wars and quarrels. . . . As Europe is our market for trade, we ought to form no partial connection with any part of it. It is the true interest of America to steer clear of European connections." Commerce, "if well attended to, will secure us the peace and friendship of all Europe; because it is the interest of all Europe to have America a free port."

Despite this inclination to avoid European connections, Americans desperately needed foreign help to win the revolution against Great Britain. The Continental Congress therefore tried to secure French aid without violating Paine's philosophy of nonentanglement. This contradiction appeared graphically in the model treaty Congress adopted to serve as a guide for all its ministers abroad. John Adams, its primary author, was so determined to avoid military or political ties with France that he was prepared to refuse French troops and naval support. The United States was to make only a "marine treaty."

America would exchange its commerce for supplies and economic aid. When the inevitable war between Britain and France resulted, the United States would promise only to refrain from support of England. The standard provisions of European alliances should be avoided: America must retain its ability to make peace separately, and should not guarantee protection of any French territory. Adams and his allies successfully resisted congressional proposals to offer France just such concessions. They warned particularly that France should be kept out of North America. Since the French wanted to break Britain's monopoly of American trade, Adams seemed confident that this alone would be sufficient incentive to make France finance the revolution.

Congress sent the model treaty to Europe with a group of talented but amateur diplomats. Because Great Britain had conducted all foreign policy for the empire, Congress had to turn to American merchants for its diplomatic corps. The secret congressional committee of correspondence, formed to secure foreign aid and intelligence, was composed largely of merchants and chaired successively by partners in one of the most influential trading houses of Philadelphia, Thomas Willing and Robert Morris. These merchants knew where and how to obtain weapons, supplies, and loans from overseas, and they took a healthy commission for their services. The first diplomat the committee sent to Paris was Silas Deane, also closely associated with Willing, Morris, and Company. Fearing British detection, Deane was melodramatically covert: He composed dispatches in invisible ink. He chose the none-too-original code name "Jones." He pledged to speak nothing but French when unsure of his company, leading French Foreign Minister Vergennes to quip that Deane had to be "the most silent man in France" because he was unable to put six French words together.

When Congress realized the need for more than material assistance, it sent Benjamin Franklin to join Deane in Paris. Franklin's name had preceded him; his scientific experiments and homespun philosophy had made him the most famous of Americans. By lobbying in Parliament as a colonial agent for Pennsylvania and Massachusetts, he had gained diplomatic experience. His list of influential contacts abroad was as lengthy as his reputation was impressive. Franklin was lionized in Paris; he frequented salons and boudoirs, charming the French ladies. He played the role of innocent rustic to his French audience, which anticipated little else from an American. To them he was a representative colonial as well as a colonial representative in the plain frontier clothing he affected. He even let them assume that as a Philadelphian, he was necessarily a Quaker, the symbol of New World simplicity.

America's greatest bargaining tool, however, was France's hatred of Britain, not its love of Franklin. France still smarted at the British victory in the French and Indian War which, in 1763, had stripped France of its North American possessions. Americans and their republican ideals did not mesmerize Foreign Minister Vergennes and the French court as they did Franklin's salon clique. Vergennes, a dedicated and conservative servant of an imperial monarchy, distrusted colonial rebels. Nevertheless, he was ready to support the American Revolution because he saw in it the opportunity to restore French supremacy in the European balance of power. Humbling Britain would not only satisfy Vergennes' desire for revenge, but also perhaps make the British more willing to cooperate with France in restraining the increasingly aggressive eastern empires, Prussia, Austria, and Russia. Those three nations had partitioned Poland in 1772 and were planning new moves against the Ottoman Empire. Vergennes saw this aggressiveness as a threat to continental stability and resented Britain's contemptuous dismissal of France's concern.

Vergennes also saw a chance for more direct gains. He might secure new West Indian islands and regain French rights in the Newfoundland fisheries. His main goal, however, would be the independence of America. He believed that the loss of the American colonies would be a devastating blow to Britain's commercial and financial strength and would undermine much of Britain's naval power. To further his larger goals, Vergennes would even renounce the chance to exploit the revolution to regain Canada. He hoped that Britain's presence in Canada would force the United States to continue to rely on French protection.

Vergennes won royal consent for covert aid to the Americans in 1776, before Franklin's arrival. Playwright-inventor Pierre Augustin Caron de Beaumarchais, author of "The Barber of Seville" and "The Marriage of Figaro," helped initiate Vergennes' project. Beaumarchais had been converted to the American cause by the Virginian Arthur Lee, whom he had met, ironically, in London. Beaumarchais and Vergennes established a bogus Spanish corporation, Roderique Hortalez et Compagnie, through which the French and Spanish governments could covertly buy arms and ship them to the American rebels. Ninety percent of the gunpowder Americans used in the first third of the war came from Europe, primarily through Hortalez. Faced with a massive British invasion force, however, Congress recognized the need for more than money and gunpowder; the United States had to have an open alliance with France. The French navy could divert British attention from America to the protection of the rest of the British Empire. But could France be lured into this arrangement without the permanent political "strings" against which the model treaty warned?

This delicate task, which fell to Franklin, called for more than friendly persuasion. Baron Turgot, finance minister to the French court, feared the costs of the war. They might lead to national bankruptcy or to taxes so exorbitant they would trigger a French revolution. Fortunately for the United States, King Louis XVI rejected this prophetic vision and Turgot resigned. Early American military setbacks also worried the French. Vergennes went so far as to halt the secret sponsorship of Hortalez and Co. for a time. Still, he was eager to help America win its independence, and he fostered a rapid building program to prepare the French navy for war. He was ready to intervene after the Americans captured a mighty chunk of the British army in the Battle of Saratoga in 1778. In case further incentive were needed, Franklin and Deane reminded the French that Britain's defeat at Saratoga might stir George III to offer new and attractive terms for peace and imperial reconciliation. A reunited British empire might then take the French West Indies. Vergennes agreed to an official alliance, but he held out for promises of no separate peace and territorial guarantees. Under the pressure of the war, the American diplomats decided to ignore their instructions and accept Vergennes' offer. Almost simultaneously, Congress prepared new orders to permit just such a pact, orders that arrived in the nick of time.

These orders coupled the concessions to the world of power politics with some audacious requests. France and the United States should take joint action against Canada, Nova Scotia, Newfoundland, and the West Indies. The United States intended to annex all but the Caribbean islands. Should the Spanish climb aboard this bandwagon, they were welcome to Florida and Portugal. Congress might bluster with such grandiose statements, but it had now accepted the kind of alliance it had disdained earlier. Neither side could sign a peace treaty without the consent of the other. America would guarantee protection of French possessions in perpetuity—but only in the Western Hemisphere, and only in a defensive war. In exchange, France would guarantee American independence and whatever borders America succeeded in wresting from the British. The accompanying treaty of commerce did reflect many of the liberal premises of *Common Sense* and the model treaty. But clearly nonentanglement had fallen by the wayside. Even John Adams praised the alliance, and Thomas Paine accepted money from the French secret service to act as a propagandist for the pact.

STRAINS ON THE ALLIANCE

The Franco-American alliance tilted the scales of war in favor of the United States. The British were put on the defensive when a joint French-Spanish force threatened invasion of southern England. After this, the British cabinet kept ships and supplies close to home rather than use them in America. The French also kept Britain occupied by harassing British colonies in the East and West Indies. Finally, in 1781, the French made a major contribution to the crowning American victory of the war. A French fleet drove off the English ships sent to rescue General Cornwallis from the Yorktown peninsula while a French army joined Washington's forces to surround Cornwallis's troops and obtain their surrender. The alliance proved indispensable, yet the allies discovered conflicting interests. The most important of these involved a new combatant in the war against England: Spain.

In April of 1779, without informing the Americans, France had lured Spain into the war by promising no peace with Britain until the French had helped Spain retrieve Gibralter from the British. This made the United States the prisoner of Spanish policy. America could make no peace without French consent; France could make no peace without Spanish consent; and Spain would refuse consent until it got Gibraltar. Spain also refused to ally itself directly with the American rebels against monarchy and imperialism, despite the fact that the two countries were fighting a common enemy. Spain feared especially for its North American colonies bordering the avaricious revolutionaries. It wanted desperately to keep the Americans away from the Mississippi River, the only means by which farmers west of the Appalachians could profitably export their crops.

Without the right to navigate the Mississippi, American settlements beyond the mountains could never be more than tiny groups of subsistence farmers which would offer no threat to the equally weak and thinly populated Spanish possessions on their borders. In hopes of pinning the Americans to the strip of land between the Atlantic and the Appalachians, Spain reconquered Florida from the British and sent expeditions up the Mississippi to lay claims as far as the Ohio Valley.

In pursuing this policy, Spain fumbled its best chance to contain the Americans. In 1780, at a particularly ominous point in the war, Congress instructed John Jay, whom it sent to Spain to gain recognition and an alliance, to part with the Mississippi if such a sacrifice was necessary to get a Spanish treaty. Reluctantly, Jay made the offer. The Spanish rejected it, confident they could hold the Mississippi with or without American consent. One reason the Spanish were so cocksure was the leverage they had over France.

France had little interest in the conflict between Spain and the United States over territory in North America, but it needed Spanish consent to conclude the war. The French were becoming desperate for peace because they had borrowed heavily to finance the war effort, and their economic situation was deteriorating rapidly as the war dragged on. They had good reason to believe that their military position might fade along with their economy. Since it seemed increasingly unlikely that they could take Gibraltar to satisfy the Spanish conditions for peace, Vergennes thought he might induce the Spanish to forfeit that hope if France successfully supported Spain's claims in the Mississippi and Ohio valleys.

America had little claim on those territories. They had not been administered by any of the thirteen colonies before the revolution and the American military expeditions to the West, notably those of George Rogers Clark, had been hit-and-run affairs resulting in no permanent occupation. French observers in the United States mistakenly wrote back to Vergennes that the Americans had no great interest in the trans-Appalachian West anyway. Vergennes consequently believed that France's guarantee of American independence and territory did not include an obligation to support America's extravagant western claims, and he tended to discourage those claims in favor of Spain's.

Some Americans were alarmed and angered by this divergence from American interests. One of these was Arthur Lee, whom Congress had sent from his post as Massachusetts' colonial agent in London to join Franklin and Deane in Paris. Lee distrusted not only the French, but his fellow commissioners as well. He wrote virulent letters to Congress calling Franklin and Deane French sycophants. He specifically accused Deane of profiting from speculations that sacrificed American interests to the French. Congress recalled Deane, and the vitriolic public debate which followed drove Deane to join the Loyalists and split Congress into bitter pro- and anti-French factions.

In Deane's place, Congress appointed John Adams, an ally of Arthur Lee and the anti-French faction. Adams was a man of deep integrity, but he was prickly, vain, and self-righteous. He already mistrusted Franklin for straying so far from Adams's own model treaty, and his outlook was not improved by closer scrutiny of the situation in Paris. Franklin, basking in French admiration, was swirling from one soirée to another. He left Adams to attend to all the drudgery and paperwork. Adams decided it was his duty to offset Franklin's indolent and compliant style. Since France was so obviously in the war for its own interests, Adams saw no reason to couch his requests for further aid in flattering terms. Vergennes bristled under Adams's continual hectoring and ultimately refused to do business with any American representative but Franklin. Vergennes was appalled, therefore, when he learned that Congress had appointed Adams as the commissioner to make peace with England. In early 1781, he instructed the French minister in America to seek Adams's dismissal.

The French had many friends in Congress, including at least one who was on their payroll. But Adams had his own allies. Instead of replacing him, Congress surrounded Adams with a new commission designed to be favorable to France. Franklin, Thomas Jefferson, and John Jay, all considered part of the pro-French faction of Congress, would share the responsibility for peacemaking with Adams and his one possible supporter, Henry Laurens of South Carolina. To further hamstring Adams, Congress instructed the commission to do nothing without the "knowledge and concurrence" of the French and "ultimately to govern" itself by French "advice and opinion." Congress then sent the mortified Adams to Holland to seek a loan.

So Franklin was alone when British commissioner Richard Oswald arrived in Paris to open peace negotiations after Britain's bitter defeat at Yorktown. Franklin dutifully informed the French of the British overture, but in his private conversations with Oswald, he disobeyed the instructions tying him to French advice. In addition to demanding absolute independence and the Mississippi River border, he recommended that Britain cede Canada to the United States. He implied that the elimination of this British threat to North America would render America's "perpetual" alliance with France obsolete. Naturally Franklin neglected to inform Vergennes of this suggestion. Shortly afterward, Franklin was joined by John Jay, who was even less concerned about French sensibilities. Jay had been known as a strong supporter of the French connection when Congress had sent him to seek Spanish recognition and alliance in 1779, but he thought he had received inadequate help from the French during his unhappy stay in Madrid. He arrived in Paris in an angry and suspicious mood, to discover that Oswald's commission empowered the British envoy to treat with the American "colonies" rather than with the independent United States. He objected strongly to this wording. Dubiously, he joined Franklin to ask Vergennes' "advice and opinion" about the matter.

Vergennes dismissed the discrepancy as trivial; only the final treaty need recognize America's independence. Vergennes also expressed support for Spanish and English claims to some of the territory east of the Mississippi which the United States sought so ardently. Franklin, true to his subtle style, seemed inclined to accept Vergennes' advice, at least on the issue of Oswald's commission, and to continue following congressional orders. But Jay would have none of it. When they returned to the American residence, Jay told Franklin they should ignore Vergennes' opinions, demand a new commission for Oswald, and negotiate independently. "Would you deliberately break Congress's instructions?" asked Franklin, as though he had not already done so himself. "I would break them like this," Jay responded, smashing his clay pipe in pieces on the brick fireplace.

Thus, at Jay's insistence, the Americans delayed negotiations with Britain until Oswald's commission could be revised. Then Jay found himself driven to further defiance. He discovered that Vergennes' secretary, Joseph Rayneval, had disappeared after ostentatiously taking leave for a short holiday in the countryside. Rayneval had been Vergennes' spokesman in support of Spanish claims in the trans-Appalachian West. Coincidentally, the British had just turned over to Jay and Franklin an intercepted dispatch from another French diplomat, one stationed in America, who urged that the United States be excluded from the Newfoundland fisheries. Jay correctly surmised that Rayneval was on a secret mission to discuss peace in London and that America's interests in the West and the fisheries might suffer. Jay ignored congressional instructions and, without telling Franklin or the French, sent his own messenger to warn the British against Rayneval. He later explained to Congress that he would have preferred to act with Franklin's consent, but that Franklin had disagreed with Jay's assessment of the situation and had felt constrained by his confidence in Vergennes and his instructions from Congress.

When John Adams joined the delegation fresh from his mission in the Netherlands, he backed Jay to the hilt.[1] He had long assumed what Jay had

---

[1] He was the only other commissioner to arrive in time to take a significant part in the negotiations. Jefferson had declined his nomination. The British captured Laurens en route to Europe

Figure 1   The American commissioners who negotiated the peace treaty with Great Britain ending the Revolutionary War—from left to right, John Jay, John Adams, Benjamin Franklin, Henry Laurens, and the secretary to the commission, William Temple Franklin. Unfinished painting by Benjamin West. Courtesy The Henry Francis du Pont Winterthur Museum.

recently decided—that the French were actively opposing American interests to keep their ally permanently under their influence. With Jay and Adams in agreement on a unilateral approach independent of France, Franklin acquiesced; henceforth the Americans excluded the French from all their deliberations and negotiations. This was a risky diplomatic strategy. The British could use the rift between the allies that Jay's messenger had revealed to play one off against the other. (Actually the British would have known of the rift anyway, if not from Rayneval himself, then from the British spy who served as Franklin's secretary throughout the negotiations.) Fortunately for the United States, the British decided to play the Americans against the French rather than vice versa. They offered the most liberal of peace terms to the United States in hopes of weaning America away from its French alliance, regaining the lion's share of American commerce, and buying off any further American contribution to the war.

While Jay's diplomacy thus seems to have had some good results, the delay caused by his insistence on a reworded commission for Oswald may have cost the United States something. During that interim, news arrived that the final French-Spanish assault on Gibraltar had failed, and the British stiffened their terms. And in all probability, the risks taken by Jay and Adams

---

and imprisoned him in the Tower of London. They released him only in time to participate in a few last-minute diplomatic details.

were unnecessary. They exaggerated France's hostility to American interests. France was caught in a Hobson's choice between the conflicting claims of its allies. Rayneval indeed implied lack of support for America's claims to the West and the fisheries during his secret mission to London, as Jay and Adams suspected. But the French did not pursue these issues seriously or maliciously. Franklin's more subtle approach to independent negotiations might well have sufficed. Certainly Jay need not have invited the British into the Mississippi area as a counterweight to Spain. He did so later in the negotiations, offering Britain joint navigation of the Mississippi River and promoting a secret article in the peace treaty that would place the Florida border at 31 degrees if Spain held the province, but farther north if the British regained it.

Fortunately for Jay and Adams, however, Jay's rash generosity cost the Americans little. The British were never able to make use of their rights to navigate the Mississippi because, as later mapping expeditions proved, the river did not cross the border into Canada. Therefore the British needed permission to cross American territory in order to reach the river, permission Britain never got.

THE TREATY OF 1783

Whatever the merits of the Americans' diplomacy, the result was a treaty so favorable to the United States that Vergennes remarked the British had bought peace, not made it. To the west, the United States reached to the Mississippi River. To the north, although America lost its first proposed border enclosing present-day Ontario, the modified line through the Great Lakes gave the United States access to that vital waterway. John Adams's advocacy won the "liberty," if not the "right," for Americans to catch and dry fish off Newfoundland. In turn the United States would put no legal impediment in the way of British collection of private debts from American citizens. The promise of a Congressional recommendation to the states that Loyalists be compensated for their war losses helped Britain save some face, but both sides knew that the states would ignore the recommendation.

While the United States won its independence and a territorial bonanza in the Peace of 1783, none of the other participants in the war fared very well. Great Britain lost the heart of its empire. The French monarchy, weakened by its war expenditures, set the stage for its own demise. The Spanish helped create for themselves an exuberant neighbor whose expanding population regarded Spain as a temporary custodian of territories destined sooner or later to be part of the United States. Americans liked to think of themselves as innocents abroad, the victims of the subtle and cynical machinations of the Old World. But occasional use of that smokescreen by Jay, Adams, and Franklin could not obscure the machinations behind their own diplomatic coup.

Vergennes was naturally chagrined by the American diplomats' conduct toward France. He had to acknowledge that technically they had not broken

Map 1 Boundary Negotiations of the American Revolution

their pledge against a separate peace, since they had not signed a final peace treaty, but a preliminary agreement to go into effect only when an official pact was signed by all combatants. Nevertheless, America had weakened the position of its allies. Britain could increase its demands against France and Spain knowing that America's belligerence on the battlefield declined in proportion to its diplomatic victory. But Vergennes could find a silver lining even in this. He could use the defection of the United States to press Spain into making peace without Gibraltar or territory in America's hinterland. When Vergennes castigated the Americans for excluding him from their negotiations, he permitted Franklin to dissuade him from any serious retaliation. Franklin blandly warned against allowing the British to flatter themselves that they had split the allies. Vergennes accepted this and even granted Franklin's request for a new loan.

Despite the negotiators' success, their conduct did not receive unanimous approval in the American Congress. A substantial portion of the pro-French faction, led by James Madison, proposed to censure the American delegation for defying its instructions and keeping the negotiations secret from the French. The taste of diplomatic triumph and Vergennes' mildness soon dampened this carping, but the issue did not die. Members of the pro-French faction—James Madison, Thomas Jefferson, and Robert R. Livingston— would soon form the Jeffersonian Republican party. During the war between Great Britain and the new revolutionary French regime in the 1790s, these Republicans would recall the diplomacy of Benjamin Franklin as justification for continued adherence to the French alliance. The opposing Federalists also would appeal to the history of the negotiations, but to remind their constituents that their Federalist compatriots, John Jay and John Adams, had rescued the Mississippi and the fisheries from the French and their compliant dupe, Franklin. Thus America's revolutionary diplomacy lived on, first as the football of politicians, later as a bone of contention among historians.

CONTROVERSIAL ISSUES AND FURTHER READING

Nationalist historians cite the diplomacy of the revolution as a prime example of successful American foreign policy. They especially praise John Jay and John Adams for taking an independent line to defend American interests against the cynical maneuverings of the French. Hard realists too appreciate the vigor and tenacity with which Jay and Adams bargained for America's desires and regard Franklin's diplomacy as too weak and compliant. Samuel Flagg Bemis, author of the classic study *The Diplomacy of the American Revolution* (2nd ed., 1957), actually thinks Jay and Adams should have taken a still harder line. [Richard B. Morris's *The Peacemakers: The Great Powers and American Independence* (1965), the most extensive account of this issue, sees Jay's position as just hard enough. Cecil Currey, in his controversial *Code Number 72: Ben Franklin, Patriot or Spy* (1972), asserts that Franklin was not just wrong but treasonous in his dealings with France and Britain.]

Restrained realists tend to favor Franklin's equally independent but more subtle defense of American interests. They condemn Jay and Adams for being excessively abrasive and taking unnecessary risks. They also regard French maneuvering as to be expected in the pursuit of national self-interest and far less malevolent than Adams and Jay had feared. [Gerald Stourzh's *Benjamin Franklin and American Foreign Policy* (1954) is the best modern defense of the Philadelphian. Stourzh calls John Adams's conduct "pretentious diplomacy of the big stick." James H. Hutson, in *John Adams and the Diplomacy of the American Revolution* (1980), says that Adams's constant mistrust of Franklin and the French was literally paranoid. The best study of the alliance itself is William C. Stinchcombe's *The American Revolution and the French Alliance* (1969). Stinchcombe discovered the list of paid American agents in the French archives and emphasized the conflicts of interest within the alliance. Jonathan R. Dull, *The French Navy and American Independence: A Study of Arms and Diplomacy, 1774–1787* (1975), argues convincingly that Vergennes' policies toward America were largely the product of military necessity and pressures from the other great powers of Europe, rather than any hostility toward the United States. The 1978 bicentennial of the signing of the French alliance inspired two collections of essays reflecting the latest thinking on the Franco-American alliance, Ronald Hoffman and Peter J. Albert, eds., *Diplomacy and Revolution: The Franco-American Alliance of 1778* (1981), and Lawrence S. Kaplan, ed., *The American Revolution and "A Candid World"* (1977). An older yet still valuable history of the alliance is E. S. Corwin's *French Policy and the American Alliance of 1778* (1916).]

The argument between nationalist and realist historians over the relative merits of Jay, Adams, and Franklin is built on a long line of quarrelsome accounts dating back to the revolution itself. In those early days, the basic issue was which of the negotiators best lived up to the sacred injunction of Washington's Farewell Address against permanent foreign alliances. Most early American historians were New Englanders who echoed and endorsed the public accusations John Adams made against Franklin and the French throughout his long life. [See, for example, Theodore Lyman, *The Diplomacy of the United States* (1826–1828).] Then, in the 1830s, Franklin's historical reputation received a powerful defense from Jared Sparks, the first professor of American history and the first American to gain access to the French archives. As a New Englander, he could hardly be accused of pro-Republican bias, and his favorable interpretation of French conduct and Franklin's diplomacy was therefore dominant for half a century. [See, for example, Jared Sparks, *The Writings of George Washington*, Vol. I (1834).] His success was somewhat surprising, because by Sparks's time, anything that implied approval of foreign alliances was suspect as heresy.

In the 1870s, George Bancroft, the greatest American historian of his day, further improved Franklin's position, bringing it more in line with Washington's admonitions against permanent foreign alliances. Bancroft discovered that Franklin himself had been the first to defy Congress's instructions to seek French advice when he secretly suggested British cession of Canada. This revelation offset an additional finding Bancroft made that might have discredited Sparks and Franklin. Sparks had blatantly distorted the French records only he had been privileged to see in order to portray the French as more beneficent than they had been. [George Bancroft, *History of the United States*, Vol. VI (1876).]

The State Department assigned Francis Wharton to issue a correct version of the diplomatic correspondence of the revolution to replace that of Sparks, but he too found support for Franklin's approach to the negotiations. He thought the record of British responses showed that Franklin might well have won Canada from the British if not for John Jay's delays in search of a properly worded commission. [Francis Wharton, *Revolutionary Diplomatic Correspondence of the United States* (1889).] Then, the Jay family struck back. John Jay's grandson and nephew separately wrote books using the newly opened French archives to demonstrate that the opposition of Vergennes and his cohorts to America's claims in the West and the fisheries might have justified Jay's suspicions and the separate negotiations. [John Jay, "The Peace Negotiations of 1782 and 1783," in Justin Winsor, *Narrative and Critical History of America*, Vol. VII (1889). George Pellew, *John Jay* (1890).]

While these opposing interpretations continue to influence histories of revolutionary diplomacy, the fading of Federalist-Republican partisanship, filial piety for the Founding Fathers, and the pride of the Jay and Adams families has muted the debate, and the gulf between assertions has narrowed. All historians now agree that Franklin was not adamantly opposed to separate negotiations, as he was the first to undertake them. No one looking closely at the British records now believes that Great Britain ever intended to surrender Canada, so negotiating delays probably had only a minor impact on the liberality of peace terms. Most of the best modern surveys of revolutionary foreign policy agree that defiance of congressional instructions was in order. They therefore tilt slightly in favor of Jay and Adams.

While nationalists and realists have built upon the old historical disputes over which American negotiators best lived up to the precepts of the Farewell Address, revisionists, with their concern for American expansionism and imperialism, have also been able to build on a foundation of older classic histories. Frederick Jackson Turner, the historian who did the most to call attention to the influence of the frontier on American history, was the first to view revolutionary diplomacy through an expansionist lens. [Frederick Jackson Turner, "The Policy of France toward the Mississippi Valley," *American Historical Review*, 10 (1905).] He inspired a longer and still worthwhile exploration, *The West in the Diplomacy of the American Revolution* (1913), by P. C. Phillips. Of course, both Turner and Phillips regarded westward expansion with favor, while the later revisionists take a considerably more jaundiced view of it. Revisionists portray the territorial demands of the Americans during the revolutionary negotiations as greedy and aggressive and find no reason why France should have been expected to support them. The best case against American revolutionary diplomacy as imperialistic is made by Richard W. Van Alstyne's *Empire and Independence: The International History of the American Revolution* (1965). Van Alstyne himself is not a revisionist, but since no radical historian has yet published a comprehensive study of the diplomacy of the revolution, revisionists cite Van Alstyne to support their imperialist image of America. [The classic work examining the foundations of American foreign policy is Max Savelle's *The Origins of American Diplomacy: The International History of Anglo-America, 1492–1763* (1967). It should by augmented by Felix Gilbert's *To the Farewell Address: Ideas of Early American Foreign Policy* (1961), and the conflicting view taken by James Hutson in his book cited above.]

CHAPTER 2

The Diplomacy of a New Nation: 1783–1800

FOREIGN POLICY UNDER THE ARTICLES OF CONFEDERATION

As the newly independent United States began to formulate its policies, Americans did not find the international atmosphere nearly as accommodating as they had expected it to be. The British and their Parliament had become increasingly disgruntled over the defeat they had suffered. They were less and less satisfied with the liberal terms by which they had secured peace from their rebellious colonists. Lord Shelburne, whose cabinet had made the peace, had hoped that generous terms, followed by a mutually advantageous trade treaty, would regain much of the economic and strategic advantage Britain had formerly enjoyed from possession of the American colonies. Not only had he been ready to offer a liberal trade arrangement between England and the United States, but he had been willing to permit continuation of America's important prewar trade with Canada and the British West Indies. This flew in the face of Britain's mercantilist policy, which closed colonies to the ships of outsiders. Many Britons feared that the West Indies trade would provide too much incentive for American commerce, shipbuilding, and naval power. They overturned the Shelburne government and abandoned his conciliatory approach: The new cabinet closed all British colonies to American ships and refused to sign a trade treaty. It counted upon the infant nation's weakness and its need for profitable trade with the British home islands, which were still open to the Americans on quite liberal terms, to prevent American retaliation.

The British also abandoned conciliation on the American frontier, angered by the discovery that the strategic forts controlling the passageways between the Great Lakes were on America's side of the Canadian border. These forts were traditional fur-trading posts for Indian tribes who trapped beaver for England's thriving hat industry. British fort commanders warned that the Indians were seething because the British government had negotiated no protection for them or their lands in the peace treaty with the United States. This left the Indians technically still at war. The United States could be expected to take advantage of this state of war to extort concessions of Indian lands in the Ohio Valley. Should the forts be given to the United States, the Indians would be dependent on the new nation and might well vent their fury on the scattered frontier population of Canada. So the British declined to turn over the posts. They justified their refusal by pointing to America's own violation of the peace treaty. The United States had neither compensated the Loyalists nor enforced collection of the private debts owed to the British. Adding insult to injury, Britain refused to send a minister to the United States in exchange for the dispatch of John Adams as the first American minister to Great Britain. Adams reported that the British expected preference over France before they would treat with the United States. In his anger he came close to agreeing with Jefferson, America's new minister to France, that the British were "rich, proud, hectoring, swearing, squibbing, carnivorous animals."

As might be expected, the Spanish were no more accommodating than their traditional enemies, the British. The Spanish had already made their decision to confront rather than conciliate the Americans when they had rejected America's offer to exchange the Mississippi River for an open alliance. There were means other than conciliation by which to limit America's westward expansion. First, Spain claimed a Florida border extending far north of the 31st parallel that the United States accepted as the proper line. Even if America prevailed in this border dispute, possession of West Florida and Louisiana guaranteed Spanish control of the river from 31° south to the Gulf of Mexico. By international law, the nation owning both banks of a river could close its portion of the waterway to foreign navigation. Spain did this by proclamation in 1784, effectively blocking the only practical route by which most farmers west of the Appalachians could send their goods to the markets of the East Coast, the West Indies, or Europe.

Spain counted on the blockade of the Mississippi to prevent westward expansion; but it also had an alternative plan. If Americans continued to migrate across the Appalachians, the Spanish hoped to lure them into secession with promises of access to the Mississippi once they had become Spanish subjects. They even paid some prominent western Americans like General James Wilkinson to help inspire secessionist sentiments. Meanwhile, like the British, the Spanish supplied neighboring Indian tribes and urged them to resist United States encroachments on their lands. And again like the British, they refused to sign a trade treaty with the United States. The Spanish trade was not nearly so important as the British, which supplied nearly 90 percent of America's imports and accounted for 75 percent of America's trade overall. But Spain was the only nation to which America exported more than it imported, making the Spanish trade the major source of hard currency. A firm trade treaty with Spain was obviously desirable.

Even the French were less forthcoming than many Americans had expected. France had no territorial conflicts with the United States, but its continuing need for Spanish aid to balance British power put France's ultimate loyalties in doubt. Franco-American trade, which Americans had expected to burgeon, instead grew rather slowly. The French did not manufacture the range of goods the British did, and contacts between French and American merchants were not as familiar and trusting as those with the British. The French merchants refused to emulate the British by extending credit or permitting American merchants to obtain goods on consignment and sell them before paying their bills. Consequently, the volume of American trade with France could never approach that with Great Britain. The French, unlike the British, did permit American ships to trade on a limited basis with their West Indies colonies. Yet ironically this trade did not much exceed that with the British West Indies, because the British islands were often thrown open to American ships by emergency decrees of the local governors in defiance of the wishes of the home government.

Many Americans could not understand why the Europeans were not more forthcoming. After all, Americans sought little more than mutually beneficial trade and security within their proper borders. Freer trade was not merely a matter of self-interest, but of justice and peace, according to the American outlook. The mercantile system was especially unjust to the United States because America was the only independent nation among the colonies of the Western Hemisphere. Colonialism barred America from trading with its neighbors and confined it to the markets of the mother countries three thousand miles away. For the European powers, on the other hand, it was their neighbors' markets that were open, and only the distant colonial ports that were closed. Surely, Americans believed, fairness and the interests of peace required the opening of colonial ports in the Western Hemisphere to the United States. This would provide profits for all and an interdependence that would encourage peace between nations. European obtuseness had to be more than mere self-interest; it had to indicate a malicious hostility to the United States and its republican system.

Americans regarded European intransigence on territorial issues as equally unjustified and spiteful. They blamed every Indian raid in the Northwest on the British, whom they accused of using the Indians to keep Americans away from the Great Lakes posts. They assumed quite correctly that the British were holding the posts for economic and strategic purposes, not just in reprisal for America's noncompliance with the peace treaty. With equal accuracy, they regarded Spanish border policy as hostile. Yet the Spanish had considerable legality and reason on their side. The administrative border of Florida had actually been moved north of 31° when the British had occupied it before the revolution. In asserting their border claims, closing the Mississippi, supporting Indian resistance, and bribing Americans to stir up secession, the Spanish were defending themselves against an attitude they knew to be common in the United States—that the Spanish colonies were empty; dominated by a corrupt, tyrannical, superstitious government; and therefore a legitimate future target for American expansion. Jefferson, for one, worried only that the Spanish might be too feeble to hold their border territories "till our population can be sufficiently advanced to gain it from them peice by peice [sic]."

As the leading political figures in the United States came to realize that the value of America's commerce would not bring the European powers hurrying to grant liberal trade treaties or to accept American domination over the Mississippi and Great Lakes systems, they began to reconsider their foreign policies. Humiliated by the lack of British and French respect, Adams and Jefferson wrote home urging more unified and vigorous action. If European powers were unwilling to adopt reciprocal trade concessions, then America must adopt reciprocal trade exclusions. John Jay, George Washington, James Madison, and Alexander Hamilton agreed.

Under the Articles of Confederation, however, the national government had no control over foreign trade. This put commercial retaliation out of the question. The Articles also prohibited most other means of diplomatic leverage. They denied Congress the power to tax or to raise an army. Congress had to request money and troops from the states, which it did with little success. Consequently, it could not build a navy adequate to protect America's shipping or guard its coasts. It could not build an army to regain the Great Lakes posts or control the Indians. It could not even enforce its own treaty obligations. State courts often defied congressional orders to enforce the collection of British debts, and state legislatures ignored congressional suggestions that they compensate the Loyalists.

Hamilton and Madison, as members of Congress, tried to win some of these powers for the national government. They proposed an amendment to the Articles of Confederation giving Congress the right to levy a tariff on imports. This would enable the federal government to retaliate commercially against hostile powers by assessing higher tariffs against them than against friendly nations. It would also provide revenue with which to build a navy and pay a militia. But a unanimous vote was required to amend the Articles of Confederation, and both New York and Rhode Island vetoed the tariff the two times it came before the Congress—New York the first time; Rhode Island the second.

If the United States did not have the power to achieve its goals, there seemed to be only one other recourse—assistance from foreign nations. No American leader considered this desirable. Even such a friend of the French as Thomas Jefferson had been made wary by the diplomatic experience of the revolution and its aftermath. When John Jay, secretary for foreign affairs, told Jefferson to seek French help against the British occupation of the Northwest posts, Jefferson declined. He preferred not to remind France that the United States had reciprocal obligations under the alliance to protect French territory. Jay had some other alternatives: The United States could ally with the British against Spain to force open the Mississippi. Or it could ally with the Spanish to remove the British from the Northwest posts. But each had its price. The British would demand the posts and American withdrawal from the West Indies trade in exchange for their help, while alliance with the Spanish would cost America the Mississippi. Despairing of any chance that the states would consent to strengthen the national government, Jay decided to bid for Spanish help. Once again, the Mississippi would be the main bargaining chip.

In 1786 Jay negotiated a preliminary agreement with Diego de Gardoqui. Spain would grant the United States a liberal trade treaty and guarantee America's borders against the British in exchange for a compromise on Florida's border, America's sacrifice of Mississippi navigation rights for twenty-five to thirty years, and a guarantee of Spanish possessions in the Western Hemisphere. Jay then went to Congress to seek approval of the agreement before negotiating the final treaty. But he told Congress only of the provisions concerning navigation of the Mississippi and trade with Spain, omitting any mention of the mutual territorial guarantees that committed Spain to help America retrieve the Northwest posts and the United States to respect and protect Spanish colonial possessions. If he had revealed these provisions, no approval would have been forthcoming.

Even so, Jay stirred up a storm that threatened the new union. Southerners accused him and his supporters of sacrificing the Mississippi to northern interests in foreign commerce. James Monroe distrusted Jay as a potential traitor from that day on. Jay encountered so much opposition to those portions of the agreement he revealed to Congress that he dropped the entire negotiation. Even so, southern delegates to the Constitutional Convention of 1787 and subsequent state ratifying conventions would cite the Jay-Gardoqui Agreement as a warning against too much power being given to a federal government that might become the instrument of the more populous North.

THE CONSTITUTION AND AMERICAN FOREIGN POLICY

But Jay's fears had been premature. The Philadelphia Convention of 1787 created a new Constitution, granting the federal government the three crucial powers it had been denied under the Articles of Confederation—the power to tax, to raise an army, and to control commerce.

Of all the constitutional provisions affecting diplomacy, contemporaries probably attributed the most importance to the commerce clauses. Americans expected commercial retaliation to be the primary weapon of their foreign policy. The South supported such action but feared that the North, with its larger voting bloc, might make southern rather than northern products the sacrificial goats. So a southern-dominated committee proposed to prohibit taxes on exports and any interference with the slave trade. It also sought to require a two-thirds vote of both houses to pass any navigation act. Northerners whittled back these demands. They secured the right of Congress to control the slave trade after 1808 and to pass navigation laws by a simple majority of the two houses. But they accepted the prohibition on export taxes. Thus the United States could wield its commercial power by taxing imports or embargoing exports, but even today it is constitutionally prohibited from taxing exports.

The members of the convention also were determined to prevent the states from flouting federal treaties, as they had under the Articles of Confederation. The first comprehensive proposal offered in the Constitutional Convention, the Virginia Plan, sought to do this by giving Congress the right to veto all state laws. This, however, was too much of an invasion of states rights for most of the convention members. Instead, the Constitution and treaties were made the supreme law of the land. In addition, the Supreme Court was given original jurisdiction over cases involving other nations, foreclosing any state control over foreign policy through the legal system.

Having increased federal power over international relations, the convention had to decide with which branch of the government that power ought to lie. The members had no difficulty deciding that the power to make war should be lodged with the legislature. It was a staple fare of British reformers and their American disciples that the people who supplied the taxes and the soldiers were far less likely to agitate for war than monarchs seeking glory and treasure. The convention made an interesting modification, however, when it permitted Congress to "declare" rather than "make" war. This would allow the president as commander-in-chief to "repel sudden attacks." In later times, of course, it enabled the president to commit the nation to full-scale wars without an official congressional declaration.[1]

The president received much of the rest of his power over foreign policy almost accidentally. The Virginia Plan granted the right to make treaties and appoint ambassadors to the Senate. Then the Great Compromise eliminated the provision that membership of both House and Senate would reflect the number of inhabitants in each state. The Senate would be composed of two senators per state, regardless of population, meaning that states with less than one-third of the population could conceivably outvote the remainder of the nation. The large states rebelled against empowering such a Senate to control foreign policy. They gave the president the right to make treaties and appoint ambassadors, leaving the Senate only the power to advise and consent by a two-thirds vote. On occasion the Senate has used this role to great effect, but its power has declined over the years.

When George Washington appeared personally in the Senate to ask for advice on a treaty, the senators asked him to leave so they could debate in private. Washington never went back. Ever since, the Senate has done more consenting than advising. More important, presidents found ways to circumvent the senatorial power over treaties. They have used joint congressional resolutions or executive agreements that require no congressional consent at all to make what are in effect treaty commitments. They have also lessened Senate power over appointments, lodging much authority over foreign policy in officials of the White House staff, such as the National Security Advisor, who unlike the secretary of state do not require senatorial confirmation.

---

[1] After such an action had led to the Vietnam debacle, Congress passed a joint resolution in November of 1973 requiring the president to secure congressional approval or withdraw American troops within sixty days if he intervened without a declaration of war.

In fact, the Constitution did not provide specifically for a cabinet or for a secretary of state, just unnamed executive departments. The first Congress created the Department of State and gave it jurisdiction over foreign policy. But diplomacy was thought a small enough task that the department could also be responsible for the mint and various domestic affairs. Thomas Jefferson, the first secretary of state, presided over a department consisting of only six employees and a handful of ministers and consuls abroad. Another of Congress's most significant decisions affecting the State Department was to reject the contention that it should require a two-thirds Senate vote to dismiss cabinet ministers as well as to appoint them. Instead, the president could fire his cabinet secretaries at will. This made the Department of State a creature of the executive, not an independent entity or a servant of the Senate. Still, the role of the cabinet remained a bit hazy. One member of Washington's administration meant to make the most of that situation. That man was Alexander Hamilton.

THE DIPLOMACY OF THE FEDERALIST ERA

John Adams, who came to hate Alexander Hamilton, called him "the bastard brat of a Scotch peddlar." Hamilton indeed had been born out of wedlock to a West Indian woman who had left her husband for a wandering Scottish laird. She bore the Scotsman two children, whereupon he unceremoniously left her. Alexander was left the breadwinner in his impoverished family, serving as an eleven-year-old clerk in a merchant firm on the island of St. Croix. This inglorious heritage produced in Hamilton a gnawing ambition. He thirsted for heroism, and what he wanted for himself, he naturally wanted for his adopted nation as well. He came to the United States under the sponsorship of a group of West Indian planters who sent him to study medicine on the condition that he would return to practice in the islands. Once in America, he became one of the revolutionaries, an officer in the artillery, and then General Washington's aide-de-camp. The childless Washington virtually adopted Hamilton as a surrogate son. Hamilton's patron permitted him to lead the charge on a critical fortified redoubt at the Battle of Yorktown and cover himself with military glory. Hamilton also profited from his connections at Washington's headquarters, marrying the daughter of the powerful Schuyler clan of New York. Upon leaving the army, Hamilton studied law and became a member of the Confederate Congress, where he teamed with James Madison to lead the movement toward a more powerful federal government.

When Washington appointed him the first secretary of the treasury, Hamilton saw himself as prime minister, and modeled his office on that of the British prime minister, who was usually the chief economic officer in his own cabinet. Hamilton thus took it upon himself to direct much of America's foreign as well as economic affairs, a task made easier by Jefferson's late arrival from France to take his position in the first cabinet as secretary of state.

Figure 2 George Washington (left) and his secretary of the treasury, Alexander Hamilton, were the key figures in making American foreign policy following adoption of the Constitution. Portraits courtesy of the National Archives.

Even after Jefferson assumed control of foreign policy, Hamilton used his private British contacts to direct diplomacy behind Jefferson's back. This might not have made much difference had Hamilton not been moving away from some of the ideas he had seemingly shared with Jefferson and Madison. All three had agitated for federal power to control trade, arguing that this would permit the United States to retaliate against British intransigence. Hamilton and Madison had even made this a central point in their famous collaborative effort in support of the Constitution, the *Federalist Papers.* But when Madison proposed such retaliation from his position as leader of the House of Representatives, Hamilton worked successfully behind the scenes to defeat it. It proved to be the first divergence among the organizers of what would become the Federalist and Republican parties.

Hamilton's goal for America was truly heroic: He wanted to build the nation's military power so that it could assume the leadership of the Western Hemisphere. Too long Europe had plumed itself as the master of the world, Hamilton wrote. The mission of the United States, therefore, was "to vindicate the honor of the human race, and to teach that assuming brother moderation." But Hamilton leavened his romanticism with a substantial dose of realism. The federal government needed money to build its power, and it was clear that a tariff on imports would have to be the primary source of federal funds. The alternative of an internal tax would be highly unpopular to a people fresh from a successful revolution triggered by Britain's attempt to impose an internal stamp tax.

The money to be derived from the tariff was crucial to Hamilton's vision. In his famous Report to Congress on the Public Credit, he proposed to use the tariff revenue to begin paying off the national and state debts. With America's credit restored, foreign governments would once again be willing to loan the nation money in case of war or emergency. The government's newly funded bonds also would circulate at full face value, giving America a much-needed money supply. Hamilton welcomed the fact that funding the bonds at face value would enrich commercial speculators, many of whom had bought the bonds at depreciated prices from needy farmers and soldiers. Farmers and soldiers would invest their profits in land and slaves; speculators were far more likely to invest in commerce and manufactures, which Hamilton regarded as the sinews of modern power. His Report also proposed a national bank, where the government could deposit excess revenue and in turn see to it that bank loans went exclusively to commercial and manufacturing projects. Finally, in a separate Report on Manufactures that Congress ultimately defeated, Hamilton advocated direct subsidies to critical manufactures. Thus, Hamilton would encourage a modern balanced economy and provide the wherewithal for a strong military and a powerful, heroic nation.

Since Great Britain supplied 90 percent of the imports on which the tariff would be levied, Hamilton argued against commercial retaliation for fear of starting a tariff war. (Subsidies rather than high protective duties would encourage American manufacturers to compete with the British.) France, Spain, and the Netherlands could not replace the immense volume of British trade because they could not furnish credit. Worse yet, a tariff war could lead to a shooting war, and Great Britain was the one European power with enough naval strength to support an invasion of the United States from its adjacent province of Canada. It would be better to appease Britain, perhaps even ally with it to force the Spanish to open the Mississippi. Then, in fifty years or so, a more mature United States could turn to the task of teaching Great Britain "moderation."

James Madison also supported a strong national government, but he did not aspire to heroism for himself or his nation. Where Hamilton strutted, Madison stooped. Where Hamilton was a dandy, Madison wore sober black. Where Hamilton was a soldier, Madison was a scholar. Madison spoke so softly his colleagues in the House of Representatives had to crowd around his desk to hear his speeches. He insisted to the House that commercial retaliation was a viable weapon. The British West Indies would starve without American foodstuffs. Manufacturers and workers in Britain's home islands would suffer terrribly if deprived of their American market. Americans would suffer far less from an interruption of the British trade because theirs was a self-sufficient agricultural economy. American citizens were virtuous, independent republican farmers who could feed, clothe, and house themselves without foreign help and who were willing to sacrifice for liberty and national dignity. The British, on the other hand, had been corrupted and made effeminate by manufacturing and trading in luxuries. They were dependent on the United States for necessities, where America got from the British only dispensable "gew-gaws."

Madison disdained Hamilton's warnings that commercial retaliation and the potential loss of tariff revenue might destroy the funding system, the national bank, and Hamilton's entire financial system. Madison would not mourn the collapse of Hamilton's financial program because he regarded it as overblown, corrupt, and inclining toward the same dependence on luxuries, speculation, and vice that plagued the British economy. Madison did not oppose trade and shipping, but he wanted only enough to carry off America's agricultural surplus and return with imported necessities. Trade in luxury goods was debilitating. To expand American shipping to the point that it would dominate the carrying trade of other nations was to invite conflict and war.

Madison did not oppose manufacturing either, but he wanted only limited home manufacturing of necessities for domestic consumption. Like many people of the eighteenth century, he asssociated large-scale manufacturing for export with extremes of luxury and aristocracy on the one hand and poverty-stricken masses and vice on the other. These ideas derived from the first large manufacturing establishments of that century, which tended to be workhouses, where minor criminals and the poor were forced to earn their keep, or royal establishments like the Gobelin factory, which produced magnificent tapestries for the French court. Madison and his friend Jefferson feared that Hamilton's attempt to subsidize manufactures would lead to the same extremes of poverty and wealth, the same division between a foppish upper class and a vicious, dependent urban laboring class as they believed already existed in England. Madison and Jefferson also did not believe that commercial retaliation would risk much harm to America. They thought Great Britain would cave in quickly, and in the meantime the few imports America truly needed could be supplied by France and Holland. British credit led only to an unhealthy dependence on British trade and an excessive volume of luxury goods.

By 1793, Madison had organized a faction of Congress in permanent opposition to Hamilton's program. This faction feared that Hamilton was forming a "corrupt squadron" in Congress made up of speculators whose financial position was in the hands of the secretary of the treasury and whose votes could be manipulated much as prime ministers like Robert Walpole had manipulated the British Parliament. Madison's allies were angry that Hamilton favored trade, shipping, and manufacturing over agriculture, and thus northeastern interests over those of the agricultural South and West. Yet so long as the issues remained complicated economic ones, they failed to strike much spark among the people at large, who preferred to trust that President Washington was doing the right thing.

Then events abroad made the issue of commercial retaliation against Great Britain dramatic and vital enough to galvanize even ordinary people into action and expand congressional factions into grassroots parties. First, the French Revolution, which all Americans had cheered in its early stages, took a sharp turn toward radicalism and violence in 1793 with the execution of the king and large numbers of the nobility. Hamilton's Federalists, some of whom had been part of the anti-French faction during the American Revolution, were generally conservatives who disliked radical and anticlerical tendencies. This attitude further reinforced their inclination to avoid offending Britain. The Republicans, on the other hand, led by members of the former pro-French faction of the Continental Congress, emphasized the kinship between the French and American revolutions, accused the Federalists of favoring Great Britain from monarchical and aristocratic sentiments, and continued to urge retaliation against the British.

Shortly after the execution of Louis XVI, France declared war on England and began still another world conflagration. American policies toward Britain and France now involved not just financial consequences or democratic sympathies, but national survival. The United States was "perpetually" bound by its treaties of alliance with France, which required America to defend French possessions in the Western Hemisphere should France request it. The alliance also gave France special privileges in American ports that were to be denied to France's enemies. Adherence to this alliance could quite easily lead to war with England; renouncing it would bring at least some danger of war with France. The vast majority of Americans still sympathized with France and its revolution; but they also wanted political isolation from Europe, the commercial benefits of foreign trade, and above all, peace. Washington, Hamilton, Madison, Jefferson, and their colleagues would have to put together a policy consistent with this rather paradoxical consensus.

Virtually the only thing they could agree upon was that the United States should remain neutral. None of the major leaders wanted to join the European fight, however strong their sympathies for England or France. The form American neutrality should take, however, became a source of bitter controversy between Federalists and Republicans. Hamilton advised President Washington to practice absolute impartiality. He wanted to renounce the French alliance and make an immediate public declaration of neutrality. This would allay the natural suspicions of Great Britain that the United States meant to go to war on the side of its French ally. Perhaps then America could avoid a break with its most important source of supplies and revenue. Jefferson, on the other hand, said America should not declare neutrality, but bargain with it. Great Britain should be threatened rather than bribed. Keep the French alliance, and when the British, who could not afford another enemy, came to beg for American neutrality, demand that they abandon the Northwest posts, open the West Indies to American ships, and respect neutral rights. If, in accordance with the alliance, the French did request American intervention to protect their Western Hemisphere possessions, there would be time enough to remind them that the United States did not have the army or navy to do so.

Washington compromised. He issued a Proclamation of Neutrality, as Hamilton wished.[2] But he refused to renounce the French alliance. Instead, he recognized the legitimacy of the new revolutionary government in France and received the new French minister, Citizen Edmund Genêt. He assumed that the Proclamation of Neutrality made it apparent to both the French and the British that the United States would not honor the alliance to the point of endangering America's peace. Jefferson and Madison remained opposed to this tepid form of neutrality, but Washington was so revered by his constituents that Jefferson and Madison could not risk a frontal attack on his policies. Their opposition had to take the form of minor quibbles about Washington's failure to consult Congress before declaring neutrality.

Jefferson and Madison had to abandon even this caviling when the tactless Genêt embarrassed them and the other friends of France. Lacking the prudence of the Republican leaders, Genêt openly defied Washington's narrow interpretation of America's obligation to its French ally. He recuited American citizens to fight against the British and used American ports to fit out captured British merchant ships as raiders. He even threatened to instigate an American uprising against Washington if the president hampered his efforts. An outraged Washington demanded Genêt's recall. The discredited French envoy wisely chose to retire quickly to New York, where he married the daughter of Governor George Clinton and thus avoided the guillotine that might well have awaited him had he returned to France.

By dampening some of America's pro-French fervor, the Genêt incident strengthened Washington's hopes for neutrality. Genêt had already boosted those hopes when he had revealed that France had no intention of asking the

---

[2] Ironically, in deference to Jefferson's opposition, the word "neutrality" was omitted from the text of the proclamation.

United States to join the war in defense of the French West Indies. The United States was far more valuable to France as a neutral. French ships and trade were largely swept from the sea by the superior British navy. The Americans, however, had the universally recognized right as neutrals to trade with warring nations. They could rescue France from economic collapse by carrying on the vital trade with the French colonies. Naturally, the British tried to interrupt this effort. They repeatedly devised legal technicalities to narrow the range of neutral rights. They knew they could rely on their navy rather than international law to protect their own commerce. The disputes occasioned by their defiance of America's concept of neutral rights destroyed all hope that the United States might enjoy an easy and profitable neutrality and soon brought the two nations to the brink of war.

France and the United States, as nations with small navies, had taken the precaution of writing a broad spectrum of neutral rights into their treaties of alliance and commerce during the revolution. They had agreed that "free ships meant free goods." Under this doctrine, a neutral ship could carry almost everything, including enemy property, to a nation at war. The British adhered to an older doctrine which gave them the right to confiscate enemy property wherever it was found. The United States protested in vain, since Britain had the bigger guns. But American shippers found a clever way around their dilemma; they bought the French property. This meant Americans were carrying neutral goods aboard neutral ships, which was legal by any definition.

The British cried "fraud" because Americans often paid far less than the goods were worth, after arranging in advance to sell them for less on arrival in France. The Americans in this way would collect only the equivalent of their shipping costs. The British then found another way to interrupt American trade. International law permitted Britain to confiscate as contraband any war materiel headed for an enemy port even if the ship and cargo were owned by neutrals. The British simply expanded their definition of contraband to classify food as war materiel because it was necessary to the enemy. To assuage American anger, they offered to pay for any food they confiscated, but the issue continued to rankle.

The British still thought too much trade was getting through to the French. So they appealed to a supposed Rule of 1756 to stop neutral ships carrying goods from the French West Indies to France. The Rule of 1756, a British creation, declared that trade closed to foreigners in time of peace could not be opened in time of war. Since direct trade between France and the French West Indies had been monopolized by France under its mercantilist system, opening it to Americans after hostilities broke out was an act of war, one the British claimed the right to counteract. Soon the Americans steered around this as well. Since trade between the United States and the French islands had been open in peacetime, as had trade between the United States and France, American ships simply detoured to America on their way between the West Indies and France. Thus they were no longer following a route that had been closed before the war.

At this point the frustrated British abandoned all niceties. They were worried by a sudden flood of supplies being sent off by French islanders trying to salvage the goods from a terrible slave uprising. In late 1793 the British declared an illegal blockade of the French West Indies. Without informing the Americans of their new policy, they swooped down upon nearly three hundred unsuspecting American ships and forced them into British ports for trial before British admiralty courts. At the same time that news of this outrage reached the American government, newspapers were printing a speech by the British governor of Canada to the Northwest Indians. He said war was imminent between England and the United States and pledged British support in expelling American settlers from the Ohio Valley.

Again Federalists and Republicans quarrelled over the proper response to these threats. Hamilton and his group urged Washington to send a friendly negotiator to Britain to iron out the differences between the two nations. Jefferson, Madison, and the Republicans argued that America should first cut off trade with the British so the envoy could bargain from strength. Federalists insisted that this would antagonize the British without accomplishing much, since the United States needed trade with Great Britain more than the British, and the British knew it. Federalists argued instead for military preparations. They especially wanted to hurry construction of six frigates already being built for use against the Barbary pirates.

Washington sided with the Federalists. He appointed John Jay, second only to Hamilton in prestige among the Federalists, to be the special envoy. Jay immediately warned Congress against any hostile commercial measures prior to the negotiations. The House of Representatives, at the urging of Madison, insisted on a nonintercourse act against Britain. Only the tie-breaking vote of John Adams defeated it in the Senate. Congress then passed a temporary embargo to prevent American ships from leaving port and so removed such targets from the seas in case of war. Since the embargo affected trade with all nations, not just England, Jay was able to approach his negotiations in the conciliatory posture he thought suitable. He would try to persuade the British that America was truly neutral and not intent on helping the French. America's measures of military preparedness would serve as subtle reminders that failure to reach agreement would mean almost certain war. He was convinced that overt threats could add nothing to this leverage and might sabotage agreement by convincing the British that America was inveterately hostile to them.

Historians ever since have wondered whether a more assertive approach might have won a better agreement than Jay was able to negotiate. The British may have thought him easy to manipulate. One British official who knew him advised the British negotiator that Jay "argues closely but is long-winded and self-opinionated. He can bear any opposition to what he advances provided that regard is shown to his abilities. He may be attached by good treatment, but will be unforgiving if he thinks himself neglected . . . almost every man has a weak and assailable quarter and Mr. Jay's weak side is *Mr. Jay.*" Jay apparently never attempted to use threats. Had he tried that approach, he would have found that Alexander Hamilton had already undermined the credibility of his major threat. The secretary of the treasury indiscreetly and secretly informed the British minister to the United States that America would not join other neutrals in Europe who were contemplating a league to resist with force British searches and seizures on the high seas.

Certainly Jay's results were less than sensational. True, the British returned the Northwest posts. They also opened the West Indies to small American ships, although they hedged the concession with so many limitations that the Senate rejected the proposition. The British also agreed to compensate Americans for illegal captures of ships during the blockade of the West Indies. The amount of damages would be set by a neutral commission. Another such commission would settle the disputes that had arisen over the location of the Canadian-American border. Of course, the greatest benefit of the Jay Treaty was that it would maintain the peace between Great Britain and the United States.

But Jay paid a high price. There was no agreement on neutral rights, so British ships would continue to disrupt Franco-American trade. Americans would be bound to pay off their prewar debts to the extent decided by a neutral commission. Above all, Jay had agreed to sacrifice the one weapon Republicans believed might have coerced a better agreement from the British—the treaty prohibited any change in the regulation of Anglo-American trade for ten years.

Historians with access to the British archives have generally agreed, however, that Jay obtained about as much as the British had been willing to give. The English could hardly undermine their war against France by bowing to the American view of neutral rights. Some figures high in the British cabinet were adamantly opposed even to those concessions Jay did win. The Republicans, nevertheless, were livid. They thought the Jay Treaty was a sellout, a purposeful attempt of pro-British Federalists to aid England by permitting interruption of the neutral trade vital to the French war effort. If the United States had used its economic weapons instead of bargaining them away for a pittance, Britain might have conceded America's neutral rights. The Federalists could only respond that unsatisfactory as the treaty was, it was better than the alternative of war. The debate ultimately stirred such emotions among the general population that it turned the two congressional factions into grassroots parties with mass followings and semi-permanent organizations.

At first the public debate was rather tentative because it was based on unsubstantiated rumors of the terms Jay had accepted in London, terms kept secret during the Senate deliberations. This changed once the Senate consented to the treaty by a vote of twenty to ten, precisely the two-thirds vote necessary. Some Republicans immediately broke the seal of silence, and newspapers published the treaty terms around the country. The treaty aroused a chorus of criticism. Congressional Republicans urged their local followers to take advantage of the situation by organizing mass meetings and signing petitions to Washington to ignore the Senate's advice and refuse ratification. Hamilton attempted to address a hostile meeting in New York and was stoned by the crowd, causing one Federalist to remark that it was the first sensible thing the Republicans had done; by dashing out Hamilton's brains, they might reduce him to an equality with themselves. Jay lamented that he could have found his way from Charleston to Boston at midnight by the light of his burning effigies.

Washington was deeply offended by the pressures the Republicans and their petitions brought on him. But he had been disappointed at the treaty himself. At the urging of Edmund Randolph, a moderate Republican who had replaced Jefferson as secretary of state, he decided to delay ratification because the British had resumed captures of American foodstuffs. Fortuitously for the Federalists, they found a way to change his mind. A British ship had recently captured some dispatches en route to France from the French minister to the United States. These dispatches seemed to implicate Secretary Randolph in a convoluted bribery scheme. The British turned them over to his Federalist enemies and they showed them to Washington. This convinced the president to fire Randolph and immediately ratify the treaty.

On the face of it, Washington's ratification should have completed the constitutional process of treaty-making. But Republicans controlled the House of Representatives and saw one last chance to defeat the Jay Treaty. Since all money bills had to originate in the House, Madison and the other Republican leaders organized an attempt to refuse the appropriations necessary to implement the treaty. Again they launched a campaign of mass meetings and petitions, hoping to influence the votes of wavering House members. This time, however, the Federalists abandoned their aristocratic disdain for such methods and matched the Republicans meeting for meeting and petition for petition. The Federalists warned that rejection of the treaty would mean a devastating war with England. Slowly they turned the tide of public opinion in their favor and used their increasing popular support to frighten some fence-sitters. The Republican majority in the House melted. One intimidated Congressman decided he had to leave the House to mail a trunk. When the Committee of the Whole took the critical vote, the result was a tie. The tie-breaking vote rested in the hands of the chairman of the committee, a Pennsylvania Republican named Frederick Muhlenberg. A passionate Federalist had warned Muhlenberg earlier that a vote against the treaty would doom the prospective match between Muhlenberg's son and the Federalist's daughter. Whether that threat had any influence or not, Muhlenberg voted for the treaty.

The treaty fight was over, but the party battle endured. The Republicans used the party organization they had developed in the struggle to promote Thomas Jefferson against Federalist Vice-President John Adams as successor to the retiring President Washington. The Federalists considered such organized opposition to be dangerous and disloyal, particularly because the French were openly supporting Jefferson in hopes of overturning the treaty with Great Britain. Washington agreed and assisted by Hamilton, composed a Farewell Address to caution his countrymen against the dangers of parties and foreign intrigue. He did not advocate violation of the French alliance, but warned against any extension of it. The United States should have as little political connection with Europe as possible. It should build its own unity and strength, steer clear of permanent alliances, and accept temporary alliances only for extraordinary emergencies. Although many Republicans were not yet convinced of the wisdom of Washington's advice, the address quickly entered the realm of American gospel. Americans printed it in children's schoolbooks, engraved it on watches, and wove it into tapestries. The Farewell Address was a ringing blow in the struggle between neutrality and foreign alliances.

Despite Washington's endorsement, John Adams found himself in a neck-and-neck race for the presidency. Gone were the days when a president could be elected unanimously. The Republicans used the emotional reactions to the French Revolution and the Jay Treaty to mobilize a large and organized vote for their candidates. But Adams could point to some Federalist accomplishments in foreign policy that were not so controversial as the Jay Treaty. Thomas Pinckney, Washington's minister to Spain, forced concessions from the Spanish by playing on their fear that the negotiation of the Jay Treaty might produce an Anglo-American alliance aimed at their North American possessions. The Spanish were susceptible to such fears because they had just withdrawn from their alliance with Great Britain to make a separate peace with France. In 1795, Pinckney concluded the Treaty of San Lorenzo with Spain, a treaty known familiarly in America as the Pinckney Treaty. It finally opened the Mississippi to American navigation and settled the boundary of Florida at 31° in line with the claims of the United States. The Pinckney Treaty was so popular that the Federalists threatened to stall its ratification as a means to force congressional acceptance of the Jay Treaty.

In addition to the Pinckney Treaty, Adams and the Federalists could brag about the victory of General "Mad Anthony" Wayne over the Northwest Indians at Fallen Timbers in 1794. This resulted in the Treaty of Greenville of 1795, which opened much of the Ohio Valley to American settlement. These two boons to American expansion, the Pinckney and Greenville treaties, along with the swing of public opinion in favor of the Jay Treaty, permitted Adams to defeat Jefferson by the slim margin of three electoral votes.

JOHN ADAMS AND THE QUASI-WAR OF 1798

With this narrow mandate, Adams faced a formidable problem. While the Jay Treaty preserved peace with Great Britain, it also came close to provoking war with France. The French economy depended on America's neutral trade. Great Britain would now interrupt a large portion of that trade with impunity because the United States had not forced British recognition of the broad spectrum of neutral rights embodied in the Franco-American treaties. In retaliation, the French announced a new version of the Golden Rule—they would do to the Americans whatever the Americans permitted the British to do. Under this rubric, they detained or captured over three hundred American ships suspected of carrying British goods.

Adams decided to treat the French just as his predecessor had handled the British. He urged naval appropriations and authority to increase the army, avoided commercial retaliation, and sent emissaries to France to negotiate. To avoid Republican charges that the diplomatic mission would be a partisan one anxious to sabotage the negotiations in order to justify war against France, Adams asked first Jefferson and then Madison to be one of the envoys. Both rejected the appointment, so Adams sent another Republican, his old Massachusetts friend Elbridge Gerry. Gerry would join two Federalists, John Marshall and Charles Cotesworth Pinckney, to demonstrate that the mission would negotiate in good faith.

Unfortunately, the French were not ready to accept the mission in a similar spirit. The new French foreign minister, the Marquis de Talleyrand, did not want war. But he thought France would benefit if prolonged negotiations allowed partisan quarrels to weaken the United States while French ships continued their plundering. He sent three underlings to inform the American delegates that they would have to explain away the Jay Treaty's supposed betrayal of the French alliance, approve an American government loan to France, and pay a bribe before they would be permitted to open official negotiations. When finally convinced that Talleyrand was serious, the two Federalists indignantly reported their reception to Adams and left the country. Gerry, however, remained in France at Talleyrand's urging to forestall a complete breakdown of relations and possible war. His was a praiseworthy effort, but one that encouraged the Republicans in Congress to suspect that the Federalists themselves had provoked the crisis. The Republicans demanded that Adams turn over the delegation's correspondence to prove otherwise. Adams confounded them by doing so, substituting for the names of the three French underlings who had requested the bribes the letters X, Y, and Z. The XYZ Affair destroyed almost all pro-French sentiment in America, discredited the Republicans, and rallied the nation around Adams, who now called for military preparations.

Yet the president did not request an immediate declaration of war. Instead, he ordered American naval vessels to retaliate against French attackers. A two-year quasi-war followed, in which there were numerous small-scale naval engagements resulting in the capture of eighty-five French ships. Meanwhile, Congress enacted additional taxes, authorized construction of ships for the newly created naval department, and voted to raise a 50,000-man army whose command Adams gave to the one man who could unite Federalists and Republicans in a war against France, George Washington. Without Adams's encouragement, Congress also passed the Alien and Sedition Acts, giving the government extraordinary powers to silence Republican dissent that might undermine the war effort and just incidentally overturn the Federalists in the next elections.

To the surprise of many, Adams never did carry through with the war. Although he was second to none in his dislike of France, he disliked Great

Britain as well. His inclination against war was further dampened when Washington insisted that Hamilton be promoted over the heads of all other officers to be inspector-general and second in command of the army. Not only was Hamilton too pro-British for Adams's taste, but Hamilton had tried to manipulate the electoral vote to elevate the Federalist vice-presidential candidate over Adams into the presidency. Then, following the appointment of Hamilton that Washington had coerced from Adams, Hamilton whirled through the capital urging Congress to appropriate less money for the navy than Adams had requested and to give it instead to the army. Hamilton dreamed of leading this army on an expedition against the Spanish border colonies and beyond, supported by the British navy and by Latin American rebels under the leadership of Francisco de Miranda.

Understandably, Adams was relieved when he heard from reliable sources in Europe, including his own son John Quincy Adams, that Talleyrand wanted peace and was ready to accept with dignity a new American negotiator. Adams immediately appointed one in defiance of his own cabinet, many of whose members were holdovers from Washington's administration and more beholden to Hamilton than to their own president. They and other "high Federalists" insisted that since France had so rudely rejected the previous emissaries, Adams should require that France send a delegation to the United States. Some of them made this demand in the hope that it would bring war with France. Hamilton's own motives are not so clear. Nevertheless, Adams's appointment of an envoy to France split his party. The peace with France also gave Americans a chance to reconsider and resent the taxes and the Alien and Sedition Acts passed in expectation of war. The way was paved for Jefferson and the Republicans to defeat Adams in the election of 1800.

Adams took his defeat hard. He left the capital immediately on the expiration of his term of office without even participating in Jefferson's inaugural. He believed he had sacrificed his political career and reputation in pursuit of the right and said he desired nothing more on his gravestone than the inscription "Here lies John Adams, who took upon himself the responsibility of the peace with France in the year 1800." Recent historians have cast some doubt on Adams's claim to transcendent moral courage. They cite evidence that public opinion was already moving toward peace when Adams made his decision, and that his defeat would have been even more likely had he taken America to war. That debate probably never will be settled. But it is indisputable that the XYZ Affair and the quasi-war ended the Republicans' emotional attachment to France. The Federalists never tired of claiming that the Republicans were the treacherous tools of French policy, but actually Republicans too were ready to accept the advice of Washington's Farewell Address.

Jefferson announced in his Inaugural Address that America sought "peace, commerce, and honest friendship with all nations, entangling alliances with none." Even the French alliance would no longer challenge this unanimous sentiment for nonentanglement. That alliance had been terminated by the Treaty of Mortefontaine, the pact that ended the quasi-war. The United States would not sign another treaty of alliance until World War II.

EXPANSIONISM IN EARLY AMERICAN DIPLOMACY

The primary theme of American diplomacy in this era was defensive, a striving for survival, independence, and respect in the relations of the United States with the formidable powers of Europe. Accompanying this was a secondary theme, the hunger for expansion. Occasionally this secondary theme surfaced in a dramatic fashion. During the Confederation period, for instance, Congress had established a format for governing new territories, the Northwest Ordinances. The ordinances imposed congressional rule on inhabitants of the territories and deprived them of full self-determination, but promised to bring them into the Union as equal states once they had achieved sufficient population and agreed to a republican form of government. This arrangement, remarkably liberal in an age when the only known means of governing new territories was an empire dominating colonies, gave Americans confidence that they could acquire new lands without breeding the same problems England had faced with its American colonies.

At least this would be the case so long as the alien inhabitants of these new lands, be they Indians or the colonists of a foreign power, were few enough that their natural resentment against the American conquerers could be overwhelmed by American settlers moving into the territory. The Northwest Territories themselves were a major arena for this expansionist process. Settlers swarmed into the Ohio Valley and intruded on Indian lands. The army inevitably followed to suppress Indian resistance and negotiate a treaty solidifying United States government control. The Department of War rather than the Department of State conducted all such diplomacy with the Indians under the assumption, dominant throughout Europe, that Indians were not totally sovereign over their lands. Indians were what the Supreme Court later called "domestic dependent nations," entitled to negotiate treaties only with the truly sovereign state whose claims were recognized as valid by the European powers.

Thus, the United States had the so-called right of preemption over the Northwest Territories, and legally the Indians of the area could negotiate only with the American government. Great Britain had maintained agents with those tribes, supplied them, traded with them, encouraged their resistance, and even sought to negotiate an Indian border state with the Americans. This project would have reserved for the Indians a broad swath of land south of the Canadian border extending from the Great Lakes to the Atlantic. The Indian border state would be guaranteed jointly by Britain and the United States. The United States resisted this British demand because the border state would have been formed entirely from land claimed by the United States, without any Canadian territory being sacrificed, and because it would permanently bar American access to the Great Lakes and the St.

Lawrence. Wayne's victory at Fallen Timbers and the near clash of his army with the British at Detroit put an end to this British project for the time being, much to the distress of the Indians, who had hoped to keep their lands.

American expansionism also showed up as a minor theme in the Constitution. One of the primary arguments of the opponents of the Constitution was that a republican form of government was appropriate only in a small area. In a small area, a homogeneous population could come to an easy consensus and make rule by elective legislatures possible. A larger area, opponents insisted, required a stronger, more arbitrary rule by a monarch to hold its disparate peoples together. James Madison countered this in his famous Federalist Paper No. 10, arguing that a republic could actually survive better in a large area than a small one. The multiple interests and factions in a large area could prevent the tyranny of a permanent majority so likely to arise in a small, homogeneous area. Some historians have seen this argument as a significant blueprint for imperialism. But Madison was not so much arguing to accommodate expansion as he was trying to convince the American people that the United States could rule that territory it already had in a republican yet efficient manner. Expansion may have been in the back of the minds of Madison and many other Americans, but survival, independence, and neutrality were in the forefront.

CONTROVERSIAL ISSUES AND FURTHER READING

The conflict between Federalists and Republicans over American foreign policy still stirs considerable passion among historians, although few go so far as to join the partisans of the 1790s and some early American historians to accuse opponents of having been the willing dupes of a foreign power. [For the rather rare examples of this, see the mid-nineteenth-century multivolume histories of the United States by pro-Republican James Schouler and pro-Federalists Richard Hildreth and Hermann Von Holst.] Increasingly, historians see these accusations as near-paranoia produced by the relative newness of the concept of a loyal opposition and the suspiciousness encouraged by libertarian thought of the time. [See John Howe, "Republican Thought and the Political Violence of the 1790's," *American Quarterly*, 19 (Summer 1967); and James H. Hutson, *John Adams and the Diplomacy of the American Revolution* (1980).] Still, many studies of this period remain rather strongly partisan in outlook.

Samuel Flagg Bemis established the standard for research in this period. His *Jay's Treaty* (1923) and *Pinckney's Treaty* (1926) thoroughly exploited foreign as well as American archives. A strong nationalist, Bemis praised the Republicans for their desire to stand up against England, but doubted the efficacy of their means, commercial retaliation. He also disapproved of their reliance on France, although he made clear that Jefferson and Madison were far from French sycophants. He disapproved even more heartily of the Hamiltonian maneuverings on behalf of Great Britain, and praised instead the prudent but sturdy independence of men like Washington and Adams, who best enabled the United States to wring American benefits from European distress.

Rather than debating whether Jeffersonian Republicans were too pro-French or Hamiltonian Federalists too pro-British, more recent historians have argued over which were the more realistic in their foreign policy. Paul A. Varg's survey, *The Foreign Policies of the Founding Fathers* (1963), portrays the Federalists as realists and the Republicans as hapless idealists. Varg is heartily seconded by Charles R. Ritcheson, *Aftermath of Revolution* (1969), based on thorough research in the British documents, and Gilbert Lycan, *Alexander Hamilton and American Foreign Policy* (1970). My own book, Jerald A. Combs, *The Jay Treaty* (1970), attempts some corrective to this interpretation by arguing that there were some realistic aspects to the Jeffersonian approach and that while Hamilton may have been a realist in some of his diplomacy, he was rash and romantic in much that he did.

Significant works by Alexander De Conde and Albert Hall Bowman take a much more Republican view of things. They praise the Jeffersonians for their idealism and claim that the Republicans managed to combine that idealism with realism, while the Hamiltonian Federalists were simply cynical and devious reactionaries. [Alexander De Conde, *Entangling Alliance* (1958) and its sequel, *The Quasi-War* (1966), and Albert Hall Bowman, *The Struggle for Neutrality* (1974). An important challenge to Bowman is William Stinchcombe, *The XYZ Affair* (1980). All these books make excellent use of the French archives.]

There have been only a few extensive radical treatments of early American diplomacy asserting that expansion rather than neutrality was the primary theme of these years. William Appleman Williams gave the expansionist interpretation of Madison's stand on the Constitution in his *Contours of American History* (1961). Jack Ericson Eblen used American territorial government to demonstrate the undemocratic, imperial tendencies of the United States in *The First and Second United States Empires* (1968). Burton I. Kaufman rather unsuccessfully sought expansionist overtones in "Washington's Farewell Address: A Statement of Empire," in Kaufman, ed., *Washington's Farewell Address: The View from the 20th Century* (1969). [For a history of this period emphasizing expansion but from a more traditional view, see Richard Van Alstyne, *The Rising American Empire* (1960), or Arthur Burr Darling, *Our Rising Empire* (1940).]

Drew R. McCoy, *The Elusive Republic* (1980), gives a fascinating analysis of the ideological and economic premises behind the clash of the Hamiltonian and Jeffersonian systems. Arthur P. Whitaker's *The Spanish-American Frontier* (1927) is still excellent on the events leading to the Pinckney Treaty. Frederick W. Marks's *Independence on Trial* (1973) is the most recent work on the role of foreign affairs in the Confederation period and the making of the Constitution. Stephen Kurtz makes the argument that John Adams was not defying but responding to popular opinion when he made peace with France in his book, *The Presidency of John Adams* (1957).

CHAPTER 3

Republican Diplomacy: The Louisiana Purchase and the War of 1812

LOUISIANA AND FLORIDA

Jefferson's dedication to "peace, commerce, and honest friendship with all nations, entangling alliances with none" was quickly put to the test. Shortly after he took office, he received disturbing information that Napoleon had forced Spain to sign a secret treaty retroceding Louisiana to France. Spanish control of New Orleans and the mouth of the Mississippi might be tolerable because Spain posed little threat to the United States. It also had committed itself in the Pinckney Treaty of 1795 to allow American navigation of the river. France in control of the Father of Waters would be an entirely different proposition. Not only was France a formidable power and Napoleon a ruthless expansionist, but there was no guarantee that France would feel itself bound by the Pinckney Treaty. Indeed, there was ominous evidence to the contrary. Spain suddenly announced that it was suspending the right of Americans to deposit goods from their Mississippi flatboats at New Orleans for transfer to ocean-going vessels. This violation of the Pinckney Treaty would render the right to navigate the river useless. Naturally, Jefferson assumed that Napoleon had instigated the Spanish decision, although historians have found nothing to indicate this in the French or Spanish archives.

The outcry from the West and Jefferson's Federalist opponents was immediate. Jefferson instructed the American minister in Paris, Robert R. Livingston, to try to purchase New Orleans from France and to acquire Florida as well if possible. This would assure American control of the Mississippi's mouth. To add to Napoleon's incentive to sell New Orleans, Jefferson indicated that upon French occupation of the city, the United States "would marry itself to the British fleet." This may not have been pure bluff; Jefferson did order America's minister in Great Britain to open negotiations for an alliance without further instructions if France took New Orleans and closed the Mississippi. Clearly Jefferson was no ideologue. He had moved rapidly from embracing the French alliance to a statement of nonentanglement comparable to Washington's, and now he was considering an alliance with Great Britain.

Few historians believe that Jefferson's threats much affected Napoleon's plans for Louisiana, but events in the West Indies did. Napoleon had ear-marked Louisiana to be the source of foodstuffs and lumber for France's im-mensely profitable sugar islands, just as the United States had served that purpose for Britain's Caribbean islands before the revolution. But the slave rebellion of Toussaint L'Ouverture on the main French island of Santo Do-mingue undermined the potential rewards of Napoleon's dream. Yellow fever and rebel attacks decimated the armies he sent to put down the revolu-tion, so Napoleon capriciously decided to get rid of his newly acquired white elephant, Louisiana. He would not return it to Spain, though his treaty of retrocession with that country required that he do so if ever France parted with it. Instead, he decided to sell it to the United States.

At first Livingston hesitated. He had instructions to buy New Orleans and Florida for $10 million, not to spend $25 million for Louisiana. But with the support of James Monroe, the newly arrived special envoy, Livingston of-fered Napoleon $15 million, and Louisiana became American territory. Liv-ingston was only chagrined that he had to share credit for his coup with Monroe. America received his unauthorized action ecstatically, and Jeffer-son's popularity soared. Even Federalist leaders like Alexander Hamilton, John Adams, and John Marshall endorsed the purchase, although a good many other prominent Federalists denounced it.

Federalist opponents doubted that a Republican government could effec-tively govern so vast an area, and they feared that the civilized East would lose its political supremacy to the barbaric West. Jefferson brushed this op-

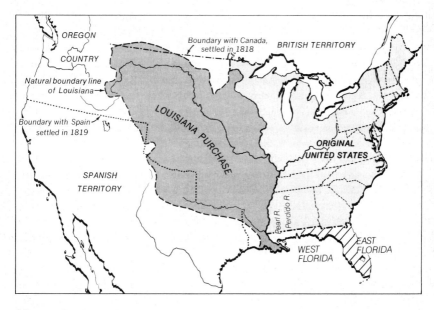

Map 2 Louisiana Purchase, 1803

position aside, along with whatever uneasiness he may have felt about the federal government acquiring territory without a constitutional amendment permitting it to do so. When Spain complained that the purchase violated France's promise not to alienate the territory to any third party, Jefferson told the Spanish to take their complaints to Napoleon. The United States, he reminded them, had never been privy to the agreement between France and Spain. He welcomed the opportunity Louisiana offered to guarantee the availability of land in the United States for years to come, thus ensuring the supremacy of agricultural interests in the political councils of the nation. He even began to contemplate the use of the purchase as leverage for further expansion.

This opportunity arose because Louisiana's borders were extremely vague. France had sold the province to America with the borders "it now has in the hands of Spain, and that it had when France possessed it." Ever since Spain had acquired Louisiana in 1763, West Florida had been administered as a separate entity. But Livingston and Monroe discovered that France had ruled the Florida territory up to the Perdido River as part of Louisiana prior to 1763. They advised Jefferson that he might use their discovery as a precedent to claim West Florida as part of the Louisiana Purchase. This required the Americans to argue that, in historian Henry Adams's pungent phrase, "Spain had retroceded West Florida to France without knowing it, that France had sold it to the United States without suspecting it, that the United States had bought it without paying for it, and that neither France nor Spain, although the original contracting parties, were competent to decide the meaning of their own contract."

The Americans seemed to make this claim without embarrassment. Talleyrand, the French foreign minister who sold them Louisiana, even encouraged them in their convoluted case. When asked the boundaries of Louisiana he professed ignorance, and archly told the American negotiators: "You have made a noble bargain for yourselves, and I suppose you will make the most of it." Jefferson did. He constantly pressed Spain to relinquish West Florida, and sought East Florida as well. At his direction, Congress established a customs district that encompassed most of West Florida. He pressed Napoleon to intervene with Spain on America's behalf and got a secret appropriation from Congress of $2 million with which to bribe the French leader. He even toyed briefly with the possibility of a British alliance to confront Spain and France should all else fail. Finally, in 1810, James Madison brought this unseemly effort to a climax. He took advantage of the invitation of a small group of American rebels in West Florida to occupy some of the area not actually garrisoned by Spanish troops. Congress excused the action on the grounds that Britain, then warring with France and Spain, might interfere in the Floridas.

Jefferson could be more straightforward with the Barbary pirates than he had been with Spain and France. Although he generally sought ways to gain American objectives without actual warfare, he was far from a doctrinaire pacifist. He had argued for using naval force against the pirates since the

Figure 3 Thomas Jefferson (left) and his secretary of state (later president) James Madison were the key figures in making American foreign policy after the Jeffersonian Republican party defeated the Federalists in 1800. Portraits courtesy of the National Archives.

1790s, taking issue with John Adams and most of the European nations, who believed that paying ransoms was easier and cheaper in the long run. Upon becoming president, Jefferson did fulfill his campaign promise to reduce naval expenditures to a minimum, even to the extent of replacing existing larger warships with ineffective coastal gunboats. But he sent the navy into the Mediterranean against the North African corsairs. After some sensational exploits, including Stephen Decatur's burning of the captured American ship *Philadelphia* in Tripoli harbor and an overland desert expedition led by William Eaton, the Barbary states accepted a temporary truce. The piratical career of those states was not finally ended, however, until after the War of 1812, when the joint efforts of the American navy and an Anglo-Dutch fleet extorted a permanent peace.

JEFFERSON AND GREAT BRITAIN: THE EMBARGO

Jefferson's difficulties with Great Britain were not so simply resolved. Relations had been pleasant enough during Jefferson's first administration for him to flirt occasionally with an Anglo-American alliance. But this happy state of affairs did not survive the resumption of the Napoleonic Wars in Europe in 1803. Once again England began interrupting America's neutral trade to France. At first these annoyances did not create a serious crisis. The Jay Treaty was still in force, and flawed as it had seemed to the Republicans, at least its terms had defined a *modus vivendi* between the two nations. Anglo-American commerce remained voluminous. The British still confiscated food as contraband, but they paid for it, so Jefferson and Madison contented themselves with nothing more than written protests. The British also allowed the United States to circumvent the Rule of 1756 and carry considerable trade between the French West Indies and France. In 1802, a British admiralty court had set a precedent in the case of the American ship *Polly* permitting French West Indies goods to be taken to France as long as they had been unloaded in America and a duty paid. The British allowed this trade despite the fact that the United States rebated almost the entire duty to the shippers when they left with their goods for France.

In 1805, British treatment of Americans stiffened. Another admiralty court decision, this time involving the ship *Essex*, set a new precedent for America's reexport trade. The court decided that any rebates given American shippers were proof that the circuitous shuttling between France, the United States, and the West Indies was a continuous voyage subject to interruption under the Rule of 1756. The *Essex* decision also transferred from the capturing vessel to the neutral ship the burden of proving that its voyage was not a continuous one. Properly interpreted, this decision only made the reexport trade more difficult; it did not stop it. But British ships enforced the decision with an overabundance of enthusiasm. Sixty-one American ships, sailing blithely in the belief that their conformance to the *Polly* case immunized them from capture, were unceremoniously hauled off to admiralty courts. American anger ran deep.

That anger intensified as 1805 also brought a substantial increase in British impressment of American seamen. The British had long used kidnapping to staff their navy, and they took British subjects as well as Americans. America had protested against the practice since colonial days, and John Jay had tried unsuccessfully to include an article against interference with American crews in his Treaty of 1794. The British, however, considered impressment essential because conditions aboard their own ships were too terrible to attract volunteers. Most earlier British impressment had been confined to crews that were ashore in Great Britain. Such seizures merely inconvenienced American shipping, however traumatic they may have been for those impressed. But when Britain began impressing men from ships already on the high seas, entire crews, cargoes, and ships suffered from being perilously undermanned. The offense to American honor and sovereignty was also more blatant. It was one thing to haul an American sailor away from a London pub; it was quite another to take him from a ship flying an American flag.

The issue was very difficult to resolve. The British never claimed the right to take American seamen, only British subjects. But the two nations disagreed on the nature of American citizenship. Britain refused to recognize America's right to make Englishmen into naturalized United States citizens. Consequently, it would not accept citizenship papers as proof of the nationality of American sailors. The United States did not want to limit its protection against impressment to sailors with citizenship papers anyway. Foreigners manned nearly 50 percent of America's merchant marine, and many of these were British deserters. To permit Great Britain to impress from aboard an American vessel any sailor who did not have citizenship papers would cripple American shipping. Thus, neither side had much incentive to compromise. The British saw impressment as a vital deterrent to desertion and a cornerstone of their naval power; the Americans saw it as a mortal insult and a threat to their prosperity.

The crisis toward which impressment and ship seizures were inevitably leading finally erupted in 1806. In a well-intentioned but maladroit action, the British cabinet of Charles James Fox sought to reduce the effects of the *Essex* decision on American trade. The cabinet announced that American ships could bring goods from the French West Indies to Europe as long as they did not try to enter French ports which the British now designated as blockaded. To pacify the hawks at home, Fox proclaimed that the blockade would extend almost the full length of Europe facing the English Channel. Quietly he let the Americans know that it would be enforced only in the narrow but strategic area bounded by the Seine and Ostend rivers. Nevertheless, the Americans were outraged by the illegal blockade. Their emotions intensified with news of the accidental killing of an American sailor by a British cannonball that had been intended as a warning shot across his ship's bow. The Republicans now faced a dilemma very similar to the one their Federalist predecessors resolved with the Jay Treaty.

Naturally they turned to the same alternative they had offered at the time of the Jay Treaty: commercial retaliation. The Republican-controlled Congress enacted the Non-Importation Act of 1806. The intention was to prohibit the importation of British goods, but the act exempted those goods the United States needed most, including cottons, cheap woolens, and iron products. Since these were also the goods Britain most wanted to sell to the United States, the Non-Importation Act would not exert much leverage. To add to this inherent weakness, the act was not to be enforced for several months. With this gesture of commercial retaliation, Jefferson was ready to bargain. He sent William Pinkney of Maryland to join James Monroe in London with instructions to negotiate a replacement for the Jay Treaty, the commercial articles of which were expiring.

Jefferson and Secretary of State Madison gave their negotiators some audacious instructions. Britain was to abandon all impressment from American ships on the high seas. The British were to treat American trade with France and the French West Indies as it had been under the *Polly* precedent. Without these concessions, there would be no agreement. Less urgently, the American negotiators were to request British adherence to "free ships, free goods" and a more limited contraband list. Jefferson even wanted the British to accept the Gulf Stream as America's boundary rather than the traditional three-mile limit. This would remove the British fleet farther from the American coast and make interruption of American trade far more difficult.

Of course Monroe and Pinkney had no hopes whatever of achieving such terms. Instead, they negotiated a severely compromised agreement, as had Jay ten years before. Britain would treat the reexport trade from the French West Indies more liberally. If West Indian goods were physically unloaded in America and a 2 percent duty paid, the goods could be reshipped to France without being condemned by the Rule of 1756. Great Britain would not make a treaty stipulation against impressment, but agreed to an official note in which it promised to use exceptional care to avoid impressment of Americans. Most of the other commercial stipulations paralleled those in the Jay Treaty, including the commitment to avoid commercial retaliation for ten years.

But half a loaf would not satisfy Jefferson and Madison, as it had their Federalist predecessors. They refused the Monroe-Pinkney Treaty of 1806 because it failed to halt impressment. They were also disturbed by a reservation the British had appended to the treaty which left Britain free to retaliate against Napoleon's new Berlin Decree, which proclaimed a blockade of the British Isles.[1] Jefferson ordered Monroe and Pinkney to renew negotiations, hoping that time and commercial pressure, such as the Non-Importation Act of 1806, would move Great Britain in America's favor.

The American envoys had no chance to negotiate a better agreement. They suspected as much, and the British records confirm their opinion. They

[1] Since Napoleon had few ships to enforce such a blockade, he would have to wait until ships that had violated the blockade and traded with England had arrived in a French-controlled port, whereupon he would confiscate them. It is interesting that Napoleon delayed enforcement of the Berlin Decree until Jefferson and Madison had rejected the Monroe-Pinkney Treaty and thereby reduced the chances of an Anglo-American settlement.

continued their bargaining, however, until the whole negotiation was interrupted by a dramatic incident that produced a fervent demand for war in the United States. In 1807, the British ship *Leopard* attacked an American naval vessel, the *Chesapeake*. The *Leopard* had demanded that the *Chesapeake* turn over four seamen suspected of being British deserters. This was the first attempted impressment from an American naval as opposed to a merchant ship. When the surprised and unprepared *Chesapeake* refused, the *Leopard* poured a series of broadsides into her hull, inflicted twenty-one casualties, and finally took the four seamen.

The British were prepared to apologize for the *Chesapeake* affair and to avoid impressment from naval vessels in the future. But Jefferson decided to use the incident to coerce Britain into abandoning all impresssment. When Britain refused to give Jefferson what it had denied to Monroe and Pinkney, the president called upon Congress to impose an embargo prohibiting all American ships and products from leaving the country. He also put the Non-Importation Act into effect. An embargo was a traditional prelude to war, a means by which a nation could retrieve and protect its shipping before the beginning of hostilities. But the Republicans, with their long devotion to commercial retaliation, also saw the embargo as a weapon in itself. It cut off trade with France as well as with Great Britain, but since both were capturing America's ships, that did not seem inappropriate. And clearly the embargo would hurt the British the most. The rival decrees of the two belligerents had already halted most trade to France, so trade with the British would be most affected. In combination with the Non-Importation Act, which was directed solely at Great Britain, perhaps the embargo would bring Britain around without the need for actual war.

Jefferson never did make clear whether he intended the embargo as a prelude to war or a substitute for it. At times he spoke as though he intended war. But he let time pass, and as the war fever dwindled in the countryside, it became doubtful that Congress would give him a declaration of war even if he wished it. Plagued by migraine headaches and indecision, he retreated to his study. James Madison, always more enthusiastic and consistent in his support of commercial retaliation, became by default the embargo's public defender. Albert Gallatin, the secretary of the treasury, became its chief administrator. Jefferson watched with disillusioned passivity as the embargo proved impotent and domestic opposition to the administration mounted.

The embargo simply did not have the desired or expected effect on the British. Great Britain's warehouses were already full of American products, and British merchants welcomed the chance to sell off their excess stock at better prices. These same products also were becoming available in South America, where Spanish colonists used their mother country's preoccupation with the Napoleonic Wars to declare their independence and open their ports to the English. In addition, so many loopholes had been left in the hastily drafted embargo that six hundred American ships left port legally in 1808, the first year of the embargo's operation. Many more departed illegally. Smuggling flourished, especially in New England, the center of opposition to

Jefferson and to the Republican idea of commercial retaliation. Jefferson, Madison, and Gallatin tried to plug the leaks, even sacrificing their devotion to civil rights by allowing widespread and arbitrary searches and seizures. Still they could not stop the hemorrhaging of the embargo despite the kind help of Napoleon, who ordered all American ships in French-controlled ports to be confiscated on the pretext that they must be embargo violators or British ships in disguise.

By 1809, most members of Congress, even Republicans, had concluded that the embargo had failed. They took advantage of Jefferson's lame-duck period, when he had completely dropped the reins of government, to replace the embargo with a far weaker measure. The Non-Intercourse Act of 1809 allowed American ships and products to leave port if not destined for territory controlled by Great Britain or France. Of course, once the ships left American waters, the United States had no effective way to ensure that they avoided these countries. Enough ships ostensibly left for the Azores to supply these islands many times over. The embarrassed Madison and Gallatin preferred war to admitting the embargo's failure, and their transparent attempts to represent the Non-Intercourse Act as the beginning of forceful measures only accentuated the American humiliation. Their warnings that they would reopen trade with the belligerents only if they respected American neutral rights rang hollow.

Yet ironically it did seem for a moment that the Republican maneuver had succeeded. The British minister to the United States, David Erskine, made an executive agreement with President Madison to stop interrupting American commerce under the Orders in Council if the United States would reopen trade with Great Britain. Not knowing that Erskine had drastically exceeded his instructions, the euphoric Republicans assumed that their advocacy of commercial retaliation had been vindicated. But the British cabinet rejected the Erskine Agreement in insulting terms and replaced Erskine with a minister obnoxious enough to ensure that the United States could not mistake the British position again.

After this new humiliation, the demoralized Republicans turned from the blackmail of the Non-Intercourse Act to the bribery of Macon's Bill No. 2. Under this act, Congress reopened trade with everyone but promised to close it to the enemy of any nation that would recognize America's neutral rights. The clever and cynical Napoleon saw the opening. He had his foreign minister, the Duc de Cadore, inform the United States that France would stop seizing American ships, "it being understood" that the United States would then force Britain to abandon its interference in American trade. Macon's Bill No. 2 had promised only to cut off trade with Britain; it could not guarantee that Britain would abandon its Orders in Council. Napoleon and Cadore had left themselves an escape hatch through which they could excuse their continuing confiscations of American ships.

As obvious as Napoleon's ruse was, Madison accepted the Cadore letter at face value. Perhaps he was duped. Or perhaps he was desperate to concentrate America's efforts on one belligerent at a time. However weak the pretext, he would close British trade while leaving that with Britain's enemy open. He hoped this would bring the British around, allowing him to turn on the French and use the British as a lever against them.

If this was his thinking, it was a wild gamble, and ultimately a disastrous one. The Cadore letter was too weak a pretense with which to pressure the British, and too flimsy an excuse to convince the American public to unite in support of confrontation with Great Britain. Yet having made the challenge, the Republicans could not back down again. Another retreat would be ruinous to the Republican party and to the nation's reputation in the world. When the Republican-controlled Congress cut off trade with Britain in response to the Cadore letter and Britain still refused to retract the Orders in Council, Madison and the Republicans could see no alternative but to declare war.

MADISON AND GREAT BRITAIN: THE WAR

In his request for war, Madison listed Great Britain's obvious offenses of impressment and interference with neutral trade to justify his course of action. Contemporary opponents of the war and later historians, however, noted some disturbing anomalies in the idea that these maritime grievances were the basic causes of the war. With few French ships challenging British control of the seas after the Battle of Trafalgar in 1805, the rate of impressment had dwindled. The United States had few instances of impressment to protest in the years immediately preceding the war. And although Britain had continued to harass American trade under the Orders in Council, the French had seized just as many American ships as the British. Ironically, Madison learned shortly after the war began that the British had already repealed their Orders in Council in the wake of a serious economic depression and the assassination of the prime minister. Yet Madison and the Republicans continued the war, supposedly to end impressment as well.

If maritime grievances were the genuine motivation for the war, why did the declaration come after the offenses had diminished so greatly? Why did the opposition to war center in the New England area, where maritime grievances were most felt, while young western war hawks like Henry Clay, John C. Calhoun, and Felix Grundy led the congressional movement for war? Why did America declare war against England rather than France, when the one had captured as many American ships as the other? Opponents of the war accused Madison and the Republican leaders of being in league with Napoleon. They also thought the Republicans had chosen to fight England rather than France because it gave them an excuse to conquer Canada and to take Florida from Britain's sometime ally, Spain. Thus opponents charged that the war was not a defense of maritime rights against British arrogance and rapacity, but an aggressive grab for territory.

There were indeed some important expansionist factors operating in the decision for war in 1812. Americans had long coveted Canada and Florida.

Frontier settlers also felt menaced by Indians they firmly believed to be supplied and supported by the British and the Spanish. The Battle of Tippecanoe dramatized the Indian problem in 1811. Two Shawnee brothers, Tecumseh and the Prophet, had been trying to organize the Ohio Valley and Southwest Indians into a confederacy. They sought solidarity to resist the corruptions of Anglo civilization and the loss of Indian lands through treaties that avaricious American settlers made with pliable village chiefs. The British did supply and encourage resistance among these Indians, but they also discouraged premature hostilities that might provoke war between Britain and the United States. Tecumseh and the Prophet established a town at the confluence of the Tippecanoe and Wabash Rivers. Governor William Henry Harrison of Indiana feared the town would be a rallying point for a British-supported Indian war against the frontier and stormed it while Tecumseh was absent on a recruiting trip to the south. Harrison then exaggerated his account of the events to claim a great victory over British-supported Indians. Consequently, Madison could mention Indian depredations and British complicity in his request for war. Later he also instructed his peace negotiators to try to acquire Canada in the settlement.

Yet it seems clear to most modern students of the War of 1812 that these expansionist factors were secondary to the maritime grievances of impressment and ship seizures. The United States had recently acquired Louisiana and still had much good unsettled land in the Northwest, so land hunger was not exceedingly strong in 1812. In addition, sectional jealousies tempered some expansionist passions. Southerners especially feared that acquisition of Canada would fuel northern political interests, and some northerners had similar reservations about Florida. Judging by the private and public comments of contemporaries, Canada was more a bargaining chip than an object of annexation. Republican leaders seemed more inclined to trade Canada for British concessions on impressment and neutral rights than to keep it. Westerners also shared the East's interest in Great Britain's maritime offenses. They may not have had many ships or seamen, but they blamed the severe depression that beset the nation's farming areas in 1811 on British interference with America's agricultural exports. Thus maritime grievances contributed substantially to the near-unanimity of western congressmen and senators in favor of war in 1812.

Nevertheless, the unsettled West could contribute comparatively few votes for war; most votes had to come from the more populous East. The maritime areas of New England did tend to oppose war, partly because merchants there were prospering in spite of European depredations on their shipping, and partly because their districts would be the most exposed to British naval bombardment or invasion. Yet representatives of other areas interested in overseas commerce, such as Philadelphia, Baltimore, and Charleston, voted for war. Thus sectional interests do not fully explain the congressional lineup. Party loyalty seems to have been more significant.

All the Federalists in the House of Representatives voted against the declaration of war with Great Britain. All but twenty-two of the Republicans voted for it, most of those dissenters hailing from states vulnerable to British attack. Such a partisan lineup makes sense. The Republicans feared that their party could not survive another humiliating retreat. Since they regarded the Federalists as antidemocratic as well as treasonably pro-British, they believed that a Federalist victory in the coming elections would doom America's experiment in republicanism. Despite their historical reputation as the party of the war hawks, most Republicans were not eager for war; they merely saw it as the best of unhappy alternatives. There was little of the buoyant belligerence one would have expected if the war had been a crusade for Canada.

Not only did the Republicans enter the war without enthusiasm, they entered without military preparations. They authorized army recruitment and naval building, but appropriated almost no money to carry them out. They detested Napoleon too much to make advances toward formal cooperation or alliance with France, yet they counted on French success in the continental war to preoccupy the British and ultimately force concession to America's neutral rights. Their calculations went awry. Within a year, Napoleon suffered a disastrous defeat in his Russian invasion. America then stood alone and unarmed against the most powerful nation left in the world.

The Federalists rushed to make political capital of the Republican plight. Before and during the war, they answered Republican denunciations of Britain with reminders that Napoleon too seized American ships and disregarded American rights. They mocked Madison's naive faith in the Cadore letter. They actually supported war preparations in the months before the declaration, but for the sole purpose of embarrassing the Republicans. Federalists hoped to pick up the political pieces when, as they confidently but mistakenly expected, the Republicans backed away from actually going to war with Great Britain. After the Republicans won the vote for war, the Federalists proposed a simultaneous fight with France and lost by only two Senate votes. Their obstructionist tactics continued throughout the war, culminating in the Hartford Convention of 1814. There the Federalists called for peace at any price, demanded constitutional restrictions on all future commercial retaliation, and hinted at the possibility of secession if the Republicans persisted in their misbegotten war.

As the American war effort stumbled from fiasco to fiasco, Federalist strength grew steadily, especially in New England. But the British saved the Republicans when they decided not to pursue the war with the United States even though Napleon had been beaten. There were many Britons who wanted to fight until they had extracted a peace that would teach the American upstarts a lesson in humility. One newspaper close to the government laid out the terms that should be required of the United States: Canada should have a new boundary giving it a monopoly of the Great Lakes–St. Lawrence system. Americans should be excluded from the fisheries and barred from trade with the British East and West Indies. The United States should be required to give a guarantee against acquisition of the Floridas. Great Britain would take New Orleans and thus ensure its domination of the

Mississippi. America should acknowledge British rules on neutral rights and impressment. And finally, the old project of an Indian border state should be revived, the area to be carved out of the American Northwest.

The Duke of Wellington warned, however, that it would take the reconquest of Lake Champlain and two years of conflict to subdue the Americans, even if he and much of his European army were transferred to North America. The debt-ridden British government thought the cost of such sweet revenge was more than its rewards, and feared that a continuing American war might weaken its position in the European negotiations at the Congress of Vienna. The cabinet decided to accept a compromise peace rather than fight to the finish.

When serious negotiations between the United States and Great Britain began at Ghent in Belgium in 1814, the British still thought it possible to secure adjustments on the Canadian border and an Indian buffer state. Twice negotiations nearly broke off on these issues, and the Americans finally convinced the British they would never accept the buffer state. The British foreign minister, Castlereagh, ordered abandonment of the demand rather than see the negotiations founder. The British negotiators insisted on a more secure Canadian border, however, claiming it was necessary to protect against American invasion. The American delegation, which included Albert Gallatin, Henry Clay, and John Quincy Adams, ingenuously professed no interest in Canada, claiming the province had merely served as a target of convenience. Meanwhile the Americans hoped anxiously that the British would not discover that their original instructions had indeed requested the cession of Canada.

When Wellington made known his opinion of the difficulties involved in an all-out invasion of the United States, the British finally decided to settle for the *status quo ante bellum.* The issues of the fisheries and British navigation of the Mississippi were to be decided later by a neutral commission, while the combatants agreed to disagree about neutral rights and impressment in the hope that the absence of world war would leave the issues moot. The war, then, had been at best a draw for the Americans. But there was reason to rejoice even at this, for British troops in occupation of American territory along the Great Lakes and in Maine would have to be removed. Certainly the terms looked good in comparison to the extensive concessions the Federalists in the Hartford Convention would have offered the British to guarantee immediate peace.

Unfortunately for the Federalists, the demands of the Hartford Convention arrived in Washington almost simultaneously with the news of General Andrew Jackson's spectacular victory over a powerful British invasion force at New Orleans, and the report from Ghent that peace had been made without major sacrifice. Jackson's victory actually was won after conclusion of the Treaty of Ghent and had no effect on the peace terms.[2] But Americans heard

[2] If the British had won this battle, however, they might have refused final ratification of the treaty and extracted significant concessions, so the victory was not totally meaningless.

of both at the same time, and many linked them indelibly in their minds. They felt they had won the war decisively, and the Federalists now appeared fainthearted if not treasonous in comparison with the Republicans.

Americans abandoned the Federalists in droves to rejoice in their apparent victory. "We have stood the contest, single-handed, against the conqueror of Europe; and we are at peace, with all our blushing victories thick crowding on us," crowed Joseph Story. To Americans, the war's end vindicated their righteous views on neutral rights and secured respect for America's honor, independence, and sovereignty. The war seemed to prove that free men, "fresh from the plow," could defeat the hired guns of European tyranny. Europeans would finally respect America's dominance in the Western Hemisphere and its right to remain unentangled in the politics of the Continent. No longer could the British or French treat Americans as underlings or dictate where and how their ships would travel and trade. The last vestiges of colonial dependence had been cast off. The war seemed a second American Revolution.

The euphoria of victory was all the greater for the depths of humiliation and incompetence that had preceded it. "Our character has been retrieved from ignominy and instead of an insulted and pusillanimous people, we rank exalted in the opinion of the surrounding world," rejoiced one pamphleteer. Nationalistic fervor reached such heights that almost no piece of furniture seemed complete without a gilt eagle perched on top of it. Europe no longer need be the center of America's diplomatic attention. The people who looked to the Atlantic as America's source of wealth and power gave way to those who faced west. The United States could pursue territorial expansion with far less concern that the major powers of Europe would interfere. Neutrality and expansion would continue to be the twin themes of American foreign policy, but their priorities were now decisively reversed.

CONTROVERSIAL ISSUES AND FURTHER READING

During the nineteenth century, the War of 1812 was popular among the general public, yet most prominent historians criticized it. This was because the historical community of that time had its roots in New England and held fast to Federalist sympathies long after they had all but disappeared from most of the country. Some Federalist histories, such as Theodore Lyman's *The Diplomacy of the United States* (1826–1828), skirted public disfavor by hinting rather gently that the war should have been avoided. If avoidance had proved impossible, Lyman said, it would have been better to have fought in 1808, immediately after the *Chesapeake* affair had united the country. By 1812, Republican mistakes had permitted the navy and army to decay, had split the nation with the embargo, and had sabotaged America's moral position by resting its challenge to Britain on the fraudulent Cadore letter. Richard Hildreth, however, the most prominent historian of this issue before the Civil War, disdained any equivocation and asserted blatantly that the war should have been avoided entirely by acceptance of the Monroe-Pinkney Treaty of 1806. [Richard Hildreth, *The History of the United States* (1849–1852).]

After the Civil War, Hildreth's Federalist view was fortified by the endorsement of the prestigious German scholar, Hermann Eduard Von Holst, in his *The Constitutional and Political History of the United States* (1876–1892). In response, Henry Adams decided to correct the view of the historical fraternity. In a review of Von Holst's work jointly written with Henry Cabot Lodge, he informed the German that Americans were not now and never had been hostile to the War of 1812. Then, in his classic *History of the United States During the Administrations of Jefferson and Madison* (1889–1891), Adams endorsed the war fully but excoriated the Republicans for being too slow to embrace it.

These historians might dispute the virtues of the Republican diplomacy that led to the war, but they did not disagree over whether maritime issues were the major causes of it. Shortly before World War I, however, historians inspired by the frontier thesis of Frederick Jackson Turner began to wonder whether western desires for Canada and Florida might not have been more influential. The most significant of these works, Julius Pratt's *The Expansionists of 1812* (1925), transformed the ideas of the majority of historians in the 1920s and 1930s. The principal debate in this era focused on whether land hunger or fear of Indian depredations most influenced the desire to conquer Canada and Florida. Regardless of this dispute, the shift to a western explanation of its causes made the War of 1812 appear far more aggressive than defensive.

Modern revisionist historians have continued to view the war as an aggressive pursuit of territorial expansion. But they have added to this a condemnation of the war as a search for commercial expansion as well. They point out that the Americans intended not just to protect the trade in their own products, but to profit from others' trade thrown their way by the war. [See, for example, William Appleman Williams, *The Contours of American History* (1961). The best discussion of this point, however, is in Burton Spivak's *Jefferson's English Crisis: Commerce, Embargo, and the Republican Revolution* (1979), which is not written from the radical perspective.]

Most recent historians have deemphasized the expansionist aspects of the War of 1812 and returned to the maritime causes. In the process, they have welded the older Federalist critiques of Jefferson and Madison to the newer realist framework which denounces the Republicans for inept, unrealistic, and partisan diplomacy that brought on an unnecessary war. [The major work initiating this trend was A. L. Burt, *The United States, Great Britain, and British North America* (1940). Bradford Perkins continued the approach in the finest work on 1812 diplomacy, *Prologue to War: England and the United States, 1805–1812* (1961) and its sequel, *Castlereagh and Adams: England and the United States, 1806–1823* (1964). Roger Brown's *The Republic in Peril: 1812* (1964) best describes the division over the war as one of parties rather than sections. Reginald Horsman's *The Causes of the War of 1812* (1962) is another outstanding realist critique. Irving Brant's biography *James Madison* (6 vols., 1941–1961) is a passionate defense of Madison and the diplomacy of the war. A more balanced defense is the recent detailed survey encompassing the most recent research, J. C. A. Stagg, *Mr. Madison's War: Politics, Diplomacy, and Warfare in the Early American Republic, 1783–1830* (1983).]

The standard portrayal of the Louisiana Purchase is that it fell into American hands like manna from Heaven. This is apparent in both E. Wilson Lyon's *Louisiana in French Diplomacy, 1759–1804* (1934), and Arthur P. Whitaker's *The Mississippi Ques-*

tion, 1795–1803 (1934). But recently Alexander De Conde has supported the revisionist view by portraying the purchase as the product of American aggressiveness and acquisitiveness in *This Affair of Louisiana* (1976). [Samuel Flagg Bemis's biography *John Quincy Adams and the Foundations of American Foreign Policy* (1949) provides the best coverage of the acquisition of Florida, but see also Arthur P. Whitaker, *The United States and the Independence of Latin America, 1800–1830* (1941), and I. J. Cox, *The West Florida Controversy* (1913). On the Barbary pirates, see Ray W. Irwin, *The Diplomatic Relations of the United States with the Barbary Powers, 1776–1815* (1931), and H. G. Barnby, *The Prisoners of Algiers: An Account of the Forgotten American-Algerian War, 1785–1797* (1966).]

CHAPTER 4

The Diplomacy of Expansion: Florida and the Monroe Doctrine

MANIFEST DESTINY

For nearly half a century after the War of 1812, the issue of territorial expansion dominated American diplomacy. Certainly this was not a new concern for the United States. Franklin, Jay, and Adams had maneuvered to increase the nation's border claims during the revolution. Jefferson had purchased Louisiana. Frontiersmen had pushed aside the Indians while the United States government abetted them with military support and coercive treaties. Jefferson and Madison had nibbled at Florida and, during the War of 1812, the United States had at least squinted at Canada.

The primary force behind American expansion throughout the early history of the United States was its enormous population growth. The American people increased at an annual rate of 3 percent, which more than doubled the population every twenty-five years. This burgeoning populace moved steadily westward. Ohio had only 45,000 people within its borders in 1800; by 1820 it had ten times as many. In 1810 no more than one-seventh of America's people lived west of the Appalachians; by 1840 one-third of the population was there.

After the War of 1812, several new factors helped make territorial expansion even more central. A revolution in transportation and communication was the most important of these. Without this revolution, much of the West would have remained remote and forbidding, doomed to isolation and poverty. The area would have supported only a few scattered subsistence farmers, and it would have been impossible to protect or govern them from Washington. But in the 1820s and 1830s Americans built many new roads. The best of these were private turnpikes that cut freight prices in half. Numerous canals were built at the same time, and their impact was even more dramatic. Water transportation was far cheaper than overland transportation, and canals cut freight costs from 20 cents per ton-mile to 2 cents. Steamboats made water transportation even more practical, since they could carry goods upstream as well as down. By the 1840s even areas that canals and steamboats were unable to reach could look forward to cheap, rapid, and safe transportation for the first time in human history. Finally, the telegraph provided almost instant communication throughout the land.

The transportation revolution made possible the territorial expansion that the population boom made desirable. American citizens could profitably bring lands within the orbit of their commercial-agricultural economy that they might otherwise have left to the subsistence economy of the Indians. White Americans increasingly coveted remote territories such as Oregon and California, which Jefferson and many of his contemporaries had considered beyond the effective reach of American governance and destined at best to be independent republics.

America's growing and increasingly mobile population exerted powerful diplomatic leverage against the thinly populated and static colonies on the nation's borders. America's performance in the War of 1812 emboldened it to shift its attention from Europe to concentrate on westward expansion. At the same time, the Europeans were on notice that they would have great difficulty defending their North American colonies from the United States. The Spanish, the British, and later the Mexicans, like the Indians, watched with apprehension as time eroded their defenses against the voracious Americans. Threats against American expansion, especially from Great Britain, now spurred rather than retarded the westward movement, for American politicians could urge that the United States had to take new territories immediately or risk losing them to British interlopers.

Moral considerations posed even fewer obstacles to American ambitions than the declining threat of European intervention. Americans found easy rationalizations for acquiring territory long claimed and occupied by others. They pointed first to the relative emptiness of the lands. What right had so few Indians, Spaniards, Britons, or Mexicans to such vast expanses of good soil? They could never make proper use of them. Cultivated properly by industrious American farmers, those lands could furnish a livelihood for millions of people. It was wrong, Americans said, that such lands should languish unused in the hands of a few backward savages or lazy Europeans. How much better that they should be brought under the sway of a people that would not only use them properly, but also give them the blessings of free institutions—democratic government, individual liberty, and Protestant Christianity.

Governor William Henry Harrison of the Indiana Territory thus defended displacement of the Indians by asking rhetorically, "Is one of the fairest portions of the globe to remain in a state of nature, the haunt of a few wretched savages, when it seems destined by the Creator to give support to a large population and to be the seat of civilization, of science, and of true religion?" He and others took care to distinguish their expansion into "empty, unused" land from European imperialism, which conquered and oppressed densely settled areas. As one newspaper put it:

> What has Belgium, Silesia, Poland or Bengal in common with Texas? It is surely not necessary to insist that acquisitions of territory in America, even if accomplished by force of arms, are not to be viewed in the same light as the invasions and conquests of the States of the old world. No American aggression can stab

the patriot to the heart . . . ; our way lies not over trampled nations, but through desert wastes, to be brought by our industry and energy within the domain of art and civilization. We are contiguous to a vast portion of the globe, untrodden save by the savage and the beast, and we are conscious of our power to render it tributary to man.

Few Americans of the early nineteenth century dissented from this view. They differed only over the pace and tactics of the westward movement. The parties of the so-called cosmopolitans, the Federalists and later the Whigs, generally favored a slower pace. The constituency of these parties included many merchants and commercial farmers who feared the disruption of their trade that might result from serious conflict with the European colonial powers. Cosmopolitans also did not want the frontier to outrun the transportation infrastructure of roads, bridges, and canals that would tie the western fringes of the country to the national commercial nexus. Remote subsistence farms and communities would do the cosmopolitans no good economically, and politically would most likely produce votes for their "localist" party opponents, the Jeffersonian Republicans and later the Jacksonian Democrats.

Excessively rapid expansion threatened the cosmopolitans culturally as well. The cosmopolitan parties generally appealed to Americans of old British stock and conservative Protestant religion who placed great store in public morality and disciplined education and who favored a strong, active government to enforce their cultural norms. They feared that remote settlers would be beyond the reach of the civilizing influences of proper churches and schools, and they often complained that the frontier was producing white savages.

Thus most cosmopolitans believed that population pressure would bring the western territories into the United States soon enough. They thought it best to wait for these lands to fall into America's lap rather than to pursue them aggressively. Let the American population flow into the borderlands, outnumber and dominate the original inhabitants, then request admission to the Union. Perhaps the colonial nations would see the handwriting on the wall and sell the borderlands to the United States peacefully, as had occurred with Louisiana. Perhaps the Indians, left alone for a time, would also move of their own accord to escape the pressures of white civilization. The Whigs could be convinced to support more aggressive expansionism if the territorial targets contained harbors, navigable rivers, or obvious commercial resources, but generally they counseled greater restraint than did their political opponents.

The "localist" parties led by Jefferson and Jackson appealed more to the subsistence farmers and those less involved in the commercial economy. Their constituencies also were composed of religious dissenters and ethnic outgroups, including such disparate people as Scots-Irish Protestants and Irish and German Roman Catholics. These people disliked strong governments with potential power to impose the cultural norms of the old stock British and conservative Protestants. They saw no reason to slow the pace of expansion to protect the trade of their political opponents, to ensure communication with the government and commercial elites in the east, or to establish "proper" schools and churches. Disliking the British, their empire, and their descendants in America, they could be aroused easily by claims that if America did not take what it wanted on the frontier quickly, the British would get it. They also had fewer compunctions about trampling on the rights of the Indians.

Another political factor increasingly affected the basic American desire for expansion—slavery. Both political parties tried desperately to keep this issue out of politics, knowing it would shatter them and divide the nation geographically rather than on a cosmopolitan-localist axis. Consequently, in the earlier years of the nineteenth century, both parties tried to avoid bringing the slavery issue into the expansionist debate. If a potential annexation stirred too much agitation over slavery to ignore, both parties generally agreed to delay the acquisition. The slave issue was powerful enough to modify the pace and tactics of American expansion, yet not powerful enough to thwart it entirely. And if even the slave issue did not stop American expansion, could anything else?

Some Americans thought geography would provide "natural" boundaries for the United States. Jefferson and many of his followers, for instance, regarded the Rocky Mountains as the natural western border of the nation. As ardent an expansionist as Senator Thomas Hart Benton once grandiloquently proclaimed that an immovable statue of the great god Terminus should be placed on the highest peak in the Rockies. The Jeffersonians visualized Oregon not as a territory of the United States, but as an independent, sympathetic republic free of European influences.

Yet if geography could erect "natural barriers" it could also provide a rationale for expansion. Americans claimed that foreign territories such as Florida and Texas were on the American side of those geographical divisions, part of America's "natural" domain. The progress of American population and transportation also expanded the perceptions of natural boundaries. As an opponent of Benton's plans for the god Terminus put it: "Gentlemen are talking of natural boundaries. Sir, our natural boundary is the Pacific Ocean. The swelling tide of our population must and will roll on until that mighty ocean interposes its waters, and limits our territorial empire." Many Americans saw the entire continent of North America as an integral unit obviously shaped by God to be ruled by a single people, and they had no doubts as to which people He had chosen to occupy it. John L. O'Sullivan, editor of the *Democratic Review,* captured this vague but powerful sense of America's supposedly predestined expansion in a vivid phrase he coined in 1845. He proclaimed that it was America's "manifest destiny" to spread over the continent allotted it by Providence.

The presence of a dense foreign population in a target area deterred American expansion more effectively than natural boundaries. If the aliens were too numerous for America's own growing population to overwhelm them, the nation would face two unpleasant alternatives. The United States could incorporate the aliens as equal voting citizens and offend the cultural and racial prejudices of most Americans. Or it could rule them as a conquered people, which had grave implications for constitutional principles. Either course would undermine America's insistence that its expansion was different from European colonialism because the United States took only "empty" areas. This conceit may have been largely rationalization, but on one level Americans devoutly believed it. For instance, after the American army conquered Mexico City during the Mexican War and gave the United States the chance to annex the entire nation, the country turned away from its brief temptation and kept only the less populated areas of the Southwest.

The power of America's neighbors set another limit to American expansion. Canada itself might be weak and relatively unpopulated, but Britain was not to be taken lightly. Americans kept their eyes on the British colonies in North America, leaving the door open for eventual acquisition, pressing successfully for portions of Oregon and some other border concessions, dabbling with revolutionary elements in Canada, but shying finally from confrontation and ultimately accepting a permanent barrier to the north.

America's other colonial neighbor, Spain, had no such power to compel respect, and its feeble hold on East and West Florida presented the most promising arena for America's territorial ambitions in the aftermath of the War of 1812.

THE ACQUISITION OF FLORIDA

The United States had long coveted Florida to round out its possessions east of the Mississippi. Florida seemed a pistol with the barrel pressed against the mouth of the Mississippi. Florida also controlled the outlets of other navigable rivers that reached up into the American South, such as the Pearl, the Perdido, and the Chattahoochee. East Florida's peninsula extended deep into the Caribbean Sea, threatening the vital shipping routes from New Orleans and other Gulf ports to the eastern coast of the United States. Florida also presented an increasing nuisance to the adjacent American territories. Escaped slaves found refuge across the Spanish border. So did marauding bands of Indians who raided American settlements, often in conjunction with some of the escaped slaves. The moribund Spanish government in the Floridas had neither the power nor the inclination to eliminate these sanctuaries, despite numerous American protests.

The United States had been nibbling at Florida since well before the War of 1812. Jefferson originally had tried to purchase Florida rather than Louisiana when negotiating for New Orleans in 1803. Then he and James Madison had begun a long series of maneuvers to extort Florida from Spain. The most decisive of these came in 1810, when Madison used the invitation of some American settlers who had revolted against Spanish rule at Baton Rouge to proclaim the occupation of West Florida up to the Perdido River. (Actually Madison sent troops only as far as the Pearl River, and thus avoided a confrontation with the Spanish garrisons at Mobile and Pensacola.) Madison feared that Great Britain, then fighting Napoleon in Spain, might preempt the

United States by taking the Floridas. The British stirred those fears further when they protested Madison's occupation of parts of West Florida.

Madison appealed to Congress, and Congress announced its "No Transfer" principle, that the United States "cannot, without serious inquietude, see any part of [Florida] pass into the hands of any foreign power." (Since it was to America's advantage that all Western Hemisphere territories either become independent or remain in the hands of a weak Spain rather than pass to a greater power, the United States later extended this "No Transfer" principle to all of Latin America as an unofficial corollary to the Monroe Doctrine.) In pursuit of this principle, Congress authorized Madison in 1810 to occupy all of Florida if necessary to thwart foreign occupation, and on the eve of the War of 1812 actually declared both Floridas annexed.

Such ringing affirmations did little to alter the fact that the United States controlled only a small portion of Florida. Nevertheless, congressional bombast gave Spain and the rest of Europe warning that the United States intended to acquire the entire territory once circumstances were favorable. Immediately after the Peace of Ghent freed America from the War of 1812, Spain made a desperate appeal to the European powers to help it preserve Florida and reclaim Louisiana. The British minister refused, with the comment that an exhausted Europe required some time for repose, and the other powers followed suit. Consequently, when Spain ordered Luis de Onís, the Spanish minister to the United States, to open negotiations with the American government, it knew there was no hope of holding Florida much longer. Spain could only stall, wear the Americans down, and extract as many reciprocal concessions as possible.

Unfortunately for Onís, the American secretary of state he hoped to wear down was John Quincy Adams, one of the most intelligent, learned, experienced, and aggressive diplomats ever to serve the United States. Adams had been minister to the Netherlands, Prussia, and Russia, had served as one of the five commissioners to negotiate the Treaty of Ghent, and then had been minister to Great Britain until James Monroe appointed him secretary of state.

Short, stout, and balding, John Quincy Adams looked much like his father and had many of the same virtues and shortcomings. An unbending integrity accompanied his learning and intelligence, but so did a strange mix of personal vanity, insecurity, and morbid suspicion of all human motivations. Unfortunately, John Quincy lacked the earthiness and humor that leavened his father's self-righteousness. John Quincy Adams, who analyzed his own failings as unsparingly as he did those of others, compared himself to Henry Clay in the following terms: "There is the same dogmatical, overbearing manner, the same harshness of look and expression, the same forgetfulness of the courtesies in society." Actually this described Adams far better than it did Clay. Clay could be arrogant, but he was also genial and outgoing, while Adams was cold and remote. Adams, for instance, was apoplectic that during the negotiations at Ghent, when he would rise before dawn to pray and read Greek and Latin, the click of poker chips and scraping of chairs from Clay's

Map 3 Continental Expansion, 1775–1867

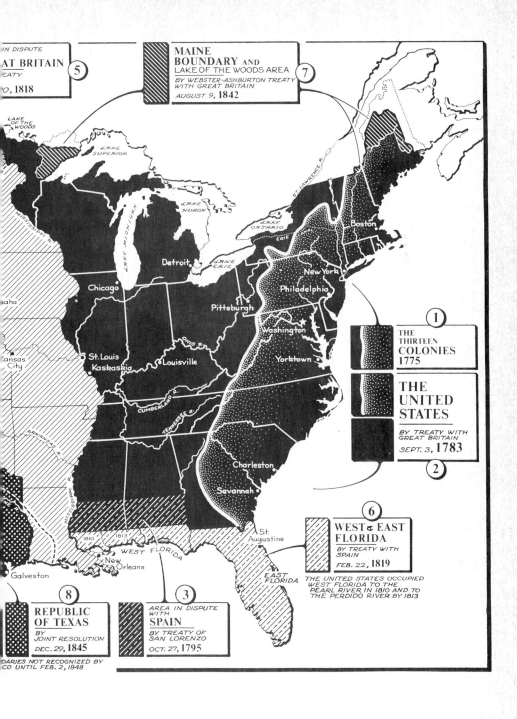

GREAT BRITAIN ⑤

IN DISPUTE

TREATY

O, 1818

MAINE BOUNDARY AND
LAKE OF THE WOODS AREA ⑦
*BY WEBSTER-ASHBURTON TREATY
WITH GREAT BRITAIN*
AUGUST 9, **1842**

① **THE
THIRTEEN
COLONIES**
1775

**THE
UNITED
STATES**
*BY TREATY WITH
GREAT BRITAIN*
SEPT. 3, **1783**
②

⑥ **WEST & EAST
FLORIDA**
*BY TREATY WITH
SPAIN*
FEB. 22, **1819**

*THE UNITED STATES OCCUPIED
WEST FLORIDA TO THE
PEARL RIVER IN 1810 AND TO
THE PERDIDO RIVER BY 1813*

⑧ **REPUBLIC
OF TEXAS**
*BY
JOINT RESOLUTION*
DEC. 29, **1845**

③ *AREA IN DISPUTE
WITH*
SPAIN
*BY TREATY OF
SAN LORENZO*
OCT. 27, **1795**

*DARIES NOT RECOGNIZED BY
CO UNTIL FEB. 2, 1848*

all-night card games in the next room would disturb him. One foreign diplomat described Adams as the most grim, unsociable, and venomous minister
he had ever met, a "bulldog among spaniels" at the court of St. Petersburg.

Onís began his negotiations with Adams by demanding the return of
Louisiana as the price of the Floridas. Spain still claimed that the purchase
had been illegal, since Napoleon had violated the provision of the retrocession that forbade him to sell the province to a third party. Adams brushed
this claim aside. He not only said that the United States would keep Louisiana, but claimed the distant Rio Grande River as Louisiana's western border.
This would have given Texas to the United States. He indicated immediately,
however, that he intended to bargain this border for the Floridas by hinting
that he would accept a border at the Colorado River. Onís's instructions anticipated such a maneuver and empowered him to retreat from his demand
that the United States give up Louisiana. In turn, however, he was to extract a
promise from the Americans to refuse aid or recognition to Spain's rebellious
Central and South American colonies.

Onís did not retreat precipitately. He put pressure on Adams by getting a
reluctant Britain to offer mediation—which, of course, the American secretary refused. The Americans in turn applied even greater pressure to Spain.
In 1818, President Monroe ordered General Andrew Jackson to cross the
Florida border in pursuit of marauding Indians. Monroe cautioned Jackson,
however, to avoid direct conflict with the Spanish garrisons if the Indians
took refuge there. Jackson immediately proposed a more aggressive course.
"Let it be signified to me through any channel (say Mr. J. Rhea) that the possession of the Floridas would be desirable to the United States, and in sixty
days it will be accomplished." Jackson later claimed that he had received
such a signal from John Rhea and had burned the message for the sake of
discretion. Monroe insisted that he had never seen Jackson's letter and denied he had authorized a conquest. Whatever the truth of all this, Monroe
had taken few steps to restrain Jackson's well-known pugnaciousness, and
Jackson did more than merely attack the Indians. He executed two British
subjects who had been suppliers to the Indians and captured the Spanish
garrisons of St. Marks and Pensacola. Jackson then asked ingenuously what
the president would like him to do with his new conquests.

John C. Calhoun and William Crawford, secretaries of war and treasury,
advised President Monroe to disavow Jackson and recall him. They expected
the British to be furious over the execution of their subjects, and they were
afraid Britain might join Spain in a war to protect Florida and punish the
United States. John Quincy Adams insisted that America should make no
apology. He even argued that the United States might keep Pensacola until
Spain could guarantee control of the Indians and escaped slaves. In the
end Monroe did recall Jackson, but he permitted Adams to justify Jackson's actions to Spain, England, and the American public on the grounds
that they were a consequence of Spanish dereliction. Adams and Monroe
may not have instigated Jackson's capture of the Spanish posts, but they
were happy to make use of the foray to force Spain into a final favorable
settlement.

Urged on by Monroe and the cabinet, Adams then offered to set the border of Louisiana at the Sabine River, in effect trading all of America's claim to Texas for the Floridas. Adams might have gotten more, for Onís's instructions permitted him to accept a boundary west of the Sabine if necessary to gain a firm border for Texas. But while Adams gave up some American claims in Texas, he acquired compensating concessions on the northwestern boundary of Louisiana. Onís agreed to accept a northern border to Spanish territories at 41° latitude, thus abandoning Spanish rights to the Oregon territory. The United States still faced competing claims to Oregon from Great Britain and Russia, but it was now considerably more likely that the United States would stretch from sea to sea. Thus the treaty has been dubbed by historians the Transcontinental Treaty of 1819.

Spain, on the other hand, gained little except a firm recognition of the border between its North American colonies and the United States, which it hoped rather forlornly would serve as a barrier to further American encroachment. Onís even failed to get a direct acknowledgment from the United States that Florida had been rightfully Spain's to turn over to the United States. Adams evaded any recognition that America's former declarations of annexation had been hot air by phrasing the Spanish cession as follows: The Spanish king would cede "all the territories which belong to him, situated to the Eastward of the Mississippi, known by the name of East and West Florida." By omitting a comma between "territories" and "which," Adams left open just which of those territories actually had been the Spanish king's property. Adams also managed to evade the Spanish demand that the treaty contain an American promise to refuse recognition of the independence of Spain's Latin American colonies.

THE INDEPENDENCE OF LATIN AMERICA

The recognition of the independence of the Latin American republics had become a very touchy issue for Monroe and his cabinet. Naturally, most Americans saw these infant nations as following nobly in the footsteps of the United States, battling colonialism and monarchy to establish free republics. Practical-minded Americans also saw commercial and strategic advantages. The ex-colonies would open their markets to the ships and goods of the United States and no longer would be potential military and naval bases for major European powers in the Western Hemisphere. Still, Monroe and Adams could not afford to grant immediate recognition to the Latin American rebels so long as the Florida negotiations were pending. Not only would recognition derail those negotiations, but it might induce other European powers to help Spain resist American pressure. In the wake of the victory over Napoleon and the French Revolution, the major European continental powers—Russia, Spain, Austria, and Prussia—had formed the so-called Holy Alliance to defend "legitimate governments" against the virus of republicanism and anticolonialism. Until the agreement with Spain was safely done, the United States could not risk defying these powers.

Monroe regretted the delay in recognition more than John Quincy Adams. Adams regarded South Americans as ignorant, racially inferior, numbed by years of ecclesiastical and military tyranny, and unlikely to form lasting republics on the model of the United States. He did not think trade with Latin America would be important, because the Latin Americans did not need the agricultural products of the United States and the United States could not afford to purchase many of Latin America's specialties. Great Britain had dominated the Latin American trade since the Spanish colonies had broken away and would continue to do so. While Adams wished the cause of Latin American independence well, he saw no reason to risk much to aid the movement. He was ready to extend the policy of neutrality to South America as well as to Europe.

Adams, however, was under great pressure to recognize the republics. Henry Clay made the issue the centerpiece of his campaign for the 1824 presidential nomination. Senator Clay embarrassed his rivals in Monroe's cabinet with continuous oratorical appeals for them to join the cause of world liberty by recognizing the republics, even though he knew the Florida negotiation required their silence.

The prospect of recognition tempted Monroe. At the president's request, John Quincy Adams dutifully sounded out the British to see if they might reduce the risks of such a policy by joining the United States in opening formal relations with the republics. The British refused. Adams judged that despite this refusal, British interests in the Latin American trade would induce them to oppose any attempt by the Holy Alliance to help restore Spain's political and commercial monopoly of the area. Still, he thought it best to delay recognition, and the British refusal helped him convince Monroe.

Once Adams concluded his treaty, everyone, including Adams himself, expected that the United States would recognize the new republics in short order. Even Clay shifted his attack away from what he thought was no longer a vulnerable flank for Adams and began bewailing the sacrifice of Texas in the treaty. But all did not go as expected. The usually punctilious Adams had overlooked a dispatch from America's minister to Spain warning him that the king had granted much of Florida's unclaimed lands to two nobles. These grants went into effect only days before the treaty made any further land distribution illegal.

The mortified Adams demanded that Spain repeal this shady proceeding, but the Spanish used the grants as leverage to gain amendments to the treaty. They again demanded that the United States promise not to recognize Spain's former colonies, and added a request for a formal guarantee of all of Spain's remaining empire in the Western Hemisphere. Clay gleefully called for Monroe and Adams to scrap the whole treaty and conquer Texas and Florida. Adams threatened Spain with just that, even though Monroe did not really want Texas because he feared that its acquisition would reopen the debate over slavery that had just been concluded with the Missouri Compromise of 1820. Under Adams's pressure, Spain finally succumbed, revoked the land grants, and ratified the treaty in 1821, two years after it had been concluded.

To help gain Spanish cooperation, Adams gave private assurances to the Spanish minister in the United States that recognition of the Latin American republics would not be immediate. So it was not until 1822 that the United States became the first nation outside South America to recognize the nations of Chile, the United Provinces of the Plata, Peru, Colombia, and Mexico. As Adams expected, Europe stood by without significant protest despite the wounded outcries from Spain. Yet no European nation joined the United States in recognition. Did Spain and Europe still harbor some hopes of regaining control of the republics?

THE MONROE DOCTRINE

That question came to a head in 1823 when France, with the support of the Holy Alliance, sent its armies into Spain to restore the authority of King Ferdinand VII over a too-independent Spanish legislature. There were fears in England and America that the French might not stop there, but mount joint expeditions with Spain to restore "legitimate" monarchical control of the lost provinces in the Western Hemisphere. As French troops poured across the Pyrenees, Richard Rush, the American minister to England, commented hopefully to George Canning, the British foreign minister, that even if France overthrew the constitutional government of Spain on behalf of Ferdinand VII, there was at least the consolation "that Great Britain would not allow her to go farther and stop the progress of emancipation in the colonies." He was startled by Canning's response: "What do you think your Government would say to going hand in hand with England in such a policy?"

A significant improvement in the relations between the two countries after the War of 1812 made possible Canning's proposal of a limited Anglo-American alliance. Trade between the two nations had become increasingly valuable. Great Britain purchased two-fifths of American exports, mostly cotton, while the Americans provided a vital market for British manufactured goods. American vessels carried almost 90 percent of Anglo-American trade, so it was especially important to the American merchant marine. Great Britain also had an added incentive to cooperate with the United States, for it was becoming clear that Canada was more a hostage to America's growing power and population than a potential staging area for a British invasion of the United States. Some hostile feelings between England and America remained, exacerbated by vituperative quarrels carried on in the newspapers and magazines of the two countries, but even confirmed British-haters like John Quincy Adams came to see the benefit of dampening Anglo-American tensions. On the British side, Canning and his predecessor, Lord Castlereagh, more than matched the growing American amicability. In this atmosphere, the United States and Great Britain settled several nagging conflicts during the years immediately preceding Canning's offer of a joint policy on Latin America.

In 1817, the Rush-Bagôt Agreement established severe limits on naval forces sailing the Great Lakes. Since land fortifications remained, this was a minor step, but it was significant in showing the willingness of the two sides to reach agreements. That same year, an arbitration commission established by the Treaty of Ghent settled the dispute over the portion of the Canadian-American border running through Passamaquoddy Bay in Maine. A few months later, the Convention of 1818 adjusted several other boundary controversies. The convention confirmed the border between the Louisiana Purchase and Canada at 49° latitude from the Lake of the Woods to the crest of the Rockies. The Oregon Territory to the west of the Rockies, however, remained a subject of argument. England insisted that the border should be the Columbia River, while the United States wanted the 49° line extended to the sea. Since the territory was so remote and unpopulated, the two sides finally agreed to defer the border settlement and allow the citizens of both nations to live there freely.

The Convention of 1818 also brought compromise on the issue of the Canadian fisheries. The British claimed that the War of 1812 had ended the American "liberty" granted by the Peace Treaty of 1783 to fish and cure their catch in Canadian waters; the Americans said that this "liberty" was equivalent to a perpetual right and could never be abridged. The convention limited slightly the areas where Americans could fish and cure, but confirmed the "liberty" forever. (The agreement would break down a decade later, but worked well for the time.) Finally, the Convention of 1818 called for arbitration of the controversy over the American slaves carried away by British troops at the end of the War of 1812.

Several issues remained to plague Anglo-American relations. The United States and Great Britain could not reach agreement on impressment, and both sides assumed that this issue would drag the United States into any future European war on the side of England's enemies. Fortunately, no general European war broke out for a century. The United States and Great Britain also continued to dispute the northern boundary of Maine. They squabbled over British prohibitions against American ships trading with the West Indies as well. The British finally opened several West Indian ports in 1821 after the United States enacted retaliatory regulations, but the United States refused to repeal all its discriminatory duties until Great Britain removed all its imperial preferences in the West Indies. This stalled the agreement until 1830. Fortunately, the breakdown of negotiations did not create a crisis because by the 1820s direct commerce between the United States and Great Britain had come to dwarf the West Indies trade.

Finally, controversy continued to swirl over the desire of Great Britain to visit and search American ships suspected of carrying on the slave trade in violation of the laws of both countries. The issue of visit and search was too sensitive even for antislavery Americans to agree readily to British visitations, although the British were willing to grant American ships reciprocal rights to search suspected British vessels.

Despite the number of these remaining quarrels, most of them seemed relatively minor in 1823, and Americans and Britons alike were impressed with the growing amity between the two countries. This allowed Canning, previously one of the most anti-American of British statesmen, to approach Richard Rush with his proposal for a joint policy on Latin America.

Britain's increasing estrangement from its erstwhile allies among the reactionary regimes of Europe also encouraged Canning to make his offer. The so-called Holy Alliance of these regimes had defied British disapproval to encourage Austrian intervention in Naples and Piedmont, along with the French invasion of Spain on behalf of Ferdinand VII. The Holy Allies had even announced that they would come to the aid of France if Great Britain interfered on the side of the Spanish legislature against Ferdinand. The pressures of Britain's estrangement from its continental allies drove Canning's predecessor, Lord Castlereagh, to commit suicide by slashing his throat with a penknife. Canning accepted the estrangement with greater aplomb. He publicly warned that Britain would fight if France tried to make its occupation of Spain permanent and added ominously that he assumed France would not try to acquire the Spanish colonies in South America. To bolster Britain's increasingly isolated position, Canning then turned to the United States. He would later brag that he had called the New World into existence to balance the Old.

Canning suggested that Great Britain and the United States jointly announce their opposition to the transfer of any of Spain's colonies to another empire. Rush was much impressed with this opportunity to enlist the British navy in defense of the "no transfer" principle, a doctrine the United States had long favored but lacked the power to enforce. Canning's proposed statement, however, coupled endorsement of the "no transfer" principle to several other assertions Rush found disturbing. For instance, Canning wanted the statement to say that the United States and Great Britain sought none of Spain's colonies for themselves. Such a self-denying pledge would prevent American acquisition of Texas and Cuba.

Cuba was the primary issue as far as Canning was concerned. In 1822, Cuban underground leaders had offered to mount a rebellion against Spain if the United States would annex the island. Americans, especially southerners, had long coveted Cuba. But President Monroe and his cabinet had not risen to the underground's bait because Cuba, like Texas, could reawaken the controversy over slavery in new territories. On the other hand, they certainly did not want a major naval power like Great Britain to take it, and they were very suspicious when the British cabinet in late 1822 sent a squadron into Cuban waters to protect commerce against the island's pirates. Monroe was ready to offer a mutual self-denial pact to Britain at this point. John Quincy Adams turned him away from it, however, because Adams wanted the acquisition of Cuba left open in case the slave issue became less volatile. Naturally the British suspected America's intentions toward Cuba as well, although they knew there were no immediate plans for American annexation. This was why Canning included the mutual self-denial in his proposed joint statement.

In addition, Canning wanted the statement to say that, although Britain and America thought Spain's hope of recovering the colonies hopeless, they would pose no obstacle if Spain sought to regain them by amicable negotiations. Britain would not join the United States in recognizing the colonies' independence, but would leave that decision for time and circumstance to determine. Rush and the United States wanted the former colonies to be free from interference by Spain as well as the Holy Allies, and so Rush renewed the former appeals to join the United States in recognizing the independence of the republics, thereby foreclosing any chance for Spain to regain them.

Rush told Canning that if Great Britain would recognize the revolutionary regimes, he would accept Canning's joint statement in the name of the United States without even asking permission from his government. He thought the benefits of committing Britain in this way would be worth the statement on Cuba, and he was willing to risk disavowal and ruin if his superiors in the United States disagreed. Nevertheless, Canning refused to risk the greater estrangement from his European allies that would result from British recognition of the revolutionary regimes. He turned instead to unilateral action. He bullied the French government into a pledge, known as the Polignac Memorandum, that France had no intention of interfering in the quarrel between Spain and the Latin American colonies. Recent research into the European archives has demonstrated that there never was a danger of such intervention, but whatever crisis there might have been was clearly ended by the Polignac Memorandum. The memorandum was not published until considerably later, however, and the American government continued to deliberate Canning's earlier offer in ignorance that the crisis was over.

When Canning refused immediate recognition of the revolutionary regimes, Rush sent Canning's original offer on to Washington, expecting that Monroe might choose to accept it anyway. Indeed, that was Monroe's first reaction. Upon receiving Rush's dispatches, he sought the advice of his predecessors, Thomas Jefferson and James Madison, and he told them "We had better meet the proposition fully, & decisively." Jefferson and Madison agreed, even though it meant giving up Cuba. "Great Britain is the nation which can do us the most harm of any one, or all on earth," Jefferson wrote; "and with her on our side we need not fear the whole world." Secretary of War Calhoun supported the inclination of the two elder statesmen. But John Quincy Adams urged that the United States make an independent statement of its policies to France and the Holy Alliance. He thought a joint statement would make the United States appear a "cock-boat in the wake of a British man-of-war."

As Adams saw it, a unilateral declaration of policy would not tie America's hands on Cuba and Texas should the inhabitants of those areas later choose to join the Union. Besides, a warning against all European interference in the Western Hemisphere would apply to Great Britain as well as Spain and the rest of the continental powers. Adams dismissed the threat of an actual European invasion of Latin America. Still, the ominous rumblings from the Holy Alliance deserved a timely response. Russia had only recently shown an aggressive posture in North America, warning foreign citizens and ships away from a huge swath of territory stretching from Alaska to the tip of

Vancouver Island, including coastal waters a hundred miles out to sea. The Russians had retreated quickly enough when Britain and the United States had protested, but the Russian minister had followed this retreat with a warning that Russia would never recognize the Latin American rebels. He had coupled this warning with smug and perhaps meaningful congratulations to the United States for maintaining its own neutrality toward them. Adams was convinced that the Russians were bluffing, but he felt that, if by some grotesque chance the Holy Allies did make a move against Latin America, Great Britain would stop them with or without the support of the United States.

Monroe accepted Adams's advice. Further dispatches from Rush confirmed him in his decision. These dispatches indicated that Canning had already cooled to the project and led Monroe to speculate correctly that Canning might have received private assurance from France. (Neither Rush nor the other Americans yet knew of the Polignac Memorandum.) In any case, Monroe decided to include a unilateral pronouncement of America's foreign policy in his upcoming message to Congress.

It was these statements of diplomatic principles scattered through Monroe's message of December 2, 1823, that later generations came to call the Monroe Doctrine. The first of these principles declared that while the United States would not interfere with European colonies already existing in the Western Hemisphere, the hemisphere was no longer open to European colonization. Adams had drafted this statement previously to apply to the Russian claims in the Northwest, but now Monroe addressed the admonition

Figure 4   James Monroe (left) and his secretary of state (later president) John Quincy Adams, the principal formulators of the Monroe Doctrine. Portraits courtesy of the National Archives.

to all of Europe. Monroe had wanted to follow this warning with a vivid declaration of American support for the Greek revolutionaries fighting their Turkish overlords and for the Spanish constitutionalists opposing Ferdinand VII. Adams talked him out of this, so the Monroe Doctrine became instead a restatement of American neutrality: "Our policy in regard to Europe, which was adopted at an early stage of the wars which have so long agitated that quarter of the Globe, . . . is, not to interfere in the internal concerns of any of its powers." This promise of abstention, which formed the second major point of the doctrine, led naturally to the third and boldest assertion—Europe must keep its hands off the independent nations of the Western Hemisphere. Any attempt to extend the European system into the Americas would be regarded as "dangerous to our peace and safety." These three points, along with the No Transfer principle that John Quincy Adams was reasserting at the same time in his diplomatic correspondence, became holy writ for later generations of Americans and ranked alongside Washington's Farewell Address as a statement of foreign policy.

Part of the Monroe Doctrine was no more than a restatement of Washington's neutralist dictum and required no further explication. But what exactly was meant by the "hands off" warning to Europe? Did the United States seriously mean to fight to protect the independence of Latin America? Was it ready to abandon neutrality toward nations in the Western Hemisphere, staying neutral only toward Europe? The answer quickly became apparent. Shortly after John Quincy Adams succeeded Monroe as president, he recommended to the Senate that it confirm two delegates to attend a conference of the newly independent Latin American republics at Panama. Those republics were considering a formal alliance against any attacks on them by outsiders. They hoped that the United States, on the strength of the Monroe Doctrine, might join. John Quincy Adams's communication to Congress made clear he had no such intention. The United States would lend moral support to the Latin Americans and would seek to enlist them on behalf of the neutral rights the United States had long championed, but it would not depart from neutrality toward all foreign nations, European or Latin American. The United States might join an all-American pact to implement the noncolonization principle, but each nation would be expected to guard its own borders.

Adams's opponents in Congress used this opportunity to attack him by insisting even more strongly than he had that the United States avoid entanglements abroad. They were not about to fight for the "hands off" policy; that policy would be a verbal warning only. They quoted Washington to Adams and delayed matters so that the American delegates, when finally confirmed and sent off, were too late for the conference. With Congress demonstrating in this way that it was even more antagonistic to entanglements in Latin America than Adams, it was clear that the United States would remain neutral toward that area for the foreseeable future unless there was an immediate threat to the United States' own territory and interests.

Yet even at this, the United States had expanded its territory and interests greatly since the War of 1812. It had acquired a transcontinental domain from Florida to Oregon. It had proclaimed unilaterally its interest in the independence of Latin America and left open the possibility of acquiring Texas and Cuba. It had backed away from a full commitment to Latin American independence and relied on the British fleet for any real enforcement necessary, but it had risked considerable embarrassment by demanding hands off Latin America. If the Holy Alliance had undertaken a Latin American invasion, the resentful British could have stood aside and let the United States put up or shut up. At the very least, the United States had laid out a path for its future ambitions as a great power.

CONTROVERSIAL ISSUES AND FURTHER READING

Until the mid-twentieth century, nationalist historians were almost unchallenged in praising the Monroe Doctrine as the outstanding example of a proper American foreign policy. The Monroe Doctrine idealistically protected republican liberty in the Western Hemisphere against European monarchy while realistically diminishing the ability of another great power to threaten the United States from a close proximity. But if early American historians could agree that the Monroe Doctrine ranked with Washington's Farewell Address as the supreme guide to American diplomacy, they agreed far less on what the doctrine meant. Isolationists argued that the Founding Fathers who formulated it intended it as reinforcement for Washington's policy of abstention. Activists argued that the Founding Fathers obviously meant the United States to intervene vigorously in Latin America to keep the Europeans out.

Although for years the histories of the doctrine's origins were among the most emotional and polemical of all diplomatic histories, for the first two decades after Monroe's message, the doctrine was almost forgotten. Only one major history or textbook mentioned it at all, and the author of that one refused to include the doctrine on his list of the major achievements of the Monroe administration. [George Tucker, *History of the United States* (1856–1857), Vol. III, pp. 361–364, 407–408.] James K. Polk revived the doctrine in the 1840s to justify American expansion against Mexico, and inspired the rebuke of one historian who insisted that the Founding Fathers had not intended to assert America's right to oppose European colonization in the Western Hemisphere if such colonization took place by "purchase, treaty, or lawful conquest," however the doctrine might have come "to be regarded in these latter days." [James Clarke Welling, "The Monroe Doctrine," *North American Review* (1856).]

When Ferdinand de Lesseps tried to build a French canal across Panama in the early 1880s, it inspired a spate of polemical historical articles debating whether the originators of the Monroe Doctrine intended the United States to intervene to prevent such a foreign intrusion into the Western Hemisphere. [John A. Kasson called for intervention in his two-part history of the doctrine, "The Monroe Declaration," and "The Monroe Doctrine," in the *North American Review* (1881). So did George F. Tucker in *The Monroe Doctrine* (1885). Arguing for restraint was H. C. Bunts, "The Scope of the Monroe Doctrine," *Forum* (April 1889).] The Venezuela Crisis of 1895 renewed the debate [Interventionist: William L. Scruggs, *The Venezuelan Question: British Aggressions in Venezuela, or the Monroe Doctrine on Trial* (1894). Restraint: William F. Reddaway, *The Monroe Doctrine* (2nd ed., 1905).]

At this time, the arguments for a restrained interpretation of the doctrine seemed to predominate in historical circles. But the pendulum swung to the interventionists after the turn of the century, when Theodore Roosevelt initiated two decades of overt military interventions in the Caribbean under the rubric of the so-called Roosevelt Corollary. [Interventionist: Albert Bushnell Hart, *The Monroe Doctrine: An Interpretation* (1916). Restraint: Hiram Bingham, *The Monroe Doctrine: An Obsolete Shibboleth* (1913).]

In the process of debating the intentions of the doctrine's originators, historians began to pit the various contributors to the doctrine's formulation against one another. The interventionist John Kassson, using John Quincy Adams's recently published *Memoirs* (1874) to discover the internal cabinet debates over the issue, insisted that Adams, along with Jefferson, had wanted a doctrine that would enlist American power for all time against European intervention in the Western Hemisphere. Monroe's caution unfortunately had brought him to make a limited declaration designed only for his own time. Kasson's opponent, Bunts, conceded that Adams had been the primary inspiration for and author of the doctrine, but argued that Adams too had wanted a limited doctrine. Credit for authorship of the doctrine was granted to Adams even more convincingly by Worthington C. Ford at the turn of the century. With access to Adams's formerly closed papers, Ford tried to demonstrate that Adams had been responsible not only for the noncolonization doctrine, but also for the renewal of America's dedication to isolation from European quarrels. It had been Adams who had insisted on a unilateral doctrine rather than a joint policy with England and had warned Monroe away from statements in support of European revolutionaries. [Worthington C. Ford, "John Quincy Adams and the Monroe Doctrine," *American Historical Review* (July 1902).] James B. Schouler insisted that Monroe should receive equal credit for the unilateral, isolationist character of the doctrine. Monroe had not needed Adams to turn him from accepting Canning's offer; Monroe had only told Jefferson he intended to "meet it fully," not accept it as it stood, and after his message had been delivered, he informed Jefferson that he had made his policy unilaterally because Rush had informed him that Canning had already cooled to the project. [James B. Schouler, "The Authorship of the Monroe Doctrine," *American Historical Association Report* (1905).]

World War I embarrassed historians who had been trying to elevate the stature of Monroe or Adams by attributing to them the doctrine's statement of noninvolvement in Europe. Albert Bushnell Hart, an avid exponent of intervention, handled this by saying that Adams had been right for his time, but America had since outgrown neutralism. John Holladay Latané, however, claimed that Adams's isolationism had been wrong from the outset, and Monroe and Jefferson had been correct in their willingness to accept the British entanglement. [John Holladay Latané, *From Isolation to Leadership: A Review of American Foreign Policy* (1918).]

After World War I, the Good Neighbor Policy made open military interventions in Latin America on behalf of the Monroe Doctrine less popular, and the immediate relevance of the doctrine faded. At this time, better researched and less polemical historical works on the doctrine appeared. The classic study of the origins of the doctrine is still that by Dexter Perkins, *The Monroe Doctrine, 1823–1826* (1927). Perkins dismissed the authorship question by crediting Adams and Monroe rather equally, and it has not been a major historiographical issue since. His research in the European archives demonstrated that there never had been any real danger of France or the Holy Alliance intervening in Latin America in 1823, and so he also dismissed all claims that the United States had saved the revolutionaries.

Walter Lippmann revived historical controversy over the doctrine by making it a centerpiece of his realist critique of the history of American foreign policy. He proclaimed that the formulators of the doctrine had been supreme realists because they had balanced their goal of security for the United States with the means available. Knowing the United States was not powerful enough to defend the Western Hemisphere alone, they devised a tacit agreement with the British to have the fleet protect against intruders despite America's unilateral pronouncement in the Doctrine. Lippmann only bewailed the fact that the formulators had not made the British alliance "permanent and binding," for later generations of Americans forgot the role of the British in the Monroe Doctrine and deluded themselves that America had defended the hemisphere unaided. This misjudgment of the nation's power and influence had led to further far-flung commitments unsupported by military force, ultimately inviting World War II. [Walter Lippmann, *U.S. Foreign Policy: Shield of the Republic* (1943).]

Many historians accepted Lippmann's realist outlook on the doctrine and America's later delusions, but disputed his specific assertion that there had been a tacit British alliance behind the doctrine. Some pointed to Edward Tatum's study, which argued that the real target of Monroe's message had been Great Britain itself rather than the Holy Alliance, since it was Great Britain which seriously threatened Cuba and Latin America. [Edward Howland Tatum, Jr., *The United States and Europe, 1815–1923: A Study in the Background of the Monroe Doctrine* (1936).] Arthur Whitaker, however, argued learnedly and persuasively that John Quincy Adams did actually pursue cooperation with the British at this time and that his desire for a unilateral declaration was simply his way of warning against an Anglo-American crusade. [Arthur Whitaker, *The United States and the Independence of Latin America* (1941).] Samuel Flagg Bemis and his student, William W. Kaufmann, then argued that Lippmann was dead wrong about the existence of a tacit British alliance, but because the British rather than the Americans had spurned the formation of a "satisfying Anglo-American entente worthy of the rights of man." Bemis condemned Lippmann for glossing over the British failure "as if it were necessary to support the cause of 1940 by a perverted historical dialectic." [Samuel Flagg Bemis, *John Quincy Adams and the Foundations of American Foreign Policy* (1949), pp. 399–401; William W. Kaufmann, *British Policy and the Independence of Latin America, 1804–1828* (1951).] Later realist works have agreed that there was no tacit British alliance, that the British had actually denounced the doctrine, but indeed had used their influence to prevent any great power other than themselves from intruding too much into the Western Hemisphere. [Bradford Perkins, *Castlereagh and Adams: England and the United States, 1812–1823* (1964); Harry Ammon, *James Monroe* (1971).]

No revisionist has written a complete study of the Monroe Doctrine, but broader revisionist surveys have emphasized its expansionist implications. They have pointed especially to the desire of the United States to win Cuba, Texas, and Latin American trade from Great Britain as the reason for rejecting the British initiative and declaring the doctrine unilaterally. Meanwhile, the only recent new interpretation of the doctrine has been that of Ernest R. May, who claimed that the doctrine was almost entirely directed at domestic partisan issues rather than the nonexistent foreign crisis. [Ernest R. May, *The Making of the Monroe Doctrine* (1975). He is disputed by Harry Ammon, "The Monroe Doctrine: Domestic Politics or National Decision?" *Diplomatic History* (Winter 1981).]

The acquisition of Florida has not been so significant a historiographical issue. For the first half-century following the Transcontinental Treaty, American historians saw little to criticize in America's expansionist course except its failure to take Texas as well as Florida. Theodore Lyman, for instance, berated the Spanish for refusing "to deliver the country" despite America's proper claim to West Florida. [Theodore Lyman, *The Diplomacy of the United States* (1826–1828).] Then Henry Adams opened criticism of America's Florida diplomacy by ridiculing the claim that the Louisiana Purchase had included West Florida. It was only the dishonesty, however, not the belligerence of America's conduct that bothered Adams. He thought the United States should have taken Texas, to which the Louisiana Purchase had given better title. Then, if Spain had resisted, America could have conquered Florida as an indemnity. Adams convinced most major historians of his era that the West Florida claim had been fraudulent, but twelve of the fourteen history textbooks of the time still insisted it was legitimate.

After the turn of the century, both the belligerence and the conniving of America's Florida diplomacy came under fire from Herbert Bruce Fuller, *The Purchase of Florida: Its History and Diplomacy* (1906), and Isaac Joslin Cox, *The West Florida Controversy, 1798–1813: A Study in American Diplomacy* (1918). The best modern work defending America's course is Samuel Flagg Bemis's biography of John Quincy Adams, mentioned above. [See also Phillip Coolidge Brooks, *Diplomacy and the Borderlands* (1939), and Charles Carrol Griffin, *The United States and the Disruption of the Spanish Empire* (1937). For a general history of American territorial expansion, see William H. Goetzmann, *When the Eagle Screamed: The Romantic Horizon in American Diplomacy, 1800–1860* (1966). For the intellectual rationales offered by Americans to justify their expansion, see Albert K. Weinberg, *Manifest Destiny: A Study of Nationalist Expansionism in American History* (1935).]

CHAPTER 5

Territorial Expansion: Texas, Oregon, California, and the Mexican War

THE UNITED STATES AND THE TEXAS REVOLUTION

Spain did not have long to enjoy the secure possession of Texas it had won in the treaty of 1819. The Mexican Revolution of 1821 ended Spanish rule in all of North America. Mexico, however, was no better able to populate, govern, and protect Texas than Spain had been. Much of the Mexican population consisted of Indians who were disaffected from the government. The Mexican people were concentrated in the central highlands, where they were surrounded by rugged mountains, malarial coastal plains, and deep gorges. This made communication with outlying territories like Texas extremely difficult.

The year before the Mexican Revolution, Spain had tried to compensate for these disadvantages and protect its recently confirmed border with the United States by establishing new settlements in Texas. Unhappily, its only reasonable source of immigrants was the United States itself, so Spain invited an American adventurer, Moses Austin, to form a community in Texas. Austin did not have time to establish his settlement before the Mexican revolutionaries had seized power, but the new government confirmed the concession. Like Spain, Mexico feared that otherwise Texas would remain an empty and inviting target for acquisition by the United States, regardless of America's treaty commitments.

In 1824, Moses Austin's son Stephen took over the colonial concession and began to settle Americans in several small municipalities in eastern Texas. Although Austin seems to have made a loyal effort to work with the Mexican government, it was probably inevitable that the American settlements would gravitate toward the United States. The American immigrants formed exclusive communities, maintained their own language and culture, and remained quite separate from the few Mexicans in the surrounding area. Although Mexican law required that the immigrants be Roman Catholic, they remained Protestants. The Mexican Constitution also implied the illegality of slavery by stating that all men were equal. Yet the American immigrants brought in their slaves to try to reproduce the cotton plantation economy of the neighboring American South. The Mexican government by and large winked at these transgressions and gave the provincial government of Texas wide latitude to deal with the American communities.

Then, in 1827 a local Texas uprising known as the Fredonian revolt frightened the Mexican government into taking measures that would lessen the danger of American settlers usurping power and joining the United States. The Mexican Congress passed a series of laws that barred further American immigration into Texas, abolished slavery, and placed high tariffs on the imports Texans required from the United States. Mexico did not strictly enforce these laws, but to many Texans they seemed ominous portents of things to come. Stephen Austin and other Texas leaders urged the Mexican government to make Texas a separate state within Mexico and thus guarantee its special privileges. The distracted Mexican government responded instead with further centralization. Even more frightening, Mexican troops under General Antonio López de Santa Anna used extreme brutality to put down a rebellion in Zacatecas against this centralization. Alarmed Texans organized militia forces, and inevitably Santa Anna marched northward to quell the uprising. In the wake of news that Santa Anna intended to repeat his Zacatecas performance, Texans met in a special convention in 1836 and declared Texas an independent nation.

Santa Anna's army of five thousand wiped out the American garrison in San Antonio at the Alamo. It then captured the defenders of the town of Goliad and executed them as traitors. But it was defeated and dispersed by Sam Houston's surprise attack at San Jacinto. Some Texan troops captured Santa Anna when he tried to slip away in disguise, and Sam Houston forced him to sign a treaty recognizing the independence of Texas. Of course Santa Anna disowned the treaty once he was out of the hands of the Texas army. He claimed Mexico had a sovereign right to reconquer its rebellious province any time it wished. Meanwhile, the Mexicans protested against the aid Americans had given the Texas rebels and warned that any attempt by the United States to annex the province would result in the severing of diplomatic relations and war.

Mexico understandably suspected the United States of complicity in the rebellion. Immigrants of American descent fomented it; American sympathizers crossed the border in droves to help Houston and his army. Large funds were collected in the United States for support of the rebels. Sam Houston was a close friend and political protégé of President Andrew Jackson. Yet there is no evidence that Jackson and Houston plotted the revolution. Jackson certainly wanted Texas. Twice before he had tried to purchase it from Mexico by pressing the claims of several American citizens against Mexico for losses they had incurred during the Mexican Revolution. He implied that the United States would assume those obligations in exchange for the cession of Texas. Still, he had shown considerable caution. He was aware of the problem Texas would pose for the slavery issue in American domestic politics, and he had advised John Quincy Adams and James Monroe to give up Texas by accepting the Sabine River border during the Adams-Onís negotiations of 1819.

When he became president, he agreed ultimately to submit the claims of the American citizens against Mexico to international arbitration rather than fight when Mexico refused to cede Texas as compensation. He also kept the American government officially aloof from the Texas rebellion, although he did nothing to discourage private American citizens from aiding Houston's rebel army, since he had neither the resources nor the desire to stop them.[1] Even after Texas defeated the Mexican army at San Jacinto, Jackson advised Congress to delay recognition of Texas as an independent nation, and he waited until the last day of his lame duck period as president to grant that recognition.

The Texas revolutionaries, however, wanted more; they wanted annexation. Thousands of Americans supported their annexation petition. Many Americans had purchased land scrip sold by the Texans to raise money for their revolution. Such speculators expected the value of their lands to rise significantly if Texas joined the Union and thus received American protection against renewed Mexican invasion. Many southerners also supported annexation because they believed they could carve several slave states out of Texas. But the issue of slavery cut both ways, as demonstrated by Jackson's uncharacteristic caution. Leaders of the political parties saw the slave issue as sure to divide the nation on geographical lines. This would shatter the party system and with it the leaders' electoral prospects. On the other hand, these leaders could not afford to oppose annexation outright. Expansion was a popular issue with Whigs as well as Democrats, so most of the party leaders hedged. They tried to cater to supporters and opponents of Texas by advocating annexation, but in the future.

Another factor complicating the Texas issue was the determination of Mexico to fight if the United States annexed the province. Antislavery northerners might accept Texas if it were acquired quickly and cheaply, but they were certain to oppose fighting Mexico on behalf of a new slave territory. Jackson's Democratic successor, Martin Van Buren, followed Old Hickory's example by rejecting Texas's repeated requests for annexation. The opposition Whigs were even more in favor of delay, and the issue temporarily receded into the political background. Rebuffed by the United States, Sam Houston and the Texans considered other expedients. One alternative was for Texas to remain an independent nation and perhaps expand its territory to the Pacific.

For the present, however, these dreams seemed grandiose even to Texans. The population was growing rapidly, but by 1840 Texas still had only 60,000 scattered inhabitants and its treasury was bankrupt. It had difficulty even maintaining its claim to the Rio Grande border, and it could mount only a few hit and run raids into that desolate area. The most important of these

---

[1] There was one exception to this. General Edmund P. Gaines did cross the Texas border with some American troops when he heard that Indians were marauding eastern Texas settlements and that neither the Mexicans nor Texans could stop them. The rumors proved false and Gaines returned to the American side of the border without having affected the Texas rebellion one way or the other.

raids, a military trading expedition of some three hundred Texans which had set off to acquire Santa Fe, ended in an ignominious surrender, the immediate execution of its leaders, and the deportation of the rest in chains to Mexico City.

Fortunately for the Texans, Mexico itself was so debt-ridden and crippled by internal disputes that it could manage only a few minor raids into its distant former province. But Houston and his fellow citizens never could be quite sure that the Mexican efforts at reconquest would continue to be ineffectual, and they had to be uneasy at the treatment meted out by the Mexicans to captured rebels. As long as Mexico posed even a distant threat, the Texans preferred American annexation to independence.

The British saw this and urged Mexico to recognize the independence of Texas. Then the Texans might abandon their desire for American annexation, benefiting Mexicans and British alike. Texas would buffer Mexico's northern border from American aggression, while the British would have in Texas a separate source of cotton, along with a potential check to American expansion. An independent Texas also would contribute to a balance of power in North America, undermining United States hegemony. With abolitionist sentiments running high in Great Britain following the outlawing of slavery in the British West Indies in 1833, some of Britain's leaders also had hopes that an independent Texas might forswear slavery.

In 1842, the British officially offered to mediate between Mexico and Texas. The British foreign minister, Lord Aberdeen, did not press his case very hard. He even gave assurances that Britain would not interfere improperly against slavery in Texas. Nevertheless, an American agent in London named Duff Green instantly wrote back to the United States that the British had concocted a plot to threaten the South by establishing an independent abolitionist Texas on its flank. He urged immediate annexation. John C. Calhoun picked up the cry and accused Great Britain of being ready to foment slave rebellions to undermine the competitive economic edge the South had acquired over Britain's West Indies since slavery had been abolished in the British Empire. Green and Calhoun induced the aged but revered Andrew Jackson to write letters warning of the British plot, which the Texas advocates used to maximum effect. The annexation issue was alive again.

GREAT BRITAIN AND AMERICAN EXPANSION

Supporters of annexation saw in the British bogey the ideal lever to revive their cause against the apathy and caution of the major political parties. There was always a generous fund of latent hostility in the United States against the former mother country, and anyone who could be portrayed as defending British interests was at a terrific political disadvantage. There were real conflicts of interest between the United States and Great Britain, but those issues were more important to the United States. The British were far more concerned with the high volume of Anglo-American trade than with peripheral areas like Texas, so many British leaders, among them Lord Aberdeen himself, were quite willing to compromise. Unfortunately, Great Britain had its own blusterers. The most powerful of these was Lord Palmerston, the great rival of Aberdeen and Aberdeen's prime minister, Robert Peel. Politicians like Palmerston were perfectly happy to exploit the British public's dislike of Americans as ignorant bullies. Such politicians helped keep Anglo-American relations in an almost constant state of agitation and made it easy for any American demagogue to further a favorite cause by linking it with an anti-British crusade.

Trivial issues had dragged America and England close to war several times in the years just preceding 1842. The most volatile of these had been the longstanding dispute over the border between Canada and Maine. The Treaty of Paris of 1783, which ended the revolution, described the border as running due north from the source of the St. Croix River to the highlands that divided the rivers flowing to the Atlantic from those flowing to the St. Lawrence, then along those highlands to the northwestern head of the Connecticut River. Unfortunately, there was no St. Croix River in the area, the term "highlands" was too vague, and no one knew which stream was the northwestern head of the Connecticut. Naturally, both the British and the Americans interpreted this description to their own best advantage, and their rival claims left some 7.5 million acres in dispute. Great Britain and the United States referred the issue to the king of the Netherlands for arbitration in 1831, but Andrew Jackson rejected the line suggested by the king because the inhabitants of Maine were adamantly opposed to any concession and Jackson's political advisers urged him to avoid alienating those voters. The issue became dangerous in 1839 when a quarrel over the control of the area around the Aroostook River brought first a posse of 200 Maine lumbermen to march on the area, followed by 10,000 Maine militia. The so-called Aroostook War ended without bloodshed after Britain offered to share control of the area, but some final settlement was necessary.

The interests involved in the Maine border dispute were not vital ones. The British did have a strategic interest in keeping the border as far south as possible to enable them to build a convenient military road from New Brunswick to Quebec for use when the St. Lawrence was frozen. The United States, on the other hand, wanted title to Rouse's Point, on which it had built a key fort to guard Lake Champlain, but which a careful survey belatedly showed to be on the British side of the border along the 45th parallel. These issues could have been settled quite easily, however, if it had not been for the violent emotions of the local inhabitants. Many of the Canadian settlers in the disputed area were descendants of loyalist refugees from the American Revolution, and they had no wish to find themselves on the American side of the border. The inhabitants of Maine were even more anxious to secure the best agricultural and timber lands available, and they rallied general American support for their cause by trumpeting that the border issue was one of national honor against British rapaciousness.

Another emotional issue between England and America concerned

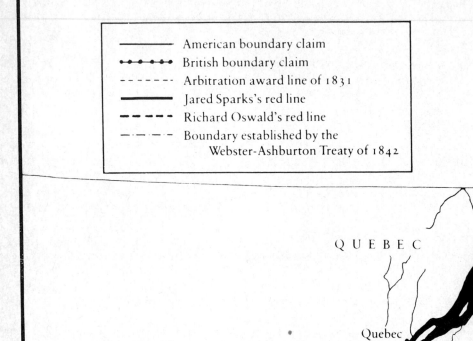

QUEBEC

Quebec

LOWER CANADA

St. Lawrence River

Montreal

45°

Rouse's Point
(Fort Montgomery)

Lake
Champlain

Hall's Stream

Indian Stream

Connecticut River

NEW YORK

VERMONT

NEW
HAMPSI

Map 4 Northeastern Boundary Problem, 1783–1842

Gulf of St. Lawrence

St. Lawrence River

Metis River

Bay of Chaleurs

Restigouche River

Lake Temiscouata

Temiscouata Portage

Lake Pohenagamook

Madawaska River

Madawaska Settlements

St. Francis River

St. John River

Fish River

Grand Falls
Fort Fairfield

Mars Hill

Aroostook River

NEW BRUNSWICK
(Part of NOVA SCOTIA until 1784)

St. John River

"narrow ← strip"

Houlton

Eel River

Fredericton

St. John River

Penobscot River

St. Croix River
[Schoodic River]

Magaguadavic River

St. John

MAINE
(Part of Massachusetts until 1819)

Kennebec

Bangor

Passamaquoddy Bay

Bay of Fundy

Grand Manan Island

NOVA SCOTIA

American aid to Canadian rebels in the area around Niagara Falls. In 1837 the *Caroline,* a ship owned by an American citizen, was supplying the rebels lodged on Canada's Navy Island just above the falls. Canadian volunteers commanded by two British officers crossed to the American side and burned the ship at its dock. An American bystander was killed in the fracas, and Martin Van Buren sent General Winfield Scott to the area and demanded redress. The British government delayed taking responsibility, which left open the possibility that the raiders had not been soldiers acting in the line of duty, but private citizens subject to trial in New York if caught. The issue died along with the Canadian rebellion when the famous Lord Durham Report to the British Parliament started Canada on the road to self-government. But it revived in 1840 when one Alexander McLeod was arrested on American territory after bragging in a tavern that he had participated in the raid and fired the shot that killed the American spectator. The British insisted that McLeod be freed, since no individual could be tried for participating in what the British now claimed as a public act for which only the British government itself could be held responsible. With local passions still high over the *Caroline* incident, the state of New York insisted on trying McLeod for murder anyway. Fortunately, the New York court acquitted him, and again the threat of war blew over.

Another issue that troubled Anglo-American relations in the 1830s and 1840s was the slave trade. Great Britain urged that the United States permit British ships off the African coast to visit and search suspected slavers flying the American flag. The United States consistently refused, remembering the humiliation of searches, seizures, and impressment that had triggered the War of 1812. The search and seizure issue was exacerbated when slaves being carried from Virginia to New Orleans aboard the American ship *Creole* killed their owner, overpowered the captain, and steered the ship into Nassau harbor in the British-owned Bahamas. The British refused to extradite the escaped slaves as mutineers or murderers, and the South joined the inhabitants of Maine and the Great Lakes area in harboring resentment against the British.

In 1842, Secretary of State Daniel Webster managed to reach agreement on these issues with a special British envoy, Lord Ashburton. The Webster-Ashburton Treaty settled the Maine border by giving the United States the best agricultural land and the fort at Rouse's Point, while at the same time keeping the border far enough south to give the British their route for the New Brunswick military road. Webster secured Maine's consent to the compromise by using government money to publish newspaper articles in favor of a settlement. He also showed Maine legislators a map discovered by historian Jared Sparks in the Paris archives on which the Maine boundary supposedly drawn by Benjamin Franklin in 1783 conformed to the British rather than the American claim. (Webster had not shown the map to Ashburton until after the settlement had been negotiated. Since there was no evidence that Franklin's supposed line was the final one rather than a preliminary proposal, the map did not mean much anyway, except as a propaganda tool.)

The Webster-Ashburton Treaty resolved several less knotty problems as well. It defined the border between Lake Superior and Lake of the Woods. It also agreed to joint British and American slave patrols in African waters. To avoid the touchy issue of visit and search, only the American ships would search suspected slavers flying the American flag. An extradition agreement in the treaty responded to the fears aroused by the *Creole* affair. It omitted any British commitment to return escaped slaves, but Ashburton signed a note promising no officious interference with American ships driven into British West Indian ports, even if they carried slaves. The British also offered an implied apology for the burning of the *Caroline* on American soil. Finally, since improved conditions aboard British naval ships made desertions less likely than in earlier years, Ashburton could afford to give private assurances that impressment was obsolete.

Although the Webster-Ashburton Treaty solved many of the problems between England and America, it did not much assuage the emotional antagonisms of the British and American peoples. These antagonisms continued to furnish a fertile field for ambitious politicians. Political opponents subjected both Webster and Ashburton to merciless criticism. Senator Thomas Hart Benton led the attack on the treaty for disenchanted American Democrats. He claimed that a map in the Library of Congress given by Benjamin Franklin to Thomas Jefferson demonstrated that America's extensive claims to Maine had been justified. When the map was brought before the Senate, the embarrassed Benton found that the line on it corresponded to the line of Sparks's map, supporting the British claim. Benton recovered to say that Webster then should not have tricked Ashburton, but the Senate overrode him and consented to the treaty.

Ashburton faced a similar attack from Palmerston, who claimed that Ashburton had given up too much, as demonstrated by the now public Sparks map. Ashburton deflated Palmerston's criticisms when he discovered still another map, this one hidden by Palmerston himself in the Foreign Office because it supported the American claim. The successful maneuvering of Webster and Ashburton saved their treaty, but Anglo-American relations remained tenuous.

Oregon

The passions that emerged in these treaty ratification debates made more ominous the failure of Webster and Ashburton to agree over the division of the Oregon Territory. Webster and Ashburton had stumbled over an obstacle to a fair division of Oregon that had plagued Anglo-American negotiations since 1818. During the 1818 negotiations the American representatives, Albert Gallatin and Richard Rush, had offered to divide the territory at the 49th parallel and thus extend the boundary between the Louisiana Purchase and Canada right through the Rocky Mountains to the Pacific. The British refused because that line would have given the United States the two most important geographical features of the Oregon territory—the mouth of the Columbia River and the Straits of Juan de Fuca. The British mistakenly thought that the Columbia River would be to the Pacific Coast what the Mississippi system was to the trans-Appalachian region, the key to the commerce and control of the whole area. Later they realized that the sand bar at the mouth of the Columbia limited the commercial value of the river.

The Straits of Juan de Fuca were another matter. They led to Puget Sound, the only decent port on the Pacific Coast outside Spanish control, and a potentially invaluable window to Asia. In addition, Great Britain's Northwest Company, soon to be merged with the powerful Hudson's Bay Company, saw the Columbia River Valley as a cornucopia for its fur-trading operation. To put all these features on the Canadian side of the border, the British proposed to divide the Oregon territory along the 49th parallel only as far as the Snake River, then go down the Snake and the Columbia to the sea. Unable to agree, the negotiators decided to share control of the entire Oregon territory for ten years.

The United States improved its claim to the Oregon Territory in 1819 by acquiring Spain's claim in the Transcontinental Treaty. The British improved theirs even more by the activities of the Hudson's Bay Company. The Americans and British tried twice more, in 1823 and 1826, to divide the territory. In those negotiations, both sides flirted with a compromise that would split the disputed rectangle between the Columbia and the 49th parallel in half. The Americans would acquire the mouth of the Columbia and several minor harbors along the Olympic peninsula, the British would get the Straits of Juan de Fuca, Puget Sound, and the right to navigate the Columbia River. The compromise failed because the Americans valued Puget Sound too highly to surrender it. On the other side, the Hudson's Bay Company pressed the British government to keep the Columbia River and valley. Consequently, despite a brief flurry of emotional rhetoric in the American Congress about establishing military forts to make good America's claim to Oregon, the British and Americans extended the joint occupation agreement indefinitely in 1826 and put the issue on the back burner.

By the time of the Webster-Ashburton negotiations in 1842, conditions in Oregon had begun to change. The British position was weakening. The Hudson's Bay Company had trapped out the Columbia basin and was planning to move its headquarters from Fort Vancouver on the Columbia to Vancouver Island. The company acknowledged in making its decision that the sand bar at the mouth of the Columbia nullified the value of the river for trade or defense. Simultaneously, thousands of Americans began to arrive in Oregon to reinforce the small contingent of some five hundred American settlers which the British fur traders had long dominated.

These immigrants were lured down the Oregon Trail by reports from American missionaries who had arrived to work among the Indians. Despite the changing balance of power in Oregon, Ashburton's hastily drawn instructions for the 1842 negotiations with Webster permitted no concessions north of the Columbia, so the joint occupation agreement was continued.

Neither envoy realized that the issue might be coming to a head in the near future.

California

During the Webster-Ashburton negotiations, Webster had suggested that if Great Britain could obtain San Francisco from Mexico for the United States, America might concede Puget Sound to the British. Ashburton offhandedly turned the suggestion aside, but Webster's proposal showed that California was joining Oregon and Texas as an arena of Anglo-American contention. Like Texas, California was a distant, weak, and disaffected part of Mexico. At the time of the Mexican Revolution in 1821, it had had a population of only 30,000, nine-tenths Indians tied tenuously to Mexican authority by the disintegrating mission system. Mexico tried to increase immigration to California by breaking up the missions and replacing them with secular *ranchos*. These ranchos soon developed a relatively profitable trade in hides with ships bound for the Far East, but the business attracted few Mexican immigrants. Instead, a handful of American and British merchants arrived to participate in the trade. Several of them became involved with disputing factions among the Californios and were deported to Mexico City on suspicion of plotting rebellion.

Like Oregon, California seemed very remote to the United States and Great Britain. Although each kept a wary eye on the other, fearing its rival might exploit the vacuum of power, neither made concerted plans to take California for itself. In 1840, Aberdeen rejected a proposal from his minister to the United States to make California a formal colony, although the United States did not know this. The United States itself had tried unsuccessfully to purchase California in 1835, and the Americans regarded the Hudson's Bay Company outpost on Yerba Buena Island in the middle of San Francisco Bay with great suspicion. Then Thomas ap Catesby Jones, the commander of America's Pacific squadron, took the British threat so seriously that in 1842 he forced the surrender of the Mexican garrison at Monterey. He did so on the basis of rumors that war was breaking out between the United States and Mexico and that the British squadron in the Pacific had moved to California to take advantage of the imbroglio. The embarrassed Jones had to haul his flag back down when the rumors proved untrue. Even the surprisingly amicable banquets he gave his former captives could not erase the suspicions his conduct had aroused among the Mexicans and British.

The Annexation of Texas

In this atmosphere of distrust arising from Anglo-American rivalry in Oregon and California and from the Webster-Ashburton Treaty, the British offer to mediate between Mexico and Texas in 1842 ignited a renewed American campaign for the immediate annexation of Texas. The leader of the campaign was President John Tyler. Unlike his predecessors, Tyler could afford to promote the Texas issue, for he had become a man without a party. Democrats detested him because he had joined his fellow southerner John C. Calhoun in deserting to the Whigs out of hatred for Andrew Jackson. The Whigs had nominated Tyler to be vice-president under William Henry Harrison as a gesture to the Calhoun rump of the party because they did not anticipate that the avid states-righter and slavery advocate could cause much trouble for the Whigs' nationalist program from that impotent office. Harrison upset their calculations by dying after only a month in office, and President Tyler promptly vetoed the Whig bill to reestablish a national bank. This veto inspired the Whigs to detest Tyler as much as the Democrats did.

With no chance of winning renomination from either major party, Tyler had no compunctions about endangering the internal unity of the parties by annexing Texas. Only by destroying the party system and reassembling a majority around himself as the hero of American expansionism could he have any hope of reelection. With this in mind, Tyler decided to negotiate a treaty of annexation with Texas. He whipped up patriotic sentiment by praising American expansion at the expense of British imperialism and Mexican degradation, and he played down the fact that annexation would increase the number of slave states in the Union.

Unfortunately for Tyler's plans, a cannon exploded aboard the battleship *Princeton* while a presidential inspection party was aboard. Tyler was below decks at the time and was spared, but the accident killed his obedient secretary of state, Abel Upshur. Tyler replaced Upshur with his old mentor, Calhoun, and charged him with completing the annexation of Texas. Calhoun did negotiate the annexation treaty, but shortly before he submitted it to a closely divided and highly emotional Senate, he sabotaged Tyler's political strategy. Inexplicably, Calhoun replied publicly to an old dispatch from Lord Aberdeen that expressed Britain's hopes for a truce between Mexico and Texas and for the abolition of slavery. Calhoun proclaimed that Britain's meddling made it imperative for the United States to annex Texas to save slavery throughout the United States. Thus, instead of portraying annexation as an expansionist issue, desirable whether slavery was affected or not, Calhoun succeeded in making slavery the primary issue. As a consequence, northern senators united against the treaty of annexation and defeated it by a two-thirds margin.

The fiasco naturally reinforced the caution of the leading candidates for the Whig and Democratic nominations, Henry Clay and Martin Van Buren. Apparently they had agreed a year earlier to avoid the Texas issue in their campaigns. On the eve of the Texas treaty vote and the party nominating conventions, both wrote public letters expressing support for eventual but not immediate annexation. A faction within the Democratic party, however, was unwilling to let the Texas issue go. These expansionists succeeded in deadlocking the Democratic convention by denying Van Buren the two-thirds vote he needed under the new party rules for nomination. They persuaded the exhausted delegates to nominate James K. Polk instead.

Polk and his expansionist Democrat supporters believed they had a way to annex Texas without arousing controversy over slavery and disrupting the unity of their party and the nation. Instead of putting off further expansion to avoid the issue, as Clay and Van Buren proposed, the United States should expand simultaneously to the north and south, bringing in slave and free territory in relatively equal measure. Their Democratic party platform called not only for annexation of Texas, but for occupation of *all* of Oregon. This included the area above the 49th parallel, presently known as British Columbia, which had been implicitly recognized as British since 1818. Polk seemed unworried that this would inevitably mean war with England. (The platform actually called for the "reannexation" of Texas and the "reoccupation" of Oregon, as though neither had ever been legitimately in the hands of anyone else.)

Running on this bold platform, Polk narrowly defeated Henry Clay for the presidency. Modern analysts of the election doubt that Polk's victory was a clear mandate for his expanionist ideas. They think it probably resulted from the natural swing back to the Democratic party of many who had voted for the Whigs in the wake of the depression of 1837, a depression many had blamed on Jackson and Van Buren. But Polk considered his election a mandate, and so did John Tyler. Tyler was now a lame duck president, but he wanted to finish the annexation of Texas. Knowing he would be unable to get two-thirds of the Senate to vote for Texas, even in the wake of Polk's electoral victory, Tyler tried to circumvent the treaty-making provisions of the Constitution and have Congress vote for annexation by a joint resolution of both Houses. This would require only 51 percent of the vote in each branch of the Congress.

The House of Representatives quickly voted for Tyler's proposal. The Senate was more wary. It was particularly worried about a potential war with Mexico over annexation. Thomas Hart Benton proposed that annexation be delayed to allow time for negotiations with Mexico. He was persuaded to water down his proposal to require only new negotiations with Texas, which might permit time for pacifying Mexico. Benton also agreed to allow the president to choose whether to annex immediately under the House resolution or delay matters under the Senate proposal.

Benton assumed that Polk rather than the lame duck Tyler would be the one to decide how to annex Texas, and he thought he had an agreement with Polk to use the Senate plan. But Tyler fooled Benton. On his last day in office, he sent messengers to Texas to annex immediately under the House resolution. Polk could have salvaged the situation by recalling the messengers and beginning negotiations for a new treaty of annexation, but he denied he had any such agreement with Benton. Mexico immediately declared the annexation an act of war and broke diplomatic relations with the United States. The Mexican government also began reinforcing its army in the north and ordered it to prepare for war with the United States.

Even then there was some chance for a peaceful settlement. Mexico was indeed deeply offended. Any Mexican government that suggested concessions on the Texas issue would face severe internal opposition and possible revolution. But Mexico's finances were in complete disarray, and the army was in terrible shape. Its commanders were more interested in taking power in Mexico City than in fighting the United States. American patience and quiet attempts to assuage Mexico's offended sense of honor might have led ultimately to an acceptance of annexation as a fait accompli, especially since Mexico itself had finally recognized the independence of Texas just before American annexation.

Polk, however, was not inclined to be gentle or patient. He was a flinty, narrow, pious man, totally lacking in charm, and known to some of his associates as Polk the Plodder. Sam Houston said the problem was that he drank too much water. Polk had only one style of diplomacy—take a hard line and extract concessions from the other side. He avowed that the only way to deal with John Bull was to look him straight in the eye. Unfortunately, he decided to look John Bull and the Mexican eagle in the eye at the same time and found himself on the brink of war with both powers simultaneously.

The Oregon Compromise

Polk began his administration with a belligerent inaugural address in which he rejoiced at the "reannexation" of Texas and demanded all of Oregon. But he followed up his Oregon bluff by renewing the old American offer to divide the territory at the 49th parallel. Lord Aberdeen had ordered his minister to the United States, Richard Pakenham, to seek a compromise. Pakenham was to accept the 49th parallel if the United States would agree to bend the border southward and run it through the Straits of Juan de Fuca. This would give Great Britain equal access to the straits, all of Vancouver Is-

Figure 5   President James K. Polk. Portrait courtesy of the National Archives.

RUSSIAN ALASKA

54° 40'

Great Divide

CANADA

O R E G O N

49°

Treaty line of 1846

Boundary with Canada, settled in 1818

Straits of Juan de Fuca

Missouri R.

Area primarily in dispute

C O U N T R Y

UNITED STATES

Colorado R.

Snake R.

42°

Boundary with Spain, settled in 1819

MEXICO

Map 5   The Oregon Settlement, 1846

land, and a decent mainland port in the lee of the island to compensate for American control of Puget Sound. Aberdeen also told Pakenham to secure Britain's right to navigate the Columbia River to its mouth.

Because Aberdeen faced domestic opposition to his proposed concessions to the United States, he asked Pakenham to get the Americans to make the compromise offer. Polk's belligerent inaugural and patronizing border proposal so angered Pakenham, however, that he forgot his instructions and rejected Polk's offer out of hand. The British rejection outraged and embarrassed Polk, since he already had betrayed his platform promises by offering a border at the 49th parallel. Polk's natural response was to become more adamant yet. He demanded 54° 40' and insisted he would offer no more compromises.

The majority of the House and Senate was not willing to play such a risky game. Congress did give Great Britain notice that the United States was terminating the joint occupation agreement, but it couched the notification in terms that invited the British to submit a compromise plan for dividing the territory. Meanwhile, Polk let it be known with a great show of reluctance that if the Senate insisted, he would consider a British request for a compromise.

Polk's blustering actually made a settlement with Britain less rather than more likely. Aberdeen was thoroughly ready to compromise. Great Britain was undergoing a severe food shortage and needed American trade. Aberdeen even secured the agreement of Lord Palmerston to abstain from attacking an Oregon compromise. Polk gravely risked this tenuous British consensus for restraint by making any British concession seem a humiliating surrender. Fortunately for Polk and the United States, Aberdeen swallowed hard and offered the 49° border that would dip to exempt Vancouver Island. Polk referred the offer to the Senate without comment, and the Senate accepted it after insisting that the British right to navigate the Columbia be only temporary. This Oregon Treaty of June 1846 saved the United States from a perilous two-front war. For by the time the British and Americans reached agreement, the armies of the United States and Mexico were already in combat.

THE MEXICAN WAR

With the danger of war looming over the Oregon issue, one might have expected Polk to operate very prudently in his dispute with Mexico. Instead, Polk moved aggressively on this southern flank as well. Prior to his election, he had pledged to protect Texas from possible Mexican retribution if it accepted annexation, even if this involved sending troops before Texas was legally a part of the United States. When Polk's agents in Texas, some of whom seem to have been bent on inviting a war with Mexico that would provide an excuse for further American conquests in the Southwest, reported that a Mexican invasion seemed imminent, Polk ordered General Zachary Taylor and three thousand troops to take a position along the "frontier of Texas . . . on or near the Rio Grande del Norte." By thus endorsing Texas's claim that its border lay on the Rio Grande rather than on the Nueces River, the acknowledged border during the time of Spanish and Mexican control, Polk was making it all the more difficult for Mexico to live with the annexation. Of course, using pressure tactics rather than restraint was Polk's natural posture in diplomatic bargaining. Besides, he wanted more than mere Mexican acceptance of the fait accompli; he wanted to compel Mexico to pay the longstanding if inflated claims it owed American citizens. He also wanted California.

According to George Bancroft, the great historian who served as Polk's secretary of the navy, Polk had confided to him at the very outset of his term of office that he intended acquisition of California to be one of the four great measures of his administration. Polk seems to have wanted California because he knew he was going to have to betray his promise to take all of Oregon. An Oregon compromise would enrage many western and northern Democrats who had seen 54° 40' as the *quid pro quo* for their support of a slave Texas. Polk may have sought a free California as compensation for his abandonment of British Columbia. Ironically, Polk later would be accused by these same Democrats of seeking California as a slave state in a plot to extend slavery throughout the United States, a charge disproved by Polk's diary.

In any case, Polk hoped to bargain with Texas's claim to the Rio Grande border and with the financial claims to pry California loose from the Mexicans. He also considered letting the inhabitants of California, many of whom had little sympathy for the central government of Mexico, revolt and invite American annexation. He preferred such pressure diplomacy to an outright war of conquest, especially since the Oregon controversy opened the possibility that Great Britain would support Mexico in a two-front war on the United States. In the last resort, however, Polk would not shy from war if necessary to accomplish his purposes.

At the same time that Polk ordered Taylor and his troops into Texas, he sent the son-in-law of Senator Thomas Hart Benton, Lieutenant John C. Frémont, on his third exploring expedition into California. Frémont took sixty soldiers and a few cannon with him. Since the Mexicans in California already were in open rebellion against their governor, Micheltorena, Polk also ordered Commodore John Sloat, commander of America's Pacific squadron, to seize San Francisco and other California ports if war broke out between the United States and Mexico. Finally, he sent instructions by way of Marine Lieutenant Archibald Gillespie to an American merchant and agent in Monterey, Thomas O. Larkin, and to Frémont, to be on guard against any attempts by the British to exploit the troubles in California.[2]

Polk then was ready to negotiate. Mexico had reluctantly agreed to accept an American "commissioner" to settle the "present dispute" between Mexico and the United States. Presumably, the "present dispute" referred to the annexation of Texas. But for Polk, the annexation was an accomplished fact; he wanted to negotiate about all outstanding issues, including the Rio Grande border, the claims, and California. He appointed John Slidell as a regular minister rather than a commissioner and empowered him to exchange the claims and $5 million for the Rio Grande border. Slidell could offer $25 million more if Mexico would sell California. Polk seemed confident that his combination of pressure and diplomacy would work. He told Slidell not to break off negotiations even if California proved unobtainable, and he wrote private letters predicting there would be no war. On the other hand, he may simply have been delaying an all-out confrontation until the Oregon issue was safely resolved.

The unstable Mexican government was under enormous internal pressure to refuse negotiations and hold firm on Texas to the point of war. It found reason to reject Slidell because of Slidell's title, "minister." To negotiate with a minister as opposed to a special commissioner implied that the diplomatic relations Mexico had broken off were now restored and that the annexation of Texas was a fait accompli. Yet even the rejection of Slidell

---

[2] Controversy still surrounds the orders Polk gave Gillespie and what Gillespie actually told Frémont. Some of Gillespie's contemporaries said he encouraged American rebellion in California. But since Polk was negotiating for California at the same time and still seemed to expect success, it is doubtful that Polk gave him such orders.

failed to save the Mexican government from rumors that it intended to abandon Texas. A coup brought in a still more adamant regime.

True to form, Polk responded aggressively. General Zachary Taylor, in response to his earlier orders to camp on or near the Rio Grande, had stopped short at Corpus Christi, just across the the Nueces River. Polk now ordered him specifically to march across the disputed territory to the Rio Grande itself. Polk followed this by telling Slidell to throw the blame for any broken negotiations on Mexico, and warned that America then would take the redress of its injuries into its own hands. At this point Polk was visited in Washington by a Mexican, Colonel Alexander Atocha, bearing a message from the exiled Santa Anna. According to Atocha, Santa Anna was ready to take power again, and for $30 million he would give California to the United States. Atocha noted, however, that no Mexican government could appear to offer such terms freely. He suggested more American pressure and threats to give Mexico an excuse to make the necessary concessions. Polk did not take Atocha's revelations at face value, but he did decide to have Slidell retire to an American naval vessel and from there issue an ultimatum. Under pressure from his cabinet, Polk delayed sending this instruction while the Oregon controversy was still in a dangerous phase. He did not know that Slidell had anticipated him and had broken off his mission.

When Polk learned that Slidell had broken negotiations, he prepared to request Congress to declare war on the grounds that Mexico had rejected Slidell's mission and had not paid America's monetary claims. He did this even though he knew Congress might well find his reasons insufficient, especially with the Oregon crisis still in limbo. Polk was rescued from his gamble by news from General Taylor that elements of the Mexican army had attacked an American scouting force north of the Rio Grande. Polk immediately told Congress that war was already underway by act of Mexico, which had shed American blood on American soil. A divided Congress finally obliged the president by declaring war on Mexico, and Polk had his excuse to acquire California.

Mexico was not blameless in this affair; there seems to have been as much war fever in Mexico as in the United States. Mexico rather than the United States broke relations and warned that the annexation of Texas was an act of war. When Taylor began his move from Corpus Christi to the Rio Grande, the Mexican president ordered two of his generals to initiate hostilities against the United States immediately. Nevertheless, Polk's pressure tactics destroyed whatever chance there might have been of settling the issue without war. Clearly he intended to get California at all costs, whether by aggressive diplomacy and purchase or through war. Polk probably did not seek war from the outset of his administration, as some historians have charged; his original instructions to Slidell contained no ultimatum. His subsequent hesitation and the obvious danger of a two-front war also indicate that he preferred other means. But he would accept war rather than forego his plans, even if there remained a risk of simultaneous war with Great Britain.

Victory and the Treaty of Guadalupe Hidalgo

Within a year after the first shots of the Mexican War, American troops had obtained everything Polk had wanted out of the conflict. California fell easily. Frémont lent support to the American residents in northern California who initiated the Bear Flag Rebellion. After the rebels took Sonoma and imprisoned the Mexican leaders, they moved on to the San Francisco Bay Area where Frémont took formal command. They then joined forces with the American naval squadron that occupied San Francisco and Monterey under Commodore Sloat. Sloat reined Frémont in somewhat, treated the Mexicans in the territory mildly, and found little opposition from them when he declared California annexed to the United States. Unfortunately, Commodore Robert Stockton replaced Sloat and issued a bombastic declaration that American military forces would crush the "boasting and abusive" Mexican leaders. Such anti-Mexican sentiments, along with the arrogance of Frémont, Lieutenant Gillespie, and some of the American troops, roused greater opposition to American occupation than necessary in a province so long alienated from Mexico. The combined forces of Frémont, Stockton, and Gillespie conquered Los Angeles, but a revolt forced their retreat. General Stephen Kearny finally pacified California in January 1847 after he had marched with an American regiment from Fort Leavenworth through Santa Fe.

While Kearny was taking California and New Mexico, General Zachary Taylor was pushing the Mexican army beyond the Rio Grande and occupying the northern Mexican towns of Monterrey and Saltillo. Once Texas and California were secure, Polk was ready to make peace. He offered a liberal payment if Mexico would concede the Rio Grande border of Texas and a line to the Pacific that would give the United States New Mexico and California as far south as San Diego. Santa Anna, who had returned to Mexico with the connivance of the Americans, forgot his offers through Atocha, rejected Polk's offer, and took command of the army fighting Taylor.

Naturally Polk exerted more pressure. He sent General Winfield Scott and an army of some 12,000 troops to occupy Vera Cruz. The troops could not stay there through the summer because of the presence of yellow fever, so Scott had to attack inland toward Mexico City. Polk hoped that Mexico would make peace before this became necessary. He sent Nicholas P. Trist, the chief clerk of the state department, to accompany Scott and negotiate a peace whenever that became possible. Polk ordered Trist to try to obtain Lower as well as Upper California and authorized him to make a cash settlement of several million dollars.

Despite Scott's victorious march toward Mexico City, the Mexican government refused to deal seriously with Trist, perhaps in part because Trist and Scott distrusted one another so openly they were not even on speaking terms. Only when Scott's army camped outside Mexico City did Santa Anna consent to a truce and begin serious negotiations. Trist was conciliatory. He agreed to accept a compromise border somewhat north of that required by his instructions if the Mexicans would propose it. The Mexican cabinet refused, and Scott's conquest of Mexico City began.

Trist's compromise offer pleased Polk even less than the Mexican government. As American victories had mounted, so had popular demands for more conquests. Some even called for the annexation of all of Mexico. Polk never committed himself to the all-Mexico movement, but he was tempted to take more than he originally had intended. He was angry that Trist had conciliated the Mexican delegation rather than confronted it. He also was suspicious when he heard that Trist had reconciled with the Whig General Scott and believed that Trist might have come under the influence of anti-expansionists. Polk recalled Trist and told him to break off negotiations.

When Trist received notice of his recall, however, he was on the verge of negotiating a reasonable peace with the fractured but moderate new Mexican government. He was afraid that if he let this chance escape, there would soon be no Mexican government left with which to deal. The United States would have to occupy and bring order to a shattered, hostile nation. He defied his orders and negotiated the Treaty of Guadalupe Hidalgo. It gave the United States the Rio Grande border of Texas, the New Mexico Territory as far south as the Gila River, and a California border that put San Diego on the American side. The United States would assume responsibility for the old monetary claims and pay Mexico $15 million.

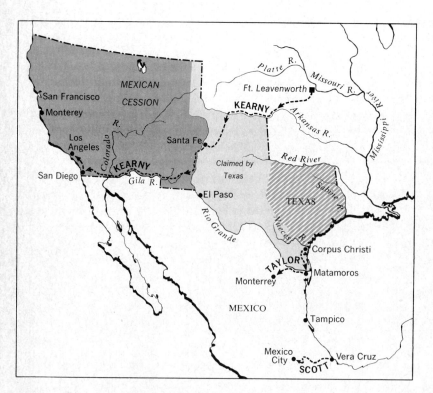

Map 6   The Mexican War, 1846–1848

Polk was indignant that Trist had defied his orders, but he could not afford to reject the unauthorized treaty out of hand. Although many Americans had been swept up in the enthusiasm of the war to demand all of Mexico, many others had remained adamantly opposed to the conflict. The Whig party, in which commercial groups who feared the impact of the war on overseas trade were very influential, opposed the war, and that party commanded a majority in the House of Representatives. Many antislavery advocates also opposed the war, including some northern and western expansionist Democrats who felt betrayed by Polk's compromise on Oregon. Ironically, these opponents were joined by some southerners who believed, along with John C. Calhoun, that any territory taken from Mexico except for Texas itself would be inhospitable to the plantation system.

Opponents of the war had never been able to defeat appropriations for the army, but they had indicated their strength and disapproval in other ways, especially in their support for the Wilmot Proviso. The Wilmot Proviso called for a prohibition of slavery in any territories conquered from Mexico in the war. If Polk were to refuse to submit Trist's treaty to the Senate, this opposition might be able to unite sufficiently to block military appropriations and undermine the war effort. Polk submitted the treaty without comment, and the Senate accepted it.

With the Treaty of Guadalupe Hidalgo, the United States had rounded out its continental empire. By annexing Texas, acquiring full control of the southern half of the Oregon territory, and conquering California and the Southwest, it had vastly increased the nation's size. To many, it seemed that the United States had reached its natural geographic limits. British Canada lay athwart any projected expansion northward, and Americans had considered and rejected further expansion into Mexico with the Treaty of Guadalupe Hidalgo.[3] Any further territorial expansion would have to be directed at territory separated from the United States by water or by other foreign territory. Many such areas were also densely inhabited by peoples of different cultures and races, making it difficult to regard acquisition as the incorporation of "empty" land and raising the specter of racial amalgamation and American colonialism in an unavoidable way.

There were some Americans willing to defy such inhibitions. They would seek further acquisition if their consciences could be assuaged by pointing to requests from the inhabitants of valuable lands for American annexation, or if the bogey of British intervention could be raised plausibly. But the only areas that seemed open to such expansion lay in Latin America, and they would undoubtedly come to the Union as slave territories. The Mexican War and the Wilmot Proviso had raised too much opposition to the spread of slavery to make such acquisitions possible.

President Polk was one of those who was thwarted. Some inhabitants of the Yucatan Peninsula who were rebelling against Mexico in the wake of the

---

[3] In 1853, the United States did purchase from Mexico an additional strip of territory on the southwestern border to facilitate the building of a transcontinental railroad, but this Gadsden Purchase was a minor exception.

Mexican War requested annexation to the United States. Polk considered the invitation and invoked the Monroe Doctrine to warn the British away, but nothing came of his interest. Polk also toyed with the idea of buying Cuba from Spain, but neither Spain nor Americans fearful of the slavery question would hear of it. Some southerners decided to take expansion into their own hands. "Filibusterers" like William Walker and Narciso López led private military expeditions to conquer Cuba, Nicaragua, and Lower California. Most of these filibusterers came to a bad end. Walker and López both were captured and executed in the lands they had come to "liberate."

This did not discourage the administrations of Polk's successors—Millard Fillmore, Franklin Pierce, and James Buchanan. They continued America's not-so-subtle attempts to acquire Cuba. Fillmore warned that the United States would oppose any attempt by another European power to relieve Spain of Cuba. When Havana seized the American ship *Black Warrior* for customs violations, Pierce unsuccessfully used the crisis to press Spain into disgorging its colony. Pierce's ministers to Great Britain, Spain, and France, James Buchanan, Pierre Soulé, and John Mason, met in Ostend, Belgium, to plot further strategy for annexing Cuba. They agreed that if Spain would not sell it, the United States would be justified in taking the island forcibly. Their confidential written conclusions, which came to be known as the Ostend Manifesto, leaked to the press and stirred a storm of controversy that destroyed any realistic hopes of annexation. Buchanan continued to agitate the question throughout his own administration, but the issue of slavery checkmated expansion until after the Civil War.

CONTROVERSIAL ISSUES AND FURTHER READING

Since the Mexican War aroused more domestic opposition than any other war in America's history with the exception of Vietnam, it is not surprising that historians have argued over it since the 1840s. In the immediate aftermath of the Mexican War, most historians treated America's diplomacy favorably. They blamed Mexican intransigence and duplicity for the outbreak of hostilities. [See, for example, R. S. Ripley, *History of the War with Mexico* (1849), and Nathan Covington Brooks, *A Complete History of the Mexican War, 1846–1848* (1849).] However, there were some dissenting histories. William Jay blamed the war on a slaveholders' plot to expand slave territory in *A Review of the Causes and Consequences of the Mexican War* (2nd ed., 1849). Albert Gallatin agreed with Jay that the United States was more at fault than Mexico, but attributed the war to the aggressive expansionism of all sections, not just that of the slaveholders. [Albert Gallatin, *Peace with Mexico* (1847). For a similar view, see Charles T. Porter, *Review of the Mexican War* (1849).]

The Civil War brought significant changes to the historiography of this question. Many northerners, led by the Republican party, blamed the expansionism of the slaveholders for the Civil War, and saw the Mexican War as early evidence of the southern conspiracy against the free northern states. The views espoused in the antebellum period by William Jay, very much a minority opinion at that time, were endorsed by every major historical study of the Mexican War written in the post-Civil War era. [Hermann Von Holst, *The Constitutional and Political History of the United States* (1876–1892); Hubert Howe Bancroft, *History of Mexico* (1883–1888); James Schouler, *History of the United States* (rev. ed., 1892–1913); James Ford Rhodes, *History of the United States from the Compromise of 1850* (1893–1906).] Even after one of these historians, James Schouler, gained access to Polk's diary, which showed that Polk was willing to see California come into the Union as a free state, Schouler did not abandon his opinion that Polk had demanded expansion because he had seen what southerners coveted. [James Schouler, *Historical Briefs* (1896).]

As the passions of the Civil War and Reconstruction subsided, younger historians challenged the slaveholder conspiracy theory. Not only did they cite Polk's diary, they also noted that some southerners like John C. Calhoun had opposed the Mexican War, fearing that the territory to be acquired in the Southwest was unsuitable for the plantation system. After 1900, little was to be heard of the slavery expansion theory, causing Hermann Von Holst to bewail the "tendency in the younger historical students to look upon the expansion of the country as the important consideration, and the slavery question as incidental." Ever since, the debate has been over whether the United States was justified in going to war and taking so much territory from Mexico.

This has blended naturally into the modern debate among nationalists, realists, and revisionists. Nationalists generally have defended American policy and blamed Mexican intransigence on the Texas issue for the war. Realists are not so likely to defend the abstract justice of the war or to deny the aggressiveness of Polk and the Americans. They see no need, however, to attribute the expansion to the capitalist ethic or extraordinary greed and rapaciousness, as revisionists do, or to try to gloss over the moral transgressions of Polk and the United States, as the nationalists do. Instead, they portray American expansion into the Southwest as the inevitable result of a growing nation on the border of a vacuum of power. Hard realists even defend Polk's tactics and credit him and a conservative coalition in Congress with harnessing the frenzy for expansion into all of Mexico to limited, realistic goals. Soft realists are inclined to believe that America could have acquired the territory with more restrained tactics.

The pendulum of historical approval and disapproval about the Mexican War has swung back and forth several times since 1900. Between 1900 and 1920, when the United States was acquiring the Philippines, intervening blatantly in Latin America, and finally participating in World War I, most significant histories supported the American side of the war. [See especially Justin Smith, *The War with Mexico* (1919), and the more moderate defense, George L. Rives, *The United States and Mexico, 1821–1848* (1913). For opposition to the American course, see Jesse S. Reeves, *American Diplomacy under Tyler and Polk* (1907).]

In the post-World War I reaction to the more blatant aspects of American imperialism, historians were more willing to see the Mexican side of the war. [N. W. Stephenson, *Texas and the Mexican War* (1921), and Richard Stenberg, "The Failure of Polk's Mexican War Intrigue of 1845," *The Pacific Historical Review* (1935). Eugene Irving McCormac's biography, *James K. Polk* (1922), supported the American side.] After 1941, America's struggle against the Axis and the succeeding Cold War brought more favor to policies that had enhanced and used American power. Polls of historians placed James K. Polk in the top ten American presidents, and Allan Nevins told the *New York Times* that "The general view of historians used to be that the war was wrong; more recently they have taken the opposite view."

Those historians who did criticize the war in the post-World War II era did not condemn American expansion per se, but criticized the tactics used and the attempts of historians to cover those tactics with a veneer of morality. [Defenses of the justice and morality of American actions can be found in Bernard DeVoto, *Year of Decision: 1846* (1943); Alfred Hoyt Bill, *Rehearsal for Conflict: The War with Mexico, 1846–1848* (1947); and Otis Singletary, *The Mexican War* (1960). Frederick Merk, *Manifest Destiny and Mission in American History* (1963), criticizes Polk's tactics. Norman Graebner wrote the best realist analyses of the war in *Empire on the Pacific: A Study in American Continental Expansion* (1955), and *Manifest Destiny* (1968). He emphasizes the importance of the Pacific ports as opposed to agricultural land in the motivation of Polk and his contemporaries and praises Polk for restraining American expansionist fever to encompass only those lands truly valuable to the United States. See also Richard W. Van Alstyne, *The Rising American Empire* (1960), for a realist view of American imperialism.]

Finally, Vietnam swung the pendulum back toward a more critical view of American policy. A good example of a moderate revisionist critique written in this era is Glenn W. Price, *Origins of the War with Mexico* (1967). The best and most balanced work on the Mexican War is David H. Pletcher, *The Diplomacy of Annexation: Texas, Oregon, and the Mexican War* (1973). [Another excellent modern work is Charles Sellers, *James K. Polk: Continentalist, 1843–1846* (1966). Nationalist defenses of America's course are Seymour V. Connor and Odie B. Faulk, *North America Divided: The Mexican War, 1846–1848* (1971), and William H. Goetzmann, *When the Eagle Screamed: The Romantic Horizon in American Diplomacy, 1800–1860* (1966).]

Other important books on special topics covered in this chapter are Frederick Merk, *The Oregon Question: Essays in Anglo-American Diplomacy and Politics* (1967); Frederick Merk, *The Monroe Doctrine and American Expansionism, 1843–1849* (1966); Howard Jones, *To The Webster-Ashburton Treaty: A Study in Anglo-American Relations, 1783–1843* (1977); Ephraim D. Adams, *British Interests and Activities in Texas, 1838–1846* (1910); J. D. P. Fuller, *The Movement for the Acquisition of All Mexico, 1846–1848* (1936); and John H. Schroeder, *Mr. Polk's War: American Opposition and Dissent, 1846–1848* (1973).

CHAPTER 6

The Civil War and Its Diplomatic Aftermath

ANGLO-AMERICAN RELATIONS ON THE EVE OF THE CIVIL WAR

The Webster-Ashburton Treaty, the Oregon compromise, and America's final victory in Texas and California had removed many of the issues disturbing Anglo-American relations in the decades before the Civil War. But serious rivalry continued between the two powers over Central America. Both England and the United States wanted an isthmian canal through Central America to facilitate trade between the Atlantic and the Pacific, and each wanted to control the vital waterway.

Nicaragua and Panama furnished the two best routes for the canal. The United States had the advantage in the contest for the Panama route, having signed a treaty in 1846 with New Granada (later Colombia) granting America transit rights in exchange for protection of the neutrality of the isthmus and of New Granada's sovereignty over it. Great Britain was in a strong position to control the Nicaraguan route, which seemed more practical than Panama in that era. Britain dominated the Caribbean side of the Nicaraguan route with colonies in Belize (later British Honduras) and the Bay Islands, along with a claimed protectorate over the Mosquito Islands. It enhanced its position in 1848 by seizing Greytown, which lay at the very mouth of the river that would serve as the Caribbean entrance to the canal. The United States responded by signing two treaties with Nicaragua. The first gave America the exclusive right to build the canal, the second permitted an American naval base on Tigre Island at the Pacific end of the canal route. The angry British made plans to preempt the United States by seizing Tigre Island before the Americans could establish their base there. With war in the offing, both sides decided a compromise was necessary.

In 1850 they negotiated the Clayton-Bulwer Treaty. They agreed that neither country would maintain exclusive control over a Central American canal nor fortify it. Each side also promised vaguely not to colonize or dominate any part of Central America. But this did not immediately end the Anglo-American contest. After the treaty was signed, the British asserted that the prohibitions against colonies did not apply to those already in existence.

They also refused any clear definition of their present possessions and set out to expand their holdings. The United States protested loudly. An American ship actually bombarded Greytown, and American filibusterers injected a further note of violence into the quarrel. The British drew back, however, partly because the Crimean War chastened them and partly because it was becoming clearer that construction of a canal would be a very difficult project. The British ceded the Bay Islands to Honduras and the Mosquitoes to Nicaragua in 1859. This laid to rest a major source of friction between the United States and Great Britain.

A revival of trade also improved Anglo-American relations in this period. The United States absorbed a quarter of Britain's exports, while the British took fully half of America's. In the meantime, the Marcy-Elgin Treaty of 1854 resolved the running quarrel over the Canadian fisheries and navigation of the St. Lawrence River. As a result, there was something of a détente between England and America on the eve of the Civil War. But this détente did not long survive the secession of the southern states.

THE DIPLOMACY OF THE CIVIL WAR

The Civil War greatly endangered Anglo-American relations, because British intervention on the side of the Confederacy was the South's great hope for survival and the greatest threat to the North's victory. For the North to win the war, it had to conquer the South; for the South to win, it had only to keep from being conquered. A key factor in the North's strategy to force the surrender of the South was a naval blockade of all southern ports. This would work a hardship on the British as well as the Confederates, however, because the British textile industry relied heavily on southern cotton. The interruption of the cotton supply would mean severe economic hardship for the owners and workers of British textile mills and for the many other enterprises whose prosperity was at least partly dependent on those mills.

The Confederates counted on Britain's need for cotton to bring British naval help in breaking the Union blockade. They also assumed that their King Cotton diplomacy would be abetted by Britain's interest in replacing United States hegemony in North America with a balance of power system. With British support, Canada and the Confederacy could check the expansive tendencies of the United States. To encourage the British in such strategic thinking, the South studiously avoided mention of its previous efforts to expand toward British interests in Central America and the Caribbean islands. Finally, the Confederates assumed that the conservative aristocrats who governed Great Britain would sympathize more with the genteel southern planters than with the supposedly money-grubbing Yankees of the North.

British sympathies assumed added significance because Napoleon III of France took his cues on American policy from the British. Napoleon inclined toward intervention on behalf of the Confederates. He detested the United

States and the Monroe Doctrine, which stood as a barrier to his ambitions in Mexico. He hoped to put a French puppet on the throne of Mexico and had just given Spain a free hand to conquer Santo Domingo in return for Spain's consent to his Mexican project. But Napoleon had to be cautious. He had just alienated the British and much of the rest of Europe by supporting Italy in a war against Austria and then, to reward himself for this effort, annexing the strategic Mediterranean provinces of Nice and Savoy. Not only had his war and annexations made Anglo-French relations delicate, they had disrupted the French economy and revived domestic liberal sentiment against him. In this tenuous economic and political situation, Napoleon would want to make sure the game was worth the candle before risking France's export trade to the United States in silks, china, wine, lace, and clocks. Unilateral French intervention would endanger Anglo-French relations and the domestic economy; joint Anglo-French intervention would avoid these problems and guarantee the intervention's success.

Actually the British were considerably more cautious than the Union, the Confederacy, or Napoleon expected them to be. British leaders certainly saw the benefits of an independent Confederacy, a secure cotton trade, and a North American balance of power. But the British people were in a wary mood because of the dangers and sacrifices they had endured during the recently ended Crimean War. The disarray in the British party system strengthened their guarded mood. Sir Robert Peel's successful leadership of the movement to repeal the Corn Laws had split his Tory party and disrupted the Whigs as well. The two parties became little more than loosely confederated factions. This required bipartisan support before any major foreign policy initiative could be undertaken.

It was difficult to get agreement on policy toward the American Civil War because the British had strong interests in the North as well as the South. British subjects were heavy investors in American canals, roads, railroads, banks, and public securities, all of which would be endangered by a vindictive policy toward the North. Also, much of Britain's trade in foodstuffs was with the North. As further incentive to caution toward the Confederacy, not only was the increasingly diversified British economy becoming less dependent on cotton textiles, but at the outset of the war Britain's warehouses were oversupplied with raw cotton.

The Confederates were overly sanguine in expecting rapid British intervention. While the British economy was still more dependent on southern cotton than on the trade of the North, the balance was closer than the Confederates acknowledged. British leaders were more sympathetic toward the genteel South than toward the Yankee North, but antislavery elements in Britain provided some counterweight to that. Thus, although the British tilted their policy slightly toward the South in the early years of the war, this owed less to their pro-Confederate sympathies than to their judgment that the North could not conquer the South. They feared that the war would drag on as an interminable stalemate, destroying the cotton trade and other American resources to the detriment of the British economy and at the continuing risk of an incident that might drag Britain into the war. Once it became clear that the North could win, British leaders abandoned all thoughts of intervention.

The Union government resented the early British tilt toward the South and dreaded the prospect of British intervention. The primary figure in shaping the Union's foreign policy to counter the possibility of British intervention was Secretary of State William H. Seward. President Abraham Lincoln maintained a general supervision of policy, but gave Seward broad authority over major decisions as well as the day-to-day activities of the State Department. Seward was a man of strong passions and flamboyant rhetoric. He was a fervent supporter of American expansion, and although he insisted that expansion be peaceful, his ambitions reached far into the Pacific and South America. He was particularly eager for naval bases and trade routes that could extend American foreign trade. His nationalism and expansionism naturally had brought him into conflict with British ambitions, and he was regarded at home and abroad as virulently anti-British and anti-European. Actually, there was a caution and hard pragmatism in Seward. Occasionally he could be carried away by his rhetoric and overreach himself, but Lincoln generally reined him in when that happened, and on the whole Seward was an effective and realistic secretary of state.

Lincoln had to restrain Seward twice early in his administration. First, Seward suggested to Lincoln a harebrained proposal to reunite the country by provoking war either with Spain, then engaged in the conquest of Santo Domingo, or with Britain and France, who were interfering in Mexico. Seward offered to take charge of the project and the government itself, since he thought Lincoln was not up to it. Some historians have seen a shred of realism in the plan, because it would have required the United States to station troops at Fort Pickens in Florida for the assault on the Caribbean, thus avoiding reinforcement of Fort Sumter. This would give some hope for a reconciliation with the Confederacy while positioning troops for an attack on the South if negotiations failed. Nevertheless, Lincoln quickly deflated Seward and his plans and saw that no mention of them leaked to the press.

Seward's second overreaction came in response to Great Britain's decision to recognize that a state of war existed in the United States and to declare British neutrality. In effect, this resolution acknowledged that the Confederates were belligerents rather than pirates or criminals. Naturally the British declaration encouraged the southerners and strengthened their determination. But it was difficult to see what else the British could have done: The North had declared a blockade of the South, which was an acknowledgment that a state of war existed. It should have been far more important to Seward and his fellow American officials that the British neither recognized the Confederacy as an independent nation nor announced any intention to disrupt the blockade. The British had warned strongly against a blockade, but had decided for the time being to respect it and to store up the precedent for use against the United States in later years when America should resume its habitual protests against British maritime practices. Britain also had taken heed of Seward's warning that recognition of the Confederacy would be an act of war.

Nevertheless, Seward took great umbrage at Britain's Declaration of Neutrality. Perhaps he did so because the British recognized Confederate belligerency before the new minister to England, Charles Francis Adams, had arrived to make the Union's case, and just shortly after the British foreign minister received a Confederate delegation. Charles Francis Adams actually considered returning home and breaking relations immediately. In the end, he decided to stay on to work against British interference with the blockade or recognition of the Confederacy's independence, but Seward threatened that any further communication whatever between the British government and the Confederacy, let alone recognition, would mean the end of Anglo-American diplomatic relations. Lincoln blue-penciled some of Seward's more strident threats, and Adams softened the dispatch even further by reading the relevant parts aloud to the British foreign minister rather than turning over the written message in its entirety. The intensity of the American reaction astounded the British minister, Lord John Russell, and he became more cautious in his policymaking, so the crisis blew over for the moment.

A far more serious crisis erupted shortly afterward in November 1861. Captain Charles Wilkes, an American naval officer, stopped a British ship and removed two Confederate diplomats on their way to Europe. These diplomats, James Mason and John Slidell, had run the Union blockade on a chartered steamer and arrived in Havana, where they boarded the British mail packet *Trent* to continue their journey. Captain Wilkes and the *San Jacinto* were in Havana harbor at the time, and Wilkes decided to capture the Confederates. Once the *Trent* had put to sea, Wilkes's boarding party removed Mason and Slidell, but disobeyed the captain's order to take the ship itself as well, so that it could be brought to a prize court and the issue adjudicated. Great Britain erupted in indignation. The cabinet composed an ultimatum demanding return of the envoys, a disavowal of Wilkes, and an apology. Prince Albert, consort of Queen Victoria, softened the ultimatum by getting the cabinet to add reminders of past Anglo-American friendship and an acknowledgment that Wilkes might have acted without instructions. Still, the British minister in America, Lord Richard Lyons, was ordered to break relations if the Americans did not bow to the ultimatum within seven days.

The British were willing to negotiate a bit further on the issue if necessary. But England was mobilizing rapidly, and a British war would ensure the victory of the South. After some soul searching, Lincoln, who had balked at releasing the envoys and was considering arbitration instead, accepted Seward's advice and released Mason and Slidell. Seward put the best face on the surrender. He announced the release in a note that blatantly defended the capture of the diplomats and asserted a wide range of belligerent rights. Seward apologized only for the failure to bring the entire ship in for adjudication by a prize court. Despite Seward's peremptory tone, Britain was glad to see the end of the crisis. The cabinet accepted Seward's half-hearted expressions of regret and noted America's defense of belligerent rights for future use.

The danger of British intervention was still not completely dispelled. The failure of Union General George McClellan's campaign against Richmond, followed by Robert E. Lee's brilliant counteroffensive in 1862, seemed to confirm the Confederacy's ability to survive and portend an unending war unless the North could be brought to see reason. Napoleon III suggested joint recognition of the Confederacy to England. The British cabinet hesitated, but several headstrong members of Parliament introduced a resolution that Britain offer its mediation. Palmerston and Russell finessed the effort by suggesting that Parliament leave the issue to them, and they began to consider intervention seriously. Then news of the Union quasi-victory at Antietam turned Palmerston away from his brief flirtation with intervention. Russell continued to mull the idea, but he too was put off when Chancellor of the Exchequer William E. Gladstone exaggerated the cabinet's inclinations toward intervention in a public speech and raised a storm of parliamentary and newspaper opposition. While Russell quietly shelved the whole project, if further southern victories had given firmer proof of the Union's inability to conquer the Confederacy, Palmerston and Russell might have revived the idea of intervention. As it turned out, however, the crisis for Union diplomacy had passed.

For years afterward, British and American popular historians attributed the cabinet's decision largely to the influence of the British mill workers, whose supposed devotion to the antislavery cause had brought them to ignore their own economic interests in the restoration of the cotton trade and protest the aristocracy's Confederate sympathies. Recent historians have put that myth to rest. Some leaders of liberal thought like John Bright and Richard Cobden had indeed been in the forefront of the protest, but the mill workers themselves, where they did express themselves in political meetings, seem to have favored the Confederacy and the restoration of the cotton trade more than the Union and antislavery. In any case, workers had little influence on parliamentary politics or cabinet decisions.

Troubles between England and Lincoln's government soon erupted again over the construction of ships for the Confederacy in British shipyards. The British cabinet was unsure of its interests and recourse in this situation. Private enterprises were building the ships. Confederate agents who commissioned the vessels carefully concealed their ownership. The ships were to leave England unarmed and be fitted out by the Confederates as armed cruisers beyond British waters. A Union agent, Thomas Dudley, spent much effort and money ferreting out information about Confederate involvement in building these ships, and he turned it over to Charles Francis Adams for use in pressuring the British government to step in. Adams insisted that the British themselves should detain the ships and investigate when there were legitimate suspicions of the intent of the builders and owners, since only the British government had access to the information necessary to prove such intent. While the British cabinet debated the issue, the recently constructed *Alabama* fled from Liverpool, fitted out in the Azores, and began a two-year campaign of fearful destruction against the Union's blockade and shipping.

Adams and the Americans howled, made dire threats, and began adding up the damages caused by the *Alabama* with the idea of suing the British government for compensation. The greatest fear of the Americans was that several other cruisers then being built in British shipyards, including two ships with metal prows for ramming Union blockaders, would follow the *Alabama* to sea. Adams went so far as to write Russell, "It would be superfluous in me to point out to your Lordship that this is war." Many historians later praised Adams for forcing the British to back down with his threat. Actually, Russell had decided to detain the rams two days before he received Adams's letter. He had been inspired less by American threats than by the fears of his cabinet and naval officials that in permitting neutrals to build ships for belligerents, they were setting a precedent that would work against their usual naval supremacy in future wars. In any case, the British government got around the legal issues involved by simply purchasing the vessels for its own use.

British concern for neutral precedents also helped defuse potentially explosive issues surrounding the later conduct of the Union blockade. The British islands of Bermuda and the Bahamas served as primary jumping off points for blockade runners trying to reach Confederate ports, and Union blockade vessels often intercepted suspect ships right outside the ports of those islands. Union ships also intercepted British ships carrying goods to Matamoros, Mexico, on the grounds that these supplies were then smuggled across the border to Brownsville, Texas, in what amounted to a continuous voyage. The British were indignant, but they were increasingly occupied by quarrels among the continental powers over Poland, Schleswig-Holstein, and Italy which threatened the European balance of power. A growing string of northern victories, accompanied by Lincoln's Emancipation Proclamation, also deterred them from intervention against the Union. The British muted their protests and took careful note of America's endorsement of doctrines favoring belligerent over neutral rights.

The events in Central Europe also distracted Napoleon III from intervention in the Civil War. Nevertheless, he continued his interest in a Confederate victory because he had undertaken a semi-permanent occupation of Mexico to which a reunited America would pose a serious threat. Napoleon began his Mexican adventure by sponsoring a joint Anglo-French-Spanish expedition to punish President Benito Juárez for suspending debt payments to his European creditors. Napoleon's army then left the troops of his erstwhile allies in Vera Cruz and marched to Mexico City to join conservative Mexican clerics and landowners in establishing a new government. Subsequently Napoleon offered the throne of Mexico to Archduke Maximilian of Austria and promised to prop him up with the French army. To protect Mexico's northern flank, Napoleon urged the British to lead the way in recognizing the Confederacy. At the same time, he was assuring the Union of his friendliness and hoping the British would bear the brunt of the American government's anger.

As hopes for a Confederate victory dimmed, he began searching for a face-saving way out of Mexico and began to withdraw some of his troops. After Appomattox, when the United States stationed on the Texas border a substantial portion of what was now the largest army in the world to protest the French presence, Napoleon abandoned Maximilian. Maximilian stayed on, however, foolishly expecting that his good intentions and support from his Mexican followers would save him. His confidence was rewarded by a firing squad at the hands of the victorious armies of Beníto Juárez.

BRITAIN AND AMERICA IN THE AFTERMATH OF THE CIVIL WAR

The attitudes and actions of Napoleon and the British government during the Civil War left Americans even more embittered and distrustful toward Europe than they had been in the antebellum years. That bitterness affected America's relations with Great Britain more than with the other European powers because American and British interests clashed more directly. Britain's presence in Canada was a constant annoyance. It also was a standing temptation to Americans and their politicians, who continued to think vaguely that North America should be the preserve of the United States. Canadian border quarrels and disputes over fishing and sealing rights in adjacent waters kept the English and Americans embroiled throughout the late nineteenth century. There were also interminable wrangles over the damages the British owed for Union losses caused by Confederate ships built in British shipyards. These damage claims served as constant reminders of the rancorous years of Civil War diplomacy. Besides, everywhere the United States turned beyond its borders—toward the Caribbean, the Pacific, the Orient, or the canal routes of Central America—it found the British Empire its predominant rival.

Many of these Anglo-American quarrels seem petty today, but they dominated the diplomatic activity of the United States at the time. Politicians searching for issues to win votes could always count on a hard line toward Great Britain to be popular—"twisting the lion's tail," they called it. Perhaps the most difficult and emotional of these Anglo-American issues was that of the damages caused by the British-built Confederate raiders. America claimed that the *Alabama* and other such cruisers had cost the Union millions of dollars worth of destroyed ships and cargoes. The British were willing to pay a moderate sum so they could use the precedent to prevent America from building ships for Britain's enemies during a European war. They signed an agreement with Seward to arbitrate the amount of damages, but Charles Sumner, chairman of the Senate Foreign Relations Committee, denounced the accord because it did not include a British apology. Sumner also insisted that the scope of the arbitration be expanded to include the costs of the last few months of the war because he figured the British-built cruisers had lengthened the conflict. He thought the British should pay $2 billion, but he hinted broadly that the United States might accept Canada in lieu of that sum. The Senate, tempted by Sumner's reasoning and looking for a way to punish President Andrew Johnson for his unpopular reconstruction policies, rejected Seward's arbitration agreement with the British.

Ulysses Grant's secretary of state, Hamilton Fish, revived the arbitration of the *Alabama* claims in 1870, when the congressional atmosphere had improved. The British attitude had softened as well because of the dangers posed by the Franco-Prussian War and other European embroilments. Fish himself helped chances for agreement by abandoning the attempt to extort Canada from the British. Fish realized that the British would never agree to Sumner's inflated figures, and he saw that the Canadians themselves had grown increasingly hostile to American absorption. They had formed themselves into a dominion in 1867 largely to protect themselves from the United States. They were embittered by the raids into Canada from American soil by the Fenians, Irish revolutionaries who hoped to free Ireland by provoking a war between Britain and the United States. Quarrels over the fisheries also alienated the Canadians. These quarrels began immediately after the Civil War, when the Americans abrogated the Marcy-Elgin agreements on mutual fishing rights and extended their fishing activities into Canadian waters. Several American fishermen had clashed dangerously with British patrol boats.

Finally, the British and Americans argued over the exact placement of the border that dipped from the 49th parallel through the Straits of Juan de Fuca to give Canada Vancouver Island. The United States insisted that the border ran north of the San Juan Islands and that those islands were therefore American. The British and the Canadians argued otherwise. The United States and Great Britain stationed rival garrisons on San Juan Island to assert their claims, and shortly before the Civil War these garrisons nearly came to blows over which had jurisdiciton in a legal case that involved a rampaging pig.

This so-called Pig War, along with the *Alabama* claims and the fisheries, were the subjects of the Treaty of Washington which high commissions from each side negotiated in 1871. The treaty referred the border issue to the arbitration of the German emperor, who gave the San Juan Islands to the United States in 1872. The Treaty of Washington also referred the *Alabama* claims to arbitration. After some tension over whether the arbitrators could consider the costs of the lengthened war, Fish devised a face-saving formula that would deny all such indirect claims (thereby protecting the United States against similar demands from the British in future wars) and would award the United States $15 million in damages.

The Treaty of Washington also gave the United States the right to purchase fishing privileges from the Canadians. But that agreement broke down over the price Canada demanded, and the fishery issue continued to roil Anglo-American relations. In the 1880s, a dispute over seals in the Pacific exacerbated the issue of the fisheries. The fur seals bred in the Pribilof Islands of the Bering Sea, which were American by virtue of the Alaskan Purchase of 1867. Congress had sold an American company the exclusive right to kill 100,000 seals annually under regulations that preserved the herd, but Canadian ships were taking the seals in open waters (a practice called pelagic sealing). This was wasteful, since the killed seals were often lost in the water before they could be dragged aboard, and the toll of pelagic sealing, when added to the land slaughter by the Americans, endangered the species. President Grover Cleveland, in righteous anger, ordered the seizure of Canadian sealing ships on the high seas. This was a flagrant violation of international law and embarrassingly similar to British seizures of American ships fishing off the east coast of Canada.

With passions running high, the Americans and British worked out a *modus vivendi* under which both sides would cease ship seizures. The agreement almost came unglued when Benjamin Harrison defeated Cleveland for reelection. One cause of Cleveland's defeat was an indiscreet letter from British minister Lionel Sackville-West recommending Cleveland over his Republican opponent. This had led to charges that Cleveland was too pro-British, and the angered lame duck president tried to prove otherwise by ordering seizures of pelagic sealers to resume. Naturally his Republican successors found it politically difficult to revoke the order. Ultimately, in 1892 the Americans and British referred the issue to arbitration, and the arbitrators, while finding the United States guilty of violations of international law, set limits on pelagic sealing that would preserve the herd.

None of these Anglo-American controversies led to the brink of war; most were minor enough to be resolved by arbitration. But they kept reminding Americans of their long and bitter rivalry with the British, and Anglo-American anger remained at a fairly high pitch throughout the later nineteenth century.

CONTROVERSIAL ISSUES AND FURTHER READING

The diplomacy of the Civil War has stirred considerable controversy. Historians writing in the aftermath of the war shared the general public's outrage at the supposedly unneutral attitudes and actions of Great Britain during the conflict. They ignored an erudite defense of British policy by Oxford don Montague Bernard, and concluded that England had been "by active sympathy favorable to the South," even to the point of grasping for "the pretext for making war." [Montague Bernard, *A Historical Account of the Neutrality of Great Britain during the American Civil War* (1870); John G. Nicolay and John Hay, *Abraham Lincoln: A History* (10 vols., 1886–1890); George Bemis, *Hasty Recognition of Rebel Belligerency: And Our Right to Complain of It* (1865); Thomas L. Harris, *The Trent Affair* (1896).] The only saving grace for Great Britain was that while the upper classes that controlled the government were "gloating" over the prospect of a divided republic, the lower classes remained staunchly Unionist because they recognized that the Civil War was a struggle against slavery. [James Ford Rhodes, *History of the United States from the Compromise of 1850* (7 vols., 1893–1906).] But by the turn of the century, America and Great Britain were drawing closer together, and historians reconsidered. Now they portrayed the attitudes of the British government and upper classes as neither particularly unfriendly nor friendly toward the Union, noting that the Confederates had regarded Lord John Russell as hostile. Also historians were not just happy but ecstatic about the support the North supposedly had received from antislavery liberals and the lower classes. [Frederic Bancroft, *The Life of William Seward* (1899–1900); James Morton Callahan, *The Diplo-*

matic History of the Southern Confederacy (1901); James Kendall Hosmer, *The Appeal to Arms, 1861–1863* (1907).]

After World War I, this trend toward sympathetic portrayals of British policy continued with two outstanding books based for the first time on thorough research in British and French archives: Ephraim Adams, *Great Britain and the American Civil War* (1925), and Donaldson Jordan and Edwin J. Pratt, *Europe and the Civil War* (1931). A dissenting view of British benevolence was offered by the book that still stands as the best on Confederate diplomacy, Frank L. Owsley, *King Cotton Diplomacy* (1931). Owsley argued that the Union's violation of the rights of neutrals during its blockade of the South set precedents very harmful to America's own attempts to maintain its neutral rights against the British in World War I. He also claimed that Great Britain had not refused to support the Confederacy on idealistic antislavery grounds, but because the grain and trade of the Union were more valuable to its economic interests than southern cotton. Owsley's blatantly pro-southern bias led to some discounting of his opinions in his own day. But recent works have swung the pendulum of historical opinion some distance back toward his view of British policy. Mary Ellison, *Support for Secession* (1973), has effectively undermined the contentions of earlier historians that the British lower classes favored the North. D. P. Crook, author of the best modern surveys of Civil War diplomacy, has concluded that British policy was marked by cynical self-regard and moral hesitations rather than lofty and generous statesmanship: "Only the rhetoric of historians who wrote during the Great Rapprochment of 1895–1930, and the wishful thinking of the apostles of Atlantic unity since, have obscured that fact." [D. P. Crook, *The North, the South, and the Powers, 1861–1865* (1974), pp. v, 371. Crook has published a condensation of this book entitled *Diplomacy during the American Civil War* (1975). Other significant modern works on Civil War foreign policy include Lynn M. Case and Warren F. Spencer, *The United States and France: Civil War Diplomacy* (1970); Frank J. Merli, *Great Britain and the Confederate Navy* (1970); Stuart L. Bernath, *Squall across the Atlantic: American Civil War Prize Cases and Diplomacy* (1970); Wilbur D. Jones, *The Confederate Rams at Birkenhead* (1961); and Gordon H. Warren, *Fountain of Discontent: The Trent Affair and Freedom of the Seas* (1981).]

CHAPTER 7

Looking Abroad: Overseas Expansion in Mid-Century

WILLIAM SEWARD AND THE ATTEMPTED RESUMPTION OF AMERICAN EXPANSION

The triumph of the North in the Civil War confronted the world with a reunited America far more capable of extending its domain and influence than would have been the case if the South had succeeded in dividing the nation. The Union victory also eliminated slavery, which had been a major stumbling block to American expansion in the antebellum period. William Seward was quick to try to take advantage of the new opportunity provided by the end of the war.

Seward shared with many Americans of the mid-nineteenth century a broad if unsystematic vision of the directions American expansion should take. He looked toward the absorption of all of North America. He hoped that in time Canada would gravitate toward the United States and that Great Britain might finally decide to let it go. He also dreamed vaguely of Mexico, although he had no firm plans for handling the knotty problem of the large and culturally different population that would undoubtedly be hostile to American annexation. Since he was anxious to avoid conflict, however, Seward was content to leave the acquisition of these countries to time and rather mild diplomacy; he devoted his attention instead to other areas that might be valuable to the United States and easier to acquire. These were places of longtime American interest, such as the Caribbean, the Central American canal routes, and Hawaii. The fate of his expansionist efforts, however, demonstrated that America's interest in expansion into these remoter areas was not yet strong enough consistently to overcome other countervailing interests. Most of Seward's expansionist proposals were thwarted in one way or another. So were those of his successors, until the 1890s ushered in a new era of American foreign policy.

One of Seward's projects that succeeded was his purchase of Alaska. The Russians were anxious to sell the territory because the Russian-American Company, which administered it, was near bankruptcy. Russia also was incapable of defending the territory against the British navy. Finally, Russia assumed that even if it were able to hold on to the area for a few years, the burgeoning American population inevitably would swarm into it and drag it

Figure 6 William Seward, secretary of state during the Civil War and ardent expansionist. Portrait courtesy of the National Archives.

into the American orbit. When the Russians hinted that they would sell Alaska, Seward offered $7.2 million for it. The Senate quickly approved the treaty, but the House of Representatives balked at appropriating such a large sum for what several congressmen were calling Seward's Icebox. Partisan politics came into play as well, with all but two of the Republicans who had recently voted to impeach President Johnson also voting against the Alaskan project of Johnson's secretary of state.

After much debate and persuasion, including, it was rumored, some strategically placed bribes from the Russian minister, the House approved the appropriation. The House was especially gratified that Alaska was not already populated by a large, hostile, "inferior" people. The House also wished to avoid offending Russia, which Americans regarded as the only country in Europe sympathetic to the North during the Civil War.[1] Finally, Senator Charles Sumner had pointed elaborately to the pressure America's possession of Alaska might bring to bear on the British position in Canada.

The surprising strength of congressional opposition to the purchase of Alaska presaged the reception the rest of Seward's proposals for expansion would receive. His other targets were not only far removed from America's borders, but also densely populated by peoples of different races and cultures. Seward negotiated the purchase of the Danish West Indies and their outstanding harbors, only to have the Senate reject the agreement as too costly. He failed in his attempts to purchase Santo Domingo, Haiti, and Cuba. He did negotiate a new treaty of privileges with Nicaragua, but a simi-

[1] A Russian fleet had taken refuge in American ports during the Civil War, fearing an outbreak of war between Russia and England; Americans mistakenly regarded the visit of the fleet as a sign of Russian support for the Union.

lar one with Colombia was turned down by the Colombian Senate. He renewed attempts to acquire Tigre Island off the Pacific coast of Nicaragua, but that also failed. Farther out in the Pacific, Seward got approval for a naval captain's seizure of the uninhabited Midway Islands. But the Senate rejected a more important reciprocal trade treaty with Hawaii which Seward regarded as a prelude to annexation. The Senate was bent on partisan revenge against Seward, fearful of racial amalgamation with the islanders, and anxious to avoid the competition of Hawaiian sugar in the domestic market.

THE OLD DIPLOMACY: ISOLATIONISM VERSUS EXPANSIONISM

The forces arrayed against Seward's expansionism continued to prevail throughout most of the rest of the nineteenth century. American politics in the post-Civil War period revolved around domestic issues, especially those of reconstruction. The sectional and racial passions that had fueled the war continued to dominate party politics, even after federal troops had been removed from the South in the 1870s. The Democratic and Republican parties remained organized around Civil War issues, with the Republicans reopening old wounds each election by "waving the bloody shirt" and calling the Democrats the party of secession and popery. Partisan rivalries permeated all aspects of American politics, and neither party showed much hesitation in voting down the foreign policy initiatives of a president or secretary of state from the opposition party. This could be done easily because the parties were evenly balanced in the size of their constituencies. Seldom in the late nineteenth century did a single party control the presidency and the majority of Congress simultaneously.

Economic issues generated by the rise of America's industrial economy also had a significant impact on politics, bringing about a reorganization of the entire party system by 1896, when William Jennings Bryan ran his famous Free Silver campaign. America's growing economy naturally had an impact on foreign affairs. Industry was anxious to encourage overseas trade in the hope that new markets would increase the demand for American products. Since half the postwar years were depression years, many Americans looked toward foreign trade as something necessary to relieve the vicious swings of the domestic economy. The concern for economic expansion would peak in the 1890s after the particularly deep depression known as the Panic of 1893.

Between the War of 1812 and the Civil War, territorial expansion had been a more significant force behind American diplomacy than overseas trade. After the Civil War, the rising industrial economy, along with the lack of any convenient, empty, contiguous territory to attract American migration, combined to make economic rather than territorial expansion the more important force. The territories Americans sought, such as the Caribbean islands, the Central American canal routes, and Hawaii, were valued more for their harbors than for their land or resources. They were steppingstones to markets.

The position of the two parties reflected this shift from territorial to trade expansion. Prior to the Civil War, the agrarian Democrats had been the most avid expansionists; after the Civil War, the Republican party, increasingly the party of industry, became the more expansionist. Many farmers also favored expansionist diplomacy in search of markets for surplus agricultural products, but by 1890 it was industry and the Republicans that led the way.

Nonetheless, in the post-Civil War era, industry and agriculture were more concerned for domestic than for overseas markets. The Republican party favored high tariffs to protect America's domestic market despite their harmful effect on the search for markets abroad. The Republicans tried to offset their protectionist stand and appeal to those anxious for overseas markets by calling for reciprocity treaties that would trade American tariff concessions for similar concessions by foreign countries. But the priority they assigned to the domestic market was demonstrated by the regular defeat of almost any reciprocity treaty brought before the Senate. Seward's reciprocity treaty with Hawaii was only the first of these defeats; other reciprocity treaties quashed by Congress included ones with Brazil, several Central American states, the Spanish colonies of Cuba and Puerto Rico, the British Caribbean islands, Canada, Germany, and Austria-Hungary.

Some revisionist historians have argued that the Democratic party's opposition to the Republicans' high tariff showed that the Democrats at least were concerned for overseas trade. But this traditional low tariff plank, stemming from the earliest days of the American Republic, reflected mostly a concern for party doctrine and for consumers seeking lower prices on imported products, not for industrialists hoping to win favor in foreign markets. Exports constituted only 6 to 8 percent of America's gross national product in the post-Civil War era, and well over 80 percent of these went to Canada and Europe rather than to the targets of America's attempted territorial expansion—Latin America, the Pacific, and Asia.

Further evidence of the relative lack of concern for aggressive diplomacy and overseas expansion can be seen in Congress's neglect of the instruments needed for such a policy—the army, the navy, and the diplomatic corps. At the end of the Civil War, the American army had been the most powerful in the world. Soon afterward it averaged only about 28,000 men, most of whom were scattered in frontier forts and Indian territories. None were serving outside the borders of the nation, as contrasted with the post-Spanish-American War period, when American soldiers would be found in Cuba, Puerto Rico, the Philippines, and China.

America also permitted the navy to decline. The United States did not make a rapid transition to warships of steel and steam, as the European powers did. It equipped some wooden vessels with steam engines, but permitted them to fall into disrepair. Many American ships could make only four and a half of their designed twelve knots. In 1885, the secretary of the navy considered the fleet an "alphabet of floating washtubs." He added four new steel-clad ships to the navy in the next two years, beginning a building program that would take the United States navy from twelfth to seventh in the world by 1893. By that year, the United States also had begun its transition from a defensive coastal navy to an offensive fleet with ships capable of ranging across the oceans. But prior to the mid-1890s, the navy was not strong enough to inspire or carry out major expansionist ventures.

America neglected its diplomatic corps even more than the armed forces. In the nineteenth century, most diplomats were selected not for knowledge and competence, but as rewards for partisan service. The State Department often sent uniform instructions to its ministers abroad, failing to differentiate between the problems faced by diplomats in Latin America or Asia as opposed to Europe. Scandal and contempt surrounded American representatives abroad. The U.S. minister to Ecuador attempted to annex the country and to assassinate the British ambassador. The minister to Japan whirled through Tokyo in a carriage with a pistol in his belt, cracking his whip at pedestrians. America's diplomats were woefully underpaid by a Congress that sometimes asked seriously whether the United States needed a diplomatic service at all.

Under these circumstances, it is not surprising that American foreign policy in this period was erratic, amateurish, and devoid of careful planning. Some secretaries of state, like Seward, Fish, and James G. Blaine, seem to have had a reasonably coherent long-range vision, but they did not have orchestrated planning or very specific goals. The presidents of this time were all far more concerned with domestic affairs. Most diplomatic initiatives did not come from Washington, but from foreigners. Many of Seward's expansionist projects and later ones as well came at the behest of substantial factions in Cuba, Santo Domingo, or Hawaii. At other times resident Americans in Latin America, Asia, or the eastern Mediterranean urged annexation, investments, diplomatic protection, or aid in opening markets.

When these suggested projects were expensive or dangerous, they were often thwarted in the same way Seward's had been. Nevertheless, the United States believed with the rest of the Western world that a nation owed protection to its citizens and their property abroad. American diplomats and naval captains were often involved in minor episodes overseas primarily to protect the lives and property of American merchants and missionaries. Usually these caused little stir. So long as the incidents did not involve great expense or the danger of a serious war, Americans assumed that such interventions were the proper function of diplomacy.

If most of these episodes seemed minor to an apathetic American public, they did not necessarily have a correspondingly minor effect on the weak and insular peoples who were their usual objects. American merchants and missionaries, like those of most of Europe, were convinced that their activities were beneficial to the people with whom they were dealing. They felt that the benefits of American industry, civilization, and religion could not help but improve peoples they regarded as backward and barbarian. Only a few among the American general public had any worries that American trade, missionary work, or even annexation could harm others. Most resistance to American intervention came from those who feared its effect on the United States. Americans did not regard their expansion as the equivalent of European imperialism, but feared that the expense and the military force needed for it would destroy economic and civil liberty at home. The nature and impact of American expansionist efforts in the post-Civil War period can be seen in a survey of the major areas at which those efforts were directed.

EXPANSION IN THE CARIBBEAN

When Ulysses S. Grant assumed the presidency, he indulged his dislike of Seward by letting Seward's agreement to purchase the Danish West Indies lapse. No sooner had he turned his back on one Caribbean venture, however, than he plunged headlong into another. The ruling faction of Santo Domingo offered to sell the island to the United States, and Grant seized the opportunity. He personally lobbied various senators and congressmen to appropriate the money, only to be forestalled by the opposition of Charles Sumner as chairman of the Senate Foreign Relations Committee. Sumner persuaded his colleagues that America should avoid imperialism because it was costly and because it would mean American suzerainty over large numbers of Catholics and nonwhites. Sumner was one of the few Americans who truly believed in racial equality and feared for the Cubans themselves, but many others were no doubt persuaded by his argument for less elevated reasons. In any case, Grant never forgave Sumner for destroying his dream. He fired Sumner's closest friend in the diplomatic corps, shook his fist when passing Sumner's house, and finally maneuvered the senator out of his chairmanship.

A bloody rebellion in Cuba in 1868 provided another opportunity for Grant to contemplate a Caribbean acquisition. Some of the Cuban rebels invited American annexation. Many congressmen urged that the United States at least recognize the rebels' belligerence. Secretary of State Fish opposed this, since he was in the midst of pressing Great Britain for damages caused by British recognition of Confederate belligerence. He and others also saw problems with annexing Cuba that were equivalent to those of the proposed purchase of Santo Domingo. When Grant finally ordered Fish to issue a proclamation of neutrality toward Cuba, Fish found a pretext to withhold it. Later, when Congress itself was ready to initiate a recognition of rebel belligerence, Fish threatened to resign, and in this way got Grant to throw his influence against the move.

As long as the Cuban rebellion continued, America teetered on the brink of intervention, stirred by the inevitable sensational incidents that roused popular emotions. Early in the rebellion, the Spanish captured and executed two Americans aboard a ship commandeered by the rebels. One of the captives wrote a highly publicized pathetic letter of farewell to his family. A more serious incident occurred in 1873, when Spanish authorities in Cuba executed fifty-three people aboard the rebel ship *Virginius*, including several

Americans. Only Spain's timely apology and compensation to the families of the dead men prevented American intervention. The danger of American involvement finally ended after an able Spanish General, Arsenio Martínez de Campos, brought the insurgents to yield in 1878 through a judicious mixture of concessions, bribery, and force. But Americans quickly moved in to buy up many of the sugar plantations that had been destroyed or abandoned during the rebellion, and this meant that American interests and emotions would be involved even more thoroughly in any new revolution.

EXPANSION IN CENTRAL AND SOUTH AMERICA

American interests in Central America stumbled over obstacles and domestic opposition similar to those involving Cuba. The completion of the transcontinental railroad in 1869 lessened the need for a canal and raised a powerful interest group that saw a canal as a threat to its prosperity. Grant did make unsuccessful attempts to negotiate new treaties with Colombia and Nicaragua. Earlier treaties with those nations had given Americans the right to cross the peninsula; Grant hoped to gain the right for America actually to construct a canal. Even though he failed, his administration sent survey teams to select the best route. They reported that Nicaragua was preferable to Panama, and for the next quarter-century American ambitions for a canal were focused on Nicaragua.

Nevertheless, the United States was very disturbed in 1879 when Ferdinand de Lesseps, the builder of the Suez Canal, announced that he would begin work on a French-supported canal through Panama. De Lesseps set up a $1.5 million fund for an American committee to purchase support for his canal in the United States, but failed to buy off President Rutherford B. Hayes, who insisted that any canal would in effect be part of the United States coastline and should be controlled by America. Hayes even sent American naval vessels to cruise off the Panama coast to show America's displeasure.

De Lesseps' canal stirred a new interest in the Monroe Doctrine. Except for Polk's references to it in the 1840s, Americans had almost forgotten about Monroe's insistence that Europeans make no new acquisitions in the Western Hemisphere. Suddenly in the 1880s, historians and publicists began debating whether the Founding Fathers had intended the Monroe Doctrine to be enforced by military action. Because De Lesseps' efforts bogged down in the mud and mosquitoes of Panama, the United States was not forced to make such a choice. But the public had been reminded of the doctrine and much more highly sensitized to the nation's interests in Central America.

At the same time that the French began building their canal in Panama, an American company secured the rights from Nicaragua to build a rival canal. But Congress, partly influenced by the transcontinental railroad interests, refused any help, and the project foundered. It also foundered because the provisions of the Clayton-Bulwer Treaty required the United States to share control of any isthmian canal with Great Britain. The American government had tried consistently to get the British to revise the treaty, but the British just as consistently refused. Chester Arthur's secretary of state, Frederick T. Frelinghuysen, decided to push the Nicaraguan project forward by simply ignoring the Clayton-Bulwer Treaty. He negotiated a treaty with Nicaragua providing for a permanent alliance with Nicaragua and a canal totally controlled by the United States. Again the Senate balked and frustrated the design, and Grover Cleveland withdrew the treaty when he took over the presidency.

American efforts in Mexico were somewhat more successful. For a brief time after Porfirio Díaz took power in Mexico in 1876, he and the United States argued over America's right to pursue bandits across the border into Mexico. Finally, under pressure from commercial interests seeking concessions in Mexico, the Hayes administration recognized Díaz's government and ended cross-border pursuits. American investments in and exports to Mexico rose markedly.

This sort of economic expansion in Latin America was a pet project of James G. Blaine, secretary of state to Benjamin Harrison after serving briefly in the same capacity for James Garfield. Blaine organized a Pan-American Conference in 1889 in hopes of establishing a customs union that would allow the nations of the Americas preferred treatment in one another's markets. This would give the United States a competitive edge over Great Britain and other European powers. He also hoped for arbitration agreements that would deter war among Western Hemisphere nations.

Blaine failed in this. The Latin American nations were interested in staving off the influence of both the United States and the Europeans. They asked endorsement of the so-called Calvo Doctrine, named after its Argentine originator, Carlos Calvo. The Calvo Doctrine would have prevented foreign nationals from appealing to their own nations to give diplomatic support for private economic interests. The Latin Americans argued that so long as they treated foreign nationals in the same way they treated their own citizens, foreigners should have no complaints. The United States and the other major powers insisted that their nationals were entitled to certain minimum standards of treatment regardless of how the Latin American nations treated their own citizens. These major powers were totally unwilling to give up their rights under international law to intervene on behalf of the lives and property of their citizens abroad. The Calvo Doctrine raised an issue that would haunt U.S. foreign policy in Latin America for the next century.

Blaine also sought naval bases in the Caribbean to further Latin American trade. He pressured the government of Haiti for Môle St. Nicholas, which controlled the vital windward passage between the islands of Cuba and Santo Domingo. Failing to get Haiti's consent, he refused to cut off supplies flowing from the United States to revolutionaries who had promised to give America the strategic harbor. When the revolutionary faction won, it reneged. Blaine applied some diplomatic pressure, but stopped short of using force. He was content to hope for peaceful annexation of Cuba and Puerto Rico in the next generation.

Blaine and Harrison also became embroiled in a civil war that broke out between the president and the legislature of Chile in 1891. Chile was much less strategically significant to the United States than Central America or the Caribbean, but its nitrate fields were important. Germany and other European nations supported the legislature in hopes of strengthening their commercial position in the country. The United States naturally supported the president. Harrison even intercepted an American ship carrying arms to the legislative faction. Nonetheless, this legislative faction won, and American relations with Chile were severely strained. Foolishly, the commander of an American naval vessel that arrived a couple of weeks later in Valparaiso, Chile, gave shore leave to over a hundred of his crew.

In the ensuing riot, one sailor was killed and six more seriously wounded. The United States demanded an apology. When Chile's foreign minister hesitated and made some rather uncivil remarks about the United States, Harrison sent an ultimatum and prepared for war. Blaine, ill and tired, delayed matters until Chile realized how close to the brink it stood and apologized. The matter quickly blew over, but the Valparaiso incident demonstrated that America's erratic and sometimes belligerent policymakers could rather easily get the United States involved in a war over very minor but emotional issues.

EXPANSION IN THE PACIFIC: HAWAII AND SAMOA

Hawaii had stirred America's imagination for a century. Britain's famous Captain James Cook made the first European contact with the islands while sailing with a grant of immunity from Benjamin Franklin during the American Revolution. America's Captain Robert Gray, who had helped lay claim to Oregon, paid a visit to the islands in 1789 on his way from the Pacific Northwest to China. American fur traders followed Gray's route to the Orient. They reprovisioned in Hawaii and picked up sandalwood to supplement their cargoes of furs. American and European contacts were an ecological disaster for Hawaii, depleting the forests of the islands and killing the inhabitants. Disease and alcohol affected the Hawaiians much as they had the American Indians. There were 200,000 Hawaiians when Captain Cook arrived in 1778; by 1890 this population had dwindled to some 35,000.

The sandalwood trade prompted the rise of mercantile establishments in Hawaii to supply the American and European traders. Four of these firms were American. As the sandalwood forests declined following the War of 1812, the slack was picked up by the shift of the whaling industry from the Atlantic to the Pacific, again led by Americans. Between 1824 and 1843, 1,400 of the 1,700 whaling ships that arrived at Honolulu were American. Missionaries sent out from New England after 1820 further enhanced American influence in Hawaii. Within a few years, they had converted much of the island population to their Calvinist brand of Christianity. In the process, missionaries also systematized a written form of the Hawaiian language, established an education system, and entered a long rivalry with the dissolute whalers and the European missionaries of other faiths. American missionaries and their descendants served as the primary advisors to most Hawaiian monarchs and chiefs. To a great extent, Hawaii became a cultural outpost of the United States.

But the British and French also had whalers, naval captains, and missionaries seeking influence in the islands. They were much in the minority, but some of the early Hawaiian kings, particularly Kamehameha III and IV, encouraged them as a counterweight to the Americans. American leaders were quick to recognize the value of Hawaii, and in 1842, Daniel Webster announced that the United States would not take Hawaii as a colony, but would oppose any attempt by the British or French to do so. Millard Fillmore renewed this declaration in 1851. The Democrats were willing to go even further: Franklin Pierce's administration negotiated a treaty of outright annexation in 1854. The treaty failed, however, because of the death of the Hawaiian monarch involved.

During the Civil War, sugar began to replace whaling as the primary economic activity of Hawaii, and most of the plantation owners were Americans or descendants of Americans. It was vital to their livelihood to have access to the American market, something domestic sugar producers opposed intensely. Secretaries of State Seward and Fish saw the benefit of tying the Hawaiian economy more firmly to the United States, since the increasing trade with China and Japan made Hawaii more and more important as a stopover on the route to East Asia. The advent of steam-driven warships also enhanced the strategic value of Hawaii. No fleet could attack the Pacific Coast of the United States without coaling in the islands. Nevertheless, the Senate defeated Seward's reciprocity treaty with Hawaii and Fish's suggestion to annex the islands fell dead in Grant's cabinet.

In some desperation, Hawaiian sugar plantation owners tried to purchase reciprocity by offering Pearl Harbor to the United States. King Kalakaua made a highly publicized tour of America in 1875 and got the reciprocity treaty. But agitation in the islands disrupted the process by forcing the Hawaiian government to withdraw the offer. Hawaii promised only to deny the port to any other country. The reciprocity treaty finally slipped through Congress anyway. Hawaiian sugar production boomed, and planters imported thousands of Asians to work in the fields to supplement the rapidly declining population of native Hawaiians. Although the reciprocity treaty tied Hawaii firmly to the American economy, some Americans worried that this Asian immigration might remove Hawaii from the American orbit. Faced with domestic opposition to a renewal of the reciprocity treaty in 1884 and forced to acknowledge that reciprocity cost the United States more than it brought in, the American government had to make the strategic importance of the islands clear if it hoped to get a renewed agreement through Congress. Consequently, the United States insisted on and finally received the exclusive right to use Pearl Harbor.

In 1890, however, American domestic sugar interests forced revision of Hawaii's preferred tariff status. Hawaiian planters now saw American annexation as the most promising means of restoring their former prosperity.

Their determination increased when King Kalakaua was succeeded by his sister, Queen Lilioukalani. Lilioukalani announced that she would proclaim a new constitution depriving the minority white planters of the special governing privileges they had won from Kalakaua. With secret encouragement from Benjamin Harrison's cabinet, Hawaii's planters resolved to secure Lilioukalani's acquiescence to American annexation one way or another. In 1893, in a nearly bloodless coup, they deposed the queen, set up a revolutionary government, and offered the islands to the United States. The United States minister to Hawaii ordered sailors from the American cruiser *Boston* ashore during the coup to maintain order and thus lent support to the revolution. He also granted recognition of the new government on his own authority. Harrison quickly negotiated a treaty of annexation and sent it to the Senate.

Grover Cleveland took office as president before the Senate took action, and he withdrew the treaty for further investigation. The commissioner he appointed reported that the American minister and the crew of the *Boston* had exercised undue influence in helping impose a government opposed by the majority of the islanders. As a consequence, Cleveland refused to resubmit the treaty, and even talked of restoring Lilioukalani to the throne. The provisional government pledged to resist any such attempt with force so Cleveland dropped that idea, but he continued to block American annexation.

Ironically, while the United States failed to annex Hawaii in the post-Civil War era, it did annex a Pacific island group far less significant to American interests. Samoa, with its harbor of Pago Pago, was a convenient steppingstone to the British colonies of Australia and New Zealand even though it was far more remote from America's Pacific Coast, far less valuable strategically, and provided access to a less desirable market area than did Ha-

Figure 7   President Grover Cleveland, who blocked the annexation of Hawaii for a time. Portrait courtesy of the National Archives.

waii. In 1872, an American naval commander signed an unauthorized treaty giving the United States an exclusive naval base in Samoa. The Senate rejected it, but President Grant was interested, and his successor Hayes concluded a nonexclusive naval base treaty six years later. The British and Germans also were interested in Samoa, and the American consul took it upon himself to agree to a three-way government of the powers over the islands. Although the American government never officially approved of the arrangement, the three consuls were the de facto government of Samoa for many years.

The dangerous entanglement involved in this arrangement became clear when in 1885 the Germans moved troops into the islands to quash native resistance. The American consul responded by announcing an American protectorate. President Cleveland disavowed the consul, but as the Germans fastened their grip more firmly, Cleveland detected an American moral commitment to the area and a German insult to American prestige. He ordered American warships to Samoa, where they joined British and German ships, all watching one another warily. The crisis subsided quickly when a hurricane sank all three fleets, killing 150 people. The German Chancellor Otto von Bismarck then called for a conference. The subsequent Treaty of Berlin of 1889 involved the United States in official joint supervision with the British and Germans over the Samoan king and brought American political entanglement in an area of little importance and great distance.

American expansion in the Pacific remained dubious and debatable to many Americans. Henry Adams, for instance, was at first a strong supporter of annexations in the Pacific. He turned away from the idea in 1893 after observing the effects of colonialism in Tahiti. He became convinced that America had no future in the Pacific, and urged instead that the United States look to Siberia. Siberia was "empty," and when Russia went to pieces, as Adams confidently expected, Siberia could be colonized and populated, in the manner of the American West. Thus the United States could avoid the problems inherent in colonizing remote areas densely populated by foreign and probably inferior peoples like the "worthless Malay types" Adams considered dominant in the Philippines. Adams's vacillation demonstrated how unsure even expansionists were as to the forms American expansion should take.

EXPANSION IN EAST ASIA: CHINA, JAPAN, AND KOREA

Just as merchants, missionaries, and naval captains entangled the United States in the Pacific, they likewise encouraged involvement in East Asia. Americans, however, had no ambitions for outright annexations in East Asia, as they did in the Pacific and the Caribbean.

Americans began trade with China immediately after the revolution. As an independent nation, the United States no longer had an obligation to respect the monopoly Great Britain had given the East India Company over the

China trade. The *Empress of China*, which sailed in 1784, was the first of many American ships that ultimately carried close to one-third of China's trade in the nineteenth century. Like other foreign merchants, of whom the British were the most dominant, Americans dealt with China under very strict Chinese rules historians generally call "the tribute system."

The Chinese visualized their territory as the center of the earth. They regarded any contact they allowed between themselves and outsiders as a privilege far more beneficial to the foreigners than to China. They did not think of dealings between representatives of foreign governments and their emperor as diplomacy between equal sovereign nations, but as inferiors paying tribute and requesting favors from a superior. They looked upon European merchants, missionaries, and diplomats as "overseas barbarians" bringing ideas, customs, and merchandise that were only marginally useful at best and positively harmful at worst. To protect their people, the Chinese emperors restricted European traders to the port of Canton and prohibited them or their fellow countrymen from venturing into China's interior. Those who violated the court's standing proclamation, especially missionaries, faced harsh punishment.

Under this system, Europeans found none of the trappings of trade and diplomacy to which they were accustomed. There were no treaties, no consulates, no diplomatic relations, and no protection of European lives and property by home governments. The consequences became clear to Americans in 1821, when the Chinese authorities in Canton demanded that an American merchant ship turn over one of its sailors, a man named Terranova. The Chinese claimed that Terranova, in carelessly dumping garbage overboard, had struck and killed a Chinese woman on a raft below. The Chinese authorities had Terranova strangled, after which they acknowledged the Americans' "proper submissiveness."

It was not such events as the Terranova incident, however, that brought the end of the tribute system; instead, it was the imbalance of trade. There was a far greater demand in Europe for Chinese products like tea and rhubarb than there was in China for the hides, furs, sandalwood, and ginseng the Europeans brought in exchange. The Europeans and Americans increasingly offset this imbalance by bringing opium to China from the British colony of India. The Chinese court had a standing prohibition against the importation of opium but did not enforce it strictly until 1839, when the volume of the trade began to threaten both the physical and economic health of China. Not only did opium ravage its addicts, the demand for it reversed the balance of trade. Silver flowed out of China to pay for the excess of European imports over Chinese exports.

By enforcing the prohibition against opium, the Chinese court threatened the whole structure of Europe's China trade. Great Britain resorted to naval force, and this Opium War of 1839–1842 resulted in a complete British victory. The British forced China to sign a treaty opening five more ports to European trade and to cede Hong Kong as a British naval base. A year later, a supplementary treaty limited China's tariffs on foreign goods. It also gave

Britain most favored nation status, meaning that England received any concession China gave to another foreign power. Finally, this supplementary treaty established the right of extraterritoriality, allowing British offenders in China to be tried not by Chinese courts, but by the British themselves.

As the treaty system replaced the tribute system, the United States moved quickly to share the spoils. In 1843, Caleb Cushing signed a treaty with China that gave the United States as well as Britain most favored nation status and extraterritoriality. The Chinese, in their traditional tactic of dividing their enemies, hoped to exploit the rivalry they vaguely recognized between Great Britain and the United States and to use the Americans to protect China against ambitious Europeans. Soon other nations, notably France and Russia, were clamoring for similar treaties, and each subsequent concession China made to these nations automatically accrued to all previous treaty countries under the most favored nation clause. China soon found itself whipsawed between the foreign powers.

At first, the Chinese did not regard the concessions under an obviously unequal treaty system as significant. It did not seem to matter that limits on China's tariff were unmatched by limits on European tariffs, for Chinese products would always be in demand. If Europeans were accountable for their own citizens in China under extraterritoriality, that relieved Chinese authorities of the task of disciplining the outsiders. And if Europeans did not furnish similar extraterritorial privileges to Chinese abroad, it served those Chinese right for abandoning the civilized world to reside in barbarian lands.

In the 1850s, however, a new Chinese emperor began to resist European pressures for further concessions. To his consternation, he found himself faced at the same time with an uprising known as the Taiping Rebellion, which ultimately cost China between 20 and 40 million lives. The Europeans used their navies to attack the distracted Chinese government. They destroyed the forts guarding the capital at Peking, burned and looted the Summer Palace, and forced new treaty concessions from the emperor.

The American administrations of Pierce and Buchanan supported treaty revision, but ordered no American use of force. They reprimanded two naval officers who participated in bombardments against their instructions. Nevertheless, they ordered American diplomats in China to partake of the benefits of treaty revision, and the United States joined in successfully pressing for the opening of eleven more treaty ports. Under the new treaties, foreigners, including missionaries, were permitted to travel anywhere in China, tariffs were limited to 5 percent, the legality of the opium trade was confirmed, and foreign diplomats were permitted to reside in Peking. Foreign diplomats, missionaries, merchants, and their property would be protected by European and American gunboats sailing not just on the coast, but up the major rivers into the heart of China. Subsequently, foreign soldiers, including two Americans and the famous British officer C. G. "Chinese" Gordon, served as leaders in the Chinese army that restored imperial authority over the Taiping rebels. In addition, the Imperial Maritime Customs Service, managed primarily by British subjects, took charge of collecting tariff revenues for China, giving foreigners control of what had become the Chinese government's primary source of revenue.

The United States had played a fairly passive role in the establishment of the treaty system. It avoided force by and large and acquired concessions by benefiting from the military activities of other European powers in what some have aptly called "jackal diplomacy." The Chinese thus tended to regard the United States as the best of a bad lot of European exploiters. At least the Americans had no territorial designs on China and opposed the inclination of some European powers to carve China into exclusive colonial outposts. Instead, the Americans supported a unified China open to the trade of all nations. The Chinese even sent an American, Anson Burlingame, as their emissary to the United States and the major European capitals in 1866.

Whatever goodwill might have existed toward the United States was thoroughly dissipated by the treatment of Chinese in the United States in the latter half of the nineteenth century. By 1868, over 100,000 Chinese had come to the United States in search of work. There was a great reaction against them, particularly in the West, where the completion of the transcontinental railroad threw many Chinese railway workers into competition for new jobs with recent Irish immigrants. Violence and lynchings erupted, and Congress responded by trying to outlaw all further Chinese immigration. President Hayes vetoed the bill because it violated the Burlingame Treaty, which permitted open immigration to both countries. Instead, he negotiated a new treaty in which China permitted the United States to suspend rather than prohibit Chinese immigration. Congress seized the opportunity by suspending Chinese immigration for ten years, with the obvious intention of renewing the suspension indefinitely thereafter. If the Chinese government had not previously bothered about the fate of Chinese abroad, the American breach of faith made it highly sensitive now. Americans continued to regard the Chinese patronizingly as friendly protégés, but time would prove that a silly conceit.

For the most part, merchants, missionaries, and a few independent-minded naval officers dominated America's relations with China in the nineteenth century. The American government itself paid little attention to diplomatic relations with the Middle Kingdom. In Japan, however, the U.S. government played the major role in opening relations.

Japan, like China, originally tried to isolate European influence. The Tokugawa shogunate opened the port of Nagasaki to Dutch traders but turned away the ships of all other Europeans, including Americans. The Japanese even treated shipwrecked sailors like criminals; they were killed or sent in cages to Nagasaki for repatriation. As Pacific whaling and trade with China expanded, the number of sailors receiving such treatment increased.

In the 1850s, Secretary of State Daniel Webster instructed Commodore Matthew Perry to lead an American naval squadron to Japan to seek protection for shipwrecked seamen and property, to open trade, and to gain the right to deposit coal for refueling ships on their way to East Asia. Perry was to warn Japan especially that any further acts of cruelty to American sailors would be severely punished. After two visits in force, Perry got Japan to sign a treaty permitting Americans to purchase supplies at two insignificant ports. The treaty also offered protection for shipwrecked mariners and accorded most favored nation status to the United States. The Japanese signed at least in part because they knew that other European powers were about to demand even greater concessions, and they hoped this moderate treaty might serve as a restraining precedent. Great Britain, Russia, and the Netherlands did sign similar treaties with Japan in short order.

Perry urged that the United States continue an active policy in East Asia. He occupied the Bonin Islands and asked the administration to make Taiwan (then known as Formosa) an American protectorate. But the government insisted that the United States' only interest should be the protection of American citizens and property in the area. The new American consul in Japan, Townsend Harris, managed to gain fresh concessions from Japan anyway. He reminded the Japanese that the Americans were more moderate than the European powers and induced them to sign a treaty which opened four new ports to American trade, gave Americans the right to reside in several areas of Japan and practice their religion, and set a limit on the tariffs the Japanese could charge. Since the European nations signing treaties with Japan had gained the right of extraterritoriality, Harris reluctantly sought and acquired that as well. Thus Japan was subject to an unequal treaty system similar to China's.

After Harris's agreements with Japan in 1857 and 1858, the United States reverted to the status of follower rather than leader of European influence in Japan. The United States cooperated with Great Britain and other naval powers in resisting attempts by some Japanese leaders to return to the old system and remove the foreigners. An American ship participated in the bombardment of areas of southern Japan to put down rebellious clans. When the Meiji Restoration of 1868 brought to power a number of Japanese modernizers who saw Western technology as essential to Japan, America returned happily to a policy of peaceful trade. By the turn of the century the United States even led the movement that ultimately ended the tariff limitations and extraterritoriality.

With China and Japan opened to Western trade by the 1850s, only the Hermit Kingdom of Korea remained closed. American naval ships tried unsuccessfully to open Korea in 1867 and 1871; Japan succeeded in doing so in 1876. Several Americans tried to follow in Japan's footsteps and negotiate a treaty with Korea, but they failed. Then in 1882, Commodore Robert Shufeldt realized that Korea wanted to use China to balance the influence of Japan. By approaching Korea through the Chinese government, he managed to negotiate a treaty that protected American sailors and gained the usual concessions of most favored nation and extraterritoriality. Shufeldt acted without instructions or support from home, and American influence might have dwindled rapidly except for the remarkable activities of the new American minister, a missionary named Horace Allen. Allen actually became a close advisor of the Korean rulers. Neither the American government nor

American merchants shared Allen's enthusiasm for Korea, however, and the American position faded as China, Japan, and Russia began to compete in earnest for the strategically placed peninsula.

Thus American diplomacy in the post-Civil War period was limited essentially to the protection of the lives and property of American citizens abroad, most of them merchants and missionaries. The navy, composed of outdated cruisers, was the primary instrument of this protection. It sought to free the seas of pirates and to remove obstacles to American navigation and trade, whether posed by the European naval powers or by the weaker countries of Latin America and Asia. A few ambitious expansionists serving as president or secretary of state initiated attempts to acquire areas important to navigation and trade. But in this era almost all such initiatives were aborted by countervailing power, apathy, and ideological distaste for incorporating or suppressing populated, noncontiguous, and culturally or racially different peoples. It would be different in the 1890s: Americans would then pursue expansion far more aggressively and successfully.

CONTROVERSIAL ISSUES AND FURTHER READING

The primary historiographical dispute over mid-nineteenth-century U.S. diplomacy has been whether to visualize it as a part of a continuous expansionist drive toward empire or as a relatively isolationist hiatus between the era of territorial expansion prior to the Civil War and the acquiring of an overseas empire following the Spanish-American War of 1898. Revisionist historians, emphasizing the concern in this period for expanding America's foreign trade and the attempts to acquire naval bases to defend it, portray the era as an age of imperialism. They tend to equate the expansion of trade with more overt forms of imperialism, such as formal territorial annexation or military intervention. They argue that America's economy has been so strong that its trade dominates and coerces other peoples almost as surely as political and military force. Often they refer to this economic expansionism as the new imperialism, informal imperialism, or neo-imperialism to differentiate between it and the more traditional military or political domination of colonies. Many revisionists advocate the development of self-sufficient national economies to avoid much foreign trade and the danger of such neo-imperialism. The most influential book asserting this view is Walter LaFeber's *The New Empire: An Interpretation of American Expansion, 1860–1898* (1963). William Appleman Williams added to LaFeber's interpretation by showing the concern of farmers as well as rising industrialists for overseas markets in *The Roots of the Modern American Empire* (1969).

More traditional historians agree that expanded trade can result in the dominance of one people by another and tempt nations to further overt military and political interventions to protect their markets, resources, and investments in weaker lands. But they are unwilling to accept the idea that this is truly equivalent to formal colonialism, or even similar enough to be called neo-imperialism. They portray the post-Civil War era, which saw the defeat of most attempts at annexation of further territory, as an isolationist contrast with the previous era of rapid territorial expansion. They contrast it also with the subsequent period when, following the Spanish-American War, the United States acquired several formal colonies and pursued other foreign interests far more aggresssively and purposefully. The careful reader of this book will notice that I agree more with these traditional historians than with the revisionists.

The best traditional works emphasizing the relative isolationism of this period and the contrast with later imperialism are Robert L. Beisner's thoughtful *From the Old Diplomacy to the New, 1865–1900* (1975), and the best survey of post-Civil War diplomacy, Charles S. Campbell, *The Transformation of American Foreign Relations, 1865–1900* (1976). Standing somewhere between these authors and the revisionists is Milton Plesur, *America's Outward Thrust: Approaches to Foreign Affairs, 1865–1890* (1971). Other important works on more limited topics are David M. Pletcher, *The Awkward Years: American Foreign Relations under Garfield and Arthur* (1962); David Donald, *Charles Sumner and the Rights of Man* (1970); Allan Nevins, *Hamilton Fish* (1937); Glyndon Van Deusen, *William Henry Seward* (1967); and a revisionist analysis of Seward, Ernest N. Paolino, *The Foundations of American Empire* (1973). For contrasting views of the tariff issue and its significance for American expansionism in this period, see Tom Terill's revisionist *The Tariff, Politics, and American Foreign Policy, 1874–1901* (1973); Paul S. Holbo's critiques of the revisionists, "Economics, Emotion, and Expansion: An Emerging Foreign Policy," in H. Wayne Morgan, ed., *The Gilded Age* (1970) and *Tarnished Expansion: The Alaska Scandal, the Press, and Congress, 1867–1871* (1983). See also Mira Wilkins, *The Emergence of the Multinational Enterprise: American Business Abroad from the Colonial Era to 1914* (1970), and an outstanding analysis of American business, naval, and missionary activities in the Mediterranean, James A. Field, *America and the Mediterranean World, 1776–1882* (1969).

The important part played by the navy in the diplomacy of this era can be traced in Kenneth J. Hagan, *American Gunboat Diplomacy and the Old Navy, 1877–1889* (1973); Harold and Margaret Sprout, *The Rise of American Naval Power, 1776–1918* (1939); and John A. S. Grenville and George B. Young, *Politics, Strategy, and American Diplomacy* (1967). Policy toward Latin America is best surveyed by Dexter Perkins, *The Monroe Doctrine, 1867–1907* (1937). See also Samuel F. Bemis, *The Latin American Policy of the United States* (1943); Karl M. Schmitt, *Mexico and the United States, 1821–1973* (1974); Russell H. Bastert, "A New Approach to the Origins of Blaine's Pan American Policy," *Hispanic Historical Review*, 39 (1959). On Hawaii, see Merze Tate, *The United States and the Hawaiian Kingdom* (1965), and Thomas J. Osborne, *"Empire Can Wait": American Opposition to Hawaiian Annexation, 1893–1898* (1981). On Samoa, see Paul M. Kennedy, *The Samoan Tangle: A Study in Anglo-German-American Relations, 1878–1900* (1974), and George H. Ryden, *The Foreign Policy of the United States in Relation to Samoa* (1933). On China, see John K. Fairbank, *The United States and China* (3rd ed., 1971); Warren I. Cohen, *America's Response to China* (1971); and Immanuel C. Y. Hsu, *China's Entrance into the Family of Nations* (1960). On Japan, see Charles Neu, *The Troubled Encounter: The United States and Japan* (1975); Akira Iriye, *Across the Pacific* (1967); and Edwin O. Reischauer, *The United States and Japan* (3rd ed., 1965). On Korea, see Fred Harvey Harrington, *God, Mammon, and the Japanese: Horace N. Allen and Korean-American Relations, 1884–1905* (1944).

CHAPTER 8

The Spanish-American War and the Decision for Empire

THE IMPERIAL SURGE, 1895–1917

It is doubtful that many Americans living in the early 1890s realized that they stood on the threshold of a new age in American diplomacy. National politics still revolved around internal questions. Americans regarded the economic issues stemming from industrialization and immigration as essentially domestic ones, despite rising concerns for foreign trade. The warnings of the Founding Fathers against foreign entanglements, military establishments, and colonial oppression still dominated popular attitudes toward foreign policy. Little of the nation's economic strength had been translated into the military or diplomatic power necessary for large-scale overseas intervention, and most Americans would have been aghast at any suggestion that the United States should involve itself in a major way in Europe or Asia. The balance of opinion was more tenuous on acquisitions closer to home, however, especially if they might be annexed without much fuss or expense. Rejections of treaties or petitions for the annexation of Santo Domingo, Cuba, Haiti, and Hawaii had been somewhat accidental, involving political partisanship, personalities, and fortuitous events that swung the balance against territorial expansion. The balance against overseas annexations and involvements was becoming increasingly precarious, ready to be altered by a major crisis or opportunity that could give it a substantial push.

The forces inclining the United States toward overseas expansion and intervention had developed rapidly in the post-Civil War period. Most important of these was America's growing power. The nation's population increased from 39 million in 1870 to 63 million in 1890. By the 1890s, America surpassed all nations in the production of coal, oil, and steel, the sinews of modern power until the atomic age. Popular writers and politicians made clear to the American people the strategic and economic benefits of acquiring Caribbean naval bases, an isthmian canal, and Hawaii. They helped translate hazy inclinations into systematic thought patterns.

The Spanish-American War supplied the catalyst to create a new national majority ready to intrude into the realm of great power politics and accept an overseas empire. The original rationale of the Spanish-American War, intervention to free Cuba from Spain, did not stretch the old diplomacy too much, especially when Congress declared its intention not to annex Cuba. But the thrill of military combat and victory broke down many of the barriers to overseas intervention and annexation. The United States took Puerto Rico, the Philippines, Guam, and Wake Island, completed the annexation of Hawaii, and asserted a protectorate over Cuba. It then acquired the Panama canal route, undertook wholesale military interventions in Central America and the Caribbean, and increased its diplomatic activity in Asia, as symbolized by the issuance of the Open Door Notes.

Even in this imperial aftermath of the Spanish-American War, Americans remained wary of European entanglements. They defended their Latin American interventions by claiming they were necessary to ward off European expansion and consequent conflict with the interests of the United States. They offered the Open Door in Asia as an alternative to European attempts to carve China further into spheres of interest, a process that might entangle the United States in European balance of power politics. Finally, however, World War I dragged the United States into the European arena. Americans became thoroughly enmeshed in global politics.

THE DIPLOMATIC REVOLUTION OF THE 1890s

Foreign nations seemed no more aware that the United States was on the verge of adopting a new diplomatic posture in the 1890s than Americans themselves. When the Turkish sultan sought to cut expenses in 1880, he decided to eliminate diplomatic missions in several minor powers, including Sweden, Belgium, the Netherlands, and the United States. The German envoy in Washington offered to take a pay cut if his superiors would transfer him to Madrid. Russia neglected to send a minister to the United States for two years after the old one had left.

These nations failed to realize that the Industrial Revolution had increased American strength tremendously. By the 1890s, the United States was manufacturing almost as much as Great Britain, Germany, and France combined. This gave the United States the means to expand its diplomatic role from a regional to a global power. Industry also provided a motive for such a change in American foreign policy, creating more need for overseas markets. By the 1890s, manufactures had surpassed agricultural products as America's main exports. Of all the nations in the world, only Great Britain outstripped the United States in the total value of its exports, and Britain's lead was clearly temporary. America's increasing desire for overseas markets naturally led to calls for a more active diplomacy.

Throughout the post-Civil War period there had been no lack of voices calling for a more aggressive military and diplomatic policy to accompany America's increasing economic strength and expanding foreign trade. Naval officers like Admiral Stephen Luce extolled the benefits of a larger, more modern navy. In the 1880s these officers succeeded in beginning a naval building program that produced long-range, steam-driven, steel-clad battle-ships. Otherwise, as we have seen, the United States pursued overseas markets, coaling stations, and strategically located colonies sporadically and ineffectually. Then, in the 1890s, advocates of an aggressive foreign policy took advantage of several traumatic events to propel America into a policy of global intervention and the acquisition of an overseas empire.

The economic panic of 1893, initiating a four-year depression more severe than any America faced until 1929, did much to turn influential Americans toward a more active pursuit of foreign markets. Fifteen thousand businesses failed in 1893, including several major railroads. Hundreds of banks went under. Three million people were left jobless, some 20 percent of the workforce. Farm production and prices plummeted. Violent strikes occurred in coal mines and railroads, and federal troops were called in to break up the great Pullman Strike. Discontented farmers flocked into the Populist party. They demanded currency inflation by unlimited coinage of silver, advocated a graduated income tax, and urged government control of railroads and utilities. Some leaders of government and industry feared that America stood on the brink of revolution.

The depression highlighted other disturbing trends that had seemed less ominous when the country was more prosperous. Large combinations of capital were becoming increasingly dominant in American business, threatening the older America of smaller competitive enterprises. Cities expanded tremendously, undercutting the power and prestige of the countryside and the older prototypical American, the yeoman farmer. Immigrants flowed into these cities at a staggering rate; over 500,000 arrived in America every year. Most of these newcomers were from Southern and Eastern Europe, bringing with them cultural mores and religious practices that clashed with the Protestantism and Anglo-Saxon culture of the dominant elite.

In addition to the problems posed by immigration, historian Frederick Jackson Turner startled the nation by publicizing the fact that the census of 1890 no longer recognized the existence of a frontier line in the West. Turner warned that the disappearance of this frontier would mean declining opportunities for internal territorial and economic expansion. Since he thought much of America's democracy had stemmed from the frontier, he feared its disappearance would have political as well as economic consequences.

All this produced in America what historian Richard Hofstadter called a "psychic crisis." Powerful and wealthy as the United States was, many Americans seem to have feared that the nation was close to blowing up, or at least entering a decline in wealth and political well-being. For some, this led to depression and apathy; but others sought to deny their own failure of confidence by embarking on a frantic crusade, motivated by the hope that if they could convince others of their virtue and virility, they could convince themselves as well.

The economic, political, and psychic crisis brought on by the depression of 1893 caused some soul-searching among leading figures in the Cleveland administration, Congress, and business. They argued that the depression resulted from a glut of American agricultural and industrial products. Since America's factories and farms were producing more than domestic markets could consume, the United States needed to pursue overseas markets more aggressively. Yet at the same time that exports came to seem so much more important to many American leaders, foreign markets seemed to be closing against American trade. European nations were carving up Africa, and in the wake of Japan's victory over China in 1895, were seeking to increase their spheres of influence in Asia as well. These European colonial powers generally erected discriminatory tariff barriers in their newly acquired territories. Even in Great Britain, the trend seemed to be toward closing markets to foreign competition. Joseph Chamberlain advocated preferential tariff structures throughout the British Empire, which formerly had been relatively open to exports from the United States.

While the depression frightened the United States into a more interventionist policy abroad, intellectual and religious currents provided a moral rationale for expansion. The surge of European imperialism in the 1880s and 1890s led to a wealth of literature praising the beneficence of European colonial government. Writers such as Frederick Fabri and James Anthony Froude spread these ideas to the attentive and cosmopolitan portion of the American public that was aware of and concerned for national policy.

Influential politicians also helped propagate the imperial gospel among Americans. Theodore Roosevelt, for instance, argued that peace could not be had "until the civilized nations have expanded in some shape over the barbarous nations. This means the cooperation of the civilized peoples of the earth to that end, whatever the cost or time." Naturally Roosevelt thought the United States the best of such civilized nations, but in areas outside America's interests, he was willing to support the imperialism of other European powers. For instance, he thought England would be doing "her duty as a civilized nation" by colonizing the Sudan. He also said it was in the interest of civilization that the English-speaking race be dominant in the Western Hemisphere.

Roosevelt did not believe such colonialism ran contrary to the traditions of the Founding Fathers expressed in the Declaration of Independence and the Farewell Address. In his best-selling book, *The Winning of the West*, he pointed out that the Founding Fathers had conquered and colonized the Indians. This had been perfectly justified, he thought, for it had been impossible "to avoid conflicts with the weaker race, unless we were willing to see the American continent fall into the hands of some other strong power," or "willing that the whole continent west of the Alleghenies should remain an unpeopled waste, the hunting-ground of savages."

A still more influential propagator of the imperial vision in the 1890s was Roosevelt's friend, Admiral Alfred Thayer Mahan. His world-famous book, *The Influence of Sea Power upon History*, extolled the benefits of Christianity and Western civilization and noted the role the British navy had played in establishing the British Empire for the mutual benefit of the British economy and these barbaric natives. He urged that the United States likewise build a strong, two-ocean navy, acquire bases and coaling stations in the Caribbean and the Pacific, build an isthmian canal, and thus extend protection to the extensive commerce that would carry American civilization to Asia and Latin America while enriching the United States. He pointed out that modern technology had brought within reach lands that the Founding Fathers had considered far beyond the realm of vital American interests. Conversely, he warned that the United States now was also within easier reach of foreign powers and would become increasingly vulnerable militarily if it did not build its navy and take a more active interest in overseas affairs.

American missionaries reinforced the inclination of the followers of Mahan and Roosevelt to seek a more activist foreign policy. Josiah Strong embodied this missionary spirit. His best seller, *Our Country*, proclaimed that the Anglo-Saxon race of America, a "race of unequaled energy, with all the majesty of numbers and the might of wealth behind it—the representative, let us hope, of the largest liberty, the purest Christianity, the highest civilization—having developed peculiarly aggressive traits calculated to impress its institutions upon mankind, will spread itself over the earth. If I read not amiss, this powerful race will move down upon Mexico, down upon Central and South America, out upon the islands of the sea, over Africa and Beyond. And can any one doubt that the result of this competition of races will be the 'survival of the fittest'?" Strong emphasized that this expansion need not be a "war of extermination . . . ; the contest is not one of arms, but of vitality and of civilization." Nonetheless, his description of international affairs as a competition of races culminating in the survival of the fittest could not help but contribute to a more aggressive American foreign policy.

"The survival of the fittest" was a catchword of the 1890s and a powerful intellectual support for the "large policy" of people like Roosevelt and Mahan. It derived from Charles Darwin's path-breaking work on biological evolution that portrayed natural selection as the means by which species had evolved from primitive forms to their present status. An Englishman, Herbert Spencer, adapted Darwin's idea of biological evolution to the realm of human social affairs. Spencer theorized that civilizations, like biological species, progressed by natural selection and the survival of the fittest. Spencer's Social Darwinism was translated by many imperialists into a formula for international relations. Nations and races competed with one another; the strong survived, the weak succumbed. Thus civilization progressed.

Some Americans found the Darwinian emphasis on survival of the fittest a convenient rationale for their own desire to participate in a glorious fight. Most of the generation alive in the 1890s had not experienced the blood and terror of the Civil War. That war appeared to them in retrospect as a great adventure fought for profound principles. It seemed far more exciting than the dreary economic concerns that dominated their own industrial America of the 1890s. They were like adolescents desperate to test their new power in a fight with an evil bully. Some even agreed with Theodore Roosevelt that "This country needs a war."

The depression, the "psychic crisis," the increased need for foreign markets, the rapid development of modern communications and transportation, the surge of European imperialism, and the development of powerful, systematic rationales for overseas expansion helped set the stage for the Spanish-American War and its imperial aftermath. But there were still strong voices for restraint, even from among those one might have expected to be in the vanguard of imperialism.

Two of America's most prominent Social Darwinists, William Graham Sumner and John Burgess, were nonetheless strong opponents of overseas expansionism. So was the historian James Schouler, who had written paeans to earlier continental expansion. Such people could agree that the United States housed a superior race and civilization, yet oppose overseas acquisitions. Like the older generations of Americans, who had an equally fervent if not so systematic belief in American superiority, they were convinced the United States best fulfilled its missionary impulse by serving as a model for foreigners rather than as a conquerer and reformer.

James Schouler summarized these ideas in an article opposing the annexation of Hawaii. He thought Americans did not "wish these islands thrown upon them, under a race conquest, like that of Cortes over the Astecs [sic] in Mexico, but must feel well assured that the Hawaiians themselves come toward us with open arms and of their own free accord, as well as resident foreigners who undertake to pledge their consent." For "notwithstanding our innate and earnest desire to diffuse the blessings of freedom which we enjoy over the rest of the globe, one would think that, with Indians not yet reclaimed, negroes emancipated only by the bloodiest and costliest of civil strifes, and, as the latest factor, Chinese disturbing our national peace of mind,—not to speak of the refuse of European nations cast lately upon us so constantly by the Atlantic tides,—this Union had enough of the problem of amalgamating races into one brotherhood to last at least for the rest of this century." Schouler thought America's present Hawaiian trade ties and coaling stations satisfied the national interest and that the United States should avoid territorial annexation and overt political rule.

THE VENEZUELAN BOUNDARY DISPUTE

The Venezuela crisis of 1895 demonstrated the delicate balance between the conflicting impulses for an aggressive and a restrained foreign policy. Grover Cleveland, the president who precipitated the crisis with his belligerent claims of American rights abroad, was the same man who had rejected the Hawaiian annexation treaty two years before. Thus he embodied within himself these competing urges. Perhaps he tipped toward intervention in the Venezuelan case because the issue involved opposition to British annexations rather than pursuit of American acquisitions, and Venezuela was a Caribbean nation rather than a Pacific one like Hawaii. Still, Cleveland's conduct in the Venezuelan crisis puzzles most historians.

Venezuela and the British colony of Guiana had never agreed on the boundary between them. For many years the conflict had been muted because the boundary ran through uninhabited and seemingly valueless land. Still the issue had the potential for serious conflict. Venezuela claimed that its proper border included nearly two-thirds of the territory Britain already ruled as Guiana, while the British insisted that the true boundary was a line favorable to Guiana established by Robert Schomburgk in a survey commissioned by the British in 1840.

The United States had expressed mild concern about the border controversy from time to time in the post-Civil War era, but the issue heated up in 1894 when an American agent paid by Venezuela, William L. Scruggs, published a vitriolic pamphlet accusing the British of open aggression and defiance of the Monroe Doctrine. Congress responded with a unanimous vote on behalf of a resolution, drafted largely by Scruggs himself, urging Venezuela and Great Britain to submit the dispute to arbitration. Venezuela wanted arbitration rather than direct negotiations with Great Britain because it knew that its large delinquent debt to Britain could be used as leverage against Venezuela's border claims in an open negotiation. Arbitration would supposedly limit the issue to the border alone.

The United States probably did have sufficient interest in the dispute to justify a call for arbitration. The largest gold nugget ever discovered came from the disputed area. Great Britain also was trying to bend the Schomburgk Line to include Point Barima, with its access to the mouth of the Orinoco River. This would give Great Britain a chance to control what some regarded as a vital trade artery into the heart of South America. The claim to Point Barima, which Britain made formally in 1895, came on the heels of several other international conflicts involving British territorial claims. The most important of these resulted when British marines temporarily occupied the Nicaraguan town of Corinto, close to the potential canal site. Because Cleveland had stayed aloof from these disputes, denying in particular that the British-Nicaraguan clash involved the Monroe Doctrine, he was roundly criticized by the Republicans for his "weakness."

Cleveland believed he had already lost one election for his supposed softness toward the British in the Sackville West incident of 1888. Facing the backlash from the Corinto incident as well as the fallout from the depression of 1893, he may have thought it salutary for the national as well as his own political interest to call a loud halt to Britain's creeping advance in South America. In any case, he proved receptive to a blustering note his new Secretary of State, Richard Olney, proposed to send to Great Britain. Olney and Cleveland decided to end the Venezuelan boundary dispute once and for all, and in the process defend the Monroe Doctrine. Thus they hoped to dash any ideas European nations might have entertained of extending their race for colonies from Asia and Africa to the Western Hemisphere.

Although Richard Olney was not a particularly warlike man, he was impatient, blunt, rigid, and self-righteous. (He banished his daughter from his home and refused to see her for thirty years even though she lived in the same town.) With Cleveland's approval, Olney told the British that the

Monroe Doctrine was well-established public law in America, and that England was violating it by seeking to expand its territory in the Western Hemisphere at the expense of Venezuela. The United States had a right to demand that Britain submit the entire matter to arbitration, since "distance and three thousand miles of intervening ocean make any permanent political union between an European and an American state unnatural and inexpedient. . . . To-day the United States is practically sovereign on this continent, and its fiat is law upon the subjects to which it confines its interposition."

The British did not realize how gravely Cleveland and Olney viewed what seemed to be a remote border quarrel. Olney's inflated language no doubt made the crisis seem a political ploy aimed at domestic voters rather than a serious diplomatic initiative. Besides, the British cabinet was preoccupied with the massacre of Armenians in Turkey and Russian pressure for Chinese concessions in Manchuria, both of which held the potential for a general European war. As a consequence, Prime Minister Lord Salisbury delayed the British answer to Olney's note for four months. Cleveland was especially irritated by the delay because he wanted to announce a resolution of the issue in his State of the Union message. He was even more irritated when the British response, handed to Olney a few days after Cleveland's congressional message, rejected out of hand any suggestion that the Venezuela dispute was covered by the Monroe Doctrine or that the doctrine was international law. Salisbury also said Britain could not risk arbitration of any territory that might result in the transfer of "large numbers of British subjects . . . to a nation of different race and language, whose political system is subject to frequent disturbance, and whose institutions as yet too often afford very inadequate protection to life and property."

Cleveland's response was to threaten war. In a sensational message to Congress, Cleveland asserted that the Monroe Doctrine was indeed international law and that it covered the Venezuela dispute. He announced that the United States would commission a study of the proper boundary which, when approved by the American government, would obligate the United States "to resist by every means in its power, as a willful aggression upon its rights and interests, the appropriation by Great Britain of any lands or the exercise of government jurisdiction over any territory which after investigation we have determined of right belongs to Venezuela."

For a few days war seemed imminent. Congress unanimously accepted Cleveland's recommendation for a border survey. But opposition quickly arose and helped dampen the flames, reasserting the balance between the urges for aggression and restraint. The famous Harvard philosopher, William James, said Cleveland had committed a political crime. Henry Adams's elder brother, Charles Francis Adams, Jr., joined James's opposition, causing Henry to wail that Charles had aligned himself with "all the other Harvard college 'mokes,' the professors of history, by talking out loud" against Cleveland's action. Businessmen joined the outcry against war with Britain when stock market prices plunged, while farmers expressed fears of losing their export markets in a war with England.

Map 7　The Venezuela–British Guiana Boundary Dispute

Britons also recoiled from war. Thousands signed petitions urging their government to arbitrate. Sentiment was so strong in both countries that the two nations agreed not only to arbitrate the Venezuela-Guiana border dispute, but to negotiate a general arbitration treaty that would cover almost all future Anglo-American disputes. Ironically, in the euphoria of their reconciliation, the United States and Great Britain excluded Venezuela from any part in the arbitration of its own border. Venezuela protested and opposed the arbitration agreement. The United States and Great Britain relented and allowed Venezuela to choose one member of the panel, although they stipulated that the member could not be Venezuelan. Venezuela reluctantly accepted the modified arbitration agreement and selected an American to serve as its representative.

The arbitration panel decided substantially in favor of the British position. It established the Venezuela border close to the Schomburgk Line, excluding only the mouth of the Orinoco and several thousand miles of trackless interior. The Venezuelans were outraged.[1] The United States and Britain, however, hailed the Venezuela arbitration with enthusiasm. Even though the Senate later rejected the general Anglo-American arbitration treaty, giving it three votes less than the two-thirds necessary for consent, the incident had clearly shocked the United States and Great Britain into a new recognition of their mutual interests.

THE ANGLO-AMERICAN RAPPROCHEMENT

In January of 1896, while the Venezuela incident still endangered the peace between Great Britain and the United States, the German kaiser sent a note of congratulation to the president of the Boer Republic of South Africa on the failure of a raid into the Transvaal by a band of Englishmen led by a Dr. Leander Jameson. This "Jameson telegram" dramatized for the British the growing challenge Germany presented to their preeminent position as a world empire and helped turn them away from the impending confrontation with the United States. Unified only two decades before the Jameson incident, Germany had rapidly become the greatest land power in Europe. The German army had beaten Austria and France in quick succession in 1866 and 1870. In the 1890s Germany began planning a navy that would threaten Britain's traditional supremacy on the seas. As a latecomer to the ranks of great powers, Germany felt left out of the earlier scramble for colonies and therefore began abrasively asserting new claims in Africa, the Pacific, and even to some extent in the Western Hemisphere.

Russia, a giant nation of immense population and potential, also was awakening to challenge British interests in eastern Europe, Turkey, and the Mediterranean. Russia was active in Afghanistan, which bordered British India, and it looked covetously toward China, where England had long been supreme. In addition, Japan demanded entrance into the exclusive club of world powers. With its policy of industrialization after the Meiji Restoration, Japan had leaped miraculously into the modern age, and it dramatized its arrival as a great power by defeating China handily in the Sino-Japanese War of 1894–95. Afterward, it too demanded a share in the exploitation of continental Asia. Russia, Germany, and France intervened and forced Japan to give up a portion of its conquests, especially the Liaotung Peninsula of China. Then they began their own scramble for new concessions from the rotting hulk of the Chinese empire. These European powers and Japan thus threatened the British position in Asia at about the same time Cleveland hurled America's challenge on Venezuela and the Western Hemisphere.

As Great Britain watched the rise of these new powers and the dangers they posed to the stability of the Pax Britannica, the British leaders decided it

---

[1] They became even more disturbed in 1949 when they discovered that the American members of the arbitration panel had made the award unanimous only because otherwise the neutral member threatened to vote for the British position. The border issue is still open and sensitive between Venezuela and the now independent state of Guiana.

was foolish to provoke the United States. Of all the rising powers, the United States posed the least danger to Britain's vital interests. The United States no longer agitated for the annexation of Canada, and the expansion of its power and interest in the rest of the Western Hemisphere did not pose an intolerable threat to Britain's growing trade and investment in Latin America. In any case, Latin America was far less important to the British than Europe, East Asia, or the eastern Mediterranean, with its Suez link to India. As Britain's policy of "splendid isolation" began to look less and less splendid, British leaders contemplated the benefits of having the United States as a friend, if not an outright ally.

Other recent events had helped pave the way for this sudden turn toward Anglo-American friendship. The British had reformed their electoral system, broadened the franchise, and brought their politics more into line with the democracy of the United States. At the same time, the new immigration into the United States had emphasized to the old stock elites of America the kinship they felt with the culture of their British cousins, as opposed to the teeming masses of Catholic Italians, Irish, and southern Europeans who threatened to displace them in the cities. The racial attitudes of the day drew attention to the shared Anglo-Saxon heritage of the two nations, and the American elites began to find attractive even the British aristocratic attitudes they had formerly so resented. They hailed the many trans-Atlantic marriages between American daughters and such British luminaries as Joseph Chamberlain, Lord Randolph Churchill, and the duke of Marlborough. Practical economics reinforced sentimental ties. Great Britain took more than half of America's exports and supplied more imports and capital than any other nation. The United States provided nearly a quarter of Britain's imports and bought more than 10 percent of its exports.

Consequently, Great Britain began to withdraw from its dominant position in the Western Hemisphere and entrust the remainder of British interests in the area to American hegemony. The submission of the Venezuelan border dispute to arbitration was only the first step in a retreat that continued through the next decade. As the British turned the Western Hemisphere over to the United States, they also sought to draw American power into East Asia. They saw in the United States a potential ally in the struggle to keep Russia, Japan, and Germany from carving China into exclusive spheres of interest that would be closed to the trade and investment of other foreigners. Britain then dominated the China trade, and left its own sphere of China relatively open to foreign trade because it was strong enough to tolerate competition. The United States was not anxious to acquire a sphere of its own, and the establishment of closed foreign spheres would hurt American trade. Noting the harmony of interests between the two nations, the British approached the United States in 1898 on a joint policy to hold the Chinese markets open. Cleveland's successor, William McKinley, refused Britain's offer.

McKinley's rejection of a limited British alliance did not stop the American movement toward cooperation with Great Britain as the United States moved toward world power. The British continued their transformation from chief rivals to best friends. Those nations that had helped America challenge British supremacy on the high seas in earlier days, such as Russia and Germany, went from friends to enemies. The United States thus played a key role in the world diplomatic revolution of the 1890s.

THE SPANISH-AMERICAN WAR

The Cuban rebellion against Spain in 1895 furnished the major catalyst for America's own diplomatic revolution. Cuba had endured nine separate rebellions since 1823, and the endemic chaos on the island worried American leaders throughout most of the nineteenth century. Americans had long coveted Cuba, and the abolition of slavery in both countries following the American Civil War eliminated the major roadblock to intervention. America's desire for Caribbean naval bases to protect an isthmian canal added to Cuba's attractiveness.

When rebellion broke out in Cuba in the 1870s, President Ulysses Grant came to the brink of intervention. Congressional opposition to the annexation of a tropical province of a different race and culture thwarted Grant for the moment, but even Grant's opponents had no wish to see a major power replace the moribund Spanish rule. Americans of both parties feared that increasing chaos in Cuba would provide an incentive for Spain to request military aid from other European powers, and the intrusion of a new European nation in Cuba would be a direct challenge to the Monroe Doctrine. The United States publicly warned Germany against acquisition of Cuba in the 1880s after rumors circulated that Germany was seeking a pretext for intervention.

By the time a new revolution erupted in Cuba in 1895, American sentiment was far readier for intervention than it had been in Grant's era. The Venezuela incident of that same year had been too ambiguous to upset the close balance between restraint and assertiveness in American foreign policy. The Cuban revolution, on the other hand, was dramatic and popular enough to swing the balance toward an aggressive, interventionist diplomacy and to help America sustain that posture for at least two decades.

Cuba certainly had enough reason to revolt against Spain. The Spanish army and civil service in Cuba were inefficient, corrupt, and arrogant. Spaniards occupied almost all positions of power and wealth. They confined most of the 800,000 white Cubans to menial labor and left the 600,000 recently emancipated blacks in conditions little better than their previous slavery. Spain monopolized Cuba's trade, and the United States compounded the problems this created by placing high duties on Cuban sugar in the Wilson-Gorman Tariff of 1894.

Americans sympathized thoroughly with the Cubans. They had regarded Spain with dislike and contempt since the early days of America's westward movement. One railroad magnate wrote his senator that "Spain is and always has been an impudent, arrogant, and barbarous nation. . . . It is quite time she was boosted out of Cuba . . . and nine out of every ten of our citizens without regard to party will agree with me." Newspapers of the time, which were just then becoming instruments of mass circulation, played on these anti-Spanish sentiments. In their battle for circulation in New York, the Pulitzer and Hearst papers tried to outdo one another with titillating horror stories about the war in Cuba. The most sensational episode in this battle of the "yellow press" was the rescue of the daughter of a former Cuban official from her Spanish cell by a Hearst reporter, who naturally made the most of his scoop. Local newspapers were perhaps even more important then the big-city yellow press in stirring American emotions. Desperate for copy, they often printed verbatim the handouts from the Cuban junta's headquarters in New York.

While the general public was enthusiastically for the rebels, the Cleveland and McKinley administrations were more interested in seeing the war come to an end regardless of the victor. They feared Spain might call in another major power to help put down the rebellion. The war was also hurting American trade and investments in the island. American exports to Cuba dropped from $20 million in 1894 to half of that in 1898. The fighting endangered some $50 million worth of American investments in Cuba. Most of these were in sugar plantations sold by frightened Spaniards during the previous revolution of the 1870s. The rebellion's impact on American business could not help but concern America's political leaders, even though most businessmen opposed military intervention in Cuba because they feared that war with Spain would threaten their far more valuable trade with Europe.

Cleveland had responded at first to the 1895 rebellion by invoking America's neutrality laws. These laws forbade organizing or recruiting men in the United States. They did not specifically bar the sale of arms, but Cleveland sought to discourage this traffic as well. Nominally this neutrality policy helped Spain more than the rebels, since only the rebels needed men and arms from the United States. Actually, neither American nor Spanish patrols could halt the aid that flowed to the revolutionaries from Cuban exiles and other sympathetic Americans, a situation which brought howls of protest from Spain.

Congress urged Cleveland to do more for the rebels. Congressional Democrats and Republicans alike saw in the Cuban issue a popular cause around which they could unite their parties. By outdoing one another in professions of sympathy for the oppressed Cubans, they hoped to paper over the deep divisions within their parties brought about by the free silver issue. Over Cleveland's protests, Congress passed a resolution urging recognition of the Cubans' belligerent status. Cleveland refused to offer that recognition and asserted that he would not use the American army in Cuba even if Congress authorized him to do so. But the situation in Cuba was becoming worse: The revolution was rapidly growing from an issue the parties could use for their own purposes to one they could not escape even if they wished.

The revolution simply demolished Cuba. The rebels saw their best chance for victory in the ruin of the Cuban economy, and with it the island's value to Spain. They burned crops and sugar refineries, tore up railroads, and made a special effort to destroy American-owned plantations. They hoped that such attacks might force American intervention and knew that America would never intervene on the side of Spain. Meanwhile, in early 1896, the Spanish appointed General Valeriano Weyler, nicknamed "Butcher" Weyler by the Hearst press, as the new commander in Cuba. Toward the end of the year, Weyler initiated the *reconcentrado* policy. People living in the country-side would be concentrated in camps where they could be defended against the rebels and also prevented from supplying or supporting them. The army would assume that all people outside these camps were rebels and would shoot them on sight.

The Spanish army had no way to supply adequate food and sanitation for these camps. By 1898, newspapers estimated that nearly 400,000 Cubans, one-quarter of the island's entire population, had died during the revolution. Later studies have shown this to have been an exaggeration. The true figure was probably somewhere between 100,000 and 200,000, but that was bad enough, and the Spaniards themselves actually believed that the number of deaths had been close to 400,000.

As reports of destruction and atrocity multiplied, even Cleveland came to believe that American intervention might be necessary. In a lame duck mes-sage to Congress, he proposed that Spain grant Cuba greater autonomy, and warned that if the war dragged on it would be the duty of the United States to halt it. His successor, William McKinley, had similar opinions. He too wished for an early end to the revolution to avoid the need for American in-tervention. But McKinley seems to have been somewhat more pro-rebel than Cleveland. Cleveland might have forced the rebels to accept a Spanish offer of limited autonomy; McKinley would not require the rebels to accept a set-tlement they thought unfavorable. Since the rebels wanted nothing less than independence, and Spain was adamant against that, the prospects for secur-ing an early end to the war were minimal.

Despite the obstacles, McKinley hoped that through diplomatic pressure he might bring both sides to settle. He instructed America's minister to Spain, Stewart L. Woodford, to inform Spain that the United States expected notice of an "early and certain peace" by November 1, 1897. Otherwise the United States would do whatever was necessary to procure that peace. McKinley reasoned that the Spanish were at the peak of their strength in Cuba during the 1897–98 campaign season. If they were unable to settle the war by the time the tropical rains forced a halt to the fighting, the prospect was for an interminable and bloody stalemate. Perhaps an American ultima-tum would force Spain to offer concessions which, along with military pressure, could bring the rebels to a settlement. Meanwhile, McKinley in-duced Congress to appropriate $50,000 for aid to the suffering Cubans and got Spain to admit these supplies duty-free. He personally contributed $5,000 to the Cuban relief fund.

Coincidentally, just as McKinley began to apply pressure, a new liberal

Spanish government succeeded that of the assassinated conservative prime minister. The liberals recalled General Weyler, alleviated the reconcentration policy, released American citizens imprisoned for rebel activity, and offered considerable autonomy to Cuba within the Spanish empire. Although these concessions were made as a result of Spain's domestic politics rather than American diplomacy, McKinley could portray them as a partial response to his initiative. He used his supposed success to keep Congress from demanding immediate intervention and hoped he still could force both sides into agreement.

The slim chance that Spain and Cuba could work out an agreement was shattered, however, when riots broke out among Spanish loyalists in Cuba against the recall of Weyler and the offer of Cuban autonomy. Many army personnel who were supposed to suppress the riots joined them instead. Opposition rose in Spain as well as in Cuba. The queen and her government feared they might be overthrown if they surrendered Cuba voluntarily. McKinley and other Americans wondered whether the Spanish government could come to an agreement with the Cuban rebels even if Spain negotiated in good faith. When the Americans read an intercepted letter written by the Spanish minister to the United States, Enrique Dupuy de Lôme, they had to wonder whether the government was negotiating in good faith in any case. De Lôme characterized McKinley as "weak and a bidder for the admiration of the crowd, besides being a would-be politician who tries to leave a door open behind himself while keeping on good terms with the jingoes of his party." Then de Lôme suggested negotiating with the Americans "even if only for effect."

Shortly after the de Lôme letter, the American battleship *Maine* exploded in Havana harbor. McKinley unwisely and hastily had sent the *Maine* to Havana during the Weyler riots to show American desire for order in Cuba. When it sank, killing 266 of the 350 crew members aboard, it made American intervention in the Cuban revolution almost inevitable.

While a naval board investigated the cause of the *Maine* explosion, McKinley tried one last time for a diplomatic solution. At his request, Congress appropriated $50 million for a defense fund that McKinley could use at his own discretion. Woodford said the appropriation stunned the Spanish government, and McKinley seemed to have considerable leverage to force a settlement. He lost much of his room to maneuver, however, when Redfield Proctor, a highly respected senator from Vermont, made an extraordinary speech on his return from an inspection of Cuba. In a calm and dispassionate voice, he recounted the horrendous scenes he had witnessed and confirmed the rumors that 200,000 Cubans had died in the reconcentration camps. His speech convinced many that Spain had simply lost control of Cuba; it could never win the struggle, but only draw out the bloody stalemate.

The report of the American naval board on the sinking of the *Maine* reinforced the assumption that Spain had lost control; the board concluded that an external rather than an internal explosion had destroyed the ship. A floating mine was a more likely culprit than a boiler room accident. Although some of the more lurid newspapers and excitable politicians of the time implied that the Spanish had sunk the *Maine*, neither the naval board nor most American leaders accused the Spanish of deliberate sabotage. Yet Spain was responsible for the safety of ships in its harbors, and the *Maine* incident convinced almost all Americans of Spain's impotence to control the colony over which it claimed sovereignty.

McKinley was under terrible pressure to do something dramatic. Failure would open the door for the Democrats to proclaim themselves the true advocates of Cuba and portray the Republicans as cowardly betrayers of freedom. The powerful Republican Senator Henry Cabot Lodge warned McKinley: "If the war in Cuba drags on through the summer with nothing done we shall go down in the greatest defeat ever known. . . . I know that it is easily & properly said that to bring on or even to threaten war for political reasons is a crime & I quite agree. But to sacrifice a great party & bring free silver upon the country for a wrong policy is hardly less odious."

McKinley had known for a week the results of the naval board's investigation. He could imagine the public reaction, so he tried to force a quick settlement of the Cuban revolution. His secretary of state, John Sherman, was senile; so McKinley bypassed him and communicated with Spain through his close friend, Acting Secretary of State William Day. On March 26, McKinley composed and Day signed a telegram to the American minister, Woodford, informing the Spanish that it was essential peace be made within a month. Spain should revoke the reconcentration order and offer the Cubans "full self-government, with reasonable indemnity." Woodford asked if this actually meant Cuban independence. Day responded that it did.

But after Woodford reported that Spain had made some tentative inquiries about an armistice in Cuba, McKinley and Day sent another telegram that clouded their earlier ultimatum. McKinley and Day told Woodford to get Spain to offer the rebels an armistice under American good offices until October 1, along with revocation of the reconcentration order, and to add "if possible: Third. If terms of the peace not satisfactorily settled by October 1, President of the United States to be final arbiter between Spain and insurgents."

A careful reading of this final telegram indicates that McKinley was still demanding Cuban independence. The rebels would never agree to a settlement before October 1 because they knew that after that date McKinley would arbitrate and he would grant Cuba independence. Still, the telegram said that the third demand was to be added only "if possible." Did Woodford understand that McKinley was still demanding Cuban independence? Did he make McKinley's position clear to Spain?

Those questions are important, because Spain ultimately conceded the unequivocal first two demands of McKinley's final telegram. It revoked the reconcentration order and offered a cease-fire to the rebels, although it offered the armistice only after refusing until the last minute, then claiming it made the offer because the pope had requested it, and finally asserting that the length and extent of the armistice would be up to the Spanish commander in Cuba. Spain said nothing of American arbitration or Cuban independence.

Woodford reported these concessions as the prelude to further Spanish surrenders and urged McKinley to delay the use of force. McKinley, however, regarded the concessions as too little, too late, and given with insufficient grace to indicate that Spain was willing to go still further and grant Cuba independence. He sent a long-contemplated message to Congress requesting authority to intervene with force if necessary to end the war in Cuba. He noted the last-minute Spanish concessions only as an afterthought.

There was no doubt Congress would grant McKinley the authority he wanted. The vast majority in Congress and the country were in favor of war, and many were criticizing the president for his procrastination. Even the business community, long opposed to armed intervention in Cuba, had come to feel that anything was preferable to the current lingering uncertainty. Thus, McKinley led a united and enthusiastic nation to war. After the war, however, when McKinley's telegrams and Woodford's advice that Spain would submit without war became public, it triggered a debate over the intervention that still continues among historians. Most concluded that the war indeed had been unnecessary, that a weak and vacillating president had bowed to partisan advantage and the war frenzy whipped up by an unscrupulous press. Like Theodore Roosevelt, they portrayed McKinley as a man with no more backbone than a chocolate éclair. Echoing Representative "Uncle Joe" Cannon, they said the president kept his ear so close to the ground that it had grasshoppers in it.

Some historians made more sinister accusations. They argued that imperialists like Assistant Secretary of the Navy Theodore Roosevelt and Sen-

Figure 8   President William McKinley, whose diplomacy leading up to the Spanish-American War still stirs controversy among historians. Portrait courtesy of the National Archives.

ator Henry Cabot Lodge had manipulated McKinley into an unnecessary war to give the United States a chance to acquire a colonial empire. Supposedly, Roosevelt and Lodge had arranged the appointment of Commodore George Dewey to the command of the Pacific squadron. Then, in the temporary absence of the secretary of the navy, Roosevelt had ordered Dewey to attack the Spanish fleet in Manila harbor. Dewey's victory would allow the United States to acquire the Philippines and gain access to the China markets.

The charge that Roosevelt and Lodge had maneuvered McKinley into an unnecessary war in order to acquire the Philippines is quickly enough dismissed. An attack on the Spanish fleet in Manila had long been part of the plan for war with Spain. That fleet was one of the two major Spanish naval forces, and its existence would threaten America's Pacific Coast as well as any expedition to Cuba. Manila's harbor defenses had been investigated by an American naval officer in civilian clothes as early as 1876, and an attack on the fleet was made part of the formal plan for a war with Spain in 1896. Roosevelt's telegram to Dewey was approved by McKinley himself.

The attack on the fleet, however, was not part of a concerted plan to conquer the Philippines. No troops were sent with Dewey to occupy Manila in the event he defeated the fleet. McKinley made preparations to send troops only after he received news of Dewey's victory and amid fears that Spain was sending another fleet to the Philippines. McKinley and the American navy did decide quickly that they wanted to keep Manila's great harbor as a window to the China market, but this was a consequence of Dewey's victory, not a motive for the attack in the first place.

It is also extremely doubtful that Spain was ready to relinquish its hold on Cuba, despite Woodford's opinion that it would do so. The Spanish government faced riots over declaration of the armistice, let alone Cuban independence. The queen feared she would be overthrown if she freed Cuba without a fight. While the Spanish government offered an armistice, it also looked about Europe, in the hope of getting other powers to intervene against Cuba and the United States. Thus there is little chance that Spain's compliance with American demands for revocation of the reconcentration order and an armistice presaged a grant of independence. It was more likely a delaying tactic. So long as America insisted on Cuban independence, war was probably inevitable.

Nevertheless, many historians continue to criticize McKinley for failing to pursue the slim chance for peace by making his demand for Cuban independence clearer and then delaying a while to see if Spain would extend its concessions. McKinley's defenders, and their number has increased substantially in the past decade, argue that the Spanish understood perfectly well that Cuban independence was necessary to prevent American intervention and that McKinley could not risk a categorical demand because the proud Spanish would have been sure to reject it. They see McKinley's diplomacy as the product not of weakness and vacillation, but of strength, subtlety, and realism. The evidence does seem to support their claim that McKinley was in full control of his policy and was not the spineless creature portrayed in earlier accounts, but it is still difficult to see why he avoided a clear statement of his purposes to Spain. Since war resulted anyway, it could not have made matters worse.

Even after war was imminent and McKinley announced the goal of Cuban independence to the American people, he studiously avoided recognition of the Cuban rebels as the successor government of the island. During the *Maine* crisis, the rebels had told McKinley: "We do not ask you to go to war; we only ask you for your neutrality, for the recognition of Cuban belligerent rights." McKinley rejected this plea. He did not think the rebels could win the war quickly without American assistance, he had no doubt Spain would declare war immediately if he recognized Cuban independence or belligerence directly, and he did not think the Cuban government was yet "capable of performing the duties and discharging the functions of a separate nation." While he implied that he might recognize Cuba later, he decided to try to stop the war as a neutral, and he asked Congress to authorize him to use force to do so.

The House of Representatives gave him the authorization he requested. But the Senate insisted on pushing him further than he wanted to go. It passed resolutions directing rather than authorizing McKinley to use force in Cuba, recognized Cuban independence and the rebels as the legitimate government (the Turpie-Foraker Amendment), and disavowed any intention of annexing Cuba (the Teller Amendment).

McKinley threatened to use his veto if the House accepted the Senate version. He insisted at least that recognition of the rebel government be dropped. A joint House-Senate resolution did so amid charges that McKinley and his followers opposed recognition because they feared this would invalidate Spain's Cuban bonds, some of which allegedly had been purchased by Americans. When McKinley signed the resolution on April 20, Spain broke diplomatic relations. Two days later, McKinley imposed a naval blockade on Cuba, and Spain declared war on the United States.

THE ACQUISITION OF AN OVERSEAS EMPIRE

John Hay, who became McKinley's last secretary of state, called the Spanish-American conflict "a splendid little war." The United States had clear military superiority over Spain, and it won a quick and decisive victory. Nevertheless, the war could have been far bloodier and more prolonged had it not been for considerable luck and Spanish incompetence. Dewey's fleet steamed into Manila harbor past the fortress island of Corregidor without suffering a single effective shot. The Spanish fleet fatalistically anchored in shallow water so its men could get to shore when the ships were sunk. These shallows were located out of reach of the shore guns in Manila that could have helped fight the Americans. Dewey won the battle with the loss of only a single man, and he to a heart attack.

The Americans were equally lucky in their invasion of Cuba. The ill-planned amphibious operation began only after a long wait in tropical Florida camps by soldiers clothed in winter woolens. The scramble to the ships was chaotic. Artillery and cavalry went aboard one ship, ammunition and horses aboard another. Fortunately, the invasion force landed unopposed on Cuban beaches because the Spanish foolishly abandoned their coastal defenses for inland positions. The American army cooperated tenuously with the Cuban rebels and together they moved toward Santiago, where the Spanish fleet had taken refuge. The famous charge up San Juan Hill put the Americans and their Cuban allies in a commanding position above Santiago, so the Spanish fleet made a forlorn dash from the harbor. The American blockading vessels pursued and sank them one by one. Americans won the war while losing only 379 men in combat (however, over 5,000 died from malaria and yellow fever).

While American troops were occupying Manila and Cuba, McKinley and his administration moved to expand and consolidate their hold on other territories in the Pacific and Caribbean. McKinley finally secured the formal annexation of Hawaii, partly by claiming that the islands were vital for getting troops and supplies to Dewey in the Philippines. Even so, to overcome Democratic opposition, McKinley had to resort to a joint resolution of Congress rather than the formal treaty procedure. American forces also took Spain's lesser colony of Puerto Rico without a fight, and no Teller Amendment required the United States to forego annexation of this Caribbean island.

It was a foregone conclusion by the end of hostilities with Spain that the United States would have an overseas empire. The only question was how big that empire would be. Should the United States keep the Philippines as well as Puerto Rico and Hawaii?

McKinley seems to have decided shortly after Dewey's victory to keep at least Manila. It was a fine port and naval base which provided access to China and the rest of Asia. McKinley also ordered seizure of the uninhabited Wake Islands and the Spanish island of Guam as steppingstones from Hawaii to Manila. He found it difficult, however, to decide what to do about the rest of the Philippines. It seemed intolerable to leave them in the hands of Spain, after seeing Spanish misrule of Cuba. He did not want to see great Britain, Germany, or Japan acquire them and use them to gain supremacy in the China trade.

He might have left them to the Philippine rebels, whose leader, Emilio Aguinaldo, had returned to the islands aboard an American ship. But McKinley did not think the rebels capable of governing the Philippines any more than he thought the Cuban rebels prepared to govern their island. He believed the Philippines would fall into anarchy, and then into the hands of one of the other great powers. While America might throw a protectorate over the islands to prevent this, the difficulties and frictions of dealing with a native government in such a situation had already been made clear in Samoa. Besides, McKinley's military advisers told him that Manila was indefensible without control of the entire island of Luzon.

McKinley's inclination to keep the entire archipelago was confirmed by a

HAWAII, THE PHILIPPINES, AND CHINA

CHINA

MANCHURIA

YELLOW SEA

RUSSIA KARAFUTO

KOREA
(JAP.)

SEA
OF
JAPAN

HOKKAIDO

JAPANESE
EMPIRE

HONSHU JAPAN

EAST
CHINA
SEA

SHIKOKU

KYUSHU

RYUKYU IS.

KURILE IS.

FORMOSA
(JAP.)

LUZON
Manila

1898
PHILIPPINE
ISLANDS
(U.S.)

MINDANAO

HALMAHERA

CERAM

NEW
GUINEA
(NETH.)

PALAU

YAP

MELANESIA

CAROLINE ISLANDS

BONIN IS.
(JAP.)

VOLCANO IS.
(JAP.)

MARIANAS
ISLANDS

TINIAN
ROTA
GUAM
(U.S.)
1898

TRUK

PONAPE

MARCUS I.

PACIFIC

MICRONESIA

1899
WAKE

ENIWETOK

MARSHALL
ISLANDS

NAURU

GILBERT
ISLANDS

OCEAN

INTERNATIONAL
DATE LINE

SUNDAY ← → SATURDAY

1867
MIDWAY

HAWAIIAN ISLANDS

1898

KAUAI
NIIHAU OAHU
HAWAII
NECKER

JOHNSTON I.
(U.S.)

PALMYRA
(U.S.)

PHOENIX
IS.

EQUATOR

1000 MILES

160°E

180°

72M

Map 8   U.S. Expansion in the Pacific, 1867–1899

campaign swing through Middle America, where mention of taking the islands drew cheers from the crowds. He returned to Washington to instruct the American peace commission negotiating with the Spaniards in Paris to insist on keeping the Philippines. After the United States assuaged Spanish protests with an offer to pay $20 million, the peace treaty was signed.

The thrill of victory brought most Americans to accept the acquisition of Puerto Rico and Hawaii, but a substantial number of influential Americans thought the Philippines were too distant, too alien, and too hostile to be annexed. Grover Cleveland, Andrew Carnegie, and Mark Twain joined the campaign againt annexation organized by the newly formed Anti-Imperialist League. They argued that America could never bring the Philippines into the Union as an equal state; the United States would have to rule the Philippines as a colony at the point of a bayonet. The precedent of bayonet rule would be as dangerous to American domestic liberty as it would be harmful to the Filipinos. Anti-imperialists insisted that the United States could expand and protect its foreign trade without resort to such imperialism. They recalled Washington's Farewell Address warning against involvement in the quarrels of European powers. But they argued in vain. Imperialists said that modern communications and American power made the Farewell Address obsolete or claimed that acquisition of the Philippines was merely the continuation of America's westward march, which Washington and the other Founding Fathers had initiated. They insisted that American rule would educate and uplift the Filipinos, not degrade or oppress them.

Republicans in the Senate supported McKinley overwhelmingly. Several had their doubts, but in the end only George Frisbie Hoar of Massachusetts and Eugene Hale of Maine could bring themselves to vote against their triumphant president. The Democrats were divided over the treaty. William Jennings Bryan thought it would be difficult to defeat a treaty that promised peace with Spain, so he urged Democrats to accept the treaty and the Philippines, then grant the islands their independence. He probably affected only one or two votes. Nevertheless, with ten out of thirty-two Democratic senators voting aye, the treaty received two-thirds approval by a single vote. Meanwhile, fighting had already broken out between American troops and Aguinaldo's rebels. It was a sign that the United States would find it far more difficult to pacify and govern its empire than to acquire it.

CONTROVERSIAL ISSUES AND FURTHER READING

The United States entered the Spanish-American War with little popular dissent. Contemporaries quarreled over the later decision to take the Philippines far more than they did over the decision to expel the Spanish from Cuba. [John Holladay Latané, *Diplomatic Relations of the United States and Spanish America* (1900); James Morton

Callahan, *Cuba and International Relations* (1899).] When the diplomatic correspondence leading to the war was published in 1901, however, and revealed Woodford's opinion that Spain would have been willing to make more concessions without war, it did generate some criticism.

Most early historical criticism of the war came from conservatives. They feared that overseas colonialism endangered American liberty at home and entangled the United States needlessly abroad, but they did not worry much about the negative impact of American rule on Cubans or Filipinos. They disliked the Cuban rebels as terrorists and thought the Filipinos would be better off under American rule. These authors did not argue that the war was the product of an imperialist plot led by Theodore Roosevelt and Henry Cabot Lodge. Instead, they saw it as the result of the yellow press, ignorant popular enthusiasm, and McKinley's weakness. [Horace Edgar Flack, *Spanish-American Diplomatic Relations* (1906), and Elbert Jay Benton, *International Law and the Diplomacy of the Spanish-American War* (1908). Both books emerged from a Johns Hopkins seminar given by W. W. Willoughby.] Even Admiral French Ensor Chadwick, a member of the naval commission that investigated the sinking of the *Maine* and the author of an encyclopedic defense of the war, moderated his stance in light of this critique. [French Ensor Chadwick, *The Relations of the United States and Spain: Diplomacy* (1909).] But until the post-World War I era, most historians continued to justify America's forcible intervention in Cuba. [See Albert Bushnell Hart, *The Monroe Doctrine* (1916); John Holladay Latané, *America as a World Power* (1907); John Bassett Moore, *The Principles of American Diplomacy* (1918).]

Disillusion after World War I brought with it a reaction against the imperial and interventionist policies initiated in the 1890s. Defenders of the Spanish-American War were few. The conservative critique of the war continued in the works of such prominent historians as James Ford Rhodes and Samuel Flagg Bemis. [James Ford Rhodes, *The McKinley and Roosevelt Administrations* (1922); Samuel Flagg Bemis, *A Diplomatic History of the United States* (1936).] But now liberal and socialist historians added their criticisms and interpretations. Walter Millis, a prominent journalist, wrote a best seller, *The Martial Spirit* (1931), which popularized the view that Roosevelt, Lodge, and other imperialists maneuvered America into a needless war to get the Philippines. Millis was very critical of the annexation of the Philippines, but less so of America's intervention in Cuba. Socialists Scott Nearing and Joseph Freeman were unsparing of this intervention as well. In their popular book, *Dollar Diplomacy: A Study in American Imperialism* (1925), Nearing and Freeman blamed big business and economic interests along with imperial thinkers like Roosevelt, Lodge, and Mahan for America's imperialism. Julius Pratt's still influential study, *The Expansionists of 1898* (1936), tried to absolve business and economic interests of the charge that they had sought war to gain an empire by showing that business had generally opposed the war. It was the imperial-minded intellectuals like Roosevelt, Lodge, and Alfred Thayer Mahan who were responsible for the needless war, he implied. Business became converted to the cause of imperialism during the war, however, and played a major role in the decision to annex the Philippines and other territories in the imperial aftermath to the war.

World War II cast interventionism in a better historical light than had World War I. Many realist historians began to praise the Spanish-American War as initiating America's necessary involvement in world affairs. Nevertheless, historians remained somewhat ambivalent about the way the United States had entered the war and the imperialism that had resulted. Richard Hofstadter and William Leuchtenberg wrote as though the war had been a needless consequence of neurotic belligerence on the part of liberals as well as conservatives, while Foster Rhea Dulles perpetuated the idea that Roosevelt and Lodge had manipulated America into the war to get the Philippines. [Richard Hofstadter, "Manifest Destiny and the Philippines," *America in Crisis*, ed. Daniel Aaron (1952); and *Social Darwinism* (1944); William Leuchtenberg, "The Needless War with Spain," *Times of Trial*, ed. Allan Nevins (1958); and "Progressivism and Imperialism: The Progressive Movement and American Foreign Policy, 1898–1916," *Mississippi Valley Historical Review* (1952); Foster Rhea Dulles, *America's Rise to World Power, 1898–1954* (1955).]

The discovery by J. A. S. Grenville and George Berkeley Young that the Navy Department had devised plans as early as 1896 to attack the Spanish fleet at Manila if war broke out over Cuba undercut the idea that Roosevelt and Lodge had ordered the attack against the wishes of their superiors. [J. A. S. Grenville and George Berkeley Young, *Politics, Strategy, and American Diplomacy* (1966).] Meanwhile H. Wayne Morgan led many historians to revise their estimate of McKinley's weakness and gullibility, arguing that McKinley was purposeful and in complete command of his administration throughout the events leading to war and the acquisition of the Philippines. [H. Wayne Morgan, *William McKinley and His America* (1963); see also Morgan, *America's Road to Empire* (1965); Margaret Leech, *In the Days of McKinley* (1959); Lewis L. Gould, *The Spanish-American War and President McKinley* (1982).] Ernest May was not fully convinced of all this, but his *Imperial Democracy* (1961) argued that Spain had been fully aware of America's demand for Cuban independence and had purposely delayed while trying to get European help against the United States. May was not sure this justified war, but said that McKinley, while he operated primarily out of a cowardly fear for the fate of the Republican party, still "conceived he had some justification for demanding a final end to the violence in Cuba."

Revisionists, of course, were far more critical of the war. Walter LaFeber's highly influential *The New Empire* (1963) argued, contrary to Julius Pratt, that business had not only been favorable to the war, but that its influence had been the primary one in McKinley's final decision to intervene in Cuba as well as take the Philippines. In the wake of Vietnam, Philip Foner argued an even more radical thesis. Using Cuban documents but citing rather thin evidence, Foner claimed that the rebels had actually opposed American intervention and had wanted only arms and munitions. McKinley intervened not to help them, but to expand the American empire. Thus, Foner said, McKinley had purposely omitted a demand for Cuban independence in his ultimatum, refused to recognize the rebel government, and meant from the outset to use the war to take the Philippines. He intended his delays merely to provide time for military preparations. When he was ready, he sent the *Maine* to Havana to create an incident that would justify war. [Philip S. Foner, *The Spanish-Cuban-American War and the Birth of American Imperialism, 1895–1902* (1972).]

Foner's views have not been widely adopted even by radical historians. The best, most judicious summary of the war is now Charles S. Campbell, *The Transformation of American Foreign Relations, 1865–1900* (1976). This book also has an excellent summary of the other events and trends chronicled in this chapter, as does Robert L. Beisner, *From the Old Diplomacy to the New, 1865–1900* (1975).

In addition to these books, the Venezuelan crisis can be studied in Dexter Perkins, *The Monroe Doctrine, 1867–1907* (1937); Gerald Eggert, *Richard Olney* (1973); and Allan Nevins, *Grover Cleveland* (1932). On the subsequent Anglo-American rapprochement, see Bradford Perkins, *The Great Rapprochement* (1968); Charles S. Campbell, *From Revolution to Rapprochement* (1974); Robert G. Neale, *Great Britain and the United States, 1895–1903* (1960). On the rise of imperialism and the anti-imperialist countermovement, see David Healy, *U.S. Expansionism: The Imperialist Urge in the 1890s* (1970); William Appleman Williams, *The Roots of the Modern American Empire* (1969); Ernest May, *American Imperialism* (1968); Robert L. Beisner, *Twelve Against Empire* (1968); and Richard Welch, *Response to Imperialism: The United States and the Philippine-American War, 1899–1902* (1979).

CHAPTER 9

The Surge into Asia: Empire in the Philippines and the Open Door in China

THE SUPPRESSION OF THE PHILIPPINE REVOLUTION

Admiral Dewey's fleet sailed into the Philippines during a recess in a revolution that was already two years old, the first modern colonial revolution in Asia. In August of 1896, the small educated Filipino middle class led an open rebellion against the Spanish. The rebels were especially angry at the Catholic friars' economic control of much of the islands' arable land. Not only did the friars hold huge feudal estates, they maintained political control of many Filipino barrios.

As the Spanish authorities and the rebels drew near to a pitched battle that would have been bloody and costly to both sides, they agreed to compromise. The rebels were not seeking outright independence; they merely wanted to reduce the power of the Church, open the economy to greater participation by the middle class, and introduce more islanders into the higher echelons of government. When Spain offered a series of reforms and a payment of $800,000 for an end to the rebellion, rebel leader Emilio Aguinaldo accepted and went into exile.

Spain never did carry out its promised reforms, and the insurrection broke out again. Aguinaldo had banked Spain's first payment of $400,000 against future contingencies, and he drew on this money to supply arms and materiel to the rebels from his exile in Hong Kong. The Americans helped him because Dewey decided that Aguinaldo and his rebels could furnish the troops Dewey lacked to give ground support to his fleet. Dewey even had Aguinaldo brought to Manila on the fleet's flagship. Aguinaldo maintained ever after that Dewey and his representatives had promised him an independent Philippine nation. Dewey swore he had made no such commitment.

When American troops finally arrived in the Philippines months after Dewey's victory, conflict quickly flared between them and the Filipino rebels. Dewey and the American army commander, General Elwell Otis, refused to permit Aguinaldo's troops to join the attack on the city of Manila, which was still held by the Spanish garrison. The Americans arranged with the Spanish defenders to have a short and harmless fire-fight for the salvation of Spanish honor, whereupon the surrender would be offered and accepted. The battle for Manila became a bit more realistic than intended when some Filipino troops joined the mock attack without authorization. Afterward, the Americans forced the Filipinos to camp outside the city, and resentment smoldered between the two occupying armies.

While American troops took Manila, Aguinaldo and his sympathizers gained control of much of the rest of the Philippines. Aguinaldo declared the Philippines independent, set up a government, and established a capital at Malolos. Nevertheless, William McKinley ignored the Filipinos. He ordered the American peace commission to demand Spanish cession of the islands to the United States. Then, before the Senate even ratified the treaty, he issued an executive order establishing American military government throughout the Philippines. This meant that the American army would have to wrest control of all but Manila from the Aguinaldo government and troops already in place. General Otis tried to disguise the full import of McKinley's order from the Filipinos by judiciously editing McKinley's proclamation before publishing it. This only made matters worse when the deception was exposed by a subordinate's inadvertant publication of the unexpurgated version.

Aguinaldo and his lieutenants were rightly suspicious, tensions heightened, and inevitably an American patrol clashed with the Philippine troops dug in around Manila. The clash came only forty hours before the Senate vote on the treaty and probably contributed to the Senate's narrow consent to it, since few senators wanted to be seen as refusing to back America's soldiers in a foreign land. The convenient timing of this incident outside Manila has led to suspicions on the part of several historians, American as well as Filipino, that McKinley provoked the incident. But there is no evidence of this, and the poor communication between McKinley and his military commanders makes it unlikely he could have contrived it even if he had so desired.

The war for the Philippines lasted more than three years and cost the Americans nearly 5,000 lives. The Filipinos suffered even more. The war cost them the lives of 20,000 soldiers and nearly 200,000 civilians. It was a savage war marked by atrocities and racial hatreds. American soldiers expressed their feelings in a song that was so offensive the American commanders tried to ban it:

> Damn, Damn, Damn the Filipinos
> Cross-eyed kakiak Ladrones,
> Underneath our starry flag,
> Civilize them with a Krag,
> And return us to our own beloved homes.

(A Krag was the army-issue rifle of the United States.)

The Americans expected a quick triumph over people they regarded as inferiors, and the protracted war exasperated them. Exasperation turned to brutality when the Filipinos refused to surrender after a series of American victories and instead dispersed to fight as guerrilla bands. "Water cures" and other forms of torture became commonplace to gain information from villagers or captives about guerrilla locations and identities. Guerrillas also fought savagely. After one especially brutal attack on unarmed American troops in a chow line, the American commander promised to make the entire surrounding area a "howling wilderness."

Ultimately the United States had to station 70,000 men on the islands to control them. The troops converted Philippine villages into garrisons in order to cut off supplies to the guerrillas, tactics reminiscent of Butcher Weyler's reconcentration policy that Americans had found so objectionable. Finally, a daring raiding party captured Aguinaldo, the Filipino middle class lost heart, other Filipino commanders surrendered their forces, and the war ground to a bitter anticlimactic end in 1902.

The war generated much controversy in America. Prominent members of the Anti-Imperialist League publicized the case against American rule in the islands. The Democratic party tried to make an issue of imperialism in the election of 1900, but other issues muddled the election and it never served as the referendum on imperialism that William Jennings Bryan proclaimed it would be. Imperialism was potentially divisive in both parties, so political leaders tended to downplay it. Only after the election did news of American as opposed to Filipino atrocities make headlines in a couple of sensational court martials. By that time the war was nearly over, and no great political movement against the occupation developed.

The relative success of America's colonial government also muted criticism in America and the Philippines. American promises of modernization, better schools, cleaner cities, more roads and factories, and improved agriculture won the grudging cooperation of the most economically progressive upper-class Filipinos, and the United States delivered on many of those promises. Nevertheless, the residual effect of the Philippine war and colonial aftermath left many Americans unsettled. Even Theodore Roosevelt came to believe that acquisition of the Philippines was a mistake. He concluded that the islands were a strategic Achilles heel: They invited attack from other powers in Asia and could not be defended. Consequently, although the United States undertook several more military interventions in the next two decades, popular acceptance of such intervention was reluctant rather than buoyant.

THE OPEN DOOR NOTES

Acquisition of the Philippines naturally prompted greater American interest in Asia. The dream of a great China market, one of the primary reasons the McKinley administration decided to annex the Philippines, now beckoned even more invitingly. American missionaries also began concentrating their efforts on China. Before the 1890s most missionaries were stationed in the

Mediterranean; only 200 were active in China. By 1900 there were over 1,000 American missionaries in China. By 1905, that figure had risen to 3,000, more than 80 percent of all American Protestant missionaries abroad.

Consequently, the McKinley administration regarded the increasing pace of European imperialism in China with a more jaundiced eye after the Spanish-American War. The acceleration of European imperialism had begun after the Japanese victory in the Sino-Japanese War of 1895. First the European powers had forced Japan to limit its spoils to the island of Formosa (Taiwan), the nearby Pescadores, and a sphere of influence in the strategic peninsula of Korea. After checking Japan, the European powers proceeded to carve their own concessions in China. Germany took financial control of the Shantung peninsula and a naval base in the port of Kiaochow. The Russians leased a naval base at Port Arthur on the Liaotung peninsula, which they had forced Japan to disgorge. Russia also secured the right to control railroads through Chinese territory to connect its Trans-Siberian Railroad with Port Arthur and Vladivostok. France extorted a naval base at Kwangchwan.

Great Britain had been no happier with these imperial ventures than the United States. Britain already controlled most of China's trade and one-third of the foreign investments in that beleaguered country. Since Great Britain was becoming increasingly preoccupied with the rising strength of Germany in Europe and wished to concentrate more of its power there, it would have been happier with the earlier status quo in China. Britain did successfully request a new concession at Weihaiwei on the Shantung peninsula, from which it could keep an eye on the Russians. Britain also made China promise not to alienate any part of the Yangtze Valley to other foreigners. But it expended its primary diplomatic effort in trying to get the other imperial powers to maintain an open door for the trade of all nations in their spheres of interest, and it warned against further dismemberment of sovereign Chinese territory.

The British knew the Americans were not in the market for their own sphere of interest in China, and so had a similar interest in restricting the imperial scramble. Prior to the Spanish-American War, the British had approached McKinley about a joint declaration in favor of the open door and the territorial integrity of China, but McKinley had turned them down. Then the victory over Spain and the acquisition of the Philippines changed McKinley's attitude. The continuing European intrusions in China brought him to accept the suggestion of a limited initiative in pursuit of America's East Asian interests.

The suggestion for the initiative came from William Rockhill, acknowledged at the time as one of the few American experts on China. He had gained the ear of John Hay, McKinley's last secretary of state. Rockhill feared that the collapse of China would set off such a scramble among the imperial powers that it might not only close out American trade, but bring world war. He knew that Hay and McKinley would balk at any American engagement to protect China's territorial integrity, but one of his acquaintances, an Englishman named Alfred Hippisley, recommended a more limited course

Map 9 China and the Imperialists

that Hay and McKinley might find acceptable. Hippisley was an official of China's semi-autonomous Imperial Maritime Customs Service, which was responsible for collecting the customs duties owed China. These tariffs constituted the major reliable source of income for the moribund Chinese government. If the European powers in China insisted on a monopoly of trade and investment in their new spheres of interest, they might prevent the Imperial Maritime Customs Service from operating there as well. This would destroy the financial underpinnings of China's government.

To forestall this, Hippisley drafted a statement for Rockhill that Hay sent off almost unchanged in September 1899 as the first Open Door note. (The British government by this time had drifted away from its earlier advocacy of the Open Door and had no role in Hippisley's initiative.) In it, the United States requested each imperial power to keep its spheres of interest in China open to trade from foreign nations. This note did not challenge acquisition of those spheres of interest or demand equality of investment along with trading rights in them.

None of the great powers was terribly anxious to accept such an open door to trade, but Russia and Japan were not nearly so concerned with the commerce in their spheres as they were with investments in such strategic enterprises as railroads and mines. Rather than offend the Americans over what they perceived as a minor issue, they and the other powers gave tentative and carefully hedged endorsements of Hay's suggestion. Hay ignored the qualifications and announced that the Open Door was now international policy. None of the nations wanted to contradict him, and his statement passed for an accepted principle among the uninitiated. Many Americans praised Hay's coup as a brilliant stroke that demonstrated America's new prestige and influence in international affairs, along with its shrewdness and idealism in protecting China against predatory powers.

The following year, Hay burnished that image even further with his second Open Door note. Hay sent this one in the midst of a crisis in China known as the Boxer Rebellion. The Society of Righteous and Harmonious Fists, or Boxers as Westerners called them, was a secret organization dedicated to eradicating foreign influence from China. At first the society also opposed the dowager empress and her Manchu court. The empress diverted their efforts exclusively toward the Europeans by quietly throwing her influence behind them and supplying them with arms. She believed the Europeans were trying to restore her son to the throne after she had imprisoned him and exiled or executed many of his advisors for excessive reformist zeal. With the secret encouragement of the empress, the Boxers murdered hundreds of Christian missionaries and their Chinese converts and laid seige to the foreign embassies and compounds in the capital of Peking.

Hay and McKinley sent 2,500 American troops from the Philippine war to join the forces of the other European powers in an expedition that set off from the China coast to rescue the besieged foreigners in Peking. The combined force plundered its way to the capital, with the American troops only somewhat less brutal than their compatriots. Almost every hut and village on the path of the expedition was destroyed. (Kaiser Wilhelm of Germany had encouraged his troops to make themselves as fearsome to the Chinse as Attila the Hun had been to the ancient world. His army obeyed, and his unfortunate turn of phrase earned the Germans an unwanted nickname that would plague them throughout World War I.)

McKinley and Hay quite naturally feared that some of the expedition's participants might be reluctant to remove their troops once their mission had been accomplished. To encourage their withdrawal, Hay sent a second Open Door note urging not just an open door for trade, but also respect for the territorial and administrative integrity of China. He uttered no threats, asked no commitments, and made none on the part of the United States. The note was simply a statement of American interests and wishes. Meanwhile, Hay worked cleverly to bolster Chinese provincial authorities who were suppressing the Boxers in the southern districts of China. He then pointed to the stability being restored there as good reason for the other powers to refrain from carving out further spheres. Once a satisfactory settlement to the Boxer Rebellion had been achieved, the United States withdrew its own troops.

Again Hay and McKinley won plaudits for what seemed a successful intervention on behalf of China. The relief of the besieged legations made a sensational story that entranced many Americans who had never given a thought to foreign policy. After Hay's death in 1905, his friends enshrined the Open Door policy alongside the Monroe Doctrine as a seemingly beneficent if vague foreign policy commandment demonstrating both America's strength and idealism. Naive Americans portrayed the United States as the protector of China, and the Chinese as grateful protégés.

While America's decision-makers did believe they were doing China a good turn in issuing the Open Door notes, their primary concern had been with America's interests in the potential trade offered by China's markets. They also understood the limitations of that interest; only 2 percent of America's exports found their way to China at the time, whatever the potential for the future. Hay and McKinley intended no major commitment to China. America's army was bogged down in the Philippines, its fleet was concentrated in the Caribbean against an imagined German threat to Latin America, and despite the defeat of the anti-imperialist campaign in the United States, the Philippine war had taken its toll on public opinion toward foreign adventures. A single expedition to China in pursuit of the traditional goal of protecting American lives and property might be popular; a significant military commitment on behalf of the Open Door or in pursuit of America's own sphere of influence in China, on the other hand, would be very risky politically as well as strategically. Consequently, Hay and McKinley were willing to support the concept of the Open Door verbally, but they had no intention of risking war.

Recognizing that the second Open Door note's call for the territorial integrity of China had no teeth and could well be brushed aside by the major powers in China, Hay prepared an alternative plan. He sent a discreet feeler to China about the possibility of America acquiring a coaling station at Samsah Bay in Fukien Province. But it was just as tentative and toothless as the Open Door notes themselves. Hay withdrew the request without even waiting for a Chinese reply when the Japanese, who already had a paramount interest in Fukien, pointedly reminded Hay of his own principles. The imperial powers thus were fully aware of the limitations of American interest in and commitment to the Open Door. They were careful of American sensitivities only because the power balance was so delicate in East Asia that for the moment even mild American action might tip the situation in favor of one side or another.

China's leaders also understood the limits of the American commitment and the essentially self-interested character of the Open Door policy. Hay never consulted the Chinese themselves about American decisions affecting their affairs. However much the principles of the Open Door and American hopes for Chinese territorial integrity may have corresponded to China's own interests, it was difficult to maintain that the Chinese should have felt much gratitude. American merchants and diplomats dealing directly with China generally urged forceful policies against supposed Chinese duplicity. Even American missionaries, idealistic as their motives may have been, were subversive of China's own culture.

They were contemptuous of Chinese authority, and their presence was made possible only by the gunboat patrols and diplomatic threats that lay behind the unequal treaty system. Also, at the very time the Americans were issuing the Open Door notes, they discriminated against Chinese residents in California and other western states. When the United States acquired Hawaii and the Philippines, it closed the door almost entirely to Chinese immigration to those islands. China's government was too weak to do anything about this, but educated Chinese who learned of these events made their displeasure known.

THEODORE ROOSEVELT, JAPAN, AND THE LIMITS OF THE OPEN DOOR

Theodore Roosevelt, who succeeded the assassinated McKinley in September of 1901, was under no illusions about the extent and nature of America's commitment to the Open Door policy. Occasionally he would bluster, as he did after the Boxer Rebellion when Russia refused to withdraw its troops from Manchuria and then erected trade barriers against American cotton exports to that area. At that time Roosevelt said he would not mind "going to extremes" with the Russians, but his actual instructions to Hay were far more restrained. Hay put the matter in perspective when he commented privately that both the Chinese and Russians knew the United States position was entirely moral. Hay suspected that neither country would pay much attention, since moral force was "mere flapdoodle."

The British also decided that America's posturing in East Asia was mere flapdoodle. They turned to Japan instead for help in restraining the Russians in China and negotiated the Anglo-Japanese Alliance of 1902. The Japanese were aching to confront the Russians. They resented Russia's role in ousting them from the Liaotung Peninsula and Port Arthur. They regarded Russia as a grave threat to their strategic interests in Korea and to their economic interests in the resources and railroads of Manchuria. Japan feared only that France might come to the aid of its Russian ally. The Anglo-Japanese Alliance protected against that contingency by pledging Great Britain to aid Japan if Japan found itself at war with more than one power. Thus fortified, Japan launched a surprise attack on Russia's Asiatic fleet and sank it while it lay at anchor at Port Arthur. The Russians immediately sent their European fleet into Asian waters, and the Japanese sank it too. Meanwhile, Japanese land forces conquered Port Arthur and Mukden after long and bloody sieges. The world looked on in astonishment as supposedly backward and inferior Asians beat a major European power.

Theodore Roosevelt was gleeful as well as astonished. Japan was doing "our work" in China, he said, and it was "bully" the way the Japanese had started the war with a surprise attack. Yet the extent of the Japanese victory gave him some pause. He did not believe it likely that the United States and Japan would ever go to war, but an increasingly powerful Japan could pose a threat to the nearly indefensible Philippines and Hawaii, perhaps even to the Pacific Coast. Japan might issue its own challenge to the Open Door in China as well. Roosevelt thought America's interest in China was relatively negligible and actually hoped Japan could be induced to spend its energies on the Asian continent rather than in the Pacific, where the United States was more involved. Still, he thought it desirable that Russia remain at least strong enough to keep some semblance of a balance of power in northern Asia.

With these interests in mind, and perhaps even more motivated by his unquenchable thirst for adventure and personal glory (Roosevelt's daughter said he wanted to be the bride at every wedding and the corpse at every funeral), Roosevelt agreed to mediate the Russo-Japanese War. He immediately found himself in difficulties. Russia was willing to make concessions in Korea and Manchuria in exchange for peace, but Japan wanted more. Unknown to most, Japan was at the end of its financial tether and desperately needed money. It demanded a large financial indemnity and the cession of Sakhalin Island. Russia was ready to break off negotiations rather than submit to these additional demands; only Roosevelt's pressure kept the bargaining from breaking down. Russia finally conceded the southern portion of Sakhalin, and Japan gave up its demand for the indemnity. Peace was made. Roosevelt won the Nobel Prize for his success, but he paid a price. The Japanese government was hard pressed to explain to the Japanese people, who had been told that their enormous sacrifices had won a great victory, why there was no indemnity to relieve their financial suffering. Naturally, the government blamed it on Roosevelt.

Nonetheless, the Japanese and the Roosevelt administration were able to compromise their respective positions in Asia. Roosevelt's special envoy to Japan, William Howard Taft, agreed to a memorandum with Japanese Prime

Figure 9   President Theodore Roosevelt stands between the Russian and Japanese delegations at Portsmouth, New Hampshire, where he helped negotiate an end to the Russo-Japanese War. Photo courtesy of the National Archives.

Minister Taro Katsura in 1905 that Japan would not challenge the United States position in the Philippines, while the United States would recognize Japanese predominance in Korea. This Taft-Katsura Memorandum said nothing about Manchuria, but it was no coincidence that a few months later Japan opened Manchuria to American trade.

In 1906 this accommodation faltered when San Francisco demonstrated its resentment of Japanese and Chinese laborers by segregating Asians in the school system. The Japanese were mortally offended. They were not like earlier Chinese governments, which had been apathetic about discriminatory practices in America. Japan encouraged emigration. It was overcrowded, and it saw emigration to the Pacific islands, the United States, and South America as a chance not only to relieve this population pressure, but also to create markets for Japanese goods. Prior to Japan's victory over China in 1895, Japanese leaders had preferred this expansion by Pacific emigration to military and political expansion on the Asian continent. The Sino-Japanese and Russo-Japanese wars had shifted Japan's emphasis toward Asia, but Pacific emigration remained a significant part of Japan's foreign policy goals.

The United States had already spiked some of these ambitions by closing the Philippines and Hawaii to Japanese immigrants and forbidding contract labor. Then riots and the segregation controversy in San Francisco led to a movement in Congress to extend the 1904 law prohibiting Chinese immigration to include Japan. Japan protested vehemently. Some American publicists panicked and warned that Japan, with its fierce military traditions and sense of honor, might declare war.

Roosevelt recognized that despite the depth of Japan's anger, the chance of war was remote, but he still thought it important to resolve the immigration and discrimination issues. When he found sentiment for excluding the Japanese too strong to be countered, he decided his only hope of avoiding a direct insult was to strike a deal. San Francisco would end its educational segregation and Congress would abandon its attempts to prohibit Japanese immigration; Japan itself would take the responsibility for preventing its citizens from emigrating to the United States. Roosevelt brought San Francisco Mayor Eugene Schmitz and the entire city school board to Washington, a major feat since Schmitz was free on bail after being charged with five counts of extortion. Roosevelt got the board to give up segregation, and a skeptical Congress dropped the bill to prohibit Japanese immigration. Japan, as its part of this so-called Gentleman's Agreement, quietly and reluctantly stopped issuing passports to laborers emigrating to the United States.

When anti-Japanese riots continued in California, Roosevelt reversed himself and concluded that war with Japan might indeed be a possibility. He decided to strengthen America's navy not only to deter Japan, but also because Britain's construction of a monster battleship, the HMS *Dreadnought*, set off a new European naval race. To stir public support for his expensive expansion of the American navy, Roosevelt sent the existing fleet on a highly publicized voyage to the Pacific Coast. Then, to impress the Japanese, he ordered the Great White Fleet to continue around the world.

Fortunately for this exposed naval task force, Japan's leaders did not contemplate war as feverishly as some American military leaders and newspaper pundits feared. A new Japanese cabinet made a formal decision to turn away from expansion by Pacific emigration and to concentrate instead on Japan's continental interests in Korea, Manchuria, and China. In this way Japan assumed that it would avoid conflict with America's domestic racism and its possessions in the Pacific. Rather than objecting to the Great White Fleet's voyage of intimidation, the Japanese cabinet invited the American ships to visit Japanese ports. The fleet received a tumultuous welcome.

Roosevelt and the Japanese moved quickly to publicize their détente and dampen war speculation. In November of 1908, Ambassador Takahira Kogoro and Hay's replacement as secretary of state, Elihu Root, exchanged notes reaffirming respect for one another's Pacific possessions, the Open Door, and the territorial integrity of China. In private conversations, the Japanese told Root and Roosevelt that they considered Manchuria, Taiwan, and Korea to be among the Pacific possessions which the United States must respect. Root and Roosevelt made no objection.

The Chinese were not nearly so pleased with Roosevelt's East Asian policies. The Chinese had hoped to make use of America's commitment to the Open Door policy to help them resist Japanese and Russian encroachments in Manchuria. The Chinese had long subscribed to the stratagem of manipulating barbarians to protect China's interests against other barbarians. By the time Roosevelt became president, China's officials were under more than usual pressure to redeem Chinese interests because a national spirit was beginning to rise among some urban and student groups. In 1905, a few Chinese nationalists even organized a boycott against American goods in response to the Chinese Exclusion Act of 1904. No longer would they permit their officials to look with indifference upon the treatment of Chinese in barbarian lands.

Roosevelt sympathized with the boycotters' anger at the indignity of Chinese exclusion. Yet he could do nothing about the law. He could only issue orders for government officials to deal fairly with the Chinese already in America. Then, unwilling to see the Chinese boycott humiliate American businessmen before the merchants of other powers, he insisted that the Chinese government suppress it. He even had America's Asiatic fleet anchor at Shanghai. Chinese officials mildy supported the boycott for a few months, fearful that the boycotters might turn their energies against the regime if it moved against them. When Chinese businessmen began to lose interest, the Chinese government finally responded to American pressure and suppressed the boycott. Roosevelt told Congress afterward that the United States had been much to blame for the conflict because "grave injustices and wrong have been done by this nation to the people of China."

Despite Roosevelt's tentative sympathy for rising Chinese nationalism, he did not make any other dramatic gestures on China's behalf. He protested vigorously when, during the boycott, the Chinese government sought to regain control of a concession it had granted the American China Development Company to build a railroad from Hankow to Canton. The stockholders of the company included such financial powerhouses as E. H. Harriman, Jacob Schiff, and the presidents of National City Bank, Chase National Bank, and Carnegie Steel. Yet by 1903, eight years after receiving its concession, the company had built only ten miles of railroad. Disturbed at the ineptitude and lethargy of the company, China took advantage of the anti-American atmosphere to try to buy back the concession from J. P. Morgan, who had assumed control after the company had passed through the hands of a Belgian consortium. Morgan was perfectly willing to sell, but Roosevelt regarded the Chinese offer as a slap at American prestige. Only after a long meeting with Morgan did Roosevelt abandon his protests and allow the financier to sell the concession back to China.

WILLIAM HOWARD TAFT AND DOLLAR DIPLOMACY IN ASIA

Roosevelt had few compunctions about putting pressure on the hapless Chinese over Morgan's railroad in southern China, but he and Root were very cautious about American activities in northern China, where Japan had its interests. Roosevelt's successor, William Howard Taft, was not so fastidious. He and his secretary of state, Philander Knox, were determined to help China. They devoutly believed that American investment in "backward" countries would aid them at the same time it fulfilled America's own interest in international stability. Taft's emphasis on financial intervention contrasted sharply with Roosevelt's greater concentration on power politics, and the newspapers began to call Taft's foreign policy "dollar diplomacy."

A group of young and vigorous American diplomats urged Taft and Knox toward financial intervention in Manchuria. These diplomats, Willard Straight, Huntington Wilson, and William Phillips, had served in East Asia and were busily and self-consciously replacing William Rockhill as the recognized American experts on the area. When the State Department was reorganized at the end of Roosevelt's administration, they formed the staff of the new Bureau of Far Eastern Affairs. In the course of their earlier duties abroad, all of them had learned to detest the Japanese. They believed it was America's mission to support China against Japan, a policy Rockhill condemned as foolhardy. Their displacement of Rockhill had little impact on such determined leaders as Roosevelt and Root, but they and their attitudes had considerable influence on the administration of Taft and Knox.

The staff of the Bureau of Far Eastern Affairs secured the support of Taft and Knox for a project of railroad baron E. H. Harriman that deeply worried the Japanese. Harriman cherished ambitions to build a round-the-world railway and was eager to acquire a Manchurian route as one link in this grandiose dream. He even induced Willard Straight to resign from the State Department and become his agent. China joined the Taft administration in

Figure 10   William H. Rockhill (left), whose loss of influence under President William Howard Taft (right) signalled a significant shift in U.S. diplomacy toward Japan and China. Portraits courtesy of the National Archives.

supporting Harriman and offered him a concession to build a railroad between Chinchow and Aigun. The Chinese hoped that such a railroad would drain business and influence from Japan's Southern Manchurian Line. When Japan objected angrily, however, the Chinese quickly aborted the project. They knew that the Americans could not protect them from Japan and that the British would not be drawn into a scheme against their Japanese allies. Undeterred, Knox proposed the neutralization of all Manchurian railways and suggested that eventually China be permitted to buy control of them with a loan from the great powers. To Japan's great relief, this scheme also failed.

Taft did succeed in wedging American capitalists into a consortium formed by British, French, and German bankers to float a loan to China. Taft and the Chinese both thought this loan might give China some strength to resist Japan. The Japanese foiled that plan by compelling the consortium to invite them and the Russians to participate as well. This ensured that the consortium would do nothing to imperil the various foreign spheres of influence in China. Yet Taft continued to cooperate; he even accepted the consortium's request to delay recognition of the Chinese Nationalist government that overthrew the Manchu dynasty in 1912. Taft's inconsistency only succeeded in making China as angry as Japan.

Although the president's dollar diplomacy offended Japan, Taft and Knox were not truly anti-Japanese. They did their best to protect Japanese rights in the United States. In 1911 they gave up America's rights under the unequal treaty system to control Japanese tariffs on American products, and they renewed the Gentleman's Agreement. They simply did not understand that Japan would regard their policies as a threat to its vital interests. They did nothing to prepare America's naval or coastal defenses in the Pacific, and they were taken by surprise when Japan drew closer to its old enemy Russia to resist the American drive on Manchuria. Theodore Roosevelt warned Taft and Knox against challenging Japan, but Knox replied that China needed Manchuria as much as Japan did and he accused Roosevelt of abandoning America's historic Open Door policy.

WOODROW WILSON AND MISSIONARY DIPLOMACY IN ASIA

Roosevelt was not the only critic of Taft's dollar diplomacy in East Asia. Many liberals refused to believe that Taft's cooperation with Wall Street bankers and European imperial powers could possibly be intended to help China. His acceptance of Japanese participation in the consortium and nonrecognition of China's new government confirmed their suspicions. In contrast to Theodore Roosevelt, these idealistic liberals thought America should do more to help China. American missionaries in China encouraged these ideas. They greatly influenced the thinking of Woodrow Wilson and his minister to China, a former college professor named Paul Reinsch.

When Wilson became president, he abruptly withdrew government support for the consortium. This caused the participating American bankers to pull out, because the government would no longer guarantee to collect the consortium's loans. Wilson had consulted none of the other nations involved in the consortium when he made his decision; he had not consulted China; he had not even consulted his own State Department. Huntington Wilson resigned in protest. But Wilson, convinced of the righteousness of his position, then announced that the United States would recognize the revolutionary government of China.

Japan argued against recognition by pointing out that the revolutionary government was on the verge of civil war. That government was an unstable coalition between the Nationalists, who had risen to control southern China in 1911, and the commander of the Manchu empire's army, Yuan Shi-kai. Yuan controlled much of northern China; by taking him into the government, the Nationalists had hoped to avoid civil war. After Yuan persuaded the last Manchu emperor to abdicate in 1912, Sun Yat-sen, whom the Nationalists had made their provisional president, stepped aside in favor of Yuan as president of the new Republic of China. Yuan secured recognition and a loan from the European powers in 1913, but many of the Nationalists disliked the terms of the loan and feared that Yuan was using the money to finance the army on which his power depended.

The Nationalists raised a second revolution against Yuan. Yuan put it down easily, and Sun and many of his followers fled to Japan. Yuan then outlawed their Kuomintang party and suspended the national and provincial parliaments. He even contemplated making himself emperor. Open civil war broke out a month after Wilson recognized the new regime. It kept China divided because Yuan could not conquer the Nationalists in the south, and the Nationalists, having no army, could not defeat Yuan in the north. To add to the chaos, Yuan lost control of his own lieutenants, who proceeded to set themselves up as independent warlords in various regions.

Meanwhile a much larger war had broken out in Europe. World War I diverted the attention of Europe and America from the Asian theater, and Japan saw an open field in a weak and divided China. Japan extorted from the European Allies the right to conquer Germany's colonies in China and the Pacific as the price for its entry into the war. Quickly Japan took Shantung and Germany's Pacific islands north of the equator (Australia and New Zealand got those south of the equator). Then, in early 1915, Japan presented China with a list of twenty-one demands. China was to ratify Japanese control of Shantung; extend Japanese concessions in Manchuria and central China; permit no further acquisition of harbors or islands on the China coast by other foreigners; purchase half its armaments from Japan; accept Japanese advisors for all its political, military, and economic affairs; and permit Japanese police to share control of critical points throughout China. In short, China would become a Japanese colony.

The Japanese told China to keep the Twenty-One Demands secret. But the Chinese leaked them to the American missionary community. Paul

Reinsch clamored from China for Wilson to do something. Initially Wilson left the affair to the State Department while he concentrated on the European war, and the State Department reacted rather coolly to China's request for help. State Department counsellor Robert Lansing said it would be "quixotic in the extreme" for the United States to entangle itself in the affair. Secretary of State William Jennings Bryan issued a statement recognizing the legitimacy of Japanese concerns in Shantung and Manchuria and expressed only mild concern for the Open Door and the territorial integrity of China. Nevertheless, other voices in the State Department, led by Paul Reinsch, warned Wilson that China's very existence was in danger.

Wilson told Bryan he wanted the United States to be the champion of China. He wrote a stern note warning that the United States would not recognize any agreement between Japan and China that impaired American rights, Chinese political and territorial integrity, or the Open Door. Great Britain joined the protest because the Twenty-One Demands infringed on its sphere in the Yangtze and Hupeh areas. This opposition, along with some internal dissent within Japan, caused the Japanese to abandon the most far-reaching of the demands. But Japan forced the Chinese to accept the rest of its ultimatum, and the Japanese now resentfully regarded the United States as their primary obstacle in Asia.

With Japan operating almost unchecked in China, Wilson swallowed hard and agreed to a new consortium to loan money to the Chinese. Japan would be a member of the consortium, but at least Wilson thought Japanese influence might be diluted if America furnished some of the loan money. In this way Wilson established a measure of superficial cooperation with Japan. As the United States entered the war in Europe in 1917, Wilson thought it important to cool the Japanese-American rivalry still further. Neither Wilson nor Japan was willing to make substantial concessions, so Robert Lansing and Japanese special minister Ishii Kikujiro agreed to a set of notes papering over the disagreements. Japan would respect the Open Door and the territorial integrity of China, while the United States would accept Japan's "special interests" there. Just what constituted Japan's special interests was left to the imagination, although a secret protocol pledged both sides to respect the status quo in China for the duration of the war.

Japanese-American relations remained strained despite the Lansing-Ishii Agreement of 1917. When Japan insisted on sending an expeditionary force into Siberia following Russia's withdrawal from World War I, a reluctant Wilson dispatched an American force to Siberia as well, in large part to keep an eye on the Japanese. Then, at the Paris Peace Conference, Wilson tried unsuccessfully to get the Allies to withdraw their cession of the Shantung Peninsula to Japan. He was also instrumental in defeating a clause Japan sought to insert into the peace treaty recognizing racial equality, a clause Wilson opposed personally and feared would prevent Senate consent. Japanese-American relations remained distrustful and contentious for the next twenty-five years.

CONTROVERSIAL ISSUES AND FURTHER READING

The Open Door policy in Asia was an immensely popular one in the United States after John Hay enunciated it at the turn of the century. Newspapers, popular magazines, and politicians praised Hay for devising a clever diplomacy that supposedly saved China from predatory imperialists while protecting American interests, all without entangling the United States in foreign alliances or war. [See, for example, A. L. P. Dennis, *Adventures in American Diplomacy, 1896–1906* (1928).] Hay knew how little influence his declaration of policy had had in the absence of any disposition on the part of the United States to enforce it. Nevertheless, he and his successors did nothing to stop the popular portrayal of the Open Door as the savior of China. Consequently, the Open Door notes rapidly acquired an aura of sanctity approaching that of the Monroe Doctrine. This popular image proved tenacious through the years, especially in those sectors of the public influenced by the reports of American missionaries in China. Even today, many Americans continue to see the United States as having been the friendly protector of China, fighting Japan in the 1940s to save China's independence, only to be betrayed by the triumph of Mao Tse-tung and the Communists in 1949.

Academic historians have never been so enamored of the Open Door or America's actions in East Asia, and they have differed strongly about their effect. The first group of historical critics in the 1920s and 1930s was isolationist. They saw the Open Door as having entangled the United States in European imperial rivalries. Then, when the Europeans pulled back, the United States was left standing alone as the primary obstacle to Japan's ambitions. Isolationists thought the United States should have avoided foreign entanglements in both Asia and Europe, and confined its military power to the defense of North America or perhaps at most the Western Hemisphere. They particularly condemned the United States for supposedly defending the interests of the British Empire by declaring the Open Door in China. [See, for example, A. Whitney Griswold, *The Far Eastern Policy of the United States* (1938), and Samuel Flagg Bemis, *A Diplomatic History of the United States* (1936).] The other great pre-World War II historian of American policy in East Asia, Tyler Dennett, wrote his major works to demonstrate that the United States should have allied itself with Great Britain and been willing to use force rather than mere words and diplomacy to ensure the Open Door and the survival of China. But by the 1930s he had come around to the isolationist view. [See Tyler Dennett, *Americans in Eastern Asia* (1922), *Roosevelt and the Russo-Japanese War* (1925), and *John Hay* (1933); and Dorothy Borg, "Two Historians of the Far Eastern Policy of the United States: Tyler Dennett and A. Whitney Griswold," in Dorothy Borg and Shumpei Okamoto, eds., *Pearl Harbor as History* (1973).]

After World War II, realist historians joined the chorus condemning America's interventionist policy in Asia, but they did not denounce American intervention in World War II in Europe, as the isolationists did. Instead, they thought the United States should have tried to stay out of the war with Japan so it could concentrate its efforts against the greater threat of Hitler's Germany. These historians pointed out that the China market never amounted to anything, that American interests in Asia were too few and unimportant to justify taking any risks for them, and that the United States would have been better off if it had allowed Japan to exert some control over China. Perhaps if the Japanese had not been threatened by American obstruction, they would have been more moderate in China and never attacked Pearl Harbor. The realists argued that the war with Japan endangered the effort against Hitler without doing China any good and without winning any real loyalty from the Chinese. China soon went Communist anyway, and the United States began its equally ineffective attempts to control communism in Asia, leading to the wars in Korea and Vietnam.

The primary quarrel among realist historians has been over which actions and leaders were most to blame for the tragic policy in Asia. Some have seen it as stemming inevitably from the decision to keep the Philippines and then issue the Open Door notes. [See, for example, Louis J. Halle, *Dream and Reality: Aspects of American Foreign Policy* (1959), and George F. Kennan, *American Diplomacy, 1900–1950* (1951).] But most realists now argue that John Hay and Theodore Roosevelt were well aware of the limitations of American interest in Asia, were quite willing to accommodate Japan, and confined their activities to diplomacy and verbal expressions of American desires. Their only fault was their failure to explain their policies adequately to their successors and the general public. These realist historians blame William Howard Taft, Woodrow Wilson, and pro-Chinese State Department officials rather than Roosevelt and Hay for America's supposedly blind and excessive attachment to China, the Open Door, and confrontation with Japan. [See Raymond A. Esthus, *Theodore Roosevelt and Japan* (1966); Charles E. Neu, *An Uncertain Friendship: Theodore Roosevelt and Japan, 1906–1909* (1967); Charles E. Neu, *The Troubled Encounter: The United States and Japan* (1975); Akira Iriye, *Pacific Estrangement: Japanese and American Expansionism, 1897–1911* (1972); Akira Iriye, *Across the Pacific: An Inner History of America–East Asian Relations* (1967); Burton Beers, *Vain Endeavor: Robert Lansing's Attempts to End the American-Japanese Rivalry* (1962).]

As realist historians dated America's overcommitment in Asia from the accession of Taft to the presidency in 1909, naturally John Hay's Open Door notes lost much of their previous significance. The significance of the notes was further undermined by historians of Chinese-American relations who pointed out that Hay did little more than confirm policies America had been supporting since its first contacts with China in the eighteenth century. Certainly Americans did not need the British to dupe them into adoption of the Open Door, especially since Great Britain was in the midst of changing its policy when Hippisley was approaching the Americans without British government authorization. [R. G. Neale, *Great Britain and United States Expansion, 1898–1900* (1966); Paul A. Varg, *Open Door Diplomat: The Life of W. W. Rockhill* (1952).]

Historians who concentrated on China have generally been less sympathetic to Japan than those realists or other historians who have concentrated on Japanese relations with the United States. They have argued that the United States never supported China to the point that it risked war with Japan or seriously threatened Japanese interests until 1940, when Japan allied itself with Germany and truly menaced American security. These historians agree that the United States could have followed a more enlightened Japanese policy before 1940, but, unlike some realists, they have little hope that a better policy would have avoided Pearl Harbor. Meanwhile, they point out that American policy was actually harmful rather than helpful to the Chinese. American diplomats and businessmen condescended to China and exploited it, while the missionaries, however good their intentions, undermined China's culture and national self-confidence. The regrets of most historians of China are not for the war against Japan, but for America's self-delusion about the supposed benevolence of its policy toward China, its sense of outrage and betrayal at the Communist revolution, and the consequent refusal of recognition and ultimate war with Mao's China over Korea. [See John King Fairbank, *The United States and China* (1958); Paul A. Varg, *Missionaries, Chinese, and Diplomats: The American Protestant Missionary Movement in China, 1890–1952* (1958); Paul A. Varg, *The Making of a Myth: The United States and China, 1897–1912* (1968); Marilyn Blatt Young, *The Rhetoric of Empire: American China Policy, 1895–1901* (1968); Warren I. Cohen, *America's Response to China* (2nd ed., 1981); Charles S. Campbell, Jr., *Special Business Interests and the Open Door Policy* (1951); Roy Curry, *Woodrow Wilson and Far Eastern Policy, 1913–1921* (1957); Russell H. Fifield, *Woodrow Wilson and the Far East: The Diplomacy of the Shantung Question* (1952); Shih-shan Henry Tsai, *China and the Overseas Chinese* (1984); Michael H. Hunt, *The Making of a Special Relationship: The United States and China to 1914* (1983); James Reed, *The Missionary Mind and American East Asian Policy* (1982).]

Revisionists dissent even more strongly from the realists who wish America had appeased Japan. They think the United States should have been far more supportive of China. They regard the Open Door as simply a policy of informal empire and economic exploitation. They argue that Americans were so confident of their industrial dominance as to believe the United States could control the Chinese economy and through the economy China itself if simply given a chance to compete openly in the China market. Americans had no real interest in China's territorial integrity or general well-being, only in the opportunity for profits. If the United States had been truly anxious to help China, it would have joined the Soviets in supporting the Chinese nationalists. This would have created a strong China capable of withstanding Japan and therefore deterring it prior to Pearl Harbor. [See William Appleman Williams, "China and Japan: A Challenge and a Choice of the Nineteen Twenties," *Pacific Historical Review*, 26 (1957), pp. 259–279; Charles Vevier, *The United States and China, 1906–1913* (1955); Thomas J. McCormick, *China Market: America's Quest for Informal Empire, 1893–1901* (1967); Jerry Israel, *Progressivism and the Open Door: America and China, 1905–1921* (1971).]

For information on the Philippine war and occupation, see Richard Welch, *Response to Imperialism: The United States and the Philippine-American War, 1899–1902* (1979); Stuart Creighton Miller, *"Benevolent Assimilation": The American Conquest of the Philippines, 1899–1903* (1982); Peter W. Stanley, *A Nation in the Making: The Philippines and the United States, 1899–1921* (1974); and for a strong revisionist denunciation, William J. Pomeroy, *American Neo-Colonialism: Its Emergence in the Philippines and Asia* (1970).

CHAPTER 10

The Surge into Latin America: Varieties of American Empire

THE NATURE OF THE AMERICAN EMPIRE IN LATIN AMERICA

Throughout its history, the United States has been wary of the idea of imperialism. Americans have prided themselves on the fact that their revolution was the first successful rebellion against European colonialism. Their political ideology has been based on the principle of government by consent of the governed. Although they have subscribed to other competing values—desire for national security, economic prosperity, and the prestige associated with great power status—they have suffered considerable discomfort when they sacrificed the principle of democracy too easily and blatantly to those other desires. Prior to the Spanish-American War, Americans found it relatively easy to rationalize the contradictions between their actions and their commitment to democratic self-determination. They ignored the Indians and visualized the westward movement as expansion into "empty lands" which they would ultimately incorporate into the Union as equal states. But it was difficult for them to conceive of making states out of the Philippines, the South Sea Islands, Hawaii, or Puerto Rico. The Supreme Court even decided in the famous Insular Cases that the inhabitants of America's new colonies were not entitled to all the basic liberties granted American citizens by the Constitution. To add to the dilemmas the United States faced in its new colonies, many Americans thought it essential to ensure stability in still other nations that were economically or strategically important.

The United States could no longer escape the fact that it was an imperial and interventionist power. In the first flush of victory, the thrill of arrival as a great world power overrode the sense of guilt and the anti-imperialist movement that had exploited that guilt. Then, as the thrill waned in the blood and atrocities of the Philippine revolution, Americans began to regard their colonial experiment and intervention in general with an increasingly jaundiced eye.

Still, intervene they did. They may not have done so enthusiastically;

they may have considered intervention only the lesser of evils; yet most came to feel that the United States had no other choice, especially in Latin America. Even many politicians and historians who opposed the annexation of the Philippines or an activist policy in defense of the Open Door in Asia were ready to defend the acquisition of colonies and protectorates in Central America and the Caribbean. They reasoned that Latin America was closer to home than Asia and believed that it was strategically vital for the United States to control the isthmian canal routes.

By the end of the Spanish-American War, the United States was well on its way to achieving the goal of an isthmian canal. America displaced Spanish rule in two critical islands guarding the Caribbean approaches to the canal routes, Cuba and Puerto Rico. Great Britain was slowly but surely reducing its power and presence in the Western Hemisphere to concentrate on the European theater. The United States wanted nothing to tempt Spain or Great Britain to return to the Caribbean or Central America, and it hoped to deter the recently united and aggressive Germany from intruding there as well.

As the strategic interest of the United States in Latin America increased, so did its direct economic stake. Cuba was especially valuable. It supplied sugar and tobacco; it served as an important market for American manufactured goods; and Americans invested heavily there in tobacco and sugar plantations, banks, railroads, and public utilities. Mexico, where Americans were developing similar markets and investments, was equally valuable. The rest of Latin America was not, although several American corporations had substantial interests in various areas and sought protection from the U.S. government. The United States had always assumed that protection of American lives and property abroad was a proper goal of diplomacy, so the government became more inclined to intervene as its Latin American economic interests increased and the obstacles posed by major rivals decreased.

Americans naturally managed to find ideological rationales for their multiplying interventions. They convinced themselves that American rule could never be like European colonial oppression because the United States would educate the native peoples for liberty. As time wore on, this took the concrete form of a decision to free the Philippines and to consider granting statehood to the largest and most compatible of the colonies. Where the United States felt compelled to intervene militarily or to exert a rather heavy-handed economic and diplomatic influence, Americans were at least half convinced that this too could work for the good of all. American trade and investments would increase the economic wealth of those nations. U.S. military power would protect Latin America against European colonial exploitation and preserve peace among the weaker nations. Political supervision could help bring stability and democracy. American influence would work against dictatorship, corruption, and the chaos that indigenous romantic nationalists or radicals might bring in their wake.

Events quickly exposed the problems and contradictions involved in colonizing or intervening in foreign areas. The clash of cultures between the native inhabitants and Americans was often bitter and ugly. Most Americans shared a condescending attitude toward non-Europeans. When Americans served abroad in positions of authority as factory owners, colonial officials, teachers, and missionaries, they often aroused nationalistic hostilities. American troops stationed in foreign countries caused special difficulties: Most soldiers were uneducated and unsophisticated. They regarded foreigners as strange and inferior and treated them as such. Consequently, American military intervention often created more problems than it solved.

The United States usually intervened in hope of establishing reasonably stable and democratic regimes. Nevertheless, those who were the targets of the intervention generally regarded any government established or supported by the United States as collaborationist. Such a government could not survive by democratic means. It would resort to oppression, invite rebellion and chaos, and tempt American intervention once again. The events of Theodore Roosevelt's administration exposed many of these problems. Roosevelt's successor, William Howard Taft, tried to circumvent the need for military intervention by substituting dollar diplomacy. By encouraging American investment to enrich and buttress weaker economies, Taft hoped he would stabilize the politics of those nations as well. But dollar diplomacy failed; American investment and trade usually enriched a few Americans and a small group of Latin Americans without raising the general standard of living.

Most Latin American countries began to concentrate on one or two cash crops or natural resources that might be exchanged in the United States for manufactured items and luxury goods. The upper classes might benefit from this trade and from the American investments and loans that made possible the railroads, port facilities, and public utilities necessary to commerce; few peasants did. The economies of these nations became almost totally dependent on the United States, whose superior economic strength permitted its citizens in large measure to control the price of both Latin American exports and imports. Latin Americans paid more for the manufactured goods they imported than they received for the agricultural products or raw materials they exported.

Woodrow Wilson recognized some of the problems with dollar diplomacy and thought they were caused by the greed of Wall Street investors. He believed that a greater dedication to democracy abroad and less concern for selfish profits in American trade and investment would resolve the difficulties. But to his chagrin, his attempt to establish just and democratic governments led to more conflict and intervention than the policies of either of his predecessors.

The dilemma Wilson, Taft, and Roosevelt faced is still with us and still generates controversy. Revisionists condemn America's historic policies toward Latin America *in toto*. Like the Latin American Left itself, they believe that the United States intervened in Latin America primarily for economic gain, to protect and increase American trade and investments. American interventions were not motivated by fears for national security, because no outside power posed a credible threat to Latin America after the British retreated at the turn of the century. The United States intervened instead to perpetuate the dictatorship of the Latin American upper classes, which have been allied with the economic interests of the United States. It has sought to protect its collaborators against indigenous revolutionaries who had no choice but to seek nationalization of land and resources because wealth was concentrated in so few hands. Obviously the United States had no interest in democracy, or it would have supported such revolutionary movements.

Restrained realists also have been highly critical of U.S. policy toward Latin America, but for different reasons. They do not believe economic interests provided the primary motivation for U.S. interventions. Instead, they think the United States intervened out of naive notions of national security and hopes for Latin American democracy. They agree with the revisionists that the United States has exaggerated the security threats to Latin America. Therefore they believe that most of the interventions have been foolish ones which generated hostility toward the United States and did little good. Most realists do not regard Latin America as terribly vital to U.S. economic or strategic interests and therefore agree that the United States should follow a much more restrained policy there. The implication of their view, however, is that the United States should not hesitate to intervene when its national security truly is at stake, even though such intervention might be harmful. They see it as inevitable that a powerful nation should influence and to some extent dominate its weaker neighbors and believe the best the United States can hope to do is to mitigate the effects of that situation.

Nationalists do not regard the Latin American policy of the United States to have been such an unmitigated failure. Like the realists but unlike the revisionists, they do not place as great an emphasis on economic motivations. Nationalists also do not believe that U.S. trade and investment have done that much harm. They argue that Latin America needed capital and would have been far worse off if the United States and its corporations had not furnished it. They are not so willing to discount the threats of outside nations to the Western Hemisphere, past or present. Nationalists also believe that the encouragement of democracy in Latin America was a sincere and worthy goal, even if U.S. intervention and influence failed to secure it in very many places. They blame the failure of democracy more on the Latin Americans themselves than on the United States and refuse to equate U.S. policy there with European imperialism.

But even nationalists find it hard to argue against the idea that the United States created at least an informal empire in Central America and the Caribbean area after the turn of the twentieth century. Along with annexing the formal colony of Puerto Rico, the United States made a protectorate of Cuba, acquired all but absolute sovereignty over the Panama Canal Zone, intervened militarily in several Central American and Caribbean nations, and exerted a profound economic influence over the rest of Latin America. Meanwhile, the United States successfully excluded all of the military and much of the economic influence of the European powers.

Map 10   The Caribbean Area, 1889–1961

PUERTO RICO: GOVERNING A COLONY

The United States had met little opposition in seizing Puerto Rico during the Spanish-American War. Americans conducted no land campaign at all. Puerto Rican revolutionaries in New York, cooperating to some extent with the Cuban junta, invited American intervention. Thus, Americans found their presence welcomed for the first two years of their occupation of the island. The Puerto Ricans had little reason to mourn the demise of the Spanish empire. Puerto Rico had shared the tragic experience of the rest of the Caribbean, including European conquest, extermination of most of the Indian population, and establishment of a brutal slave system by absentee owners of large sugar plantations. The African slaves ultimately had been emancipated, but the society remained fixed in a rigid class system with a small upper class dominating a large mass of landless, racially mixed peasants. In 1898, only 21 percent of Puerto Rico's land was under cultivation. There were no banks and only two or three roads.

Nevertheless, this was no "empty land" available for mass American immigration. The island was already overpopulated as well as poverty-stricken. Americans would come to Puerto Rico as colonial officials, entrepreneurs, missionaries, or tourists, not as farmers and settlers. Some American capital did flow into the island, and Americans replaced Spaniards as absentee landlords. They shifted Puerto Rican agricultural enterprise even more toward sugar, away from the cultivation of coffee produced by the smaller and relatively independent farmers of Puerto Rico's interior. The United States had abundant supplies of coffee from elsewhere and saw sugar as more profitable.

By 1930, American absentee owners controlled more than half of Puerto Rico's sugar, 80 percent of its tobacco, 60 percent of its banks and public utilities, and under special government protection, 100 percent of its shipping. Some 70 percent of the profits from Puerto Rico's large enterprises went to foreigners, including Americans. Much of the other 30 percent went to rich Puerto Ricans, who in turn spent it on manufactured and luxury goods from the United States. Lower-class Puerto Ricans had to buy food from the United States at tariff-protected prices or produce their own on small, inadequate farms. Existence was possible only at a low subsistence level. Many fled to the cities or to the United States itself to escape their dilemma, so no middle-class farming population developed. The Puerto Rican middle class was essentially a set of bureaucrats or lower-level managers in the larger enterprises and almost totally dissociated from the peasants.

Meanwhile, the Anglo-Calvinist civilization of the United States conflicted with the Catholic Spanish-Creole culture of the island. Puerto Ricans, themselves ambivalent and uncertain in their attitudes toward race, were shocked to find themselves considered black by their American masters. The middle and upper classes considered themselves white and looked with disdain and some alarm at what they considered to be the shallow imported materialistic culture of their supposed racial superiors. This economic and cultural scenario was repeated to a lesser or greater extent throughout Central America and the Caribbean.

The impact of the United States was somewhat different on Puerto Rico than on the rest of Latin America because Puerto Rico was a formal rather than an informal colony. The Insular Cases dictated that the United States did not have to govern Puerto Rico and the Philippines with the expectation that they would become states, as had been the rule with previous American territories. The Organic Act of 1900 gave Puerto Rico a territorial government that allowed election of Puerto Rican representatives, but guaranteed an American governor and an American majority on the governing council. Various American administrations usually reserved these offices for loyal party workers, without regard to their knowledge of Puerto Rico or the Spanish language. Often these officials did little to disguise their patronizing attitudes.

The United States did extend citizenship to the Puerto Ricans in 1917. Americans improved sanitation, utilities, and roads, although the primary benefits of these went to the cities and larger agricultural enterprises rather than to the ordinary peasant. Americans also did much for education on the island. Puerto Rico's literacy rate rose to better that 80 percent, compared to Haiti's 15 percent or the Dominican Republic's 26 percent. Still, this did not offset the growing resentment of the Puerto Ricans toward their American overlords.

It was not until the early 1940s that Puerto Rico tenuously accepted its position within the American empire. During those years, a remarkable Puerto Rican leader, Luís Muñoz Marín, organized a political party that finally convinced the United States to allow Puerto Rico to elect its own governor. Muñoz Marín then gained commonwealth status for Puerto Rico, corrected some of the most glaring of the island's economic inequalities, lobbied successfully for large economic benefits from Congress, and attracted considerable private capital. Yet Puerto Rico's consent to its United States connection remained unstable and laced with considerable hostility. This boded ill for U.S. relations with the rest of Latin America, where the problems raised by the overwhelming North American presence were not balanced as they were in Puerto Rico by the investment of some $500 million between 1898 and 1945 and by the right of free passage to the United States.

CUBA: SHAPING A FORMAL PROTECTORATE

William McKinley committed the United States to abstain from annexing Cuba when he accepted the Teller Amendment, but he also avoided recognizing the Cuban rebel government. This left him free to set the ground rules under which Cuba could remain independent. He forced the Spanish to surrender Cuba to the U.S. military, not to the Cuban rebels. The United States then established a temporary military government and managed to disband the Cuban army by making liberal payments to its commanders and soldiers.

After complaints from Cubans and Americans alike that the first U.S. governor was too liberal toward the defeated Spanish, McKinley appointed General Leonard Wood to succeed him. Wood was a medical doctor who was able, confident, energetic, and sympathetic to the "large policy" of his friends Theodore Roosevelt and Henry Cabot Lodge. Wood did much to improve sanitation, eradicate yellow fever, establish public schools, and bring a measure of efficiency to Cuba's government and public services. Yet he distrusted Cuban abilities and always put North Americans in charge of these projects. He even established a paternalistic code of discipline that prescribed public whippings for violaters of his new civic codes.

Wood and Secretary of War Elihu Root formulated the terms on which the United States would turn Cuba over to an indigenous government. Wood and Root wanted a stable Cuba that would protect U.S. trade and investment and that would welcome a U.S. military presence to defend the island, the approaches to the Caribbean, and the peninsular canal routes. To achieve this, Root circumvented a congressional prohibition against permanent economic concessions in Cuba by granting supposedly temporary ones instead. He and Wood also worked through Senator Orville Platt of Connecticut to attach the so-called Platt Amendment to the Army Appropriations Bill of 1901. This prohibited Cuba from granting foreign economic concessions without U.S. permission or doing anything to impair independence. The Platt Amendment required Cuba to keep its debt at a low level, grant the United States sites for military and coaling stations, and permit the United States to intervene if necessary to protect Cuban independence and maintain stability.

To persuade a Cuban constitutional convention to accept these stipulations, Root promised that the United States would intervene only in the most extreme circumstances. Wood proclaimed that the U.S. occupation force would not leave until Cuba accepted the terms of the Platt Amendment. The Cubans reluctantly acquiesced, and in 1902 Wood turned over the government to a newly elected Cuban president. U.S. troops left, but in conformance with a treaty negotiated on the basis of the Platt Amendment, the U.S. navy moved into the strategic port of Guantánamo to establish its major Caribbean base. A reciprocal trade treaty was also part of the bargain. Cuba received tariff concessions on exports of sugar to the United States and gave U.S. products special privileges in Cuban markets. U.S. investments also increased rapidly. In 1898 U.S. citizens had some $50 million invested in Cuban sugar; by 1920 that figure was $1.25 billion.

Cuban stability did not last very long. President Tómas Estrada Palma refused to accept the verdict of the polls when he was defeated for reelection. His opponents announced a revolution, and Estrada Palma begged for U.S. support. Theodore Roosevelt sent an American warship to Havana, but decided Estrada Palma himself was the major problem. Roosevelt appealed to the Cubans to resolve the issue fairly to avoid American intervention. No one wanted a repetition of the Philippine war. On the other hand, Roosevelt and his special envoy to the island, William Howard Taft, did not want to turn the government over to rebels and thus reward armed insurrection. They preferred that Estrada Palma stay on temporarily while new and fair elections were held.

Estrada Palma and the rebels, however, refused to negotiate. They both angled for U.S. intervention in hopes that Roosevelt would support their position. Estrada Palma resigned rather than accept a new election, and Roosevelt sent Taft, supported by the landing of 5,000 American troops, to establish himself as head of a provisional government. The U.S. provisional government itself held new elections while Roosevelt warned the Cubans that "if the elections become a farce, and if the insurrectionary habit becomes confirmed in the Island, it is absolutely out of the question that the Island should continue independent." Taft's successor as governor, Charles Magoon, tried to encourage reform and strong political parties, but the parties had few roots among the people. Party leaders were mostly intent on the spoils of office. They felt little responsibility because they knew they could induce U.S. intervention in a crisis by threatening revolution and chaos.

After Taft's elections established a new government, the United States withdrew its troops in 1908, some two years after it had intervened. Nevertheless, the Cuban political system remained unstable, corruption increased, and the army set up by the new government became an expensive source of political favoritism and boodle.

In 1912, the United States intervened once again in Cuba. President Taft sent 500 marines to support the Cuban regime against a rebellion of army officers and blacks who were protesting political discrimination. Woodrow Wilson denounced such interventions, but he too felt compelled to threaten intervention to deter a revolt against the incumbent Cuban regime on the eve of U.S. entry into World War I. His action won the consent of a grateful Cuban government to station U.S. troops on the island to guard against any potential German threat. The crisis of World War I temporarily silenced opposition in the United States to Wilson's action, but it was increasingly clear that military intervention in Cuba was self-defeating.

THE PANAMA CANAL: ACQUIRING A FORMAL ENCLAVE IN AN INFORMAL COLONY

By establishing a colony in Puerto Rico and a protectorate over Cuba, the United States took two major steps toward securing control of the Caribbean access to any canal built through Central America. The strengthened U.S. position affected Great Britain as well as Latin America. The United States had been trying for years to rid itself of its obligations under the Clayton-Bulwer Treaty of 1850 to share control of any Central American canal with Great Britain, and in December of 1898, the British decided to open new negotiations on the issue.

After a year of hard bargaining, Secretary of State John Hay and British Ambassador Lord Julian Pauncefote concluded a pact that gave the United States sole control of the potential canal, but ensured its neutrality by forbidding the canal's fortification. Theodore Roosevelt and his "large policy" cohorts campaigned against this first Hay-Pauncefote Treaty because it prohibited fortification, and the Senate responded by mangling the treaty so thoroughly that it had to be renegotiated. By the time the second Hay-Pauncefote Treaty was signed in January 1902 Roosevelt himself was president, and the British were ready to retreat still further from Latin America. This second treaty was silent on fortification, implicitly according to the United States the right to full military control of the canal.

All that remained was for the United States to choose between Nicaragua and Panama as the canal route. A commission appointed by McKinley, the so-called Walker Commission, had reported in favor of Nicaragua in 1901. The commission's engineers admitted that Nicaragua's river system might be too shallow for easy construction, but the Panama route had an even more serious drawback. The successor to De Lesseps' bankrupt New Panama Canal Company demanded the exhorbitant sum of $109 million for the purchase of its works and concessions. The House of Representatives accepted the Walker Commission report and authorized construction through Nicaragua.

William Nelson Cromwell, a remarkable U.S. lobbyist for the New Panama Canal Company, refused to accept this House action as final. He convinced the Panama Company to reduce its demand from $109 million to $40 million. Then he persuaded the U.S. Senate to authorize the money and to urge the negotiation of a treaty with Colombia for canal rights through Panama with the proviso that if negotiations failed, Roosevelt would return to the Nicaragua option. Cromwell got his way in Congress through liberal application of money. His allies distributed Nicaraguan stamps showing an erupting volcano to counter Nicaraguan claims that its route would be perfectly safe.

The Roosevelt administration quickly negotiated the Hay-Herrán Treaty with Colombia, which gave the United States a ninety-nine-year lease on a canal zone six miles wide in exchange for an initial payment of $10 million plus $250,000 annually. But the Colombian Senate balked. It wanted an increase in payments and greater acknowledgment of Colombian sovereignty over the canal zone. Colombia had reason to stall. The New Panama Company's concessions ran out in 1904, and Colombia would then receive the money for De Lesseps' works as well.

The stall enraged Roosevelt. He might have turned to Nicaragua, but instead he resolved to get the better of the "contemptible little creatures in Bogotá." You could no more make a binding agreement with them than you could "nail currant jelly to the wall," he later complained. When an influential Panamanian suggested that Panama might rebel against its Colombian overlords and sign its own treaty with the United States, Roosevelt was ready to listen. Roosevelt knew rebellion was endemic in Panama. The United States, in its role as guarantor of transit rights across the isthmus of Panama, had intervened four separate times in recent years to protect the railroad against rebel attacks. The man who suggested that a convenient rebellion might break out again was Philippe Bunau-Varilla, an official of the New Panama Canal Company who was desperate to strike a deal before the company's concession ran out.

Bunau-Varilla wanted the United States to protect the revolution against Colombian reconquest by using its rights as guarantor of transit to block Colombian landings or use of the Panamanian railway. Panama needed the help because its revolutionary forces consisted of a fire brigade, a few local police, and a small contingent of Colombian soldiers whose commander had been bribed. Roosevelt told Bunau-Varilla that he could not encourage revolution, but he let John Hay inform Bunau-Varilla that the American ship *Nashville* was steaming toward the isthmus. Roosevelt later commented that Bunau-Varilla would have been a very dull man not to have known what America would do in case of a revolution.

Bunau-Varilla was not dull. He delayed the revolution until the *Nashville* was lying off Colon. When the revolution began, however, the commander of the *Nashville* failed to prevent the Colombians from landing an invasion force because orders to do so had been too late in arriving. A quick-thinking railroad supervisor saved the day. He had already sent all the rolling stock to the Pacific side of the isthmus, stranding the Colombian force. He then invited the Colombian commanders aboard one of the last available trains and sent them off also, leaving the troops leaderless. The *Nashville* landed some U.S. sailors to "keep the peace," and the revolution was secure.

Panama's new leaders gratefully authorized Bunau-Varilla to negotiate a canal treaty with the United States. They told him at the same time to protect Panama's sovereign rights over the canal, but Bunau-Varilla was so anxious to guarantee the American Senate's approval of the treaty that he gave away even more than Hay requested. Hay wanted American control of a canal zone six miles wide for ninety-nine years. Bunau-Varilla insisted the United States govern "as if it were sovereign" a ten-mile zone in perpetuity. In return, the United States would protect the sovereignty of Panama, especially against Colombia. The Panamanian leaders protested Bunau-Varilla's giveaway, but accepted it rather than face Colombia alone.

The treaty with Bunau-Varilla ran into considerable opposition in the United States from the press and Congress. The Democrats particularly denounced Roosevelt's unscrupulous tactics. They argued that America should have turned to the Nicaraguan route rather than encouraging the Panamanian revolution. The Senate could not resist the handsome concessions the president had won, however, and it accepted the treaty by a vote of 66 to 14. Roosevelt defended his actions as perfectly legal. When he asked his cabinet if he had successfully vindicated himself, Elihu Root replied that he certainly had: "You have shown that you were accused of seduction and you have conclusively proved that you were guilty of rape." Later, in 1911, Roosevelt was quoted as telling an audience at the University of California: "I took the Isthmus." His alleged comment triggered a congressional investigation, and Woodrow Wilson subsequently apologized to Colombia while trying to get Congress to appropriate $25 million as an indemnity. Roosevelt succeeded in getting his Republican friends in Congress to defeat Wilson's move, but two years after his death in 1919, Congress did grant Colombia the indemnity.

Ironically, as Colombia became mollified, Panama became less so. The United States completed the canal in 1914 and eliminated yellow fever in the process, but it established the canal zone as a protected enclave against the Panamanians themselves. The American flag gradually replaced the Panamanian flag. The Americans set up separate schools and commissaries. They made English the language of the zone and imported English-speaking West Indians to replace Panamanians in jobs on the canal. The United States officially segregated the canal zone by race and grouped the Panamanians with the West Indians as blacks. American labor bosses, often white southerners, treated the Panamanians and West Indians as they had treated blacks at home. Discrimination even extended to the currency in which laborers were paid. American citizens received gold, while the Panamanians and West Indians were paid in less valuable silver. The United States also exerted tremendous authority in Panama outside the zone. It controlled all lakes and streams necessary to the operation of the canal; it had a monopoly of all communications and utilities; and it tied Panama's economy to the American dollar.

Although the United States maintained the right of direct intervention in Panamanian politics and foreign policy, it tried to leave this sphere to the Panamanians as much as possible. Panamanian politics degenerated into a struggle for power within an economic elite of older families that considered themselves "white" and whose main goal was protection of their private interests. If this political system did little for the mass of Panamanians, it permitted efficient and uninterrupted operation of the Panama Canal by the United States.

THE ROOSEVELT COROLLARY: STAKING OUT AMERICA'S SPHERE OF INFLUENCE

As the United States strengthened its hand in the Caribbean through acquisition of formal colonies and protectorates in Cuba, Puerto Rico, and the Panama Canal, Theodore Roosevelt reconsidered America's policies toward the other independent nations of the area. At first he did not seem to think that anything more than the traditional adherence to the Monroe Doctrine was necessary. In 1902, when Great Britain and Germany approached him with a plan to use naval power to force Venezuela to pay its long-overdue debt, Roosevelt made no objection beyond warning that the venture must lead to no territorial acquisitions by the two European powers. He even wrote the German ambassador that if any South American country misbehaved toward a European country, the European nation should "spank it." He had a change of heart, however, after Britain and Germany sank several Venezuelan gunboats, blockaded the Venezuelan coast, and proceeded to bombard several coastal forts.

When the Venezuelans offered to submit the debts to international arbitration, Roosevelt urged a reluctant Germany and a somewhat less reluctant Great Britain to accept. In 1915, at the height of Roosevelt's fight to bring the United States into the world war against Germany, the former president even declared that he had sent an ultimatum to the kaiser that had finally forced the Germans to accept arbitration. There is no record of such an ultimatum in German or American archives, but Roosevelt had deployed the fleet in Latin American waters and used leaks to the press to threaten Germany.

This second Venezuela crisis stirred some soul-searching in many nations. Financial chaos, indebtedness, and political instability were endemic throughout Latin America. Other crises like the one in Venezuela were bound to arise. Sooner or later, a major European power would acquire control of a Latin American country, either by conquest or by gaining command over its economy and finances. This would pose a direct challenge to the Monroe Doctrine, which Roosevelt and the United States took far more seriously after the Spanish-American War.

Roosevelt considered two alternatives beyond the enforcement of the traditional injunctions of the Monroe Doctrine. The first of these was suggested by the Argentine foreign minister, Dr. Luís Drago. He proposed a new international principle: Public debts should not justify the use of force or territorial occupation. This Drago Doctrine, however, contradicted the European and American diplomatic tradition that a nation had the right to protect the lives and property of its citizens abroad. Roosevelt was willing to accept the Drago Doctrine, but he insisted that if a debtor nation refused to submit the issue to arbitration, then force was justified. He supported this modified Drago Doctrine at the Hague Conference of 1907 and the conference accepted it.

Many Latin American nations refused to sign the Hague modification of the Drago Doctrine because they rejected forcible collection of debts under any circumstances. The United States also had an incentive to ignore the Hague agreement. In the arbitration of the Venezuelan debt following the second Venezuelan crisis, the arbitrators favored the debts of the British and Germans over those of the United States. Since the British and Germans had used force to secure their debts while the United States had not, Roosevelt feared this precedent would undermine whatever authority was left to the Drago Doctrine after so many Latin American countries had refused to sign it.

Roosevelt turned to a very different alternative. He declared that if worse came to worst, the United States itself would intervene in Latin America to see that Latin American nations behaved justly toward their European creditors. U.S. intervention would eliminate any pretext for European intervention. This policy of "preventive intervention" became known as the Roosevelt Corollary to the Monroe Doctrine.

The occasion for Roosevelt's announcement was a crisis in the Dominican Republic. The Dominican Republic was the scene of continuous political and economic chaos. In seventy years, it had had nineteen revolutions and fifty-three presidents. The latest civil war had broken out in 1903, while European creditors were clamoring for payment of their debts and their war vessels sailed Dominican waters. In 1904, the harassed Dominican president asked the United States to intervene by sending arms, guaranteeing Dominican sovereignty, and paying its debts. Roosevelt had no desire for a new territory. He said he would as soon annex the island as swallow a porcupine wrong-end to.

He suggested instead that the United States take over Dominican customs collections, pay off creditors, and turn the remainder of the revenue over to the Dominican government. The suspicious Dominicans accepted out of fear of the Europeans, but the U.S. Senate recoiled after hearing Roosevelt claim that in cases of "chronic wrongdoing, or impotence" among Western Hemisphere nations, the United States "however reluctantly" would have to exercise "an international police power." Roosevelt seemed ready to extend the Platt Amendment to the whole of the Caribbean and Central America.

Roosevelt established the Dominican customs house receivership on his own authority until the balky Senate finally accepted the treaty with the Dominican Republic in 1907. Yet he hoped to keep the intervention limited and to avoid any further ones. He managed to do so until the end of his term; his successors were not so fortunate.

WILLIAM HOWARD TAFT AND DOLLAR DIPLOMACY

Taft tried to avoid interventions under the Platt Amendment or the Roosevelt Corollary by stabilizing Latin regimes through the infusion of private American capital. The new bureaucracy in the State Department advocated this dollar diplomacy in Latin America just as it did in China. And just as in China, it brought little but trouble.

Roosevelt had tried to promote stability in Central America by sponsoring a tenuous treaty arrangement among the fractious republics of the area. Taft tried to secure the area further by negotiating a customs receivership in Honduras to stave off potential British intervention. The arrangement was frustrated by the objections of the U.S. Senate and by various Honduran governments and agencies embroiled in their own civil wars.

In Nicaragua, Taft used greater force to accompany his dollar diplomacy. Nicaragua was meddling in other Central American states, including Honduras, and had contracted major loans with British institutions. Taft and Knox threw their support to a rebellion that promised a more pliant regime. They landed U.S. marines in rebel-held territory to protect North American property and lives, which just incidentally deterred the government from reconquest. After many twists and turns, the U.S.-sponsored government took power, and it accepted an American loan and a customs receivership to guarantee repayment. The U.S. Senate delayed its consent to the arrangement, but under Knox's urging, U.S. banks funded the loan anyway. These North American financiers also established the Bank of Nicaragua and chartered a corporation for operating Nicaragua's rail and steamship lines, all in defiance of the Nicaraguan constitution, which forbade special concessions to foreigners. U.S. marines then helped to put down another rebellion that charged the incumbent Nicaraguan regime with selling out to Wall Street. As the marines withdrew, leaving behind a one-hundred-man legation force to help keep order, Taft and Knox proclaimed their policy of stabilizing Central American economies a success.

WOODROW WILSON AND MISSIONARY DIPLOMACY

Woodrow Wilson disagreed with Taft's proclamation that dollar diplomacy had been successful. As he had criticized such diplomacy in Asia for its self- ish economic motivations and its favors to Wall Street, so he denounced the loans and customs receiverships in Nicaragua and Honduras. Wilson apol- ogized to Colombia for Roosevelt's "taking" of Panama and tried to get Con- gress to appropriate $25 million as compensation. He also announced that the United States would never seek another foot of territory in Latin America.[1] Although neither Roosevelt nor Taft had sought more territory, Wilson's pledge, along with his denunciation of dollar diplomacy as unwar- ranted interference in the affairs of sovereign nations, implied that he would seek a less interventionist policy than his predecessors.

Yet for all of Wilson's denunciations of dollar diplomacy, he still as- sumed that an orderly free economy open to "legitimate" U.S. trade was a vital part of the proper democratic system every nation should enjoy. This devout belief in democratic political procedures and a free economy actually gave Wilson more incentive to intervene in the affairs of the Caribbean and Central American nations than had the more overt strategic doctrines of Roosevelt or the dollar diplomacy of Taft. That Wilson's missionary diplo- macy would override his initial commitment to nonintervention was demon- strated most graphically on the island of Hispaniola. The two nations that shared the island, Haiti and the Dominican Republic, both endured long mil- itary occupations initiated by Woodrow Wilson.

The most systematic and extensive intervention took place in Haiti. That country had had a long history of suffering and turmoil since the legendary slave revolt led by Toussaint L'Ouverture at the turn of the nineteenth cen- tury. American ships and marines had intervened there eight times between 1867 and 1900 to protect American lives and property. A thin upper class of French-speaking Creoles arbitrarily and rather contemptuously ruled a great mass of peasants. The elite was tied to France by culture, religion, and the exchange of Haitian coffee for French tobacco. An influential coterie of Ger- man merchants also resided in Haiti. U.S. economic interests were less im- portant than those of France or Germany until 1900. Then a rapid rise of activity brought the United States control of 60 percent of Haiti's import

---

[1] Apparently he did not regard purchasing the Virgin Islands from Denmark under threat of seizure, as he did in 1916, to be in violation of this pledge.

market by 1910. With State Department support, U.S. bankers pried their way into a French and German consortium that controlled Haiti's national bank. The 50 percent share they acquired allowed America to dominate Haiti's customs office, since the bank was empowered to collect customs duties.

Before the Spanish-American War, Haiti's fine port at Môle St. Nicholas had given the country strategic importance, and the United States had tried to secure the harbor several times. After the United States had acquired Puerto Rico and Guantánamo in Cuba it seemed less important. But the United States still did not want to see Môle St. Nicholas fall into the hands of a rival European power like Germany. The continuing turmoil in Haiti thus led to considerable sentiment for intervention in the state and war departments of the United States. American bankers also encouraged such interventionist sentiments in hopes of gaining government protection for their financial concessions.

Racial prejudices inclined American officials to think the worst of Haiti's potential for stable and humane government. These prejudices were reinforced by the fact that between 1911 and 1915, seven of Haiti's presidents were assassinated or forcibly removed from office, one of them by being blown up in his palace. The final straw came in 1915 when the president tortured and executed 167 political prisoners and in turn was dismembered by angry revolutionaries.

The United States had already made the decision to intervene if fighting broke out in the capital because a staunch opponent of U.S. influence seemed prepared to overturn the government. Wilson sent in marines, established martial law, and installed a hand-picked government. The marines forced this government to accept a treaty empowering the United States to supervise Haiti's customs collection and finances, establish schools, build roads, and train a national guard. The marines and their national guard protégés then carried on a running battle with bands of Haitians who were menacing the roads the Americans were building with conscripted labor. Americans also began buying land in Haiti after forcing repeal of Haiti's constitutional provision prohibiting foreigners from owning property.

U.S. military courts constituted the Haitian judicial system until 1929. The Americans improved government efficiency and established roads and schools, but at great cost. A rebellion in 1919 cost 3,000 Haitian lives. American racism was rampant and bred much resentment. The second U.S. commander in Haiti, U.S. Marine Colonel Littleton W. T. Waller, expressed his disgust with "bowing and scraping to these coons." The Haitian national guard, organized by the United States to maintain order, became a force of its own. The guard continued the conscription of labor after the U.S. occupiers had formally abandoned it and waited in the wings to take control when the United States left.

A year after U.S. marines landed in Haiti, they occupied the neighboring Dominican Republic. The United States had operated the Dominican Republic's customs since 1905, and this helped maintain financial and political stability there while satisfying the country's European creditors. Such stability demonstrated the virtue of the customs receivership to many Americans. The United States failed to recognize how much Dominican stability owed to that nation's powerful president, Ramón Cáceres. When Cáceres was shot in 1911, the country became a revolving door for presidents, each of whom gutted the treasury before he abandoned office. The Dominican Republic was left with no public sanitation, a 90 percent illiteracy rate, only sixty-five kilometers of roads, and not a single public school. Bandits roamed the interior, and even the capital city became a wasteland.

The Taft administration intervened briefly in 1912 to end one civil war by helping to install a provisional president. The civil war resumed immediately after the U.S. ship left, however, and the provisional president resigned. Wilson's administration pressed the Dominican factions to end the turmoil and insisted that the United States be given supervisory control to ensure free elections and clean government. When even the factions most sympathetic to the United States resisted, the marines landed. After a brief effort to find a compliant government, the American military took full control. It tried to confiscate all private weapons, and it replaced the politicized national guard with a new independent one officered primarily by Americans. Again the United States built roads, established schools, provided public sanitation, and reformed government finances, but the occupation also raised almost universal resentment against the U.S. overlords. In addition to the racism that plagued the U.S. reputation everywhere it intervened, the occupation authorities established a particularly noxious press censorship. And, as in Haiti, Cuba, Panama, and Nicaragua, the local guard established under U.S. auspices overran its bounds.

MISSIONARY DIPLOMACY IN MEXICO

Wilson's intervention in Mexico was more sensational than his interventions elsewhere, but Mexico's size and the power of its nationalist resistance also made the intervention much shorter and more embarrassing. In the thirty-five years before the Mexican Revolution of 1910, General Porfirio Díaz's dictatorship had given the United States little reason to consider intervention. Díaz's ruthlessness had provided order and rapid economic growth, and he had invited U.S. businessmen to share the profits. The United States was the market for 75 percent of Mexico's exports. Europeans shared more equally in Mexico's import markets, investments, and loan portfolios, but Americans dominated the railroads and communications. Americans owned many of Mexico's mines and much of its agricultural land; after 1901, they invested heavily along with the British in the extraction of oil.

Foreign economic domination naturally roused nationalist antagonism in Mexico. Resentment was especially strong toward the United States, the most prominent foreign presence and the well-remembered despoiler of Texas, California, and the Southwest. Even Díaz, who generally welcomed foreign investment, disliked the dominance of foreign technicians and the use of English as the official language on the railroads. He began to buy out foreign investors. When his grip on the country faltered, there was a reservoir of anti-American nationalism ready to be tapped by the revolutionary contenders for his power.

A loose alliance of local leaders headed by Francisco Madero finally overthrew Díaz in 1911. Fighting then broke out between Madero and his erstwhile allies, who included Francisco "Pancho" Villa, Bernardo Reyes, and Emiliano Zapata. Madero had to rely on the regular army, led by Victoriano Huerta, to suppress these local rebellions. Huerta ultimately joined Madero's enemies, overthrew and murdered him, and then made himself provisional president.

President William Howard Taft and Secretary of State Philander Knox followed a cautious policy toward the revolution. Madero had considerable sympathy in the United States, and Taft and Knox had no desire to get entangled in Mexican politics. On the other hand, their ambassador to Mexico, Henry Lane Wilson, had no such compunctions. He regarded Madero as a visionary and wrote urgent and distorted analyses of Madero's supposed radicalism and anti-Americanism. Before Huerta overthrew Madero, Huerta worked out an agreement with the other rebel leaders at the American embassy under the auspices of Henry Lane Wilson. The ambassador also did nothing to prevent Madero's murder.

Henry Lane Wilson's policies and actions came under strong criticism from American liberals and certain sectors of the press, who pointed out the ambassador's connections to American investment interests that had long opposed the Madero family. Taft consequently resisted the ambassador's urging to recognize Huerta's government immediately and left the touchy issue to the new American president, Woodrow Wilson. Woodrow Wilson came to office with little knowledge of Mexico but with strong liberal commitments to legitimate democratic practices at home and abroad. He decided to make Mexico an example of the virtues of democracy. He told Huerta that the United States would withhold recognition of his government until Huerta established a cease-fire and held proper elections in which he would refrain from running. When Huerta balked, Wilson dismissed Ambassador Wilson and cut off arms to Huerta's government. Huerta persuaded President Wilson to cut off arms to his opponents as well by hinting that he would not run in the coming elections. As Huerta saw his power slipping, however, he arrested most of his congressional opponents, declared the subsequent election void, and stayed on as provisional president.

Woodrow Wilson responded by trying to induce the European powers to withhold recognition and arms. Then he settled down to a policy he called "watchful waiting" as various Mexican rebel groups under the umbrella title of Constitutionalists carried on the fight against Huerta. The Republican party ridiculed Wilson's policy and demanded vigorous military intervention in Mexico to ensure stability and protect American economic interests. As the turmoil in Mexico continued and Republican political pressure mounted, Wilson removed the embargo on arms to the Constitutionalists.

Then he found the opportunity for an even more sensational gesture. In

April 1914, an American naval vessel patrolling Mexico's Gulf coast sent a whaleboat ashore to purchase gasoline, only to have the crew arrested by Mexican soldiers for trespassing. The Mexican commanding officer released the eight crewmen with an apology in a couple of hours, but the American fleet commander demanded far more—a written apology, a court martial for the arresting officer, and a twenty-one gun salute to the American flag. President Wilson supported him and ordered the Atlantic fleet to Mexico. He did not want a confrontation; but he insisted on the twenty-one gun salute, and he let it be known to Huerta that the United States would return the salute. When Huerta continued to hesitate, Wilson ordered the occupation of Vera Cruz, Mexico's second city.

After a bloody invasion costing 100 American and 500 Mexican casualties, Americans took the city. But Wilson did not know what to do with it. American intervention had strengthened Huerta's position with his countrymen rather than weakened it. Wilson wanted to withdraw as quickly as possible, yet saw no way to do it gracefully. His chance came when the ABC powers—Argentina, Brazil, and Chile—offered mediation. Wilson accepted but insisted that the settlement include replacement of Huerta's government by the Constitutionalists until new elections could be held. Even the leader of the Constitutionalists, Venustiano Carranza, refused such direct interference in Mexico's internal affairs. Carranza took power on his own two weeks after the ABC mediation had offered a meaningless declaration to paper over the Mexican-American dispute. He refused to hold elections or cater to America in any way—and he left the embarrassed Wilson still with no graceful way out of Vera Cruz.

Finally, Carranza found himself in desperate need of the port at Vera Cruz to defeat the rebellions of Pancho Villa and Emiliano Zapata. He pledged to avoid reprisals against collaborators and political opponents in Vera Cruz, and with this face-saving concession in hand, Wilson withdrew the American forces. Carranza immediately arrested or fired everyone who had cooperated with the Americans in Vera Cruz.

When Carranza's forces gained the upper hand over those of Villa and Zapata in the following year, 1915, Wilson decided to recognize the Carranza government. He also cut off arms to Carranza's opponents. Pancho Villa retaliated angrily: His troops massacred seventeen Americans while robbing a Mexican train, and Villa himself led a raid across the U.S. border on the New Mexican town of Columbus in March 1916. Against the protests of Carranza, Wilson sent a military force under General John Pershing into Mexico in pursuit. Pershing found himself fighting not just Villa's forces, but Carranza's troops and the populace of several towns as well. After one particularly fierce fight with Carranza's troops at Carrizal, open war between Mexico and the United States seemed probable. Perhaps it was prevented only by the growing conflict with Germany that ultimately led the United States into World War I. In February 1917, the distracted Wilson withdrew Pershing's troops unilaterally.

Relations between Mexico and the United States remained strained in the

Figure 11 Pancho Villa (top) and his pursuers—General John (Black Jack) Pershing is fourth from left. Immediately to his right is George Patton, who would make his reputation in World War II. Photos courtesy of the National Archives.

succeeding years. Germany even proposed an alliance to Mexico if the United States entered World War I on the Allied side. Germany offered the reconquest of Texas and the Southwest as a reward. Mexico did not consider the offer seriously, but when the famous Zimmermann telegram proposing the alliance came to light, it reemphasized the tenuous state of Mexican-American relations. The constitution adopted by Carranza's revolutionary government damaged relations even further. It established a liberal labor code to be enforced against foreign as well as Mexican employers. The constitution also gave the Mexican government the right to expropriate any property necessary for the good of the Mexican society. Carranza could take over foreign investments in Mexico's mines, agricultural land, and oil fields. He began by imposing a royalty tax on oil drillers. Thus he directly challenged America's commitment to protect the property of its citizens abroad.

Wilson protested but kept a low profile to avoid war, since the United States was deeply involved in the European conflict and needed Mexican oil. Wilson's dilemma in Mexico illustrated the basic issues that would bedevil American relationships with the Third World in the twentieth century. America's interest in foreign trade and investment would often conflict with indigenous economic interests, beget dislike of economic dependence on the United States, and lead to conflict if the United States adhered to its historic belief in the right of a nation to protect the property of its citizens abroad. American insistence on stability and to a lesser extent on democratic procedures in nations of strategic or economic importance would lead to military interventions. American racial and cultural prejudices, borne by its military forces, merchants, missionaries, or travelers, further aroused nationalist resentments.

Some of these difficulties were no doubt inevitable. Relationships of weaker to stronger nations cannot help but be tinged with a degree of dependency and consequent resentment. Even the most enlightened nations and peoples have radiated a degree of cultural smugness and disdain for foreign ways. Regardless, many people will agree that a serious threat to vital national strategic and economic interests may justify forcible intervention. Yet it seems clear in retrospect that Germany, Great Britain, and Japan did not really jeopardize vital American interests in East Asia and Latin America. With the possible exception of the isthmian canal, it is difficult to find interests in East Asia and Latin America that the United States could rightly consider vital. Neither the strategic threats nor the economic trade and investments in those areas were significant enough to justify the extent and forcefulness of America's interventions in this pre-World War I era. A more restrained diplomacy could have protected most American interests without breeding the resentment that America's imperial surge did.

CONTROVERSIAL ISSUES AND FURTHER READING

American historians writing in the post-Spanish-American War era almost unanimously supported American intervention in Central America and the Caribbean as necessary to national security. None were very enthusiastic about it, but almost none could bring themselves to oppose it outright. They often demonstrated their reluctance by accompanying their defense of the Roosevelt Corollary or dollar diplomacy with ironic asides about the self-righteousness of Americans in denying their imperialistic tendencies. [See, for example, Archibald Cary Coolidge, *The United States as a World Power* (1918).] Their reluctance also could show up in partisanship. Democrat historians often limited their criticisms of intervention to those undertaken by Republicans, especially Roosevelt's "taking" of Panama. Republicans, on the other hand, praised Roosevelt's interventions while ridiculing Woodrow Wilson for trying to remove the problems of Latin American republics by "removing their independence." [For criticism of Roosevelt's intervention, see John Holladay Latané, *America as a World Power* (1907); for defenses of Roosevelt accompanied by criticisms of Wilson, see Albert Bushnell Hart, *The Monroe Doctrine: An Interpretation* (1916).] Still, historians were clearly in the interventionist camp. [Chester Lloyd Jones, *Caribbean Interests of the United States* (1916).] Some even condemned Wilson for being too restrained in his policy toward Mexico. [See, for example, Frederick A. Ogg, *National Progress, 1907–1917* (1918).] The author of the only full condemnation of American intervention written in this period, Hiram Bingham, recanted only a few years later by saying that the United States owed it "to the progress of the world . . . to see to it that the republics of Tropical America behave." [Hiram Bingham, *The Monroe Doctrine: An Obsolete Shibboleth* (1913). For his recanting, see Thomas L. Karnes, "Hiram Bingham and his Obsolete Shibboleth," *Diplomatic History* (Winter 1979).]

Following World War I, there was a general acknowledgment in the United States that military interventions in Latin America were undesirable and in many cases had been mistaken. This trend would culminate in the Good Neighbor Policy of the 1930s. Among historians, it would lead to a widespread belief that restraint toward Latin America was necessary, but significant divisions remained over the reasons for such restraint and over evaluations of America's past and present policies.

Nationalist historians generally defended America's past interventions as necessary under existing conditions to prevent the chaos that could have invited intervention by Germany or other European powers. Nationalists were ready to show more restraint following World War I because they said that the Latin American nations themselves were becoming more stable and capable of self-defense. This made American intervention less necessary. They implied, however, that if instability were again to invite intervention by outside powers hostile to the United States, strategic interests would require the United States to resume its interventionist policy. [The classic work of this genre is Samuel Flagg Bemis, *The Latin American Policy of the United States: An Historical Interpretation* (1943). Another broad text with a similar outlook is J. Lloyd Mechem, *A Survey of United States–Latin American Relations* (1965). Works in this vein restricted to the Caribbean are Chester Lloyd Jones, *The Caribbean since 1900* (1916), and Howard C. Hill, *Roosevelt and the Caribbean* (1927). On Cuba, see Russell Fitzgibbon, *Cuba and the United States, 1900–1935* (1935), and two modern works which argue that the United States abandoned its occupation too soon, Allan R. Millet, *The Politics of Intervention: The Military Occupation of Cuba, 1906–1909* (1968), and

James Hitchman, *Leonard Wood and Cuban Independence, 1898–1902* (1971). Not many other recent historians are willing to defend America's post-Spanish-American War interventions, but Julius W. Pratt's survey *America's Colonial Experiment: How the United States Gained, Governed, and in Part Gave Away a Colonial Empire* (1950), is considerably more sympathetic to the occupations than one might have expected from his earlier books.]

Most historians since World War I have been more critical of America's military interventions. They have argued that neither Germany nor any other power posed a serious threat to American security in the Western Hemisphere in the early twentieth century. Therefore American interventions were generally mistaken overreactions to imaginary threats that did great harm to the image of the United States in the minds of Latin Americans. But most also have implied that if ever there had been or was to be a true threat to American security, however remote the possibility, the United States would have to intervene. Liberal internationalists hoped the unpleasant necessity might be mitigated by making intervention a cooperative enterprise through international or regional organizations like the Organization of American States or the United Nations. [See, for example, Dexter Perkins, *A History of the Monroe Doctrine* (1963), and J. Fred Rippy, *The Caribbean Danger Zone* (1940).] Realists urged that the United States simply face up to the fact that although it needed to use far more restraint in Latin America, "A nation which has tremendous economic strength and world-wide strategic concerns must develop a political philosophy which will take account of unavoidable dependency, whether it be economic or strategic, or as it sometimes must, political as well." [Whitney T. Perkins, *Denial of Empire: The United States and Its Dependencies* (1962), pp. 351–352.]

As in the case of historians of U.S. Asian policy, these realist historians are generally less critical of Theodore Roosevelt's frankly power-oriented interventions than of Taft's idealistic dollar diplomacy or Wilson's even more idealistic missionary diplomacy. Also they do not believe American interventions were much motivated by narrow economic interests, but harshly condemn the few instances they find. [Broad surveys that criticize the United States from a realist outlook are Edwin Lieuwen, *United States Policy in Latin America: A Short History* (1965), and Donald Dozer, *Are We Good Neighbors?* (1959). A better and more recent survey, although slightly more restricted in its coverage, is Lester Langley, *The United States and the Caribbean, 1900–1970* (1980). The classic survey of American policy toward the Caribbean is Dana G. Munro, *Intervention and Dollar Diplomacy in the Caribbean, 1900–1921* (1960). Another excellent work emphasizing the political aspects of American intervention is Whitney Perkins, *Constraints of Empire: The United States and Caribbean Interventions* (1981). For Theodore Roosevelt's policies, see Howard K. Beale, *Theodore Roosevelt and the Rise of America to World Power* (1956). For Taft's dollar diplomacy, see Walter V. Scholes and Marie V. Scholes, *The Foreign Policies of the Taft Administration* (1970). For Wilson's missionary diplomacy, see Arthur Link's multivolume biography, *Woodrow Wilson* (1947–   ). For Mexico, see Karl M. Schmitt, *Mexico and the United States* (1974); P. Edward Haley, *Revolution and Intervention: The Diplomacy of Taft and Wilson with Mexico, 1910–1917* (1970); Kenneth J. Grieb, *The United States and Huerta* (1969); and Robert E. Quirk, *An Affair of Honor: Woodrow Wilson and the Occupation of Vera Cruz* (1962), an excellent book. For Cuba, see Lester D. Langley, *The Cuban Policy of the United States* (1968).]

Although some of these realist analyses of U.S.–Latin American relations can be quite critical of American intervention, revisionist analyses are generally more so. Revisionists do not regard American policy as having been motivated by benevolent if mistaken liberalism or concerns for imaginary security threats. They see it as intentional rapine motivated mostly by economic greed. [One of the oldest of these analyses is that of Scott Nearing and Joseph Freeman, *Dollar Diplomacy: A Study in American Imperialism* (1925). A somewhat milder book, and an excellent one, is Leland H. Jenks, *Our Cuban Colony: A Study in Sugar* (1928). The most recent critical surveys of U.S.–Latin American relations are Cole Blasier, *Hovering Giant: United States Responses to Revolutionary Change in Latin America* (1978), and Gordon Connell-Smith, *The United States and Latin America: An Historical Analysis of Inter-American Relations* (1974). For a look at Cuba from this point of view, see Jules Robert Benjamin, *The United States and Cuba: Hegemony and Dependent Development, 1880–1934* (1977). A milder revisionist account is David F. Healy, *The United States in Cuba, 1898-1902: Generals, Politicians, and the Search for Policy* (1963). The best recent work on Panama is Walter LaFeber, *The Panama Canal: The Crisis in Historical Perspective* (1979). For Haiti, see Hans Schmidt, *The United States Occupation of Haiti, 1915–1934* (1971). A mild revisionist account of U.S. relations with Mexico is Robert F. Smith, *The United States and Revolutionary Nationalism in Mexico, 1916–1932* (1972). Gordon Lewis's excellent work, *Puerto Rico* (1963), is written in a similar spirit.]

CHAPTER 11

Europe, America, and World War I

GERMANY DISRUPTS THE EUROPEAN BALANCE OF POWER

The rise of the United States and Japan at the end of the nineteenth century challenged the stability of the international system and resulted in three potentially disruptive conflicts: the Sino-Japanese, Russo-Japanese, and Spanish-American wars. But at least the United States and Japan intruded into areas relatively remote from the existing major powers of Europe. No similar power vacuums cushioned the rise of Germany in the late nineteenth and early twentieth centuries. When Germany joined the roster of world powers, it threatened the heart of Europe and disturbed the precarious balance that had been the basis of peace since the defeat of Napoleon.

In 1860, Germany had been little more than a geographical expression, thirty-nine principalities sharing a heritage of German language and culture but little sense of political or economic unity. The central plain of Europe offered few natural boundaries, and Germans were mixed liberally into surrounding areas such as Schleswig-Holstein (Denmark), Alsace-Lorraine (France), Luxembourg (Holland), Switzerland, Austria, Poland, and the Baltic fringes of Russia.

The architect of modern Germany was the chancellor of Prussia, Otto von Bismarck. Using the small but efficient Prussian army, he combined with Austria to seize Schleswig-Holstein from Denmark. Then he turned on his Austrian ally in a contest for influence over the numerous principalities that lay between the two Germanic rivals. Bismarck won this war at the Battle of Sadowa in 1866, but he refrained from occupying Vienna and managed to avoid alienating Austria permanently.

Five years later, Bismarck's rising Germany shocked Europe by attacking and defeating France. Bismarck was not as successful in reconciling France to its defeat as he had been in pacifying Austria. His military commander, the great Prussian general Helmuth von Moltke, refused to accept the easily defended Rhine River as Germany's western border. Instead, he insisted on annexing Alsace-Lorraine, with its large French population, in order to secure the province's resources of iron ore and a defensive perimeter in the Vosges

Mountains. The annexation all but guaranteed permanent Franco-German enmity. To sustain the memory of its lost territory, France draped black veils over the statues in Paris's Place de la Concorde that represented the capital cities of Alsace and Lorraine.

Following the Franco-Prussian War, Bismarck set out to protect his new Germany by juggling the balance of power among the major European states. After winning an alliance with Austria in 1879, he lured Russia into the arrangement by emphasizing the common interest of the emperors of Germany, Austria, and Russia in resisting France. Although France had lost most of its revolutionary fervor domestically, it continued to advocate liberalism and nationalism in the rest of Europe. French-encouraged nationalism in Poland worried the three empires especially, since they had divided Poland among them in the previous century.

Bismarck had to work mightily to hold the Three Emperor Alliance together. Russia and Austria could agree on Poland and France, but they were bitter antagonists in the Balkans. There Russia encouraged the rebellions of its kindred Orthodox Slavs against the rule of Ottoman Turkey, "the sick man of Europe," in order to extend the czar's sway through the Balkan Slavs to the Dardenelles. These straits would give the Russian navy access from the Black Sea into the Mediterranean. Austria feared that the independence movements Russia was encouraging would spread to Slavic groups within the Austro-Hungarian Empire and rip that multi-ethnic state to shreds. Bismarck dampened some of this Balkan rivalry between his allies by acting as an "honest broker" in the area and by encouraging Russia to direct its expansion toward China and India, where it would not conflict with the interests of Austria or Germany.

Bismarck's convoluted policy began to unravel when Kaiser Wilhelm II came to the German throne in 1888. Wilhelm found Bismarck's policy too conservative and constraining. He dismissed the Iron Chancellor and permitted the treaty of alliance with Russia to lapse. France leapt at the chance to end its isolation in Europe, loaned money to the czar, and in 1898 began a series of contracts and agreements that led to a military entente. Europe looked on aghast as the autocratic czar of Russia bared his head at the playing of the *Marseillaise,* the anthem of revolutionary France. Kaiser Wilhelm naturally drew closer to Austria. Then both Germany and France began casting half-apprehensive, half-inviting glances at Great Britain.

Great Britain stood aloof from most of this maneuvering. So long as no European nation threatened the British Isles directly, Great Britain preferred to concentrate on its overseas imperial interests, especially the Suez Canal, India, China, and southern Africa. These interests brought the British more frequently into conflict with France and Russia than with Germany or Austria. France, whose citizens had built the Suez Canal, challenged Britain for control of Egypt and the Mediterranean, Britain's lifeline to India. France and Great Britain came within a hair's breadth of war in 1898 when rival military expeditions confronted one another at the small Egyptian-Sudanese outpost of Fashoda. France, finding itself at a military disadvantage, withdrew, but the Fashoda Incident was almost enough to make France forget Alsace-Lorraine and turn to Germany for help against Britain. France's ally Russia also posed a major threat to Britain. Its push toward the Dardenelles made Britain fear for its control of the Mediterranean and Suez. Russian pressure on Persia and Afghanistan threatened the British colony of India. Russian movement into Manchuria, Korea, and northern China challenged the British position in southern China as well.

Compared to Britain's problems with France and Russia, Bismarck's cautious probes for colonies in Africa and the Pacific (such as Samoa) seemed minor and temporary irritants. Neither Bismarck nor Kaiser Wilhelm looked on Great Britain with any special enmity, although both German statesmen found it necessary to protect the imperial throne and the aristocratic class structure against rising German liberalism by appealing to German nationalism with bold foreign policy adventures that challenged the position of Britain and its empire.

Bismarck had managed to keep his expansionist initiatives limited enough to avoid provoking a permanent alliance of offended powers against him. The kaiser did not. He angered London by demanding that it leave railroad concessions in Turkey to Germany, and he began to build a railroad to Baghdad. He sent his flamboyant Jameson telegram of support to the Boers of South Africa and in it denied British claims to the Transvaal. To support his push for overseas colonies, he began a huge naval building program in 1897 and extended it in 1900. The fleet he built in his North Sea ports seemed aimed particularly at Great Britain's traditional naval supremacy. At the instigation of the kaiser's chief naval advisor, Grand Admiral Alfred von Tirpitz, Germany constructed battleships capable of taking on the British fleet, rather than fast cruisers that might raid colonial commerce. The kaiser and Tirpitz drummed up domestic support for their heavy naval expenditures with shrill anti-British rhetoric.

A surge of German industrial and military growth accompanied all these developments. For two centuries France had been the major continental power, but by 1910 Germany towered over its rival. Germany led France in population by 65 to 39 million, in coal production by 222 to 38 million tons, in steel by 14 to 3 million tons. The German army also replaced that of France as the most powerful in Europe. Germany pioneered the efficient general staff system, the development of elaborate contingency war plans, and the use of masses of trained civilian reserves to supplement professional troops. After 1910, Germany sought to improve on its advantages by doubling its military appropriation. None of its neighbors could afford to match this expenditure.

Even before 1910, the British began to fear that Germany could overrun France and the Low Countries, which would make possible a successful invasion of England. Since Germany's industrial output surpassed that of Great Britain as well as France, and since Germany's navy seemed intent on challenging British supremacy, Britain grew nervous about its policy of "splendid isolation" and the emphasis on imperial affairs. To counter Germany's threat to the European balance of power, the British sought to resolve their conflicts with the United States. Great Britain accepted a secondary status in the American sphere and returned its Western Hemisphere fleet to home waters to guard against the German threat from the Continent. It concluded an alliance with Japan in 1902 to protect British interests in East Asia, thus enabling it to bring home major elements of its Asian fleet as well. It began a bitter internal debate over whether it was necessary to abandon its open market policy in the British Empire to protect British commerce from the rising economic power of Germany. Finally, in 1904, Great Britain and France determined to put aside the bitterness of the Fashoda Incident and move toward a closer understanding. France traded its claims in Egypt for British support of the French colonial position in the rest of North Africa.

THE UNITED STATES AND THE EUROPEAN BALANCE OF POWER: THE ALGECIRAS CONFERENCE

The reconciliation between Great Britain and France shocked Germany. Leading German diplomats wanted to disrupt the Anglo-French entente before it could be extended from a minor colonial agreement to a continental alliance aimed against Germany. They believed that if they challenged French control of Morocco, where Germany also had some treaty claims, Great Britain would back away and expose the hollowness of its support for France. The German army approved the timing of this challenge because France's ally, Russia, had been at least temporarily shattered by its humiliating defeat in the Russo-Japanese War of 1904 and the subsequent abortive revolution of 1905. The German navy, however, opposed the Moroccan maneuver because its fleet was not ready to confront Great Britain. Even the kaiser was reluctant to trigger a crisis at that moment. Nevertheless, his foreign policy advisors bullied him into a visit to Morocco, where he delivered a speech encouraging the sultan to resist French supervision and make an independent agreement with Germany. Caught between the great powers, the sultan appealed for an international conference to resolve the issue.

Although the United States had stood apart from these European struggles, Kaiser Wilhelm sought the support of Theodore Roosevelt for the German position on Morocco. Wilhelm appealed to America's time-honored dislike of European colonialism and desire for open doors for trade by insisting that Germany sought nothing more than equality of treatment for all nations in Morocco. He warned that war might result if France disregarded German rights and interests in North Africa, and that the victors might then partition China to America's disadvantage. The German ambassador to the United States, Roosevelt's personal friend Speck von Sternburg, tried to give further emphasis to the kaiser's goodwill toward the United States by writing Roosevelt that the kaiser would accept any advice Roosevelt chose to give him for a settlement. (Sternburg had been authorized only to say that the foreign ministry would urge the kaiser to abide by Roosevelt's suggestions.)

Roosevelt responded to this extraordinary expression of Germany's respect with much flattery and words of sympathy. But after the Venezuela crisis, Roosevelt harbored some concern for the growth of German power and intentions in the Western Hemisphere. He was more favorably disposed toward Great Britain because the British had removed the last barrier to Anglo-American friendship in 1903 by accepting the decision of an American-stacked commission on the disputed border between Canada and Alaska. So Roosevelt determined to use the influence Sternburg's indiscreet letter had given him to back France and preserve the Anglo-French entente in the face of German threats. He persuaded France to accept the call for a conference by promising that the United States would participate and support France against any German demands that Roosevelt considered unreasonable. Roosevelt hoped the conference would avoid war and at the same time maintain the balance of power against Germany's growing strength.

America's official delegates to the Algeciras Conference of 1906 operated strictly as observers. Behind the scenes, however, Roosevelt persuaded a reluctant Kaiser Wilhelm to accept French dominance in Morocco by threatening to publish Sternburg's letter, which supposedly committed the kaiser to abide by Roosevelt's advice. Afterward, Roosevelt ingenuously congratulated the kaiser on a diplomatic triumph. Thus Roosevelt had helped avert war and maintain the Anglo-French entente. But, to his great frustration, he had to keep the full extent of his role in the outcome secret because he knew he had no support from the American people for meddling in European politics.

ISSUE OF NEUTRAL RIGHTS ON THE EVE OF WAR

Roosevelt did not have to be so secretive about his role in the Second Hague Peace Conference of 1907. Like the First Hague Conference of 1899, the second conference was called by the Russian czar to discuss means of preventing or limiting war, and the American public approved of such efforts. But the results were disappointing. The conferees could not agree on military budget limitations, restrictions on the size of ships, reduction of army enlistment terms, or the composition and powers of a world court. They did agree on a modified version of the Drago Doctrine prohibiting forcible debt collection unless the debtor state refused arbitration, but most Latin American nations refused to sign.

In the Second Hague Conference's one concrete accomplishment, the conferees managed to set up an International Prize Court of Appeals to judge cases involving neutral rights on the high seas. Unfortunately, they could not agree on the neutral rights it was supposed to enforce. They scheduled a conference for the following year to devise such a code, and surprisingly the British reversed their naval policy of centuries to agree to a broad range of neutral rights. The resultant formulation of international law, embodied in the Declaration of London of 1909, seemed to eliminate the issue that had driven Great Britain and the United States to war in 1812 and had hung over Anglo-American relations ever since.

But the Declaration of London masked internal disagreements over maritime issues in both nations, disagreements that would play a vital role in America's entry into World War I. Just as American diplomats were winning the long struggle for neutral rights at the Hague and London conferences, Alfred Thayer Mahan and some other important naval officers had changed their views of America's interest in that struggle. Since the United States had become a major naval power, they wanted to avoid restrictions on the navy's operations and adopt the old British view of belligerent rights. (Some of these officers had the inflated notion that the Union navy had won the Civil War for the North by invoking the doctrine of continuous voyage to prevent neutrals from trading with the Confederacy through Mexico and thus circumventing the Union blockade.) For once Theodore Roosevelt ignored such strategic balance of power arguments and nonchalantly instructed his delegates to the London conference, including Mahan, to continue their traditional advocacy of neutral rights. The other delegates overcame Mahan's obstructionism and negotiated the London agreement.

The British delegation endorsed the Declaration of London amid almost equal confusion. The British navy supported the declaration's provisions on neutral rights because the admirals no longer thought it necessary to stop all neutral trade with Europe in wartime. If war broke out with Germany, the British navy planned only a limited blockade sufficient to draw the German battle fleet out of port so it could be destroyed. Thus Great Britain would not need to invoke the doctrine of continuous voyage to stop neutral trade from reaching Germany through nonbelligerent neighbors like the Netherlands. The British navy also was willing to restrict the contraband list, for the British Isles were far more dependent on imported food than they had been in Napoleonic times, and the declaration would prohibit the confiscation of food shipments as contraband.

A number of British leaders, however, challenged this strategy. These leaders, who came to be known as Continentalists, worried that the French might abandon the entente if the navy strategy were followed. It would leave France the entire burden of fighting the Germans on land. Besides, most Continentalists assumed that the war would be over quickly, like the Austro-Prussian, Franco-Prussian and Russo-Japanese wars. (They assumed that the only exception to the rule of short wars in the previous half-century, the American Civil War, had degenerated into a lengthy war of attrition only because American military men were inept amateurs.) In such a short land war, a naval blockade, which took a long time to be effective, would be irrelevant.

The naval strategists and the Continentalists fought continuously among themselves and never fully rationalized British strategy. The Continentalists, with their assumption that the next war would be too brief for a blockade to be effective, had little more objection to the neutral rights protected by the Declaration of London than their naval rivals. But the bickering between the two groups made it possible for those outside either clique to make their voices heard. Many of these outsiders in Parliament and the press denounced the declaration for giving up too many belligerent rights, while others condemned it for placing too few restrictions on the capture of food as contraband. Even politicians who considered such objections silly had difficulty resisting the political gains to be made by attacking the declaration. Consequently, Parliament deferred ratification time and again. When war finally came in 1914, the British still had not formally ratified the declaration, and as the war dragged on they once again turned to a rigid blockade that violated the neutral rights the Americans and the Germans had both assumed would be universally accepted.

THE OUTBREAK OF WORLD WAR I

While the Second Hague Conference and London Conference were seeking international agreement, Great Britain came to its own private arrangement with its long-time antagonist, Russia. Great Britain had believed it necessary to find some common ground with the ally of its entente partner. Russia, after its defeat at the hands of the Japanese, was ready to forego the Asian ambitions that clashed with British interests and return its attention to European questions, particularly the Balkans. In this atmosphere, the British successfully urged the reconciliation of the interests of their Japanese ally with Russia, reached an accommodation with Russia on the Persian approaches to India, and tabled their historic opposition to Russian ambitions for the Dardenelles. This Anglo-Russian Entente of 1907 quickly brought cries of "encirclement" fron Kaiser Wilhelm and his allies.

But the two great European alliances were not yet facing one another with unalloyed enmity. Russia and Austria even worked out a secret Balkan deal. Russia would stand by while Austria annexed Bosnia; Austria would not object when Russia took the Dardanelles. Suddenly, Austria double-crossed its rival in the Balkans by annexing Bosnia before Russia was ready to move. This added to the legacy of bitterness between the two nations. Tensions increased during the Second Balkan War of 1912–1913 in which Serbia, a Russian client and the chief Balkan instigator of the Slavic nationalism that threatened to destroy the Austro-Hungarian Empire, acquired another great bite of Turkey's territory. When the heir to the Austro-Hungarian throne, the Archduke Franz Ferdinand, and his wife were assassinated in Bosnia's capital city of Sarajevo by Bosnian dissidents who had entered Sarajevo with help from the Serbian secret police, the stage was set for calamity.

Austria used the occasion to send an ultimatum to Serbia with demands for control over its internal affairs. Austria purposely made the demands harsh enough to force a Serbian rejection and provide a reason for war. Foolishly, Kaiser Wilhelm gave Austria a "blank check" and promised support for whatever action Austria thought necessary in the wake of the assassination of the Hapsburg heir. Russia, having already been humiliated once by Austria in the Bosnian annexation affair, believed it could not afford to stand by again while Austria swallowed Russia's Serbian protectorate. Russia mobilized its troops along the Austrian border, then extended the mobilization along its German border as well.

Mobilization in that era constituted a threat almost guaranteeing war, for a mobilized nation using modern transportation could conquer an unmobilized nation before any resistance could be mounted. So Germany mobilized against Russia. But Germany's plan for war with the entente, the so-called Schlieffen Plan, called for a holding action on the eastern front, where Germany thought the backward Russians would be very slow in bringing their potential force to bear, while an all-out invasion quickly conquered a more formidable France. Consequently, Germany mobilized against the French as

Map 11   Alignment of the European Powers in World War I

well as the Russians, and the French responded with their own mobilization.

As the Continent plunged toward war, Great Britain wavered. The British cabinet appealed desperately for a mediated peace. It had forsworn British interests in the Balkans and might have stayed out of the war entirely if the conflict had remained limited to that area. But when the German armies slashed through neutral Belgium, threatening the conquest of France and the destruction of the continental balance of power, Great Britain honored its treaty obligations, declared war, and sent its expeditionary force to France.

The French and British finally managed to stop Germany's westward drive in the great Battle of the Marne. In turn, Germany thwarted a Russian invasion of Prussia. The war settled into a long and bloody stalemate. At the outset, the British had launched their long-planned attempt to draw the German fleet into battle by instituting a limited blockade of Germany. Then, as World War I degenerated into a prolonged war of attrition, Britain's allies pressed for a total blockage of trade to their enemies. The British never declared an official blockade. That would have required them to station ships directly at the mouth of German harbors, a suicidal action after the invention of long-range artillery and submarines. But the British found other ways to stop almost all trade to the Central Powers.

They turned away the United States request that all belligerents abide by the unratified Declaration of London. They extended the contraband list to include such American exports as copper, oil, lead, rubber, aluminum, and ultimately cotton. They declared food contraband on the pretext that the German government had nationalized all food distribution, even though the rumor of nationalization proved false. They used the doctrine of continuous voyage to extend their blockade to neutral Holland, arguing that food sent to the Netherlands was destined for Germany. The British navy even sowed mines northward from Scotland into the open ocean to block the approaches to the North Sea. These actions did more than contravene the unratified Declaration of London; they violated doctrines of international law that even Britain had accepted over the past two centuries.

WILSONIAN NEUTRALITY

Woodrow Wilson watched in horror and surprise as the world around him exploded into war. The first inkling that the Sarajevo crisis might bring general war did not reach him from his ministers abroad until the very day the shooting started. He had remarked on his accession to the presidency how ironic it would be if he, with all his preparation for presiding over domestic reforms, were called upon to lead the United States in a foreign war. Like all Americans, he was determined to stay out of the conflict. He told his countrymen to remain neutral in deed as well as name, impartial in thought as well as action.

Wilson's call for neutrality and his sincere desire to stay out of the war did not mean that he was personally impartial, however. He was a profound admirer of Great Britain's parliamentary tradition, and he regarded Germany as militaristic, brutal, and a threat to civilization. If Germany won the war, he feared it would "change the course of our civilization and make the United States a military nation." He told the British ambassador to the United States, "Everything that I love most in the world is at stake." These sentiments might not have been strong enough to push Wilson into immediate war with Germany, but they certainly determined him to avoid a clash with Great Britain over neutral rights. He did not want conflict between American exporters and the British fleet to bring the United States into the war on the wrong side, as Wilson believed had happened in 1812. Wilson did not suspect that the United States could be drawn into the war in any other way. Germany had neither the fleet nor the geographical proximity to clash with American interests or retaliate for America's tolerance of the British blockade. Wilson saw a conciliatory policy toward the British as the best way to gratify his desire to check the ambition of militaristic Germany and keep America out of the conflagration.

Despite Wilson's strong feelings about Great Britain and Germany, he did not immediately take full charge of American policy toward the war. His wife died a day after Great Britain declared war on Germany, and he spent much of the energy that remained to him shepherding his domestic reform program through Congress. He did not think it necessary to worry about the intricacies of neutral rights under international law in any case. He assumed, along with the Europeans, that the war would be over before the posture of the United States could have serious consequences.

With Wilson preoccupied, the task of shaping American policy fell largely to William Jennings Bryan, the ill-prepared secretary of state, and Robert Lansing, a narrow and somewhat devious international lawyer who served as the chief legal advisor to the State Department. Bryan left the technicalities of international law to Lansing and set out to restore peace in Europe. He offered immediate American mediation between the belligerents. Bryan either did not understand or did not think it important that immediate mediation would enable Germany to demand large concessions from the Allies, since the German invasion force had occupied much of Belgium and northern France in its march toward Paris. The shocked Allies rejected Bryan's mediation proposal and held their breath. If the Central Powers accepted, Germany might appear to the United States as the advocate of peace and win American public opinion.

Fortunately for the Allies, the German chancellor, Theobold von Bethmann Hollweg, rejected Bryan's offer. Bethmann would have been happy to have accepted and escaped from the war with minimal annexations, but his country was split. The right wing was buoyed by the early German victories and demanded that the war be pursued until the Allies conceded Belgium, Poland, the Baltic states, parts of France, and the dismemberment of much of the British Empire. The German left wing, having debated furiously within itself whether its duty to the international laboring class and peace out-

Figure 12   Secretary of State William Jennings Bryan (center) and his State Department staff on the eve of World War I. Photo courtesy of the National Archives.

weighed its duty to support the fatherland, had assuaged its conscience after deciding for war by insisting that the conflict was purely defensive and should end with no annexations. Bethmann tried to pacify the two sides with a "diagonal policy," contriving to agree with both and remaining silent on war aims until the progress of the war brought some hope of agreement between the factions. His rejection of Bryan's mediation proposal bought him some time, but at the cost of sacrificing his best chance to ensure that the most powerful of all noncombatant nations did not come into the war against Germany.

If Bryan did not understand the significance of his actions, another of Wilson's entourage did. "Colonel" Edward M. House held no official position in Wilson's administration, but he was the president's closest confidant and advisor. He was a wily, soft-spoken, somewhat effeminate man who managed to remain close to the strong-willed president by listening well, avoiding any contradiction of Wilson, and accompanying all suggestions with abundant flattery while insinuating that his ideas were mere rephrasings of Wilson's own. He played on Wilson's idealism and vanity with great virtuosity. This honorary Texas colonel felt even more strongly than Wilson that the Allies were fighting a war for civilization. He was not anxious to see Germany totally defeated and the balance of power in Europe destroyed, but he certainly did not want to see a German victory of any sort. He warned Wilson against Bryan's mediation approach, and Wilson privately agreed to entrust Colonel House with any further attempts at mediation. House henceforth would be sure to clear all diplomatic initiatives with the Allies before presenting them to the Central Powers. This would ensure that the United States would never be lined up with Germany, pressing the Allies to accept unwanted peace terms.

Meanwhile, Robert Lansing was trying to devise a response to Great Britain's announcement that it intended to ignore or revise parts of the Declaration of London in order to stop German commerce. Lansing composed a rather stiff note of protest. Colonel House told Wilson that the note was exceedingly undiplomatic, and Wilson decided to pursue private negotiations with the British to remove any bones of contention that might bring conflict. During a month of quiet contacts, Wilson and his advisors tried to induce the British to make at least sufficient gestures to America's neutral rights to avoid raising a popular outcry among the American people that might force the government into a hostile posture. The British refused to do anything that might restrict their naval warfare, so Wilson and Lansing finally issued a blunt official protest to Britain's policies. But they made clear in subsequent contacts that they would not push a general protest to the breaking point. Instead, they would protest each individual case of interference with American ships or goods as it came up and would be willing to accept a settlement after the war.

The relieved British continued to tighten their blockade and to funnel all American goods to themselves and their allies. Wilson's protests were muted, and so were those of American shippers and exporters. Accelerated trade with Great Britain more than offset the loss of potential trade with Germany. Vast exports of food, raw materials, and arms to the British revived an American economy that had been in a recession since 1911.

Meanwhile, Wilson made several other decisions that encouraged the growth of this one-sided trade with the Allies. At the outset of the war, Wilson and Bryan had decided to forbid private citizens from making loans to the belligerents. Soon it became clear that Great Britain would not have the ready cash to continue its volume of purchases. Without credits from American suppliers and banks, the booming trade that was lifting the United States out of recession would dry up. Wilson, with Bryan's reluctant consent, quietly removed the ban on private loans. There was nothing legally unneutral about the decision; international law did not forbid loans to belligerents from neutrals. Germany itself agitated for removal of the ban, unaware as yet that the Allied blockade would be effective enough to prevent supplies Germany might buy on credit from reaching the Central Powers.

In another significant decision concerning his nation's neutral stance, Wilson refused to prohibit exports of arms to the nations at war. Again, this was no violation of neutrality: All belligerents would have the right to purchase American arms, and Germany did not argue with the decision at first. Only after it became clear that the British blockade would ensure that the

Allies alone benefited from neutral armaments did Germany object. Wilson refused to change his mind. He believed that a ban on arms shipments would encourage militarism, since the neutral arms trade would benefit primarily nations that had not made prewar preparedness a fetish. Wilson also argued that to revise America's neutral stance in midwar after the course of combat had made it disadvantageous to one or the other of the belligerents would itself be unneutral.

Finally, Wilson refused to order a strong protest against the British mining of the North Sea approaches. Since American ships preferred the English Channel route, the mines did little or no harm to American trade, and Wilson did not think the issue warranted the risk of conflict with Britain.

THE GERMAN RESPONSE: SUBMARINE WARFARE

Throughout the last months of 1914, the Germans protested long and loud against Great Britain's illegal interference with neutral trade to the Central Powers and against Washington's refusal to enforce those rights at the risk of conflict with the Allies. The German navy was particularly frustrated. Its battle fleet was too weak to meet the British navy head-on; it had to remain in port and watch helplessly as the British fleet swept up German merchant ships and then proceeded to stop neutral vessels headed for Germany or any other nation that might trade with the Central Powers. The only ships in the German navy that did anything at all in the early days of the war were a few submarines which, through a combination of luck and British carelessness, managed to sink four aged British warships. The German navy formerly had regarded U-boats as experimental and auxillary craft, but these early successes seemed to promise a chance for the navy to help win the war. The submarines might turn the tables on Great Britain and blockade the British Isles. Great Britain was far more dependent on overseas commerce than Germany, and an effective blockade would be devastating to the Allied cause.

Unfortunately for Germany, an attempt to blockade England with submarine warfare inevitably would run afoul of international law. International law permitted enemy warships to be sunk on sight, but required that merchant or passenger ships be warned and that safety be provided for their crew and passengers before they could be sunk. Submarines were unable to fight under such rules. Even small weapons could penetrate their thin hulls, and a merchant or passenger ship was perfectly capable of ramming a U-boat if the submarine surfaced to give warning.

Germany could afford to ignore such niceties in its dealings with the British, since the British already were doing as much harm to Germany as they could. But Germany could not afford to offend the United States to the point that it joined the Allies. Submarine warfare had the potential to do just that. Under international law, citizens of neutral nations had the right to work or travel aboard belligerent merchant or passenger vessels. If Germany violated international law by failing to warn civilian belligerent ships and provide for the safety of passengers and crew, it might kill American citizens as well as British subjects. Germany also had to fear that submarines, operating under conditions that made visibility very difficult, might sink American ships by mistake. British ships often used the ruse of sailing under an American flag, which increased the chances of mistaken sinkings even further.

Chancellor Bethmann Hollweg thought these were reasons enough to avoid the use of submarines against British commerce. He believed that American entry into the war would be fatal to Germany's hope for victory. And he did not think the submarine could effectively blockade the British Isles in any case. In early 1915, Germany possessed a grand total of twenty-one submarines, of which only about half could be on station at any one time. This was far too few to sink the hundreds of ships carrying goods to the Allies. Germany had estimated before the war that it would take 221 submarines to mount an effective blockade. But German naval officers maintained that a U-boat campaign could frighten ships from even attempting to reach Great Britain. These officers ignored the disparity between the force they previously had insisted would be necessary and the U-boat fleet they actually had. They wanted to get the German navy into the war. Admiral von Tirpitz warned his fellow officers: "If we come to the end . . . without the fleet having bled and worked, we shall get nothing more for the fleet, and all the scanty money that there may be will be spent on the army."

Tirpitz orchestrated a colorful newspaper campaign on behalf of submarine warfare and raised considerable sentiment for it among the right and center parties in the German Reichstag. The admiral also made use of his privilege as a military leader to carry his argument directly to Kaiser Wilhelm without having to go through the civilian chancellor. Tirpitz finally won over the emperor to a declaration of U-boat warfare in February 1915. That declaration established a war zone around Great Britain in which enemy merchant ships would be sunk without warning. Germany suggested that neutrals keep their citizens and goods off belligerent vessels, and also warned that neutral ships might be sunk in cases of mistaken identity. Germany acknowledged that its actions went beyond the customary rules of warfare, but argued that this was justified as reprisal against Great Britain's flagrant violations of international law and neutral rights.

WILSON'S TEMPORARY VICTORY: "HE KEPT US OUT OF WAR"

Woodrow Wilson had several options when he realized that Germany's declaration of submarine warfare would endanger American citizens and ships. William Jennings Bryan urged him to do nothing that would endanger America. He advised Wilson to treat Germany as he treated Great Britain—protest, but reserve settlement until after the war. He further asked Wilson to warn American passengers and seamen away from belligerent vessels and to couple his protest to Germany with one to Great Britain against its violations of neutral rights. Thus Wilson would be able to retreat from his protests by claiming that both belligerents violated American rights and that neither was worthy of American sacrifice.

Although none of Wilson's advisors suggested it, later critics of Wilson and American entry into World War I have argued that there was a better way to avoid the war. Wilson could have forced Great Britain to respect American neutral rights and to abandon much of the blockade by embargoing supplies and credits to the Allies or convoying neutral ships and goods to Germany. Internal British cabinet reports and memos indicate that the British probably would have backed down rather than face a confrontation with American convoy escorts or loss of American materiel. But wartime emotions made the British response unpredictable, and an embargo or convoys could have led to war with Great Britain. It also is doubtful that enforcing neutral rights would have deterred Germany's decision for submarine warfare. Germany did not embark on submarine warfare in retaliation for the British blockade or American lack of neutrality; it did so because German leaders gambled that the submarine could win the war. Only the threat of war with the United States kept the German navy from sinking any ships sailing toward Great Britain. To avoid confrontation with Germany, Wilson would have had to keep all American vessels and citizens away from the waters around Great Britain or to overlook it when submarines attacked them.

Wilson was not willing to do that. He regarded submarine warfare on civilian vessels as a drastic and barbaric challenge to international law and humanity. He sent a stiff note to Germany warning that the United States would take "any steps necessary to safeguard American lives and property" and would hold Germany to a "strict accountability" for the actions of its U-boats.

Wilson's "strict accountability" note bristled like an ultimatum but it fell short of one. It did not say whether Germany would be held accountable before or after the war, and Bryan signed the note thinking it meant afterward. Wilson encouraged Bryan's hopes that "strict accountability" did not presage war when he sent a parallel protest to Great Britain, albeit a far weaker one, warning against the use of the American flag as a ruse by British ships. His policy in the weeks following issuance of the note cast further doubt that Wilson was prepared to enforce his protest at the risk of war. The United States sent a note to Germany suggesting that the Germans trade their submarine warfare on merchant ships for a British promise to permit foodstuffs to reach Germany. As Wilson and the State Department wrestled with the new and complex issues surrounding the use of undersea weapons, protests against German sinkings that affected American ships or property were delayed and muted. During a brief period of German fright at the "strict accountability" note, Bethmann urged revocation of the submarine order to prevent American entry into the war. But the Germans soon concluded that Wilson was not prepared to fight. The kaiser then instructed submarine commanders to stop risking their own ships in the attempt to identify the nationality or nature of potential target vessels.

Sinkings increased. The British steamer *Falaba* went down, taking an American citizen with it. Another German submarine mistakenly torpedoed the American ship *Gullflight.* Wilson waited three weeks before protesting the *Falaba* incident and was still wrestling with the *Gullflight* issue when the destruction of the *Lusitania* abruptly ended his hesitation.

The *Lusitania* was a giant British passenger liner carrying over 1,900 people from New York to England. On May 7, 1915, a German submarine torpedoed it off the coast of Ireland, and it sank within twenty minutes. Nearly 1,200 passengers drowned, including 124 Americans. The Germans had posted signs in New York warning people not to sail on the ship, and they correctly claimed that the vessel carried some arms and ammunition. Germany thus felt the sinking was justified, and some Germans even celebrated it by declaring a school holiday.

Wilson and America were horrified at the deaths of over a thousand civilians; they were not yet accustomed to the routine killing of civilians in war. The British enhanced the shock of the *Lusitania* by releasing a report signed by the famous and respected British commentator on American life, Lord Bryce, which detailed and exaggerated German atrocities during the "rape" of Belgium.

At first Wilson reacted somewhat tentatively. He announced that America was a nation "too proud to fight." But then he sent a protest note to Germany harshly condemning the sinking of the *Lusitania* and calling for an end to submarine warfare against civilian ships. To strengthen the note even more, he deleted an indication that the United States might defer compensation until after the war. When Germany delayed its response, he sent a second and still harsher note. He rejected Bryan's advice to couple his notes with parallel protests against the British, even though the British had exploited the period of outrage against the sinking of the *Lusitania* to tighten their blockade drastically. Wilson also refused the suggestion of his secretary of state that he order Americans off belligerent ships and out of the war zone. Bryan refused to sign the second *Lusitania* note and resigned on June 8, complaining, "Colonel House has been Secretary of State, not I. I have never had your full confidence."

Wilson's reaction to the *Lusitania* convinced Bethmann that Germany had to stop torpedoing passenger ships or it would face a new and powerful enemy on the battlefield. The Army Chief of Staff, General Erich von Falkenhayn, agreed that the danger of American intervention outweighed the benefits of U-boat warfare, and he refused to support the adamant naval officers in a ferocious debate before the kaiser. The kaiser finally permitted Bethmann to prohibit submarine attacks on large passenger liners and to order greater caution against sinking neutral vessels, but Wilhelm insisted that the order be kept secret so Germany would not be seen as retreating. Since Wilson could not know that his protests had had some effect, he continued to press the case and relations remained tense. Then a German U-boat mistakenly sank the British passenger liner *Arabic,* and two Americans died in the attack. Wilson could only see this as an obdurate refusal to heed his warnings. Failure to take strong action would expose his protests as hollow and destroy both his own prestige and that of his nation.

Still, as in the *Lusitania* crisis, Wilson was willing to exert some patience. Rather than issue an immediate public ultimatum, he had his new secretary of state, Robert Lansing, privately inform the German ambassador that the United States would sever relations with Germany if it did not stop submarine attacks against innocent ships and passengers. The German ambassador, Count Johann von Bernstorff, violated his orders and informed Lansing of the earlier secret instructions against attacks on large passenger liners. He said the *Arabic* sinking was a mistake and promised compensation. Confusion and hesitation on the part of Berlin in confirming Bernstorff's promises caused new concern and consternation, but after another struggle between the navy and Bethmann for the mind of Kaiser Wilhelm, the German government gave a further public pledge that no passenger liners of any kind would be sunk. Bethmann also issued secret orders to withdraw all submarines from the west coast of England, where passenger liners most commonly traveled. Temporarily, Bethmann had managed to stifle the threat of American intervention. But the German navy and its political allies were merely biding their time. Winter and the shortage of U-boats would have rendered submarine warfare relatively ineffective for the following months anyway. The return of operational weather and the growth of the U-boat fleet would inevitably bring new pressures on the German chancellor.

Wilson could not know of the debates within the German hierarchy, but he was aware of how fragile America's peace was. He had staked the prestige of the nation on his warnings against illegal submarine warfare. If Germany embarked again on all-out U-boat warfare, he would face a choice between humiliating retreat and measures almost sure to bring war. Britain added its own reminders of possible future conflict with America: It placed cotton on the contraband list. As usual, the British waited until a German-American crisis could divert attention from the blow and issued the order immediately after the sinking of the *Arabic.* Britain also signed a contract to purchase large amounts of U.S. cotton to support the market price and pacify American farmers. Still, Wilson and Lansing felt they had to respond with a long and detailed protest against British policies toward neutral trade.

Such tensions convinced Wilson that the only sure way the United States could stay out of the hostilities and maintain its honor was to end the war. He approved a plan offered to him by Colonel House that involved an enormous gamble to bring the war to an end through American mediation. Wilson would call for a peace conference and threaten war against whichever side refused. But first House would consult with the Allies and, by promising that American mediators at the conference would be sympathetic to Allied war aims, ensure that they would not be the ones to refuse. House went to London and induced the British cabinet to accept this plan, as embodied in the so-called House-Grey Memorandum.

Wilson would wait until the Allies informed him that the military situation was propitious. Then he would issue a call for a peace conference. If Germany refused, the United States *probably* would join the Allies in the war. If Germany agreed to the conference but then rejected reasonable terms of peace, the United States *probably* would leave the conference a belligerent on the side of Great Britain. (Wilson personally added the "probablies" to this memorandum of understanding, the first before House negotiated it with the British, the second afterward.) Meanwhile, House tried to tempt the Germans to accept the call for a peace conference by telling them that Great Britain was unlikely to accept. At the same time, he assured the Allies that the peace conference was nothing but a gimmick to pave the way for American intervention on the side of Britain and France.

Wilson's wait for the British signal to call the conference and mediate a peace was interminable. The British never did decide the time was propitious. David Lloyd George, the new British prime minister, later claimed that Wilson's "probablies" undermined the whole plan. No doubt he worried even more that Wilson's ideas of reasonable terms could never satisfy the war aims the Allies had developed during a year of bloody warfare. France would not be satisfied without moving Germany out of Alsace-Lorraine and all other lands west of the Rhine. Great Britain would insist on the reduction of the German fleet. Both would want Germany weakened so it could not attack through Belgium again. Russia insisted on concessions in the Balkans. Only a complete Allied victory, not a Wilson-mediated peace, could achieve those goals.

Wilson became desperate for Britain to give him the signal to call the conference, because by the time House returned to America in February of 1916, the danger of American intervention had increased drastically. On February 10, Germany had announced resumption of submarine warfare against armed merchant ships. Bethmann thought he could get away with this because while House had been bouncing around Europe, Secretary of State Lansing had been trying to work out a *modus vivendi* between Germany and Great Britain. Lansing wanted the British to cease arming merchant ships in return for Germany abandoning submarine sinkings of unarmed ships without warning. The British rejected this trade of a practice long sanctioned by international law for a submarine warfare they regarded as totally illegal. Bethmann thought this British rejection would dispose Wilson and Lansing to accept resumption of U-boat attacks on armed merchants.

But German U-boats "mistakenly" sank many neutral merchants and one Dutch passenger liner. It was only a matter of time before a ship went down with American passengers or a submarine sank an American merchant vessel. Many members of Congress tried to forestall the crisis by promoting the Gore-McLemore Resolutions, warning Americans off armed merchant ships or ships carrying contraband. Wilson defused this movement with a letter to the chairman of the Senate Foreign Relations Committee refusing to accept a single abatement of American rights. Then, on March 24, a submarine attacked the French channel steamer *Sussex*. The *Sussex* did not sink, but eighty people died and four of the twenty-five Americans aboard suffered serious injury.

Wilson sent the Germans a public ultimatum. The United States would break relations if Germany did not halt all submarine attacks on passenger and freight-carrying ships, armed or unarmed. Bethmann had anticipated such a crisis. He had convinced the kaiser that since the German navy did not possess enough U-boats to blockade Great Britain effectively, continuation of submarine warfare was not worth the risk of war with the United States. Bethmann also had maneuvered the resignation of Admiral von Tirpitz. This enabled him to answer Wilson's protest with amazing concessions. The German note conceded that the attack on the *Sussex* had been wrong and promised no further sinkings without warning. This *Sussex* pledge was a remarkable victory for Wilson's diplomacy. Wilson campaigned for and won the presidency in 1916 with the slogan, "He kept us out of war."

AMERICA ENTERS THE WAR

In the euphoria that followed the *Sussex* pledge, few noticed that Germany's *Sussex* note claimed the right to resume submarine warfare if the United States did not compel Great Britain to respect international law. No one in America could know that the German navy was continuing to build U-boats with the intention of reopening the issue when it had enough to enforce an effective blockade of Great Britain. Nor could Americans know that Bethmann was losing his power to resist the naval campaign. General Paul von Hindenburg had replaced Falkenhayn in command of the German armies, and he and his chief subordinate, General Erich Ludendorff, had enough influence with the kaiser to override Bethmann on the U-boat if they chose. The Centre party also gave up its opposition to the submarine campaign, depriving Bethmann of his parliamentary majority in the Reichstag. Bethmann decided his only chance to prevent all-out submarine warfare in the near future was to make peace.

Bethmann had at least a slim chance to succeed in getting American support for a peace conference. Once the *Sussex* pledge seemingly ended the crisis with Germany, Wilson had turned harshly on Great Britain. He was disillusioned by Britain's refusal to ask him for mediation in line with the House-Grey Memorandum, and he was increasingly angered by British contempt for American neutral rights. He was prepared to offer neutral mediation and call for peace terms from both sides without preconditions, a dangerous course for the Allies so long as Germany had the military advantage and occupied Allied territory.

Wilson recognized this danger and it caused him to hesitate, especially after Germany began to deport Belgian civilians to work in German factories.

In the interim Bethmann asked the neutral powers, including the United States, to communicate to Great Britain an offer of a peace conference. Wilson proposed his own mediation as a substitute. He claimed that the objects for which each side said it was fighting were "virtually the same" and invited the belligerents to send him their peace terms. Bethmann refused to take this last chance to split America and the Allies. He distrusted Wilson and the Americans, so he refused Wilson's mediation offer and insisted on talking directly to the Allies.

The British did not make the same mistake. They were greatly offended that Wilson could equate their objectives with those of the German militarists and they feared that Wilson's mediation offer was part of a German plot, but they were coaxed to give an answer by Secretary of State Lansing. Lansing had no desire to see the British refuse to answer and cast themselves as the enemy of Wilson's ambition to be a peacemaker. Lansing believed the true policy of the United States should be to "join the Allies as soon as possible and crush the German Autocrats." He assured the British and French that Wilson's mediation offer was not part of the German proposal and that the president preferred the democracies enough to support any demands they might devise. Lansing even encouraged the Allies to make their peace terms as extreme as they wished. Lansing's unauthorized maneuvers helped convince Great Britain to spell out its war aims, and it was even more encouraged to do so when Germany refused to state its own terms.[1]

The Allies insisted on restoration of all territories conquered by the Central Powers, by which it turned out they meant Alsace-Lorraine as well as Belgium, Serbia, Montenegro, and parts of France, Russia, and Rumania. They also demanded liberation of the nationalities dominated by the Austro-Hungarian Empire and Turkey, along with reparations for war damages. Wilson considered these demands a bluff and continued private negotiations with the belligerents. He added pressure to his peace initiative by making a dramatic speech to the Senate in which he appealed brilliantly for "peace without victory," a peace that would replace the balance of power with a community of power. The peace settlement would be based on the concepts of national self-determination, government by consent of the governed, arms limitations, and freedom of the seas. He promised that the United States would contribute its power to a league of nations designed to maintain this peace.

Wilson did not know that his great appeal for mediation and peace was doomed before he set foot in the Senate. The British believed that there could be no return to the *status quo ante bellum* and that only an Allied victory could produce the world Wilson desired. They also feared they might lose the war unless the United States intervened soon on their side. They essen-

---

[1] Historians still debate why Lansing wrote such strong protest notes against the British blockade early in the war if he was so pro-Allied. Opponents of American entry like Charles Tansill have speculated that he changed his policy to conform to the opinion of Colonel House in hopes of furthering his own career. Others, like Daniel Smith, argue that his initial response was simply that of a narrow legal mind confronted with violations of international law.

tially ignored Wilson's initiative and hoped it would go away. The Germans too believed that the war must end in a victorious rather than a compromise peace, and they too feared they would lose the war if it continued much longer. But they knew the United States would not enter on their side to save them. They put their faith instead in their submarines.

By January 1917 Germany had nearly a hundred U-boats, and the navy claimed that if given free rein, these submarines could reduce Great Britain to starvation in six months. Germany's leaders realized that renunciation of the *Sussex* pledge would mean American intervention, but they gambled that they could win the war before the United States could do much to help the Allies. The choice seemed to be between winning the war quickly with the submarine or losing without it. The kaiser secretly decided on January 9, nearly two weeks before Wilson's "Peace without Victory" speech, to launch unrestricted submarine warfare. On February 1, the German government announced that its U-boats would sink without warning all ships sailing in the war zone around Great Britain, including neutral vessels. This was the first time Germany had declared it would sink American ships purposely. The United States would have to fight or back down ignominiously from the stand it had taken since the sinking of the *Lusitania.*

Wilson immediately broke relations with Germany and pressed the Germans to go back to the *Sussex* pledge. But he did not ask Congress for a declaration of war; he told the Senate he would wait for "overt acts" before taking extreme measures. Three weeks later, the British turned over to the United States a telegram to Mexico from the German foreign secretary, Arthur Zimmermann. Zimmermann proposed an alliance between Germany, Mexico, and Japan against the United States if America joined the war, and he offered to help Mexico regain the territory it had lost in the Mexican War. This Zimmermann telegram convinced Wilson that Germany preferred war to abandonment of its submarine campaign. Two days later, Wilson asked Congress for permission to arm American merchant ships to resist German attacks. A Senate filibuster by what Wilson condemned as "a little group of willful men" blocked the measure. So Wilson ordered this interim step toward war on his own authority. He hoped arming American merchant vessels might be enough to protect American ships and avoid full-scale war. But within two weeks he received news that German submarines had sunk three American ships with the loss of fifteen lives. After two more days of mental agony and soul-searching, he accepted the advice of his cabinet and asked Congress for a formal declaration of war.

Wilson accepted that tragic alternative with immense sorrow, but with one great consolation. If the United States was an active and powerful participant in the war, Wilson would have great influence over the peace settlement. He would have the opportunity to create a just peace that would promote democratic government and eliminate the causes of war that had plagued the Old World for so long. Since the February Revolution in Russia had just overthrown the czar and installed a democratic socialist government, Wilson could portray the war against Germany to himself and the American people as one of free nations against militaristic tyrannies. In ringing tones he asked Congress to enlist the United States in a crusade to "make the world safe for democracy."

CONTROVERSIAL ISSUES AND FURTHER READING

The vast majority of historians of Wilson's day, like the vast majority of Congress and Americans at large, approved Wilson's decision for war and had no doubts about the reasons behind it. They agreed that Wilson had tried to be neutral. They approved Wilson's refusal to do more than protest British illegalities, for to have done more might have made Americans participants in the war on the side of Germany. This was unthinkable; Germany's violation of Belgian neutrality, its subsequent atrocities in that unhappy country, and its brutal submarine campaign confirmed that Germany was "a horrible menace to civilization" which, if it won the war, would form a great empire that would "dominate Europe and imperil the safety of the Americas." [John Bach McMaster, *The United States in the World War* (2 vols., 1918–1920). See also John Spencer Bassett, *Our War with Germany* (1919); Christian B. Gauss, *Why We Went to War* (1920); Carleton J. H. Hayes, *A Brief History of the Great War* (1920).] Historians who criticized Wilson argued only that he had not entered the war soon enough. Frederick A. Ogg censured the president for leading Americans to believe that they were unconcerned with the causes and objects of the Great War "until he and the country were rudely awakened by what had become clear to many much earlier—that this was a contest between democracy and autocracy," that the United States would have to fight imperialistic Germany alone if "the Teutonic powers" were victorious. John Holladay Latané shuddered to think that if Germany had not violated international law so flagrantly with its submarines, Wilson would have permitted a German victory and its grave consequences for the security of the Americas. [Frederick A. Ogg, *National Progress, 1907–1917* (1918); John Holladay Latané, *From Isolation to Leadership: A Review of American Foreign Policy* (1918). There was only one significant book criticizing Wilson for entering the war at all, socialist Scott Nearing's *The Great Madness* (1917).]

Within five years after the end of the war, historical opinion began to change. The refusal of the European powers at the Paris Peace Conference to abandon the more self-interested of their war aims in the interest of America's ideas of a just peace undermined the conviction that America had joined a crusade for democracy. Revelations from the historical archives of the defeated powers destroyed the Allies' accusation that Germany and Austria had purposely plotted world war. This raised further questions about why the United States should have intervened. Early critics of American intervention took a rather conspiratorial view of Wilson's decision for war. They accused munitions makers of pushing the Wilson administration into the conflict as a means of increasing their war profits. They charged that Wall Street bankers had maneuvered America into war to prevent the Allies from losing and then defaulting on the vast loans granted them by American financial institutions. Critics claimed that a vicious British propaganda campaign had twisted facts, created German atrocities out of whole cloth, and made use of Britain's control of the single communications cable to the United States to delude American opinion into supporting intervention on the side of the Allies. [John Kenneth Turner, *Shall It Be Again* (1922); C. Hartley Grattan, *Why We Fought* (1929); Harry Elmer Barnes, *The Genesis of the World War* (1927); Frederick Bausman, *Let France Explain* (1922) and *Facing Europe* (1926).]

Later, World War I revisionist critics returned a broader indictment. Charles Beard pointed out that America's high volume of trade with the Allies and the loans that encouraged it tied the prosperity of all Americans, not just big business, to the survival of the Allies. The original mistake of encouraging this trade gave the United States no choice but to intervene to save the British and French from defeat. Charles Tansill was not so ready to let big business off the hook in the most extensive of these revisionist studies. He argued that big business had influenced Wilson to encourage trade with the Allies in the first place and to violate America's neutral duties by refusing to make an effective challenge to Britain's illegal blockade. An embargo or convoy system would have broken the blockade easily and without danger of war with the dependent Allies. Germany would not have had to use the submarine, and America could have continued neutral. [Charles A. Beard, *The Devil Theory of War* (1936); Charles C. Tansill, *America Goes to War* (1936). See also Walter Millis, *The Road to War: America 1914–1917* (1936), and C. Hartley Grattan, *Preface to Chaos* (1936). These World War I revisionists, as opposed to the modern revisionists writing in the Cold War era, were very diverse politically. Turner and Grattan were socialists; Barnes, Beard, and Millis were disillusioned liberals; Tansill and Bausman were right-wing conservatives who detested the British Empire, partly because of their nineteenth-century American nationalism and, in Tansill's case at least, ethnic sympathies with the Irish and Germans. But their books did not reflect these political divisions. The socialists and liberals denounced British propaganda and America's pro-British bias as ardently as the conservatives, and the conservative Tansill denounced the influence of big business on intervention as thoroughly as those historians on the left.]

These World War I revisionist histories had a great impact on American opinion in the years before World War II. They helped lead Congress to pass a series of neutrality acts to prevent the United States from being drawn into World War II in the ways the revisionist historians claimed it had been drawn into World War I.

But Wilson had many defenders among historians as well as the population at large. These defenders argued that Wilson was the last person to have been influenced by big bankers or munitions makers. Wilson had defended neutral rights with no initial expectation that this would bring war, and then felt the United States could not abandon its stand in midwar without itself being unneutral. They agreed with Wilson that Germany's offenses were more heinous that Britain's, since submarine warfare destroyed people as well as property. If Wilson had instituted an embargo or convoy system, destroying American prosperity while risking war with Britain on the side of Germany, he would have provoked a revolt against his administration. Nothing Wilson could have done would have kept Germany from resorting to submarine warfare anyway. Germany had to stop all British trade to win the war, and this required either sinking or terrorizing neutral ships as well as Allied ones.

Yet even Wilson's defenders in this pre-World War II era no longer asserted, as the wartime historians had, that the United States had had to intervene to protect itself from invasion by a ruthless Germany bent on world conquest. They agreed that Wilson had intervened not to protect American security, but to defend America's neutral rights and prestige against submarine warfare. All agreed that Wilson had tried to maintain American neutrality and had joined the war only reluctantly. But one of his most prominent defenders, his official biographer and former press secretary Ray Stannard Baker, accused Wilson's advisors House and Lansing of disloyally trying to maneuver the president into the war. [Ray Stannard Baker, *Woodrow Wilson: Life and Letters* (6 vols., 1927–1937). Charles Seymour, *Woodrow Wilson and the World War* (1921), *American Diplomacy during the World War* (1934), and *American Neutrality, 1914–1917* (1935); Newton D. Baker, *Why We Went to War* (1936).]

World War II revived American fears of Germany as a menace to civilization and made the next generation of historians more willing to believe that American intervention in World War I had been essential. Walter Lippmann wrote a highly influential book during World War II in which he bewailed the naïveté he had shared with the American people and urged a return to a realistic foreign policy based on national interest and power politics. In the course of his argument, he claimed that Wilson had intervened in World War I on these realistic grounds, had recognized that unlimited submarine warfare would cut Atlantic communications, starve Great Britain, and leave the United States to face a "new and aggressively expanding German empire which had made Britain, France, and Russia its vassals, and Japan its ally." [Walter Lippmann, *U.S. Foreign Policy; Shield of the Republic* (1943).]

Other realist historians like George Kennan and Robert Osgood accepted the contention that Wilson should have intervened in the war to protect Britain and the balance of power. But they did not believe that Wilson or the American people had done so for that reason. Osgood conceded that House and Lansing might have thought intervention necessary to American security, but pointed out that Wilson paid his advisors little heed. In any case, most American interventionists, including the leaders of the preparedness campaign, had not thought of security in terms of the subtle interest the United States had in the European balance of power. They spoke instead of the chimerical threat of a direct German invasion of the United States or the Western Hemisphere.

Neither Wilson nor most Americans took the threat of a direct invasion seriously. Osgood pointed out that at the time Wilson and Congress made their decision for war, no one in the United States believed the U-boat campaign would break the great stalemate and defeat the Allies. It was only months later, when Great Britain was weeks from running out of food, that the prospect of German victory became imminent. Thus Wilson had chosen war because he was offended by German conduct, not because he thought it posed a threat to American survival. Wilson's failure to understand and explain America's self-interest in joining the war to preserve the European balance of power left the American people open to the suggestion that the United States had fought for no good reason at all, that it had been duped into rescuing the Allies by British propaganda and international bankers. Psychohistorians bolstered these contentions as they attempted to explain the strange quirk of character that had led Wilson to deal in rigid moralistic and legalistic terms with matters he should have handled pragmatically in terms of power and self-interest. [Robert E. Osgood, *Ideals and Self-Interest in American Foreign Policy: The Great Transformation* (1953); George Kennan, *American Diplomacy, 1900–1950* (1951). The best of the psychohistorical biographies is Alexander L. and Juliette L. George, *Woodrow Wilson and Colonel House: A Personality Study* (1956). The worst is by Sigmund Freud himself, with William C. Bullitt, *Thomas Woodrow Wilson: A Psychological Study* (1966). See also John M. Blum, *Woodrow Wilson and the Politics of Morality* (1956).]

A plausible defense of Wilson against this realist onslaught was slow to emerge. Even Arthur Link, most prominent of all Wilsonian scholars and defenders, at first accepted the realist contention that Wilson had ignored the hard-headed advice of

Lansing and House and gone to war because submarine warfare violated American neutral rights. He differed only in that he believed this reason was good and sufficient. [Arthur S. Link, *Woodrow Wilson and the Progressive Era, 1910–1917* (1954).] But Edward Buehrig noted Wilson's subtle recognition of the European balance of power in the president's hopes for a negotiated peace that would avoid total defeat of either the Allies or the Central Powers. Buehrig thought this showed Wilson was realistic, even though Wilson often said the peace should transcend balance of power considerations. [Edward H. Buehrig, *Woodrow Wilson and the Balance of Power* (1955).] Link seized on Buehrig's point. He admitted that Wilson might have contented himself with armed neutrality after Germany's declaration of unlimited submarine warfare if Germany had avoided sinking American ships. Thus he might have permitted a German victory. Yet his decision for war when German submarines did sink American ships represented more than just a defense of neutral rights; Wilson knew that failure to react strongly to the German provocation would have sacrificed all America's prestige and leverage abroad, giving him no chance to influence the peace. With what Link called a "higher realism," Wilson intervened at least in part to ensure that the peace would be a just one that did not sow the seeds of future war by inciting revenge or disrupting the balance of power. [Arthur S. Link, *Wilson: The Struggle for Neutrality, 1914–1915* (1960); *Wilson: Confusions and Crises, 1915–1916* (1964); *Wilson: Campaigns for Progressivism and Peace, 1916–1917* (1965); *Wilson the Diplomatist: A Look at His Major Foreign Policies* (1957), revised as *Woodrow Wilson: Revolution, War, and Peace* (1970).]

Most recent historians have accepted Link's formulation of Wilson's motivation. Their differences are subtle ones, except in their evaluations of Wilson's advisors. Some modern historians praise House and Lansing for their realism. Most follow Link (and Ray Stannard Baker of the earlier era) in arguing that House and Lansing were disloyal and devious. [Favorable to House and Lansing are Ernest May, *The World War and American Isolation, 1914–1917* (1959), still the best one-volume history of American intervention; Daniel S. Smith, *Robert Lansing and American Neutrality, 1914–1917* (1958), and *The Great Departure: The United States and World War I, 1914–1920* (1965). Closer to Link's view of House, Lansing, and Ambassador Walter Hines Page are Patrick Devlin, *Too Proud to Fight: Woodrow Wilson's Neutrality* (1975), which agrees that Wilson fought primarily to protect America's prestige but regards this motive with a more jaundiced eye than Link; Ross Gregory, *The Origins of American Intervention in the First World War* (1970), which diminishes Wilson's desire to shape the peace as a motive for his intervention; John Milton Cooper, Jr., *Walter Hines Page: The Southerner as American* (1977); and Julius W. Pratt, *Challenge and Rejection* (1967).]

Curiously, modern revisionists have not made much attempt to revive the earlier revisionist critiques of Wilson. [One exception, Sidney Bell's *Righteous Conquest: Woodrow Wilson and the Evolution of the New Diplomacy* (1972), is rather ham-handed and has generally been disregarded by recent historians.] John W. Coogan, however, has argued strongly that Wilson never was truly neutral by proper standards of international law, that he undermined the entire system of international relations by his favoritism toward Great Britain, and that even though it may have been to America's interest to prevent Germany from defeating the Allies, it was even more to America's interest to defend American neutrality, prevent a crushing victory by either side, and maintain both the balance of power and the prewar structure of international law. [John W. Coogan, *The End of Neutrality: The United States, Britain, and Maritime Rights, 1899–1915* (1981).]

Coogan also presented interesting new information on negotiations and strategic planning in Europe prior to World War I. [For further information on the plunge of Europe into the war, see Paul Kennedy, *The Rise of Anglo-German Antagonism* (1980); A. J. P. Taylor, *The Struggle for Mastery in Europe* (1954); Laurence Lafore, *The Long Fuse* (1965); Dwight E. Lee, *Europe's Crucial Years: The Diplomatic Background of World War I, 1902–1914* (1974); Samuel R. Williamson, *The Politics of Grand Strategy: Britain and France Prepare for War, 1904–1914* (1969); and Gerhard Ritter, *The Schlieffen Plan* (1979). On American-European relations prior to the Wilson administration, see Howard K. Beale, *Theodore Roosevelt and the Rise of America to World Power* (1956); Raymond Esthus, *Theodore Roosevelt and International Rivalries* (1970); Frederick Marks, *Velvet on Iron: The Diplomacy of Theodore Roosevelt* (1979); Calvin Davis, *The United States and the First Hague Peace Conference* (1962), and *The United States and the Second Hague Peace Conference* (1975). Richard Challener investigated American military planning and influence in *Admirals, Generals, and American Foreign Policy, 1898–1914* (1973), while Holger Herwig wrote of German planning for war with the United States in *The Politics of Frustration: The United States in German Naval Planning, 1889–1914* (1976).]

CHAPTER 12

The United States and the Peace of Versailles

AMERICA AND THE ALLIED VICTORY

The European Allies welcomed America's entry into World War I with a sigh of relief. American intervention seemed to assure their victory. They turned out to be correct, but by a far closer margin than they or the United States expected. The German submarine campaign proved frighteningly successful. U-boats sank one out of every four British merchant ships that left harbor. At one point in the early summer of 1917, Great Britain had on hand only a six-week supply of food. After much anguished debate, the British decided to change their naval tactics. They abandoned their attempts to sneak widely dispersed ships past the U-boats and instead concentrated them in convoys protected by destroyers. This convoy system, enhanced by America's contribution of destroyers, merchant vessels, and supplies, broke the back of the German submarine campaign.

In declaring war on Germany, Americans had expected to play a role as supplier, financier, and naval adjunct to the Allies. They had not expected to have to send large numbers of troops to fight the land war in Europe. At the time the United States intervened, the Allies seemed to have a comfortable edge in manpower over the Central Powers. The British and French armies on the western front commanded more than 2.5 million men against only 1.5 million Germans. That ratio changed, however, when the Bolsheviks took power in Russia in November 1917 and shortly afterward abandoned the war. The peace treaty Germany forced on Russia at Brest-Litovsk not only gave Germany access to the wheat fields of the Ukraine and the oil fields of the Caucasus to supply the continuing war against the western Allies, it also permitted the Germans to transfer a million men from the eastern to the western front.

With these reinforcements, Hindenburg and Ludendorff launched an all-out offensive to conquer France and win the war. The United States poured men into Europe to help stop it. While many of the 2 million Americans ultimately sent to Europe got there too late to be part of the major campaigns, their imminent arrival permitted France and Great Britain to throw their reserves into the final battles with confidence that replacements were on the way. Those Americans who arrived early fought valiantly in the battle that stopped the German offensive just short of Paris and then joined the counteroffensive that broke the German lines.

As the German armies reeled back toward their own territory, Ludendorff panicked. He beseeched the German government to negotiate an armistice immediately and save his army from disaster. Shortly thereafter, the Allied attack outran its supplies and communications, the counteroffensive bogged down, and Ludendorff realized he had time to establish a new line of defense. He did an abrupt about-face and demanded that the German government call off its peace initiative. But it was too late: The armies and the home front were demoralized. A moderate socialist government took control of Germany to make peace. In all probability, the continuing Allied blockade and American buildup would have forced a German surrender in a few more months. Ludendorff and the army, however, insisted they could have prevented defeat had they not been sold out by socialist and Jewish peacemongers at home. The German army shelled its own peace delegation as it returned from signing the armistice. The bitterness spawned within German ranks by the myth of the Jewish and socialist "stab in the back" held ominous implications for the future.

CONFLICTING PLANS FOR THE PEACE: WILSON'S "NEW DIPLOMACY" VERSUS EUROPE'S "OLD DIPLOMACY"

When the Germans sued for an armistice, they did not approach their old enemies, the British or the French; they turned instead to Woodrow Wilson. They quite rightly believed Wilson would be willing to give them better terms. Before the war, Wilson had made himself the supreme symbol of the idea of peace without victory, a peace of justice rather than revenge. To emphasize the distinction between the purposes of the United States and those of the Allies (as well as to cater to the historic American aversion to alliances), Wilson insisted that America was merely an "associate power" rather than one of the formal Allies.

Wilson reinforced his idealistic stance when the Bolsheviks announced that they were going to publish the secret territorial treaties the czar and the Allies had made among themselves. Publication promised to be a terrible blow to the domestic unity of the Allies, since many liberals in Great Britain, France, Italy, and the United States had supported the war only because they believed the Allies represented the ideals of democracy and peace against the aggressiveness and autocracy of the Central Powers. Wilson thought it essential to restore Allied idealism and asked the Allies to abandon their secret treaties and territorial demands. The Allies refused despite Colonel House's threat that the United States might make a separate peace. Consequently, on

January 8, 1918, Wilson unilaterally issued a lofty statement of war aims, the Fourteen Points.

The Fourteen Points and Wilson's later elaborations on them galvanized liberal opinion in America and the world. Wilson appealed for an end to the practices liberals believed were the basic causes for war—secret diplomacy, barriers to free international trade and navigation of the seas, arms races, and colonialism that took no account of the desires of the indigenous populations. Wilson also called for territorial adjustments in Europe designed not to cripple Germany, but to honor the wishes of the many different peoples of Europe for national self-determination. Under the rubric of self-determination, Wilson specified the return of Alsace-Lorraine to France, German evacuation of Belgium and Russia, adjustment of Italy's frontier with Austria according to nationality, autonomy for the peoples of eastern Europe long ruled by the Austro-Hungarian, Russian, German, and Ottoman Turkish empires, and the establishment of an independent Poland with access to the sea.

Most important, Wilson called for an international organization of nations to supervise the settlement. This League of Nations could provide a peaceful means of revising the final war settlement if that proved necessary. If some discontented nation tried to overthrow the treaty settlement by force, the League would provide an international alliance of powers to protect the independence and territorial integrity of the victim. No aggressor would ever be able to stand against such a force. Collective security would eliminate the need for secret treaty arrangements, contests for strategic borders, and all the other accoutrements of balance of power politics.

Wilson had a negative as well as a positive reason for seeking a generous policy toward the defeated Central Powers. He feared that a harsh peace would so demoralize the beaten Germans, Austrians, and Hungarians that they would be easy prey for Bolshevik revolutionaries. Wilson thought the best way to prevent Bolshevik revolutions in the ravaged nations of Europe was to eliminate the conditions that drove people to such desperate measures. He urged the Allies to lift the blockade during the armistice and get food to the starving people of the Central Powers. Meanwhile, the Allies would offer a generous peace on the condition that the defeated nations replace their militaristic governments with democratic ones. Wilson firmly believed that liberal democratic institutions and national self-determination offered the world the best protection against the war and suffering produced by the imperialism of the old aristocratic orders and against the revolutionary tyranny of the Bolsheviks.

Georges Clemenceau, the premier of France, came to symbolize European opposition to Wilson's New Diplomacy. Clemenceau remarked cynically, "God gave us the Ten Commandments, and we broke them. Wilson gives us the Fourteen Points. We shall see." He told Colonel House: "I can get on with you. You are practical. I understand you, but talking to Wilson is something like talking to Jesus Christ!" He was not willing to trust the League of Nations or the United States to prevent Germany from launching another attack on

France. He wanted Germany weakened to the point that it could not break the peace even if it wished. He called not only for the return of Alsace-Lorraine to France, but also for a buffer state along the Rhine under French domination and French control of the Saar Valley.

These acquisitions would give France Germany's most productive iron and coal mines, along with much of its industrial capacity. French occupation of the Rhine would prevent the Germans from fortifying that natural barrier to a French invasion. Clemenceau also demanded huge reparation payments from Germany, both to weaken that nation and to help pay for the enormous destruction France had suffered. All the fighting on the western front had taken place on French rather than German soil, and since the Germans had flooded the French coal mines before retreating, Clemenceau had no doubt that France was justified in compensating itself at the expense of the enemy.

Clemenceau was all the more determined to weaken Germany because the Bolshevik Revolution in Russia had removed a major prop from the old balance of power. Without a Russian ally to threaten Germany from behind, France could not afford to have Germany return to its previous strength. France's preferred solution was not only to weaken Germany, but forcibly to overthrow the Bolshevik regime and bring Russia back into the family of Western nations. Unfortunately for Clemenceau, only the United States had enough troops and resources left to make intervention in Russia successful. Clemenceau tried to inveigle the United States into providing the wherewithal, but when Wilson proved reluctant, the French decided their best alternative was to support and enlarge the tier of new nations in eastern Europe that were emerging out of former German, Austrian, and Russian territories.

The French could expect American help in this enterprise because Wilson saw such nations as Poland, Czechoslovakia, Rumania, Yugoslavia, Latvia, Lithuania, and Estonia as embodying his principle of national self-determination. Thus France hoped to erect a *cordon sanitaire* against the spread of bolshevism from Russia and to build an alliance of eastern European nations to contain and oppose Germany from behind. When Wilson warned that such a punitive peace might drive Germany, Austria, and Hungary to bolshevism, Clemenceau argued that the best way to prevent this was not food and generosity, but bayonets.

Clemenceau's approach to peace found substantial support from the Allies, whose war aims could be satisfied only by stripping the Central Powers. Great Britain was not so concerned about the continental territorial settlement as France was, but it wanted many of Germany's colonies, and it especially wanted to confiscate the German navy. Italy had entered the war because the Allies had promised to revise its boundaries with Austria. Italy would acquire the Brenner Pass and with it a strategically defensible border at the crest of the Alps. It also would get the important Adriatic port of Trieste. Italy insisted that these commitments be fulfilled even though the new border violated the principle of national self-determination and incorporated the German-speaking Tyrol. Later, the Italians went even further to demand the port cities and strategic islands of the Dalmatian coast that were to have been vital outlets to the Adriatic Sea for the new nation of Yugoslavia. Italy could justify its desire for such ports, especially the city of Fiume, on the grounds that many Italians lived there, surrounded by the Slavic inhabitants of the interior. But Italy's major purpose was absolute control of the Adriatic.

Japan too insisted on its pound of flesh from Germany. The Allies had promised to give the Japanese control of the German colony on the Shantung peninsula of China, along with Germany's Pacific island colonies north of the equator (those south of the equator would join Australia and New Zealand in the British Empire). Great Britain, Italy, and Japan also largely agreed with Clemenceau that the spread of revolution in Russia and Central Europe should be countered by force rather than generosity.

INTERVENTION IN RUSSIA

The old diplomacy of Clemenceau and the new diplomacy of Wilson fought a preliminary battle before the peace conference, as Wilson and the Allies heatedly debated the proper approach to the revolution in Russia. The French and Italians, with support from many prominent Britons like Winston Churchill, wanted a full-scale intervention to overturn the Bolsheviks. Their primary goal was to restore the eastern front.

In the spring of 1917, a moderate socialist government originally had taken power in Russia after the overthrow of the czar, and it had obliged the Allies by pursuing the war. But it had lost thousands of men in an abortive campaign on the Austrian front, bringing total Russian deaths in the war to 1.7 million. The Bolsheviks then denounced the war and rode to power in the autumn of 1917 on a wave of popular disgust with the suffering and fruitless slaughter incurred by the inept leaders of both imperial and post-imperial Russia. The Bolsheviks kept their promise to end the war by accepting the costly peace of Brest-Litovsk in March 1918 and abandoning Estonia, Latvia, Lithuania, Finland, Poland, and the Ukraine to German control or influence. Since Lenin had arrived in Russia after the czar's overthrow aboard a sealed German train, some Allied officials feared the Bolsheviks not only as a menace in their own right, but also as potentially active contributors to the German war effort.

The European Allies sent economic aid, weapons, and some military advisors to the scattered anti-Bolshevik forces in Russia, but only the Americans and perhaps the Japanese could supply the troops necessary for full-scale intervention. Wilson opposed such an effort. The European Allies nonetheless cajoled him into sending American troops to participate in the occupation of Murmansk and Archangel, the two northern Russian ports through which the Allies had sent supplies while Russia was still in the war. Because of the inefficiency of the railroads that connected those ports to the Russian interior, some 160,000 tons of supplies furnished on credit to the

Russians had piled up in Archangel, and the Allies feared that the Russians would turn them over to Germany. The Allies planned to take back the supplies and keep the ports out of German hands. Some five thousand American troops moved into northern Russia under orders to protect the ports. World War I ended three months later, but winter trapped the occupying forces until they could be withdrawn in 1919. After they left, the Bolsheviks shot between ten and thirty thousand collaborators.

Wilson and the Allies occupied a third major Russian port as well, the Pacific harbor of Vladivostok, which served as the eastern terminus of the Trans-Siberian Railroad and housed an Allied stockpile four times greater than Archangel. Again Wilson was reluctant. But the Japanese were not, and Wilson feared that a unilateral Japanese intervention on the heels of Japan's Twenty-One Demands on China would result in Japanese control of Manchuria and the Trans-Siberian Railroad. The plight of the Czech Legion, 40,000 Czech soldiers who had been fighting on the eastern front alongside the Russians and had been trapped there when Russia left the war, also influenced Wilson.

The Czechs were riding the Trans-Siberian Railroad to the Pacific, where they expected to be ferried back to Europe to join the war on the western front. They were bitterly anti-Bolshevik and were busily fighting various Bolshevik units along the way. A portion of the Czechs reached Vladivostok and occupied the city, but a Bolshevik force blocked the railroad and stranded the remainder two thousand miles up the line in Siberia. Wilson got the idea that nearly a million German and Austrian prisoners of war held in Siberia had been released by the revolutionaries and were attacking the Czech Legion. The Allies had long feared that the Germans might use these prisoners to take control of eastern Russia. Wilson sent an American contingent of 7,000 American troops to join the Japanese in occupying Vladivostok.

In joining the Siberian intervention, Wilson did not understand the intentions of the Allies. They did not intend to withdraw the Czechs, but to encourage them to stay and fight. The Czechs in Vladivostok actually linked up with their compatriots on the Trans-Siberian Railroad two days before the Americans arrived. The Americans then stayed in Vladivostok while the Japanese occupied the Manchurian portion of the railroad. A British unit of a thousand men helped clear the railway and then took up garrison duty in the Urals in support of the anti-Bolshevik effort of Russian Admiral A.V. Kolchak.

As had been the case at Murmansk and Archangel, the Americans stayed on in Vladivostok for a year and a half, even though the war ended a few weeks after their arrival. Wilson did not want to withdraw them during the peace conference. But he did hope to find means other than force to combat bolshevism in Russia and elsewhere.

During the peace conference, Wilson and British Prime Minister David Lloyd George wanted to invite the Bolsheviks and their leading domestic opponents to Paris to try to work out an arrangement under the guidance of the major Western powers. Clemenceau refused to have the Bolsheviks in

France, but consented to such a meeting on the island of Prinkipo in the Turkish Sea of Marmara. Clemenceau's consent was deceptive, however, for he successfully encouraged the Russian Whites to reject the invitation to meet with the Bolshevik Reds.

Surprisingly, the Bolsheviks had expressed a willingness to come to Prinkipo even though it meant sitting down as mere equals with numerous Russian factions that could not compare in power and influence with the Bolshevik government. Since the Prinkipo meeting was off, Colonel House thought the Bolsheviks' positive response made it worthwhile to send a mission to talk with Lenin. With Britain's silent approval, House delegated William Bullitt to explore the possibility of exchanging Allied withdrawal from Russia for amnesty toward those who had collaborated with the Whites and the Allies. Lenin, who evidently was fearful of a major Allied offensive in the spring, offered Bullitt a truce with all sides continuing to occupy their present positions. But he insisted on a reply within two weeks.

The excited Bullitt met a wall of apathy on his return to Paris. Lloyd George, under heavy attack from conservatives at home for even considering recognition of the Bolsheviks, denied ever endorsing the Bullitt mission. Wilson evidently regarded the mission as a mere fact-finding expedition; he had no more interest than Lloyd George in according recognition to the Bolsheviks. He turned instead to a plan offered by Herbert Hoover, the former director of the American relief effort in German-occupied Belgium, to undertake a food distribution program in Russia designed to wean the Russian people away from bolshevism.

Hoover thought Lenin might be desperate enough to accept a truce, turn over Russian railroads to a neutral commission for distribution of the food, allow local elections to choose the domestic distributors, and all this without any commitment to Allied withdrawal. Lenin was not that malleable. In any case, Clemenceau and other conservatives considered the Wilson and Hoover plan appeasement and stalled it because Kolchak's Whites seemed for a short time to be winning.

In the end, however, the scattered White contingents failed to coordinate their efforts, alienated many Russians with their forced conscription of troops, and fell apart before the Red onslaught. The Allies withdrew ignominiously, having done enough to confirm the Bolsheviks in their hatred and distrust for the capitalist nations, but far too little to overturn them.

PRESSURES ON THE PEACE FROM LEFT AND RIGHT

During the peace conference in Paris, Wilson, Clemenceau, and the Allies had to deal with Communist revolutions in the defeated Central Powers as well as in Russia. Since defeat in the war had discredited the old orders in Germany, Austria, and Hungary, politics swung to the Left. In Hungary, a moderate socialist government displaced the old Hapsburg Empire. But Czech and Rumanian troops took much of Transylvania from the helpless

Hungarians, while the Yugoslavs appropriated Hungary's last anthracite mines. This demonstration of Wilson's inability to keep his promises of a just peace, along with the food shortage produced by the continuing Allied blockade, undermined Hungary's successor government just as the military defeat had undermined the old imperial regime. The moderates threw up their hands and turned the government over to the Communists, headed by Bela Kun. Bela Kun's government lasted only 133 days, but it threw a major fright into the peacemakers in Paris.

To add to Allied concern, a Communist government took power briefly in Bavaria. Even Vienna trembled on the brink of revolution. Most critical, the moderate socialist government in Germany, facing the harsh demands of the Allies, found itself under siege from the radical Left and its charismatic Sparticist leaders Karl Liebknecht and Rosa Luxemburg. But Hindenburg and the German army remained loyal to the government and threw its weight against the radical Left. The Freicorps, unofficial organizations of returning soldiers, crushed a radical-led general strike in Berlin and summarily executed Liebknecht and Luxemburg. Ultimately the moderate government survived, but it continually pointed to the danger of revolution as reason for the Allies to moderate the peace terms.

Clemenceau refused to be deterred by such considerations. As he had urged intervention in Russia, so he insisted that the Allies should take what they wanted from the Central Powers and forcibly quell any radical attempt to exploit the situation. His approach found increasing support throughout the Allied nations. As defeat turned the Central Powers to the Left, victory turned the domestic politics of the Allied nations to the Right. Marshal Foch and France's President Raymond Poincaré demanded that Clemenceau be even harder on the defeated enemy. England's Prime Minister Lloyd George won reelection on the eve of the conference by promising to squeeze the Germans "until the pips squeek," and thus encouraged the British Right to demand that he secure large reparations from Germany. The moderate premier of Italy, Vittorio Orlando, was under immense pressure for annexations from his foreign minister, Baron Sonnino, and from populist right-wing groups led by the noisy demagogue Benito Mussolini.

Even Wilson faced a rising rightist tide at home. During the off-year election of 1918, Wilson had appealed for the election of more congressional Democrats to support his approach. The Republicans denounced Wilson for breaching the bipartisan approach to foreign policy that ostensibly had prevailed during the war, and won narrow victories in both houses of Congress. With their two-seat margin in the Senate, the Republicans would be able to reorganize that body's entire committee structure. This included the Senate Foreign Relations Committee, to which Wilson would have to submit his peace treaty. The most likely candidate for chairman of the committee was the president's worst political enemy, Henry Cabot Lodge. Just as Wilson left for the peace conference, Lodge proclaimed that the Allies should be permitted to dismember Germany and exact heavy reparations from it. In effect, he and his fellow Republicans told the Allied leaders they could afford to ignore

Wilson's grandiose plans because Wilson had been repudiated by his own people in the election of 1918.

NEGOTIATING THE TREATY OF VERSAILLES

The electoral defeat of 1918 was not the only factor that undercut Wilson's position; the terms of the armistice agreement weakened Wilson's bargaining power as well. Wilson personally handled the first stage of the negotiations when the Germans approached him rather than the other Allies with an offer to make peace on the basis of the Fourteen Points. Wilson spent the month of October 1918 clarifying the terms of the armistice in the face of steady complaints from Republicans like Theodore Roosevelt that peace should be made by hammering guns rather than clicking typewriters. Wilson let the Germans know that a democratically governed Germany might receive better terms than the kaiser's militaristic regime, and the German Reichstag dutifully installed a democratic government. (The kaiser abdicated and fled to Holland, where he lived for twenty-three years "unwept, unhonored, and unhung.")

When the British and French objected that Wilson was conducting these preliminary negotiations unilaterally and expressed reservations about the Fourteen Points, Wilson secured German approval for Britain's rejection of the point concerning freedom of the seas and for France's insistence on specific recognition of its right to reparations for civilian damages. Then, on the assumption that the Fourteen Points with these minor reservations would serve as the basis for a final peace, Wilson turned the negotiations over to the Allied military command.

Marshal Foch, with the full support of America's General John Pershing, insisted on terms that would ensure the Germans could not resume the war. He demanded that the Germans turn over half their machine guns, a third of their artillery, and all of their battle fleet. The Germans also had to permit the Allies to occupy bridgeheads over the Rhine. The Germans bridled at the terms, but by this time felt incapable of further resistance. The British interned the German fleet at Scapa Flow, its major naval base, where the German crews ultimately scuttled their own ships. The Allies left the blockade in force and did not remove it until seven months later, when the final peace had been concluded. The Allied ground forces improved their position with each periodic renewal of the armistice and left the Germans with no geographical position to defend even if they had had the weapons to do so. Thus Germany could exert no military leverage to ensure a just peace; the Germans could only point to the moral obligation of the Allies to live up to Wilson's pre-armistice agreement and threaten to collapse into Bolshevik arms.

While the disarming of Germany and the electoral defeat of 1918 undermined Wilson's bargaining power, his reception on his arrival in Europe seemed to restore it. The president received a tumultuous welcome in the cities he visited on his way to Paris and the peace conference. Wilson as-

Figure 13   The United States delegation to the Peace Conference—"Colonel" Edward House, Robert Lansing, President Woodrow Wilson, Henry White, and General Tasker Bliss. Photo courtesy of the National Archives.

sumed that the people in these huge emotional crowds sympathized with his peace plans. No doubt many did; but many others welcomed him as another victor, rather than an angel of mercy. Wilson was wrong to assume that the nationalistic demands of the European leaders at the conference went beyond the sentiments of their constituencies.

Wilson did have another element of strength. Prior to his departure for Paris, Wilson had Colonel House assemble a group of academic experts, dubbed The Inquiry, to investigate the various territorial, ethnic, political, and economic issues that would come up in the negotiations. The Inquiry helped make the American delegation the best informed at the conference. But the makeup of the negotiating delegation itself was not nearly so strong. Wilson, of course, was the chief delegate. Colonel House, who held no official position in the government and was heartily disliked by almost all except Wilson, was a second delegate. Secretary of State Lansing, who was not in full sympathy with Wilson and was seldom consulted by the president, was the third. General Tasker Bliss served competently as a military representative, although his liberal Wilsonian outlook was far out of line with that of General Pershing and much of the rest of the military establishment. Finally, Wilson ignored William Howard Taft and Elihu Root, the two most powerful Republican party advocates of an international peacekeeping organization, and chose Henry White instead as a Republican representative on the delegation. White was a career diplomat with no influence whatever over the congressional Republican regulars who stood in the way of Wilson's peace objectives. One periodical portrayed the delegates as follows:

Name	Occupation	Representing
Woodrow Wilson	President	Himself
Robert Lansing	Secretary of state	The executive
Henry White	None	Nobody
Edward M. House	Scout	The executive
Tasker H. Bliss	Soldier	The commander-in-chief

The Paris Peace Conference, which began meeting in January 1919, was a huge affair, with 27 national delegations forming some 50 commissions and holding over 2,000 separate meetings. One observer described it as a "riot in a parrot house." The Allies did not invite Germany to join the deliberations; they decided to negotiate terms among themselves and then present them as a *fait accompli* to the Central Powers. Russia did not participate in the treaty-making either. It remained to be seen whether a peace settlement could be maintained when two of the six major world powers were not party to it.

Great Britain moved quickly to secure the German colonies it wanted, supported by the Japanese, French, and Italians, who also received parts of the German Empire. Wilson, in conformity with the strictures against colonialism in the Fourteen Points, tried to moderate the colonial partition and succeeded at least in getting the German colonies nominally assigned as wards of the League of Nations, to be administered by the colonial powers as temporary mandates.

The League of Nations itself was Wilson's great passion. He used his prestige to make it the first order of business, and got himself appointed chairman of the commission assigned to draw up the League charter. He drove himself and the commission mercilessly and managed to formulate a draft in only ten days. The League would consist of an Assembly, in which all members would have one vote, and a Council, composed of the Big Five as permanent members, with several temporary elected nations. Under Article X of the League covenant, the League would provide united international action to preserve the independence and territorial integrity of all its members. The League also would be an integral part of the peace treaty. Wilson proudly proclaimed that "a living thing is born." Then, on Feburary 24, 1919, he boarded his ship for a three-week return to the United States to sign pending congressional bills and prepare domestic public opinion for participation in the new international organization.

The president quickly ran into trouble. Many members of Congress resented Wilson's failure to consult them or keep them informed of the important proposals he was making to the peace conference. The Senate and House committee members Wilson summoned to discuss the League with him greeted the president's advocacy with sullen silence. Senator Henry Cabot Lodge circulated a so-called Round Robin petition, which harshly criticized the League, and thirty-nine members of the recently elected Senate signed it. This was more than enough senators to prevent Wilson from getting the two-thirds vote necessary to consent to the treaty. Wilson responded defiantly that the League covenant would come back to the United States so intertwined with the rest of the peace treaty that it could not be removed without ruining the entire structure of the settlement. Evidently he never dreamed the Senate might reject the whole treaty to rid itself of the League.

Despite Wilson's bold response, he knew he had to modify the League covenant if he expected to win Senate approval. Even some senators friendly to the idea of a League of Nations worried that the covenant did not specifically recognize the Monroe Doctrine, exempt domestic issues like immigration and tariffs from its purview, or provide a means for a nation to withdraw from the organization. Wilson would have to make concessions to the other Allies to win their consent to these changes.

Wilson returned to Paris in mid-March to find his bargaining position even weaker than he had expected. He had left Colonel House in charge of the American side of the negotiations and had told House he did not want the work of the conference held up by his own absence. But he did not expect that Colonel House actually would try to speed up the conference and bring many matters close to settlement before he returned. In House's haste to get a settlement, he consented to a French plan to include some substantive peace issues in a temporary military settlement, thus providing immediate relief from uncertainty and chaos in large areas of Europe, while leaving only the more controversial issues to the lengthy negotiations that would lead to a final treaty. In the discussion over this temporary military settlement, House tentatively had implied American willingness to concede some of France's territorial and reparations demands. Worse, from Wilson's point of view, this preliminary settlement would not include the League of Nations. Since Wilson had fought France to get the covenant included in the peace treaty itself, he assumed that House had fallen for a European plot to kill the League. He decided to nip this supposed plot in the bud by publicly announcing that the League would be an inextricable part of the treaty, and then set about trying to retrieve the ground he blamed House for losing.

He faced an uphill battle. Clemenceau inspired a virulent French press campaign against Wilson, accusing the president of delaying the peace treaty so as to invite the Bolsheviks to take advantage of the resulting chaos. During this time of extreme stress, Wilson fell seriously ill and had to conduct his campaign from a sickbed. At one point he ordered his ship to be ready to take him back to America and threatened to sign a separate peace with Germany if the Allies continued to demand harsh terms. In the end, however, he compromised more than his adversaries.

Lloyd George extorted a commitment from Wilson that the United States would not build up its navy to rival that of the British. In exchange, the British consented to an amendment to the League covenant recognizing the Monroe Doctrine. Lloyd George also joined Clemenceau in pressuring for a huge reparations settlement, and ultimately they got Wilson to turn the question over to a reparations commission. Wilson wanted to put a limit on the amount the commission could award, but under Allied pressure he left the sum open. In addition to this blank check for the reparations commission, Wilson agreed to the French demand that veterans' pensions be considered civilian war damages and added to the reparations bill, a serious distortion of the pre-armistice discussions Wilson had conducted with Germany.

Since Lloyd George already had won Britain's major goals, he joined Wilson to secure a compromise on French territorial demands. France recovered Alsace-Lorraine. The French also would occupy the strategic Rhineland for fifteen years, after which it would become a demilitarized zone of Germany. The League of Nations would administer the Saar Valley, while France took over the area's coal mines. After fifteen years the inhabitants of the Saar would conduct a plebiscite to determine whether they would rejoin Germany. All assumed they would vote to do so. In exchange for Clemenceau's agreement not to remove the Saar and Rhineland from Germany permanently, Great Britain and the United States signed a separate security treaty with the French in which they promised to intervene if a revived Germany attacked France. (The Senate ultimately declined this security pact as well as the Treaty of Versailles. The French felt betrayed, since they received neither the Rhineland nor the security treaty.)

The reparations and western border settlements were not the only ways in which the peace settlement weakened Germany. The Allies gave Poland a corridor through East Prussia so it could have access to the sea. As a concession to the German character of the port city of Danzig (now Gdansk), which lay at the corridor's terminus, the Allies made Danzig a free city rather than a formal part of Poland. Czechoslovakia acquired the Sudetenland, with its German minority of some 3 million. The Treaty of Versailles reduced German armed forces to what was essentially a police constabulary, and accompanied this with a vague promise that the Allies would soon disarm. The

Figure 14   The Big Four at the Paris Peace Conference—seated from left to right, Vittorio Orlando of Italy, David Lloyd George of Great Britain, Georges Clemenceau of France, and Woodrow Wilson of the United States. Photo courtesy of the National Archives.

settlement prohibited any German tie to Austria. Wilson and the Allies also reluctantly permitted Italy to take full advantage of its wartime treaty to acquire Austria's southern Tyrol, with its strategic Brenner Pass and its German population.

Italy was not so fortunate in its drive to acquire Fiume and the other Adriatic ports the Allies had promised to Yugoslavia. Wilson even appealed over the heads of the Italian delegation to the Italian people, asking them to repudiate the demands of their leaders. Orlando and Sonnino left the conference huffing that Wilson was trying to restore his lost virginity at Italian expense. To Wilson's great chagrin, the Italians gave Orlando tumultuous support for his stand on Fiume. But Wilson remained adamant, and Italy ultimately regarded the loss of its demands as reason to join Germany and other dissatisfied powers in their drive to revise the Treaty of Versailles.

If Wilson's stand on Fiume did not endear him to the Italians, it did temporarily revive his prestige among liberals in the United States and the rest of Europe. But his support quickly dissipated when Wilson backed away from another confrontation with Japan and conceded Japanese control of Germany's former Chinese leasehold, the Shantung Peninsula. Japan in turn abandoned its drive to include a specific recognition of racial equality in the treaty, a provision Wilson knew would make ratification that much more difficult at home. The Japanese also promised to return the Shantung Peninsula to nominal Chinese sovereignty in the future and keep for themselves only the railroads and other economic concessions in the area. (This they did in 1923.) China objected to this arrangement and refused to sign the treaty. Wilson's liberal supporters despaired at yet another violation of the principle of national self-determination. Conservatives meanwhile found in the unpopularity of Wilson's decision to favor the Japanese over America's beloved China another weapon to use against Wilson's treaty.

After the Allies had shaped their bundle of compromises, they called the Germans to the palace of Versailles to receive the completed treaty. The Germans balked at the terms and especially at a clause that admitted Germany's guilt for starting the war. They complained that since they had not surrendered but only agreed to an armistice, they should be permitted to negotiate the peace, not have it imposed on them. The Allies made a few minor adjustments in response to their complaints. For instance, they allowed a plebiscite in Upper Silesia instead of awarding the province outright to Poland. But then the Allies threatened to march on Berlin unless Germany signed. On June 23, 1919, the Germans grudgingly accepted the Treaty of Versailles.

THE SENATE, THE LEAGUE, AND THE TREATY OF VERSAILLES

Wilson returned home to a barrage of criticism. Henry Cabot Lodge, recently appointed chairman of the Senate Foreign Relations Committee, made the committee a forum for every variety of denunciation available. Disillusioned

Map 12   Central Europe and the Balkans

liberals like William Bullitt testified against the treaty on the grounds that Wilson had betrayed the Fourteen Points and imposed a "Carthaginian" peace on Germany. Liberals worried that the crushing reparations imposed on Germany along with the fragmentation of eastern Europe would make Central Europe's economic recovery impossible. Disillusioned liberals also opposed American participation in a League of Nations whose purpose, according to Article X, would be the preservation of boundaries and territorial entities that were products of an unjust peace. Why should the United States protect Italy against the natural resentments of Germans and Slavs, or Japan against a rightfully offended China? Irish-Americans joined the chorus against the League. They feared it would require American support of Britain's territorial integrity against the legitimate aspirations of the oppressed Irish, whose Easter Uprising the British had crushed in 1916.

Lodge also encouraged the testimony of conservative opponents of the League. Conservatives did not concern themselves much about the harsh treatment of the Central Powers, whom they would just as soon have beaten into total surrender and impotence. Conservatives worried instead about the threat of the League commitments to America's historic tradition of independence, isolation, and unilateralism. On the League issue they were joined by a few senators whose liberalism took the form of isolationism rather than Wilsonian internationalism.

Wilson and defenders of the League pointed out that Article X of the League covenant was a moral rather than a legal commitment. They reminded Americans that some concessions to the desires of the Allies had been inevitable. They insisted that at least Wilson's presence and persistence had moderated Allied goals. Germany had lost only about 13 percent of its territory and 10 percent of its population, and much of both had historically been French or Polish.

At first a clear majority of both the Senate and the American people at large favored the treaty and the League. But Lodge managed the opposition very adroitly. Six of the ten Republicans he appointed to the Foreign Relations Committee were irreconcilably against the treaty, and he struck a deal with them whereby they would support his attempts to attach amendments and reservations to the treaty before voting against the whole package. At first, the majority of the committee attached forty-five amendments and four reservations. When it became apparent that the Senate would reject such a package, in part because the amendments would require Wilson to renegotiate the entire settlement, Lodge fell back on a set of fourteen reservations. Three of the four great powers would have to accept these reservations, but there would be no need to renegotiate the treaty itself. The most significant of these Lodge reservations disavowed the obligation to defend victims of aggression unless Congress approved. Many of the other reservations were irrelevant or redundant.

Wilson regarded Lodge's proposals as dire threats to the League's integrity. Ignoring his doctor's warnings following his bout with illness in Paris, Wilson embarked on a cross-country train tour to drum up support for the

League. After a speech in Pueblo, Colorado, he collapsed. He was rushed back to Washington, but several days later a massive stroke paralyzed half of his body and left him an invalid, confined to his bedroom. His second wife, Edith, guarded his time and privacy so he could not aid in the battle for the League or keep his finger on the pulse of public opinion. The stroke also seemed to drain his small store of political flexibility. Even though he constructed four reservations of his own for possible use by the Democrats to counter Republican opposition in an emergency, he refused to compromise at all with Lodge. He insisted that the Lodge reservations "emasculated" the League and ordered Democrats to vote against the treaty if those reservations were attached. Democrats joined the irreconcilables to defeat the treaty with the attached Lodge reservations, 39 senators voting for it to 55 against. Then the irreconcilables and Republicans defeated the Democrats' attempt to pass the treaty without reservations, 38 to 53.

Public outcry and the fact that four-fifths of the Senate supported the League in some form forced Lodge and the Senate to reconsider. Lodge actually began to meet with some Democrats and Republican "mild reservationists" to work out a compromise. But the irreconcilables threatened to disrupt both Lodge's career and the Republican party, and he abandoned the discussions. Wilson proved no more cooperative. He continued to insist that his loyal Democratic followers reject the treaty if the Lodge reservations were attached. In the final vote on the Peace of Versailles, twenty-one Democrats who realized that the choice was between the treaty with reservations and no treaty at all deserted Wilson and voted for it. But twenty-three Democrats joined the irreconcilables, and the treaty fell seven votes short of the two-thirds majority necessary to consent to ratification.

Wilson, despite his perilous physical condition, hoped to run again for president in 1920 and make the election a referendum on the treaty. A public mandate might still make it possible to bring the United States into his beloved League. But the Democratic party nominated Governor James Cox of Ohio. Cox and his running mate, Franklin Delano Roosevelt, campaigned on a platform that supported the League, but they did not make the League the centerpiece of their effort. The Republican nominee, Warren G. Harding, purposely muddied the issue. Many prominent Republicans, including Elihu Root and Herbert Hoover, insisted that a vote for Harding was a vote for a modified League. Irreconcilables insisted that Harding opposed the peace settlement. Harding uttered vacuous platitudes that could be interpreted either way, and won by promising to return the country to quiet and "normalcy." He made no attempt to revive the League during his administration; he said it was dead as the dodo. In 1921 he signed a separate peace with Germany and left the shrunken League to its own devices.

CONTROVERSIAL ISSUES AND FURTHER READING

In the wake of the Senate's defeat of the Treaty of Versailles, participants and historians rushed to assess the blame for the failure of the peace. Even those who defended the treaty did so tepidly and spent most of their time discussing who was to blame for its shortcomings.

Although the greatest opposition to Wilson's League came from conservatives, there were very few published critiques of Wilson's diplomacy from that point of view. Henry Cabot Lodge's own memoirs of the Senate fight, *The Senate and the League of Nations* (1925), constituted the most thorough conservative analysis. Lodge insisted that Wilson should have told the Allies that "the boundaries to be fixed in Europe were nothing to us, that we wanted a peace which would put it beyond Germany's power for many years to attempt again to destroy the peace of the world and the freedom and civilization of mankind. . . ." He blamed Wilson's rigidity for the Senate's rejection of the League, but admitted he did not regret the League's ultimate defeat.

The memoirs of Wilson's secretary of state, Robert Lansing, also contributed to the conservative critique, even though Lansing favored ratification of the treaty with all its defects. Lansing criticized Wilson's attempt to make Europe's borders conform to the principle of popular self-determination, because that principle often conflicted with strategic and economic interests and imperiled national safety, "always the paramount consideration in international and national affairs." Lansing pronounced himself favorable to the League of Nations only if it preserved America's right to a unilateral foreign policy. He believed Wilson was wrong to reject the treaty with the Lodge reservations. He reproved Wilson for attending the conference personally, and further argued that Wilson should have paid more attention to the advice of his fellow delegates. All these criticisms would become subjects of later historiographical disputes. [Robert Lansing, *The Peace Negotiations* (1921).]

These conservative criticisms probably had more impact on general popular opinion than the complaints of the disillusioned liberals, but the disillusioned liberals had more influence than the conservatives on historians and intellectuals. Most historians in the post-World War I era followed the liberals and bewailed Wilson's failure to achieve his aims rather than criticizing the aims themselves. John Maynard Keynes, the prominent English economist and a member of the British delegation to Paris, published a famous book called *The Economic Consequences of the Peace* (1920). In it he called Wilson's supposed negotiating collapse "one of the decisive moral events of history." Although he said most of Wilson's advisors were "dummies," he claimed that Colonel House had had far more knowledge and wisdom than the president and wished Wilson had heeded him more. He especially flayed Wilson for refusing to admit the shortcomings of the treaty and claimed that the sanctimonious Presbyterian president had tried to disguise his sellout by using the "subtlest sophisters and most hypocritical draftsmen" to clothe the pact with insincere language.

Wilson's chief defender in the two decades after World War I was his aide and press officer, Ray Stannard Baker, whom Wilson authorized to publish the presidential papers. Even Baker, however, began his defense by admitting the shortcomings of the peace settlement. His primary argument was that others were to blame for them. The Europeans had refused to abandon the precepts of the "old diplomacy." Secretary of State Robert Lansing had given aid and comfort to the treaty's adversaries because of his dislike of the principles of national self-determination and his continuing belief in an isolated America devoted to its own "selfish development." The pliable Colonel House had caved in to the pressure of the Europeans during Wilson's absence and advanced a long way toward a preliminary peace that conceded many of the Allies' unjust demands while leaving out the League covenant. Wilson temporarily saved the League from this "plot" by making his "bombshell" announcement that the League would be tied inextricably to the treaty, but never had been able to regain the ground House had lost. [Ray Stannard Baker, *What Wilson Did at Paris* (1919), and *Woodrow Wilson and World Settlement* (3 vols., 1922).]

Colonel House cooperated with Yale historian Charles Seymour to defend himself against the charges that he had been responsible for Wilson's concessions at Paris. House and Seymour insisted that the concessions were inevitable. Not only had Wilson's concern for the League made it necessary to defer to the Allies on other issues, but Wilson had undermined his domestic position by rejecting House's advice to avoid a partisan appeal during the election of 1918 and refusing to add more prominent Republicans like Elihu Root or William Howard Taft to the negotiating delegation. The need to make concessions had "suddenly appeared" during Wilson's absence, but House committed Wilson to no concessions and certainly had not been part of a plot to sidetrack the League. Throughout the book, House spoke of "Wilson's compromises" and professed himself distraught that Wilson had made them. [Charles Seymour, ed., *The Intimate Papers of Colonel House* (4 vols., 1926–1928).]

Meanwhile, Wilson's defenders turned their fire on Henry Cabot Lodge and the Senate. D. F. Fleming claimed that Lodge deliberately sabotaged the treaty. First Lodge undermined Wilson's bargaining position by forcing the president to seek amendments to the League covenant on his return to Paris. Then Lodge conspired with the irreconcilables to defeat the treaty in the Senate. Fleming rejected Lodge's claim that he had favored the League so long as reservations were attached to it. Fleming saw the attachment of the reservations strictly as a partisan maneuver to kill the peace. Fleming's analysis brought agreement from W. Stull Holt, who studied the Treaty of Versailles and other treaties defeated by the Senate and argued that the Senate's role in treaty-making should be reduced. [D. F. Fleming, *The United States and the League of Nations, 1918–1920* (1968; originally published 1932); W. Stull Holt, *Treaties Defeated by the Senate* (1933).]

In 1933, another Englishman turned his attention to Wilson at Versailles. Harold Nicolson, who had served as a minor functionary in the British delegation, echoed Keynes's argument that Wilson was a fanatical and obsessed Presbyterian true believer who convinced himself that he had not compromised his principles. Nicolson agreed that Wilson's peace program was better than continued dependence on the dangerous and provocative balance of power in the European system. But unlike Keynes, Nicolson concluded that Wilson's hopes had been impossible from the beginning. Neither Wilson's domestic opponents nor the European Allies would permit a generous peace. That being the case, Nicolson said, perhaps a Carthaginian peace would have been better than the hypocritical compromise that emerged. If the peace was not to be generous, better that it crush Germany rather than wound it and leave it powerful enough to act on its resentment. [Harold Nicolson, *Peacemaking, 1919* (1933).]

Nicholson's analysis had a tremendous impact in the United States. The rise of Hitler and the outbreak of World War II seemed to validate his argument. Many popular pronouncements in Europe and the United States blamed the Treaty of Versailles for World War II. But no major historian in the United States concluded that the treaty should have been more Carthaginian. All influential books on the peace settlement assumed that a generous peace gave a better promise of avoiding war, and all argued that the Treaty of Versailles was not that bad. Paul Birdsall's *Versailles: Twenty Years After* (1941) pointed out that despite the concessions to the Europeans, which Birdsall blamed primarily on Colonel House, the treaty established at least some degree of international responsibility for colonial possessions and provided much self-determination for Europe. If boundaries were not fully compatible with ethnic loyalties or economic rationality, there was little Wilson or the other powers could have done about it. The collapse of Germany and Russia allowed the eastern European nations to occupy boundaries that could only have been altered by the peace conference through the use of force. Thomas A. Bailey's *Woodrow Wilson and the Lost Peace* (1944) and *Woodrow Wilson and the Great Betrayal* (1945) treated Wilson's decisions and concessions more caustically than Birdsall, but still said the treaty was worthy of ratification. Birdsall and Bailey saw World War II more as the consequence of the League's failure to enforce the Treaty of Versailles than as a product of the treaty provisions themselves.

Robert Osgood incorporated the views of Birdsall and Bailey into the realist critique of the post–World War II era. Accepting the argument that the Treaty of Versailles was not a bad peace settlement, Osgood blamed Wilson for raising the people's expectations with excessive appeals to idealism, leading them to imagine that no deviations from American desires would be necessary. Wilson also foolishly presented the League "as a substitute for the balance-of-power system, not as a supplementation or extension of it." In the absence of any explanation of the nation's self-interest in the League, the American people's enthusiasm waned rapidly. Without American participation, Europe could not enforce the peace terms against Germany, and Hitler could march Germany toward World War II. [Robert Osgood, *Ideals and Self-Interest in America's Foreign Relations: The Great Transformation* (1953). George Kennan's realist tract, *American Diplomacy, 1900–1950* (1951), was more critical of the peace, but the trend was against him.]

Several prominent historians defended Wilson against the realist charges that he had negotiated unrealistically and had raised excessive expectations in the American people. David Trask studied Wilson's war strategy and concluded that the president understood the connections between military dispositions and the settlement that would follow, while Lawrence Gelfand's study of The Inquiry led him to believe that Wilson was more realistic than his advisors. [David F. Trask, *The United States in the Supreme War Council: American War Aims and Inter-Allied Strategy, 1917–1918* (1961); Lawrence E. Gelfand, *The Inquiry: American Preparations for Peace, 1917–1919* (1963).] Wilson's defenders also revived Ray Stannard Baker's charge that many of the treaty's shortcomings were the result not of Wilson's lack of realism, but of Colonel House's undermining of Wilson's diplomacy. [See Inga Floto, *Colonel House in Paris* (1973); Arthur S. Link, *Woodrow Wilson: Revolution, War, and Peace* (1979).]

Generally, however, realists and Wilsonians moved toward a loose consensus. The realists admitted that Wilson's negotiations and the treaty terms were not so bad as the previous era had asserted. The Wilsonians admitted that Wilson had conducted himself too rigidly in the battle to get Senate consent for the League. Debate continued over why Wilson had been so rigid, however. Alexander L. and Juliette L. George, *Woodrow Wilson and Colonel House: A Personality Study* (1956), published a highly influential psychoanalytical analysis of Wilson that traced the president's lack of flexibility to his relationship with an overbearing father. Arthur Link, basing his judgment on a medical study by Dr. Edwin A. Weinstein, claimed Wilson's rigidity was a consequence of the physical impairment connected with several strokes. [Edwin A. Weinstein, *Woodrow Wilson: A Medical and Psychological Biography* (1981); Arthur Link, introduction to Inga Floto, *Colonel House in Paris* (1973). For a contrary medical view, see Michael F. Marmor, "Wilson, Strokes, and Zebras," *New England Journal of Medicine* (August 1982).] As historians came to agree that Wilson had mismanaged the Senate fight, the reputation of Wilson's opponents tended to revive. [See Warren F. Kuehl, *Seeking World Order: The United States and International Organization to 1920* (1969); Ralph A. Stone, *The Irreconcilables* (1970); and William C. Widenor, *Henry Cabot Lodge and the Search for an American Foreign Policy* (1980.)]

Even as the realists and Wilsonians approached their consensus, revisionists began to shift the focus on Wilsonian diplomacy. Arno J. Mayer and N. Gordon Levin portrayed Wilson's plan for a moderate peace and the League of Nations more as a conservative attempt to combat Russian bolshevism and the radical European Left than an altruistic step toward forgiveness of past enemies and the spread of democracy. They saw Wilson's program as expansionist—a search for an open door world that would permit American economic and cultural expansion and forestall the advance of the rival Leninist system. [Arno J. Mayer, *Politics and Diplomacy of Peacemaking: Containment and Counterrevolution at Versailles, 1918–1919* (1967); N. Gordon Levin, Jr., *Woodrow Wilson and World Politics: America's Response to War and Revolution* (1968). William Appleman Williams opened discussion of some of these themes as early as 1952 in his *American-Russian Relations, 1781–1947* (1952).] While Wilsonians and realists admitted some aspects of the revisionist view, they resisted this inversion of Wilson's priorities from a benevolent peace toward Germany to combatting Russian bolshevism. They pointed to studies of Wilson's reluctant participation in the Russian intervention as evidence of his opposition to a crusade against communism abroad. [Among the studies documenting Wilson's reluctance to intervene in Russia were George F. Kennan, *Russia Leaves the War* (1956), *The Decision to Intervene* (1958), and *Russia and the West under Lenin and Stalin* (1960). See also Betty M. Unterberger, *America's Siberian Expedition* (1956); and John Thompson, *Russia, Bolshevism, and the Versailles Peace* (1966).]

CHAPTER 13

America's Retreat from Internationalism: Foreign Policy Between the World Wars

WAS WORLD WAR II INEVITABLE?

Many Europeans and Americans who witnessed the creation of the Treaty of Versailles predicted that its provisions would make a second world war inevitable. Those critics who survived until 1939 no doubt felt vindicated in their judgment. They saw Germany use the Polish corridor the Allies had carved out of East Prussia as the excuse for the invasion of Poland that triggered World War II. Germany already had raised international tension to an intolerable pitch by successfully sweeping aside the other hated provisions of the Versailles settlement—reparations, disarmament, the demilitarization of the Rhineland, the prohibition against German-Austrian union, and the border with Czechoslovakia.

Yet most modern historians wonder whether the admitted instability produced by the Versailles settlement might have been overcome had it not been for the Great Depression of 1929. The Depression drastically exacerbated the despair and fanaticism already present in Germany and paved the way for Adolf Hitler. The moderate governments that preceded Hitler sought treaty revision, just as Hitler did. Like Hitler, the moderates agitated for rectification of Germany's eastern borders with Poland and Czechoslovakia and the right to have German armed forces. But their tactics were cautious and peaceful. Europe could have accommodated them without war. Hitler, on the other hand, pursued treaty revision ruthlessly and used it to enlist domestic support for such grandiose ambitions that he indeed made war inevitable.

A similar situation existed in Japan. The Japanese had insisted throughout World War I that Japan had to have secure access to the resources and markets of Manchuria and China. After World War I, however, a series of moderate Japanese governments was willing to pursue Japan's goals in conjunction with the Western imperialists. These governments sought especially to avoid a clash with the United States, because American trade was extremely valuable to Japan. Moderates restrained the young officers of the

Japanese military who, emboldened by their unbroken string of victories in the Sino-Japanese War, Russo-Japanese War, and World War I, believed Japan should take what it needed in Asia by military force without regard to the desires of the West, let alone of the Chinese. When the Depression cut off much of Japan's trade with the West, it removed a major rationale for the moderate approach. The military and its allies took power and began to move along the road to Pearl Harbor.

These developments led historians to wonder whether the West could have propped up the moderate German and Japanese regimes in the 1920s to the point that they might have survived the political and economic impact of the Depression. It would have been no easy task. The moderate governments in Germany had a very tenuous credibility with the German people. These successor regimes rather than the kaiser's government and army bore the onus of Germany's defeat because Wilson and the Allies had invited democratically inclined Germans to overturn the kaiser, then made them responsible for signing the harsh Versailles Treaty. The combined votes of the extreme nationalists and Communists in the German Reichstag always outnumbered those of the centrist parties. If the extremists of Right and Left could forget their hatred of one another long enough to vote together, as they did after the Depression, they could topple any moderate regime whenever they pleased. Likewise, extremists could thwart the moderates in Japan, because by 1930 the military had direct access to the emperor and the right to full and independent control of all matters pertaining to high strategy.

Yet there was still some slight chance that an enlightened and determined policy on the part of France, Great Britain, and the United States might have enabled moderate governments to survive in Germany and Japan. The United States especially had the leverage to influence the course of events. It emerged from World War I with extraordinary economic power. At the outset of the war, the United States had owed other nations $3.7 billion; at the end of the war, other nations owed the United States $12.5 billion. (By 1930 they would owe America $21 billion.) In 1919 the United States produced nearly half of the world's manufactured goods, sent out one-sixth of the world's exports, and took one-eighth of its imports. By 1929 the U.S. gross national income was greater than that of Great Britain, France, Germany, Canada, Japan, and the next eighteen wealthiest nations combined. The American army demobilized rapidly after World War I, but the American navy was second only to that of Great Britain. At the peace conference, Wilson had promised to slow America's naval building program in exchange for Lloyd George's promise to amend the League covenant so as to recognize the Monroe Doctrine. But since the United States had refused to ratify the Treaty of Versailles, it was theoretically free to resume naval building.

The Republican administrations of Warren Harding, Calvin Coolidge, and Herbert Hoover recognized American power and knew what they wanted in Europe. Under the influence of bankers and businessmen who dealt regularly with Europe, the Republicans abandoned the earlier inclination of Henry Cabot Lodge and his colleagues to crush and punish Germany.

Most Republicans in the 1920s agreed with Wilson that a prosperous Germany was essential to the economic and political health of Europe, including the health of that implacable enemy of German revival, France. But the Republicans were not as willing as Wilson to take political risks or make sacrifices to support French security and thus allow France to tolerate if not welcome a more prosperous and powerful Germany.

Harding refused to resubmit the Treaty of Versailles to Congress. He also went along with the earlier rejection of the separate French security treaty Wilson had negotiated in Paris. For a while Harding declined even to recognize the existence of the League, going to the absurd length of refusing to open League mail addressed to the American government. More important, the Republicans rejected several chances to promise that the United States might suspend its neutral right to trade with an aggressor nation in wartime. Such a promise might have encouraged the British to a firmer support of French security against a revanchist Germany, since the British would not have had to fear another conflict with American neutrality policy. (Democratic President Roosevelt abandoned a similar initiative early in his administration.)

Warren Harding and the Republicans were determined to avoid any political entanglements with Europe. When they finally agreed to send observers to meetings of the League and its various committees, they carefully insisted that these observers were unofficial. The Republicans relied instead on private economic diplomacy to promote American ideas and interests abroad. American bankers, with only tacit government endorsement, served as unofficial foreign envoys and performed valuable tasks, such as extending bank loans where American national interests were involved and securing reductions in the reparations burden placed on Germany.

But private economic diplomacy proved unequal to the task of preventing Europe's plunge into World War II. The refusal of the United States to ratify the Treaty of Versailles left Washington without an official representative on the Reparations Commission that set Germany's final bill. Without the threat of an American veto, the commission decided to charge Germany the exorbitant sum of $33 billion. American bankers serving as unofficial government representatives to succeeding conferences on reparations managed to scale down the bill. Still, reparations hung like a black cloud over Europe. Germany probably had the capacity to pay the $33 billion, since by the late 1930s it had spent far more than that on armaments alone. But many Germans, reeling from the drastic inflation of the mark in 1923 and again from the Depression of 1929, naturally looked upon the drain of reparations from the German economy as the cause of their ruin.

Meanwhile, France and England relied on German reparations to pay French and British war debts to the United States. Whenever the Americans asked for a reduction of the German reparations bill, the French and British demanded that the United States compensate by reducing Allied war debts. After all, France and Great Britain had made far greater contributions in blood and suffering than the United States. America ought to regard the loans as its own contribution and forgive the debts. But Wilson had refused to link war debts and reparations in the Paris conference, and the Republican administrations of the 1920s followed suit. Calvin Coolidge allegedly remarked, "They hired the money, didn't they?"[1] Congress howled whenever there was a hint that the war debts might be linked to reparations. The Europeans would simply spend the money they saved on armaments, Americans complained.

Instead of forgiving the war debts, American bankers, urged on by the Republican administrations, floated huge loans to Germany to help it restore its economy while paying out reparations. In effect the United States loaned money to Germany, which Germany paid in reparations that came back to the United States as war debt payments. This revolving money machine functioned so long as Germany's economy continued to expand and give promise of an eventual ability to pay off both reparations and American loans. But when the German economy faltered in 1928 and 1929, American bankers stopped loaning money, Germany stopped paying reparations, and Great Britain, France, and all other countries with the exception of Finland stopped paying American war debts. This was a major cause of the collapse of the world economy in 1929.

The Republicans' refusal to make any political commitments in support of French security and their rejection of any linkage between war debts and reparations were not their only contributions to the undermining of European prosperity and moderate governments. They also insisted on a high tariff to protect American manufactures and farmers against foreign competition. The Fordney-McCumber Tariff of 1922 and the Hawley-Smoot Tariff of 1930 effectively closed the American market to the very countries that needed to sell products to enable them to pay war debts or reparations.

While postwar America would undertake no political and only informal private economic commitments abroad, it participated vigorously and publicly in efforts to reduce armaments. Certainly Americans were right to believe that arms races contributed to international tension and war. But Wilson's successors did not pay sufficient attention to the need for better political understandings to go hand in hand with arms reductions. America's reliance on the idea that disarmament alone might produce peace ultimately boomeranged. By 1939, the poorly prepared Western democracies faced rearmed and aggressive totalitarian regimes determined to rule or ruin.

The Republican regimes that permitted this state of affairs deserve a large measure of blame, but there were important mitigating circumstances. Wilson's unsuccessful and bitter fight with the Senate over the Treaty of Versailles had left a sour political atmosphere in which statesmanlike conduct

---

[1] This was only one of many stories that floated around in the 1920s to illustrate the terse and laconic Coolidge style. "Silent Cal" was famous for long naps and short statements. When one lady sitting next to him at dinner told him that she had a bet with friends that she could make him say more than two words at dinner, Coolidge told her, "You lose." When his wife asked the topic of the sermon at a church service Coolidge had attended, Coolidge supposedly said, "Sin." His wife asked what the preacher had said about it, and Coolidge replied, "He was against it."

was very difficult. Congressional Democrats vied with their Republican colleagues in denouncing the slightest move toward linking war debts and reparations. America turned inward in its search for domestic prosperity and gave little thought to the effects abroad of a creditor nation, untouched by the devastation of war, closing its markets to foreign products. Historical revisionism in the 1920s, which disproved the Allied theory that Germany alone was guilty of starting World War I, left disillusioned Americans with little justification for sacrificing their comforts to protect foreigners from the consequences of their own greed and cynicism. Of course Americans operated without foreknowledge of the militaristic regimes that would emerge in Germany and Japan in the 1930s. But when those regimes did take power, the first response of Americans was even greater withdrawal.

The pattern of partial withdrawal in the 1920s and 1930s extended beyond America's relations with Europe and Asia to its relations with Latin America as well. In the case of Latin America, however, historians have praised this partial withdrawal as vociferously as they have denounced it in Europe. Most historians have wondered not whether the United States should have retreated in Latin America, but whether it retreated far enough.

THE WASHINGTON NAVAL CONFERENCE OF 1921

The Washington Naval Conference epitomized much of the postwar Republican approach to foreign policy, and the stunning success of the conference seemed to bode well. Although many Republicans, including President Harding, wanted to complete Wilson's naval building program and make the United States the world's leading sea power before considering naval limitations, a British suggestion for a conference to discuss naval and East Asian affairs offered a tempting opportunity to achieve several goals. The British at the time indicated a willingness to accept American naval parity, and for the United States to gain parity while still reducing government expenditures would be a great political triumph. The British also indicated a willingness to modify their alliance with Japan if that could be done gracefully. A naval limitation conference might enable the United States to strip Japan of its British support and ensure American naval supremacy over Japan at the same time. If the United States could achieve all those goals while avoiding political entanglements, the Washington Conference could serve as a worthy Republican alternative to Wilson's League of Nations.

An agreement with the British and Japanese seemed all the more attractive in 1921 because tensions with both countries were high. The British were excluding American oil companies from their recently acquired League mandates in Iraq and Palestine. The British navy was determined on a naval arms race if the United States, freed from Wilson's pledge to slow American naval building by the Senate's rejection of the Treaty of Versailles, resumed the building program Congress had authorized in 1916 and 1918. British association with Japan in the alliance of 1902 created much anger in the United

States because Japan's relations with the United States had become quite hostile during and shortly after World War I.

In the wake of the Wilson administration's stand against Japan's Twenty-One Demands on China and Wilson's opposition at the Paris Peace Conference to Japan's desire for the Shantung Peninsula, a new wave of anti-Asian agitation swept the American West. The Democratic and Republican parties both adopted Japanese exclusion planks in their 1920 platforms. Japan also contributed to U.S.–Japanese estrangement when it increased the number of its occupation troops in Manchuria from the expected 7,000 to 72,000, and kept control of eastern Siberia after the United States withdrew its contingent from Vladivostok on April 1, 1920. Finally, a dispute over American rights to establish a cable station on Yap Island led the United States to agitate against all the Pacific mandates Japan had acquired at the Paris Conference. The American navy believed rumors that Japan was building fortifications on the Pacific islands, contrary to the terms of its mandates, and worried that those fortifications, combined with Japan's accelerated naval building program in 1920, might give Japan control of Asia.

Harding's secretary of state, Charles Evans Hughes, after extending invitations for the Washington Naval Conference to all the major nations of the world except the Soviet Union, startled the diplomats with a dramatic and very specific proposal for naval limitation. After a period of hard bargaining, the powers agreed to freeze the number of capital ships for ten years at the following ratio: The United States and Great Britain 5, Japan 3, France and Italy 1.75. At Japanese insistence, the United States agreed not to increase fortifications in Guam and the Philippines, knowing Congress probably

Figure 15   The Washington Naval Conference. From left to right at the head of the table are Aristide Briand of France, Senator Oscar Underwood, Elihu Root, Senator Henry Cabot Lodge, Secretary of State Charles Evans Hughes, and Lords Balfour and Lee of Great Britain. Photo courtesy of the National Archives.

would refuse appropriations for them anyway. In exchange, the Japanese gave up any further fortifications of their outlying island mandates. The Japanese assumed that the limitations on American fortifications in the western Pacific, along with America's need to spread its superior navy over two oceans, would permit Japanese naval supremacy in East Asian waters.

Fearing that Britain would refuse to fight the United States regardless of the provisions of the Anglo-Japanese Alliance, the Japanese also agreed to terminate that treaty. A Four Power Treaty between the United States, Japan, Great Britain, and France replaced the Anglo-Japanese Alliance, with the four signatories merely promising to consult one another if any of their possessions were endangered. A supplementary Nine Power Treaty committed the powers to respect China's territorial integrity and the Open Door policy. None of the signatories would seek special concessions at the expense of the citizens of other nations. Japan additionally gave the United States the right to establish its cable station on Yap, withdrew Japanese forces from Siberia, and promised to return Shantung to Chinese sovereignty.

The Washington Conference was a remarkable step toward world peace and stability. But it was just a first step; it left some major questions and dissatisfactions. Only continued progress toward political amicability would allow it to hold up. Moderates in Japan, for instance, assumed that the dictum in the Nine Power Treaty against infringement on any nation's rights in China validated Japan's existing special position in Manchuria and northern China. The United States, on the other hand, regarded the dictum as the beginning of a new Open Door order in Asia. The Japanese armed forces bridled at the inferior naval status granted them by the Washington Conference and remained ready to attack the moderates if the West's policies endangered Japanese hegemony in Manchuria.

The French were even more disturbed than the Japanese. They felt they had given up much of their naval security and then had been denied an agreement on land armaments that would solidify their position on the Continent. The French believed that since their navy had to defend coastlines on both the Atlantic and the Mediterranean, France should have received parity with Japan rather than Italy. Italy required only a Mediterranean fleet, and France's need to station some of its ships in the Atlantic would give Italy an edge in the Franco-Italian rivalry over North Africa. As a consequence, France had opposed extending the Washington Naval Limitation Agreement beyond capital ships to smaller cruisers, destroyers, and submarines. Great Britain found reason to avoid such limitations as well. Thus the treaty covered only capital ships, and the race for supremacy in auxiliary ships continued.

The naval race over auxiliary ships especially strained relations between Great Britain and the United States. In 1927 the powers met again at Geneva to try to extend the Washington agreement to auxiliary ships, but the conference foundered. France and Italy boycotted the meeting because they refused to separate the issue of naval disarmament from that of land armaments. The Japanese demanded that their ratio of auxiliary ships be raised above the ratio they had received for capital ships to compensate for their earlier concessions. The British and Americans could not agree over whether the treaty should be slanted to allow a few large ships with long cruising ranges, which the United States needed to defend its wide-spaced possessions, or more and smaller ships, which the British wanted to defend their more numerous colonies.

The British, the Japanese, and the Americans tried again for agreement in the London Naval Conference of 1930, and this time they succeeded. Ramsay MacDonald, the British Labour government's new prime minister, defied his admirals and declared to the United States: "What is this bother about parity? Parity? Take it, without reserve, heaped and flowing over." The British and Americans agreed to accord Japan the higher ratio on auxiliary ships it had demanded, and all seemed well. But Japanese militants assassinated the minister who made the agreement, and the Japanese military prepared to take things into its own hands to secure Japanese power in Asia.

Meanwhile, the European powers failed to make any progress toward reductions in land armaments. Germany was especially distressed and protested that it had accepted disarmament under the Treaty of Versailles only because other powers had promised they would soon join Germany in disarming. France wanted some guarantee of joint military action against aggression before it would consent to arms reductions, but the United States objected. The United States had already rejected participation in a Geneva Protocol of 1924 that would have required joint military action against any nation that refused to submit a quarrel to arbitration. Secretary Hughes even claimed the United States might regard the League of Nations as a potential enemy if it took action in the Western Hemisphere under the Geneva Protocol. A full-scale land disarmament conference did not meet in Geneva until 1932. President Herbert Hoover tried to duplicate Hughes's dramatic Washington Conference coup by proposing that all nations reduce their arms by one-third. Germany welcomed the proposal, but France insisted on security guarantees before reducing its military edge, and the conference stalled.

In 1933, British Prime Minister Ramsay MacDonald proposed a new plan to the Geneva Conference. European nations would equalize the size of their armies and, along with the United States, pledge to consult with one another to identify any aggressor who broke the peace. The new president, Franklin Roosevelt, agreed that the United States would join the consultations and would not insist on its neutral right to trade with the aggressor if America agreed with the outcome of the consultations. The new German chancellor, Adolf Hitler, welcomed Roosevelt's initiative. But the old irreconcilable senators William Borah and Hiram Johnson opposed any economic discrimination against aggressors. They attached to a neutrality bill pending before Congress an amendment prohibiting any discriminatory embargoes. The preoccupied Roosevelt accepted it, only to have Secretary of State Cordell Hull point out that this amendment violated Roosevelt's pledge to the Geneva Disarmament Conference. Without the right to enact discriminatory embargoes, the United States would not be able to stop neutral trade with an aggressor. Roosevelt then sidetracked the entire neutrality act. Hitler, who was pledged to German rearmament anyway, cynically denounced the negotiations and withdrew Germany from both the Geneva Conference and the League of Nations.

ECONOMIC DIPLOMACY TOWARD EUROPE

By the time Hitler pulled out of the Geneva meeting and the League of Nations, he and the Depression had destroyed more than America's hopes for disarmament; they also destroyed the Republican belief that the United States could maintain a stable and peaceful Europe through unofficial economic diplomacy without political or military commitments. While rejecting the League and the World Court, Republicans had participated eagerly if unofficially in European economic negotiations.

The first major flurry of Republican unofficial economic diplomacy occurred in the early 1920s. This was a time of severe economic and political crisis in Europe. Germany was challenging the terms of the Versailles Treaty; it published great volumes of documents to disprove its war guilt and urged reduction of its reparations bill. When France, feeling itself vulnerable and betrayed by America's rejection of the League and of the supplementary security treaty, insisted that Germany obey every jot and tittle of the Treaty of Versailles, Germany turned to another outcast nation, the Soviet Union. The governments of Germany and Soviet Russia detested one another, but they saw a rapprochement as a means of frightening their common adversaries. They signed the Treaty of Rapallo in 1922, restoring diplomatic relations between them and promising consultation on economic matters. Russia was already secretly permitting Germany to train soldiers with heavy weapons on Russian territory, thereby circumventing the Versailles strictures against German rearmament.

The French saw the Treaty of Rapallo as part of a dangerous trend toward German militarism. Freicorps toughs operated freely in Bavaria under the protection of the right-wing Bavarian government that had overthrown the short-lived Communist regime. The Nazi party of Adolf Hitler, then rising in Bavaria, encouraged Freicorps activities. Armed bands assassinated two moderate German leaders in 1921 and 1922, Matthias Erzberger and Foreign Minister Walter Rathenau. Amid the economic and social chaos that still pervaded Germany three years after the war, the German government fell into the hands of businessmen who were profiting from the inflation by extending their businesses in Germany, salting away their money in foreign currency and banks, and refusing to pay taxes for reparations.

Germany defaulted on reparations payments, and France, in the absence of support from its former allies, took matters into its own hands. In January 1923, the French army marched into the Ruhr to take over the mines and factories there and collect France's own reparations. The German workers laid down their tools and sabotaged French collections by passive resistance.

The German government paid the striking workers out of government funds and inflated the currency to the point that Germans rushed to buy goods whose prices might triple during the time they were standing in line. The British protested the French action, and the Americans withdrew their last troops from the occupied Rhineland as a sign of disfavor.

As inflation wiped out the savings of most of the German middle class and ravaged the economy, a new moderate government under Gustav Stresemann took power and moved to end the crisis. He called off the passive resistance campaign in the Ruhr and put down revolts from Right and Left, including Hitler's abortive Beer Hall Putsch. The French, whose own currency was being undermined by the German economic collapse, in turn consented to a conference on reparations. Secretary of State Hughes decided the United States should try to help in this crisis. Although he still adamantly refused to link reparations and war debts, he sent two prominent American businessmen, Charles G. Dawes and Owen D. Young, to serve as "unofficial" American delegates to the conference. Because Americans could provide the loans to make a reparations plan work, Dawes and Young played a prominent role. They helped formulate the Dawes Plan, which supplied loans from the old Allies to stabilize the German currency, temporarily scaled down German reparation payments, and secured French withdrawal from the Ruhr.

France left the Ruhr convinced of the futility of occupying Germany to force reparations payments. The French economy required at least a minimally healthy German economy, and every time France threatened to strangle Germany, Germany threatened to die. So France cast around for other ways to maintain its security against a reviving Germany.

Through the League of Nations, France proposed a treaty that would require all signatories to give armed support to any victim of aggression on their continent. The British balked because they had possessions on almost every continent and conceivably could be required to fight anywhere in the world. The United States warned that it would not tolerate interference with its right as a neutral to trade with any nation at war. As this hope for a collective security treaty collapsed, France, Germany, and Great Britain turned to a more limited form of security guarantee. They signed the Treaty of Locarno in 1925.

All agreed to guarantee the French-German border, thus confirming Alsace-Lorraine to France. They also agreed that the Rhineland would be demilitarized permanently. Germany became part of the League of Nations and promised to solve its problems peacefully. But the treaty gave no guarantee of Germany's eastern borders, and Stresemann made clear German intention to rectify them sometime in the future. France could only console itself that Stresemann usually advocated peaceful means of treaty revision and had demonstrated his sincerity by giving tacit consent for France to sign new security treaties with Czechoslovakia and Poland. At the same time, however, Germany signed a neutrality treaty with Russia, demonstrating that it was not abandoning the leverage of Rapallo.

By 1927, France had given up all hope of getting the United States to sign an official security treaty. Yet Aristide Briand, the French foreign minister who had been one of the architects of the Treaty of Locarno, thought he might at least involve the United States unofficially. He proposed that the United States and France sign a pact outlawing war between the two nations. He hoped that such a treaty would deter the United States from clashing with France and its League allies if they applied sanctions against an aggressor. Perhaps this would relieve British fears of a conflict with the United States and encourage England to consider more favorably potential sanctions against Germany. President Calvin Coolidge and the old irreconcilable Senator William E. Borah expressed some interest in the idea. Borah, however, soon retreated to the idea of a pact that would include all nations and would say nothing denying American neutral rights to trade with an aggressor. Secretary of State Frank Kellogg agreed. Briand had no interest in such a watered-down pact, but he decided there would be no harm in signing a treaty renouncing war. In July of 1928, all the great powers except Russia signed the Kellogg-Briand Pact. That treaty outlawed all wars but those of self-defense.

In the wake of this emotional paean to peace, the new Republican administration of Herbert Hoover sent Owen Young, one of the American negotiators who had shaped the Dawes Plan of 1924, back to Europe to negotiate a new and more permanent reparations settlement. The Young Plan of 1929 reduced German reparations still further. But neither the Young Plan nor the paper promises of the Kellogg-Briand Pact could survive the tumultuous emotions and events brought about by the depression that struck late in 1929.

At first Hoover and the Republicans tried to cope with the Depression by using strictly domestic means, including raising tariff rates with the Hawley-Smoot Tariff of 1930. But the drastic economic situation in Germany and Great Britain as well as the United States brought Hoover in mid-1931 to suggest a one-year moratorium on both reparations and war debt payments, thus finally making the link that Washington had tried so hard to avoid. Unfortunately, the Depression proved too powerful for Hoover's initiative to lead to a permanent solution. France, which got more in reparations than it paid out in debts, refused to accept the moratorium unless Germany diverted money from armaments to its reparations bill. France also insisted that the United States reduce its debt demands. Germany refused to make political concessions unless the Treaty of Versailles was revised. The United States would not reduce its debt demands unless France, which was the least affected by the Depression of all the major powers, proved its incapacity to pay. Finally, at Lausanne in Switzerland, the European powers agreed to reduce Germany's reparations by 90 percent if the United States would make a similar concession on war debts. Hoover was furious, because this politically explosive proposal came on the eve of the presidential election. He refused, but he went down to defeat at the hands of Franklin Roosevelt anyway.

In his lame duck period, Hoover gingerly tried to get Roosevelt to join him in accepting the linkage of debts and reparations along with the inevitable political flak that would result, but Roosevelt dodged his requests.

Hoover therefore demanded that Great Britain and France make their 1932 debt payments on time. When the French government tried to do so, the French Assembly overturned it. One by one the other European nations followed France in defaulting. Shortly afterward, German President von Hindenburg invited Adolf Hiter to accept Germany's chancellorship.

THE UNITED STATES, JAPAN, AND THE NEW ORDER IN ASIA

In Asia as well as in Europe, the postwar Republican administrations tried to maintain a stable and peaceful environment without drastic action or political commitments. They found in Japan, as they had in Germany, a moderate government that maintained only tenuous control over militant and dissatisfied elements of its population. Japanese moderates were willing to defend Japan's interests in China in cooperation with the other imperial powers, as they did at the Washington Conference, rather than resort to such provocative measures as the Twenty-One Demands. Ironically, however, the moderates tried to cooperate with the European imperial system just as that system was crumbling.

The Washington Conference dealt one telling blow to the cooperative imperial system: That conference nominally replaced the imperial system with America's long-sought Open Door. Japan signed the Nine Power Treaty, thus recognizing the principles of the Open Door, but insisted that its existing rights in China were not affected. Instead, the Lansing-Ishii Agreement of 1917, by which the United States recognized Japan's special position in Manchuria, remained in force. Harding and Hughes, on the other hand, argued that the Nine Power Treaty superseded the Lansing-Ishii Agreement and invalidated Japan's special position.

Hughes told the Japanese that if they insisted that the Lansing-Ishii Agreement still pertained, the United States would have to publish the agreement's secret protocol. That protocol pledged both powers not to seek privileges in China which would abridge the rights of other nations. Japan had insisted it be kept secret for fear of arousing its own militants. The Japanese finally agreed to renunciation of the Lansing-Ishii Agreement but went on to proclaim that their special rights in China existed without need for express recognition in diplomatic documents. Hughes replied he was happy that the Japanese did not claim special rights prejudicial to China or the other imperial powers. Just as in the past, the United States and Japan talked past one another when discussing the Open Door and Japan's special position in East Asia.

Perhaps, as the Republicans hoped, time would resolve the Japanese as well as German issues peacefully. In the case of Asia, these Republican hopes were thwarted not only by the Depression, but by another powerful agent as well, the rise of nationalism in China.

The emergence of Chinese nationalism dealt a far greater blow to the imperial system and Japan's special position in China than America's mild attempts to implement the Open Door. Chinese nationalism made itself felt at the Washington Conference when a Chinese delegation showed up with ten demands, including an end to extraterritoriality and the elimination of foreign control over China's tariff. But the Washington conferees were more concerned with eliminating the rivalry between the imperial powers than in accommodating China. At the instigation of the Americans, the powers promised to hold future conferences on the tariff and extraterritoriality. For the present, however, they would only return control of the postal service to China, and that with strings attached. The powers regarded China as too chaotic to provide adequate security for the lives and interests of foreigners and refused to abandon the unequal treaties until order could be guaranteed.

China was indeed a chaotic land of warring factions. The authority of the government extended only to those provinces controlled by semi-loyal warlords. The Peking government's primary opposition came from Sun Yat-sen's Kuomintang or Nationalist party, which controlled portions of South China from its capital of Canton. Sun Yat-sen demanded that the imperial powers recognize him as the ruler of China and revise the unequal treaty system. When the powers refused, he turned to the one nation that had offered to give up its special privileges in China, the Soviet Union. At the urging of his major military leader, Chiang Kai-shek, Sun accepted Soviet advisors and merged the Chinese Communists with his Kuomintang. Then he embarked on a campaign to unite China under Nationalist rule and at the same time force the imperial powers to give up their unequal treaty system. When Sun died of cancer in 1925, Chiang took over and marched his armies northward to try to unite China by military force.

The Nationalists' northern campaign brought several clashes with the citizens of the treaty powers. The British insisted that their subjects should be protected against the fighting and in one instance bombarded the city of Wanshien, killing many civilians. The Americans opposed the use of force but sent 5,000 marines to join the British in defending foreign nationals in Shanghai. Fortunately, the Nationalists took Shanghai without incident. In Nanking, however, Nationalist soldiers killed several foreigners, including the American vice-president of Nanking University and a Japanese officer.

Throughout these clashes, the United States remained relatively aloof and continued to offer concessions to the Chinese. In 1925, a year before the northern campaign, the United States, Great Britain, and Japan had agreed that China would have tariff autonomy as of 1929. During the northern campaign, the United States and Great Britain offered to make further concessions if the Chinese developed a government with which the Western powers could negotiate. The Americans and British became even more conciliatory when Chaing Kai-shek turned against Russia and his Communist allies in the bloody purge of 1927. The Americans and British saw Chiang as a moderate who might restrain the most militant anti-Westerners in his party. Chiang confirmed their view by marrying an American-educated wife and converting to Christianity later in 1927. When Chiang consolidated his hold on China in 1928, the United States quickly recognized his government. Many American observers warned, however, that the Kuomintang had lost its ideals and maintained only a fragile control over China through bribery, corruption, and alliances with various warlords and large landowners.

The Japanese were not so accommodating. They regarded American policy as "hypocritical humanism" and denounced it for undermining the prestige of the Japanese and other foreigners in China. They had much more at stake than the United States; over 40 percent of their trade and investments depended on Manchuria and Inner Mongolia, and they believed their Manchurian railroad and mining concessions along with the cotton textile mills in China to be vital to Japan's existence. They disliked the idea of Chinese tariff autonomy because tariff revision might make Chinese-owned cotton mills competitive with their own. Nationalist-inspired strikes and riots also threatened the Japanese mills and railroads in China. Before Chiang purged his Communist allies, those Communists had added fuel to the Nationalist strikes while Chiang's link to Russia had posed a strategic threat to the Japanese position in Manchuria and Inner Mongolia.

The Japanese responded to the Nationalist threat by trying to induce the warlord who controlled Manchuria, Chang Tso-lin, to separate himself from China and accept Japanese tutelage. But Chang resisted, so when Chiang Kai-shek turned against the Communists, the Japanese government decided to try to work out an arrangement in harmony with the other imperial powers. Even when former General Giichi Tanaka took over as Japanese prime minister and pledged a more "positive" policy in Manchuria, he continued to try to work with Chiang's government.

The Japanese army in Manchuria was not so sanguine as the civilian government. Both the army and navy considered war with the United States inevitable and believed that Japan had to secure a self-sufficient empire that would include Manchuria. The army saw Chiang's northern campaign as a threat to Japan's position in Manchuria despite Chiang's protestations to the contrary. When Prime Minister Tanaka ordered Japanese army units to march from Manchuria to the Shantung peninsula to protect Japanese citizens and interests there from Chiang's troops, one of the officers exceeded instructions and occupied the town of Tsinan, directly in the path of the advancing Nationalists. After a clash between Japanese and Chinese soldiers, the Japanese military decided to use the opportunity to make war. With the support of Tanaka, Japanese officers formulated an ultimatum too harsh for the Chinese to accept, then expelled the Chinese army from the Tsinan area and ruled by terror for a year. Meanwhile, Japanese officers in Manchuria assassinated Chang Tso-lin, the Manchurian warlord, in hopes of creating chaos that would require full military occupation of Manchuria.

This was going too far even for Tanaka. While he still pressed Chang Tso-lin's son to maintain a degree of autonomy from the rest of China, Tanaka recognized Chiang Kai-shek's government as the ruler of all China including Manchuria, and resigned when the army refused to court-martial Chang's assassins. A more moderate government succeeded Tanaka's. It moved toward greater cooperation with the imperial powers at the London Naval Conference of 1930 and in negotiations to modify extraterritoriality in China. But the Depression destroyed this process. The silk market in the United States dried up, and silk prices plummeted 75 percent. The level of Japanese exports to the United States sank 40 percent and the Hawley-Smoot Tariff of 1930 reduced them still more. As the incentives for cooperation with the West declined, many of the people hardest hit by the Depression in Japan sided with the military's desire for a stronger policy in China. They denounced the concessions made at the London Naval Conference, and fanatics even attempted to assassinate the prime minister, who died of his wounds six months later.

With rising public support and continuing problems in China, the Japanese army decided to act on its own. In September of 1931, officers in Manchuria blew up some of the railroad track on the Japanese-controlled South Manchurian Railroad north of Mukden, blamed the explosion on Chinese dissidents, and used this so-called Mukden Incident to justify military occupation of all of Manchuria. The Japanese civilian government accepted the *fait accompli* and formed the puppet state of Manchukuo with the heir to the old Manchu dynasty as regent.

THE STIMSON DOCTRINE

The United States responded cautiously. Hebert Hoover's secretary of state, Henry Stimson, told the Chinese that the Americans were "playing no favorites." He thought the Chinese were partly at fault for violating their treaties with Japan. He also hoped the incident was just another military mutiny, and that if the West avoided sanctions against the Japanese which might strengthen the fanatics, the civilian government might get the army officers to crawl "back into their dens." The Japanese did consent to an investigation by a neutral commission headed by the Earl of Lytton, but they continued to seize strategic points in Manchuria.

Stimson reluctantly and belatedly associated the United States with a League of Nations initiative that reminded Japan and China of their obligations under the Kellogg-Briand Pact and requested that the Japanese withdraw in one month. But he withheld endorsement of the Lytton Commission investigation even though the Japanese had consented to it. Only after Japan continued to consolidate its hold on Manchuria did Stimson take action. He announced that the United States would not recognize any infringements on American rights, the Open Door, China's territorial integrity, or any changes brought about by force in violation of the Kellogg-Briand Pact. This nonrecognition statement came to be known as the Stimson Doctrine.

The Japanese disregarded the Stimson Doctrine and, in response to a Chinese boycott of Japanese trade, bombarded Shanghai with its navy. The indiscriminate slaughter outraged public opinion in the West: The United States and Great Britain sent troops to Shanghai to protect their own nationals; the League of Nations adopted a resolution, similar to the Stimson Doctrine, that refused to recognize Japanese gains in Manchuria. But both Hoover and the British rejected Stimson's suggestion of economic or military sanctions. Stimson could only state that Japan's violation of the Washington Conference agreements freed the United States from its pledge not to fortify its Pacific possessions.

This empty threat did nothing to deter Japan. When the League of Nations adopted the Lytton Commission report, which mildly condemned the Manchurian invasion while blaming China for some of the actions that provoked it, Japan announced its withdrawal from the League. Japan also continued to fortify and expand its control of all Chinese territory north of the Great Wall. It even forced China to accept a broad demilitarized zone south of the wall. Japan's attempts to cooperate with China or the other imperial powers were over.

THE GOOD NEIGHBOR POLICY IN LATIN AMERICA

The American post-World War I reaction against intervention took effect more slowly in Latin America than it did in Europe and Asia. Secretary of State Charles Evans Hughes, to whom Harding delegated control over Latin American policy, made no such dramatic initiative in Latin American affairs as he had with the Washington Naval Conference. This seems surprising, since World War I ended whatever small chance there had been of European intervention in Latin America. Not only was Europe weaker, but many Latin American countries had grown stronger. The United States could no longer invoke the Roosevelt Corollary to cover its intervention. It was too obvious that postwar interventions would be designed not to prevent European intervention, but to protect U.S. economic and political interests.

By the turn of the twentieth century, Latin Americans had come to fear U.S. intervention far more than any possible European invasion. But the Harding and Coolidge administrations failed to change the interventionist policies of Theodore Roosevelt, Taft, and Wilson. Hughes withdrew American troops from the Dominican Republic in 1924, but kept the customs house and therefore Dominican finances in U.S. hands. The Dominican Republic remained an American protectorate ruled by the dictatorial Trujillo family, whose power stemmed from the U.S.-trained National Guard. Coolidge and his new secretary of state, Frank Kellogg, withdrew American marines from Nicaragua in 1925, but sent them right back in the following year when civil war broke out. In response to criticism of America's continuing presence, Coolidge proclaimed: "We are not making war in Nicaragua any more than a policeman on the streets is making war on a passerby." Herbert Hoover and his secretary of state, Henry Stimson, finally decided to withdraw the marines permanently in 1932 when they became embarrassed by the comparison of America's position in Nicaragua with Japan's conquest of Manchuria. As in Santo Domingo, American withdrawal left power in the hands of the National Guard and a dictatorial family, in this case the Somozas.

Wilson's Republican successors faced an even more dangerous and delicate situation in Mexico. Under Article 17 of Mexico's 1917 constitution, the Mexican government claimed all rights to subsoil resources in its territory. It also restricted surface land ownership to Mexican nationals except under special conditions, and any foreigners permitted to own land would have to subscribe to the Calvo Doctrine by promising not to appeal to their home governments for diplomatic assistance. Under these constitutional provisions, Mexican President Venustiano Carranza threatened to confiscate American oil company holdings. This gave new impetus to the hostility between the United States and Mexico that had nearly led to hostilities prior to World War I. The United States protested on behalf of the oil companies and Carranza gave none-too-credible assurances that the law would not be used retroactively against the companies. Meanwhile, he used the law to tax the companies in ways the companies thought were punitive.

In 1920, Álvaro Obregón overthrew Carranza, but the dispute with the United States continued. The United States withheld recognition of Obregón because he would not sign a treaty guaranteeing the property rights of U.S. citizens. Finally, in 1923, Obregón agreed to an informal understanding rather than a public treaty on property rights, and the United States recognized his government. But expropriations continued under Article 17. Mexico also imposed harsh restrictions and punishments on the Catholic Church and clergy, raising a strong outcry from American Catholics. To strain relations even further, Mexico extended aid to opponents of American occupation in Nicaragua. Kellogg went so far as to denounce Mexico for abetting a Bolshevist plot on Latin America. But public opposition to U.S. intervention in Mexico and Central America remained high, and ultimately Coolidge backed away from confrontation. He sent Dwight Morrow to Mexico as ambassador with instructions to avoid war. With the aid of Mexican judicial decisions that sided to some extent with the oil companies and with a diminution of the Mexican government's anticlerical policies, Morrow managed to smooth relations. Many historians pointed to this as the beginning of the Good Neighbor Policy.

Herbert Hoover took several additional steps toward a more cooperative and less interventionist policy in Latin America. He made a tour of Latin America in 1928 as president-elect and emphasized his wish to avoid further interventions. He abandoned to a large extent the manipulation of U.S. recognition policy to force changes on Latin American governments. After considerable hesitation, he endorsed a memorandum by Undersecretary of State Reuben Clark that repudiated the Roosevelt Corollary. Secretary of State Stimson explained Hoover's decision by pointing out that "the Monroe Doctrine was a declaration of the United States versus Europe—not the United States versus Latin America." But Hoover coupled his repudiation with a defense of the right of the United States to intervene in case of actual European threats or to protect American lives and property. He also signed, albeit reluctantly, the Hawley-Smoot Tariff, whose high rates were a formidable blow to Latin American economies. Thus Latin Americans were not too impressed by Hoover's professed friendliness, even when he withdrew American marines from Nicaragua, accelerated marine withdrawal from Haiti, and avoided further intervention into the tumults that followed the Depression in Panama, Honduras, and Cuba.

Franklin D. Roosevelt was far more successful than Hoover in convincing the Latin Americans that the United States had retreated from interventionism. He made the Good Neighbor policy his own in the eyes of most people, South and North American alike. In a 1928 article for *Foreign Affairs,* Roosevelt had denounced unilateral intervention by the United States in Latin America, although he endorsed joint intervention with other American powers. He also appointed Cordell Hull to be secretary of state, and Hull was an ardent supporter of reciprocal tariff reductions.

Roosevelt's turn toward nonintervention did not start auspiciously. A series of coups in Cuba in 1933 resulted in a leftist government headed by Dr. Ramón Grau San Martín. Roosevelt sent his personal friend, Undersecretary of State Sumner Welles, to Cuba as ambassador and troubleshooter, and Welles suggested sending troops to overthrow Grau. Roosevelt refused, but he did send several naval ships to Havana harbor and he withheld recognition from Grau. Welles then encouraged Fulgencia Batista, the military strongman behind Grau, to withdraw his support. Batista did, Grau was overthrown, and the United States recognized the new government in five days.

In the midst of this Cuban imbroglio, Cordell Hull met with the other countries of the Western Hemisphere at the Montevideo Conference of 1933. Under strong criticism for America's interference in Cuba, Hull surprised the conference by accepting a pledge against any nation interfering in the internal affairs of another Western Hemisphere country. Hull inserted a reservation that the United States did not give up its right to protect the lives and property of its citizens abroad. He also narrowly defined intervention as military rather than economic or diplomatic interference. But it seemed to many at the time a substantial step forward.

The Roosevelt administration followed the Montevideo pledge with further symbols of its good faith. In 1934 it abrogated its right to intervene in Cuba under the Platt Amendment. Roosevelt said nothing, however, of the right of the United States to intervene under other provisions of international law. That same year of 1934, Roosevelt withdrew the marines from Haiti three months ahead of Hoover's schedule, although the United States kept control of Haitian finances. In 1936, Roosevelt signed a new treaty with Panama that ended America's special rights of intervention. Unfortunately, the Senate refused consent until 1939, when an exchange of notes guaranteed the right of American intervention in an emergency. In 1940, Roosevelt relinquished the right to intervene unilaterally (but not jointly) in Santo Domingo.

As one can tell from all the qualifications to these treaties and pledges, the Good Neighbor policy did not mark a wholesale abandonment of intervention. Not only did Roosevelt insist on America's continuing right to intervene to protect American lives and property, he also sought mechanisms to permit joint intervention with other Latin American countries. Thus, at the Buenos Aires Conference of 1936, he accepted a new pledge that broadened the prohibition against intervention to "direct and indirect" interference, but saw to it that this prohibition extended only to intervention by "any one state," not a combination of countries. Roosevelt coupled this qualified commitment to yet another pledge that required all Pan American nations to consult with one another if there were a threat to peace.

Shortly afterward, in 1937 and 1938, Bolivia and Mexico tested Roosevelt's noninterventionist intentions by expropriating American oil companies. Roosevelt deferred the issue in Bolivia by requiring Standard Oil to exhaust all Bolivian court remedies before seeking U.S. government assistance. The Mexican situation was more difficult. Roosevelt feared that Mexican President Lázaro Cárdenas might invite Germany, Italy, or Japan to help run the confiscated oil equipment and resources. Josephus Daniels, ambassador to Mexico, still urged Roosevelt to be accommodating. Daniels had the ear of the president, for he had been secretary of the navy while Roosevelt was assistant secretary, and they both had come to regret their part in Woodrow Wilson's occupation of Vera Cruz. Roosevelt urged Mexico to submit the oil companies' claims of $450 million to arbitration. Cárdenas refused, but his more conservative successor agreed with Roosevelt to submit the claims to a two-man mixed arbitration commission. When the commission awarded the oil companies $24 million, Roosevelt accepted the decision and refused to back the companies in further action.

World War II brought further U.S. attempts to tighten its ties to Latin America and increase U.S. security. The Pan American foreign ministers, at American instigation, issued the Declaration of Panama in September 1939. It established a neutrality zone three hundred miles around the Western Hemisphere where belligerent ships were prohibited to sail. All the belligerents ignored it. But in Havana in the following year, 1940, the foreign ministers endorsed the "no transfer" principle. This prohibited Germany from acquiring French and Dutch colonies in the Western Hemisphere after it had conquered the mother countries. Since Germany never attempted to take the colonies, that declaration too was a dead letter. Even more illustrative of the growing Pan American cooperation on hemispheric defense, the Havana Conference of 1940 agreed that an attack by a non-American state on an American nation would be regarded as an attack on all.

There remained much contention in the Western Hemisphere, however, despite the Good Neighbor policy and the threat of World War II. Argentina sympathized with the Nazis, while many other nations wanted no part of the European war. Western Hemisphere countries resented the attempts of the FBI to ferret out subversives in Latin America. Many also resisted American desires to place troops in strategic areas of Latin America, remembering all too well past U.S. military interventions. The United States nonetheless stationed some 100,000 troops in Latin America during World War II, most of them in Central America and the Caribbean area to guard the Panama Canal.

The United States also sent $475 million in lend-lease aid to Latin America and supported Export-Import Bank loans to strengthen the Latin American economies, which made available more strategic materials from those nations to help the war effort. Since the Depression devastated the economies of Latin America, this wartime aid and trade, along with the few reciprocal trade treaties Hull managed to negotiate, tied Latin American finances even more tightly to the United States. In addition, the war closed many of Latin America's alternative markets. The U.S. wartime demand for raw materials thus distorted Latin American economies, and these economies faced major difficulties when the end of the war reduced U.S. demand. Meanwhile, the U.S. leaders most responsible for the relative restraint of Roosevelt's policy toward Latin America left the stage one by one. Sumner Welles, an important architect of the Good Neighbor policy once he had returned from his aggressive embassy in Cuba, had to resign when political enemies threatened to publicize an alleged incident of homosexual solicitation on a railroad train. Cordell Hull, an adversary of Welles but a supporter of the Good Neighbor approach, left office shortly before Franklin Roosevelt died of a stroke on the eve of victory in Europe. The faltering steps the Good Neighbor policy had taken toward cooperation and less intervention in Latin America would be undone by new leaders facing the challenge of the Cold War.

CONTROVERSIAL ISSUES AND FURTHER READING

The primary debate between historians over this period has been whether it truly constituted a retreat from internationalism. Certainly Americans of the time thought there was, and most approved of it. Historians were more divided. Many of them kept their Wilsonian sympathies and regretted America's lack of cooperation with the League of Nations, along with the country's refusal to be involved in European security affairs. [See, for example, Denna F. Fleming, *The United States and World Organization: 1920–1933* (1938). For a collection of pre–World War II opinion, see Quincy Wright, ed., *Neutrality and Collective Security* (1936).]

World War II converted Americans and their historians almost en masse into critics of what they still perceived as America's retreat from internationalism in the 1920s and early 1930s. Most historians laced their writings with harsh denunciations of the silliness and irresponsibility of Americans and their leaders, who failed to see that peace, disarmament, and economic diplomacy had to be linked to considerations of security, politics, and the balance of power. [See, for instance, the works of Robert Ferrell on this period: *Peace in Their Time: The Origins of the Kellogg-Briand Pact* (1952); *American Diplomacy in the Great Depression* (1957); *Frank B. Kellogg and Henry L. Stimson* (1963). Other works on important topics that took this view were Selig Adler, *The*

Isolationist Impulse (1957) and *The Uncertain Giant* (1965); Alexander DeConde, ed., *Isolation and Security in Twentieth-Century American Foreign Policy* (1957); Alan Nevins, *The United States in a Chaotic World* (1950); John D. Hicks, *The Republican Ascendancy* (1960); Gordon A. Craig and Felix Gilbert, eds., *The Diplomats, 1919-1939* (1963); John Chalmers Vinson, *The Parchment Peace: The United States Senate and the Washington Conference, 1921-1922* (1955) and his biography, *William E. Borah and the Outlawry of War* (1957); Marian C. McKenna, *Borah* (1961); L. Ethan Ellis, *Frank B. Kellogg and American Foreign Relations* (1961); Joseph Brandes, *Herbert Hoover and Economic Diplomacy: Department of Commerce Policy, 1921-1928* (1962); Raymond G. O'Connor, *Perilous Equilibrium: The United States and the London Naval Conference of 1930* (1962); Armin Rappaport, *Henry L. Stimson and the Japanese, 1931-1933* (1963); and Herbert Feis, *The Road to Pearl Harbor* (1950), and *Diplomacy of the Dollar* (1950).]

A few historians stood outside this post-World War II consensus. Richard N. Current's revisonist *Secretary Stimson* (1954) condemned Stimson for his interventionism. William Appleman Williams's seminal revisionist article, "The Legend of Isolationism in the 1920s," *Science and Society* (1954), denied that the Republican era had been isolationist in any case. He pointed especially to American economic expansion abroad to disprove the idea that the United States had truly retreated from internationalism after World War I. The Vietnam war, by undercutting sympathy for interventionist policies, moved many historians to join these earlier critics. Leading the historiographical movement were the so-called corporatist historians, who combined a mild version of Williams's revisionist emphasis on American economic expansionism with an insistence that Republican diplomacy was a continuation of at least one aspect of Wilsonian internationalism. [See especially the works of Joan Hoff Wilson, *American Business and Foreign Policy, 1920-1933* (1971), and *Herbert Hoover: Forgotten Progressive* (1975); Carl Parrini, *Heir to Empire: United States Economic Diplomacy, 1916-1923* (1969); Michael J. Hogan, *Informal Entente: The Private Structure of Cooperation in Anglo-American Economic Diplomacy, 1918-1928* (1977); and an especially good work, Melvyn Leffler, *The Elusive Quest: America's Pursuit of European Stability and French Security, 1919-1933* (1979).]

Other important recent works on American relations with Europe in this era include two broader surveys, L. Ethan Ellis, *Republican Foreign Policy, 1921-1933* (1968); and Arnold Offner, *The Origins of the Second World War* (1975). [For developments in Europe, the best survey is Raymond Sontag, *A Broken World, 1919-1939* (1971). On Harding, see Robert K. Murray, *The Harding Era* (1969), which is excessively favorable, and Eugene P. Trani and David L. Wilson, *The Presidency of Warren G. Harding* (1977). On Charles Evans Hughes, see Betty Glad, *Charles Evans Hughes and the Illusions of Innocence* (1966), a harsh critique. Older but milder treatments of Hughes are Dexter Perkins, *Charles Evans Hughes and American Democratic Statesmanship* (1956); and Merlo J. Pusey, *Charles Evans Hughes* (2 vols., 1951). An excellent character study is Elting E. Morison's biography of Stimson, *Turmoil and Tradition* (1960). Robert Schulzinger examines the State Department at this time in *The Making of the Diplomatic Mind: The Training, Outlook and Style of United States Foreign Service Officers, 1908-1931* (1975).]

Works on American relations with Asia also have become milder in tone and conclusion than they were in the immediate aftermath of World War II. [The most significant work on American-Japanese relations in this era is Akira Iriye, *After Imperialism: The Search for a New Order in the Far East, 1921-1931* (1965). See also Dorothy Borg, *American Policy and the Chinese Revolution, 1925-1928* (1947); and Dorothy Borg and Shumpei Okamoto, *Pearl Harbor as History: Japanese-American Relations, 1931-1941*

(1973). On the various naval limitation conferences with Japan, see Thomas Buckley, *The United States and the Washington Conference, 1921–1922* (1970); Roger Dingman, *Power in the Pacific: The Origins of Naval Arms Limitation, 1914–1922* (1976); Gerald E. Wheeler, *Prelude to Pearl Harbor: The United States Navy and the Far East, 1921–1931* (1963); and Stephen Pelz, *Race to Pearl Harbor: The Failure of the Second London Naval Conference and the Onset of World War II* (1974). For British policy toward the United States and the Far East, see William Roger Louis, *British Strategy in the Far East, 1919–1939* (1971); and Christopher Thorne, *The Limits of Foreign Policy: The West, the League, and the Far Eastern Crisis of 1931–1933* (1972). For a Japanese view, see Saburo Ienaga, *The Pacific War: World War II and the Japanese, 1931–1945* (1978); Sadaka Ogata, *Deviance in Manchuria: The Making of Japanese Foreign Policy, 1931–1932* (1964); and Takehiko Yoshihashi, *Conspiracy at Mukden* (1963). James B. Crowley takes a harsh view of Japan in *Quest for Autonomy: National Security and Foreign Policy, 1930–1938* (1966). For American responses to the rise of nationalism in China, see Russell D. Buhite, *Nelson T. Johnson and American Policy toward China, 1925–1941* (1968).]

In contrast to historical works on American policy toward Europe and Asia, there have been few historians who have argued for American interventionism in Latin America. Contemporaries welcomed the Good Neighbor policy, and most post-World War II historians continued to praise it, arguing only over whether Franklin Roosevelt or his Republican predecessors deserved credit for it. [For examples of works praising the Good Neighbor policy, see Edward O. Guerrant, *Roosevelt's Good Neighbor Policy* (1950); Bryce Wood, *The Making of the Good Neighbor Policy* (1961); Irwin F. Gellman, *Good Neighbor Diplomacy: United States Policies in Latin America, 1933–1945* (1979); Dana G. Munro, *The United States and the Caribbean Republics, 1921–1933* (1974); Kenneth J. Grieb, *The Latin American Policy of Warren G. Harding* (1976), which argues that Harding truly initiated the policy of restraint toward Latin America; Alexander DeConde, *Herbert Hoover's Latin American Policy* (1951); and Donald Dozer, *Are We Good Neighbors?* (1959), which sees World War II as bringing an increase in intervention and undermining the restraint of the Good Neighbor policy.]

Revisionists have seen the Good Neighbor policy as a mere change of tactics rather than a retreat from American empire. They emphasize America's increasing economic penetration of the Latin American nations. Although Franklin Roosevelt did not resort to military interventions as often as his predecessors, military intrusions were an ever-present threat and ultimately would become necessary to protect the increasing economic stake in Latin American stability. For revisionists, then, the Good Neighbor policy was no more than a blip on the continuing history of America's economic expansion. [David Green, *The Containment of Latin America; A History of the Myths and Realities of the Good Neighbor Policy* (1971); Jules Robert Benjamin, *The United States and Cuba: Hegemony and Dependent Development, 1880–1934* (1977); Robert F. Smith, *The United States and Revolutionary Nationalism in Mexico, 1916–1932* (1972); Dick Steward, *Trade and Hemisphere: The Good Neighbor Policy and Reciprocal Trade* (1975); Lloyd C. Gardner, *Economic Aspects of New Deal Diplomacy* (1964); and Joseph Tulchin, *Aftermath of War: World War I and U.S. Policy toward Latin America* (1971).]

Recent American policies toward Latin America seem to have influenced even nationalists and realists to take a harsher view of U.S. policy and the supposed success of Good Neighbor diplomacy. Many of these historians are almost as critical of American policy as the revisionists, but they place somewhat less emphasis on economic motives and are somewhat more fatalistic about the influence a great power will have over a smaller one. [See, for instance, Gordon Connell-Smith, *The United States and Latin America* (1974); Cole Blasier, *The Hovering Giant: U.S. Responses to Revolutionary Change in Latin America* (1976); Michael Grow, *The Good Neighbor Policy and Authoritarianism in Paraguay* (1981); William Kamman, *A Search for Stability: United States Diplomacy toward Nicaragua, 1925–1933* (1968); Hans Schmidt, *The United States Occupation of Haiti* (1971); Stanley E. Hilton, *Brazil and the Great Powers, 1930–1939* (1975); and Stephen J. Randall, *The Diplomacy of Modernization: Colombian-American Relations, 1920–1940* (1977).]

CHAPTER 14

Franklin D. Roosevelt and the Coming of World War II

APPEASEMENT: 1932–1939

Franklin Roosevelt had been a champion of the League of Nations while serving as Wilson's assistant secretary of the navy and again when running for vice-president on the Democratic ticket in 1920. But as public opinion recoiled from Wilson's vision in the 1920s, Roosevelt grew more cautious. Then, during his campaign for the presidency in 1932, Roosevelt bowed to the pressure of the powerhouse Democratic publisher, William Randolph Hearst, and publicly renounced the League of Nations.

Nonetheless, Roosevelt's internationalist opinions occasionally peeked through during his first administration. In November 1933, Roosevelt broke with the policy of nonrecognition toward the Soviet Union initiated by Wilson and continued by the succeeding Republican administrations. Wilson, his Republican successors,and the American Congress held aloof from the Soviets in part because the Bolsheviks had repudiated over $600 million in debts Russia owed to the United States and in part out of revulsion against the Soviet Communist system. Ironically, American business had not stayed so aloof from the Soviets. Several large American corporations, like General Electric, DuPont, and International Harvester, had contracts in the 1920s to provide technological aid to the Soviet Union. Henry Ford, the arch capitalist, spent millions helping to set up a factory in Russia to produce Model A cars and trucks. Thus, Roosevelt could count on support from much of the American business community for his decision formally to recognize the Soviet government. Roosevelt also hoped that the Soviets might be of aid in resisting Japanese expansion on the Asian continent.

Roosevelt showed other internationalist proclivities in early 1934 when he contemplated the desirability of an international trade boycott against Nazi Germany. Two years later, when Hitler marched his troops into the demilitarized Rhineland, Roosevelt confided to a British visitor that he thought the choice was between war immediately or five years later. But Roosevelt would not pursue any internationalist action that posed the slightest threat to the domestic consensus he needed to pull the United States out of the Depression. He demonstrated this in two sensational 1933 decisions.

The first of these decisions, mentioned in the preceding chapter, was to accept the attachment of an amendment prohibiting discretionary embargoes to the pending neutrality bill. As we have seen, this contradicted Roosevelt's pledge to the Geneva Disarmament Conference that the United States would avoid challenging collective economic actions against an aggressor. Even more sensationally, Roosevelt disrupted the London Economic Conference of 1933 by choosing domestic over international priorities. The European delegates to the London Conference wanted the United States to forgive the war debts, lower its tariffs, and agree to a plan that would stabilize the exchange rates between national currencies. Roosevelt refused from the outset to permit any discussion of war debts. (In the Johnson Act of 1934, Congress went further and prohibited new loans to any nation that had defaulted on its debts.) Roosevelt also refused to permit Cordell Hull, the leader of the American delegation, to pursue his cherished program of reciprocal tariff reductions. Roosevelt feared lower duties would undermine his hopes to raise domestic prices.

The president initially remained vague about the third European goal, monetary stabilization. But when White House advisor Raymond Moley, whom Roosevelt had sent to London in midconference amid a splash of publicity and wounded outcries from Hull, recommended a stabilization agreement, Roosevelt sent the assembly a "bombshell" message. The United States would accept no stabilization agreement whatever. Like tariff reduction, stabilization would interfere with his desire to raise domestic prices.

Roosevelt's priorities remained the same even as Europe and Asia marched toward war. He believed he had little choice, for most Americans regarded the approach of a foreign war as reason for further withdrawal rather than intervention to prevent it. Roosevelt was very sensitive to public opinion; he commissioned poll after poll to test it. He commented once in the late 1930s that it was a "terrible thing to look over your shoulder when you are trying to lead—and to find no one there."

The apathetic public mood was a compound of events and personalities—not only the reaction to the sacrifices of World War I, the Senate defeat of the League and Treaty of Versailles, the Depression, and the rise of totalitarian governments, but also the highly publicized activities and opinions of isolationist politicians, historians, and activists. In 1934, Senator Gerald P. Nye conducted hearings on the causes of American entry into World War I which publicized the idea that munitions makers, bankers, and British propagandists had maneuvered the United States into the conflagration. Revisionist historians like Harry Elmer Barnes, Walter Millis, and Charles A. Beard reinforced the idea that intervention had been a mistake, if not an evil plot.

A strong pacifist movement supported isolationist sentiments. Uncompromising organizations like the National Society for the Prevention of War and the Women's International League for Peace and Freedom condemned the League of Nations and any sort of international sanctions on the grounds that disarmament was the only road to peace. They challenged the older peace organizations that had supported the League and collective security, organizations such as the World Peace Foundation and the Carnegie Endowment for International Peace.

This groundswell of isolationist opinion had a powerful impact on Congress and the president. In 1935, isolationist Senators William Borah, Hiram Johnson, George Norris, and Robert LaFollette engineered the congressional defeat of an inocuous proposal for the United States to join the World Court. At the same time, Roosevelt suggested that Congress formulate a new neutrality act to prohibit the activities that Americans believed had dragged them into World War I. The United States should embargo loans and the shipment of arms to belligerents and prevent American citizens from traveling aboard belligerent vessels. Unfortunately, this immediately raised the issue that had sidetracked the Neutrality Bill of 1933. Should an arms embargo extend to all belligerents, or just to the aggressors?

Roosevelt and the internationalists wanted the president to be able to embargo arms to an aggressor while supplying them to the victim. They argued that the best way for the United States to stay out of a war was to deter it in the first place by joining collective security agreements. Isolationists, on the other hand, insisted on an impartial arms embargo against all belligerents, without any discretion for the president to punish a supposed aggressor. Senator Nye successfully filibustered against the discriminatory clause, and the Senate finally included an impartial arms embargo in the Neutrality Act of 1935. Roosevelt got a six-month limit put on the bill, announced it was entirely satisfactory to him, then warned while signing it that it might do more to push the United States into war than to avoid it.

Behind Roosevelt's vacillation there seems to have lain a hidden agenda. He accepted the Neutrality Act for six months because he saw how he might manipulate it to punish Italy for its aggression toward Ethiopia. Benito Mussolini, whose Fascist regime had taken power in Italy in 1922, had been agitating to incorporate Ethiopia into Italy's existing North African empire for more than a year. Immediately after Roosevelt signed the Neutrality Act of 1935, Mussolini followed up his bluster with an invasion, complete with tanks, artillery, and poison gas ranged against spear-carrying Ethiopian warriors on horseback. Roosevelt immediately invoked the Neutrality Act. He embargoed arms to the nations at war, warned Americans off belligerent ships, and told his countrymen that they traded with Italy and Ethiopia at their own risk. As Roosevelt had foreseen, the supposedly impartial Neutrality Act worked entirely against the Italian aggressors. Ethiopia had no passenger vessels and no submarines to threaten Italian liners. Roosevelt's decree affected only Italian ships. Likewise Ethiopia had no way to get trade from the United States, so the act affected only trade with Italy. As Hull pointed out, invoking the Neutrality Act was a "gratuitous affront" to Italy.

Roosevelt's circuitous attempt to punish Italian aggression presented a golden opportunity for the League of Nations and the United States to align their policies. Tragically, they missed their chance. The League condemned Mussolini's invasion and embargoed a long list of goods to Italy. But it omitted oil from the embargo list, the one thing that might have given Mussolini pause. Great Britain and France feared that embargoing oil might lead Italy to declare war and fall into Hitler's waiting arms. Roosevelt also moved cautiously. He would not risk joining the League embargo formally, especially since the omission of oil made it ineffective. He did ask American business voluntarily to observe a "moral embargo" on trade with Italy, but despite his request the volume of Italian-American trade went up rather than down.

Meanwhile, in December of 1935, British Foreign Secretary Sir George Hoare and French Foreign Minister Pierre Laval decided to offer Mussolini control of most of Ethiopia if he would end his invasion. Public outcry aborted this Hoare-Laval deal and forced Hoare's resignation, but Mussolini completed his conquest without further interference. England, France, and the United States drew still further apart with mutual recriminations over who was at fault for the collapse of resistance to Italy.

This situation precipitated further American withdrawal from European affairs. Congress extended the Neutrality Act into 1937 and added to it a ban on private loans to belligerents, a provision that had fallen out of the original act in the 1935 revision. In the debates over extension of the Neutrality Act, Roosevelt asked once again for some presidential discretion. He wanted to be able to bar trade in strategic materials other than arms to aggressors while continuing such trade with the victims. Once again he failed. This time congressmen who wanted an impartial embargo found allies among those who wanted no embargoes on strategic materials at all. These latter members of Congress insisted on vigorous and impartial enforcement of America's neutral right to trade with all belligerents. They thought truly impartial trade rather than abstention was the proper means to keep America out of war. In the face of this opposition, Roosevelt dropped his request for flexibility and signed the bill without comment. One week later, March 7, 1936, Hitler's troops marched into the demilitarized Rhineland.

Hitler's move was an enormous gamble. It violated both the Treaty of Versailles and the Treaty of Locarno. It posed a grave strategic threat to France, for it put German troops in a position to attack France once again through Belgium. This would outflank the elaborate Maginot Line the French had been building on the German border since 1929. Not only did France have an incentive to resist the German move, it had the capability. Germany's army was just rebuilding, and the French had an enormous military superiority. They easily could have forced a German retreat, and Hitler's government would probably not have survived the fiasco. The French general staff, however, advised against resistance. The British, having already signed a treaty with Hitler recognizing Germany's right to a navy so long as it did not exceed 35 percent of the British navy, told the French they could expect no help from Great Britain if they attacked. The beleaguered French did nothing but strengthen the Maginot Line.

The German occupation of the Rhineland demonstrated the bankruptcy of British and French foreign policy. Hitler's bold success made his political position in Germany unassailable, and he began immediately to fortify Germany's west wall. This confirmed the French in their defensive strategy. They ignored the advice of General Charles de Gaulle to build offensive weapons such as the tank, airplane, and submarine. Instead, they relied on the defensive weapons of fortifications, machine guns, heavy artillery, and infantry to make themselves invulnerable to another German attack. They also counted on their eastern European allies to force a two-front war on Germany if Germany attacked France. By adding 30 million Poles and 12 million Czechs to France's own population of 40 million, the Allies would outnumber Germany's population of 65 million.

Unfortunately, the French did not anticipate that Germany, adopting modern offensive weaponry and *blitzkrieg* (lightning war) tactics, would so easily sweep aside their defensive preparations. Even more inexcusably, they failed to anticipate that Germany might attack eastward and eliminate Polish and Czech resistance before invading France. France had no way to respond to an invasion of its allies because of its defensive posture. Great Britain, with its navy, might have had the capacity to land an expeditionary force to aid Poland and Czechoslovakia. But the British were unwilling to defend the eastern borders created by the Treaty of Versailles against what they believed was inevitable German revision. Great Britain's commitment to France was limited to joining it in a *defensive* war. That meant that if Germany attacked Poland or Czechoslovakia and France responded by attacking Germany from the rear, Great Britain would regard it as an offensive war and feel under no obligation to aid the French.

Roosevelt also remained aloof in the Rhineland crisis. He refused the French plea for a moral condemnation of Germany and declined to send observers to the League discussion of Germany's challenge to the Versailles system. With the Europeans themselves rejecting a strong stand against Germany, Roosevelt saw no reason for the United States to leap into the fray.

On the heels of the Rhineland crisis, civil war broke out in Spain. Royalist General Francisco Franco and the Spanish army launched a campaign to overthrow Spain's republican government. Great Britain and France asked the United States and other nations to deny arms to both sides and thus prevent the war from spreading. Roosevelt heeded their plea. But Germany and Italy provided invaluable support for Franco. When the Spanish navy refused to ferry Franco's troops from North Africa to Spain to join the fight, German planes did the job. The Soviet Union tried to counter the Fascist support for Franco by sending arms and advisors to the Spanish government, and American liberals emotionally demanded that the United States join the Russians in aiding the Loyalists. After all, they pointed out, the Neutrality Act did not prevent the United States from sending arms to a legitimate government for use against rebels. Roosevelt personally favored the Loyalists, but pressure from American Catholics in support of Franco along with the desire to cooperate with Britain and France froze Roosevelt's policy until Franco's triumph in 1939.

The Spanish Civil War triggered renewed discussion of the Neutrality Act, the provisions of which were due to expire in 1937. Many members of Congress expressed fear that ordinary trade with nations at war could drag the United States into a war as easily as trade in armaments. They suggested extending the arms embargo to all commerce with belligerents. Others argued that this abandoned too many of America's neutral rights and would threaten American recovery. Financier and sometime presidential advisor Bernard Baruch suggested an alternative that could save American trade and avoid war at the same time. He would permit belligerents to buy American goods, but require them to use their own ships to transport them home. Thus, if the ships and goods were attacked, the United States would have no stake in them and would not be obliged to fight. Roosevelt supported this "cash and carry" provision because he saw it would aid Great Britain and France to the exclusion of Germany. British control of the sea would ensure that the Germans would not be able to get their ships to America to take advantage of cash and carry. The British remained disturbed that the impartial arms embargo remained in the Neutrality Act of 1937, but they were grateful for the opportunity to obtain other goods.

Cash and carry did not work so fortuitously in Asia. A few weeks after Congress passed the Neutrality Act of 1937, the Japanese army clashed with Chinese soldiers at the Marco Polo Bridge just south of Peking, and Japan immediately took the opportunity to embark on a war of conquest into southern China. If Roosevelt recognized the state of war and invoked the Neutrality Act, as he was expected to do, Japan would benefit because it had the navy to take advantage of cash and carry. Again Roosevelt showed his ingenuity in using isolationist laws to benefit interventionist causes. He refused to recognize the state of war and thus permitted American trade with China to continue. Still, the volume of trade with Japan, especially in critical materiel such as oil and scrap iron, far exceeded that to Japan's victim.

Japanese aggression seemed all the more ominous because Japan was moving toward an alliance with Germany and Italy. The latter had signed a treaty eliminating obstacles to cooperation between them in October 1936, during their joint venture in the Spanish Civil War. A month later, Japan signed an Anti-Comintern Pact with Germany which promised mutual aid if either were attacked by the Soviet Union. Italy joined the Anti-Comintern Pact the following year, 1937. Roosevelt began to contemplate some sort of gesture against what he privately called these "bandit nations."

He made a sensational splash in late 1937 when he spoke publicly of "quarantining" aggressors. He also joined Great Britain and France in condemning Japan's war as a violation of the Washington Conference treaties and agreed to send an American delegate to a meeting in Brussels to discuss the conflict in China. But nothing came of any of these gestures. Roosevelt had no firm plan in mind when he gave his quarantine speech, and neither he nor any other Western leader was prepared to risk being dragged into the war in Asia. When Japanese planes attacked the American gunboat *Panay* on the Yangtze River in late 1937, Roosevelt accepted the Japanese apology and let the matter drop.

The president was too weak domestically in 1937 and 1938 to do much more than make gestures on foreign policy. His attempt to "pack" the Supreme Court had failed and generated charges that he was becoming a dictator on the model of the European Fascists. His refusal to break several prolonged sit-down strikes in 1937 cost him considerable support among middle-class voters. Most devastating of all, the economy plunged down-ward in 1937 to destroy much of the painfully slow recovery that had been made under the New Deal. Conservative Democrats in Congress deserted the New Deal coalition and joined the Republicans to try to defeat further re-form legislation and deter Roosevelt from seeking a third term in 1940. One group of congressmen told Roosevelt: "For God's sake, don't send us any more controversial legislation." Roosevelt tried to improve his position in the 1938 elections, but his attempts to replace conservative Democrats with lib-erals in the primaries failed, while the Republicans picked up eighty-one seats in the House along with eight in the Senate during the subsequent gen-eral elections.

With the strengthened bipartisan conservative coalition stalemating most of Roosevelt's political initiatives, the president could do little more than watch as Hitler forced Austria to select a Nazi prime minister and then got him to invite German troops across the border to prevent violence and bloodshed. Hitler then demanded that Czechoslovakia turn over the Sude-tenland. The Sudetenland contained 3.5 million Germans whom Hitler had encouraged to make extortionate demands on the Czech government. Roo-sevelt briefly considered joining France and Great Britain in supporting the Czechs. But Czechoslovakia succumbed to British and French pressure and agreed to give the territory eventually to Germany, so Roosevelt lost heart. When Hitler arrogantly demanded that Czechoslovakia cede the territory immediately or he would march, Roosevelt made public appeals for peace. He wired British Prime Minister Neville Chamberlain, "Good man!" when Chamberlain arranged a meeting with Hitler at Munich to head off the crisis. At Munich, Chamberlain, French Prime Minister Edouard Daladier, Musso-lini, and Hitler agreed that Germany would occupy the Sudetenland in ex-change for Hitler's promise that he would seek no further territory in Europe. The relief of the world was short-lived, for six months later Hitler flagrantly broke his promise and occupied the remainder of Czechoslovakia.

The shock of Czechoslovakia stirred Roosevelt to try once again to revise the Neutrality Act. He wanted to be able to lift an arms embargo against the victim of aggression while leaving it on the aggressor. But the Senate stalled and the House defeated the discriminatory provision by four votes. Roose-velt called the Senate leaders to the White House to try to reverse the defeat. After his emotional appeal, Vice-President John Nance Garner polled the group and told Roosevelt: "Well, Captain, we may as well face the facts. You haven't got the votes, and that's all there is to it." Not until Europe was ac-tually at war would the United States begin to abandon its isolationist course.

AMERICA'S MARCH TOWARD WAR IN EUROPE

After Hitler completed his invasion of Czechoslovakia, he quickly revealed further ambitions in the east. First he occupied Memel at the expense of Lith-uania. Then he demanded that Poland turn over the free city of Danzig and permit a German railroad across the corridor to East Prussia. Great Britain already had begun a substantial arms-building program after Hitler's betrayal of his Munich promises. Then, when Hitler made his demands of Poland, Neville Chamberlain responded by making a defensive alliance with the beleaguered Poles and other eastern European states. Hitler was shocked. He had hoped to seize eastern Europe without interference from the West. France seemed sufficiently intimidated, but Hitler told his commanders that he wanted to avoid war with Great Britain at least until 1943.

The key to the situation was the Soviet Union. After Great Britain made its guarantees to Poland and Poland's neighbors, Chamberlain and the French approached Russia for a pact that might further deter Germany's eastward march. But Stalin distrusted the British and the French. He professed to believe that Britain and France purposely had conceded Hitler's demands on Czechoslovakia to keep Hitler pointed eastward and ultimately embroil Germany and Russia in a war. Stalin demanded that any pact with the West should involve a guarantee of the independence of eastern Europe's regimes even if they did not want such a guarantee. He also insisted that a military pact precede a political agreement, and that the military pact should include the stationing of Russian troops in Poland and elsewhere to meet an invading Germany well short of the Soviet border.

Poland was adamant against Russian troops on its soil, and other nations were reluctant as well. The British were especially suspicious of Stalin's purposes after the Russian leader told Estonia that any concession Estonia might make to Germany would result in an end to Russia's nonintervention pledge. Stalin's program seemed to be a prelude to Soviet occupation of eastern Europe. This made the British and French hesitant and vacillating in their negotiations with the Soviets.

Hitler showed no such hesitation. As often as he had railed against Russia and communism, he was ready to make a nonaggression pact with the Soviets. He believed this would not only prevent Soviet opposition to his intended conquest of Poland, but demoralize the Western powers and deter their intervention as well. To achieve the stunning Russo-German Non-Aggression Pact of August 1939, Hitler conceded eastern Poland, Finland, Estonia, Latvia, and the Bessarabian portion of Rumania to the Soviet sphere of influence. (The Russians added Lithuania to their sphere a month later.)

Freed of the fear of Russian intervention, Hitler sent his armies plunging into Poland on September 1, 1939. To his surprise and chagrin, the British and French declared war even though they had no means to resist Germany's advance into eastern Europe. While Germany's blitzkrieg tactics demolished and conquered western Poland, the Soviets moved into eastern Poland to claim their share, and then turned to attack Finland. The Finns put up a surprising battle, and this Russo-Finnish War absorbed American attention for several months because the Germans paused after conquering Poland. Hitler had denuded his western borders of troops to concentrate them in Poland, and he had to return them before striking at France. But France did not exploit the opportunity to attack. After a minor sally into the Saar Valley, most of the French army hunkered down in defensive positions along the Maginot

Line to await a German offensive. Hilter used this opportunity to capture Denmark and Norway. Then he ended the period of "phony war" or *sitzkrieg* with a surprise attack through the Ardennes Forest that broke the French lines, forced France's surrender in little more than a month, and sent the British Expeditionary Force scurrying back across the Channel from the collapsing pocket around Dunkirk.

Hitler's invasion of Poland stirred deep anger in the United States. Roosevelt invoked the Neutrality Act with the comment that he regretted ever signing it. In contrast to Woodrow Wilson's appeal on the outbreak of World War I, Roosevelt asked for neutrality in action but not in thought. He then called for repeal of the arms embargo. Roosevelt knew repeal would favor Britain and France, but he portrayed it simply as a return to traditional international law. Although this failed to avert a terrific debate betwen isolationists and internationalists in Congress, repeal finally passed.

The fall of France then shocked Congress into a still more vigorous response. Under Roosevelt's urging, Congress increased the military budget for 1940 from $2 to $10.5 billion. Public opinion also changed drastically. Prior to France's collapse, 82 percent of Americans expected the Allies to win the war and thus saw no particular reason for the United States to aid them. After Germany had swatted aside French resistance, a majority of Americans polled feared that Germany would win the war. Therefore 80 percent favored extending aid to Great Britain, even though 65 percent expected this to lead to American involvement. And yet 82 percent still opposed American military intervention.

Roosevelt read the message these polls delivered. Americans wanted Britain to win the war and were willing to aid it, but they did not want to enter the war themselves. Consequently, Roosevelt portrayed every action he took to aid Great Britain as designed to prevent American intervention by helping the British to win on their own. Roosevelt undoubtedly realized that Britain would require American military intervention to win, but he never said that directly to the American people. He would not take a divided nation into a major war. Instead, he urged aid to the Allies in hopes either that a miracle would allow them to win or that Hitler would retaliate and galvanize Americans into a united determination to fight and defeat the Nazis.

Roosevelt was anxious to prevent a Nazi conquest of Europe because he knew this would give Hitler the resources to threaten the United States. He especially worried that Hitler might capture the British navy intact. He had no doubt that once Hitler had the capability to extend his power to the Western Hemisphere, he would have no trouble finding a rationale for doing so.

Despite Roosevelt's deviousness and proclamations that he would never send Americans to fight a foreign war, polls showed that Americans had few illusions about what the president was doing. In fact, most historians who have criticized Roosevelt have accused him of moving too cautiously toward intervention. They argue that the polls show Roosevelt to have been behind public opinion rather than ahead of it. Hitler seemed to understand Roosevelt's intentions as well. He refused to respond to Roosevelt's provocations and create an incident that would bring America into the European war. He remembered too vividly the miscalculation Germany had made in World War I. In hopes of diverting the United States from Europe, he encouraged the Japanese to expand. Even if this led to war with the United States, America would have to fight on two fronts, and Hitler could continue his triumphant march of conquest.

Once Hitler had defeated France, he began to soften up England for an amphibious invasion. His air force bombed port facilities and Royal Air Force bases, then foolishly switched to terror bombing of English cities to try to break British morale. At the same time, German submarines began sinking vast numbers of British cargo ships. The cash and carry provisions of America's Neutrality Acts prevented Roosevelt from using American ships to carry the goods. But after three months of hesitation, Roosevelt decided to respond to British Prime Minister Winston Churchill's pleas and give Great Britain fifty destroyers to help guard the convoys. Roosevelt softened the impact of this "destroyer deal" by trading the overage destroyers for leases on British naval bases in the Western Hemisphere and a British promise not to let their navy fall into German hands. The British regarded this as a hard bargain, but it permitted Roosevelt to portray the deal as a strengthening of American defenses rather than aid to the Allies. Public opinion polls showed wide support for Roosevelt's action, but still he took no chance of congressional interference. He concluded the destroyer deal as an executive agreement rather than as a treaty that would require consent of two-thirds of the Senate.

Roosevelt remained cautious as he approached the election of 1940, in which he sought a third term as president. He stayed aloof from the battle in Congress for a Selective Service Act, and signed it without fanfare in September of 1940, the same month he announced the destroyer deal. When the Republicans rejected isolationist Robert Taft and nominated Wendell Willkie, a fervent supporter of aid to Britain, Roosevelt thought he would be permitted to continue his ambiguous course. On the eve of the election, however, Willkie succumbed to temptation and attacked Roosevelt for secretly maneuvering the United States toward war. Roosevelt responded by promising an Irish isolationist crowd in Boston: "I have said this before, but I shall say it again and again and again: Your boys are not going to be sent into any foreign wars." His advisors had warned against this unqualified pledge and reminded him that the Democratic platform had promised to stay out of war "except in the case of attack." Roosevelt blithely disregarded this advice with the remark: "Of course we'll fight if we're attacked. If somebody attacks us, then it isn't a foreign war, is it?" Willkie was not so blithe. "That hypocritical son of a bitch! This is going to beat me," he complained. He was right; Roosevelt won 55 percent of the vote.

A month after his electoral victory, Roosevelt faced another crisis. Britain's RAF had won the Battle of Britain by defeating the German air campaign and forcing Hitler to call off his invasion. But Hitler accelerated submarine wolfpack attacks on British convoys to starve the British into submission. Churchill informed Roosevelt that Great Britain was running out of money to buy American supplies and ships to carry them. He asked Roosevelt to find a way to expand the American supply effort.

The Neutrality Acts prohibited loans of money to belligerents. The Johnson Act of 1934 prohibited loans to any nation that had defaulted on its war debts. Roosevelt decided to circumvent these prohibitions with the ingenious program he called Lend-Lease. America would loan Britain war materiel rather than money, and Great Britain would return it after the war. It was like lending a neighbor a garden hose to put out a fire, he told the American people. It was far more like loaning chewing gum, one of his opponents said. After the neighbor had used it, you did not want it back. Senator Burton Wheeler claimed that Lend-Lease was another Agricultural Administration Act—it would plow under every fourth American boy. Roosevelt called this the rottenest remark made during his political life. He argued that the United States had to become the "arsenal of democracy." This was a serious risk, for if Great Britain lost, American equipment needed for the defense of the United States would fall into German hands. Nevertheless, the Senate and House followed changing public opinion and passed the Lend-Lease Act by overwhelming majorities.

Winston Churchill called Lend-Lease the most unsordid act in history but, as with the destroyer deal, the United States demanded a quid pro quo. The British had to exhaust their financial holdings in the United States to demonstrate to the American people their need for aid. The British also had to reduce the barriers to outsiders trading with Britain's colonies.

At this time, Roosevelt permitted British and American military officials to plan strategy for joint operations if America entered the war. These officials decided that the Allies would concentrate their primary efforts in Europe to defeat Hitler while maintaining a holding operation in Asia, where the less powerful Japanese posed much less of a threat to Western security and vital interests. Roosevelt also moved to extend American naval protection to British convoys near American shores. At the outset of the war, the United States and Latin America had proclaimed a neutrality zone of three hundred miles from their coasts. In April 1939, Roosevelt extended that zone to incorporate Greenland. American ships patrolled the defense area and radioed the position of German submarines to both convoys and British sub-hunting planes. But American ships could not fire at the German submarines, so the German wolfpack war remained a grave danger to Britain's North Atlantic supply route.

While Hitler was expanding his submarine war, he also was expanding his effort on land. He sent troops to the Balkans and North Africa to rescue his floundering Italian allies. Then he launched an invasion of Russia. Roosevelt's advisors told him that the Soviet Union could survive for only a few months and they urged him to increase aid to Great Britain while Germany was tied up in Russia. At first Roosevelt seemed to move in that direction. After maneuvering an invitation from Iceland, Roosevelt occupied that nation. Then he prepared to escort British vessels with the American convoys supplying Iceland. But he backed away from those convoys at the last minute. Then, as the USSR proved more resilient than anyone had expected after its inept performance in Finland, Roosevelt decided to gamble and extend lend-lease to Russia. He found surprising support for this move. While Americans hated communism, they did not yet fear Russian power and admired Russia's brave stand against the Nazis. They hoped that Russian resistance just might help defeat Hitler without the United States having to join the fight. Their reluctance to fight showed up in the close congressional vote to extend the terms of men serving under the Selective Service Act; it passed the House by a single vote in August 1941.

That same month, Roosevelt took another step toward intervention by meeting Winston Churchill in Argentia Bay off Newfoundland. In addition to issuing a joint declaration on the purposes of the war to defeat fascism, Roosevelt and Churchill agreed that the United States should finally begin convoying British ships as far as Iceland. Despite this agreement, Roosevelt hesitated until a German submarine attacked the American destroyer *Greer.* Roosevelt did not reveal that the *Greer* had been trailing the submarine and radioing its position to a British patrol plane, but announced that this "unprovoked" attack was indicative of Germany's plan for world conquest by force, terror, and murder. He announced that American ships would protect convoys in the neutrality zone as far as Iceland and would fire on German submarines to do so. A subsequent attack on the American destroyer *Kearney* provided the impetus for repeal of the Neutrality Act's prohibition against arming merchant ships and sending them into combat zones. The United States now was free to escort convoys all the way to Great Britain.

Hitler still did not order attacks on American ships. He told Admiral Raeder such incidents would have to be avoided at least until October. Probably he was waiting to be sure that the Japanese would fight and force the United States to face a two-front war.

THE MARCH TOWARD WAR IN ASIA

The Manchuria incident of 1931–1932 turned out to be the beginning rather than the end of more militant Japanese actions aimed at dominating China and Asia. In 1934, Japan formally renounced the Washington Treaties of 1922 and their naval ratios. In 1935, it walked out of the London Naval Conference when the other powers refused to give Japan full naval parity with Great Britain and the United States. Meanwhile, the Japanese infiltrated China's northern provinces and made plans for severing them entirely from China. The Japanese military steadily increased its power over more moderate politicians who wished to achieve Japanese hegemony in Asia by pressure diplomacy rather than war.

Military rebels assassinated three high cabinet officials in 1936 for lack of militancy, and they missed the prime minister only because they killed his brother-in-law by mistake. The Japanese army put down the rebels, but forced the prime minister to agree that only high-ranking military officers could serve as ministers of war and navy. This gave the military the power to bring down any government. The war and navy ministers could threaten to resign with the assurance that no other officer would accept the positions, and thus could prevent the formation of a new cabinet. In 1936, Japan also signed the Anti-Comintern Pact with Nazi Germany. Although ostensibly an agreement to combat Communist subversion and propaganda, secret protocols made it a defensive alliance, and the rest of the world suspected as much.

Despite these signs of increasing Japanese militance, the United States and the League of Nations were shocked in 1937 when Japan escalated a clash with Chinese soldiers at the Marco Polo Bridge into a full-scale war. The Japanese were responding not only to the Marco Polo Bridge incident, but also to a bizarre agreement between Chiang Kai-shek and the warlord Chang Hsueh-liang, whom the Japanese had expelled from Manchuria. Chiang had visited the Manchurian warlord to arrange for another campaign against the Chinese Communists. Chang then kidnapped the Nationalist leader and insisted that he concentrate his efforts against the Japanese rather than the Communists. Chiang Kai-shek agreed, and Chang not only freed him, but accompanied him back to Nanking as his prisoner.

The Japanese heartily disliked this alliance. They made use of the incident at the Marco Polo Bridge to reinforce their armies, occupy Peking, and seize most of northern China. Chiang Kai-shek broadened the war by attacking the Japanese garrisons in the southern city of Shanghai, perhaps hoping to force the Western nations to intervene to protect their own nationals and interests. But the United States and the League of Nations were preoccupied with the crisis in Europe. Roosevelt briefly raised Chinese hopes by delivering his quarantine speech, but dashed them again by rejecting sanctions. The most he would do was make use of Japan's unwillingness to declare a formal state of war to avoid invoking the Neutrality Act. This permitted American-owned companies to ship weapons and supplies to China without the restrictions of an arms embargo or cash and carry provisions. The League of Nations met in Brussels to consider the China situation, but they also refused sanctions and chose appeasement.

Japan stirred another flurry of anger when its planes sank the American gunboat *Panay* and damaged several other American and British boats during a rapacious siege of the Nationalist capital at Nanking. Even when it became apparent that the Japanese pilots had deliberately attacked the boats and that it was not a case of mistaken identity, the United States and Great Britain accepted Japanese apologies, and the incident blew over.

Japan, seeing that China would receive no support from the Western powers, continued its relentless advance. By 1938 it controlled all the railroads, industries, and major cities of northern and central China. In November, it announced that the war would not end until a reformed China accepted a New Order in Asia. China would have to accept Japanese troops wherever necessary to combat communism. China also would have to coordinate its military, economic, and cultural life with Japan. Outside powers would no longer have an open door, but would have to recognize Japan's special position in China. Hitler withdrew his aid and military advisors from China and in effect gave his blessing to the New Order. It soon became public knowledge that Germany and Japan were discussing an expansion of the Anti-Comintern Pact into a general military alliance.

Still, Roosevelt and his advisors hoped that Japanese moderates might resume control and restrain Japan's expansion within tolerable limits. Roosevelt made gestures against the Japanese advance in China, but he did not interfere with the extensive American trade to Japan in scrap iron and oil. These materials were vital to Japan's war machine, and an embargo of them would have created a crisis. Instead, Roosevelt loaned China $25 million and unofficially embargoed airplanes to Japan. As public anger against the Japanese continued to mount, Henry Stimson led an organized campaign to impose an embargo on all trade to them, including scrap iron and oil. Roosevelt circumvented the demand by giving Japan notice that the United States would terminate the Japanese-American Trade Agreement of 1911.

Japanese reaction to this notice was angry, but both Japan's anger and the American agitation for an embargo were shortcircuited when Hitler invaded Poland and began World War II in Europe. Hitler's action not only turned American attention away from Asia toward Europe, it forced Japan to reconsider its entire policy. The Nazi-Soviet Agreement of 1939 that preceded the invasion of Poland undermined Japan's Anti-Comintern Pact with Germany and shocked the Japanese army. The army regarded the Soviet Union as its greatest enemy in Manchuria and had suffered over 50,000 casualties in a 1939 clash with Soviet troops along the Manchurian border. The Japanese military dreamed of expansion into Siberia at Soviet expense once the China Incident was settled. Siberian oil and natural resources would relieve Japan of its dependence on American oil and scrap iron. But with Russia the partner of Germany, Japan turned its attention even more strongly toward Southeast Asia, especially the oil of the Dutch East Indies and the rubber, rice, and tin of French Indochina and British Malaya. These targets became even more tempting when Germany conquered the Netherlands and France and put their colonies up for grabs.

Immediately after the French and Dutch fell to Hitler, the Japanese successfully demanded that the French stop supplies from reaching Chiang Kai-shek through Indochina. The Japanese also forced Dutch authorities in the East Indies to ensure a more rapid flow of oil and trade to Japan. Finally, they pressed the isolated British into closing the Hong Kong and Burma Road supply routes to China for three months.

On the advice of Ambassador to Japan Joseph Grew, Roosevelt and Hull briefly tried to wean Japan away from Germany following Germany's betrayal of the Anti-Comintern Pact. They offered to negotiate a new commercial agreement that might accept Japanese de facto control of Manchuria and North China. But Japan demanded that the United States also recognize its candidate to replace Chiang Kai-shek as ruler of all China, and the negotiations foundered. As Japan pressed southward, Roosevelt decided to keep the American fleet in Hawaii, where it had been on maneuvers, rather than signal weakness by withdrawing it to San Diego's better staging and repair facilities. A month later, on July 25, 1940, Roosevelt imposed an embargo on the shipment of aviation fuel and the highest grades of steel and scrap iron to Japan on the grounds that they were needed for America's own defense.

These warning gestures did not deter the hard-line Japanese cabinet that had taken power three days before Roosevelt announced his limited embargo. Japan forced the Vichy government, which nominally ruled France after Hitler's conquest, to permit the stationing of Japanese troops in France's northern Indochina colony. As Japanese troops moved across the Indochinese border, the United States also learned that Japan was about to sign a formal military alliance with Germany. Ambassador Grew reversed his earlier advice to avoid confrontation and, in what came to be called the "green light" telegram, urged Roosevelt to adopt economic sanctions as a "show of force" to deter further Japanese aggression. Roosevelt responded by deciding to embargo oil and steel. But Hull warned that this would bring war, and Roosevelt modified the order to omit oil. A day after this embargo on all grades of iron and scrap steel, September 27, 1940, Japan signed the Tripartite (or Axis) Pact with Germany and Italy.

Germany, Japan, and Italy hoped that the Tripartite Pact would intimidate the United States and prevent it from aiding Great Britain in either Asia or Europe. It had exactly the opposite effect. It stiffened American opinion by dramatizing what seemed to be a united and global totalitarian threat. Still, Roosevelt and Hull considered Germany a far greater threat than Japan, and they desperately wanted to delay war until America was better prepared. While they were not willing to make major concessions to Japan or engage in an "Asian Munich," they hoped to "baby the Japanese along" until the United States was better armed and more unified or until, by some stroke of fortune, the British finished the war in Europe.

Thus, Roosevelt and Hull walked a narrow line. Roosevelt permitted secret joint naval planning with the British on Asia. He extended a further $100 million loan to Chiang's government in China. In his "arsenal of democracy" defense of Lend-Lease, he included Japan as part of the unholy alliance that sought to "dominate and enslave the human race." He privately concluded that he could not afford to let the Japanese strip the British of their colonies in Asia and thus undermine Britain's war effort in Europe, yet he was afraid to make a firm public commitment to defend the European colonies in Asia.

There was some chance that Roosevelt could have saved the colonies by conceding Japan a free hand in China. Some historians have argued that Roosevelt should have conceded that free hand to avoid a two-front war and concentrated on the greater threat in Europe. If such a concession had involved merely American abstention, Roosevelt might have accepted that unpleasant alternative. But the minimum demand of moderates as well as militants in Japan required the United States not just to abandon the Nationalists, but to guarantee the flow of oil and steel necessary to supply Japan's brutal war in China. Roosevelt feared that such a betrayal would undermine the American people's moral opposition to aggressive dictators in Europe as well as Asia.

Rejecting both major concessions and confrontation, Roosevelt saw no alternative but to make small incremental additions to the embargo list and use American defense needs rather than Japanese provocations as justification. He hoped Japan would become frightened of a total interruption of American trade and draw back from its advance in Asia. But just as Japan's Axis Pact with Germany and Italy provoked stiffer American resistance, so Washington's tightening of trade restrictions provoked more rather than less Japanese military expansion. Each tightening of the American trade noose brought the Japanese army to make stronger demands for the conquest of areas with the oil and metal resources that would render the Japanese empire self-sufficient.

The Japanese navy was slightly less militant, but the navy and most Japanese politicians as well would fight the United States rather than abandon the war in China and their dreams of Asian hegemony. The Japanese militants realized that the United States had the resources to win a war with Japan. Rather than retreat from China, however, they would take the calculated risk of a quick strike to conquer the western and southern Pacific and establish a naval defense line through the chains of Pacific islands. They hoped that the United States, faced with a *fait accompli* and diverted by the war in Europe, would be unable to summon the determination or accept the sacrifices necessary to destroy the Japanese empire.

Some Japanese moderates hoped to avoid such a dangerous gamble. They made contact with Roosevelt and Hull in January of 1941 through two Catholic Maryknoll missionaries serving in Japan, Bishop James E. Walsh and Father James M. Drought. Walsh and Drought, known in the interests of secrecy as the John Doe Associates, told Roosevelt and Hull that the Japanese were willing to withdraw from the Axis Pact and remove their troops from China if the United States would guarantee the flow of critical supplies. Roosevelt and Hull doubted that the Japanese government truly was willing to do this, but they asked the missionaries to continue their private contacts and get the Japanese proposal in writing. The Japanese government sent Colonel Hideo Iwakuro of the War Ministry to consult with the missionaries, and together they drew up a proposal.

Colonel Iwakuro ensured that the proposal was far more favorable to Japan than the missionaries had led Hull and Roosevelt to believe it would be. Japan would not withdraw from the Axis Alliance. It would only promise not to fight the United States unless the United States were the aggressor in an attack on Germany. The United States also would have to request China to make peace and form a coalition government with the Japanese-sponsored regime. Then some Japanese troops would be removed, but others would stay behind for "joint defense against communistic activities and economic cooperation."

Hull was very disappointed. Instead of breaking off negotiations, however, he told the Japanese ambassador, a moderate admiral favorable toward the United States named Kichisaburo Nomura, that he would be willing to negotiate on the basis of this draft proposal if Japan would pledge itself in advance to four principles: the territorial integrity of China, noninterference in the internal affairs of other nations, equality of commercial opportunity, and the status quo in the Pacific. Unfortunately, the Japanese ambassador misunderstood Hull. In transmitting the draft agreement he not only omitted Hull's four principles, but portrayed the Maryknoll draft as an American offer rather than an informal Japanese initiative. The Japanese naturally drafted a counterproposal that was even more favorable to themselves, and the negotiations were stalemated.

Japanese Foreign Minister Yosuke Matsuoka opposed negotiations with the United States anyway; he favored defying America and taking what Japan needed in Southeast Asia. Ignoring Hitler's hints that the Russo-German pact might be less than permanent, Matsuoka negotiated a nonaggression pact with the Soviets in April 1941. Thus Japan's northern flank was protected if and when it moved into Southeast Asia. But in June Hitler invaded Russia and urged Japan to take the opportunity to attack Siberia. In a momentous series of cabinet meetings in June and July of 1941, the Japanese refused the invitation. They decided to continue southward to build the Greater East Asia Co-Prosperity Sphere. They would expand from north into south Indochina preparatory to invading British Malaya and the Dutch East Indies. They specifically stated that they would not be "deterred by the possibility of being involved in a war with England and America."

The United States knew of this decision almost immediately because in the spring of 1941, naval intelligence had broken the Japanese diplomatic codes and could decipher messages between Tokyo and the Japanese embassy in Washington. Hull broke off his talks with Ambassador Nomura and, after Japan made public its demands on Vichy, warned against the Japanese plans. The Japanese ignored Hull and moved their troops into southern Indochina. Roosevelt then froze all Japanese assets in America. If strictly enforced, this freeze order would establish a total embargo on the Japanese by denying them the means to pay for any further purchases in the United States.

Evidently Roosevelt and Hull did not intend to enforce this total embargo: Roosevelt ordered the release of enough blocked funds for Japan to make oil purchases at the prewar level. But Dean Acheson of the State Department thwarted Japanese oil purchases by stalling the issuance of export licenses. When Hull learned of this, he sanctioned Acheson's maneuver rather than show weakness to Japan by retreating from the de facto oil embargo. The British and Dutch also embargoed oil to Japan. This left the Japanese with no further sources of petroleum and only an eighteen-month supply in reserve. Since the Japanese calculated it would take a year to conquer the East Indies and restore the flow of oil from there, this left Japan with six months to accommodate the United States and restore its American supply line or conquer another source.

Prime Minister Prince Fuminaro Konoye decided to make one last stab at a peace settlement with the United States. He proposed a summit meeting with Roosevelt. The Japanese military consented grudgingly, but only on the condition that if Konoye failed to get the United States to accept Japanese dominace in Asia by October of 1941, he would have to be prepared to lead a war against the United States, Great Britain, and the Dutch East Indies.

American Ambassador Joseph Grew urged that Roosevelt accept the meeting with Konoye. He thought the prime minister would risk assassination to make a compromise agreement with the United States once he was out of Japan. Konoye sent a personal message to Roosevelt promising that Japan would withdraw from Indochina at the conclusion of the China Incident and would not invade Southeast Asia if the United States would cease its aid to China and assure Japan an adequate supply of raw materials. Roosevelt was anxious to meet with Konoye. But he believed that if he sold out China, it would undermine America's willingness to resist totalitarianism. Also, meeting with the prime minister of Japan, the ally of Hitler, might leave the British fearing they would have to go it alone in Asia as well as Europe. At Hull's urging, Roosevelt decided to insist on further guaranteed concessions before taking such a political risk.

Through the months of August and September, Roosevelt and Hull delivered several messages to Konoye. They insisted on Japanese acceptance of the four points Hull had communicated to Ambassador Nomura, expressed fears of Japan's obligations under the Tripartite Pact, opposed Japanese discriminatory trade policies in China, and asked for a "clear-cut manifestation" of Japan's intention to withdraw its troops from China and Indochina. They tried to string out the negotiations and gain time for defensive preparations. They also sent a squadron of B-17 bombers to the Philippines in hopes of intimidating the Japanese. Konoye pressed his war minister, General Hideki Tojo, to accede to the American demand for troop withdrawals from China to break the stalemate. But Tojo held Konoye to the agreed October timetable for a decision on war and suggested Konoye resign. Konoye did so, and the emperor appointed Tojo to take his place.

Tojo was not absolutely bent on war. He was determined, however, to make a final decision on it. Roosevelt quickly learned through the MAGIC code-breaking operation that the United States would have to restore trade by November 25 or face a rupture of negotiations. A later message from Tojo's government to the Japanese embassy in Washington extended the deadline to November 29, after which "things would automatically begin to happen." Roosevelt assumed this meant an invasion of the Dutch East Indies or British Malaya. He suspected the Japanese might also attack the American-held Philippines. He had no idea that the automatic happening would be the departure of the Japanese fleet for an attack on Pearl Harbor in Hawaii.

The Japanese decided to present their final peace terms in two plans, A and B. Plan A would be a long-term settlement. If the United States would restore trade to Japan and force China to make peace, Japan would withdraw

Figure 16   President Franklin D. Roosevelt and Secretary of State Cordell
Hull. Photo UPI/Bettmann News Photos.

its troops from China and Indochina after a suitable interval. Japan also
would permit equality of commercial activity in China so long as the open
door program would be adopted in the colonies of other nations as well. The
chances of an open door throughout the world were so slim as to vitiate this
Japanese concession. In addition, MAGIC intercepted a message to Nomura that although Japan would agree to evacuate troops from China after
peace was made, actually Japan would only shift areas of occupation. "We
will call it evacuation; but . . . in the last analysis this would be out of the
question." Finally, Tojo refused to cancel the Tripartite Pact. Japan expected
the United States to reject this offer, and it did.

Plan B visualized a short-term truce. Japan would promise no new moves,
while the United States would restore trade and end its support for China.
Again MAGIC intercepted a rebuke to the Japanese negotiating team in the
United States for suggesting that Tojo eliminate the requirement that the
United States cease aid to China. Hull and Roosevelt had been working on a
modus vivendi as an answer to plan B—a three-month truce during which the
United States would sell some oil and raw materials to Japan if Japan would
withdraw from southern Indochina and make no new moves while further
negotiations were in progress. But Chiang Kai-shek objected "hysterically."
Churchill also objected; he warned that Chiang had been on a "thin diet" and
might drop out of the war.

When Hull received news that Japanese ships were moving toward Indochina and the message that "things would automatically begin to happen"

after November 29, he decided it was hopeless to stall further. He and Roosevelt decided to "kick the whole thing over." They discarded the *modus vivendi* and sent Japan a ten-point reply essentially demanding that Japan leave China. On November 27, Washington sent "war warnings" to the American commands in the Philippines and Hawaii. On December 3, Roosevelt finally made a firm commitment to Great Britain. If the Japanese attacked the British or Dutch colonies, the United States would give "armed support." He continued to worry, however, whether he could bring a united America into a war for British colonies if the United States was not directly attacked.

He need not have worried. At that very moment, Japanese carriers were steaming through the northern Pacific toward Hawaii. Pressure rose in Washington on December 6 as MAGIC intercepted thirteen parts of what was said to be a fourteen-part message to the Japanese embassy. The message warned the embassy that nothing was to be communicated to the Americans until the fourteenth portion arrived the following morning. Roosevelt told Harry Hopkins: "This means war."

Many Americans have wondered why, then, the Japanese were able to surprise the Pacific fleet at Pearl Harbor, where they destroyed five battleships, four cruisers, almost all of the war planes in Hawaii, and killed 2,403 Americans while wounding an additional 1,178. Some isolationists and historians have suspected that Roosevelt deliberately sacrificed the fleet to get America into war by "the back door" when his attempts to provoke Hitler had failed. Why had Hawaii been unprepared when the United States had broken the Japanese code and received other indications of a possible attack? Why had the fleet been lined up in such close quarters rather than dispersed? Why had the carriers been absent, and only obsolete battleships left in the harbor?

These questions have been answered to the satisfaction of almost all historians. MAGIC had told Washington approximately when the Japanese would move, but not where. All Japanese ship and troop movements pointed to Southeast Asia. The Pearl Harbor attack fleet left Japan under radio silence and moved toward Hawaii north of regular shipping channels. American intelligence personnel assumed that radio silence from these carriers indicated they were still in home waters, using low-frequency radios that would not be picked up by long-range American monitoring equipment. The American army and navy commanders in Hawaii received war warnings on November 27, but had too little aviation fuel to mount round-the-clock aerial surveillance. The naval commander feared sabotage from local Japanese rather than a surprise air attack, so he kept his ships close together to guard against infiltration.

Scattered warnings that the Japanese might strike Pearl Harbor as well as Southeast Asia drowned in the "noise" of thousands of other conflicting signals. A report to Joseph Grew from the Peruvian embassy in Japan that the Japanese would attack Hawaii seemed of little worth, since no one could understand how the Peruvians would know. A warning of an attack on Pearl Harbor from a German double agent inexplicably stopped at the desk of FBI

Director J. Edgar Hoover. Americans observed the Japanese burning papers at their consulate in Hawaii, but this gave no clue that the Japanese would strike Hawaii, only that war was imminent. The Americans already knew that.

Perhaps the best evidence against a Roosevelt conspiracy is that it made no political or strategic sense. If Roosevelt had wanted to galvanize American opinion to fight the Axis, he did not have to sacrifice the fleet; a Japanese attack on an empty harbor would have sufficed. No one knew at the time that the battleships and cruisers lost at Pearl Harbor would prove obsolete and that the carriers would be decisive in the naval war to come. Besides, Roosevelt did not want war in the Pacific; he wanted to fight the far greater threat of Hitler in Europe. There was no guarantee that Pearl Harbor would bring America into the European conflict. It might even have diverted American public attention to the Pacific and made a declaration of war against Germany all the more difficult. Fortunately for Roosevelt, he did not have to request war against Germany as well as Japan. Hitler cheered Pearl Harbor and declared war on the United States. He had avoided provoking conflict while Roosevelt extended aid to Britain, but evidently he had concluded that war was inevitable. Roosevelt had waited until his hand was forced, but now Americans were united in their commitment to World War II.

CONTROVERSIAL ISSUES AND FURTHER READING

American entry into World War II caused far less historical controversy than entry into World War I. World War I revisionists Charles A. Beard, Charles Tansill, and Harry Elmer Barnes survived to write parallel denunciations of World War II, but historians dismissed them far more quickly than they had the earliers ones. (These World War I and World War II revisionists are to be distinguished from the more modern revisionists writing since the advent of the Cold War.) Beard, Tansill, Barnes, and their revisionist compatriots denied that either Germany or Japan had posed a serious threat to American interests or security. They admitted that Hitler had been a dangerous neurotic, but his major goal had been the destruction of the Soviet Union. If Roosevelt had stood aside, Hitler and Stalin would have demolished one another. If, in the process, Germany and Japan destroyed the British Empire as well, that was no concern of the United States.

Unfortunately, the revisionists claimed, Roosevelt wanted war to ensure his re-election, preserve the British Empire, and expand American markets abroad. Thus, he supported appeasement at Munich at a time when the Allies were strong enough to defeat Hitler. Roosevelt did not want war then because the Allies would have won it too quickly to permit Roosevelt to get the United States into the conflict. Only after he had helped destroy the Allied defensive potential did he support resistance to Hitler. Once combat was safely underway, he undertook to "lie America into war because he could not lead it into war." He steadily and often secretly extended unneutral aid to the Allies in hopes of provoking Hitler to strike the first blow. He knew this was the only way to get the American people to support the war. But Hitler would not accommodate him. The postwar capture of German war plans demonstrated Hitler had no plans to attack the United States and actually was trying to avoid an American conflict.

When Roosevelt failed to lure Hitler into an attack, he decided to take the "back door to war" by provoking Japan. He brushed aside reasonable offers from the Maryknoll priests, Prince Konoye, and General Tojo. He knew from the MAGIC intercepts that this meant war. Revisionists cited as proof of their contentions Hull's remark that he was washing his hands of the Japanese problem and turning it over to the military. They also quoted Secretary of War Henry Stimson's famous remark: "The question was how we should maneuver them into firing the first shot without allowing too much danger to ourselves."

Finally, World War II revisionists claimed that Roosevelt purposely invited Japanese attack on Pearl Harbor. Roosevelt made sure only obsolete battleships were there, withheld MAGIC information from the commanders, and then, while Japanese planes butchered thousands of Americans, "In the quiet atmosphere of the oval study in the White House, with all incoming telephone calls shut off, the Chief Executive calmly studies his well-filled stamp albums while Hopkins fondles Fala, the White House scottie. At one o'clock, Death stood in the Doorway." [The final quotation is from Charles Callan Tansill, Back Door to War: The Roosevelt Foreign Policy, 1933–1941 (1952), p. 652. Other major revisionist studies include Charles A. Beard, American Foreign Policy in the Making, 1932–1940: A Study of Responsibilities (1946), and Beard's more elaborate work, President Roosevelt and the Coming of the War, 1941 (1948). Harry Elmer Barnes, ed., Perpetual War for Perpetual Peace: A Critical Examination of the Foreign Policy of Franklin Delano Roosevelt and Its Aftermath (1953), includes brief summary articles by many of the following authors: George Morgenstern, Pearl Harbor: The Story of the Secret War (1947); William Henry Chamberlin, America's Second Crusade (1950); Frederick C. Sanborn, Design for War: A Study of Secret Power Politics, 1937–1941 (1951); Rear Admiral Robert A. Theobold, The Final Secret of Pearl Harbor: The Washington Contribution to the Japanese Attack (1954); Husband E. Kimmel, Admiral Kimmel's Story (1955); Anthony Kubek, How the Far East Was Lost: American Policy and the Creation of Communist China, 1941–1949 (1963).]

The conspiracy charges of the World War II revisionists naturally excited many replies, and the replies have been convincing enough to discredit these revisionists entirely in the historical profession. [John Toland tried to revive the Pearl Harbor plot thesis in Infamy: Pearl Harbor and Its Aftermath (1982) by offering supposedly new evidence from anonymous sources that Roosevelt knew the attack was coming at Pearl Harbor, but he was not convincing. The general antiwar atmosphere after Vietnam inspired Bruce M. Russett to reconsider the wisdom of American abstention from World War II in No Clear and Present Danger: A Skeptical View of the United States Entry into World War II (1972). But those are about the only flickers of World War II revisionism in recent times.] Historians could not swallow the revisionist contention that the Axis posed no threat to American security. Historians searching the German documents did not turn up a Nazi plan for the conquest of the Western Hemisphere, but they almost all concluded that Hitler would have threatened America if he had acquired the British fleet and the vast resources of Europe and Russia. [Hans L. Trefousse, Germany and American Neutrality, 1939–1941 (1951); Saul Friedlander, Prelude to Downfall: Hitler and the United States, 1939–1941 (1963; English translation 1967); James V. Compton, The Swastika and the Eagle: Hitler, the United States, and the Origins of World War II (1967); Alton Frye, Nazi Germany and the American Hemisphere, 1933–1941 (1967).]

Historians also recoiled from the vitriolic portraits of a scheming Roosevelt offered by the World War II revisionists, although historians admit Roosevelt was devious, and a good many argue that he was far more devious than he needed to be. They maintain that public opinion was prepared for a far stronger response to the Axis than Roosevelt permitted. If he had provided clear and vigorous leadership instead of hesitant limited actions covered by uncandid remarks, the United States might have been much better prepared for war when it came and might have intervened before the Allies teetered dangerously on the brink of collapse. [Walter Lippmann made this argument during the war in *U.S. Foreign Policy: Shield of the Republic* (1943). It was made far more extensively in what is still the most complete and in many ways the best history of American entry, William L. Langer and S. Everett Gleason, *The Challenge to Isolation, 1937–1940* (1952), and *The Undeclared War, 1940–1941* (1953). For similar views, see Robert A. Divine, *The Reluctant Belligerent: American Entry into World War II* (1965), and *The Illusion of Neutrality: Franklin D. Roosevelt and the Struggle over the Arms Embargo* (1962); Arnold Offner, *American Appeasement: United States Foreign Policy and Germany, 1933–1938* (1969), and *The Origins of the Second World War: American Foreign Policy and World Politics, 1917–1941* (1975); Michael Leigh, *Mobilizing Consent: Public Opinion and American Foreign Policy, 1937–1947* (1976).]

Many other historians have defended Roosevelt's pace and tactics in bringing America to intervention. They maintain that isolationism was far too strong and dangerous to permit the direct and rapid actions that seem so necessary in retrospect. [Dexter Perkins made this argument during the war in *America and Two Wars* (1944). The best work from this point of view is Robert Dallek, *Franklin D. Roosevelt and American Foreign Policy, 1932–1945* (1979). See also Basil Rauch, *Roosevelt: From Munich to Pearl Harbor* (1950); Donald F. Drummond, *The Passing of American Neutrality, 1937–1941* (1955); William E. Kinsella, Jr., *Leadership in Isolation: FDR and the Origins of the Second World War* (1978); T.R. Fehrenbach, *F.D.R.'s Undeclared War: 1939–1941* (1967); Gloria J. Barron, *Leadership in Crisis, FDR and the Path to Intervention* (1973); John E. Wiltz, *From Isolation to War, 1931–1941* (1968).]

Historians discredited the plot thesis of Pearl Harbor and the back door to war as thoroughly as they discredited the World War II revisionist position on the intervention in Europe. [Admiral Samuel Eliot Morison, "Did Roosevelt Start the War–History through a Beard," *Atlantic Monthly* (August 1948); Roberta Wohlstetter, *Pearl Harbor: Warning and Decision* (1962); Gordon W. Prange, *At Dawn We Slept: The Untold Story of Pearl Harbor* (1981); Robert Ferrell, "Pearl Harbor and the Revisionists," *Historian* (Spring 1955); Herbert Feis, "War Came at Pearl Harbor: Suspicions Considered," *Yale Review* (Spring 1956).]

While historians dismissed the Pearl Harbor plot thesis, they continued to debate whether Roosevelt's policy in the Far East had been wise. Roosevelt certainly had many prominent defenders who argued that the United States had little choice but to oppose Japanese expansion into Asia. The United States simply could not continue to supply war materiel to permit Japan's conquest of China, and nothing short of that would have deterred the Japanese from conquering the European colonies in Asia necessary to the war effort against Hitler. Perhaps more flexible American diplomacy could have delayed war a few more weeks, but that was all. [In addition to the general surveys of Roosevelt's diplomacy already cited, see Herbert Feis, *The Road to Pearl Harbor: The Coming of the War Between the United States and Japan* (1950); Robert J. C. Butow, *Tojo and the Coming of the War* (1961), and *The John Doe Associates: Backdoor Diplomacy for Peace, 1941* (1974), which deals with the Maryknoll initiative; Samuel Eliot Morison, *The Rising Sun in the Pacific, 1931–April, 1942* (1948); James H. Herzog,

Closing the Open Door: American-Japanese Diplomatic Negotiations, 1936–1941 (1973).]

A good many historians, however, questioned whether war in the Pacific had been necessary. These were not revisionist or isolationist historians who opposed American entry into World War II; they were realists who believed that the United States could and should have avoided war with Japan and concentrated all its effort against the greater threat to America and the world balance of power, Germany. These realists based their contention that America could have avoided war with Japan on the memoirs of Ambassador Joseph Grew. [Joseph C. Grew, *Ten Years in Japan* (1944), and *Turbulent Era: A Diplomatic Record of Forty Years, 1904–1945* (2 vols., 1952).] Grew believed that the German attack on Russia had discredited the Japanese militarists and the Tripartite Pact. This gave Konoye a chance to break with Germany, galvanize moderate sentiment, and come to a dramatic settlement with the United States if only Roosevelt had met with him.

Even without the meeting, Japan had signaled its willingness to abandon the march southward and to leave the European colonies intact if the United States would permit some Japanese control over China. The realists thought this a price worth paying to ensure the defeat of Hitler in Europe. Chiang was incapable of unifying China even with American help; elimination of the Japanese presence simply created a vacuum of power into which the Chinese Communists and the Russians could move. The diversion of resources from the European theater not only prolonged the war, but permitted the Soviet Union to move farther into western Europe than it might have done had the Allies invaded Normandy earlier. [Paul W. Schroeder, *The Anglo-American Alliance and Japanese-American Relations, 1941* (1958); David J. Lu, *From the Marco Polo Bridge to Pearl Harbor: Japan's Entry into World War II* (1961); F. C. Jones, *Japan's New Order in East Asia: Its Rise and Fall, 1937–45* (1954).]

Many other realists were not so sure that actions taken as late as 1941 could have prevented war. But they sympathized with the idea of avoiding confrontation with Japan to concentrate on Europe and argued that America might have contributed to a peaceful situation in Asia with a friendlier policy toward Japan in earlier years. [See the works of such realists as Nicholas Spykman, *America's Strategy in World Politics: The United States and the Balance of Power* (1942); and George F. Kennan, *American Diplomacy, 1900–1950* (1951). See also the historiographical discussion following Chapter 8 in this book.] In 1968, John Wiltz wrote that the ideas of realists like Paul Schroeder on the war with Japan had "found little response among other non-revisionist historians." [Wiltz, *From Isolation to War*, p. 120.] But in a conference between American and Japanese historians only a few years later, Richard Leopold noted that American contributors to the conference "look back on the Pacific war as a mistake, one that led to many of the intractable problems confronting the United States today," while ironically the Japanese contributors viewed "that conflict somewhat fatalistically, as perhaps the only instrument by which the incubus of fascism and militarism could have been exorcised." [Richard W. Leopold, "Historiographical Reflections," in Dorothy Borg and Shumpei Okamoto, eds., *Pearl Harbor as History: Japanese-American Relations, 1931–1941* (1973).]

The revulsion against interventionism that followed the Vietnam war had less impact on the historiography of World War II than on any other interventionist episode. There have been only a couple of new revisionist accounts, and they attack America's motives rather than the intervention itself. [Lloyd C. Gardner, *Economic Aspects of New Deal Diplomacy* (1964); Jonathan G. Utley, *Going to War with Japan, 1939–1941* (1984); Robert Freeman Smith, "American Foreign Relations, 1920–1942," in Barton J. Bernstein, ed., *Towards a New Past: Dissenting Essays in Ameri-*

can History, 1968).] In the second edition of *Reluctant Belligerent,* published in 1979, Robert Divine noted that, under the influence of Vietnam, he had softened the strictures against Roosevelt's slowness to intervene he had presented in the 1965 edition. Isolationists also have received a slightly better press than immediately after World War II. [For typical earlier denunciations of isolationism, see Walter Johnson, *The Battle Against Isolation* (1944); Selig Adler, *The Isolationist Impulse: Its Twentieth-Century Reaction* (1957); John E. Wiltz, *In Search of Peace: The Senate Munitions Inquiry, 1934–1936* (1963). Wayne S. Cole has been more sympathetic to the isolationists in his *Roosevelt and the Isolationists, 1932–1945* (1983); *America First: The Battle Against Intervention, 1940–1941* (1953); *Senator Gerald P. Nye and American Foreign Relations* (1962); and *Charles A. Lindbergh and the Battle against Intervention in World War II* (1974). Recent works that sympathize at least with some of the motives of the isolationists include Manfred Jonas, *Isolationism in America, 1935–1941* (1974); and Geoffrey S. Smith, *To Save a Nation: American Counter-subversives, the New Deal, and the Coming of World War II* (1973).]

The only other significant recent trend in the historiography of American entry into World War II has been an increased emphasis on Anglo-American rivalry, a trend encouraged primarily by the opening of diplomatic and treasury documents in Great Britain. [See, for example, the works of Arnold Offner mentioned above, along with James Leutze, *Bargaining for Supremacy: Anglo-American Naval Collaboration, 1937–1941* (1977). For continued emphasis in the popular press on Anglo-American cooperation and friendship, see Joseph P. Lash, *Roosevelt and Churchill, 1939–1941: The Partnership That Saved the West* (1976). For an excellent work on Lend-Lease aid to the British, see Warren F. Kimball, *The Most Unsordid Act: Lend-Lease, 1939–1941* (1969).]

CHAPTER 15

The Diplomacy of World War II and the Seeds of the Cold War

ROOSEVELT, CHURCHILL, AND STALIN: COMPETING STRATEGIES FOR THE GRAND ALLIANCE

Immediately after Pearl Harbor, Winston Churchill arrived in Washington, D.C., for the Arcadia Conference with Roosevelt and Soviet Ambassador Maxim Litvinov. With great fanfare, the three allies announced that their war goals would be the defense of "life, liberty, independence and religious freedom," along with "human rights and justice."

Even as they were preparing this United Nations Declaration, the Russians confronted Roosevelt and Churchill with a demand that was thoroughly embarrassing to the high ideals they were ready to proclaim. The Soviets wanted immediate recognition of the borders they had possessed just before the Nazi invasion. Thus the West would endorse the Soviet absorption of Latvia, Lithuania, Estonia, eastern Poland, and a portion of Rumania, areas the Soviets had won by virtue of their 1939 pact with Nazi Germany and their subsequent war against Finland in 1940. These all were provinces the Soviets felt had been unjustly stripped from them after World War I, but they also were areas of intense nationalist sentiment.

The suppression of national independence in these areas would seem a cynical flouting of the principles enunciated in the United Nations Declaration. Churchill and his foreign minister, Anthony Eden, expressed some willingness to concede the Soviets a free hand in this eastern European sphere of influence, but Roosevelt and Cordell Hull refused. They saw Russia's request as too reminiscent of the secret treaties of World War I that had wrecked Woodrow Wilson's hopes for a just peace. Anything that smacked of Europe's "old diplomacy"—the acquisition of new colonies, the establishment of spheres of influence, or cynical manipulation of the balance of power—could revive isolationist opinion in America. Not only would this undermine America's immediate war effort, but it might destroy popular support for American participation in postwar international arrangements. Roosevelt and Hull feared that World War III then would follow World War II as surely as World War II had followed World War I.

Yet Roosevelt and Churchill also wanted to avoid offending Stalin; they needed a willing Russia in the war. Ever since Hitler had turned away from the Battle of Britain to invade Russia, the Soviets singlehandedly had confronted the major portion of the German war machine. The Allies could not afford to have the Soviets make another separate peace like Brest-Litovsk or the Nazi-Soviet Pact and leave Germany free to concentrate on Western Europe. Roosevelt wanted Stalin not only to help win the European war, but to join the fight against Japan once the European phase was over.

For these reasons, Roosevelt tried to avoid controversy over Stalin's border demands. He asked Stalin to agree that the Allies would defer all territorial claims until after the war. This would avoid disputes that might threaten the Allied war effort. It would also give Roosevelt a chance to win Stalin's confidence. If the Soviets could see they had nothing to fear from the West, they might not feel the need to impose an iron hand on Eastern Europe to guarantee their own security.

As a first step, Roosevelt and Churchill reaffirmed their earlier agreement on a "Europe first" strategy. This was the most important decision of the war, and it took some courage on Roosevelt's part to make it. Many Americans were angrier at Japan after Pearl Harbor than at Germany and demanded that the United States concentrate its war effort in Asia and the Pacific. Roosevelt realized that Germany was the far greater threat: Japan could never conquer the United States, but Germany might be able to do it if it gained control of Europe's resources and Britain's fleet. Consequently, Roosevelt pledged to Churchill and Stalin that the United States would give top priority to the European theater and relegate the Pacific to a holding action until Hitler was defeated.

Roosevelt went even further than this at a meeting with Soviet Foreign Minister V.M. Molotov in Washington the following May. Against the better judgment of Churchill and some of his own American military advisors, Roosevelt promised that the United States and Great Britain would take the pressure off Russia by opening a second front in Europe as early as 1942. This was an almost impossible task; the United States had only begun to mobilize, and the Allies were very short of landing craft. Churchill refused to go along with Roosevelt's promise. He remembered too well the devastations of trench warfare in World War I and was determined to avoid a repetition. Besides, since an early European second front would be set up before full American mobilization, British ships and soldiers would bear the brunt of the effort. And even the Americans admitted that an early European landing would be a "sacrificial one." Churchill favored a peripheral strategy. He wanted to delay a cross-Channel invasion until an air bombing campaign had softened the Germans up sufficiently to guarantee success. Meanwhile, British and American forces would attack the Mediterranean periphery of the German empire—first North Africa, then the Mediterranean islands, and finally the "soft underbelly of Europe," Italy and the Balkans.

Churchill claimed that such diversions would make the ultimate cross-Channel invasion even more likely to succeed. It would also protect the British lifeline to India and Asia through the Mediterranean and the Suez Canal.

It might even give the Western allies a chance to get to the Balkans and some of Eastern Europe before the Russians. Of course, while it would mean limited fighting and casualties for Great Britain and the United States, it would increase the time the Russians would be engaged with the bulk of the German army. Stalin and the American military chiefs came to suspect that Churchill would avoid a frontal attack on France entirely if he could.

Stalin complained often and bitterly of this, and generally Churchill responded with concern for Stalin's natural desire to see pressure taken off the Russian front. Churchill was anxious to aid Russia, if only to keep it in the war. He knew that the Red Army was the primary hope of defeating Hitler. But he was not ready to jeopardize the British armed forces, economy, and empire on behalf of the Russians. When Stalin became too insistent, Churchill reminded him with some asperity that the Soviets had left the British to fight the Germans alone until 1941.

THE DIPLOMACY OF THE WAR: 1941–1943

Churchill and the American military chiefs, led by George Marshall, finally succeeded in convincing Roosevelt that an invasion of Europe in 1942 was impractical. At this point, Churchill and Marshall parted company. Churchill pressed Roosevelt to undertake a limited invasion of North Africa to help the British defend their Mediterranean-Suez lifeline, then threatened in Egypt by the army of Marshal Erwin Rommel, known as the Desert Fox. Marshall and the American military high command opposed any peripheral operations that might divert effort from a cross-Channel invasion in 1943. They correctly feared that an invasion of North Africa would occupy the landing craft and troops essential to the cross-Channel invasion and delay it until 1944. Roosevelt decided in favor of Churchill. He thought it politically necessary to involve American troops in the Atlantic theater immediately. Otherwise, public pressure to turn to the Pacific might become irresistible. He ordered Marshall to substitute a North African operation for the European invasion he had promised Stalin.

At almost the same time, Roosevelt and Churchill felt compelled to halt convoys bearing lend-lease aid to the Soviet Union because the Germans were sinking more than half the ships sent into the Baltic. On August 12, 1942, Winston Churchill flew off to Moscow to inform Stalin personally of the painful North African and lend-lease decisions and to try to allay the Russian's anger. Churchill said he felt as though he was "carrying a large lump of ice to the North Pole." He emphasized to Stalin that the North African invasion would occupy at least some German troops. Stalin, only slightly mollified, expressed bitterness that the British and Americans were unwilling to accept the kind of casualties the Russians were suffering.[1]

---

[1] After the North African invasion, Cordell Hull still worried about the potential casualties in a cross-Channel invasion and mentioned to the Russians the 200,000 casualties America already had suffered. The Russians told him: "We lose that many each day before lunch. You haven't got your teeth in the war yet."

Operation Torch, the invasion of North Africa, turned out to be a military success. The British and Americans defeated Rommel, captured many of his troops, and pushed the remainder back across the Mediterranean. Yet the operation occupied relatively few German forces, while the Russians faced massive invasions aimed at Leningrad, Stalingrad, and the Caucasus oil fields. Operation Torch also raised some serious political complications. Roosevelt and the commander of Torch, General Dwight D. Eisenhower, decided to make an arrangement with a notorious Nazi collaborator, Admiral Jean Darlan, the ranking French naval officer in North Africa. Darlan promised that the Vichy French military forces would not resist the American invasion if he were left in charge. While the Darlan Deal did limit resistance in many areas, it did not keep the French from scuttling their fleet at Toulon or eliminate the fighting in Tunisia. Meanwhile, the United States was seen to be cooperating with a regime that was imprisoning Jews and hunting down Frenchmen opposed to the Nazis.

The Darlan Deal soured relations between Roosevelt and General Charles de Gaulle, commander of the Free French. Roosevelt refused to believe that de Gaulle had much support in France itself, and he tried consistently to relegate the general to a back seat. When Darlan was assassinated, the Americans unsuccessfully tried to force de Gaulle into a subsidiary role behind General Henri Giraud. After de Gaulle cleverly manuevered Giraud into a lesser position, it was only with great reluctance that Roosevelt permitted de Gaulle and the Free French to take a significant part in the liberation of France. Roosevelt thought de Gaulle's vision of the postwar French Empire inflated. FDR openly opposed any return of Indochina or Dakar (in Africa) to the French and hoped instead for some sort of international administration that would permit an American military presence in those areas.

THE CASABLANCA CONFERENCE: 1943

The successful completion of the North African operation in early 1943 left 500,000 Allied troops unoccupied. With the number of troops and landing craft still too few to guarantee a successful cross-Channel invasion, Churchill urged that they be used to invade Sicily and Italy in hopes of forcing the weakest member of the Axis out of the war. Roosevelt and Churchill met at Casablanca in January 1943 to settle these plans. The American military chiefs continued to urge an invasion of France in 1943. Since the majority of ships and troops in Europe at this time were still British rather than American, however, the chiefs reluctantly accepted Churchill's plan for a limited invasion across the Mediterranean in exchange for a firm British promise to support a cross-Channel invasion in 1944.

Stalin refused to join Roosevelt and Churchill at Casablanca because he feared that a decision to defer a major second front might be imposed on him. Knowing Stalin would object, Roosevelt and Churchill put off notifying him officially of the deferral until much later in 1943. In the hope of sweetening the bitter pill and counteracting the squalid aftermath of the Darlan Deal, Roosevelt announced at the end of the Casablanca Conference that the Allies would demand unconditional surrender of the Axis powers. This would reinforce the decision to postpone territorial arrangements until after the war and reassure Stalin that his allies would not make a separate peace. "Unconditional surrender" also implied the total destruction of German power to avoid what was thought to have been a mistake at the time of the first world war. The Russians would not need to fear future invasions from a weakened Germany, and Roosevelt hoped this might bring Stalin to abandon his demands for a rigid security sphere in Eastern Europe.

After the Casablanca Conference, dissension increased among the Allies over the second front strategy. Churchill feared that the Americans wanted to divert supplies and troops to the Pacific theater. The Americans tried to limit the Mediterranean operation in preference to building and planning the 1944 cross-Channel invasion. Stalin kept up a running denunciation of the efforts of both his allies to relieve the Russian front. Meanwhile, the Allied invasion of Sicily and Italy quickly forced Italy's surrender, and this caused further Allied dissension. Great Britain wanted to deal with the Italian king and Marshal Pietro Badoglio, whom the British believed were best able to keep Italy from falling apart. Roosevelt preferred to replace these Fascist collaborators with a more centrist government headed by Count Carlo Sforza. Stalin complained that the Russians were being ignored entirely in arranging the surrender. Hitler rendered much of the debate moot when he sent crack German troops to stop the Allied advance through Italy and then set up a new Italian regime with Mussolini as its nominal leader.

Great Britain and the United States faced another vital question while they were debating the second front—the development of the atomic bomb. At the beginning of the war, Great Britain had offered to share its atomic technology with the United States. Roosevelt and Churchill agreed that the bomb would be built in the United States, where the industrial capacity existed and there was less danger of the facilities being overrun. As work on the manufacture of the bomb progressed, however, American military leaders began to withhold some information from their British partners. Churchill protested, but Roosevelt's advisors told him he should share only information that could be used during the present war and hold all the rest secret. Roosevelt rejected their advice and ordered full collaboration on atomic weapons, but only after Churchill had once again firmly committed the British to a cross-Channel attack in 1944.

Once Stalin was satisfied that Churchill and Roosevelt would invade Europe in 1944, he finally agreed to a summit meeting of the three leaders. He even gave some preliminary pledges of his own. He promised to enter the war against Japan once the European war was over. He also accepted Roosevelt's argument that China should be included with Great Britain, the Soviet Union, and the United States as one of the Big Four to police the postwar peace.

Roosevelt had boosted China for a position as one of the Big Four ever since America's entry into the war. He knew that the regime of Chiang Kai-shek was hollow, dictatorial, and corrupt, and that China was far from being a major power. Nevertheless, he thought China's vast population gave it the potential to be a great power in twenty-five to fifty years, and he wanted it to be on America's side. He also wanted to appeal to the popular American image of China as a suffering, democratic, friendly protégé. Americans might be more willing to join a postwar international organization that included China. Meanwhile, China could be used as an alternative occupying power in Korea, French Indochina, and parts of the British Empire as these areas were recaptured from the Japanese. This would give the United States a chance to reduce the European empires in Southeast Asia and to stave off Russian penetration in northern Asia.

Chiang, despite Roosevelt's backing, was not very cooperative. He actually did very little against the Japanese. He employed his best troops to surround the Communist forces of his domestic rival Mao Tse-Tung in the north at Yenan. Chiang refused to contribute to the reopening of the Burma Road through which Allied supplies might reach him, yet demanded that the Allies fly supplies to him "over the hump" of the Himalayas in ever-increasing amounts, despite the dangers involved. He so exasperated his American military advisor, General "Vinegar Joe" Stilwell, that that acerbic soldier referred contemptuously to him as "Peanut" and told Roosevelt that he should press Chiang to turn over control of China's military forces to Stilwell himself.

Roosevelt was unwilling to push Chiang too hard, however. He saw no alternative to Nationalist rule, and he certainly did not want China to collapse. Roosevelt believed China would be essential as a launching pad for an eventual invasion of Japan. With his Europe First strategy, he could not afford to send much help to China anyway. He tried instead to pacify Chiang with morale-building gestures. He invited Chiang to meet with him and Churchill at Cairo in November 1943, immediately before he and Churchill were to meet together for the first time with Stalin at Teheran. Chiang used the opportunity to press for more supplies and less harassment from Stilwell, but his timing was poor. With Russia's pledge to enter the war against Japan, Roosevelt felt less need of China. Roosevelt put Chiang off with a few promises of support for a Burma campaign and a statement that China should regain the islands and territories Japan had seized earlier.

From Teheran to Yalta: 1944

Following the Cairo Conference, Churchill and Roosevelt flew to Teheran in Iran to meet Stalin. Roosevelt tried to charm Stalin; he even baited Churchill about the British Empire to win Stalin's approval. He joined Stalin in rejecting Churchill's desire for a Balkan invasion to supplement the invasion of Normandy. Roosevelt and Stalin also agreed in opposition to Churchill that France should not be rebuilt into a major power or its empire returned. Fi-

Figure 17 Roosevelt, Churchill, and Stalin at Teheran, 1943. Photo courtesy of the National Archives.

nally, Roosevelt and Stalin discussed dividing Germany into five separate provinces, while Churchill wanted to preserve some German strength by dividing it into no more than two. Churchill actually challenged Stalin directly by asking if he contemplated a postwar Europe of small, weak states.

On the other hand, Stalin and Churchill found more agreement with one another than with Roosevelt on the shape of postwar international arrangements. They were thinking in terms of regional organizations of nations. Roosevelt objected that this smacked too much of spheres of influence. He advocated instead one organization dominated by the Big Four to police the world at large, although he agreed that each of the Big Four would have primary responsibility in its own area of the globe. To disarm any Soviet suspicions that the United States might try to use such a world body to dominate areas critical to Russian security, Roosevelt warned that American troops would probably remain in Europe no more than a year or two after Germany's defeat and asked that the United States be given only limited occupation duties.

Ominously, however, Stalin found himself somewhat isolated on the issue of Eastern Europe. Roosevelt tried to reassure Stalin by acknowledging Russia's historic and strategic interest in the area and suggesting the internationalization of the Baltic waterways so vital to the Soviet Union. He asked in return that Stalin recognize the importance to American opinion of self-determination in Eastern Europe. Stalin objected bluntly. The question of self-determination had not come up when the czar had controlled the area, he said. He told Roosevelt that some propaganda work should be done to reconcile the American people to the Soviet position. Stalin was particularly adamant about Poland; he insisted that Russia should regain eastern Poland, and that Poland should be compensated with portions of eastern Germany. Stalin also refused to have anything to do with the exiled Polish government in London.

The London Poles refused to acknowledge Russian demands for border adjustments, and demanded a Red Cross investigation into the Katyn Forest massacre. The London Poles knew that thousands of Polish officers and class enemies had been put in Soviet camps following the Russian occupation of eastern Poland in 1939. They also believed, on good evidence, that the mass graves discovered by the Germans in the Katyn Forest contained the bodies of 10,000 of those Poles executed by the Russians. (The fate of the remainder of Russia's Polish prisoners is still unknown.)

Roosevelt and Churchill had both tried unsuccessfully to get the London Poles to reconcile themselves to Soviet power while urging Stalin not to set up a rival Communist government. Churchill reminded Stalin that Britain had gone to war over Poland and that for the Allies to recognize different Polish governments would be a major blow to hopes for the continuing unity of the alliance. Roosevelt spoke of the importance of the Polish voters within the United States. Roosevelt and Churchill implied acceptance of most of Russia's 1941 borders, but Roosevelt said he would make no commitments until after the 1944 election, and both made clear the need for compromise on the status of the London Poles and East European elections.

Returning to the United States, Roosevelt was optimistic about the Teheran agreements. He assured the American people in a fireside chat that the United States would get along with Stalin and the Russian people "very well—very well indeed." Churchill, on the other hand, returned in a funk. He told his physician that they would have to do something with the "bloody Russians."

Stalin appeased Churchill's funk somewhat when he cooperated with the Normandy invasion in June of 1944 by launching a simultaneous attack on the eastern front. Once the Normandy invasion forces finally broke out of the beachhead at the end of the summer, and began their race across France toward Germany, victory was in sight. The imminence of victory forced the Allied diplomats to begin their own race to create a comprehensive plan for postwar Europe. The Bretton Woods Conference of August 1944 established much of the postwar economic structure. In a bucolic resort hotel at the foot of Mt. Washington in New Hampshire, the United States won the endorsement of the representatives of forty-four allied countries for measures designed to encourage world trade by ensuring stable currency exchange rates, reducing tariffs, and providing reconstruction loans. The conference created an International Monetary Fund that would use the contributions of gold and currency from its members to support the exchange rates. The IMF would loan money to nations whose deficits threatened the value of their currency, but only if the deficit countries followed policies the other members thought necessary to ensure fiscal stability. Since the United States was the major contributor to the fund, it received weighted votes that gave it the dominant voice in determining the loans the IMF would make. On the other hand, the United States did consent to rules that would require it to dispense some of the vast surplus of gold and dollars it had acquired as a result of the war. This lessened the burden of debtor and deficit states. The Bretton Woods Conference also established the World Bank to loan money to weaker nations for reconstruction and development projects. Again, the United States had the dominant voice in determining World Bank loans.

The British joined these arrangements with some trepidation. Britain's political Left feared that the open world of international trade contemplated by the Bretton Woods arrangements would prevent domestic control of the British currency and tariff rates. This would make it impossible to guarantee full employment by protecting British enterprises against the competition of the powerful American economy. The British Right feared that opening the British Empire to world trade would permit the more powerful United States to replace British influence in British colonies. To allay these fears, the United States promised to help the exhausted British pay their enormous war debts and modernize their industrial plant. With this concession, the British chose to join the open and expanding system of world trade promised by Bretton Woods.

The Russians were less amenable. The Soviets ran a closed economy; the government conducted all trade and set the value of the national currency by fiat. Despite this obstacle, the Soviets attended the Bretton Woods Conference and agreed to join the IMF and the World Bank. The Roosevelt administration saw this step as a considerable concession on the part of the Soviets and was much encouraged. U.S. Treasury officials even began to consider a separate $10 billion loan to Russia. (In late 1945, however, the Soviet government decided not to ratify the Bretton Woods Agreement.)

A month after Bretton Woods, representatives of the Allied nations met at Dumbarton Oaks near Washington, D.C., to establish the United Nations. The Soviets were far less cooperative in these negotiations, which were designed to build an international political structure to accompany the Bretton Woods economic structure. The USSR demanded sixteen votes in the General Assembly, one for each of the Soviet Socialist Republics. The Soviets also demanded the right of a permanent member of the Security Council to veto a discussion of any topic, not just the final decision. Despite personal appeals from Roosevelt, they refused to budge. The conference finally adjourned without resolving these critical questions.

While Soviet demands at Dumbarton Oaks raised British and American hackles, Stalin's conduct toward Poland created far darker suspicions. Prior to the Bretton Woods and Dumbarton Oaks conferences, Stalin set up the Lublin Committee, a group of Poles loyal to the Soviet Union, as a potential rival to the Polish government in exile in London. Still, he did not officially recognize the Lublin Committee as the legitimate government of Poland and shut the door completely on the London Poles. Roosevelt and Churchill did not yet despair of an amicable settlement. Then, in July 1944, Soviet army radio appealed to the pro-London Warsaw underground to rise against the

Nazi occupiers and aid the advancing Red Army's entrance into the city. Warsaw began its uprising on July 31, but the Russian army halted on the outskirts of the city. The Germans proceeded to slaughter the underground fighters.

It is possible that German resistance and the logistical problems of crossing the Vistula River halted the Russian advance, as Stalin claimed. Stalin raised strong suspicions of his motives, however, when he prevented the British and Americans from air-dropping supplies to the beleaguered Warsaw garrison until it was too late. Shortly afterward, Averell Harriman, America's ambassador to the Soviet Union and previously a sympathetic director of lend-lease aid to the Russians, warned Roosevelt that the Soviet Union was inclined to be a "world bully." He advised Roosevelt henceforth to demand a *quid pro quo* for any concessions he made to Stalin.

In this troubled atmosphere, Roosevelt met Churchill at Quebec in September 1944. He listened sympathetically to Churchill's complaints about Soviet actions in Rumania and Bulgaria and to Churchill's argument that if the war in Italy was concluded soon, American and British troops should be sent into the Balkans through Trieste in hope of beating the Russians to Vienna. Roosevelt also agreed with Churchill that they should continue to withhold atomic information from the Soviet Union. Roosevelt had known for a year that Russian spies were keeping Stalin informed of Anglo-American progress on the bomb, and he had been advised by physicist Niels Bohr that he had nothing to lose and much to gain by offering to share atomic technology with the Russians. Nevertheless, Roosevelt apparently wanted a firmer demonstration of Russian cooperation before he risked sharing atomic secrets with the Soviets, particularly since he knew Congress would be extremely hostile. He let Bohr believe he might consider sharing in the future, expecting that Bohr would get the message to the Soviets, and accepted instead Churchill's advice to withhold collaboration.

Despite this decision, Roosevelt had not given up his attempts to cooperate with the Russians. His secretary of the treasury, Henry Morgenthau, convinced him that the Soviets wanted the destruction of Germany to avoid ever facing a German invasion again. Morgenthau devised a plan for "pastoralizing" Germany by eliminating its industrial as well as its military potential. Roosevelt abruptly and casually recommended this plan to Churchill at Quebec. Churchill said he looked upon the Morgenthau Plan with as much favor as he would "chaining himself to a German corpse." He thought German productivity was necessary for the revival of Europe. Morgenthau and Roosevelt argued that Britain would prosper more when relieved of German competition. The issue was probably decided by Churchill's desperate need for American aid after the war. When Roosevelt promised to continue lend-lease, Churchill accepted the Morgenthau Plan.

Both agreements came unglued almost immediately after the Quebec Conference. The State Department, which considered Morgenthau's Treasury Department a usurper in taking over planning for a German settlement, argued that Churchill had been perfectly correct in saying that Europe needed the products of Germany's Saar and Ruhr valleys. Even the Russians were anxious for reparations that a pastoralized Germany could never provide. Finally, Roosevelt admitted that Morgenthau had "pulled a boner" and said he did not see how he had ever initialed it. As he backed away from the Morgenthau Plan, he also heeded congressional opposition to postwar lend-lease aid for Britain and reduced the level of support he had promised the English.

In one final agreement at Quebec, Roosevelt and Churchill decided to send a joint note remonstrating with Stalin about his lack of cooperation. Afterward, Churchill had second thoughts and chose to meet with Stalin personally in October 1944. The British prime minister found this meeting encouraging. After he protested the ruthless Soviet conduct in Rumania and Bulgaria, Stalin agreed to a broad division of influence in the Balkans. The Russians were to have 90 percent of the authority in Rumania, 85 percent in Bulgaria, and 75 percent in Hungary, while Great Britain would have 90 percent control in Greece. They would divide influence in Yugoslavia 50–50. This agreement substantially broadened an earlier tentative arrangement reached just before D-Day in which they had exchanged Russian control of Rumania for British control of Greece. Roosevelt remained wary of these spheres of influence agreements. He had accepted the first one only after being assured it was a temporary military measure, and he avoided commitment to the second by announcing in advance that he would not be bound by any decision made by Churchill and Stalin at their Moscow meeting.

The ambiguity in the arrangements on the Balkans might not have raised serious problems if the Allies had been able to reach agreement on the far more critical issues of Poland and Germany. Stalin was determined to have a friendly regime in Poland. It was his corridor to Germany as well as Germany's invasion route into Russia, and the Poles would be behind his lines as he undertook the final thrust into Berlin. The British also felt strongly about Poland. They had gone to war over Poland, had fought alongside the military forces commanded by the Polish government in exile, and were anxious that the Poles have some degree of self-determination. The United States, with a large number of Polish immigrants, also felt a sentimental attachment to Poland. Roosevelt acknowledged that the Soviets had a greater stake in the Polish settlement and had the troops in place to see that their will was done. But he insisted on at least enough self-determination for the Poles to pacify American public opinion.

Churchill came away from the Moscow meeting with Stalin believing progress had been made on the Polish issue. The situation fell apart, however, when the London Poles refused to accept the Russian claim to eastern Poland up to the so-called Curzon Line, and the prime minister of the government in exile, Stanislaus Mikolajczyk, resigned in protest over his colleagues' intransigence. To the dismay of Roosevelt and Churchill, Stalin then officially recognized the Lublin Committee as the government of Poland. Although Roosevelt and Churchill were willing to encourage Poland to accept Stalin's border demands, they did not believe the Lublin Committee represented anywhere near a majority of Poles.

Fearing that Stalin's actions might trigger another American retreat to isolationism, Roosevelt called for another climactic meeting of the Big Three. Roosevelt had incentives in Asia as well as in Europe for requesting a summit conference. He naturally wanted confirmation of the date for Russian entry into the war with Japan. But he also wanted Stalin's cooperation in forcing the Chinese Communists into a coalition with Chiang Kai-shek's National-ists. Chiang continued to resist U.S. pressure to send his best troops into battle against the Japanese. When Japanese forces attacked Nationalist-held areas containing critical Amercian air force facilities, Chiang left their de-fense to inexperienced local militia totally incapable of stopping the Japanese offensive. Chiang would not contribute to the campaign to open land supply routes to China through Burma or aid the British in their defense of India against a Japanese invasion from Southeast Asia.

Roosevelt tried everything, including an ultimatum, to get Chiang to fight. He demanded that Chiang turn over command of his entire army to General Stilwell and combine with the Communists to oppose the Japanese. Chiang continued to stall. Finally, with Russia's firm commitment to enter the Pacific war and the capture of some islands close enough to serve as air bases for the bombing of the Japanese homeland, Roosevelt decided he would not need China to defeat the Japanese after all. He quit trying to force Chiang to fight and even gave in to the generalissimo's insistence that he re-call Stilwell.

Some of Roosevelt's more knowledgeable advisors thought the United States might do better to aid the Chinese Communists rather than Chiang. The Nationalist regime was doomed anyway, and Mao's might be kept inde-pendent of the Russians by American cooperation. Roosevelt, however, needed a truly friendly regime in China for his postwar plans, even if he did not need Chinese help against the Japanese. He also knew that the fall of Chiang's government would raise a hue and cry in America against both Roosevelt and continued American participation in world politics. Conse-quently, he tried to save Chiang by arranging a truce and coalition between Chiang and Mao. With Stilwell removed, he sent General Patrick Hurley as his personal representative to negotiate between the Nationalists and the Communists.

Hurley was an ignorant blusterer who arrived in China wearing an army uniform with every campaign ribbon except that for Shays's Rebellion, ac-cording to one observer. He failed totally to overcome the resistance of Chiang and Mao to a coalition. With Hurley's failure, Roosevelt turned to Stalin in the hope that he would force Mao to accept a subsidiary position in a coalition with Chiang.

THE YALTA CONFERENCE: FEBRUARY 1945

Roosevelt, Churchill, and Stalin arranged to meet at the Russian resort town of Yalta in the Crimea. Each came with a separate agenda of priorities. Roo-sevelt wanted Stalin to help defeat Japan and push Mao toward a coalition with Chiang Kai-shek. He knew he had to agree to a settlement in Poland that would provide a regime friendly to Stalin because Russian troops occupied the country, but he still hoped to salvage something of the Poles' right to self-determination. He wanted similar settlements in the rest of Eastern Europe, but these were of less public interest to the West and less strategic interest to the Soviets. Most important, he wanted an agreement on Germany that would permit it to remain strong enough economically to contribute to Europe's recovery and prosperity. He had abandoned the Morgenthau Plan completely. In addition, he had accepted Churchill's argument that France should regain its position as a great power. He was ready to support France's position as a permanent member of the United Nations Security Council with a veto and to give France an area of occupation in Germany.

At Yalta, he would also abandon his attempts to dismantle the French Empire. Under pressure from Churchill, who had the fate of the British Empire in mind, Roosevelt would agree that the United Nations should be given trusteeships only over colonies of the defeated Axis powers, not over any colonies of the Allies. Thus, Roosevelt was ready to permit the French to reassume their control of Indochina once the Japanese were defeated. Finally, Roosevelt wanted to maintain cordial relations with the Soviet Union and keep it engaged with the United States in a United Nations that would be attractive to American public opinion.

Stalin's primary goal at Yalta seems to have been the guarantee of Soviet security through the establishment of friendly regimes receptive to Soviet troops in strategic areas of Eastern Europe, especially Poland and Rumania. He wanted to ensure that Germany would never again be in a position to invade and devastate Russia. He also needed some source of funds to help rebuild his shattered nation. No doubt he wanted Communist regimes in Western Europe, or at least weak nations in that area. But whatever his future ambitions for expansion, they were subordinated to his immediate desire for security and recovery. Thus, Stalin gave no great help or encouragement to the Communist uprisings in Greece, Italy, or China, and he posed no serious objections to the revival of France.

By the time of Yalta, Roosevelt was seriously ill. He had very high blood pressure and a weak heart; he was gray with fatigue, and his hands trembled. Critics of the Yalta agreements have often argued that physical illness might have been a major reason Roosevelt supposedly gave away so much to the Russians. The men who attended Yalta, however, have testified that Roosevelt was alert and competent. If he tired easily, he also recovered quickly. The Yalta agreements seem to bear out Roosevelt's competence, for they were quite consistent with his priorities on the eve of the conference.

Roosevelt, Churchill, and Stalin concurred rather easily on most aspects of a settlement with Germany. They divided Germany into four occupation zones, with Stalin consenting to a French zone so long as it was carved out of the British and American territories. They divided Berlin, which lay deep in

Map 13   Germany in defeat.

the Russian zone, into its own four occupation zones, with what turned out to be rather minimal guarantees of Western access to the city through Soviet-occupied Germany. The Big Three then agreed to give Poland a portion of eastern Germany in compensation for Poland's loss of some of its eastern territory to the Soviet Union. But they hedged the most critical question concerning Germany.

Stalin wanted vast reparations from Germany. Churchill and Roosevelt objected. They remembered the debacle brought about by the reparations settlement following World War I. They also feared that the size of the reparation settlement demanded by Stalin would prevent Germany's recovery and contribution to the revival of Western Europe. Despite these fears, Roosevelt finally accepted a figure of $20 billion in German reparations as the basis for future discussion, $10 billion of which was to go to the Soviet Union. Churchill complained that the figure was beyond reason and perhaps even beyond possibility, but he reluctantly acquiesced.

Accord on Poland was more difficult to reach. The Big Three disagreed over whether Poland's western border should be moved as far into Germany as the western branch of the Neisse River, as Russia insisted, or should go no

Map 14   Poland after Yalta

farther than the eastern Neisse, as Roosevelt and Churchill maintained. The
conferees ultimately deferred the decision until a final peace treaty conference could be held, a conference all assumed would take place in the near
future. Roosevelt wanted the postponement because he feared the Senate
would revolt at any territorial settlements he might make outside the regular
treaty process. Churchill also thought it "would be a pity to stuff the Polish
goose so full of German food that it died of indigestion." He knew that the
more German territory Poland had, the more dependent Poland would be on
the Soviet Union to protect it from German revanchism.

The makeup of the Polish government was even more controversial. Stalin was adamant that the Lublin Poles should form the basis of the government. He had neither objected to de Gaulle's elevation in France without an
election nor interfered in Greece, he pointed out. He promised that the Polish
government would be reorganized on a broader democratic basis to include
other Poles from abroad and that this government would hold "free and un-
fettered" elections shortly after the war was over. Yet it was clear that Stalin
would decide how much reorganization would take place and which Poles
would be considered democratic. He rejected a proposal that an Allied com-

mission, including representatives of the United States and Great Britain, be permitted to observe and report on the elections.

Admiral William Leahy, one of Roosevelt's aides, warned the president that "this is so elastic that the Russians can stretch it all the way from Yalta to Washington without ever technically breaking it." "I know, Bill," Roosevelt replied; "I know it. But it's the best I can do for Poland at this time." Roosevelt and Leahy might have expressed the same sentiments about the Declaration on Liberated Europe. In this case, the Yalta conferees publicly promised the creation of governments in occupied territories that were "broadly representative of all democratic elements in the population and pledged to the earliest possible establishment through free elections of governments responsible to the will of the people."

On the United Nations, Stalin finally reduced his demand for Russian votes in the General Assembly from sixteen to three. He also abandoned his insistence on the right of a permanent member of the Security Council to veto discussion as well as final action. In turn, the United States and Great Britain were ready to abandon their wish that the permanent members be prohibited from voting on issues that directly involved them and be allowed to veto any substantive decision. Roosevelt reserved the right to have three American votes in the General Assembly to match the Soviets if this proved necessary to win congressional approval (the United States never exercised this option). They all further agreed to hold an organizing conference for the United Nations in San Francisco in April.

The Big Three also came to a settlement on East Asia at Yalta, although this was kept secret because the Soviet Union was still officially neutral in the Pacific war. Stalin promised to enter the war against Japan within three months of the conclusion of the war in Europe. He also promised to recognize Chiang Kai-shek as the head of the Chinese government and to push Mao to join a coalition with the Nationalists. In turn, Roosevelt promised to see that the Soviet Union regained the territory and rights it had held in Asia before the Russo-Japanese War of 1904–1905. The USSR would receive southern Sakhalin Island, the Kuriles, recognition of the Soviet satellite regime in Outer Mongolia, management of China's Manchurian railroads, and control of the warm-water ports of Darien and Port Arthur. Although Roosevelt guaranteed that these conditions would "unquestionably be fulfilled," he also inserted a clause that Chiang would have to concur in those provisions that concerned Chinese territory. Thus Roosevelt made himself responsible for getting Chiang's consent. He did not think this would be too difficult: He had plenty of leverage over Chiang, and besides he incorrectly expected that Chiang would be happy to exchange the Yalta concessions for Stalin's help with Mao.

Still, these agreements and many other aspects of the Yalta accords were fragile. Chiang might kick up a public fuss about the concessions of Chinese territory, and this would be sure to raise tumultuous opposition to Roosevelt in the United States. American public opinion might also be aroused by the acceptance of an only slightly modified Lublin government in Poland if Stalin used too heavy a hand there. Finally, if Russia was to receive $10 billion in reparations from Germany, much of it would have to come from the British, French, or American zones, since they included the rich Ruhr and Saar areas.

Roosevelt might have tried to explain to the American people that the presence of Russian troops in Eastern Europe and the need for Russian help against Japan had made concessions necessary. He might have pointed out that the United States and Britain had no choice but to accord the Soviet Union its sphere of interest, despite the fact that Stalin would impose arrangements all Americans would find distressing. Candor, however, had never been one of FDR's virtues. He always put on a hearty exterior, but he confided in few people, and even to those few he told contradictory things. Secretary of War Henry Stimson and Chief of Staff George Marshall complained that he spoke with the frivolity and lack of responsibility of a child. General Stilwell said more to the point that he was just a "bag of wind." Roosevelt often avoided issues by talking nonstop. (His advisors used to compete to join him at meals in the hope that they might get a word in when the president's mouth was full.) He could rarely bring himself to say "no" to anyone. Rather than disappoint, he would pretend to agree. He would not fire officials with whom he was displeased, but would appoint parallel officers. He even had to have his wife fire his barber. When two antagonists left his office together and smiling, his secretary remarked that one would later find his throat cut.

After Yalta, Roosevelt probably feared that an open and frank acknowledgment of the differences between the Western Allies and the Soviets would be offensive to Stalin and at the same time arouse domestic opposition to further cooperation with Communist Russia. He still thought that cooperation was essential, since it required a unanimous agreement among the five major powers for the Security Council of the UN to act. For these reasons, he kept secret both the arrangement for the Soviets to have three votes in the United Nations and the agreement concerning East Asia. The effect of this secrecy ultimately was very unfortunate. Shortly after Roosevelt had reported on Yalta to Congress, the arrangement on the UN leaked out and caused a public outcry. Cordell Hull's successor as secretary of state, Edward Stettinius, tried to defuse the issue by telling the press that no further secret Yalta agreements remained undisclosed. Suspicions of a secret deal on East Asia remained, however, and when these agreements leaked out a year later, some opponents of Roosevelt's policies accused the late president of treason.

Roosevelt not only kept secret several of the Yalta agreements, but he also made a dramatic speech to Congress on his return in which he claimed that the Yalta accords would eliminate unilateral national action, exclusive alliances, spheres of influence, balance of power politics, and "all other expedients that had been tried for centuries—and have always failed." Roosevelt must have realized that the Russians would do as they pleased in their sphere. He probably hoped that Stalin would be discreet and operate with some appearance of democratic method. Perhaps if Stalin could be brought to trust his Western Allies sufficiently, he might even be satisfied with a strong influence rather than absolute control of Eastern Europe.

But this was not to be. Negotiations on the reorganization of the Polish government stalled on Stalin's post-Yalta insistence that a couple of London Poles would simply be grafted onto the existing Lublin regime and no full reorganization would take place. Worse, Andrei Vishinsky arrived in Rumania two weeks after Yalta with an ultimatum. If the Communists were not given power within two hours, Russia would not be responsible for the continuance of Rumania as an independent nation. While Stalin shattered hopes that he would abide by the Declaration on Liberated Europe, he made clearer his distrust of his allies. American and British military leaders were meeting with representatives of the German commander in Italy to try to arrange a surrender of the German army there. The Allied commanders had refused Stalin's request for a Russian observer to be present. Stalin bitterly accused Roosevelt of betraying the alliance, of seeking to arrange a separate peace, and of permitting the Germans to shift their troops from Italy to the eastern front.

Roosevelt responded indignantly. He was disturbed by the virulence of Stalin's suspicions, and he was increasingly distressed by Soviet actions in Poland and Rumania. He remarked to a friend that Averell Harriman had been right; the United States could not do business with Stalin because he had broken every promise he had made at Yalta. Yet Roosevelt continued to hope. In his last cable to Churchill, he said he would minimize problems with the Soviets, since difficulties arose every day and most of them straightened out. Thus it is unclear how he would have reacted to the continuing mixture of heavy-handed oppression and occasional surprising concession that Stalin meted out over the next year. When Roosevelt died of a massive cerebral hemorrhage in the last days of the war in Europe, he left that task to his successor, Harry S Truman. Unfortunately, Roosevelt had not explained the reasoning behind his policies to Truman any more than he had to the American people.

CONTROVERSIAL ISSUES AND FURTHER READING

It was not long after Roosevelt's death that hostility between the United States and the Soviet Union rose to such a pitch that it was dubbed the Cold War. The praise Roosevelt had received for his wartime success in cooperating with the Russians quickly melted away, to be replaced by harsh critiques for his supposed lack of realism in trusting the Soviets. Memoirs of participants in wartime diplomacy emphasized his naïveté in thinking he could win Stalin over. They claimed he had disregarded the political ramifications of his military strategy. He had ignored his State Department advisors and listened only to his military chiefs, who were intent on winning the war as quickly as possible without regard to the political consequences. He had refused Churchill's plan for a Balkan invasion that might have met the Soviets farther east. He had refused to demand Russian guarantees of self-determination in Eastern Europe as a price for opening the second front. He had demanded unconditional surrender from the Axis and brought about the destruction of the only two countries in Europe and Asia, Germany and Japan, that might have balanced Soviet power.

Roosevelt's demand for unconditional surrender from the Japanese also eliminated any hope that Japan could be defeated without an all-out invasion of its home islands. Such an invasion required Russian help, and to get it Roosevelt had been forced to make concessions to the Soviets in Eastern Europe and Asia. Some historians wondered why Roosevelt had made so many concessions to get the Soviet Union into the war against Japan when he supposedly knew the atomic bomb would be available to force Japan's surrender without Soviet help and without an invasion. A few right-wingers decided that there had been more than naïveté involved in these concessions. They were not sure if Roosevelt himself had been treasonous, but they were convinced that advisors like Alger Hiss and Harry Dexter White had been Communist agents steering American policy toward appeasement of Russia. [The early memoirs criticizing Roosevelt for his naïveté included those of Winston Churchill himself, *The Second World War* (6 vols., 1948–1953). Also William C. Bullitt, "How We Won the War and Lost the Peace," *Life* (August 30 and September 6, 1948); Robert E. Sherwood, *Roosevelt and Hopkins* (1948); Robert Murphy, *Diplomat among Warriors* (1964); and Arthur Bliss Lane, *I Saw Poland Betrayed: An American Ambassador Reports to the American People* (1948). Elements of these critiques were picked up by some of the early realist historians, including Hans Morgenthau, *In Defense of the National Interest: A Critical Examination of American Foreign Policy* (1951), and *Politics among Nations: The Struggle for Power and Peace* (1948); Hanson Baldwin, *Great Mistakes of the War* (1954); Louis J. Halle, *Civilization and Foreign Policy* (1955), and *Dream and Reality: Aspects of American Foreign Policy* (1959); and Anne Armstrong, *Unconditional Surrender: The Impact of the Casablanca Policy upon World War II* (1961). Right-wingers who took these criticisms to an extreme included William Henry Chamberlin, *America's Second Crusade* (1950); Anthony Kubek, *How the Far East Was Lost: American Policy and the Creation of Communist China, 1941–1949* (1963); and Edward Rozak, *Allied Wartime Diplomacy: A Pattern in Poland* (1958). For good summaries of right-wing thought and activities, see George H. Nash, *The Conservative Intellectual Movement in America since 1945* (1976), and Athan C. Theoharis, *The Yalta Myths: An Issue in U.S. Politics, 1945–1955* (1970).]

These criticisms of Roosevelt's diplomacy made a bigger impact on popular opinion than they did on historians. Careful historical research discredited the practicality of many of Roosevelt's supposed alternatives. Herbert Feis agreed that Roosevelt had failed to take into consideration some of the political implications of his unconditional surrender formula, but said it had made little difference. Popular opinion would have revolted at too many concessions to the Axis. Germany and Japan would have fought to the end anyway, the Germans because they knew that retribution awaited them if they lost, the Japanese because their culture inspired fanatical resistance. [Herbert Feis, *Churchill—Roosevelt—Stalin: The War They Waged and the Peace They Sought* (1957).] Meanwhile, military historians argued that Roosevelt had acted properly with regard to the second front. An earlier invasion of Europe would have been very difficult militarily and might well have failed. An invasion of the Balkans might have bogged down in the mountainous terrain, as had the campaign in Italy. The Red Army would then have gone over the top of the Allied penetration to occupy all of Germany and France. [Kent Roberts Greenfield, *American Strategy in World War II: A Reconsideration* (1963); Maurice Matloff and Edwin M. Snell, *Strategic Planning for Coalition Warfare, 1943–1944* (1959); Forrest C. Pogue, *The Supreme Command* (1954); Samuel Eliot Morison, *Strategy and Compromise* (1958).]

Finally, historians defended Roosevelt's policies at Yalta. With the Russians already occupying much of Eastern Europe, Roosevelt had no leverage to get a better settlement. No one realized the atomic bomb would be as important as it later became. Scientists estimated it would be no more powerful than a single flight of conventional bombers already operating over Germany. Thus Roosevelt had needed continued Soviet cooperation in Europe and Asia and had not conceded the Soviets anything in either theater that they were unable to take on their own if they wished. [John Snell, *Illusion and Necessity: The Diplomacy of Global War, 1939–1945* (1963).] Most historians concurred that however desirable a more realistic attitude on the part of Roosevelt might have been, it would have made no substantial difference in the position of Russia and the Western Allies after the war. [Gaddis Smith, *American Diplomacy during the Second World War, 1941–1945* (1965); William L. Neumann, *Making the Peace, 1941–1945* (1950).]

Realist historians then shifted their ground. If Roosevelt's concessions to the Russians had been a product of inescapable military necessity, then the United States should have granted the Soviets their sphere of influence and avoided fatuous efforts to promote liberty or self-determination there. It was wrenching to abandon the Poles, East Germans, and the Balkan and Baltic peoples to Soviet tyranny, but there was no alternative short of World War III. Conceding the Soviets their sphere might at least have kept East-West tensions from exploding. Meanwhile, however, the realists believed the United States should have extended political, economic, and military aid to its allies around the Soviet periphery to "contain" any Soviet hopes for further expansion. [George Kennan, *American Diplomacy, 1900–1950* (1951). For the shifts in the realist outlook, compare Hans Morgenthau's *In Defense of the National Interest*, esp. pp. 109–112, with his essay in Lloyd D. Gardner, Arthur Schlesinger, Jr., and Hans J. Morgenthau, *The Origins of the Cold War* (1970). Compare also Louis Halle's *Civilization and Foreign Policy* with his *Cold War as History* (1967), and William Neumann's *Making the Peace* with his *After Victory: Churchill, Roosevelt, Stalin, and the Making of the Peace* (1967). See also Herbert Feis, *Between War and Peace*, p. 38. An early advocate of this spheres of influence strategy was William Hardy McNeill, *America, Britain, and Russia: Their Cooperation and Conflict, 1941–1946* (1950).]

Many historians who looked with favor upon this spheres of influence approach to the Soviets ultimately concluded that Roosevelt had actually followed just such a policy. They pointed to his early conception of the United Nations as a big-power policing organization, quite different from the universalism of Wilson's League of Nations. They argued that he had fully intended to grant Stalin control of Poland and the rest of Eastern Europe and had only wanted enough gestures from Stalin to make this palatable to American public opinion. They criticized Roosevelt not for naïveté, but for dissembling, for continuing to portray his foreign policy to Americans as a universalist pursuit of democracy without explaining the realistic, spheres-of-influence, balance-of-power politics that truly lay behind it. Thus the deluded American people felt betrayed when Stalin quite naturally took full control of his sphere. After Roosevelt's death, the United States overreacted to Stalin's actions and helped initiate the Cold War. [The best of these books, and the best book on Roosevelt's diplomacy in general, is Robert Dallek, *Franklin D. Roosevelt and American Foreign Policy, 1932–1945* (1979). James MacGregor Burns, *Roosevelt: The Soldier of Freedom* (1970), sees Roosevelt as somewhat less realistic. See also Raymond G. O'Connor, *Diplomacy for Victory: FDR and Unconditional Surrender* (1971); Robert A. Divine, *Roosevelt and World War II* (1969), and *Second Chance: The Triumph of Internationalism in World War II* (1967); John Lewis Gaddis, *The United States and the Origins of the Cold War, 1941–1947* (1972); George C. Herring, *Aid to Russia, 1941–1946: Strategy, Diplomacy, and the Origins of the Cold War* (1973), dealing with lend-lease; Martin F. Herz, *The Beginnings of the Cold War* (1966), emphasizing the Polish issue; Lynn Etheridge Davis, *The Cold War Begins: Soviet-American Conflict over Eastern Europe* (1974); Lisle A. Rose, *Dubious Victory: The United States and the End of World War II*; Hugh Di Santis, *The Diplomacy of Silence: The American Foreign Service, the Soviet Union, and the Cold War, 1933–1947* (1980), examining the role of the State Department; and finally, three excellent works that argue Roosevelt should have bargained harder with Stalin before granting the Soviets their sphere: Adam Ulam, *The Rivals: America and Russia since World War II* (1971); Vojtech Mastny, *Russia's Road to the Cold War* (1978), written from Soviet and East European sources; and William Taubman, *Stalin's American Policy* (1981).]

However much these realists criticized Roosevelt for not explaining the actual motives behind his concessions to the Soviets, they still portrayed Stalin and the Soviets as the primary instigators of the Cold War. Russian tyranny in Eastern Europe had done far more to sour relations than any mistakes Roosevelt or Truman may have made, they believed. But the revisionists felt otherwise; they argued that the Americans had been more at fault for the Cold War than the Russians.

Most of the early revisionists, however, exempted Roosevelt from this blame. They argued that Roosevelt had truly cooperated with the Russians, and that at Yalta he had indeed accorded the Soviets their sphere in Eastern Europe. Then, on Roosevelt's death, Truman had gone back on Roosevelt's bargain. He had tried to force Stalin to open up Eastern Europe to the economic and political influence of the United States and the West. Thus Truman was at fault for the Cold War. [The earliest of these revisionist accounts was Denna Frank Flemming, *The Cold War and Its Origins: 1917–1960* (2 vols., 1961). The most recent and best is Daniel Yergin, *Shattered Peace: The Origins of the Cold War and the National Security State* (1977). Gar Alperovitz, *Atomic Diplomacy: Hiroshima and Potsdam* (1965), argues that the atomic bomb gave Truman the confidence to reverse Roosevelt's policy. Thomas J. Paterson, *Soviet-American Confrontation: Postwar Reconstruction and the Origins of the Cold War* (1973), emphasizes economic rather than atomic blackmail as the major goal of Truman. Thomas M. Campbell, *Masquerade Peace: America's UN Policy, 1944–1945* (1973), sees Truman's rejection of Roosevelt's policy coming in the United Nations. Stephen E. Ambrose, *Rise to Globalism: American Foreign Policy since 1938* (2nd ed., 1980), surveys the whole of U.S. military and strategic policy from this moderate revisionist point of view.]

More radical revisionists rejected the idea that Truman had reversed Roosevelt's course. Roosevelt too had sought a world open to capitalist expansion and had done his share to initiate the Cold War. Gabriel Kolko's *The Politics of War: The World and United States Foreign Policy, 1943–1945* (1968) was the most strident of these works. He said Roosevelt and his advisors had calculated the political consequences of their actions very carefully. They had delayed the second front purposely to hurt Russia, then invaded Normandy and raced eastward because France and Germany were more important than the Balkans. Roosevelt had temporarily supported the Morgenthau Plan not as a sop to the Soviets, but because he did not want Germany to be able to supply reparations to Russia. By denying Russia reparations, he would make the Soviets dependent on the United States instead. Roosevelt abandoned the Morgenthau Plan only when he saw the need of the Western economies for a revived Germany. But he made sure to direct Germany's economic productivity westward rather than toward the Soviets. Then he used lend-lease and other economic leverage to try to pry the Soviet and Eastern European economies open to American exploitation. Meanwhile, Roosevelt had refused to share atomic technology with the Russians, inducing still further distrust between the two powers. [Books agreeing with Kolko's insistence on the continuity of American economic expansionist diplomacy from Roosevelt to Truman, although usually stated in milder terms, include Walter LaFeber, *America, Russia, and the Cold War* (4th ed., 1980); Bruce Kuklick, *American Policy and the Division of Germany: The Clash with Russia over Reparations* (1972); Diane Shaver Clemens, *Yalta* (1970), which is a bit ambiguous on this question, supporting one view in the text and another in the conclusion; Lloyd Gardner, *Architects of Illusion: Men and Ideas in American Foreign Policy, 1941–1949* (1970); Barton Bernstein, ed., *Politics and Policies of the Truman Administration* (1970). Martin J. Sherwin is not in political agreement with this group of revisionists, but does argue that Roosevelt initiated the atomic policy Truman later followed. See his *A World Destroyed: The Atomic Bomb and the Grand Alliance* (1975).]

Kolko also attacked the image of Anglo-American cooperation during the war. Traditional accounts had noted some strain between Britain and America over second front strategy and questions involving the British and French empires. But they had emphasized the rapport between Churchill and Roosevelt, along with the unprecedented and successful merging of the two countries' military commands during the war. [In addition to Churchill's memoirs and the military histories already cited, see Richard Gardner, *Sterling-Dollar Diplomacy* (1956), and Joseph P. Lash's later *Roosevelt and Churchill, 1939–1941: The Partnership That Saved the West* (1976).] Kolko, on the other hand, portrayed a rapacious America bent on using Britain's weakness to force that nation into economic dependency and take over its empire by breaking down imperial barriers to American trade.

Recent works, exploiting the opening of British archives, have struck a balance between these two portrayals, seeing essentially a cooperative relationship but one that did involve more competitiveness than earlier historians had acknowledged. [See Armand Van Dormael, *Bretton Woods: Birth of a Monetary System* (1978); Alfred E. Eckes, Jr., *A Search for Solvency: Bretton Woods and the International Monetary System, 1941–1971* (1981); Christopher Thorne, *Allies of a Kind: The United States, Britain, and the War against Japan, 1941–1945* (1978); William Roger Louis, *Imperialism at Bay, 1941–1945: The United States and the Decolonization of the British Empire* (1978). Brian Loring Villa, "The Atomic Bomb and the Normandy Invasion," *Perspectives in American History*, 11 (1977–78), pp. 233–245, argues that Roosevelt extorted final agreement on the second front by withholding atomic sharing. On the second front, see also Mark A. Stoler, *The Politics of the Second Front: American Military Planning and Diplomacy in Coalition Warfare, 1941–1943* (1977). See especially for the Anglo-American relationship, Warren F. Kimball, ed., *Churchill and Roosevelt: The Complete Correspondence* (1984).]

For diplomacy with China during World War II, see Herbert Feis, *The China Tangle* (1953); Akira Iriye, *The Cold War in Asia* (1974); Tang Tsou, *America's Failure in China, 1941–1945* (1963); Barbara Tuchman, *Stilwell and the American Experience in China* (1970); Warren I. Cohen, *The American Response to China* (2nd ed., 1980); and Michael Schaller, *The United States Crusade in China, 1938–1945* (1979).

CHAPTER 16

Harry Truman and the Onset of the Cold War

TRUMAN TAKES OVER

If Franklin Roosevelt had survived the second world war, he would have faced a monstrous dilemma of his own making. He would have had to reconcile his vague promises to Stalin of a Soviet sphere with his assurances to the American people that the Allies were fashioning an open, democratic world. Even a master politician like Roosevelt might have faltered. How much more difficult, then, was it for Harry Truman? Truman did not even understand that he faced a dilemma. He did not know that FDR had all but conceded the Soviets their sphere in Eastern Europe, just as he did not know that the United States was close to exploding its first atomic bomb. In his profound ignorance of the status of Roosevelt's diplomacy, he naturally turned to FDR's State Department advisors. He did not realize that Roosevelt had largely ignored them and relied instead on his military advisors or kept his own counsel. After years of plucking fruitlessly at the sleeves of those in power, the State Department grabbed its chance to explain to Truman that Roosevelt had trusted the Russians too much.

Averell Harriman returned to Washington from his post as ambassador to the Soviet Union to tell Truman that Soviet conduct in Poland and the rest of Eastern Europe posed a threat to American interests. Harriman and other advisors recounted for Truman the Soviet clampdown in Eastern Europe and the betrayal of the Warsaw uprising. They warned that once the Soviet Union had control of Eastern Europe, its hostility toward capitalist nations would tempt it to penetrate adjacent areas. Harriman urged Truman to be firm and use Russia's desperate need for reconstruction funds as economic leverage.

Truman accepted this advice "with an alacrity that unsettled even those who had given it."[1] When Soviet Foreign Minister Molotov was passing through Washington on his way to the United Nations Organizing Conference in San Francisco, Truman called him in and told him in unvarnished

[1] John Lewis Gaddis, *Strategies of Containment: A Critical Appraisal of Postwar American National Security* (New York, 1982), p. 15.

316

terms that Soviet-American relations would no longer be a one-way street. Molotov complained that he had never been talked to like that in his life. "Carry out your agreements and you won't get talked to like that," snapped Truman.

Truman loved to project this image—a quick, decisive man of plain common sense. "The buck stops here" proclaimed a plaque on his White House desk. Quick and decisive he was. One State Department official bragged that Truman had gone through fourteen problems in less than a quarter of an hour. But Truman seems to have used this air of decisiveness to cover a deep uncertainty. He often made snap decisions without much information and then had to rescind them with considerable embarrassment. When the war in Europe ended, he signed an order cutting off further lend-lease aid to the Soviet Union. This was in accordance with the letter of the lend-lease law, and many congressmen had made clear they wanted to stop the program immediately after a German surrender. But the abruptness of the cutoff, turning ships around in mid-ocean, was a gratuitous slap at an ally the Americans hoped would join the war against Japan. Stalin could not help but see Truman's lecture to Molotov and this sudden termination of lend-lease as an indication of a changed American policy. The Russian dictator complained bitterly and Truman lamely apologized that he had not read the directive he had signed. He ordered the ships to turn around again and return to the Soviet Union.

Truman also had second thoughts about what he had called his straight one-two to Molotov's jaw. "Did I do right?" he plaintively asked Joseph Davies. When Davies and others explained Russia's side of several of the questions bedeviling Soviet-American relations, Truman decided to try a more amicable approach. He and Eisenhower, for example, refused to accept Churchill's advice to violate the Yalta agreement and hold Prague until Stalin became more cooperative. The president also sent on special missions two men who were identified with a relatively benign view of Soviet intentions. He dispatched Joseph Davies to London to explain Truman's position to Churchill, and Harry Hopkins to Moscow to deal with Stalin.

Hopkins dragged himself from what would be his deathbed to carry out his mission, and Stalin appeared impressed by this demonstration of America's intent. The Soviet leader assured Hopkins that Russia would enter the war against Japan and reaffirmed his endorsement of Chiang Kai-shek in China. He and Hopkins also agreed on a list of non-Lublin Poles Stalin would invite to Moscow for consultations on revision of the Lublin Polish government. Stalin even claimed Poland would be governed in a manner similar to Belgium, Holland, or Czechoslovakia. If Hopkins was inclined to believe such an exaggeration, he would have been disabused of it by Stalin's refusal to release sixteen Polish underground leaders he had already arrested. Hopkins mused at the conclusion of his mission that Stalin would never understand America's interest in a free Poland as a matter of principle. The Russian leader viewed everything in terms of power.

This bothered Truman as well. His vacillation mirrored the confusion most Americans felt about Soviet intentions, even those high in government councils and supposedly knowledgeable about foreign affairs. Were Stalin and the Soviets still Communist revolutionaries bent on world conquest, ready to use any Western concessions as steppingstones to further aggression? Or was Stalin truly willing to give up world revolution in favor of communism in one country, seeking more traditional Russian national interests such as security from attack through Eastern Europe? Truman and most Americans were ready to judge Soviet intentions by their conduct in Eastern Europe. If Stalin were willing to compromise with the West on arrangements there and permitted a modicum of freedom as Americans understood that word, then Truman would assume Stalin's goals were limited and defensive. Failure to compromise in Eastern Europe would be seen as evidence of Stalin's aggressive intent elsewhere.

Unfortunately, such a test not only failed to take into account the fact that no freely elected regime in Eastern Europe would be friendly to the Soviet Union, but also that Stalin might be ruthless and cautious at the same time. Stalin directed his ruthlessness almost entirely toward the most strategically vital areas in Eastern Europe, a sphere he may well have believed Roosevelt had conceded to him. It was true that he was merciless in Poland, Rumania, and Bulgaria, and it was natural that Truman and many of his advisors should worry that this was indicative of Stalin's intentions for any other areas he sought to control. Yet Stalin did permit a degree of self-determination in less strategic countries such as Hungary and Czechoslovakia so long as Communists loyal to the Soviet Union controlled key posts within those governments. Later he would be even more accommodating toward Finland and Austria. He insisted only that their foreign policies be neutral rather than hostile to the Soviets.

Truman and his advisors may have been confused as well about Stalin's intentions because they regarded Josip Tito's relatively independent regime in Yugoslavia as a faithful satellite of Stalin. They assumed that Tito made his militant demands for control of Trieste and the surrounding area at the head of the strategic Adriatic Sea at Stalin's instigation. They missed Stalin's subtle signals that he placed a higher priority on the Balkans. They also blamed Stalin for instigating the Communist rebellion against the British-backed regime in Greece. Actually Stalin was trying to restrain Tito from supporting the rebels and interfering in the sphere that Stalin had accorded the British.

During this early postwar period, Stalin also restrained Communists in other areas of the West. The Communist parties of Italy and France were still under orders to cooperate with the regimes established by the Western Allies. So was the American Communist Party. But when the head of the American party, Earl Browder, went so far as to proclaim that this cooperation would continue for the foreseeable future, the French Communist leader Jacques Duclos denounced this as heresy and insisted that class war was a permanent condition. In retrospect, Duclos's public rebuke to Browder in April 1945 seems to have been a reassurance to international Communists that they could continue to collaborate as Stalin was instructing them to without giving up their ideology. Many contemporary observers in the West, however, saw it as Stalin's own proclamation of the end of the cooperation with the West that the exigencies of World War II had forced upon the Soviet Union.

Amid these swirling events and conflicting signals, Truman remained confident for a time that the United States could control matters regardless of Russia's intentions. The Red Army in Europe might be larger than that of the Western Allies and its position would grow even stronger as America withdrew its troops to finish the Japanese war, but the Soviets seemed in desperate need of economic support. The USSR had lost one-quarter of its capital equipment, 1,700 towns, 70,000 villages, 100,000 collective farms, and 20 million dead. By early 1945 it was clear that Congress was not going to extend lend-lease into the postwar era, so Truman would not be able to offer that as bargaining leverage to get Russian concessions. But Henry Morgenthau's suggestion of a multibillion-dollar loan was still alive in the State Department, if only barely. Congress might approve the loan if Russian conduct was more reassuring. In addition, Truman could still arrange for Germany to supply reparations to the Soviets. Here certainly was something for which the Soviets would be willing to bargain. They already were busy looting the industries of their own sector of Germany, but the Western Allies controlled the great bulk of German's industrial facilities. Russia would have to win Western consent to gain access to them.

Stalin seems to have misjudged this economic situation just as he did the Western response to his suppression of liberty in Eastern Europe. Stalin assumed that the capitalist world faced a postwar depression and that the West was desperate for new overseas markets for its goods. Stalin thought he was doing the United States a favor by accepting postwar aid and credits, thus furnishing an outlet for American products and postponing the inevitable crisis of capitalism. Certainly he needed and wanted Western economic assistance, but even some Western experts recognized that this was not as vital to Stalin as it appeared to most Western leaders.

Many intelligence reports claimed that American aid would speed Russian reconstruction by only a matter of months. Besides, Stalin was counting on the economic crisis of the capitalist world to permit a cautious but persistent expansion of communism in the future. Apparently he was unwilling to risk a major war or confrontation with the West, but certainly he would take what he could get cheaply, as of course would the West in the Soviet sphere. America's economic lever thus worked far less effectively in bargaining with the Soviets than Truman, Harriman, and many other American advisors expected.

Truman, however, had another reason for believing he could force Russian cooperation. The first test of an atomic explosion was nearly ready when he took office. He listened only fifteen minutes to the report on the bomb given by Secretary of War Henry Stimson and General Leslie Groves. He then appointed an interim committee to advise him on its use and accepted

Stimson's recommendation to try to postpone his summit meeting with Stalin at Potsdam until a successful test demonstrated the bomb's feasibility. He would not brandish it at Potsdam or threaten the Russians directly, but he would not offer to share it either. He would inform Stalin of the explosion as casually as possible and turn aside any question of shared control. Even with sole possession of the bomb to go along with American economic leverage, Truman knew he could not get all he wanted from the Soviets. But he concluded that he should be able to get 85 percent or so.

FROM POTSDAM TO THE TRUMAN DOCTRINE: THE TRANSITION FROM QUID PRO QUO DIPLOMACY TO CONTAINMENT

News of the first successful test explosion of an atomic device near Alamagordo, New Mexico, reached Truman in the midst of the Potsdam Conference. Churchill immediately noted an increased confidence in Truman. Yet that confidence did not do the United States or Britain much good. Stalin passed over Truman's remark that the United States had acquired a tremendous new weapon with an offhand wish that it would be used on the Japanese. If Stalin was little moved by the implied threat of the bomb, he seemed even less so by Truman's attempt prior to the meeting to conciliate him with an abrupt recognition of the slightly reorganized Polish government. (Truman had given Churchill only a few hours notice of his intention to recognize the Lublin government and then ignored British protests.) The little progress that was made at Potsdam seemed to be accomplished through hard bargaining and reciprocal concessions. The Big Three agreed that Germany should be administered as a single unit by a four power control council composed of military commanders. There harmony ended. The Americans insisted that German assets and production should go first to assuring Germany's own economic survival, and only what was left over should go for reparations. When the Soviets objected, the Americans said each side should just take reparations from their own zones. Again the Russians protested that this would destroy the agreement to administer Germany as a single unit. Since Germany's primary assets were in the West, a division would make it impossible for the Russians to obtain their $10 billion worth of reparations.

Finally, the Big Three worked a trade. The Western Allies acceded to Soviet desires and recognized the Polish-German border at the Western Neisse. The USSR agreed to take most of its reparations from its own zone of Germany and acquire only a small amount of additional capital equipment from the Western zones deemed "unnecessary" to German recovery. The Russians were unhappy, but realized they would get nothing from the Western zones if there was no agreement. Meanwhile, the Big Three established a council of foreign ministers to draw up the peace treaties with Germany's ex-allies. Again a trade was evident. Stalin made sure that the fate of the treaty with Italy was linked directly with the fate of the treaties with Rumania, Bulgaria, Hungary, and Finland.

Another proposed Potsdam "deal" did not come off. Stalin demanded military bases, territorial concessions, and other guarantees from Turkey to give the Soviets effective control over the Dardanelles, the bottleneck that controlled Russia's access to the Mediterranean from the Black Sea. Truman argued instead that the Dardanelles and the whole Danube River ought to be under international control. Stalin responded with the suggestion that the Suez and Panama canals be treated the same way. Several Americans saw this as solid evidence of Russia's aggressive, expansionist desires. That impression was reinforced by Stalin's requests for control of Japan's Hokkaido Island and portions of Italy's colonies in North Africa. The Soviet desire for part of Libya particularly disturbed those American officials knowledgeable about the atomic bomb, for they saw Libya as a steppingstone toward the Belgian Congo, the source of most of America's uranium ore.

Potsdam ended with many unsettled questions and considerable American suspicion of the Soviets. Truman told a sailor on the ship home that he thought Stalin was an "S.O.B." But then, he added, Stalin probably thought he was one too. Truman still seemed to hope he could strike a deal with Stalin on a quid pro quo basis. He also seemed to hope, however, that the bomb would make Russian participation in the war against Japan less necessary and remove the opportunity for the USSR to fulfill all its ambitions in Asia.

Truman never seems to have had a second thought about using the atomic bomb on Japan. Some of the scientists who had worked to develop the bomb urged that the United States demonstrate it to the Japanese in some uninhabited place, but Truman's interim advisory committee, headed by Stimson, rejected the idea. The committee recommended instead that the two bombs in America's arsenal be dropped on relatively untouched Japanese cities. This might eliminate the need for an invasion of the Japanese home islands, which General George Marshall estimated would cost 500,000 American casualties.

Some high-ranking naval and air force officers argued at this time that Japan might be forced to surrender without an invasion or use of the bomb. These officers believed that a naval blockade, continued conventional bombing, and a promise that the Japanese could keep their emperor might be sufficient. Stimson seems to have dismissed these claims as posturing by rival armed services, and Truman probably never saw their estimates at all. Nevertheless, some historians believe Truman and Stimson had blacker motives for ignoring the possibilities these officers raised. They argue that Truman and Stimson wanted to drop the bomb on Japan with maximum horror and destruction in order to demonstrate it to Russia, to make the Soviets more manageable.

Most historians, however, see the decision more as one of bureaucratic momentum and wartime callousness. American leaders had assumed since the inception of the Manhattan Project that the bomb would be used when ready, and only a major reevaluation by Stimson or Truman could have re-

Figure 18 President Harry Truman and Secretary of War Henry Stimson, the men most responsible for the decision to drop the atomic bomb on Japan. Photo courtesy of the National Archives.

versed that course. Stimson was not ready to change his assumptions on the use of the bomb, and Truman was never inclined to thorough evaluations anyway. They were already inured to the horror and civilian casualties involved in modern war by the Nazi rocket-bombing of London, the suicidal Japanese stands on the Pacific islands, the kamikaze raids on American ships, and their own massive bombing raids on cities like Dresden and Tokyo.[1]

On August 8, 1945, two days after the first atomic bomb had fallen on Hiroshima and the day before the second wiped out Nagasaki, Russia opened its attack on Manchuria. The combination of these shocks finally drove the Japanese to surrender. The Soviets moved quickly to occupy the areas they had been promised at Yalta, and they kept their own word by signing a treaty with Chiang Kai-shek pledging him exclusive moral support and military aid.

As the war in the Pacific came to an end, Henry Stimson was moved to reconsider the advice he had given Truman on the use of the atomic bomb. Contemplating the lack of progress at Potsdam, he concluded that carrying the bomb conspicuously on the American hip made the Soviets resentful and stubborn rather than malleable. Stimson was also mindful of the estimates of America's atomic scientists that the Russians would probably have the

[1] The firebombing of Tokyo caused more casualties than the atomic bombing of either Hiroshima or Nagasaki.

bomb within one to five years. An American atomic monopoly of such short duration would provide little incentive for Russia to make major concessions. Stimson advised Truman to promise not to use the bomb and to share the technology for peaceful application of atomic energy with the Soviets in exchange for a Russian promise not to build the bomb in the first place.

Truman's new secretary of state, James F. Byrnes, opposed such an approach. He rejected scientific estimates of a one-to-five-year monopoly, and believed instead the calculation of General Leslie Groves, head of the Manhattan Project, that the Soviets would not have the bomb for fifteen to twenty years. Thus Byrnes saw the atomic "secret" as a valuable counter in negotiating with the USSR. (Actually General Groves did not base his estimate on any technological secrets, but instead on a top-secret program he had undertaken during the war to monopolize the world's sources of uranium ore. He was unaware that the Russians had plentiful supplies of uranium in East Germany.)

Several members of the recently formed Joint Congressional Committee on Atomic Energy supported Byrnes in his opposition to sharing even peaceful atomic technology and advised Truman to keep the secrets of the bomb. A public opinion poll also showed the vast majority of Americans in favor of keeping the bomb secret even if the monopoly could be expected to last only one to five years. After some vacillation, Truman decided to go along with Byrnes rather than Stimson. From a speech on atomic energy, he deleted a sentence warning that no amount of secrecy could keep foreigners from drawing abreast of American atomic technology in a "comparatively short time."

The threat of the bomb played a significant role in the London Conference of Foreign Ministers, which met from September to October of 1945 to draw up the final peace treaties with Italy, Rumania, Bulgaria, Hungary, and Finland. When Byrnes pushed for more representative governments in the Soviet sphere, Molotov demanded a greater say in Japan, Italy, and the Italian colonies. In the midst of this argument, the dour Molotov asked with a studied attempt at humor if Byrnes had an atomic bomb in his side pocket. Byrnes replied with equally studied humor that he did and if Molotov did not become more cooperative he would "pull it out and let him have it." When neither side would budge, Molotov suddenly denounced the participation of the Chinese foreign minister in European questions and used it as a pretext to break up the conference.

Byrnes's highly publicized failure at the London Foreign Ministers Conference caused him to reconsider his strategy. He decided that the Soviets would neither be intimidated by the bomb nor succumb to economic blandishments. He asked them for another foreign ministers meeting, and this time prepared to offer international control of the atomic bomb to gain Russian concessions. Republican Senator Arthur Vandenberg and Democratic Senator Tom Connally, members of the Congressional Committee on Atomic Energy and vital figures in Truman's hopes to conduct a bipartisan foreign policy, went to the president to protest Byrnes's secrecy and independent policymaking. Truman responded by ordering Byrnes to secure safeguards before offering to share atomic technology with the Russians.

Byrnes ignored the president. He had been a more prominent senator than Truman and had expected to be selected over him for the vice-presidency in 1944. He still considered himself more qualified to conduct American foreign policy than this accidental president, and tended to treat Truman somewhat condescendingly. Therefore, at the Moscow Conference of Foreign Ministers in December 1945, Byrnes conceded that UN control of atomic energy might be lodged in the Security Council, where Russia could veto enforcement measures, rather than in the General Assembly, where Truman had wanted it. In return for Byrnes's concessions on atomic policy and acceptance of Russian practices in Eastern Europe, the Soviets accepted American domination of occupation policy in Japan, added two non-Communists to the Bulgarian government, and agreed to new elections in Rumania. They had already permitted elections in Hungary that gave the Communists only 17 percent of the vote. Byrnes returned to the United States and scheduled a triumphant speech to the nation before even reporting to the president.

Truman was enraged both by Byrnes's concessions and his failure to keep him informed. He had just read a report on Eastern Europe compiled by Mark Ethridge, a liberal newspaperman and friend of Henry Wallace, whom Byrnes had sent to check on State Department reporting in the Soviet sphere. Ethridge had surprised Byrnes by describing Soviet actions in Eastern Europe as oppressive and warning that the Russians harbored aggressive intentions for Turkey and Iran as well. Byrnes withheld this report and gave it to Truman only on the eve of his departure for the Moscow Conference.

To add further to Truman's increasing distrust of Byrnes and Russia, General Patrick Hurley resigned from his special mission to China with a report that Stalin was hindering Nationalist attempts to occupy Manchuria in favor of Mao's Communists. Hurley further claimed that Soviet strategy was being abetted by American diplomats. At the same time, Truman learned that Canada had broken up a spy ring aimed at America's atomic technology. More sinister, there was a suspicion that at least one member of the State Department had been in league with the Canadian spies. Truman remained calm about these revelations; he knew that there was no great secret to be discovered. But the revelations no doubt made him more receptive when Senator Vandenberg denounced Byrnes's offer on atomic sharing at the Moscow Conference as "another typical American giveaway."

After Byrnes returned from Moscow, Truman called him in and announced that he disapproved entirely of the secretary's approach. Eastern European governments would not be recognized until they had become truly representative, the president said. He bewailed Soviet pressure on Turkey and Iran, and proclaimed he was "tired of babying the Soviets." A month later, on February 9, 1946, Joseph Stalin made a speech that indicated he might be tired of babying the West as well. He called for a series of five-year plans aimed at a rapid military-industrial buildup and spoke of the wartime alliance as a thing of the past. This address shocked many American leaders. Supreme Court Justice William O. Douglas called it a declaration of World War III. Equally alarmed, the State Department asked George Kennan, its foremost expert on Russia, for an explanation of Soviet policy. Kennan wired an 8,000-word reply from Moscow that came to be known as the Long Telegram.

Kennan told American leaders in Washington that their policy to date had been built on a false assumption. Americans assumed that Soviet conduct could be affected by outside influences. Thus Roosevelt had thought the USSR could be won to cooperation by open-handedness. Byrnes had sought to alter Soviet policies by horse trading. Actually, Kennan said, Soviet foreign policy was dictated by internal necessities so strong that nothing but the threat of force could limit or alter Soviet ambitions. The Soviets' Marxist-Leninist persuasion made them inevitably hostile and suspicious of the West, and nothing the United States could do would alter that. More important, Russian leaders knew no other way to govern their people than by a heavy-handed dictatorship. They needed to conjure up an external threat to justify the suffering they imposed upon their people.

Kennan was not terribly clear about what the United States should do to deal with Soviet behavior. His program would develop over the next year and culminate in what came to be called the doctrine of containment. But one implication stood out: The United States should cease offering concessions to win Stalin's confidence. The United States had a perfect right to resent and denounce Soviet conduct in the areas controlled by the Red Army, but neither threats nor concessions would change that conduct. All the United States could do was draw a line around the Soviet sphere and put itself in a position to resist any further Soviet penetration. The American people had to be alerted to the situation and rallied to support a long and difficult effort to contain Communist expansion.

Kennan was relatively optimistic about the outcome if this policy were followed. He would argue over the coming year that the Soviet regime was cautious and weakened by World War II. Therefore it would not challenge the American position if it meant risking all-out war. If the Soviet regime could be contained for a while, it would inevitably mellow or be overthrown, for no people could sustain its intensity or bear its oppressiveness for an extended period of time.

Kennan's Long Telegram received an enthusiastic welcome throughout much of the American government. Byrnes, already pushed toward a stronger line by Truman, abandoned his *quid pro quo* approach and adopted a program of "patience and firmness." Government officials began to publicize their quarrels with the Soviets for the first time. Truman invited Winston Churchill to speak in the United States on Soviet policy and sat on the platform at Fulton, Missouri, on March 5, 1946, as Churchill warned that the Russians had dropped an "iron curtain" around the territories they had conquered. Byrnes and Truman had gone over Churchill's speech before the former British prime minister gave it, but Truman was not yet ready to associate himself

fully with Churchill's draconian view of the Soviet threat or with his suggestion of an Anglo-American "fraternal association" to counter it. Consequently, Truman denied that he had known what Churchill was going to
say.

Public opinion began to push Truman in Churchill's direction, however,
when the Canadian spy scandal burst into the headlines. A crisis in Iran also
came to a head only days after Churchill's speech. Iran had long been an
arena of competition between Great Britain and Russia because it controlled
access to the Persian Gulf. The discovery of oil in Iran in the early twentieth
century added to that nation's value. In the 1920s, the British government
obtained majority control of the Ango-Iranian Oil Company that monopolized exploitation of the oil fields of southern Iran. The shah of Iran, the former commander of Iran's armed forces who seized control on the eve of the
second world war, began to look to Germany to counter the overwhelming
British presence in southern Iran and continuous Russian pressure on the
nothern border. When the British and the Russians became allies in 1941,
they forestalled Germany by occupying Iran and deposing the shah in favor
of his son. The United States joined the occupation in order to use the major
Iranian railroad as a means of getting lend-lease aid into Russia. Because the
Americans worried that Great Britain or the Soviet Union might try to make
their occupations permanent, the United States instigated a treaty in 1942
which committed all occupying powers to withdraw their troops within six
months after the end of the war.

The young shah saw the opportunity to use the United States as a permanent counterweight against Britain and Russia. The Soviets were especially
troublesome. They restricted travel in their northern zone of occupation, encouraged dissident ethnic and religious groups against the new shah's central
government, and hindered the movement of the Iranian army to suppress
these dissidents. In hopes of checking the Russians, the shah requested the
American government to send advisors to Iran and invited American oil
companies to seek concessions. The United States complied, but it was more
interested in keeping Iran as a strong buffer for America's existing oil concessions in Saudi Arabia than in acquiring new ones in Iran. Consequently
Roosevelt agreed to Churchill's proposal in 1944 that the United States
would not make "sheeps' eyes" at Iranian oil, while the British would stay
away from Saudi Arabia. To check the Russians, the United States and Britain then supported the shah's decision to defer any new Iranian concessions
until after the war. All occupation troops would be withdrawn by then, and
the shah would be able to resist demands for concessions from its near and
feared neighbor to the north.

The Russians accepted the deferment of oil concessions with bad grace.
Ominous troop movements and heavy-handed propaganda roused Iranian,
British, and American fears that the Soviet army would not leave Iran as it
had promised. These fears were justified. The British and Americans withdrew their troops before the March 2 deadline, except for a few American
advisors asked to stay by the Iranian government. The Soviets, however, an-

nounced that their troops would remain "pending examination of the situation." Even more frightening, these troops were deployed for full-scale combat. Byrnes angrily decided to give it to the Soviets "with both barrels." He personally joined the Iranian delegation at the United Nations to denounce the Soviet deployment in northern Iran. The Russian ambassador indignantly walked out of the UN deliberations, but the Soviet government did finally withdraw its troops.

Truman and many American leaders now believed they had the key to dealing with Russia—firmness. Acting on this assumption, Truman took a hard line in 1946 when Russia sent an ultimatum to Turkey demanding joint control of the Dardanelles. "We might as well find out whether the Russians are bent on world conquest, now as in five or ten years," he declared. As in the Iranian crisis, the Americans registered a harsh protest. More important, they dispatched a naval task force to the eastern Mediterranean that quickly became a permanent presence in the area. Again the Soviets failed to follow up their threats.

Meanwhile, the Americans moved to shore up their line in Western Europe. At a meeting of foreign ministers in Paris, Byrnes tried one more test of Russian intentions by offering a four power treaty that would guarantee German demilitarization for twenty-five years. If the Russians truly were motivated by security rather than ambition, Byrnes assumed they would accept this, because it would eliminate the fear of another German invasion and the need for a security zone in Eastern Europe. But Molotov turned it down. The United States then began to unite the Western zones of Germany and integrate them into the Western European economy. The commander of the American occupation troops had halted reparation payments from the American zone in May of 1946, although he had aimed his action more at France than at the Soviets. Byrnes extended the ban on reparations and approved a merger of the American and British zones to take effect on January 1, 1947. Since this so-called Bizonia was expected to establish its own economic rules and currency, it was a significant move away from joint control with the USSR over a unified Germany.

At the same time that Byrnes consolidated the Western sphere, he moved toward acceptance of Russian domination over its own sphere. Byrnes and his advisors thought there might be less contention between the Soviets and Americans if they disengaged from as many common problems and joint enterprises as possible. At the Foreign Ministers Conference in Paris in October 1946, Byrnes signed the final peace treaties that recognized the legitimacy of the governments of Rumania, Bulgaria, Finland, and Hungary, while Molotov did the same for Italy. Truman made it clear, however, that he did not intend this recognition to signify a softer line toward Russia. After this Paris Peace Conference, he accepted Byrnes's resignation. He had already fired Henry Wallace from the cabinet for making a speech critical of the hard line toward Russia, a speech which Truman had inexplicably approved before Wallace delivered it.

Throughout 1946, the United States was also trying to devise a safe plan for international control of atomic energy. American leaders recognized the dangers of a nuclear arms race. They were ready to give up the American atomic monopoly if they could be assured that a peaceful and stable world would result, but they were increasingly distrustful of Soviet goals. If the Soviets really intended to take over Western Europe, there was little in the way of conventional military forces to stop them. The American army, which had had 12 million men at the end of the war, had dwindled to 3 million by mid-1946, and would be down to 1.5 million a year later. Western Europe was devastated and nearly bankrupt. It could not provide the troops necessary to counter the Red Army stationed in or near Eastern Europe. World War II had already demonstrated to the satisfaction of most American leaders that American security was dependent upon a balance of power in Europe. What but the atomic bomb stood in the way of the Russian forces?

The American government's scientific advisors tried to counter such strategic thinking. Led by J. Robert Oppenheimer, they placed first priority on avoiding a nuclear arms race rather than defending Europe against what might turn out to be a nonexistent threat. They knew that the USSR could not be far from developing its own bomb, so they drew up a simple and direct plan for turning atomic energy over to the United Nations. Dean Acheson and David Lilienthal, who were in charge of devising an American plan for international control of atomic energy, were less sanguine. They wanted the turnover to go through four stages, with inspections after each one to ensure that no nation was holding out a potential nuclear threat.

In this process, the UN would survey all sources of radioactive ores and atomic industrial facilities before the United States would actually turn over its bombs and technology. This might deter Soviet acceptance of the plan, because the United States could wait until the survey had been completed and all Russia's military secrets had been exposed, then find an excuse to refuse to turn over the bomb itself. Regardless, Acheson and Lilienthal thought inspection was necessary. Besides, if the Soviets were willing to make such concessions, it would indicate that they did not really have aggressive intentions in Western Europe or elsewhere and the United States would be justified in abandoning its atomic monopoly.

After Acheson and Lilienthal had formulated their plan, Byrnes and Truman appointed Bernard Baruch to present it to the United Nations. Baruch had an undeserved reputation as an astute and experienced advisor to past presidents, and Byrnes counted on Baruch's clout to bring public and congressional approval for atomic sharing. Baruch agreed with General Leslie Groves that America's atomic monopoly would be a long-lasting one and that the United States should demand a great price for giving it up. He insisted on adding a provision to the Acheson-Lilienthal plan which would prevent any great power from exercising a veto over actions the UN might take to enforce the atomic agreement. (He and Groves actually visualized a UN force with the power to drop atomic bombs on any nation violating the UN accords.) Baruch also insisted that the plan should be offered to Russia and the UN on a take-it-or-leave-it basis. There would be no compromises and no negotiations. Byrnes complained later that the appointment of Baruch had been his greatest mistake.

Debate on the Baruch Plan in the UN dragged on from July until the end of 1946. Finally, as might have been predicted, the Soviets rejected it. Probably they would have spurned any plan and continued to build their own bomb, but the Baruch Plan afforded little real chance to assess their intentions. With the failure of the Baruch Plan, the United States had committed itself to a strategy that depended on American nuclear superiority to offset Russia's superior conventional forces in Europe. But the full ramifications of such a strategy were not yet clear to most American leaders, military or civilian. The secrets of the atomic program were closely held within the government and even the joint chiefs of staff did not know that as of 1947, the United States possessed only about a dozen bombs. In fact, those few bombs were unassembled, and the firing mechanism for them had never been tested. The United States was not adding much to this arsenal either, because after the war most of the personnel involved in the project had left the military for civilian life.

In ignorance of all this, the joint chiefs' war plans remained vague and unrealistic. In early 1947, American planning was still based on the presumption that war with Great Britain was as likely as war with the USSR. If war did break out with the Soviets, the joint chiefs assumed that the United States would use the atomic bomb on some twenty Russian cities and the Russian oil fields in the Caucasus. Yet many of the twenty targeted cities were out of range of American bombers. The joint chiefs also had to acknowledge that bombing would do nothing to stop the Russian army from overrunning Europe. They planned to evacuate the American occupation troops in Germany, Austria, and Trieste rather than order them to stand and fight against hopeless odds. Ironically, they did not have the transportation facilities to carry out the evacuation part of their plan either.

Containment of the Red Army in Europe thus rested essentially on the psychological threat of the bomb rather than any true Western military capacity. Truman and many other Americans were relatively content with this. As long as the United States had its atomic monopoly, even the vague menace of such a powerful weapon seemed a cheap and effective way to counter the Russian threat to Europe. With America's fears of a postwar depression and the desire for reduced taxes, there was strong sentiment for avoiding large military expenditures. Men like George Kennan, who became director of policy planning for the State Department in mid-1947, regarded the primary Russian threat as political rather than military in any case. Kennan thought the United States should concentrate on bolstering the economic and political systems of the Western European nations. This would be the best defense against political subversion, which he saw as a far more likely Russian tactic than overt military invasion.

George C. Marshall, Byrnes's successor as secretary of state, played a crucial role in promoting American acceptance of Kennan's policy of containment. Marshall no sooner assumed office than he was faced with what seemed to be a major crisis. The British announced that they were no longer financially able to support the Greek government in its civil war against Communist rebels. Both Great Britain and the United States assumed that the rebels were being encouraged by the Soviet Union as part of Russia's expansionist program. Actually, many of the rebels were motivated by opposition to the foreign-born king, who was supported by Greek right-wing forces and the British. Other rebels were simply involved in a traditional Greek vendetta, a vendetta based on old family and regional feuds and exacerbated by the brutalities of all sides during and after the war.[2] In addition, although the West did not understand at the time, Stalin was urging Yugoslavia to stop giving sanctuary and arms to the rebels.

Nevertheless, Truman and Marshall saw the British withdrawal from Greece as a serious matter. They had known for some time that Britain's financial weakness might bring such a retreat. They had already loaned the British $3.75 billion to help them cope with their financial emergency and had decided to give some aid to Greece. Still, American government leaders were surprised by the abruptness of the British decision and galvanized into action by it. Truman went before Congress to request $300 million for Greece. While he was at it, he asked $100 million more for Turkey. Fearful of residual isolationism and antitax sentiment in the Republican-controlled Congress, Truman defined the issue in stark terms. The struggle in Greece was only part of a global struggle between alternative ways of life, Truman said. The United States must "support free peoples who are resisting attempted subjugation by armed minorities or by outside pressure," he proclaimed. The press quickly dubbed this proclamation the Truman Doctrine.

While Truman announced his doctrine, Secretary of State George Marshall was in Moscow with the other big power foreign ministers trying to complete the peace treaties for Germany and Austria. He had gone into the conference with the conviction that one could not really negotiate with the Russians—"It is either yield to them or tell them 'no,'" one briefing paper had advised him. Russian conduct at the conference confirmed him in that belief. The Soviets repeatedly insisted upon $10 billion worth of reparations in their usual negotiating style, "the same fruitless arguments about minor matters, the same distortions and the same blaring propaganda," according to Marshall. The secretary and his advisors assumed that the reparations demands actually were an attempt to divert resources from Germany and Western Europe, keeping both areas weak and preparing the way for a Communist upheaval and Russian takeover.

The Americans said "no" to reparations. They would continue their course toward a divided Germany. Neither the West nor the Soviets could afford to see a unified Germany throw its weight to the wrong side, and neither trusted the other not to make an attempt to win over Germany once unification was an accomplished fact. In the absence of mutual confidence, a

[2] For instance, the Leftist guerilla forces had taken 30,000 hostages in Athens during their flight from the reoccupying British forces, and had killed some 4,000 of them. The right-wing Greek government, in turn, arrested and executed thousands when it established control.

divided Germany was safer for both sides. Since both sides assumed that the German people would support whichever nation could guarantee them a reunified country, however, neither wanted to be seen by the Germans as responsible for a permanent division. Thus the United States later refused recognition of East Germany even when, during the various Berlin crises, it recognized that the question threatened to bring it to the verge of nuclear war.

Marshall returned from the Moscow Conference with nothing settled except his conviction that the Soviets wanted to bring about the disintegration of Western Europe. That disintegration already seemed well on its way by early 1947. Wheat production was only half what it had been in 1938. The diet of people in some areas of Germany had fallen as low as 900 calories a day. Supplies of coal were dwindling. Inflation had boosted wholesale prices in France some 80 percent. When Great Britain had made its pound sterling convertible to dollars, a rush of investors from pounds to dollars had undermined the British economy. The United States had loaned Britain $3.75 billion and France $600 million, but obviously more was needed. America had an economic as well as a strategic stake in offering aid: The United States had an export surplus of $12.5 billion, and Europe was running out of money to buy American goods.

On June 5, 1947, America's secretary of state spoke at Harvard University and outlined what would be known as the Marshall Plan. The United States would offer some $20 billion for European relief if the European nations themselves would devise a rational, integrated plan for the recovery of the area as a whole, including West Germany. Surprisingly, Marshall also offered to extend the aid to the Soviet Union and its Eastern European satellites. This offer was strictly a ruse designed to avoid the appearance that the United States was responsible for the division of Europe. Marshall and his advisors hoped against hope that the strings America attached to the aid would cause the Soviets to reject it. Marshall was afraid the Soviets would sabotage European negotiations for an integrated plan and that the U.S. Congress would reject the plan if it included large grants to Russia. The gamble worked. The Soviets were not about to make the economic disclosures necessary to joint planning or permit the Americans to judge the uses to which they would put the aid. Neither would they integrate their economy and that of Eastern Europe into the much stronger economy of the West and subject their citizens to the lure of American abundance. When the Americans rejected the Russian proposal that each nation draw up its own plan and request for aid, the Soviets abandoned the conference and ordered their satellites to do likewise.

As the Western European nations decisively formulated a combined plan for economic recovery, the American Congress demonstrated its support of the Marshall Plan by granting $600 million in interim funds. Once the plan was officially prepared, Congress appropriated $4 billion for the first year of operation in 1948. By 1952, the United States had contributed $13 billion to the near-miraculous revival of the Western European economy.

FROM THE MARSHALL PLAN TO THE WAR IN KOREA: THE HARDENING OF CONTAINMENT

The Truman Doctrine and the Marshall Plan formed the keystones of what came to be known as the policy of containment. The word "containment" was derived from an article published in the prestigious journal *Foreign Affairs* and signed by a Mr. X. Enterprising journalists quickly discovered that Mr. X was George Kennan, director of policy planning for the State Department. Thus the article seemed a semi-official rationale for the policy embodied in the Truman Doctrine and the Marshall Plan. In this condensed version of his "long telegram," Kennan reiterated his belief that Russia was driven by its own internal dynamics to conjure up an enemy and expand against it until it was met by superior force. Since a balance of power in Europe was necessary to America's own security, and since World War II had destroyed the ability of Britain, France, and Germany to maintain that balance against Russia, the United States would have to intervene. If this were done, Kennan continued to hold out hopes that the Soviet regime would either mellow or be overthrown from within.

As Kennan would later admit, the article was carelessly phrased and failed to convey some of the subtleties of his thought. His article spoke of containing Russia at every point it might seek to expand and made no distinction between areas of vital and those of marginal interest to the United States. Yet Kennan believed the United States should limit its concern primarily to the major industrial powers of Europe and Japan. Those nations had the capacity to support a significant military force, while many of the governments outside Europe and Japan were neither stable nor popular with their own people and had little real sympathy for Western democratic and moral values. Kennan had been one of the few in the administration to warn against the Truman Doctrine portraying temporary aid to Greece and Turkey as part of a global commitment to defend against communism everywhere.

Likewise, Kennan's article failed to make clear that he believed containment should emphasize economic and political rather than military measures. Kennan thought that an overt Soviet military invasion was unlikely. The Russians were hurt and cautious. Even though their army might be able to sweep over Europe, they would be unable to digest the Western European nations, and they knew it. Their more likely tactic was political and economic subversion that would prepare Western Europe for a more peaceful takeover.

Finally, Kennan's article portrayed containment as a justifiably hostile policy toward Soviet aggression and tyranny. Certainly it was hostile. But it also was predicated on some assumptions the Russians could have been expected to welcome. Containment implied the concession of the Soviet sphere, and this probably had been Stalin's primary goal all along. In later years, Kennan would emphasize this more positive side of containment and regret that it had been hardened into a rigid prescription for fighting a Cold

War. At the same time, however, Kennan's own emphasis had been much more on the shamefulness of the United States having to abandon the Eastern Europeans to Russian tyranny.

Walter Lippmann, the prominent and respected columnist, wrote a highly publicized critique of the X article making many of these same points. Kennan writhed privately. He wanted desperately to answer and clarify his essential agreement with many of Lippmann's arguments, but in mid-1947 it did not seem that these subtle distinctions would turn out to be so important. Containment was pursued in a limited, flexible manner. The emphasis was political and economic, rather than military. Marshall's undersecretary of state, Dean Acheson, told a congressional committee that the Truman Doctrine did not mean an automatic American commitment to any nation on the globe resisting communism. Each situation would be evaluated independently, and aid would be primarily economic and political. His words were borne out, as Marshall Plan dollars flowed most generously to the major industrial powers of Europe, while aid to Chiang Kai-shek in China was severely limited. The State Department was still flexible enough to recognize that Mao Tse-tung did not represent as great a threat to American interests as Russia did in Europe. It was also flexible enough to extend aid to Tito's Communist regime in Yugoslavia when Tito showed in 1948 that he was resisting Stalin's dictates.

These subtle limitations on containment were fragile, however, and no one is quite sure how clearly Kennan himself held to them, let alone the other members of the government. Such restraint and flexibility could not survive the shocking events of the next two years—the Soviet crackdown on Czechoslovakia, the Berlin blockade, the triumph of Mao in China, the explosion of the first Russian atomic bomb, and the North Korean invasion of South Korea. Steadily the United States moved toward a more militant version of containment, and it seemed at the time to be a natural extension of Kennan's policy rather than a violation of it. Any doubts Kennan expressed were drowned out by the rising accusations of many, especially Republicans, that containment was an immoral and cowardly policy that was soft on communism.

Kennan and Marshall had expected the Soviets to react strongly against the Marshall Plan, but the extent and violence of that reaction surprised them. First, the Soviets forced the nations they had warned away from the Marshall Plan to sign a series of trade treaties they called the Molotov Plan. These treaties ensured that the satellite economies remained oriented away from the West toward the USSR. Stalin also revived the Communist Information Bureau (Cominform) to coordinate the strategy of the Communist parties of Europe. Through it, he ordered the Italian and French parties to cease collaboration with the bourgeois regimes in power. The French and Italian parties began a series of strikes to disrupt the reviving European economies. Many observers began to fear that the Communists could win the 1948 elections. Truman and Marshall publicly warned that Marshall Plan aid depended on the victory of non-Communist regimes in both nations, and in Italy the recently organized Central Intelligence Agency distributed secret funds to the centrist parties.

The Communist parties of France and Italy both lost the elections of 1948. Perhaps the most important factor in that loss was not the manipulation of American economic aid, but Stalin's brutal suppression of the relatively independent Czechoslovakian regime. The Western-oriented Foreign Minister Jan Masaryk fell to his death from a small bathroom window of a high building while in custody of the Russians. The Soviets proclaimed it a suicide, but the most thorough investigation to date concludes that Masaryk was murdered. Masaryk's death was just the beginning of a series of purges, show trials, and mass executions that continued until Stalin's death in 1953. This did a great deal to discredit the Communist parties in Western Europe.

It also did a great deal to frighten the West. With American encouragement, Great Britain organized a mutual defense pact that included itself, France, Belgium, the Netherlands, and Luxembourg. This Brussels Pact of March 17, 1948, proclaimed that an attack on one member would be an attack on all. It anticipated that both Western Germany and the United States would be incorporated into the arrangement, and the American Senate quickly expressed its approval by passing the so-called Vandenberg Resolution. America's revolutionary decision to sign an entangling alliance with European powers paved the way for the expansion of the Brussels Pact into the North Atlantic Treaty Organization in April 1949. NATO incorporated the United States, Canada, Turkey, and Greece, along with the original Brussels Pact members.

The original purpose of the Brussels Pact and NATO, however, was not a significant military buildup; it was more a political and spiritual rallying against the possibility of Soviet aggression. The Soviet Union had thirty divisions in Eastern and Central Europe. The combined American, British, and French forces in Europe totaled only ten divisions, and Western intelligence reports assumed that Russia could sweep through all of Western Europe in a few weeks. Yet for the time being, the United States and its allies did little to build up their conventional capacity to resist. It was clear that beyond the spiritual rallying of the NATO alliance and the economic and political revival brought about by the Marshall Plan, the military defense of Europe rested with America's atomic deterrent.

Yet the United States had little capacity to carry out its assigned part. The Czech crisis caught the United States still without an operational war plan, an adequate supply of bombs, or bombers capable of reaching their targets in the Soviet Union. A breakthrough in technology in early 1948 increased the supply of bombs, so that at the end of the year the United States could plan to retaliate against a Russian attack by obliterating seventy Russian cities with 133 bombs. But the delivery capability was still in doubt. In a mock raid on Dayton, Ohio, in 1948, not a single bomber got through.

The navy and air force urged Truman to undertake massive rearmament programs to correct this. The air force wanted to build some seventy air groups shaped around the new B-36 bomber. These bombing groups would be stationed on bases the United States would acquire from its allies around the periphery of the Soviet Union. The navy wanted to build supercarriers that would carry smaller atomic bombers within striking range of Russia. Truman resisted all these rearmament programs. He was not certain atomic bombs could actually be used in warfare. If they were dropped on the Russians, they would not stop a Red Army invasion of Europe, and the horror they inflicted would make the Russians too angry ever to accept a compromise settlement short of total victory or defeat. The bomb could not be dropped on the invading force because it would destroy the very nations America was trying to protect. The cost of building a conventional force that might oppose the Russians without use of the atomic alternative seemed astronomical, especially when added to the navy and air force plans to make the atomic alternative workable in the first place. Finally, Truman was determined to hold the defense budget under $15 billion. He believed this necessary to maintain a healthy domestic economy during the difficult postwar adjustment.

Thus, more by default than by careful planning, the United States and its European allies continued to depend on economic and political measures to contain Russia. As late as April 1949, when the NATO Pact was signed, there was no specific provision to incorporate the American atomic umbrella in the defense of Western Europe.

The Soviet blockade of Berlin that began June 24, 1948, highlighted the significance and vagueness of that atomic umbrella. The Western occupying powers had given up any real attempt to establish a cooperative four power rule in Germany. They were convinced the Soviets would simply stall discussion and action until either the German economy crumbled or the Russians were given $10 billion in reparations. The United States was not about to pour Marshall Plan aid into Germany so Russia could drain it out in reparations. Instead, the Americans, British, and French combined their zones, established a separate currency to stop the inflation and hoarding that plagued the German economy, and permitted a German assembly to begin work on a constitution for a separate West Germany. To assuage French fears of this revived Germany, the United States promised to keep occupation troops in Germany indefinitely.

The Soviet Union responded that if Germany was indeed going to be divided, then the rationale for four power occupation in West Berlin no longer existed. Since the city was deep in the Russian zone, the Soviets announced they would no longer permit overland travel to Berlin from the West. They also cut off West Berlin's electricity. Truman considered this a direct violation of American rights, but was chagrined to find that there was no written agreement guaranteeing Western access by road or rail. Some military leaders proposed sending an armed column to defend the earlier oral arrangements. Truman decided instead to try to supply Berlin by plane through the air corridors that were guaranteed in writing. With a plane touching down at Templehof Airport every ninety seconds, the resulting airlift succeeded in bringing in more supplies than the 2 million inhabitants of West Berlin actually needed.

To reinforce this signal of American determination, Truman negotiated an agreement with Great Britain permitting the United States to station B-29s on its soil within striking distance of Russia's major cities. In a great show of force, Truman sent sixty B-29s to British airfields. It was all bluff. America's atomic bombs were kept at home, disassembled and under civilian control. Besides, most of the planes had not been modified to carry atomic bombs, despite Truman's statement that they were "atomic capable."

Some historians have believed that this atomic threat was the primary factor in Stalin's ultimate decision to lift the blockade. But it is now clear that Russian spies like the British diplomat Donald MacLean were in a position to know it was a bluff. Stalin seems to have lifted the blockade instead because it was costing him more than he was gaining. The blockade frightened Western Europe into greater unity, added to the discredit the Western Communist parties had suffered from the Czech crisis, and led to a counterblockade that denied East Germany supplies from the West. It also helped drive American occupation in Japan from a concentration on reform to one emphasizing recovery so Japan could contribute to the anti-Soviet economic bloc. In May of 1949, almost a year after Stalin had announced the Berlin blockade, he gave it up.

American relief was short-lived. In September 1949, an American plane detected traces of radioactivity from a Russian atomic explosion. America's atomic monopoly had ended. How would the U.S. atomic umbrella defend Europe against superior Russian conventional forces if the Soviets acquired an equal atomic capacity to retaliate? American scientists like Edward Teller and Ernest Lawrence proposed an answer. The United States could maintain its nuclear superiority by building a hydrogen bomb, a bomb so powerful that the atomic bomb would be a mere trigger to set it off.

Other scientists, like J. Robert Oppenheimer, objected. They did not argue that the bomb was impossible to build, but that it would wipe out humanity. George Kennan wrote an eighty-page paper and numerous memos for the administration incorporating this scientific objection with his political objections. He saw no political use for the bomb. There were only a couple of targets in all of Russia that could not be obliterated by a single smaller atomic bomb. An H bomb could never be used to accomplish a political purpose, only to annihilate. Kennan argued that the United States would be better off renouncing first use of the bomb and seeking solid international controls. This might leave Western Europe somewhat vulnerable to an invasion by the superior Russian army, but better that than to rely on a weapon that could not be used without endangering the very existence of humankind. Even if the United States built the hydrogen bomb, the USSR would soon have it too. Then America would face the same dilemma, but at an even more ominous level of potential destruction.

The USSR had no intention of invading Western Europe anyway, Kennan argued; containment had succeeded. Now it was time to think of negotiations aimed at a mutual guarantee of European neutrality and withdrawal of most foreign troops from Western and Eastern Europe. The Soviet crackdown on Czechoslovakia and the Berlin blockade indeed had been vicious, but they had been defensive attempts to shore up the Russian sphere in the face of the Marshall Plan and the rebuilding of an independent West Germany. A negotiated withdrawal might be possible. If such negotiations failed, the United States could build up a conventional force with NATO to deter a Russian invasion. Prior to negotiations, however, the United States should avoid militarizing containment; it should not build the H bomb or a powerful NATO army.

Dean Acheson, who had replaced George Marshall as Truman's secretary of state, did not agree. He saw the United States as operating from a position of weakness rather than strength. He did not trust talks with the Russians, and thought that the United States should build a superior force before opening any negotiations. America should base its military plans on Russian capacity, not its intentions. If the Soviets got the hydrogen bomb when the United States did not have it, this would be a terrible blow to the courage and morale of America and Western Europe. (In fact, we now know the Russians already had begun work on their H bomb.) So Acheson withheld Kennan's analytical paper from Truman and other presidential advisors.

It was unlikely to have changed Truman's mind anyway. The political atmosphere was poisoned by the conviction of diplomat Alger Hiss for lying about his membership in the Communist party and by the arrest of atomic physicist Klaus Fuchs as a Soviet agent. Truman had to fear the political consequences if the Soviets exploded a hydrogen bomb and it was revealed he had decided not to build one. He made his decision to go ahead with the H bomb in a seven-minute meeting.

Truman accompanied his decision with an order for a thorough study of America's entire strategic program, a study that was embodied in the National Security Council's Memorandum 68. NSC-68 was written by Kennan's successor as head of policy planning for the State Department, Paul Nitze. It conformed to Acheson's insistence that the United States plan to counter Soviet capabilities rather than its intentions. It defined American national security in global terms. NSC-68 called for U.S. military power capable of responding to any Russian threat anywhere in the world. Finally, NSC-68 urged that the United States build a greater conventional warfare capacity, thereby reducing dependence on atomic weapons and decreasing the likelihood of nuclear war. NSC-68 would require a defense budget of between $30 billion and $50 billion, double or triple the $15 billion to which Truman was already committed. Truman's economic advisors insisted that America could afford the increase because government spending would boost economic productivity and generate more tax revenue, but Truman withheld approval of NSC-68 pending firmer financial estimates. It would take another foreign policy shock, the North Korean invasion of South Korea, to drive the United States to the fully militarized containment visualized in NSC-68.

THE COLD WAR IN EAST ASIA

On October 1, 1949, one month after the United States had detected the Soviet atomic explosion, the Chinese Communists celebrated their victory over the Nationalists by announcing the formation of the People's Republic of China. Although the American State Department had expected Chiang's defeat since mid-1948, the flight of Chiang and his army to the island of Taiwan still came as a shock. But the "fall" of China did not immediately eliminate all flexibility in America's policy toward East Asia. The "old China hands" of the state department, like O. Edmund Clubb, John S. Service, and John Paton Davies, had recognized and reported the corruption and fragility of Chiang's rule and knew his fall was inevitable if he did not reform his regime. His Nationalist government relied heavily on landowners, military warlords, and the urban commercial community. After 1927, Chiang had alienated the Communist wing of the nationalist revolution by slaughtering all the Communists he could find. In the 1930s, the Japanese invasion pushed him and his armies into the countryside and forced him to abandon his supporters among the urban bankers and middle classes who stayed behind in the Japanese-occupied cities. Finally, the remnant of the Chinese Communists that had survived the Long March to escape Chiang's purge had won the standard of Chinese nationalism by a more vigorous prosecution of the war against the Japanese. With land reform and promises of industrial modernization, the Communists gained support among the peasants and the urban population. They kept that support with an efficient government organization.

Stalin had lived up to his Yalta promises to recognize Chiang's government, but he had prevented Nationalist troops from landing at Darien and Port Arthur to occupy Manchuria. Instead he had permitted the Communists to disarm the Japanese, claiming he thought they were part of Chiang's army. Then he had reversed himself abruptly and welcomed the Nationalists into the remainder of Manchuria. Obviously he was more interested in keeping China weak and distracted by civil conflict than in aiding Mao, and the Chinese Communists strongly resented this action. America's "old China hands" knew that Mao would still remain friendlier to the Soviets than to the Americans, but they thought he would retain sufficient distrust of Russia to accept some American support as a check to Soviet influence. They urged that diplomatic channels to the Communists be kept open.

By and large, Truman's State Department followed their advice. In late 1945, shortly after taking office, Truman had sent George Marshall to arrange a coalition government between Chiang and Mao. Marshall had failed. Mao was not about to give up his arms and accept a secondary office under Chiang, as Marshall proposed. Mao remembered too well Chiang's earlier purge of the Communists and the continuing hostility during the war with Japan. Chiang also was adamant against accepting Communists in his government. He rejected Marshall's warning that he was likely to lose a civil war. Ultimately the Communists withdrew from the talks, Marshall flew home to become secretary of state, and the Chinese civil war resumed.

Despite the disgust of Marshall, Acheson, and most of the State Department with Chiang, they were not willing to abandon him. They still feared Stalin's connection with Mao, and they believed they still had some leverage over the Communists. Even if Mao defeated Chiang, America's China hands thought Mao would have as many difficulties governing the unwieldy Chinese nation as Chiang and his predecessors. In order to hold China together and maintain some independence from Russia, Mao would need American help. Thus America would not have to abandon Chiang or woo Mao to have reasonable relations with a victorious Communist regime.

Unfortunately, these reasoned attitudes were eclipsed by partisan politics. The Truman administration was getting increasing political pressure to do more to fight communism in China. Members of Congress with ties to Chinese missionary and merchant circles—the China Lobby—were urging more aid for Chiang. The Republican party, stung by its unexpected defeat in the 1948 elections, saw the loss of China as an attractive campaign issue to use against the Democrats. They threatened to hold up aid to Europe unless aid to Nationalist China was included. Many American military leaders also were urging more aid to Chiang. They did not want American troops sent to China, but once Chiang had escaped to Taiwan, they wanted an American fleet stationed off the China coast to prevent a Communist invasion from the mainland. Finally, an obscure Wisconsin senator, Joseph McCarthy, began to revive Patrick Hurley's old charges that disloyal State Department advisors were responsible for the "loss of China." This particularly hurt Dean Acheson, who had announced after Alger Hiss's conviction for perjury that he would not abandon him.

Under this political pressure, Truman, Marshall, and Acheson walked a tightrope in their policy toward China. Limited aid continued to flow to Chiang. The United States delayed recognition of the Communist regime while quarrelling with it about the treatment of American diplomats and property in areas conquered by Mao's troops. But Truman did not station the American fleet off Taiwan, and he agreed that the question of China's admission to the United Nations was a procedural rather than a substantive one, which meant it was not subject to an American veto. Meanwhile, Acheson released a mammoth government report, the so-called *China White Paper*, to demonstrate that Chiang himself rather than the Yalta Agreement or supposed later betrayals were responsible for the collapse of his regime.

Acheson and the State Department also tried to rearrange America's policy toward the rest of Asia in the light of the Communist conquest of China. Acheson was fearful that another quick Communist takeover elsewhere in Asia might lead to the collapse of all non-Communist regimes in the area. He and Truman sent John Foster Dulles, the most prominent Republican expert on foreign affairs, to negotiate a peace treaty with Japan that would exclude Soviet participation and leave American troops stationed there for the indefinite future.

The Truman administration also began sending direct aid to the French in Indochina for the first time. Until 1950, the administration had looked askance at the French war against Ho Chi Minh in Vietnam. But the United

States had needed French power and cooperation in Europe to help balance the Soviet threat, and Marshall Plan aid had flowed into France even though the Americans knew that some of it was diverted to the war in Vietnam. Then Mao's victory in China made Truman and Acheson vigorous rather than reluctant supporters of the French effort in Indochina. They had no wish to see another Communist victory in that region. They did continue to irritate the French by urging them to promise independence for Vietnam. They believed that a truly nationalist regime would be far more likely to resist the Communist advance than the thinly disguised French colonial regime headed by the puppet emperor Bao Dai. But when pressed, they would choose French colonialism over the Vietminh.

Acheson spelled out the Truman administration's overall policy toward Asia in a speech he made to the National Press Club on January 12, 1950. Acheson said that the bulk of America's limited resources had to go to the area of primary interest, Europe. In Asia, the United States would use its preeminent naval and air power to defend a ring of islands around the mainland, including the Aleutians, Japan, and the Philippines. He did not include Korea or Taiwan, but he said that rising nationalism would lead China and the other nations of Asia to resist Soviet attempts to take them. In the unlikely event of an overt invasion beyond America's defense perimeter, the United Nations undoubtedly would aid "people who are determined to protect their independence." His confidence was about to be tested in Korea.

THE KOREAN WAR

The Allies had treated Korea as an afterthought during World War II. They did not make arrangements for its occupation until the Soviet Union entered the Pacific war, only days before Japan's surrender. The Soviets and Americans hastily agreed that Russia would temporarily occupy that portion of Korea north of the 38th parallel, while the United States occupied the south. The United States assumed that Korea would quickly be united and turned over to an indigenous regime, after which both occupying powers would withdraw their troops.

The American occupation commander, General John R. Hodge, soon found that an acceptable Korean government was not so easy to come by. Japan had formally annexed Korea in 1910 after expelling Russia in the Russo-Japanese War five years before. There simply was no easily legitimized government of Korean nationalists available. A group of Koreans who had taken refuge with the Nationalist Chinese claimed the status of a provisional government, but it had very shallow roots among the Korean people themselves. Another group of Koreans who had stayed to fight the Japanese during the war formed a People's Republic in Seoul and claimed recognition, but Hodge mistakenly believed it was a puppet regime of Russian and Chinese communism, so he refused to work with it.

The American occupiers found themselves dependent on individual Koreans who could speak English to communicate between the American occupying government and the Korean people. Most of these English-speaking Koreans were elite conservatives or former policemen and collaborators with the Japanese. Naturally they were not terribly popular with many of their countrymen. The most prominent of these right-wing English-speaking Koreans was Syngman Rhee, who had spent the war in Washington lobbying for himself as leader of a liberated Korea. Rhee was a clever politician with strong ties to the Korean police forces who managed to divide and rule the various conservative factions in South Korea. He used his position to exclude the centrist politicians Hodge was trying to bring into the new parliamentary system. This caused Hodge to explode that Rhee was a pain in the neck. In the midst of the factional squabbles and popular riots that plagued South Korea, the American occupiers made very little progress toward land or economic reform.

The Russians had better luck in their zone. Their occupying army brought Korean Communist exiles with them and installed them as the government of North Korea. The USSR strictly regulated all contact between North Koreans and the outside world, built a strong North Korean army to aid the Red Army in maintaining control, and established an extensive land reform program that helped win some local support despite the oppressions of the new regime.

As the Russians and Americans sought to build friendly regimes in their own occupation zones, they naturally had difficulty in agreeing on how to unify the peninsula. The Russians insisted that consultations for forming a provisional unified government be held only with Koreans friendly to themselves. The Americans insisted on peninsula-wide elections. Since two-thirds of Korea's population was in the south, the Russians feared such elections would result in a regime favorable to the Americans. When negotiations for a unified Korea broke down, the United States appealed to the United Nations. At that time, the majority of UN members were favorable to the Western powers, so the United States was able to win a call for unifying elections similar to the American plan. When the Soviets rejected the UN plan, the United States and the UN held elections in the south anyway. These elections resulted in the formation of the Republic of Korea in August 1948, with Syngman Rhee as its leader. By mid-1949, the United States had withdrawn the last 7,500 of its occupation troops. This left Rhee's government dependent on an unpopular constabulary with a Japanese collaborationist reputation. Worse yet, it left a small, disorganized army accompanied by a few American military advisors to face a well-trained, well-armed North Korean army of over 150,000 men. The South's weakness did not keep Rhee from claiming his government was the legitimate ruler of all of Korea. He began to build his military forces and to send raids north of the 38th parallel.

American officials were not optimistic about the chances for Rhee's regime. They estimated that 30 percent of the people in South Korea supported Leftist policies and were sympathetic to the North. Guerrilla activities were a constant source of concern. The Americans doubted the ability of the fractious, bull-headed Rhee to unify South Korea. They were willing to give only minimal economic and military aid to Rhee on the slim hope that he might be able to preserve an independent, Western-oriented South Korea. American troops and economic aid were needed too desperately elsewhere, particularly in the more critical theater of Europe, for the United States to be able to afford a massive commitment to Korea.

American military officials especially wanted American troops out of Korea. They believed there was no way the United States could win a major conflict on the mainland of Asia. Even General Douglas MacArthur, as committed to Asia as he was, proclaimed that anyone advocating such a war should have his head examined. MacArthur wanted troops stationed in Japan and in the Philippines, the island periphery of the Asian mainland from which the United States could exert its naval and air power. He was disturbed, however, when the troops withdrawn from Korea during the Berlin blockade crisis were earmarked for European rather than Asian-oriented missions. His disagreement with the Truman administration's Europe First policy would soon cause a public uproar.

If the United States was prepared to tolerate a slow erosion of Rhee's position in South Korea, it was not at all prepared to accept the direct and massive North Korean invasion of South Korea in June of 1950. The North Korean invasion was a direct challenge to American prestige. In shock, members of Truman's administration speculated that the invasion was a Soviet attempt to skirt the containment line the United States had drawn in Europe. Truman was still smarting from his administration's "loss" of China and could not turn away from what he saw as a direct Communist challenge to American credibility. He was already under attack from Senator Joseph McCarthy's crusade against Communists in government, and Congress had just overridden his veto of the ominous McCarran Internal Security Act. Thus, despite his administration's long avoidance of a major commitment to South Korea, Truman decided without congressional consultation to defend Rhee's regime against the invasion.

The United States first took the issue to the United Nations and received the sanction of the Security Council to defend South Korea. The Americans were fortunate that the Soviets were boycotting the UN at this time to protest the exclusion of the People's Republic of China. This meant the Soviets had no chance to veto the Security Council's action. Truman quickly grasped the opportunity to send supplies and air cover to aid the South Koreans. When that proved inadequate to stem the invasion and after it was clear that there were no major uprisings in the South to challenge Rhee's control, Truman decided to commit American troops to the battle. Finally, the combined forces of South Korea and the United States managed to stop the North Koreans at the Pusan perimeter and cling to a small foothold at the southern tip of the Korean peninsula.

Before dispatching American troops, Truman and his administration had looked carefully to see if Russian or Chinese soldiers were involved in the invasion. If they had been, he probably would have avoided sending American ground forces into Korea, where they were at so much of a strategic disadvantage. He then would have challenged the Soviets elsewhere. Since Russian and Chinese troops were not directly engaged in the fighting, he assumed he could commit American soldiers without risking a great power confrontation. He was as puzzled by the Russian role in the war as later historians have been. If the North Korean invasion was instigated by the Russians as an end run around American containment and a test of American credibility, how could the Soviets have failed to be present at the UN to protect the North Korean position with the veto?[3] Or had North Korea gone off on its own? If so, could the United States do more than just resist the invasion? Could it actually push north of the 38th parallel, destroy the regime of Kim Il Sung, and unite Korea under Syngman Rhee's pro-American government without risking a confrontation with Russia or China? This would be a fitting punishment for Communist aggression and a demonstration of the credibility of the containment policy.

The Truman administration entertained this vision even while the South Korean and American forces were in headlong retreat toward the Pusan perimeter. On September 11, after the perimeter had been stabilized and plans approved for a counterattack, Truman signed National Security Council Directive 81, which empowered MacArthur to conduct operations north of the 38th parallel to destroy the North Korean forces and reunify Korea if this could be done without the risk of war with the Soviet Union or China. Truman would have to assess the risk of Soviet and Chinese intervention when American troops approached the 38th parallel and make the final decision at that time.

Meanwhile, Truman increased arms shipments to aid the French effort in Indochina and sent a portion of the Seventh Fleet from the Philippines to the Taiwan Straits to deter Mao from capturing Taiwan. He still showed some restraint, however, in rejecting the suggestion of MacArthur and others that the United States use the opportunity of the war in Korea to destroy communism in China and all the rest of Asia. He made clear that aid to Taiwan was a temporary military measure to protect the flanks of Korea. When General MacArthur met Chiang Kai-shek and implied a permanent American commitment to the Nationalist regime on Taiwan, Truman sent Averell Harriman to remind MacArthur that he was to avoid such pledges. Then Truman announced publicly that the Seventh Fleet would be withdrawn from the Taiwan Straits after the Korean war. He even considered demoting MacArthur after the headstrong general released a public statement condemning malicious misrepresentations "by those who invariably in the past have propagandized a policy of defeatism and appeasement in the Pacific."

---

[3] Nikita Khrushchev wrote in his memoirs that Stalin had indeed approved the invasion at the importuning of Kim Il Sung after Mao had assured him that the United States would not intervene.

CONFLICT IN KOREA, 1950–1953

RUSSIA

Vladivostok

CHINA

MANCHURIA

Yalu R.

Chosin
Reservoir

NORTH

KOREA

Farthest penetration of U.S
northward, Nov. 24, 1950

Pyongyang

Armistice line, July 27, 1953

38th parallel

Inchon   Seoul

SOUTH

KOREA   Pusan perimeter
(farthest penetration
of North Korea southward)
Sept. 15, 1950

YELLOW

SEA   Pusan

SEA

OF

JAPAN

Tokyo

JAPAN

PACIFIC

OCEAN

Map 15   Conflict in Korea, 1950–1955

Any inclinations Truman and Acheson might have had toward restraint were overwhelmed when MacArthur engineered a brilliant amphibious invasion behind the North Korean lines at Inchon. With the North Korean army in frantic retreat, Truman euphorically approved MacArthur's wish to pursue the enemy beyond the 38th parallel and destroy the Communist regime. MacArthur insisted that the Chinese would never intervene and that the Americans would defeat them easily if they did. Even the more reluctant members of Truman's administration agreed that if the Chinese or the Russians had intended to intervene, they would have done so earlier when American forces were still distant enough to be able to avoid a confrontation.

MacArthur made the most of his authorization. He ignored orders to send only Koreans, not Americans, close to the Yalu River that formed Korea's northern border with China. He did not halt even after his troops made contact with Chinese units. He assumed that the 200,000 Chinese troops were in Korea only to protect a *cordon sanitaire* around their border. He split his attacking forces and dispersed them thinly throughout the broad part of the North Korean peninsula. He was a sitting duck when the Chinese army began its offensive: His forces reeled backward as fast as they had advanced and barely managed to stabilize a defensive line close to the 38th parallel. MacArthur publicly raged that the United States should carry the war into China, bomb beyond the Yalu, "unleash" Chiang's troops to attack the mainland, and even use the atomic bomb if necessary. The chastened Truman fired MacArthur instead, accepted a limited war, and opened negotiations that dragged on for two years before a tenuous truce could end the conflict.

Truman's acceptance of a limited war opened him to harsh criticism from the Right in American politics. MacArthur returned home after his dismissal to a hero's welcome. His moving farewell to Congress made him a unifying symbol for those who abhorred the Democrat's Europe First strategy. Republicans reminded Americans that Acheson had omitted Korea from the U.S. defense perimeter in his National Press Club speech and argued that this had invited Communist aggression. They often supported MacArthur's insistence that the object of war was victory, not a stalemate, and urged that the United States replace the doctrine of limited war with one of total war for total victory. They were freer to criticize than they might have been because Truman had refused to ask Congress for an official declaration of war, something the Republicans would have supported fully at the outset of the conflict. In the absence of an official congressional commitment, the Republicans could call Korea "Truman's war."

Truman and Acheson may have been more moderate than MacArthur and many of their Republican critics, but their decision to push beyond the 38th parallel after the Inchon landings already had escalated the Cold War. Had they stopped at the 38th parallel and negotiated a peace, the war would have ended after only three months and would have cost a minimum of casualties, yet would have demonstrated the determination of the United States to resist overt military aggression. The decision to go north extended the war almost three years. It cost America 30,000 lives, and the South Koreans many more. It also cost the United States much of the support of its allies. Nations like Great Britain and India had supported the United States and the UN decision to resist the North Korean invasion, but they objected strongly to the extension of the war beyond the 38th parallel.

They objected even more strongly to the increased American commitment to Chiang's Nationalist regime on Taiwan that accompanied the extension. With China now an overt enemy in Korea, all flexibility disappeared on the issues of Taiwan, recognition of Mao's government, and admission of China to the United Nations. America's previously reluctant aid to the French conflict in Indochina had become enthusiastic and overt. The United States urged even greater effort than the French themselves were willing to expend and set the stage for America to pick up the war when the French left it. NSC-68 was fully implemented. American defense expenditures tripled from less than $15 billion before Korea to $44 billion in 1952 and $50 billion in 1953. The successive shocks of Czechoslovakia, the Russian atomic bomb, the Berlin blockade, and finally Korea had brought the Cold War to a dangerous pitch that would continue for another generation.

CONTROVERSIAL ISSUES AND FURTHER READING

Harry Truman received very favorable treatment from most historians throughout the 1950s and early 1960s. They saw him as a feisty and decisive underdog who had been called upon to fill the gigantic shoes of Franklin Roosevelt and had done a remarkably good job. They praised him especially for overcoming America's historic tendency toward isolationism and rallying the American people to stop the aggressive expansion of Stalinist Russia. They saw the Truman Doctrine, the Marshall Plan, and the formation of NATO as landmarks of American foreign policy, wise decisions that prevented the collapse of Western Europe and restored the world balance of power. They believed American intervention had avoided the tragic results of the appeasement policy of the 1930s. At the same time, they generally argued that Truman's common sense had kept him from overreacting to the Communist threat. His firing of MacArthur had marked his acceptance of the doctrine of limited war and a sustained, moderate policy of containment. Most historians regarded this as a mature alternative to the natural but simplistic American desire for total war to achieve total victory. [See, for instance, the earlier editions of surveys like John W. Spanier, *American Foreign Policy since World War II* (1960); John Lukacs, *A History of the Cold War* (1961); Walt Whitman Rostow, *The United States in the World Arena* (1960); Desmond Donnelly, *Struggle for the World: The Cold War, 1917–1965* (1965); William G. Carleton, *The Revolution in American Foreign Policy: Its Global Range* (1963); and Eric F. Goldman, *The Crucial Decade and After* (1960). See also Louis J. Halle, *Civilization and Foreign Policy* (1955); Robert E. Osgood, *NATO: The Entangling Alliance* (1962); Norman Graebner, *The New Isolationism* (1956); Herbert Feis, *Between War and Peace: The Potsdam Conference* (1960); David Rees, *Korea: The Limited War* (1964); John W. Spanier, *The Truman-MacArthur Controversy and the Korean War* (1959); Richard H. Rovere and Arthur M. Schlesinger, Jr., *The General and the President* (1951); Trumbull Higgins, *Korea and the Fall of MacArthur* (1960); and Allen Whiting, *China Crosses the Yalu* (1960).]

During the 1950s and early 1960s, the primary criticisms of Truman came from the Right. Republicans claimed that Truman and the Democrats were "soft on communism," just as FDR had been. [See William Henry Chamberlin, *America's Second Crusade* (1950), and James Burnham, *Containment or Liberation? An Inquiry into the Aims of United States Foreign Policy* (1952–1953).] Since most of the attacks on Truman came from the Right, he and his defenders countered by emphasizing their toughness rather than their restraint. [See especially Truman's *Memoirs* (2 vols., 1956); James F. Byrnes, *Speaking Frankly* (1947), and *All in One Lifetime* (1958).]

By the early 1960s, and especially after the escalation in Vietnam in 1965, Truman was under increasing attack from the Left. Moderate revisionists might disagree with radical revisionists over whether Roosevelt had instigated the Cold War, but both could agree that Truman merited blame for his anti-Russian policy. Gar Alperovitz accused Truman of dropping the atomic bombs on Japan long after it was clear the Japanese could be forced to surrender without such horrors, and claimed Truman's purpose had been to make the Soviets more compliant. [Gar Alperovitz, *Atomic Diplomacy: Hiroshima and Potsdam* (1965).] Gabriel Kolko disputed Alperovitz's contention about the bomb, but only to insist that Truman had pursued his nefarious policy with economic rather than atomic weapons. [Gabriel Kolko, *The Politics of War: The World and United States Foreign Policy, 1943–1945* (1968); and Joyce and Gabriel Kolko, *The Limits of Power: The World and United States Foreign Policy, 1945–1954* (1972).] Thomas M.

Campbell accused him of sabotaging the United Nations. [Thomas M. Campbell, *Masquerade Peace: America's UN Policy, 1944–1945* (1973).] Bruce Kuklick blamed him for the division of Germany. [Bruce Kuklick, *American Policy and the Division of Germany* (1972).] Richard J. Walton compared Truman unfavorably to Henry Wallace. [Richard J. Walton, *Henry Wallace, Harry Truman and the Cold War* (1976).] Lloyd Gardner extended this condemnation to Truman's advisors. [Lloyd Gardner, *Architects of Illusion: Men and Ideas in American Foreign Policy, 1941–1949* (1970). Barton J. Bernstein edited a collection of revisionist essays on Truman, *The Politics and Policies of the Truman Administration* (1970). The best survey of the Cold War from a revisionist viewpoint is Walter LaFeber, *America, Russia and the Cold War* (4th ed., 1980). For other revisionist accounts, see the historiographical essay in the previous chapter.]

Realists increasingly joined the rising chorus of criticism aimed at Harry Truman's Cold War policies. George Kennan began to clarify his essential agreement with Walter Lippman's earlier critique of containment as being too universal in scope, too ideological, too oriented toward military rather than economic and political measures, and too rigid in avoiding negotiations with the Russians. [Walter Lippmann, *The Cold War* (1947). George Kennan, *Russia, the Atom, and the West* (1958), and *Memoirs* (2 vols., 1967–1972).] Other historians also began to move toward this "soft" or "restrained" version of realism. They too contended that Truman had overreacted to communism and argued that he should have accorded the Russians their sphere without so much strife. [John Lewis Gaddis, *The United States and the Origins of the Cold War, 1941–1947* (1972); Herbert Feis, *The Atomic Bomb and the End of World War II* (1966), and *From Trust to Terror: The Onset of the Cold War, 1945–1950* (1970); Louis Halle, *The Cold War as History* (1967); Lynn Etheridge Davis, *The Cold War Begins: Soviet-American Conflict over Eastern Europe* (1974); Lisle A. Rose, *After Yalta* (1973), and *Dubious Victory: The United States and the End of World War II* (1973); Martin F. Herz, *The Beginnings of the Cold War* (1966); David F. Trask, *Victory Without Peace: American Foreign Relations in the Twentieth Century* (1968); and Alonzo L. Hamby, *The Imperial Years: The United States since 1939* (1976).]

On American strategic policy in this era, see Gregg Herken, *The Winning Weapon: The Atomic Bomb in the Cold War, 1945–1950* (1981); John Lewis Gaddis, *Strategies of Containment: A Critical Appraisal of Postwar American National Security Policy* (1982); and Alexander George and Richard Smoke, *Deterrence in American Foreign Policy* (1975). For analyses of some of the personalities involved in the Cold War, see John C. Donovan, *The Cold Warriors* (1974); Richard K. Betts, *Soldiers, Statesmen and Cold War Crises* (1977); and Hugh DeSantis, *The Diplomacy of Silence: The American Foreign Service, the Soviet Union, and the Cold War, 1933–1947* (1980); Robert L. Messer, *The End of an Alliance: James F. Byrnes, Roosevelt, Truman and the Origins of the Cold War* (1982); Robert H. Ferrell, *George C. Marshall* (1966); Richard F. Haynes, *The Awesome Power: Harry S Truman as Commander-in-Chief* (1973); and Richard Barnet, *The Roots of War* (1972). For critics of the Cold War, see Thomas G. Paterson, ed., *Cold War Critics* (1971), Ronald Radosh, *Prophets on the Right: Profiles of Conservative Critics of American Globalism* (1975); James T. Patterson, *Mr. Republican: A Biography of Robert Taft* (1972); and J. Samuel Walker, *Henry A. Wallace and American Foreign Policy.*

On Soviet-American relations, see Adam B. Ulam, *The Rivals* (1971); Milovan Djilas, *Conversations with Stalin* (1962); Vojtech Mastny, *Russia's Road to the Cold War* (1978); Isaac Deutscher, *Stalin* (1967); and William Taubman, *Stalin's American Policy* (1981).

On Anglo-American relations in this period, see Terry H. Anderson, *The U.S., Great Britain and the Cold War, 1944–1947* (1981); and Robert M. Hathaway, *Ambiguous*

Partnership: Britain and America, 1944–1947 (1981); D. Cameron Watt, *Succeeding John Bull: America in Britain's Place, 1900–1975* (1984). On the Mediterranean, see Bruce Kuniholm, *The Origins of the Cold War in the Near East* (1980); G. M. Alexander, *The Prelude to the Truman Doctrine: British Policy in Greece, 1944–1947* (1982); and Lawrence Wittner, *American Intervention in Greece, 1943–1949* (1982). On Europe, see Joseph A. Jones, *The Fifteen Weeks* (1955); John Gimbel, *The American Occupation of Germany* (1968), and *The Origins of the Marshall Plan* (1976); Lawrence S. Kaplan, *A Community of Interest: NATO and the Military Assistance Program, 1948–1951* (1980); Escott Reid, *Time of Fear and Hope: The Making of the North Atlantic Treaty, 1947–1949* (1977); and Timothy P. Ireland, *Creating the Entangling Alliance: The Origins of NATO* (1981).

On the Far East, see Akira Iriye, *The Cold War in Asia* (1974); Russell D. Buhite, *Soviet-American Relations in Asia, 1945–1954* (1982); Dorothy Borg and Waldo Heinrichs, eds., *The Uncertain Years: Chinese-American Relations, 1947–1950* (1980); Nancy Bernkopf Tucker, *Patterns in the Dust: Chinese-American Relations and the Recognition Controversy, 1949–1950* (1983); and Robert Blum, *Drawing the Line: The Origins of the American Containment Policy in East Asia* (1982). Several significant books on Korea have appeared recently. See William Whitney Stueck, Jr., *The Road to Confrontation: American Policy Toward China and Korea, 1947–1950* (1981); Bruce Cumings, *The Origins of the Korean War* (1981); Joseph Goulden, *Korea: The Untold Story of the War* (1982); and Charles M. Dobbs, *The Unwanted Symbol: American Foreign Policy, the Cold War, and Korea, 1945–1950* (1981).

CHAPTER 17

The New Look of Dwight D. Eisenhower

THE NEW LOOK

Although Dwight David Eisenhower ran for president as a Republican, he had no quarrel with the interventionist foreign policy of Harry Truman and the Democrats. Eisenhower entered the race for the Republican nomination in part because his concern for collective security clashed with the isolationism of the conservative wing of the Republican party and its favorite, Senator Robert A. Taft. But Eisenhower shared Taft's fear that the free-spending ways of the Democrats would bring the United States to bankruptcy and weaken its international position. His desire to cut the budget could not help but influence his foreign policy. He was appalled that the defense expenditures Truman projected in accordance with NSC-68 would result in a $44 billion deficit over the next five years.

In his search for an alternative foreign policy, Eisenhower turned for help to John Foster Dulles. Dulles, the Republican party's leading foreign affairs expert, had managed to stay in favor with the Taft wing of the party even while espousing an interventionist policy. In a widely read article for *Life* magazine, he had suggested that reliance on the threat of strategic nuclear weapons would be a cheaper and more effective way of deterring Soviet aggression than the Democrats' buildup of expensive conventional land forces. Dulles also had said the United States should seek the liberation of the Soviet satellites and not be content with Truman's "defeatist treadmill policy of containment."

Eisenhower permitted Dulles to write the foreign policy portions of the Republican platform, appointed him secretary of state, and left in his hands the technical implementation of American diplomacy. Pundits of the day came to believe that Dulles actually ran the administration's foreign policy. But the recent availability of Eisenhower's classified and private papers has demonstrated that Eisenhower kept the major decisions of the administration in his own hands. He preferred to operate behind the scenes and leave the details, the partisan battles, and much of the blame for any unpopular or unsuccessful maneuvers to his subordinates. He was ready, however, to rein in his advisors if they went off the track.

Figure 19   President Dwight Eisenhower (left) and his secretary of state, John Foster Dulles. Photos courtesy of the National Archives.

Eisenhower generally approved of Dulles's policies, but told him he did not see how wholesale threats of nuclear retaliation could be a credible deterrent to low-level Communist nibbling at neighbor nations. When Dulles nonetheless included the term "retaliatory striking power" in the Republican platform, Eisenhower fumed, "I'll be damned if I run on that." The platform phrase was quickly revised. Likewise, Eisenhower qualified Dulles's platform condemnation of the "negative, futile and immoral policy of 'containment'" by publicly insisting that any "liberation" of the satellites would have to come by "peaceful means." He became irked at the rumors that Dulles controlled him and once caustically remarked that there was "only one man I know who has seen *more* of the world and talked with more people and *knows* more than [Dulles] does—and that's me."

Eisenhower used his reputation as a statesman above the party battle to good effect, notably in his campaign pledge to "go to Korea." Such a pledge committed him to no particular policy, yet allowed him to imply that with his authority and experience he would be able to end the war. Thus, he finessed the conservatives' demand that he end the war by winning it and the liberals' insistence that he end it by compromising. After winning the election but before taking office, Eisenhower paid a three-day visit to Korea. On his return he apparently let the Communists know he was considering the use of atomic weapons if progress toward peace was not made quickly. Abruptly the Chinese dropped the demand that was stalling the truce negotiations, that even unwilling POWs be repatriated. China's policy shift may have resulted more from the uncertainties following Stalin's death than Eisenhower's veiled atomic threat, but Eisenhower and Dulles considered the subsequent truce in Korea proof of the effectiveness of their nuclear strategy.

As Dulles explained it, such use of the "deterrent of massive retaliatory power" would enable the United States "to respond vigorously at places and with means of its own choosing." This would be far less expensive than the NSC-68 strategy of trying to defend against every possible type of aggression the Communists were capable of mounting. Instead of reacting to a threat on the enemy's own terms, the United States could shift the nature and location of the confrontation to correspond to America's strengths and its adversary's weaknesses. Dulles and Eisenhower acknowledged that nuclear weapons were inappropriate for minor, low-level conflicts; they would devise supplementary strategies for such "brushfire wars." Nevertheless, the nuclear threat would always lurk in the background.

Eisenhower and Dulles purposely wanted to keep potential aggressors off balance. The Communists would be confronted with the certainty of an American response, but uncertainty as to its nature. Dulles acknowledged the danger of enemy miscalculation inherent in this strategy, but declared: "You have to take chances for peace just as you must take chances in war. The ability to get to the verge without getting into the war is the necessary art. If you cannot master it, you inevitably get into a war. If you try to run from it, if you are scared to go to the brink, you are lost."

Reporters listening to Dulles's explanations dubbed administration diplomacy "massive retaliation" and "brinksmanship." Despite Dulles's objections to this characterization of his policy, the press was not far off the mark. Intercontinental bombers capable of carrying the newly developed hydrogen bomb became operational early in Eisenhower's administration. With only twelve NATO divisions facing a hundred Soviet formations, Eisenhower and Dulles made no secret that they would rely on nuclear weapons to prevent or fight a Soviet invasion of Western Europe. They also briefly considered the use of nuclear weapons in Korea and Indochina, and they publicly threatened to use them in the two crises over the Nationalist-occupied islands of Quemoy and Matsu. But if Eisenhower and Dulles were willing to consider use of nuclear weapons far more readily than Truman, they were very cautious in their actual use. They were interested in deterrence, not war. Eisenhower believed it would be nearly impossible to keep nuclear war limited. He estimated that 65 percent of the American population would need medical aid in case of a nuclear strike on the United States, and little or none would be available.

These defense policies did save money. Eisenhower reduced Truman's 1954 projected budget from $41 billion to $36 billion, and to $31 billion for the following year. All the services took some cuts, but the air force, with its primary responsibility for strategic bombings, suffered only slightly. The army faced the most reductions. It went from 1.5 million to 1 million men, and from twenty to fourteen divisions. In future conflicts, the United States would contribute air and sea power, but would rely on overseas allies for most of the troops.

Reliance on foreign troops sent Dulles in search of more and firmer overseas alliances. He extended America's alliance system to only four more nations than Truman had, but Dulles pushed neutrals harder to abandon their nonaligned status for the Western-oriented alliance system. He condemned neutrality as "immoral," and publicly maintained that nations had to be for America or against it. Privately, Dulles was a bit more flexible, and Eisenhower was even more so. They sent aid to Tito's Yugoslavia to help it maintain its neutrality against Soviet pressure. They felt sympathy for non-Communist independence movements and nationalism in the Third World and hoped that gradual independence might produce stability and prosperity in former Western colonies. They realized communism was not monolithic and considered means to exploit the strains they perceived in the Soviet-Chinese alliance.

Publicly, however, they were not as flexible. Eisenhower and Dulles generally supported right-wing regimes, such as those of South Korea, Saudi Arabia, Iran, the Philippines, and Pakistan. Dulles continued to portray Left-leaning neutrals, notably Nehru's India, as part of a monolithic Communist conspiracy. He considered pressure rather than sympathy the best way to keep nations out of the Soviet orbit. Thus, he continued to talk of liberation and rollback in Eastern Europe even when he knew the United States would not risk any major action in Russia's security sphere. (Indeed, when strikes and rebellions broke out in East Germany, Poland, and Hungary, the United States stood by while the Russians crushed them.) He also continued to put pressure on China. He refused it recognition, opposed its admission to the United Nations, and threatened to "unleash" Chiang Kai-shek for an attack on the mainland. Dulles hoped that this would force China to call upon the Soviets for more economic aid and military support than they were willing to supply and thus break up the Sino-Soviet alliance. Perhaps he succeeded. When the Russians refused to provide as much nuclear technology as China wanted, Mao expelled most Russian technicians.

Dulles aimed his anti-Communist rhetoric at Americans as well as potential foreign enemies. He caved in to Senator Joseph McCarthy's opportunistic and malicious attempts to purge the State Department of its supposedly Communist tendencies. Dulles fired many loyal officers, including the Old China Hands the right wing had denounced for losing China. He even ordered supposedly Leftist books removed from American government overseas libraries.

Thus, the New Look relied on massive retaliation, foreign alliances, indigenous troops, and political pressure to maintain its commitments abroad while reducing defense expenditures on conventional land forces. The New Look also placed increased emphasis on covert activities to deal with low-level threats to American interests. Under Eisenhower and Dulles, the CIA helped overthrow the governments of Iran and Guatemala, planned unsuccessful coups in Indonesia and Cuba, and considered or attempted the assassinations of Chou En-lai, Fidel Castro, Patrice Lumumba of the Congo, and Rafael Trujillo of the Dominican Republic. The extent of Eisenhower's knowledge of the CIA's assassination plots is still uncertain, as is that of his successor John F. Kennedy, but it is doubtful that the agency would have attempted such things without a broad mandate from the president.

EISENHOWER, THE SOVIET UNION, AND WESTERN EUROPE

On March 5, 1953, Joseph Stalin died. Shortly afterward, the apparent victor in the struggle for succession within the Kremlin, Georgi Malenkov, called for peaceful competition and coexistence with the United States. Eisenhower briefly considered calling a summit meeting and offering some concessions to see if the Cold War might not be moderated. Dulles, however, urged caution. Eisenhower accepted this advice and asked the Soviets to demonstrate their desire for peace with a few concrete steps. The Soviets might allow free elections throughout Germany (which undoubtedly would result in a pro-Western unified Germany), sign a peace treaty with Austria, end the Korean war, or free the East European satellites. Before any further progress toward a summit could be made, the more erratic and belligerent Nikita Khrushchev replaced Malenkov.

Later critics have wondered what might have happened if Eisenhower had met Malenkov's offer more fully, agreed to a summit conference, and offered to avoid any armament of West Germany in exchange for Soviet concessions. Eisenhower and Dulles, however, believed it was better to press the Soviets than to try to propitiate them. They desperately wanted to build up Western Europe's conventional forces, and West Germany seemed the natural source for more soldiers. In addition, Eisenhower and Dulles were wary of any show of weakness on the German issue. They felt they had to support the West Germans' hopeless passion for reunification under Western auspices, or West Germany might accept the Soviet offer of reunification in exchange for German neutrality and disarmament. Since West Germany's potential military and economic contribution to Western Europe was far more critical than East Germany's to the Soviet sphere, Eisenhower and Dulles feared a neutralist Germany would cripple Western Europe and make its defense almost impossible.

The United States moved quickly to rearm West Germany and tie it irrevocably to Western Europe. But a revived and rearmed Germany was a fearful prospect to France as well as to the Soviets. In order to reassure the French, the Western European allies devised a plan for a European Defense Community (EDC) that would incorporate small units of German soldiers into an integrated European army. Dulles warned the balky French that if they did not go along, the United States might have to undertake an "agonizing reappraisal" of its policy in Europe. Nevertheless, in August 1954, the French National Assembly voted to table EDC without even debating it.

What seemed like a terrible blow to Western unity was turned around with amazing ease. The British, who had held aloof from the continental army contemplated by EDC, stepped in to mediate. The French quickly consented to the integration of German forces into NATO, which would mean that the German troops would be subject to the control of the United States and Great Britain, as well as the weaker continental powers. Rapid strides toward the further economic integration of Europe followed, and the Common Market and Euratom were formed by 1957.

Meanwhile, in 1955, the Soviets countered the military and economic integration of Western Europe with their own organization in Eastern Europe, the Warsaw Pact. At the same time they moved to lessen tensions and draw the United States into a summit meeting. They unexpectedly agreed to a peace treaty with Austria that provided for that nation's neutrality and the mutual withdrawal of Western and Soviet occupation troops. They also recognized West Germany. The Soviets even offered a nuclear disarmament plan that included carefully hedged but significant concessions to the Western point of view. They agreed to discuss the reduction rather than the elimination of nuclear weapons and to accept some very limited forms of inspection.

With these hints of Soviet flexibility on the critical Cold War issues of nuclear weapons and a European settlement, Eisenhower finally agreed to meet the new Soviet leadership at Geneva in July 1955. The results of this Geneva summit were disappointingly meager. The participants could agree to little more than a vague formula for continuing discussion on a German settlement. The USSR was adamant against a reunified and rearmed Germany linked to the West, while the United States and its allies rejected a neutral Germany ruled by a coalition of West Germans and the East German Communists. Eisenhower did offer a so-called Open Skies plan to permit aerial inspection of all nuclear powers as a means of inspiring the trust necessary to a nuclear disarmament treaty. But the Soviets, who already had access to most of the details of American nuclear production and deployment, who regarded secrecy as an important enhancement of their own inferior nuclear capability, and who knew of the technologically superior American U-2 spy plane, saw Eisenhower's proposal as one-sided and rejected it. About all that came out of the summit was a fragile atmosphere of goodwill briefly hailed as the "spirit of Geneva."

The Suez crisis and the contemporaneous Soviet suppression of the Hungarian rebellion of 1956 shattered that spirit. Egypt's Gamal Abdel Nasser triggered the Suez crisis by taking control of the Suez Canal. Nasser and his fellow Egyptian army officers had overthrown King Farouk and persuaded the British to withdraw their troops by 1956. The Suez Canal, however, was not to come under Egypt's control. An international combine dominated by the British and other European users would run it.

Shortly after the last British troops had left, Nasser began accepting arms from the Soviets. An outraged Dulles consequently withdrew American offers of financial support for the Aswan High Dam, a project Nasser saw as the key to Egypt's economic development and his own prestige. Nasser responded by seizing the Suez Canal and proclaiming that he would use the revenue generated by the canal to finance the Aswan Dam. Without informing the United States, Great Britain and France immediately began plotting with Israel, Egypt's enemy in the Middle East, to retrieve the canal. In October 1956, Israel would launch an attack on Egypt. Britain and France would then seize the canal on the pretext that the Israeli-Egyptian war endangered navigation there.

Israeli-British-French military operations succeeded, and a British parachute force actually landed in Egypt to capture a portion of the canal. But Nasser blocked the canal by sinking ships in its navigation channels. Syria backed Egypt by cutting off the oil pipeline that traversed its territory on the way to the Mediterranean. The British Labour party denounced the invasion and undermined domestic support for Prime Minister Anthony Eden. The Soviets rattled their rockets and threatened nuclear retaliation.

Far more critical than any of these obstacles to the success of the operation, Eisenhower and Dulles proclaimed the opposition of the United States and took the issue to the United Nations. The United States also began selling off massive amounts of British pounds sterling, which exerted tremendous pressure on the British economy. Finally, Eisenhower refused to ship Western Hemisphere oil to Europe to replace that lost by the closing of the Suez Canal and the disruption of the Syrian pipeline. Such measures finally forced Great Britain and France into a humiliating retreat. The Western alliance lay in tatters. As the French and British continued to retreat, the United States was left increasingly alone to try to maintain some Western influence in the Middle East and Asia.

At this nadir of Western unity, the Hungarians rose up against Soviet control. The Soviets hesitated briefly and actually withdrew their tanks. Then, at the height of the Suez crisis, Soviet forces surged back into Hungary and crushed the Hungarian freedom fighters. The Eisenhower administration, after encouraging East European resistance to communism in Voice of America broadcasts and talking of "liberation," could only stand by with its disillusioned and fractious European allies and watch.

A year later, in October 1957, the Soviet Union launched the first space satellite, Sputnik. The missile that carried Sputnik into space obviously was capable of carrying a nuclear warhead from Europe to North America. This first potential intercontinental missile frightened many Americans and led to calls for crash programs to catch up to the Russians. Eisenhower agreed to expand America's ICBM production slightly and to station intermediate-range missiles in Europe. But he resisted the panic calls for a crash program that emanated even from within his own administration. He was convinced that the United States had sufficient power to deter a Soviet nuclear attack and that it would be foolish and outrageously expensive to build beyond that. He even offered to suspend nuclear testing if the Soviets would agree to a mutual moratorium and enter negotiations at Geneva for a formal test ban treaty. The Soviets accepted.

Eisenhower was able to make these decisions because of a top-secret program of U-2 flights over the Soviet Union. Those flights could pick up any evidence of a major Soviet nuclear test that violated the moratorium. The U-2 also sent back information that the Soviets were not deploying large numbers of ICBM missiles. Khrushchev had decided to wait for the second generation of missiles before installing a full-fledged intercontinental nuclear strike force.

Nevertheless, Khrushchev tried to capitalize on Sputnik and the supposed Soviet strategic lead. In November 1958, he announced that the Soviets would sign a peace treaty with East Germany in six months unless there was a negotiated settlement with the West by that time. Since the Soviets already recognized West Germany, recognition of East Germany would complete the process of restoring sovereignty to the conquered Germans. Occupation rights would cease, and foreign troops would have to be withdrawn from West Berlin. Khrushchev offered to make Berlin a free demilitarized city, but he knew that the expulsion of the Western powers would put an end to German hopes of a unified and rearmed Germany allied with the West. It would also put a stop to the flow of refugees into West Berlin, a drain that had cost East Germany nearly 3 million of its most productive citizens since 1949.

Eisenhower and the West were at an enormous strategic disadvantage in Berlin. They did not have the conventional forces to defend West Berlin against the Russians and East Germans, and the Soviets could wipe out Europe if the United States resorted to nuclear weapons. Yet Eisenhower was determined not to abandon Berlin or to negotiate under Khrushchev's six-month ultimatum. He announced that the United States would not try to shoot its way into Berlin or to fight a ground war in Europe, and he made clear his desire for a negotiated settlement. But he implied he would resort to nuclear arms if all other alternatives failed and the Soviets initiated hostilities. He could only hope that Soviet uncertainty would lead Khrushchev to seek a peaceful solution.

After several weeks of growing tension, Khrushchev offered to drop the six-month deadline if Eisenhower would attend a summit meeting. Eisenhower balked at this, but invited Khrushchev to an informal meeting at Camp David following the Soviet leader's whirlwind tour of the United States. At Camp David, Eisenhower finally agreed to a formal summit, and Khrushchev abandoned his deadline for solving the Berlin issue. They set the summit for May 1960 in Paris.

Just before the Paris meeting convened, the Soviets shot down an American U-2 over their territory. Eisenhower had approved the flight because intelligence sources were reporting that the Russians had begun construction of their first operational ICBM base, and Eisenhower thought U-2 confirmation was worth the risk of endangering the summit. When the Russians announced that they had shot down the U-2, the Americans issued a cover story that it was a weather plane blown off course. Eisenhower was then thunderstruck to hear that the Soviets had actually recovered the plane's wreckage and its pilot, Francis Gary Powers. Khrushchev offered Eisenhower a way out by saying he was sure Eisenhower had been unaware of these flights. Eisenhower, however, accepted personal responsibility. Khrushchev then demanded that Eisenhower halt all further U-2 flights over the USSR and apologize for past ones. Eisenhower said he had already halted the flights, but would not apologize for defending American security. Khrushchev stalked out of the summit and proclaimed he would wait to negotiate with Eisenhower's successor. It was a sad and ignominious way for Eisenhower to end his presidency.

THE DILEMMA OF THE MIDDLE EAST

As the Cold War reached its height in the 1950s and 1960s, the United States found itself increasingly embroiled in what was for it a relatively new arena, the Middle East. Prior to World War I, the American presence in the Middle East had been limited to a few missionaries and traders who received minimal support from American diplomatic or naval officers. During World War I, Woodrow Wilson briefly asserted an American role in the Middle East by urging Great Britain and France to grant independence to the Arab provinces whose rebellions against the Ottoman Turks the Allies had aided and abetted. Unfortunately, Wilson's influence evaporated in the battle over the Versailles peace terms, and the United States could only watch as the British and French divided the remnants of the Ottoman Empire between them. Great Britain received a League of Nations mandate to legitimize its wartime occupation of Iraq and Palestine. It also used the opportunity to strengthen its control of Egypt and the Sudan. France obtained a League mandate for Syria and Lebanon to go along with its existing North African colonies in Algeria, Tunisia, and Morocco.

American oil industry experts and government officials were especially disturbed when Britain and France announced that they intended to monopolize all oil resources in their Middle Eastern mandates. Experts feared that U.S. oil reserves had been badly depleted by World War I and that the remaining domestic resources would be exhausted within a decade or two. The Wilson and Harding administrations protested loudly that the oil concessions should be open for competition. The British and French adamantly refused such an open door policy until 1928, when they reluctantly invited some American oil companies to join their international cartel as junior partners. In return, these American companies had to abide by the co-called Red Line agreement, formulated by Britain and France at the San Remo Conference of 1920. The Red Line agreement provided that none of the members of the cartel could undertake independent or competitive operations in the mandates.

By the time the American companies were admitted to the cartel, the urgency had passed for the American government. Major oil discoveries in Texas, Oklahoma, and California had produced a petroleum glut in the

United States. But some oil companies did not lose interest. Standard Oil of California, which had not joined the cartel and therefore was not bound by the San Remo agreement, acquired independent concessions in Bahrain and Saudi Arabia when those nations managed to throw off some of Britain's control. Shortly before World War II, Standard Oil of California invited several other American companies to help exploit its concessions. Standard Oil and these companies formed their own cartel, the Arabian-American Oil Company (Aramco).

By the end of World War II, the Middle East possessed two-thirds of the world's proved reserves, and American oil companies controlled 40 percent of them. There had been some wartime rivalry between Great Britain and the United States over this oil, but Churchill and Roosevelt had agreed not to make "sheeps' eyes" at one another's concessions, and they had turned together to face what they regarded as the greater threat of Soviet expansion into the area.

Increasingly the United States found itself bearing the primary responsibility for Western influence in the Middle East. France's defeat by Germany in 1940 had caused it to lose its grip in Syria and Lebanon, and after the war France granted the two nations their independence. France also faced rising nationalist movements in its North African colonies. Meanwhile, Great Britain had been forced to turn over its responsibilities for the defense of Greece and Turkey to the United States and its Truman Doctrine in 1947. Britain had its own difficulties with rising nationalism in Egypt, and it faced a nearly insoluble problem of Arab-Jewish rivalry in Palestine.

The United States tried to ease its way into the Middle East by reminding Arab nationalists of the favorable opinion Woodrow Wilson and Franklin Roosevelt had had of Arab independence. Truman argued that the greatest threat to Arab independence came from the Soviet Union, and he tried to establish a Middle East Command that would formally ally the Arab countries with the United States, Great Britain, and France to combat Soviet expansionism. The Arabs, however, worried far more about Jewish Zionist ambitions in Palestine than about Soviet Russia, and they regarded the United States and Great Britain as the primary supporters of the Zionists. Arab nationalists thus increasingly ranged themselves against the Western powers.

The Zionist movement to establish a Jewish state in Palestine had crystallized in the late nineteenth century when the rise of nationalism in Europe accentuated the differences between European Jewish communities and the increasingly self-conscious nationalities that surrounded them. Theodore Herzl and the World Zionist Organization led the movement. They encouraged European Jews to emigrate to Palestine and asked that the great powers recognize a Jewish state in the area. The British, who were seeking Palestine as a mandate for themselves during World War I, saw a chance to enlist Jewish support for their position. On November 2, 1917, they issued the Balfour Declaration. This proclaimed British support for "the establishment in Palestine of a national home for the Jewish people . . . it being clearly understood that nothing shall be done which may prejudice the civil and religious rights of existing non-Jewish communities in Palestine. . . ." Of course there was no way to establish a Jewish homeland in Palestine without disturbing the rights of the Muslim inhabitants. Nevertheless, the Balfour Declaration and its basic internal contradiction were written into the British mandate for Palestine.

Arab riots against the growing Jewish population in Palestine erupted as early as 1921. They did not become serious until the late 1930s, however, when Nazi persecution provoked a flood of Jewish immigration. The Arabs of the territory called a general strike in 1936 and attacked both Jewish settlements and British authorities. In 1939, the beleaguered British issued a White Paper declaring they would permit only 100,000 more Jews to enter Palestine. The White Paper quota threatened to choke off the flow of Jewish refugees even as the Nazis were beginning their program of genocide.

The United States had never formally endorsed Zionism, although Woodrow Wilson had given a private and reluctant consent to the Balfour Declaration and Congress had passed a joint resolution endorsing a Jewish homeland in Palestine. Throughout the 1930s and 1940s, popular sentiment in America generally favored the Zionist idea, and the Democratic and Republican parties regularly included a Zionist plank in their platforms. In addition, American Jews were the primary financial support of the Jewish communities in Palestine.

But for all the sympathy Americans had toward the Jewish victims of Nazi persecution, the United States did little to provide a refuge for them. The Depression had encouraged a strong anti-immigration sentiment in the American body politic which Roosevelt and the State Department were reluctant to challenge. The State Department additionally feared that Fascist fifth columnists and Communist agitators might slip into the United States in the flow of immigrants. Consequently, while the British requested the United States to absorb more Jewish refugees, the Americans urged the British to open Palestine to further immigration. Neither relented until 1944, when Roosevelt finally formed a War Refugee Board outside the jurisdiction of the State Department. The board vigorously sought to rescue the remaining Jews of Europe, but by then it was too little, too late.

In 1942, the desperate Jews of Palestine began to attack the British and the Arabs to force permission for further immigration. They also smuggled their European compatriots into Palestine in violation of the quota. A sympathetic Roosevelt called for a Jewish state in Palestine, but he also promised King Ibn Saud of Saudi Arabia that he would take no action hostile to the Arab people. Ibn Saud and other Arab leaders had made clear to Roosevelt that the Arabs would fight to stop further Jewish immigration or the formation of a Jewish state in Palestine.

Harry Truman was the unfortunate heir of Roosevelt's ambiguous policy toward this insoluble problem. Truman was under pressure from his State and Defense departments to avoid alienating Arab opinion. They pointed to the potentially disastrous consequences of Zionist sympathies for U.S. interests in Middle Eastern oil and hopes for resistance to Soviet expansion in the area. But Truman sympathized with the plight of the Jews. He also saw political benefits to a pro-Zionist stand. Since Jewish lobbies and votes were critical to elections in several key states, and since there was no domestic constituency for the Arabs, a pro-Jewish stand seemed pure political gain. Thus, he decided in 1945 to urge the British to revise their White Paper quota and permit 100,000 more Jewish refugees into Palestine.

The British, fearful of losing Suez and their oil concessions to angry Arabs, caustically rejected Truman's suggestion. Foreign Minister Ernest Bevin commented that the Americans were moved less by sympathy than by their desire to avoid more Jews in New York. Truman went on in 1946 to endorse a Jewish state in Palestine, and the British blamed him for the failure of their already doomed plan for a federated Jewish-Arab state to relieve them of their mandate. Thwarted at every turn, the British handed the issue over to the United Nations.

Meanwhile, tensions rose in Palestine as Jewish settlers ignored a new British quota of 1,500 immigrants per month and smuggled increasing numbers of refugees into Palestine. When the British captured groups of these illegal immigrants, they interned them on the island of Cyprus in concentration camps built by German POWs. In this explosive atmosphere, the United Nations, with the support of a Soviet bloc that wished to see the British out of the Middle East, agreed to partition Palestine between independent Jewish and Arab states. The Arab nations angrily announced they would destroy any independent Jewish state. The Syrians threatened to cut their oil pipeline. The British warned that they would not enforce any arrangement that did not have the consent of both Arabs and Jews, and they insisted they would abandon the mandate in May 1948.

Truman, fearful of the chaos and war that were impending, suddenly intervened and called for a truce and delay of partition. But the Jews insisted that it was now or never for the creation of Israel; the Arabs refused a truce unless there was a unified Arab state in all of Palestine; and no UN member offered to help the United States enforce a truce. Partition took place as scheduled, and on May 15, 1948, the Jewish state of Israel was born. Truman regained the support he had lost in the American Jewish community with his truce proposal by recognizing the new nation within minutes after it had been proclaimed. The Arab states, on the other hand, invaded Israel.

The United Nations tried with only sporadic success to impose a cease-fire on the combatants. Finally, in 1949, Israeli troops surrounded much of the Egyptian army and Egypt had to request an end to the fighting. The other belligerent Arab states soon followed suit, but the situation remained volatile. The Israelis were unhappy with their borders, even though they had expanded them during the war with the Arabs. The Israelis thought their territory was too small to absorb the flood of immigrants they expected. Many Jews claimed the biblical right to restore all of Palestine to Jewish rule by annexing the West Bank area of the Jordan River, the part of Palestine the UN had allotted to the Arabs but which Jews knew as the old biblical provinces of Judea and Samaria. Absorption of the West Bank also would give the Israelis defensible borders. They were particularly worried that if the Arabs attacked Israel at its narrowest point, they would have to drive only 9 miles to the sea to split Israel in half.

The Arabs were even more distressed. Some 750,000 people, nearly half the Arab population of Palestine, had fled or been forced from their homes to become refugees in miserable camps within the Arab states bordering Israel. Those who stayed behind became second-class citizens in a Jewish religious state. The displaced Palestinian Arabs posed a prickly problem for the Arab nations of the Middle East, especially for Trans-Jordan, the country that annexed the Arab portion of Palestine. The Palestinians were an energetic and relatively well-educated people. If Israel's neighbors tried to absorb them, the Palestinians might actually displace the indigenous leadership. So, rather than absorb them, most of the Arab border states left Palestinian refugees in temporary camps and encouraged them to devote their energies to restoring Arab rule in Israel. The British abetted the process of Arab-Israeli enmity by discouraging tentative peace moves toward Israel made by King Abdullah of Trans-Jordan and King Farouk of Egypt. The British feared that Israel, which was then neutral and derived substantial support from the Soviet Union, might try to lead the Arab world away from its Western orientation.

The British miscalculated badly. The continuing Arab-Israeli conflict stirred the Arab peoples to an extraordinary emotional pitch, and they became enraged at the incompetence, venality, and half-heartedness of their leaders' efforts against Israel. Nationalistic army officers overthrew the Syrian regime in 1949. King Hussein, Abdullah's successor in Jordan, barely survived a Palestinian coup. A group of Egyptian army officers overthrew King Farouk in 1952, and one of them, Colonel Gamal Abdel Nasser, soon became the rallying point for the revival of Arab nationalism throughout the Middle East. As such, Nasser threatened not only Israel, but the British position in Egypt and Suez, the remaining French colonies in North Africa, the vital Western oil holdings in the Middle East, and the large military bases the United States had recently established in Libya and Morocco.

To the still greater discomfort of the West, the rise of Nasser coincided with a change in Soviet policy toward the Middle East. Stalin had regarded the Arab nationalists as bourgeois reactionaries and had done as much as the United States to aid Israel during the Arab-Israeli conflict. After Stalin's death, however, Nikita Khrushchev announced Soviet support of Arab wars of national liberation.

To further compound Western disturbance, the Middle Eastern oil nations began to realize the strength of their position and to demand greater profits from oil operations in their countries. In the pre-World War II days, the oil companies had held the whip hand. They had had the technological expertise and the capital to invest in risky enterprises, while the oil nations had been unable to drive a hard bargain either because they were not free agents (like the British mandates of Iraq and Kuwait), or because they were in desperate need of money (like Saudi Arabia and Iran). Consequently, the oil companies had paid their host nations very low fees and had received exemption from taxation.

The worm began to turn in 1948, when Venezuela imposed a 50 percent tax on oil company profits and got away with it. Saudi Arabia and Kuwait quickly demanded similar arrangements. The Truman administration encouraged the oil companies to concede to the demands, for although the United States was still self-sufficient in petroleum, its Western European allies were dependent on imported oil. The State Department proceeded to work out a deal whereby Saudi Arabia and Kuwait would receive 50 percent of the oil companies' profits on operations in their countries, while the United States would compensate the companies by exempting these payments from American taxation. In effect, the $50 million increase in Ibn Saud's profits came from American taxpayers. The State Department had made the oil companies the "paymasters of the Arab states." The Truman administration hoped the subsidies might hold the Arabs in line despite America's support for Israel. It also realized that subsidizing the oil companies to pay the Arabs would circumvent the need to ask a pro-Israeli American Congress for direct appropriations to Israel's enemies.

The British-dominated Anglo-Iranian Oil Company, however, was unwilling to make a similar deal with Iran. The Iranians began to clamor for nationalization of the oil industry. By the time the Anglo-Iranian Company came around to offer a 50–50 split in oil revenues, it was too late. In 1951, Mohammed Mossadegh took over as Iranian prime minister and nationalized Anglo-Iranian's holdings. Great Britain then withdrew its technical personnel and imposed a boycott on Iranian oil with the aid of the American oil companies. The Truman administration tried to find a compromise between the Iranians and the British company and provided some aid to keep the Iranian economy afloat. But Mossadegh would not compromise on nationalization; the Iranian economy crumbled without its oil revenues; and Mossadegh threatened to turn to the Soviets for help.

Eisenhower and Dulles despaired of the Mossadegh regime and decided that nothing the United States could do would successfully prop up the regime to keep it out of the hands of the Communists. Eisenhower and Dulles turned to the CIA to promote a coup that would restore power to the shah and pro-Western elements in the Iranian army. In 1953, Kermit Roosevelt, the grandson of Teddy Roosevelt, arrived in Iran with $1 million and dispensed $100,000 of it to recruit pro-shah demonstrators from the athletic clubs and slums of Teheran. Unfortunately for the CIA, Mossadegh anticipated the coup, arrested some of the opposition leaders, and aroused a tremendous demonstration in his favor that sent the frightened shah into headlong flight to Rome.

Still, there was a strong current of discontent with Mossadegh's policies in Iran. Not only had he increased Iran's dependence on the communist Tudeh party, he had dissolved the legislature and personally assumed almost all government power. When Mossadegh finally had to call out police and soldiers to control the more violent acts of his demonstrating supporters, the army and police pushed the Tudeh party off the streets, chanting: "Long live the Shah, death to Mossadegh." Then Kermit Roosevelt's mob put in its appearance. Supported by the army and police, it attracted a cheering throng of thousands of Teheran residents. Mossadegh went to prison in tears; the shah returned to power; and the legislature installed a retired general as prime minister.

The new government imprisoned or executed hundreds of Tudeh party members and Mossadegh supporters. It also worked out a compromise on oil with the Western powers. Iran retained ownership of the oil fields and refineries and shared half the revenues from oil sales with a new Western oil consortium that included five American firms, along with Britain's Anglo-Iranian Company. The intrusion of the five American firms into the previously exclusive domain of Britain's Anglo-Iranian Company was yet another sign that the United States was replacing Britain throughout the world.

Meanwhile, the Western oil companies believed they had succeeded in making an example of Iran that would deter other oil nations from pushing their advantages too far. The companies even worked out a way to minimize the gains the oil nations had already made. Since the oil cartels in Iran, Saudi Arabia, and elsewhere were selling Middle Eastern oil to their own parent companies back home, they charged themselves very little. This left the oil nations with 50 percent of very low prices, while the oil companies made their big profits on retail sales, which they did not have to share with the producer nations. But the oil company victory was far from permanent. The resentful nations formed the Organization of Petroleum Exporting Countries (OPEC) in 1959 to gain a better share of the profits from their oil resources. In the 1970s they would turn the tables on the oil companies and the Western powers.

Like the oil companies, the CIA and the American government also viewed Iran as an object lesson. They saw how easily a handful of CIA operatives with a trunkful of cash had thwarted a dangerous nationalist movement in a Third World country. Eisenhower and the CIA mistakenly assumed that they could repeat this success whenever it seemed necessary. CIA chief Allen Dulles, for instance, turned on one State Department official who had defended Nasser's nationalistic conduct and snarled: "If that colonel of yours pushes us too far we will break him in half!"

Eisenhower, however, hoped to deal with Nasser and Arab nationalism less drastically. In 1955, he and Dulles helped organize the Baghdad Pact, which allied Turkey, Iran, Pakistan, Iraq, and Great Britain to block any Soviet advance into the Middle East. Eisenhower continued Truman's policy of indirectly subsidizing the oil-producing nations by offering tax exemptions to the oil companies. He also extended Truman's policy of blocking the Justice Department's attempt to prosecute the oil companies for antitrust activities in the Middle East. He was appalled at the potential effect on Arab nationalist emotions of the British-French-Israeli attack on Suez and compelled their retreat.

But once Eisenhower had secured the British and French withdrawal from Suez, he knew he had shattered their prestige in the Arab world. He thought it essential that the United States move dramatically to ensure that the Soviet Union did not take advantage of the power vacuum. In 1957, he secured congressional approval not only for economic and military aid to the Arab nations, but also for the so-called Eisenhower Doctrine. The Eisenhower Doctrine permitted the president to use armed force to protect any Middle Eastern nation that requested aid against "overt armed aggression from any nation controlled by international communism."

Eisenhower made use of that authority quickly. He sent the Sixth Fleet and $10 million to King Hussein of Jordan to help Hussein and his Bedouin supporters beat back an attempt by Palestinian-led nationalists to dethrone him. When a revolution in Iraq overthrew the Westward–leaning monarchy, Eisenhower sought to prevent the spread of the virus by landing over ten thousand American troops in Lebanon. Great Britain, meanwhile, sent equivalent forces to Jordan.

Thus, Eisenhower aligned the United States more and more overtly with the most conservative forces in the Arab world, even though most Arab nationalists did not want all that much to do with the Soviets or communism. Nasser actually outlawed the Egyptian Communist Party and imprisoned or executed many of its members. The Soviets consequently remained wary of Arab nationalism, despite paying lip service to wars of national liberation. So Eisenhower's excessive interventionism probably pushed Arab nationalism closer to the Soviets than was necessary. Still, the United States had rather little room to maneuver in the Middle East as it tried to balance its moral commitment to Israel, its need for oil, and the probability that the Soviets would accept whatever influence or territory might be thrown their way by anti-Western Arab nationalists.

EISENHOWER AND LATIN AMERICA

Eisenhower ranged the United States against nationalism in Latin America as well as the Middle East, and for the same reason. He feared that Latin American nationalists would invite Soviet influence into another area of strategic and economic importance to the United States. The United States focused most of its attention on Europe and the Far East during the Cold War, but it could not remain oblivious to the continuing strategic value of the Panama Canal, the naval bases of the Caribbean, and the large reserves of oil and copper in Latin America. Besides, after World War II Latin America's market for U.S. exports came to equal that of Europe and to surpass those of Asia, Africa, and Oceania combined. Thirty-five percent of U.S. imports came from Latin America as well, and the United States had more foreign investments in Latin America than any other foreign area except Canada.

Harry Truman had tried to protect the U.S. position in Latin America by extending minor amounts of economic and technological aid through his Point Four program, by giving some military aid ($38 million in 1951), and by signing the Rio Pact of 1947 with the nations of the Western Hemisphere. The Rio Pact promised reciprocal assistance if Soviet intervention threatened any Western Hemisphere nation. These measures, however, did little to cope with the rise of revolutionary nationalism in Latin America. When the Eisenhower administration feared that a nationalist movement in Guatemala might invite Soviet influence into the hemisphere, it turned to the same sort of covert intervention that had been successful in Iran.

Guatemala was a nation and society ripe for revolution. Two percent of its people owned 70 percent of the land. Foreigners, led by the United Fruit Company of the United States, owned most of the big latifundias (plantations) that produced Guatemalan bananas and coffee for export. United Fruit also controlled the nation's railroads and its major Caribbean ports. It made sure that no Pacific port and no other railroads were built to compete with company-controlled facilities. The Maya Indians, who composed two-thirds of Guatemala's population, were left with 15 percent of the least arable land. This was insufficient to provide even a subsistence living for them. With 90 percent of the nation's agricultural production in bananas and coffee intended for export, Guatemala had to import food, and the lower classes, deprived of the ability to produce their own, had to buy it at very high prices. Yet half of United Fruit's land lay fallow and unused as the company sought to avoid overproduction of its export crops.

In 1944, a middle-class revolution brought Juan Jose Arévalo Bermej to power. Arévalo was supported mainly by the 30 percent of the Guatemalan population known as Ladinos, those who had adopted European languages and ways. Arévalo forced United Fruit to rent out some of its fallow lands, imposed rent control and a labor code on the latifundias, and eliminated forced labor. United Fruit convinced the Truman administration that Communists influenced the revolution. Consequently, Truman withheld aid and instituted an arms embargo. But he did little else. Arévalo, after surviving twenty-five coup attempts in six years, was succeeded by Jacobo Arbenz Guzmán, who won 60 percent of the vote in the 1950 election.

Arbenz sympathized with the workers' strikes plaguing United Fruit and began expropriating and redistributing United Fruit's fallow land, paying the company in compensation the low price United Fruit had set on the land for purposes of taxation. United Fruit howled bitterly that Communists had taken over in Guatemala. It had ready ears in the Eisenhower administration, since Secretary of State John Foster Dulles and his brother, CIA Director Allen Dulles, had been members of the company's law firm. When Arbenz made a deal for Soviet arms, the suspicions of the CIA and the FBI seemed confirmed. The United States secured a reluctant condemnation of the Arbenz regime from the Organization of American States (the Caracas Declaration) and then organized a coup in Guatemala.

The CIA settled on General Carlos Castillo Armas to lead an invasion from neighboring Honduras in 1954. That invasion comprised a total of 150 soldiers, 150 advance agents, a few minor air raids (some bombs were thrown out of planes by hand), a CIA-run radio station that broadcast threats of a huge invasion force, and a great deal of bluff. Arbenz had difficulty calling the bluff, however, because he commanded a disloyal army. He also had little support from the peasants, because they had not benefited from his reforms.

Arbenz was even afraid to order his planes to scout the invasion force because he feared the pilots would accept the CIA radio invitations to desert. Thus, he could not know how small Castillo Armas's army was or that Castillo Armas had halted it when he was only 6 miles into Guatemala. Arbenz simply panicked and fled.

Once again the CIA had demonstrated to itself how easily nationalist movements in Third World countries could be manipulated. But others were deriving lessons from Iran and Guatemala as well. Cuban rebels Fidel Castro and Che Guevara saw how important it was to rally the peasants and not just the moderate middle class to their revolution. They realized that the Iranian and Guatemalan CIA-sponsored coups had won by luck and bluff. When the CIA tried to repeat its Iranian and Guatemalan successes in Cuba, it found the outcome much different.

Meanwhile, the half-secret CIA role in Guatemala further alienated Latin American nationalists from the United States. South Americans picketed, threw rocks, and spit on Vice-President Richard Nixon during a highly publicized tour in 1958. Riots broke out in the Panama Canal Zone. Eisenhower tried to win back some non-Communist nationalists by creating the Inter-American Development Bank and subscribing $500 million to it in 1959. But this made little impact on either the problems or the sentiments of Latin Americans.

EISENHOWER AND ASIA

Eisenhower and Dulles approached revolutionary nationalism in Asia with the same assumptions they did nationalism in the Middle East and Latin America. They were determined that Soviet and Chinese communism should not benefit from turmoil in strategic areas. Once the Korean war ended, Eisenhower was particularly concerned about the French war in Indochina. He believed that a Communist victory in Indochina would mean not only the loss to the West of the area's rice, tin, and rubber, but the fall of Indochina's neighbors like a row of dominoes—Burma, Thailand, Indonesia, and perhaps even Japan, Taiwan, and the Philippines.

Eisenhower thought the French were handling the Indochina war very badly. He believed their military tactics were foolish. He thought their refusal to guarantee Vietnamese independence and self-government was destroying the hope of a nationalist alternative to communism. When the Communist Vietminh surrounded a French army at Dienbienphu in 1954 and threatened to exterminate it, Eisenhower regarded the debacle as the culmination of France's disastrous and expensive strategy.

The French asked for American help, but Eisenhower doubted the Americans could rescue Dienbienphu whatever they might do. He and Dulles were primarily concerned with saving what would remain of the Western position in Indochina. Eisenhower set several preconditions for any help he might give the French and their beseiged troops at Dienbienphu. The

French would have to make public their request to the United States for aid; America's allies, especially Great Britain, would have to contribute; Congress would have to give its consent; and the French would have to share future control of their political and military operations in Indochina with the United States, grant Vietnam its independence, and prosecute the war more vigorously.

The French refused to share control, Great Britain declined to participate, and Congress proved reluctant. Senator John F. Kennedy proclaimed that an American war in Indochina would be "dangerously futile and self-destructive." Lyndon Johnson warned against "sending American GIs into the mud and muck of Indochina on a bloodletting spree." Eisenhower let the matter drop and permitted Dulles to blame his decision on Britain's refusal to participate.

Nevertheless, Eisenhower warned Communist China that any attempt to expand into Indochina might call forth a nuclear response from the United States. He then sent Dulles to observe as the French, Vietnamese, and British tried to work out a negotiated settlement at Geneva. Russia and China pressed North Vietnam's reluctant leader, Ho Chi Minh, to accept a truce, and the Geneva Conference decided that Vietnam would be divided temporarily at the 17th parallel until elections for a unified nation were held two years later in 1956. The United States did not formally accept the Geneva Agreement, but "took note" of its provisions, promised not to disturb them by force, and warned that it would intervene if anyone else tried to break them.

After the Geneva Conference of 1954, Eisenhower and Dulles set out to replace French influence in South Vietnam and build a non-Communist regime there capable of winning the 1956 elections. (Eisenhower admitted that Ho Chi Minh and the Communists would win 80 percent of the vote if the elections were held in 1954.) The United States supported Emperor Bao Dai's appointment of Ngo Dinh Diem as the new prime minister of South Vietnam and funneled American aid through Diem rather than through the French. Diem was a Catholic refugee from North Vietnam who had spent much time in the United States as the guest of several Catholic monasteries and institutions. Many Americans, including the family of John F. Kennedy, regarded him as an ideal nationalist alternative to communism or colonialism who could protect Western interests in the Third World.

As further protection against Communist expansion, Dulles organized the Southeast Asia Treaty Organization (SEATO). SEATO allied the United States, Great Britain, France, Australia, and New Zealand with the non-Communist Asian nations of Thailand, the Philippines, and Pakistan. Although the Geneva Agreement of 1954 prohibited South Vietnam, Cambodia, and Laos from participating in an alliance, a protocol of SEATO extended the alliance's protection to Indochina. But SEATO was as weak a reed as Ngo Dinh Diem and the South Vietnamese government turned out to be. SEATO included no major Asian power like India or Indonesia, and it had no automatic provisions for collective action against aggression.

Map 16 Indochina, 1953–1954

One further crisis in Asia bedeviled Eisenhower and Dulles. The Communist Chinese periodically bombarded the offshore islands of Quemoy and Matsu, which were occupied by Chiang Kai-shek's Nationalists as outposts of their refuge on Taiwan. Quemoy and Matsu were not necessary to the defense of Taiwan, and it seemed ridiculous to risk a major war over them. But Chiang was determined to hold them as launching pads for his projected return to the mainland, and Eisenhower and Dulles did not want to demoralize their Nationalist allies or give in to Communist pressure. Eisenhower therefore announced with studied ambiguity that the United States would defend Quemoy and Matsu if an attack on them seemed to be a prelude to an invasion of Taiwan, and he hinted broadly that this defense would not be limited to conventional weapons. Ultimately the Chinese reduced their pressure and shelling and agreed to informal negotiations. Democrats and other critics roundly condemned Eisenhower for risking World War III over such a trivial issue. The Quemoy-Matsu issue faded, but the Indochina war remained to plague the administrations that succeeded Eisenhower.

CONTROVERSIAL ISSUES AND FURTHER READING

Until well into the 1970s, historians treated John Foster Dulles as the primary figure behind the foreign policy of the Eisenhower administration. Some praised Dulles for his strong anticommunism, for being a "Patriot, Statesman, and Unflinching Warrior in the Struggle Against Appeasement." [William Henry Chamberlin, *Appeasement; Road to War* (1962). The best book on Dulles from this perspective is Louis Gerson, *John Foster Dulles* (1967).] Others condemned him for his anti-Communist rigidity. [Townsend Hoopes, *The Devil and John Foster Dulles* (1973).] As hard-line anti-communism started to go out of fashion in the wake of Vietnam, some tried to emphasize Dulles's private flexibility and realism. [Michael Guhin, *John Foster Dulles: A Statesman and His Times* (1972).] A few right-wingers had thought they detected this flexibility even earlier and condemned it as weakness in the face of Communist aggression. [See George H. Nash, *The Conservative Intellectual Movement since 1945* (1976).] But all agreed that Eisenhower had deferred to Dulles's supposedly greater expertise. Even defenders of Eisenhower admitted this and regretted that Eisenhower had not asserted his own more moderate views over the ideological rigidity of his secretary of state. [Emmet John Hughes, *The Ordeal of Power: A Political Memoir of the Eisenhower Years* (1963); Sherman Adams, *Firsthand Report: The Story of the Eisenhower Administration* (1961).]

In the late 1960s, a few journalists began to revise this view. They asserted that Eisenhower had controlled his own foreign policy and that his restraint in foreign affairs contrasted favorably with the sort of activism that had led Kennedy and Johnson to escalate the Vietnam war. [Murray Kempton, "The Underestimation of Dwight D. Eisenhower," *Esquire* (September 1967); Garry Wills, *Nixon Agonistes: The Crisis of the Self-Made Man* (1969).] As historians delved into the recently opened archives of the Eisenhower Library in Abilene, Kansas, they largely agreed. Like the journalists, most of these "Eisenhower revisionists" praised Eisenhower for his restrained foreign policy, but even those who criticized him as just another cold warrior agreed that he had dominated his administration. [Herbert S. Parmet, *Eisenhower and the American Crusades* (1972); Robert A. Divine, *Eisenhower and the Cold War* (1981). A less flattering analysis of Eisenhower's foreign policy is Peter Lyon, *Eisenhower: Portrait of the Hero* (1974). A hostile revisionist critique, and not a very good one, is Blanche Wiesen Cook, *The Declassified Eisenhower: A Divided Legacy* (1981). See also the works of Stephen Ambrose, a moderate revisionist with considerable respect for Eisenhower—*Rise to Globalism* (1980); *Eisenhower: The President* (1984); and, with Richard H. Immerman, *Ike's Spies: Eisenhower and the Espionage Establishment* (1981). Another revisionist view is Burton I. Kaufman, *Trade and Aid: Eisenhower's Foreign Economic Policy* (1982).]

On the Eisenhower-Dulles strategy, the New Look, see John Lewis Gaddis, *Strategies of Containment* (1982); Charles Alexander, *Holding the Line* (1975); and Douglas Kinnard, *President Eisenhower and Strategy Management* (1977). On nuclear issues, see George Kistiakowsky, *A Scientist at the White House* (1976); James R. Killian, *Sputnik, Scientists and Eisenhower* (1978); Chalmers M. Roberts, *The Nuclear Years: The Arms Race and Arms Control, 1945–1970* (1970); George H. Quester, *Nuclear Diplomacy: The First Twenty-Five Years* (1970); and Robert A. Divine, *Blowing on the Wind: The Nuclear Test Ban Debate, 1954–1960* (1978).

On Khrushchev and the Soviets, see Strobe Talbott, translator and editor, *Khrushchev Remembers* (1970), and a supplement, *The Last Testament* (1974). See also Edward Crankshaw, *Khrushchev: A Career* (1966), and Michael Tatu, *Power in the Kremlin: From Khrushchev to Kosygin* (1969). On Europe, see Alfred Grosser, *The Western Alliance: European-American Relations since 1945* (1980); and Michael M. Harrison, *The Reluctant Ally: France and Atlantic Security* (1981).

On the dilemma of the Middle East, there are four recent surveys: George Lenczowski, *The Middle East in World Affairs* (1980); Seth P. Tillman, *The United States in the Middle East* (1982); Philip Groisser, *The United States and the Middle East* (1981); and Robert W. Stookey, *America and the Arab States: An Uneasy Encounter* (1975). On early American relations with the Middle East, see James A. Field, *America and the Mediterranean World, 1776–1882* (1969); and John A. DeNovo, *American Interests and Policies in the Middle East, 1900–1939* (1963). On American interest in Middle Eastern oil, see Aaron D. Miller, *Search for Security: Saudi Arabian Oil and American Foreign Policy, 1939–1949* (1980); Irvine H. Anderson, *Aramco, the United States, and Saudi Arabia* (1981); Burton I. Kaufman, *The Oil Cartel Case* (1978); Anthony Sampson, *The Seven Sisters: The Great Oil Companies and the World They Shaped* (1975); Benjamin Shwadran, *The Middle East, Oil, and the Great Powers* (1973); and Edward A. Chester, *United States Oil Policy and Diplomacy: A Twentieth-Century Overview* (1983).

On the United States and Israel, see Nadav Safran, *The United States and Israel* (1963), *Israel: Embattled Ally* (1978), and *From War to War: The Arab-Israeli Confrontation, 1948–1967* (1969). On the United States reaction to the Jewish refugee problem during World War II, see Yehuda Bauer, *American Jewry and the Holocaust* (1981); Saul S. Freidman, *No Haven for the Oppressed* (1973); and Henry L. Feingold, *Politics of Rescue* (1970). Truman's decision to recognize Israel is analyzed in John Snetsinger, *Truman, the Jewish Vote, and the Creation of Israel* (1974), and Evan M. Wilson, *Decision on Palestine: How the U.S. Came to Recognize Israel* (1979). On the Suez crisis, see Chester Cooper, *The Lion's Last Roar: Suez, 1956* (1978); Hugh Thomas, *Suez* (1967); Anthony Nutting, *No End of a Lesson: The Inside Story of the Suez Crisis* (1967); and Herman Finer's unflattering view, *Dulles over Suez* (1964). On the Iranian coup, see Barry Rubin, *Paved with Good Intentions: The American Experience in Iran* (1980); Michael K. Sheehan, *Iran: The Impact of U.S. Interests and Policies, 1941–1954* (1968); and the memoirs of the CIA operative in the coup, Kermit Roosevelt, *Countercoup: Struggle for the Control of Iran* (1980). The Eisenhower Doctrine and subsequent intervention is handled in Cecil V. Crabb, Jr., *The Doctrines of American Foreign Policy: Their Meaning, Role, and Future* (1982), and Fahim I. Qubain, *Crisis in Lebanon* (1961).

Eisenhower's policy toward Latin America is covered in three critical histories: Cole Blasier, *The Hovering Giant: U.S. Responses to Revolutionary Change in Latin America* (1976); Samuel L. Bailey, *The United States and the Development of Latin America* (1976); and Walter LaFeber, *Inevitable Revolutions: The United States in Central America* (1983). On the coup in Guatemala, see Richard H. Immerman, *The CIA in Guatemala: The Foreign Policy of Intervention* (1982), and Stephen Schlesinger and Stephen Kinzer, *Bitter Fruit: The Untold Story of the American Coup in Guatemala* (1982).

The best works dealing with Eisenhower and the war in Indochina are George Herring, *America's Longest War* (1979); Paul Kattenburg, *The Vietnam Trauma in American Foreign Policy, 1945–1975* (1982); Melvin Gurtov, *The First Vietnam Crisis: Chinese Communist Strategy and U.S. Involvement, 1953–1954* (1967); Robert R. Randle, *Geneva 1954: The Settlement of the Indochinese War* (1969); and Richard H. Immerman, "Between the Unattainable and the Unacceptable: Eisenhower and Dienbienphu," in Richard Melansen and David Mayer, eds., *Eisenhower Revisited: American Foreign Policy in the 1950s* (1984).

CHAPTER 18

The Path to Vietnam: Kennedy, Johnson, and Flexible Response

JOHN F. KENNEDY AND THE STRATEGY OF FLEXIBLE RESPONSE

John F. Kennedy personified the Democrats' campaign against the supposedly old, tired, and muddled Eisenhower Republicans. Kennedy was young, vigorous, and glamorous. While Eisenhower golfed, Kennedy and his people played touch football. While Eisenhower was balding, Kennedy had a great shock of hair. While Eisenhower seemed to stumble through his answers at press conferences, Kennedy responded sharply with grace, wit, and a touch of irony. When Kennedy and his beautiful wife Jacqueline returned from France where she had made a hit by speaking French on public occasions, the president introduced himself as the man who had accompanied Jackie to Paris. Asked how he enjoyed being president, he replied, "I have a nice home, the office is close by and the pay is good." He claimed that on taking office, what surprised him most was that things were just as bad as he and the Democrats had been saying they were.

Kennedy surrounded himself with men whose reputations were similar to his own—young, bright, witty and well educated. The news media kept count of the number of authors and Rhodes scholars among them. Kennedy quipped at a reception for the new administration's appointees that he was holding it because he wanted to see some of the names he had been reading about in the papers. Vice-President Lyndon Johnson was in some awe of the sophisticated Ivy Leaguers he encountered at the first meeting of the cabinet, but when he described them to his old political mentor, Speaker of the House Sam Rayburn, Rayburn replied: "Well, Lyndon, you may be right and they may be every bit as intelligent as you say, but I'd feel a whole lot better about them if just one of them had run for sheriff once."

Kennedy promised to get the country moving again. He called for a new determination and sense of purpose in the Cold War. He promised in his inaugural address that the United States would "pay any price, bear any burden, meet any hardship, support any friend, oppose any foe in order to assure the survival and the success of liberty."

The price Kennedy thought needed to be paid started with an addition of $2 billion to Eisenhower's defense budget. Kennedy argued that the Republicans had made a serious error by relying on massive retaliation to keep the defense budget down. "We intend to have a wider choice than humiliation or all-out nuclear war," he proclaimed. Bluff and ambiguity were insufficient to deter the Russians. The Soviets had to know they would face a superior force wherever they might probe.

He proceeded to strengthen America's military and diplomatic positions across the board. He started with an acceleration of the deployment of Minuteman intercontinental ballistic missiles and submarine-launched Polaris missiles. This he said was to counter a "missile gap" between the post-Sputnik Soviet forces and those built under Eisenhower. Kennedy also sought to increase America's capability to fight conventional wars. He doubled the number of combat-ready army divisions, enlarged the Marine Corps, and added fifteen ships to the navy. He particularly emphasized the development of an American capacity to fight irregular guerrilla wars in case Khrushchev followed through with his threat to instigate and support wars of national liberation. The Green Berets became the symbol of his concern for these "special forces."

Kennedy promised a more flexible approach to diplomacy as well as to defense. "Let us never negotiate out of fear, but let us never fear to negotiate," he said. So long as the United States was strong, it could afford to be civil. It could seek agreements to reduce arms and deal more generously with the Third World. Kennedy criticized Eisenhower and Dulles for their hostility toward neutralism. The United States should welcome diversity and nationalism, Kennedy said. America simply should make sure such nationalist movements did not fall into the hands of Communists who might join the Soviet sphere. Kennedy thought that keeping Third World countries nationalist rather than Communist was better done with economic and technical aid, such as that which would be provided by Kennedy's Peace Corps, than by empty anti-Communist rhetoric, formal alliances, and denunciations of neutrality. As a senator in the 1950s, Kennedy had dramatized this position by criticizing the French empire in Algeria and Vietnam.

By emphasizing his interest in building American strength and lessening world tensions through negotiations, Kennedy was undertaking a very delicate balancing act and leaving himself vulnerable to domestic opposition. When he denounced Eisenhower for neglecting preparedness, Kennedy was attacking a true expert on military affairs. When Kennedy stressed his willingness to negotiate with the Soviets and to tolerate neutralist nationalism in the Third World, he was leaving himself open to Republican charges that he was "soft on communism." Consequently, when his presidential opponent, Richard Nixon, declared that Kennedy's campaign opposition to a hard line on Quemoy and Matsu showed he was weak, Kennedy returned the charge by denouncing the Republican administration's inactivity in the face of Fidel Castro's revolution in Cuba.

THE BAY OF PIGS AND ITS AFTERMATH

Actually, Eisenhower was not inactive on Cuba. The CIA was secretly planning an invasion of Cuba by a 1,400-man army of Cuban exiles based in Florida. When Kennedy found out about the project, he decided to go ahead with it.

The invasion at the Bay of Pigs in April 1960 was an absolute disaster. The landing area was swampy and easily cut off from the rest of the island. Although the CIA originally planned the operation with the expectation that most Cubans were unhappy with Castro and would rise in support of the exile army, by the time the invasion actually took place it was clear to the planners that no such uprising could be expected. They went through with it anyway on the wild gamble that Castro could be bluffed from office like Arbenz of Guatemala or Mossadegh of Iran. The Cubans quickly surrounded the invasion force and sank the vessel carrying all its reserve ammunition. Kennedy canceled a planned second strike by American airplanes to support the force and abandoned the exile army to its fate.

The president took the blame for the invasion himself, much as Eisenhower had done in the U-2 incident. He then ordered an investigation of the operation along with a shakeup of the CIA. (Tragically, distrust of the CIA aroused by the fiasco would lead Kennedy and Johnson to discount the CIA's accurate and pessimistic reports on Vietnam.) The Kennedy administration also permitted a continuation of CIA attempts to assassinate Castro. Meanwhile, the Bay of Pigs loomed over Kennedy's attempts to establish his credentials as the friend of independent nationalism in the Third World and especially in Latin America.

Khrushchev Challenges Kennedy

The Bay of Pigs also undercut the image of strength and determination Kennedy thought necessary to project to the Soviet Union before he could negotiate a proper peace. Thus, Kennedy approached his summit meeting with Khrushchev, scheduled for June 1961 in Vienna, with a sense of weakness. He hoped, however, that he might compensate for the effect of the Bay of Pigs by a personal display of competence, confidence, and firmness. He intended to win what Eisenhower had sought at the aborted summit of 1960, a nuclear test ban and the end of Soviet ultimatums on Berlin.

Khrushchev had his own policy imperatives. He desperately wanted to eliminate the thorn of a high-living West Berlin stuck deep into East Germany. He knew he had the local conventional military superiority to take West Berlin, but he also knew that his decision to defer deploying ICBMs left the Soviets strategically inferior to the United States if Berlin triggered World War III. His solution to this problem was to frighten the Americans by bluster and erratic behavior. Perhaps they would back away despite their strategic superiority if they thought that Khrushchev was illogical enough to launch a suicidal nuclear attack on the United States. Thus, he had broken up the 1960 summit over the U-2 incident. That same year, at a UN meeting, he had banged his shoe on his desk and shouted insults at the British prime minister. He bragged continually that Sputnik demonstrated Soviet nuclear superiority over the United States. He announced support for wars of national liberation and threatened to "take the American imperialists by the scruff of their neck [and] give them a good shaking."

As one historian put it, Khrushchev was like a person "who seeks to have a friendly chat with a man next door, . . . [but] instead of knocking politely on the door of the apartment, climbs on the window ledge outside, makes ferocious faces through his neighbor's window or loudly bangs at the door, threatening to break it down. In the interval, he explains that all he wants is friendship and neighborly comity."[1]

At the Vienna summit Khrushchev continued his intimidating behavior, perhaps hoping he could rattle his neophyte opponent. He declared he would turn control of West Berlin's access routes over to East Germany in six months, and he followed this ultimatum with a substantial increase in the Soviet defense budget.

Kennedy and the Missile Gap

Kennedy must bear some share of blame for the crises that followed the Vienna summit. The crash missile program he initiated must have seemed ominous to Khrushchev. Kennedy may not have been sure by the time of the Vienna summit that the missile gap was nonexistent, but he had good reason to believe it. The U-2 planes had found no evidence of the deployment of ICBMs until the last two flights Eisenhower ordered. It is unclear how much of the U-2 information Eisenhower revealed to Kennedy before Kennedy's inauguration, but within a month of taking office, Secretary of Defense McNamara hinted that there was no missile gap. Kennedy may still have wished to err on the side of caution because it was possible that the U-2 had missed something. But by September of 1961, pictures taken by the newly launched American satellites combined with strategic information offered by the turncoat Soviet Colonel Penkovsky convinced Kennedy that the United States did indeed have strategic superiority. In October, during a particularly tense moment in the Berlin crisis, Kennedy publicly informed Khrushchev he knew there was no missile gap.

Yet America's missile building program continued. Kennedy and McNamara dropped the missile gap as justification for the acceleration and argued instead that the United States needed strategic superiority of from 2:1 to 4:1 over Soviet missiles in order to give the United States a flexible and credible response to a nuclear threat. Kennedy and McNamara refused the strategy of "minimum deterrence," advocated by the army and navy, that would have built fewer but invulnerable missiles. Such a force would deter a Soviet first strike because it would permit enough missiles to survive to destroy Russia's

[1] Adam Ulam, *The Rivals: America and Russia since World War II* (New York, 1971), pp. 285–286.

Figure 20   Premier Nikita Khrushchev and President John Kennedy at the Vienna Conference. Secretary of State Dean Rusk stands above at the left. Photo courtesy of the National Archives.

major cities. Kennedy and McNamara wanted far more missiles to survive. They no longer planned for a force that would deter a Soviet attack by surviving a first strike and having missiles left over to destroy Russia's cities. After absorbing a Soviet first strike, they wanted to be able to destroy all Russia's remaining strategic missiles and then hold Russia's cities hostage. Such a "counterforce" strategy might inspire the USSR to spare American cities and limit the damage involved in a nuclear exchange.

There were a great many problems with this strategy. Could a nuclear war be fought with such control and rationality? And why should the Russians not suspect that America's nuclear superiority implied that the United States itself was contemplating a first strike? American superiority might tempt the United States to presume it could wipe out all of Russia's missiles before Russia could retaliate.

Kennedy and McNamara could have avoided this situation by cutting back the missile program once it was clear there was no missile gap. But they reasoned that they had to plan for the worst contingency. After all, the Soviets might intend to build a huge strategic force of missiles even if they were not deploying one at the moment. Neither Kennedy nor Congress was ready to give up America's nuclear superiority and permit Soviet strategic parity. They depended on this superiority to deter an attack by superior Russian conventional forces in Europe. Besides, it would have been politically embarrassing to reverse course after Kennedy had made such strong criticisms of Eisenhower's strategy.

In any case, Kennedy and McNamara thought a cutback of the missile program might be interpreted as weakness in the face of Khrushchev's continual threats. Consequently, they planned and built a force of more than a thousand Minuteman ICBM missiles to be deployed in hardened silos. They also built hundreds of Polaris missiles for stationing aboard forty-one nuclear submarines. These Minuteman and Polaris missiles carried smaller payloads than the Russian missiles but were designed for greater accuracy and invulnerability, as befitted McNamara's "counter-force, no-city, protracted warfare" strategy.

The Berlin Wall

In this atmosphere of menace, Kennedy gloomily contemplated his options in responding to Khrushchev's Berlin ultimatum. He did not want to make major concessions under the Soviet threat because, with President Charles de Gaulle of France and Chancellor Conrad Adenauer of West Germany urging him to firmness, he thought retreat would destroy the unity of Western Europe and NATO. Yet there was no means to defend Berlin short of general war. With the sinking feeling that the chances of a nuclear exchange were about one in five, in July 1961 he ordered $3.25 billion added to the defense budget, called up some reserve and National Guard troops, and enlarged civil defense efforts.

Within a month, the world watched astounded as the East Germans began building a wall to seal off East from West Berlin. Khrushchev announced that the wall's purpose was to prevent Western spies from infiltrating the East, but he clearly intended it to stop the hemorrhage of refugees to the West. Looking back, it is clear that this was a defensive move by Khrushchev to end the Berlin crisis, but at the time Kennedy thought it might be the opening move in an attempt to drive the West entirely out of Berlin.

Some advocated that Kennedy knock down the wall. He believed this would mean war, so he limited his action to a show of support for West Berlin. He ordered an American battle group to march from West Germany to the city and sent Vice-President Lyndon Johnson to Berlin to meet the American troops. Khrushchev did not try to block access to the battle group, and in October 1961 he defused the crisis by deferring the deadline for a peace treaty indefinitely. He warned one American privately, however, that he regarded West Berlin as the West's exposed foot and planned to stamp on its corns from time to time. He also accompanied his deferral of the deadline with an announcement that the Soviet Union was breaking the moratorium on nuclear tests to begin a series of giant nuclear explosions in the atmosphere. The biggest of these was well over fifty megatons. Kennedy responded by resuming American testing in the atmosphere as well.

THE CUBAN MISSILE CRISIS AND ITS AFTERMATH

As the test of wills between Kennedy and Khrushchev continued, Khrushchev decided in 1962 to try to improve Russia's standing in the strategic balance of power by secretly installing intermediate-range missiles in Cuba. By then the Soviet Union had hundreds of intermediate missiles aimed at Europe, but only thirty ICBMs capable of reaching the United States. The United States, on the other hand, had some 300 ICBMs and 144 Polaris missiles capable of reaching the Soviet Union.

After weeks of rumors about missiles being installed in Cuba, a U-2 flight brought firm confirmation. Kennedy convened an emergency executive committee to survey the possible responses. Some members urged an invasion of Cuba. Others advocated "pinpoint" bombing to take out the installations. Some, including Adlai Stevenson, suggested trading the withdrawal of America's obsolete Jupiter missiles in Turkey for Soviet removal of missiles in Cuba. (Kennedy maliciously leaked to a reporter that Stevenson had wanted another Munich.)

Kennedy was determined to see the Soviet missiles removed and felt something must be done before they became operational. At the urging of his brother Robert, who said the president should not bomb with the risk of killing Russian soldiers and being compared to Tojo at Pearl Harbor, Kennedy chose to blockade Cuba and stop Russian ships from carrying any further missiles or warheads to the island. Since it would be a couple of days before any Soviet ships arrived to test the quarantine (the word preferred to "blockade," since under international law a blockade was an act of war), Khrushchev would have time to ponder and negotiate. If at all possible, Kennedy wanted to leave Khrushchev a way to back down gracefully, not paint him into a corner where he would face a choice between humiliation and nuclear war.

Tensions mounted as the Soviet ships approached the American naval picket line. If an American ship had to sink a Soviet vessel to enforce the quarantine, there seemed little chance that war could be averted. President Kennedy estimated that the chance of nuclear war was somewhere between "one out of three and even." Just before the first Soviet ships carrying missiles and equipment were due to reach the quarantine line, they stopped dead in the water. Secretary of State Dean Rusk remarked, "We're eyeball to eyeball, and the other fellow just blinked." But work continued on the Cuban missile sites. Would the Soviets remove the missiles already in Cuba, or seek to make them operational? The tension broke as a letter from Khrushchev arrived in Washington pledging to remove the missiles if the United States promised not to invade Cuba. Kennedy and his advisors were willing to accept the deal and were drafting a positive reply when a second Khrushchev letter arrived that raised the stakes. The United States would also have to remove its Jupiter missiles from Turkey. At the suggestion of Robert Kennedy, the United States agreed to the first letter as though the second one had never existed. Khrushchev acquiesced and ordered the missiles dismantled. The world had stepped back from the nuclear brink.[2]

The Cuban missile crisis ironically pushed the United States and the Soviet Union toward a relaxation of Cold War tensions. Khrushchev abandoned his bullying tactics. Kennedy emerged from the crisis as a hero whose firm but flexible and rational policy had applied the minimum of force, kept open a series of rational options, and provided the Soviets with a graceful means of backing down. Kennedy, having proved his strength and competence, could now afford to negotiate and make concessions without being branded as soft on communism.

Thus, in 1963 Khrushchev and Kennedy signed a formal ban on all but underground nuclear tests. By barring testing only where compliance could be ascertained through satellite surveillance, the Test Ban Treaty circumvented the thorny issue of on-site inspection. The Cold War antagonists also agreed to install a "hot line" that would allow the leaders of the United States and the Soviet Union to communicate directly in case of a crisis and thus perhaps head off a nuclear exchange.

Kennedy, de Gaulle, and Europe

Unfortunately, there was considerable negative fallout from the Cuban missile crisis as well. Kennedy had not consulted with his NATO allies during the crisis; he had taken on himself the decisions that could have incinerated the world. Charles de Gaulle had loyally supported Kennedy during the crisis, but he saw the lack of consultation as reinforcement of his long-held belief that a revived Western Europe should separate itself somewhat from the Atlantic-oriented Americans and British. Europe should establish itself as a Third Force in world politics under French leadership. De Gaulle recently had managed to withdraw France from its debilitating war with the Algerian revolutionaries, and now that it was free of most of its colonial entanglements in Africa and Indochina, de Gaulle was ready to take charge of European affairs. This led to considerable tension with the United States, particularly over the issue of nuclear weapons.

By the 1960s, France and Great Britain both had developed an independent nuclear capacity to support their positions as world powers. Great Britain generally coordinated its nuclear policy with the United States as part of the on-again, off-again pattern of nuclear partnership that had existed since World War II. The United States was anxious that France coordinate its nuclear strike force in the same way. To accomplish this, some of Kennedy's advisors were pushing for a Multi-Lateral Nuclear Force (MLF) that would assign several Polaris submarines to NATO to be manned by crews of mixed

[2] Even though the Kennedy administration had been unwilling to accept publicly Khrushchev's additional demand for removal of the obsolete missiles in Turkey, evidently Robert Kennedy gave the Soviets informal assurances that they would be removed, and in a few months they were.

nationalities. These crews would include not only the French and British, but also the West Germans. Advocates of the MLF hoped it would integrate and control the nuclear deterrent of Western Europe, give confidence to the Western Europeans that the United States would indeed risk its own existence to protect its allies, and hopefully sidetrack any thoughts West Germany might have of becoming an independent nuclear power.

De Gaulle disdained such integration. He pointed out that the MLF plan still gave the United States a veto over the use of nuclear weapons assigned to NATO. His disdain increased when the United States offered Great Britain but not France unilateral control over some Polaris missiles as compensation for canceling the Skybolt missile program that was supposed to have furnished vital launchers for Great Britain's independent nuclear force. De Gaulle saw this as one more aspect of the special relationship between the Anglo-Saxons that excluded France from the club of world powers. Consequently, he vetoed Great Britain's belated request for admission to the European Common Market, refused to support a nuclear nonproliferation treaty that the United States and Great Britain were trying to negotiate with the Soviets, and signed a treaty of cooperation with West Germany as the initial building block of his European Third Force. His effort culminated when he announced that France would withdraw its troops and facilities from NATO's joint command in 1967.

One other factor in de Gaulle's disillusionment with American policy had been Robert McNamara's attempts to lessen the chances of nuclear war in Europe. McNamara advocated a flexible response policy for Europe as well as the United States. He wanted to build up Europe's conventional forces to deter or fight a Soviet invasion without early recourse to nuclear weapons. McNamara thought this possible because his calculations showed the Soviet conventional superiority to Europe to be less overwhelming than previously thought. Russia's more numerous divisions were only a third as large and effective as the NATO divisions that opposed them. De Gaulle, however, saw McNamara's argument as an attempt by the United States to "decouple" its defense from Europe's to avoid a nuclear strike that might put the American homeland at risk. For de Gaulle, America's emphasis on conventional defense against a Soviet attack on Europe proved that the United States would not risk New York for Paris. After de Gaulle's withdrawal from NATO in 1967 eliminated French opposition within the organization, the other Western European allies accepted flexible response as official NATO strategy. Nonetheless, they continued to worry about decoupling and they resisted furnishing the number of conventional forces Washington thought necessary to deter a Soviet invasion.

The Soviet Drive toward Nuclear Parity

The Cuban missile crisis had a significant impact on Soviet as well as Western European affairs. Many Soviet leaders were disillusioned by Khrushchev's reckless gambles and his slowness to deploy the Soviet nuclear force. They overturned Khrushchev in 1964 and began a rapid missile buildup. The new leadership, headed by Leonid Brezhnev and Alexei Kosygin, installed 224 ICBMs by 1966. By 1968, they were approaching the equivalent of America's 1,054 land-based ICBMs and were deploying some submarine-launched missiles as well.

The Cuban missile crisis, the disarray in NATO, and the increase in Soviet nuclear power forced Kennedy, McNamara, and ultimately Lyndon Johnson to rethink their nuclear strategy. Despite the praise Kennedy and McNamara had received after the Cuban missile crisis for a supposedly masterful use of minimum force with options for a gradually escalated response, they realized that they had relied on the threat of a massive strike on the Soviet Union if it came to nuclear warfare, not a limited, controlled attack. The growth of Soviet nuclear power made Kennedy and McNamara even more doubtful that a future nuclear war could be limited or rationally controlled.

Thus, shortly before Kennedy's assassination, McNamara began to talk not only about flexible response in Europe, but also about a new strategy that would be premised on Russian nuclear parity rather than American superiority. He called this strategy "mutually assured destruction" (MAD). MAD would deter war because both sides knew the other could absorb a first strike and still devastate the other's vulnerable population.

The acceptance of Soviet nuclear parity and the strategy of mutually assured destruction opened the possibility of an arms control treaty with the Soviet Union. The United States could afford to make concessions because, as McNamara stated publicly in 1967, America's missile force was "both greater than we had originally planned and in fact more than we require." The Soviets, who previously had rejected all efforts at arms control because an agreement would have frozen Russia in an inferior strategic position, were willing to consider a treaty based on parity. In 1968, Johnson and Kosygin signed a Nuclear Non-Proliferation Treaty and announced that they would begin negotiations for limitations on strategic weapons.

The Soviet Union short-circuited this progress toward limitation when it invaded Czechoslovakia in the spring of 1968. The Czechs had frightened the Soviets by attempting to liberalize their Communist regime and permit greater freedom of speech and opposition. The Soviets justified their invasion with the Brezhnev Doctrine, which declared that the Soviet Union had a right to intervene in any socialist country to forestall counterrevolution. In the sour atmosphere that followed the crushing of the Prague Spring, Richard Nixon denounced Johnson for considering abandonment of America's nuclear superiority. Johnson already was reeling from opposition to the war in Vietnam, so he deferred the strategic arms negotiations until after the election of a new president. In this way Nixon inherited both the problem of Vietnam and the Soviet drive toward strategic parity.

KENNEDY AND THE NATIONALIST ALTERNATIVE IN THE THIRD WORLD

While John F. Kennedy devoted most of his attention to the critical issues that threatened to bring a direct confrontation with the other world superpower, his administration did make some halting attempts to break away from what Kennedy saw as the sterile antineutralist policies of the Eisenhower administration toward the Third World. Kennedy tried to support nationalist rather than old colonialist or reactionary regimes as counters to communist movements in developing nations. He extended economic aid to encourage peaceful and democratic reforms as alternatives to the revolutionary socialist model of nation-building and modernization. The intent of Kennedy's initiatives, and their failure, can be illustrated in three countries: the Dominican Republic in Latin America, the Congo (later Zaire) in Africa, and Laos in Asia.

The Dominican Crisis

In Latin America, Kennedy faced the prickly problem of appealing to the area's nationalism while trying to destroy Castro's Cuban regime at the same time. In March of 1961, Kennedy dramatically announced to Latin American diplomats gathered at the White House that the United States was ready to contribute the lion's share of $20 billion to encourage development in Latin America. The members of the Organization of American States adopted this Alliance for Progress in August 1961 and pledged to carry out internal reforms that would permit equitable distribution of the benefits of the alliance. But the program faltered from the outset.

Even moderate nationalist politicians in Latin America came from families that would be hurt badly by progressive taxation or land redistribution. Yet the only alternative internal source of funds to win over the dispossessed classes would be the confiscation of foreign enterprises. Such nationalization was not likely to win favor in the United States unless so much compensation were paid the foreign owners as to eliminate the net financial gain. In any case, much of the money from the Alliance for Progress went to the military, which the Kennedy administration believed offered one of the few hopes for an efficient nationalizing force in Latin America. The Alliance for Progress also required that most of the aid be spent on U.S. goods, further diminishing the benefits of the program to the poorer Latin American nations. Latin Americans complained that much alliance money went simply to pay their debts to the United States.

Kennedy's political initiatives in Latin America had little more success than his economic ones. The showcase for his strategy of the nationalist alternative in Latin America was the Dominican Republic. Dictator Rafael Trujillo, one of the most hated men in Latin America, had taken power in the wake of the U.S. occupation in 1930. At a 1959 OAS meeting, even other authoritarian Latin American regimes urged sanctions against Trujillo. The Eisenhower administration opposed these sanctions and found itself in the unfamiliar position of defending nonintervention in the Caribbean.

Kennedy changed U.S. policy. At an OAS meeting in 1960, the Latin American nations resumed their call for sanctions. Venezuela was especially angry that Trujillo had tried to have its president assassinated. The Kennedy administration at first urged free elections in the Dominican Republic as an alternative to sanctions, but ultimately gave in to the other OAS members. In January 1961, the Kennedy administration even added some new sanctions of its own. Opposition groups within the Dominican Republic took heart at this show of U.S. determination and requested help from the CIA in overthrowing Trujillo. The CIA agreed to supply some arms. Three pistols and three rifles reached the rebels before the United States backed away from the plot in the aftermath of the Bay of Pigs. This did not prevent the rebels from assassinating Trujillo in May 1961.

Following Trujillo's assassination, the Kennedy administration used its influence to secure free elections and prevent either a return to military dictatorship or a Castro-like revolution. In December 1962, the Dominican Republic elected a writer, Juan Bosch, its first constitutional president in thirty-eight years. The United States immediately recognized the new government and increased its aid. Unfortunately, Bosch proved to be "the best short-story writer and the worst politician in the hemisphere," according to Venezuelan ex-president Romulo Betancourt. Within a year, the Dominican military threw him out of office. Kennedy denounced the coup and recalled the U.S. ambassador. Ultimately, however, he recognized a pseudocivilian government set up by the military and restored some Alliance for Progress aid to the beleaguered nation.

The denouement in the Dominican Republic came in April 1965. A group of pro-Bosch officers overthrew the nominally civilian Dominican government. In the ensuing turmoil, Ambassador W. Tapley Bennett reported that American lives were in danger and that Communists were attempting to seize control. Lyndon Johnson sent in the marines. At first he said this was necessary to protect American lives and property, but a few days later he justified his action with a list of several Communists who were purported to have influence over the rebels. He then proclaimed the Johnson Doctrine: No Communist government would be permitted to take power in the Western Hemisphere. There would be no more Cubas if the United States could help it.

Johnson's intervention helped secure power for an American-leaning regime of military men headed by a former Trujillo lieutenant, Joaquin Balaguer. Johnson also got Balaguer to remove his most reactionary adherents from the government. But the Johnson Doctrine revived Latin American fears of the Monroe Doctrine and the Roosevelt Corollary. When Johnson sought retroactive OAS approval for his actions, he had great difficulty getting the two-thirds vote necessary. Ultimately, however, the OAS sent an inter-American force to join the U.S. marine contingent in Santo Domingo, both of which were withdrawn in 1966.

The Dominican Republic illustrated the difficulty of trying to find democratic regimes and support gradual peaceful modernization in the Third World. The stark division between the elites and the poor left little room for a moderate center. The United States increasingly faced a choice between reactionary and radical regimes. In the Latin America of the 1960s, reactionaries seemed to be winning. Military coups overthrew governments in Brazil, Argentina, Peru, Guatemala, Ecuador, and Honduras as well as the Dominican Republic between 1962 and 1965. In former times the United States could at least have consoled itself that reactionary regimes tended to be pro-American, but that too was changing. Even military dictatorships began to see their interests aligned with other Third World nations. Latin America joined African, Asian, and Communist countries in the UN to condemn the policies of the United States and the other Western industrialized powers.

Chaos in the Congo

Kennedy's search for democratic nationalist alternatives to radicals and reactionaries was no more successful in Africa than in Latin America. The site of Kennedy's most dramatic African initiative was the former Belgian Congo, soon to be called Zaire. It had significant mineral resources and the largest proportion of wage earners in Africa, but few internal markets for its products. It relied instead on exports and imports, which were managed and consumed by a thin crust of elites while the decaying traditional tribal cultures, deeply divided within themselves, remained unintegrated into the developed part of the society.

The Congo won its independence from Belgium in 1960 and installed a parliamentary government that was a very uneasy alliance of numerous tribes and factions. The new prime minister of the Congo was a Left nationalist named Patrice Lumumba. The Eisenhower administration initially welcomed Lumumba because he seemed to have the best chance to hold the Congo together. Lumumba's constituency was the urban elite and the most detribalized elements of the interior, tribes so scattered that they would look to a strong national government to protect them against local majorities. Then Eisenhower soured on Lumumba when the prime minister announced to the Belgian representatives at the independence day celebration: "From today we are no longer your monkeys." Within five days of independence, several army units mutinied against their Belgian officers and began attacking Europeans. Lumumba at first gave Belgian units permission to help put down the mutinies. But when Moise Tshombe proclaimed the independence of Katanga Province in the midst of the crisis, Lumumba portrayed the whole situation as a Belgian plot to reoccupy the country. He appealed for help from the UN and warned he would summon Soviet help if the Belgians were not out of the country in 72 hours.

Katanga's secession was an especially sensitive issue because that province's copper, cobalt, diamonds, and tin contributed one-third to one-half of the economy while containing one-third of the Congo's European population. No Congo government could survive without it. Belgium surreptitiously helped Tshombe and Katanga because it feared that Lumumba might disturb Belgian access to the Congo's vital resources. The Eisenhower administration, repelled by Lumumba and wanting to keep support in Europe against Soviet expansionism, leaned toward Belgium and tried to delay UN action to put down the Katanga rebellion. Eisenhower said the UN should not be drawn into an internal dispute.

An increasingly desperate Lumumba turned to the Soviets. One hundred twenty-five Soviet technicians arrived in Leopoldville, and the Soviets made plans to fly Lumumba's troops to Katanga to put down the secession. Lumumba's troops attacked four Canadian soldiers with the UN forces that had been sent to Katanga, and Lumumba worried aloud that white UN troops would simply substitute for Belgian colonialists.

At that point, the Congo army, headed by Joseph Mobutu, took over the government and arrested Lumumba. Lumumba's captors took him to Katanga and murdered him. (The American CIA had plans for Lumumba's assassination, but evidently was not responsible for the murder.) Lumumba's ally, Antoine Gizenga, fled to the Congolese city of Stanleyville and established a rival regime which quickly won at least verbal backing from the Soviets, Nasser's United Arab Republic, and Guinea.

Kennedy was inaugurated shortly after Lumumba's death and ordered a full reappraisal of American policy in the Congo. "We must ally ourselves with the rising sea of nationalism in Africa," he announced. Colonialists and reactionaries were driving nationalists into Communist hands. Kennedy shifted to support the bloc of Afro-Asian nations that was urging the United Nations troops to get other foreign and paramilitary personnel out of the Congo, reconcile the Stanleyville and Mobutu governments, and use force as a last resort to prevent civil war with Katanga. Against noisy opposition from conservatives who supported Tshombe as a bulwark against communism, Kennedy furnished American planes to ferry UN troops into Katanga. At the same time, the CIA purchased votes in the Congolese national parliament to ensure that Gizenga and the Leftists of Stanleyville would be submerged in a government headed by a liberal labor union politician, Cyrille Adoula. Thus, Kennedy would have his liberal, anticolonial, anti-Communist nationalist alternative.

Adoula's narrow and vulnerable parliamentary majority would not hold, even with CIA bribery, unless he ended the Katanga secession. When the mere presence of UN troops failed to cow Tshombe, Adoula and the UN ordered a march on the Katanga capital of Elizabethville in December 1962. As the UN troops occupied Elizabethville and marched onward, Tshombe finally collapsed.

But the conquest of Katanga did not end Adoula's troubles. Many Congolese peasants remained disenchanted with the national government. The government confiscated their tribal lands for parks and mines. It relocated them to combat sleeping sickness. It forced farmers to grow export crops, such as cotton, and thus pushed them into the cash economy under very disadvantageous conditions. Secret societies organized fragmented opposition to the government and the white oppressors. Adoula and liberalism had no answer to this rural radicalism. Adoula could only arrest Gizenga, purge the Lumumbists who might lead the rural disaffection, and become totally reliant on the military to remain in office. And the military of Joseph Mobutu only made matters worse. It lived off the land and exerted its control with great brutality. Eighty-five percent of the government's budget went to pay the salaries of the army and state employees, leaving little for economic development. Corruption and profiteering were rampant.

The rebellion also turned brutal. As fetishes and incantations withered before modern weapons, villagers abandoned the rebels and the rebels resorted to terror tactics. In 1964, they captured Stanleyville and controlled most of the eastern Congo. They also took hundreds of European hostages to deter American and European support for the government, now ironically headed by the former Katanga rebel, Tshombe.

Since the UN had withdrawn its troops from the Congo earlier in 1964, Tshombe turned to South Africa and various white mercenaries to spearhead his attack on the rebels. Lyndon Johnson contributed American planes and over fifty paratroop advisors. A series of parachute drops and an accompanying ground operation freed 2,000 European hostages and crushed the rebels. But the rebels executed 300 hostages and the Congolese army committed many of its own atrocities. While the operation saved a pro-Western government for the Congo, that government was weak and corrupt, and many African states protested the intervention of Americans, Europeans, and South Africans. Kennedy's hope of associating the United States with the rising nationalist tide in Africa evaporated.

A Flimsy Settlement in Laos

In Laos, an unhappy Kennedy accepted a settlement that went beyond his tolerance for nationalist anti-Communist alternatives to colonialism. He consented to a neutralist coalition government that included the Pathet Lao, the Laotian Communist Party. He did so only because anti-Communist alternatives were limited in Laos and, as one Kennedy administration official put it, "Laos was not all that goddamned important."

Laos was a small and divided nation. Its population of only 3 million was split into forty-two tribal clusters and five different language groups. The most powerful tribe, the Lao, comprised 40 to 50 percent of the population. It dominated the southern and lowland areas and used its authority to prohibit minority languages and schools. But poor communications made it impossible for the Lao to extend firm control over the upland and northern areas. Laos had few roads, and even where they were passable, they carried little trade among the inward-looking tribes. Laotians paid so little attention to affairs beyond their own tribal lands that in 1956 fewer than half of the people knew the name of their own nation and only 10 percent knew the name of the prime minister. National politics consisted of a struggle for leadership among twenty families with an active constituency of only about 2,000 people.

When the French began to evacuate Laos and the rest of Indochina following the 1954 Geneva Accords, they left behind three major groups vying for power. The Pathet Lao, headed by Prince Souphanouvong, controlled the northern and upland areas. Although nominally Communist, the Pathet Lao represented the ambitions of minority tribes more than international Marxism, and it permitted minority languages and schools in its territory. A right-wing anti-Communist group, ultimately led by General Phoumi Nosavan and Prince Boun Oum, bitterly opposed the Pathet Lao. Between these two groups stood a neutralist faction led by Prince Souvana Phouma, Souphanouvong's half-brother.

Although the French tried to leave Souvana Phouma as their successor, the right wing took over and the Pathet Lao withdrew its cooperation from the central government, effectively partitioning the country. For the time being, however, conflict remained at a low level. The Laotians were a peaceful people and accepted whatever government ruled them, be it colonial or Communist, with considerable passivity. The neutralists even regained power in 1957.

Change was underway, however, as American advisors and money poured into Laos to replace French influence. The American mission in Laos went from one person in 1954 to one hundred in 1957. At first this did not drastically change conditions in Laos. Much of the growing American mission's effort went merely to maintain its own personnel rather than to influence the Laotians, because conditions in Laos were very difficult for Westerners. One CARE official remarked: "There are only two kinds of Americans in Laos—those who have amoebic dysentery, and those who don't know it." In addition, the American mission was split during most of Eisenhower's administration. Some State Department officials favored the French approach of a restrained policy and support for Souvana Phouma's neutralists. The CIA and many lower-level diplomatic officials in Laos, however, feared that a coalition between Souvana Phouma and the Pathet Lao would result in another Czechoslovakia. They threw their money and efforts behind the right wing.

Then, in 1959, American congressional conservatives decided that Laos was a prime example of the corruption in America's foreign aid program and cut the Laos appropriation drastically. Souvana Phouma's neutralist coalition fell to a right-wing government, and the army of Phoumi Nosovan took the opportunity to conduct an anti-Communist purge. Neutralist troops, led by a young officer, Kong-Le, rebelled against the government and put Souvana Phouma back in power as prime minister. Phoumi Nosavan refused to submit, and the strife escalated into civil war.

After much debate within the administration, Eisenhower threw his weight behind Phoumi and the right, to the great consternation of the French, the British, and his own ambassador in Laos. Souvana Phouma, Kong-Le, and the neutralists then began to accept supplies from a Soviet airlift through

North Vietnam. When the armies of Phoumi and the right proved thoroughly incompetent, Eisenhower began to reconsider his policy. But he still insisted to incoming President Kennedy that Laos could not be allowed to fall to the Communists.

As in the cases of the Dominican Republic and the Congo, Kennedy made a reappraisal of policy toward Laos. He was slow to accept neutralization, but he quickly saw that the military option was foreclosed when he learned that sending 10,000 troops to Laos would exhaust America's strategic reserve. Finally, he announced he would accept a conference to neutralize Laos if the USSR would end its airlift. He told Averell Harriman, America's roving ambassador charged with negotiations over Laos: "I want a negotiated settlement. I don't want to put troops in."

Negotiations at the Geneva Conference of 1962 dragged on for months. Harriman and Kennedy put pressure on the Communists by sending 3,000 American troops to neighboring Thailand. They pushed Phoumi Nosavan and Boun Oum by withholding American aid payments. Finally, in June, Harriman got his agreement. Souvana Phouma would head a neutralist coalition government with the Pathet Lao and the Right. Foreign troops would withdraw, and Laos would not be used as a base for attacks on other countries.

This agreement kept strife at a relatively low level in Laos for some seven years, but none of the factions lived up to the full terms of the accord. North Vietnam withdrew only 40 of its 6,000 troops and continued to use the Ho Chi Minh Trail complex through northern Laos to get supplies to the Vietcong in South Vietnam. The United States withdrew its 666 advisors, but extended aid to Souvana Phouma and to Kong-Le when he fell out with the Communists and fought them. About all that survived of the agreement within months of its negotiation was Souvana's government and a tacit understanding: The Pathet Lao would not challenge for control of the southern Mekong area, so vital to Laos, Cambodia, and South Vietnam, while America's supporters would not challenge Pathet Lao control of northern Laos.

This fragile agreement simply could not survive the overwhelming events in the rest of Indochina. Laos, as Secretary of State Rusk said, was "only the wart on the hog of Vietnam." The Pathet Lao began to push Kong-Le's troops off the strategic Plain of Jars, and Lyndon Johnson initiated a secret war in Laos. First, Johnson gave American financial and technical assistance to Laotian air strikes on Pathet Lao territory and the Ho Chi Minh Trail. Then he sent in secret American bombing raids. Meanwhile, the CIA led the Meo tribes of the mountains in attacks on Communist territory. Richard Nixon continued this secret war, and by 1972 American aid to Laos was $350 million, ten times the Laotian budget and 75 percent larger than the entire Laotian gross national product. In 1971 Nixon also authorized a South Vietnamese invasion of Laos to eliminate North Vietnamese and Vietcong sanctuaries. This invasion ended in an embarrassing rout of America's allies, and in 1975 Laos fell to the Pathet Lao about the same time Vietnam and Cambodia fell to their Communists. The Pathet Lao then completed the destruction of the country so well begun by North Vietnamese intrusions and American bombing.

AMERICA IN VIETNAM

John F. Kennedy did not live to see the collapse of his Laotian initiative. In fact, he remarked shortly before his death: "Thank God the Bay of Pigs happened when it did. Otherwise we'd be in Laos by now—and that would be a hundred times worse." Tragically, he did not say the same of Vietnam. Averell Harriman and Chester Bowles urged him to conclude a neutralization pact on Vietnam as he had on Laos, but in the wake of the Bay of Pigs and the Laotian compromise, Kennedy believed he could not afford another retreat. Besides, a fact-finding commission that included Vice-President Lyndon Johnson, chief military advisor Maxwell Taylor, and National Security Council member Walt Whitman Rostow, which he sent on a fact-finding mission to Vietnam, reported that the war could be won. Consequently, Kennedy flatly rejected a negotiated settlement. Yet he never established a firm policy of support for Vietnam either. He refused Maxwell Taylor's recommendation to send American troops. He remained as cautious and indecisive as he had in Laos, improvising from day to day.

Kennedy, Diem, and Ho Chi Minh

The Kennedy administration talked bravely of South Vietnamese Prime Minister Ngo Dinh Diem as Vietnam's nationalist alternative to communism. Kennedy also reinforced the public image of South Vietnam as a bastion of freedom and progress against the spread of communism from the north. He recalled the exodus of thousands of refugees from North to South Vietnam after the Geneva Conference of 1954 ratified Communist control of the North. This seemed to most Americans proof of Vietnamese hostility to communism: The Vietnamese had "voted with their feet." American leaders failed to note publicly the reverse flow of 100,000 southern Vietminh from the South to the North. These American leaders also failed to point out that the vast majority of refugees from the North were Catholics fleeing as much for religious as political reasons.

The Catholic exodus actually made things easier for Ho Chi Minh. Not only was he rid of a disruptive minority, but the exodus made available land for redistribution in his drastic reform program. Perhaps the windfall tempted him to go too far, for he almost destroyed his popularity. Although 98 percent of North Vietnamese farmers owned their own farm plots, Ho insisted on redistributing them. He issued a Population Classification Decree that divided the countryside into five categories, ranging from landlord to agricultural worker. People's Agricultural Reform Tribunals then ordered some 50,000 landlords and rich peasants to be shot, sent twice that many to labor camps, and gave their property to the lower strata. Since property already was relatively equitably distributed, this sometimes meant that the difference between a friend and an enemy of the revolution was as little as a quarter of an acre or an extra pig. Ho's redistribution program often produced farm plots too small to support families. By late 1955, he backed away from his population classification and land redistribution and moved toward the collectivization of agriculture. Considerable unrest remained in the countryside for several years, but Ho had moved soon enough to avoid the complete destruction of his popularity and to tower over Diem as the symbol of Vietnamese nationalism.

Diem stood little chance of exceeding Ho's popularity and influence anyway. As a northerner and a Catholic, he was an alien to many southerners. He aggravated the situation by choosing northern Catholics as advisors and sending his cronies to replace the traditional elected headmen of local villages. His own land reform program actually resulted in undoing much of the land redistribution that had taken place in Vietminh-controlled areas prior to the Geneva Conference of 1954. Two percent of the people still owned 45 percent of the land when he was through, while 72 percent of the people had to survive on 15 percent of the land. American aid did little for these villages. It supplied consumer goods that benefited Saigon but were unaffordable or of little benefit to the 90 percent of the population that lived in the countryside. More than 75 percent of American aid was military rather than economic anyway.

Thus, Diem built an army without a political structure to support it. He made up for this lack of political support with bribery and repression. A fierce Catholic and mandarin, he viewed any kind of opposition as subversive. He established a rigid censorship; enacted morality laws against contraception, dancing, prostitution, and occultism; relied heavily on his secret police; and centralized government administration to the point that all forty provinces reported directly to Saigon. It even took a presidential decree to get a divorce.

Eisenhower and Kennedy were aware of Diem's foibles. Eisenhower came close to dumping Diem in 1955, but Diem surprisingly defeated the combination of religious sects, criminal gangs, and private armies that had created chaos in southern Vietnam for years. John Foster and Allen Dulles convinced Eisenhower that this feat proved Diem's potential to establish a viable non-Communist government in the South, and so the Eisenhower administration began lavishing aid on Diem. Diem ratified his right to rule by holding an election in which he managed to turn out a 98 percent vote for himself. Then, with Eisenhower's support, he blocked the Vietnam-wide election the Geneva Conference had set for 1956 by insisting that the vote in North Vietnam be "free and open" as the West defined those terms.

After it became apparent that Diem would not permit reunification of Vietnam through the promised election of 1956, open rebellion broke out in the South Vietnamese countryside in late 1957. Part of this rebellion was a natural reaction to Diem's misrule; part was the product of Vietminh cadres who had buried their arms after the Geneva Conference and remained behind for just such a contingency. North Vietnam gave little support at this stage, since it was preoccupied with the problems of its own revolution. Diem responded to the rebellion with greater repression. He dislodged villagers from their homes and the graves of their ancestors to concentrate them in "agrovilles," where they might be better protected by the army. This only increased alienation in the countryside.

By the time Kennedy took office, the Diem government was near collapse. Nevertheless, Kennedy decided Vietnam was more important than Laos and that Khrushchev was testing him. The United States would have to support Diem whether he was a good ruler or not. Perhaps the problem was Eisenhower's strategy in Vietnam. In the quiet period between the Geneva Conference and the outbreak of rebellion in 1957, Americans had trained and equipped the South Vietnamese army to fight a conventional war such as the one in Korea. Kennedy hoped to redeem the situation by developing antiguerrilla capabilities. He set up the Green Beret special forces, sent 16,000 advisors to Vietnam, urged Diem to reform his government, tried to get aid directly to the villagers, and supported construction of villages called strategic hamlets, a program reminiscent of Diem's agrovilles.

After a brief surge of success following these new infusions of American aid, the situation began to fall apart again. Not only did the Vietcong regain the initiative, but new resistance to Diem's government sprang up among anti-Communist elements in South Vietnam as well. The Buddhists spearheaded this resistance. To protest religious persecution by Diem's Catholic officials, Buddhist monks even set themselves afire on the public streets. In the face of spreading antigovernment demonstrations, Diem relied more and more heavily on punitive actions by his secret police under the command of his brother-in-law, Ngo Dinh Nhu. Meanwhile, Diem's wife, Madame Nhu, callously offered to supply the gasoline and matches for more monkish "barbecues." Finally, in direct violation of Diem's promise to try to conciliate the Buddhists, Ngo Dinh Nhu launched massive raids on Buddhist temples throughout Vietnam. Nhu's forces ransacked the pagodas and arrested some 1,400 people.

Not only did Diem ignore American advice to reform his regime, he began talking publicly of American ignorance and arrogance in trying to impose its policies on him. Kennedy also learned that Diem had opened secret contacts with North Vietnam. Thus, when a group of South Vietnamese generals informed the Americans in August 1963 that they were contemplating a coup, Kennedy did nothing to discourage them and kept the information secret from Diem. The coup fell apart, but it triggered still another reevaluation of American policy in Vietnam. Kennedy sent a two-man team to survey the situation, and it returned with a divided report. One member told Kennedy to seek reconciliation with Diem, the other that there was no chance to defeat the Vietcong as long as Nhu remained in the government and the regime remained unreformed. An exasperated Kennedy exclaimed, "You two did visit the same country, didn't you?"

Map 17   South Vietnam and the Ho Chi Minh Trail

In the midst of the reevaluation, Robert Kennedy finally broached the question of whether the United States should withdraw entirely. Perhaps the president considered it; some of his advisors claim he did. Before he was assassinated, he actually approved a plan for removing American advisors by 1965. But probably Kennedy would have been unwilling to quit. His plan to remove the advisors assumed that the South Vietnamese government would be making progress in combatting the Vietcong, not disintegrating. He dismissed his brother's suggestion of a withdrawal and reacted angrily to Senator Mike Mansfield's independent and pessimistic report on the situation in South Vietnam. At the very least, Kennedy wanted to put off withdrawal until after he was safely reelected. He told Mansfield that to withdraw earlier would play into the hands of his conservative rival for the presidency, Barry Goldwater, and perhaps set off a new wave of McCarthyism.

Johnson Takes Charge

Kennedy's policy drifted until November 1, 1963, when, with JFK's tacit approval, a revived military junta overthrew Diem's government. The soldiers who captured Diem and Nhu killed them in the back of an armored truck. Three weeks later, John Kennedy himself was assassinated.

Kennedy left to his successor, Lyndon Johnson, a South Vietnam in chaos. The new military junta was squabbling within itself and proving totally incapable of governing the country. Presidential advisors told Johnson there was a 50–50 chance the war would be lost in the next six months unless the South Vietnamese government operated more efficiently. But if there was some question of withdrawal in Kennedy's mind, there was none in that of Lyndon Johnson. As vice-president he had been part of the mission to Vietnam early in Kennedy's administration that had advocated stronger support for the war effort. He could not stand the thought of being the first American president to lose a war. He remembered the consequences for the Democratic party of "losing" China in 1949. He also feared that a foreign policy debacle would destroy his ability to push through Congress his treasured Great Society program.

Johnson, like his native state of Texas, was larger than life. His intelligence was as powerful as his physique. Publicly, in his attempt to avoid looking like a hick, he appeared stiff, stilted, and programmed with empty, maudlin slogans. Privately he was razor-sharp, raucous, and friendly as a St. Bernard trying to crawl into someone's lap. He was fearsomely persuasive in a one-on-one situation, slapping backs, "pressing the flesh," shamelessly flattering, horsetrading, and never letting up until he had his commitment. But he also could be vulgar and intimidating. He once said of Gerald Ford that he was so dumb he couldn't fart and chew gum at the same time. He grabbed a Canadian official who had made statements against the Vietnam war, pinned him against a wall, and shouted in his face: "You pissed on my rug." He said that the Organization of American States "couldn't pour piss out of a boot if the instructions were written on the heel."

Figure 21 The Vietnam Quagmire—President John Kennedy explains U.S. policy toward Vietnam in 1961 (top). President Lyndon Johnson shakes hands with South Vietnam's Premier Nguyen Cao Ky in background while Secretary of Defense Robert McNamara and Secretary of State Dean Rusk greet Chairman Nguyen Van Thieu at a meeting in March 1967 (bottom). Courtesy the National Archives.

Johnson was the last person to accept defeat in Vietnam. He wanted "the coonskin nailed to the wall." He understood, however, that outright victory was either impossible or too costly, so he resolved at least not to lose. To keep from losing, he began to escalate the American effort in South Vietnam. He threw American backing behind General Nguyen Khanh after Khanh took power in another coup on January 19, 1964. Johnson increased American advisors from 16,000 to 23,000, appointed General William Westmoreland to replace the optimistic and ineffectual Paul Harkins as commander of the advisors, and initiated covert joint commando raids on North Vietnam. He also ordered contingency plans for graduated pressure against North Vietnam, including air strikes. Yet he turned down the recommendation of the joint chiefs of staff for all-out air and ground attacks on the North.

On August 1, 1964, the American destroyer *Maddox* was conducting electronic surveillance of North Vietnam in Tonkin Gulf waters recently vacated by a South Vietnamese squadron that had conducted a covert raid. North Vietnamese torpedo boats attacked the *Maddox*. The destroyer, with the aid of planes from a nearby carrier, drove the torpedo boats away and damaged at least one. An angry Johnson ordered the *Maddox* to return to those same waters the following day accompanied by a second destroyer, the *C. Turner Joy*. Both destroyers reported another attack by torpedo boats, although bad weather conditions made the radar sightings and other evidence of the attack problematical. Johnson ordered retaliatory attacks against North Vietnamese torpedo boats bases and contiguous oil storage dumps. He also got congressional approval of a resolution, drawn up during the earlier contingency planning for air strikes on North Vietnam, which gave the president the power to take "all necessary measures to repel any armed attacks against the forces of the United States and to prevent further aggression."

Johnson did not intend to use this Tonkin Gulf Resolution as a blank check for escalation. He hoped to continue limited warfare and merely retaliate for North Vietnamese actions. After he had safely won reelection, however, the Khanh government fell apart and the South Vietnamese war effort declined still further. Johnson decided to extend his retaliatory policy to one of continuous bombing of North Vietnam. Using a February 6 attack on U.S. barracks at Pleiku as the provocation, Johnson initiated this bombing program and called it Rolling Thunder. Johnson intended Rolling Thunder as a slow squeeze, a gradual escalation of pressure to destroy the North's morale, revive morale in the South, cut off North Vietnamese supplies to the insurgents in the South, and do all this without provoking intervention by the Soviets or the Chinese. With the help of the Kennedy advisors who stayed on in his administration, Johnson tried to emulate the realist, flexible strategy of the Cuban missile crisis—using carefully calibrated and limited power to show the enemy it could not win, while providing the opponent with a face-saving way to retreat. Thus, Johnson would force the Communists to negotiate while he avoided either total war or appeasement.

When Johnson's initial bombing produced no immediate effect, he extended the bombing targets northward. He also approved the use of napalm.

Then, in March 1965, he ordered American ground troops to guard the airfields necessary to stage the bombing raids. A month later, he decided to send 40,000 more troops to protect population enclaves, although he rejected the requests of the joint chiefs and Westmoreland for still larger infantry contingents.

All the while, Johnson denied that his actions constituted a change of policy and continued to justify them as retaliatory. The government issued a White Paper blaming the war in the South on North Vietnamese aggression, even though it was clear to policymakers that to this point the revolt was mostly indigenous and fought with captured American weapons far more than Russian- or Chinese-supplied arms. Johnson also refused to seek a firm mandate from Congress and the country for full-scale war. In this, as in his attempt to fight a limited war, he imitated Harry Truman in Korea. He used the Tonkin Gulf Resolution as authority for his actions. He failed to report that American escalation was designed not so much to win as to improve South Vietnam's morale and prevent that nation's imminent collapse. He refused to risk opposition by raising taxes to support the war. (The combination of increased domestic spending along with the escalation of military expenses produced budgetary deficits that ultimately helped lead to devastating inflation in the 1970s.) He consciously emulated Franklin Roosevelt in trying to lead America into what he thought was a necessary war by indirection and disingenuousness.

Johnson also tried to disarm critics by making dramatic peace initiatives. He ordered several bombing pauses and offered unconditional discussions. He even tried to bribe the enemy with talk of a gigantic economic development program for the Mekong Delta on the scale of the Tennessee Valley Authority. Yet Johnson's final terms remained the preservation of an independent non-Communist South Vietnam. Neither the Vietcong nor North Vietnam were willing to accept that, so the peace talk of both sides remained hollow public relations efforts.

Johnson's efforts to disarm his critics and his escalated war effort in Vietnam both failed. China and especially the Soviet Union increased the amount and sophistication of the weapons they sent to Vietnam. Coups and countercoups continued to paralyze the South Vietnamese government until the rise of two strongmen, Air Marshal Nguyen Cao Ky and General Nguyen Van Thieu, produced a modicum of stability. Johnson met Ky at Honolulu and, with an exuberant bear hug, threw the weight of the United States behind his government. Then, in July 1965, with confidence that North Vietnam would have to retreat before the might of a superpower, Johnson sent another 100,000 troops and permitted General Westmoreland to change the mission from guarding enclaves to pursuing the enemy in "search and destroy" operations. Johnson refused to permit bombing of North Vietnam's primitive industrial base, the capital of Hanoi, or the main harbor at Haiphong, but he ordered B-52 saturation bombing raids on suspected enemy territory in South Vietnam.

Yet by 1967, with almost half a million American soldiers fighting in Vietnam, with the air force having dropped more bombs than in all the theaters of World War II, with the expenditure of $2 billion a month, with the destruction of over half of South Vietnam's timberlands by defoliants, South Vietnam and the United States were no closer to victory than they had been two years before. The United States could not send enough troops to occupy all of South Vietnam, and the South Vietnamese government could not control it either.

Meanwhile, domestic American criticism of the war escalated along with the military effort. University students and faculties held all-night teach-ins. Civil rights leaders like Martin Luther King denounced the war as not only unjust, but a diversion from domestic racial and economic reform. Newspaper and television reporters challenged administration "body counts" and reports of progress. Opposition even arose within the administration. Secretary of Defense Robert McNamara, a major architect of Johnson's policy, concluded that most targets in North Vietnam were already destroyed and that no further escalation would be profitable. He advised scaling back America's war effort when he resigned in 1967. The president found himself trapped in the White House, unable to travel or speak without triggering massive demonstrations.

The crisis came in January of 1968. Taking advantage of the holiday laxness during Tet, the Vietnamese lunar new year, the Vietcong and North Vietnamese regular units launched surprise attacks on thirty-six of South Vietnam's forty-four provincial capitals, five of the six major cities, sixty-four district capitals, and fifty hamlets. One daring team of rebels even penetrated the walls of the American embassy in Saigon and laid seige to it for more than six hours until all were killed or captured. The Communists suffered horribly in the attacks. American forces and a surprisingly effective South Vietnamese army repelled most attacks within hours or days, although liberation of the old imperial capital of Hue took nearly three weeks. The Communists suffered some 40,000 casualties, while the United States and South Vietnam lost about 3,500 men. No general uprising took place to overthrow the South Vietnamese government or to welcome the Communists as liberators. Shattered Communist units broke up into smaller groups to resume guerrilla tactics in the villages and jungles. From then on, regular North Vietnamese army units carried the major burden of the Communist war in South Vietnam.

Even though the Tet offensive may have been a tactical defeat for the Communists, it came as a devastating surprise to most Americans that the enemy could launch such a widespread attack at all. Television anchorman Walter Cronkite remarked: "What the hell is going on? I thought we were winning the war." The devastation portrayed on the television screens shocked Americans—the Saigon police chief summarily executing a captured guerrilla, the Saigon embassy in ruins, an American officer remarking of one liberated village, "We had to destroy the town to save it." Government claims of progress and pacification seemed a mockery in the face of thousands of civilian casualties and nearly a million new refugees. Feeding and housing the refugees became impossible. Civilians were all the more reluctant to cooperate with the Americans and the South Vietnamese army after the Vietcong and North Vietnamese executed thousands of collaborators during the brief time they held Hue and other territories. Promises that the Americans or South Vietnamese could provide protection from guerrilla retribution had proved empty.

Westmoreland blamed the defeatism that followed Tet on media distortions. He prepared to urge Johnson to send reinforcements to exploit the Communist defeat. But Westmoreland permitted himself to be convinced by Army Chief of Staff General Earle Wheeler to ask for reinforcements of 206,000 men not as part of a new offensive strategy, but as necessary to stave off further disaster. Wheeler hoped to push Johnson to declare a state of emergency, mobilize the reserves, and replace his gradualist strategy with an all-out effort to win the war.

Wheeler's strategy backfired. Johnson was not greatly shocked by Wheeler's grimly pessimistic report of the Tet offensive and the state of the war. He was insulated by Westmoreland's earlier portrayal of Tet as an American victory and by full knowledge that the United States had been barely staving off defeat since 1963. But he never communicated his true view of the war to the rest of the country. Johnson calmly turned the request for reinforcements over to Secretary of Defense Clark Clifford. The president was prepared to send the troops necessary to prevent defeat, but expected the number needed to be rather few.

Clifford, under the influence of Pentagon civilians who had been largely responsible for the conversion of Robert McNamara, came to question the entire basis of the war in his report to Johnson. The secretary recommended gradual disengagement. An enraged Johnson refused this recommendation, but decided to send only a few new troops and avoid a major escalation. To counter the demands for disengagement coming from Clifford and a rising chorus outside the government, he also called together an outside commission, dubbed the Wise Men, on the assumption that such hard-nosed elder statesmen as Dean Acheson and McGeorge Bundy would support his determination to continue the war. He was shocked when a substantial majority of the Wise Men reacted as Clifford had to the same briefings and information Johnson had been getting. "Someone poisoned the well," Johnson railed.

Eugene McCarthy dealt Johnson and the war another blow when he polled 42 percent of the vote in the New Hampshire Democratic primary against the incumbent president. Although many of those voting for McCarthy were hawks who were protesting American defeats rather than demanding withdrawal, they indicated Johnson's weakness. When Robert Kennedy jumped into the race to take advantage of the nation's antiwar sentiment, Johnson realized he was painted into a corner. In a dramatic speech to the nation on March 31, 1968, he ordered an end to bombing in almost all of North Vietnam and named Averell Harriman to undertake a new effort at peace negotiations. To emphasize the sincerity of his move, he announced his withdrawal from the race for reelection.

Johnson, however, did not reduce operations in South Vietnam. He was not ready to compromise much for peace, and he did not think North Vietnam or the Vietcong were either. He hoped to maintain public support for South Vietnam by proving the insincerity of the Communists in negotiations. South Vietnam feared a sellout, however, and stalled the negotiations in the hope that it would get a better deal from the new president, whom South Vietnamese leaders correctly predicted would be Richard Nixon.

THE IMPACT OF VIETNAM

Vietnam did more than devastate the presidency of Lyndon Johnson. It challenged the whole constellation of thoughts and feelings about foreign affairs that had prevailed in the United States since World War II. Vietnam came to replace Munich as the most potent symbol of what America should avoid in foreign policy. The charge of "appeasement" or "soft on communism" no longer automatically threw the burden of proof on those who questioned proposals for foreign intervention. One poll taken early in the 1970s showed a majority of Americans unwilling to intervene anywhere abroad except in the case of an invasion of Canada.

Vietnam thus raised powerful challenges to the realist ethos and Kennedy's concept of flexible response, with their emphasis on limited wars, graduated responses, fine-tuned interventions, and carefully orchestrated programs of diplomatic persuasion and military coercion that were aimed at circumscribed goals within rationally balanced power systems. How could any president mobilize popular opinion for such wars? Who would die willingly and heroically for such abstractions as the balance of power when principle and morality were not involved? If it were possible to mobilize opinion for such a war, how could public emotions of hatred and revenge be kept in check as the deaths, mutilations, and atrocities that inevitably accompanied war multiplied? Once these emotions were released, how could the war effort be adjusted without upsetting the power balance? And how could a president retreat when it became apparent that victory required an effort greater than the interests involved were worth?

The challenge to the Munich analogy and flexible response came from many different directions, however, and did not result in unification around any coherent alternative. Radicals portrayed Vietnam as the inevitable result of capitalist aggression and called for a new American internal revolution as the only way to prevent more Vietnams. Liberal moralists denounced Vietnam as a product of moral blindness and urged election of less evil officials. "Soft" realists argued that realist precepts should continue to guide American foreign policy, but be applied with more intelligence and restraint. "Hard" realists feared that the experience of Vietnam would lead to a new isolationism and prevent future necessary interventions. A great many conservatives and military men argued that the problem was not the original intervention in Vietnam, but the doctrine of graduated response and limited war that rejected a fight for total victory and tied the hands of America's armed forces. Perhaps the most typical reaction of ordinary citizens was a confused distaste for the war, a desire to end it but also an unwillingness to accept defeat. They demanded that the United States both win and get out.

CONTROVERSIAL ISSUES AND FURTHER READING

The best general survey of the Vietnam war is George Herring, *America's Longest War: The United States in Vietnam, 1950–1975* (1979). Another good one is Stanley Karnow, *Vietnam* (1983).

Early histories of the war in Vietnam generally agreed with the Johnson administration that the policy of gradual escalation, limited rather than total war, and offers of unconditional negotiations were proper extensions of the realist containment policy and the doctrine of flexible response. They likened the war in Vietnam to other successful instances of containment—the Marshall Plan, NATO, the Korean war, and the Cuban missile crisis. They accepted the Johnson administration's contention that the war was a product of North Vietnamese aggression rather than internal South Vietnamese dissent. South Vietnam seemed to these historians a testing ground for the Communist attempt to circumvent containment by resorting to wars of national liberation in place of direct conventional attacks. [For official administration positions, see *State Department White Paper*, publication 7839 (February 1965), and the testimony of Dean Rusk before the Senate Foreign Relations Committee in *The Vietnam Hearings*, introduced by J. William Fulbright (1966). For historical analysis, see Wesley R. Fishel, ed., *Vietnam: Anatomy of a Conflict* (1968). See also Frank N. Trager, *Why Vietnam?* (1966); Chester A. Bain, *Vietnam: The Roots of Conflict* (1967); and Maxwell D. Taylor, *Responsibility and Response* (1967).]

Ironically, while Dean Rusk, Lyndon Johnson, and their historian defenders relied on the rhetoric of restraint and realism to justify their policies, some of the war's earliest critics were among the primary formulators of the realist perspective on diplomatic history. George Kennan, Hans Morgenthau, and Walter Lippmann opposed the Vietnam war as an excessive commitment to an area that was not essential to the balance of power or to America's vital strategic, economic, or cultural interests. They believed that the nations of Southeast Asia were too culturally and politically diverse to fall like dominoes if the Communists won in Vietnam. These nations were even less likely to be faithful satellites of Russia or China. The realists also doubted that the United States could do much to stave off the Communists even if that were to its interest. The people of South Vietnam were too estranged from their American-backed government. Hans Morgenthau pointed out that a guerrilla war, "supported or at least not opposed by the indigenous population, can only be won by the indiscriminate killing of everybody in sight—by genocide."

At first the realists did not advocate immediate withdrawal, since the original intervention had committed American prestige. Instead, they favored the so-called enclave strategy, limiting the war effort to the protection of population enclaves while negotiating for a coalition or even a neutralist Communist government. Then, after the Tet offensive demonstrated that the United States could not even protect enclaves for any length of time, these "restrained" or "soft" realists urged unconditional withdrawal. [Hans J. Morgenthau, *Vietnam and the United States* (1965); George F. Kennan, testimony before the Senate Foreign Relations Committee in *The Vietnam Hearings* (1966). Lippmann offered his opinions in numerous syndicated columns, which are best summarized in Ronald Steel, *Walter Lippmann and the American Century* (1980).]

While "soft" realists were among the early opponents of the Vietnam war, their previous advocacy of containment, limited wars, and pragmatic considerations of power and interest over moralism were so much a part of the rationale for American policy toward Vietnam that many historians decided Vietnam was more than a mistaken instance of overzealous and overmilitarized containment. They began to argue that realism and containment were intrinsically flawed and inevitably brutalizing policies. They maintained that moral considerations had to play a greater role in foreign policy. Most of these liberal moralists were journalists rather than scholars, and they did not formulate a full philosophy of foreign relations or place the role of morality in context. They simply recited the numerous horrendous atrocities that resulted from the Vietnam war and showed how realist principles had led to them. [David Halberstam, *The Best and the Brightest* (1972); J. William Fulbright, *Old Myths and New Realities* (1964), as compared with his *The Crippled Giant* (1972); Frances Fitzgerald, *Fire in the Lake: The Vietnamese and the Americans in Vietnam* (1972).]

Meanwhile, the very few Western academic experts on the Vietnamese people helped undermine the government position on Vietnam. One of those experts was Joseph Buttinger, who wrote the best history of Vietnam in the English language. Buttinger said all but two authors worthy of inclusion in his bibliography were "critical or firmly opposed to the Vietnamese war." [Joseph Buttinger, *Vietnam: The Unforgettable Tragedy* (1977); *The Smaller Dragon: A Political History of Vietnam* (1958); and *Vietnam: A Dragon Embattled* (2 vols., 1967). See also Bernard Fall, *The Two Vietnams* (1963). Before Fall was killed in Vietnam, he also contributed *Vietnam Witness: 1953–1966* (1966) and, with Marcus G. Raskin, *The Vietnam Reader* (1965).] Works by American government officials also helped undermine the official American view, sometimes inadvertently. Douglas Pike, a government analyst, published an extensive description of the Vietcong that belied government claims that the Communists in the South were weak and dependent on the North. [Douglas Pike, *Viet Cong: The Organization and Techniques of the National Liberation Front of South Vietnam* (1966).] Chester Cooper, a member of the CIA, wrote pessimistic assessments of the war from within the government and publicly summarized them in his book, *The Lost Crusade* (1970). But probably *The Pentagon Papers*, a government study leaked to the *New York Times*, did most to discredit the Vietnam war. [Neil Sheehan et al., *The Pentagon Papers as Published by the New York Times* (1971).] *The Pentagon Papers* revealed, among other things, the covert operations that had provoked the Tonkin Gulf incident and the contingency planning for bombing the North that Johnson had ordered even while he was running against Barry Goldwater in 1964 on a campaign of restraint in Vietnam.

The atrocities of Vietnam and the disingenuousness of American leaders made the mild criticisms and prescriptions of the restrained realists and liberal moralists almost laughable to an increasing number of radical historians. These new revisionists regarded Vietnam as far more than a mistake resulting from understandable misapprehensions about communism or overzealous applications of necessary realistic prescriptions for the Cold War. Revisionists portrayed the war as the inevitable outcome of tragic evils built into the very foundation of America's political and economic capitalist system. They saw Vietnam as the result of America's driving need to dominate the Third World to provide the United States and its clients with ever-expanding markets and sources of raw materials. Gabriel Kolko provided the most rigorous economic determinist explanation of the war. [Gabriel Kolko, *Roots of American*

Foreign Policy (1969).] Moderate revisionists like Richard J. Barnet agreed with much of this. Yet they ranked other factors like the bureaucratic momentum of the national security elite and American racism alongside economic considerations as important in dictating American intervention. Moderate revisionists also were more likely to note distinctions between Vietnam and some of America's earlier wars, rather than portray them all as economically selfish and wrongheaded. [Richard J. Barnet, *Roots of War* (1972).]

By the 1970s, the volume of opposition to the U.S. role in Vietnam and America's ultimate defeat left few in the academic or historical world to defend the war. Lyndon Johnson maintained in his autobiography, *The Vantage Point* (1971), that he really had not lost the war, that Tet had been a disastrous defeat for the Communists, and that Westmoreland had had enough troops to win the war even without reinforcements at the time Johnson left office. [See also Walt Rostow, *The Diffusion of Power* (1972).] But not even General Westmoreland agreed with Johnson. Westmoreland and much of the military argued that they could have won the war had it not been that Johnson's misguided gradualist policies tied their hands. [William C. Westmoreland, *A Soldier Reports* (1976); Dave Richard Palmer, *Summons of the Trumpet* (1978); Harry G. Summers, *On Strategy: The Vietnam War in Context* (1982).]

The military found at least partial support from the "hard" realist view of such academic analysts as Guenter Lewy. Lewy insisted that the Vietnam war had been no more brutal than most wars. Moral criticism of the war had gained a foothold only because American interests in the conflict had not been clearly demonstrated and the South Vietnamese government had been corrupt and ineffectual. Lewy feared that the reaction to Vietnam would lead to an unwillingness to intervene where it was necessary to contain Communist expansion. The lesson of Vietnam, in his view, was simply to ensure that American interests were substantially involved and potential allies capable of doing their part before the United States intervened. [Guenter Lewy, *America in Vietnam* (1978).]

The vast majority of historians, however, rejected Lewy and moved toward the "soft" realist view that Vietnam had demonstrated the need for less American interventionism. Partisans of John F. Kennedy tried to demonstrate that Kennedy had been properly restrained, had understood the limits of America's interests and ability to affect the course of events in Vietnam, and would have withdrawn rather than escalate as Johnson did. They blamed Robert McNamara, Dean Rusk, and the military for presenting Kennedy with a false rosy picture of the progress of the South Vietnamese government and the war effort, thus leading him further into the war than he was inclined to go. [Arthur Schlesinger, Jr., *The Bitter Heritage: Vietnam and American Democracy, 1941–1966* (1967), and *A Thousand Days: John F. Kennedy in the White House* (1965); Roger Hilsman, *To Move a Nation: The Politics of Foreign Policy in the Administration of John F. Kennedy* (1967); Robert L. Gallucci, *Neither Peace nor Honor: The Politics of American Military Policy in Vietnam* (1975).]

Leslie Gelb, who had compiled the Pentagon Papers while a member of the government, convinced most historians that neither Kennedy nor Johnson were misled into Vietnam. He showed that Kennedy and Johnson both had good information. He thought both had escalated because politically they could not afford to accept defeat in a war. Gelb argued that Congress should be given a stronger voice in foreign policy to permit American withdrawal when circumstances dictated it but a president was too politically committed to bring himself to admit defeat. [Leslie H. Gelb, with Richard K. Betts, *The Irony of Vietnam: The System Worked* (1979). See also Warren I. Cohen, *Dean Rusk* (1980); Larry Berman, *Planning a Tragedy* (1982); and George Herring, *America's Longest War*, mentioned at the beginning of this essay.]

A careful study of the North Vietnamese side of the war by Wallace Thies provided further arguments against the interventionist propensities of flexible response. Thies inferred from the North Vietnamese materials available to Western scholars that there had been a bitter bureaucratic battle within North Vietnam in the early stages of American intervention. Militants in favor of all-out aid to the Vietcong had won out over moderate Premier Pham Van Dong and General Vo Nguyen Giap, who had wanted to restrict such aid and perhaps come to some compromise with the United States to avoid destruction of their hard-won industrial and economic progress. Once the militants had triumphed, for them to have accepted a compromise peace under American pressure would have been to admit error and destroy their internal political position. In such circumstances, gradual escalation had little chance of success. [Wallace J. Thies, *When Governments Collide: Coercion and Diplomacy in the Vietnam Conflict, 1964–1968* (1980).]

On popular response to Vietnam, see Thomas Powers, *The War at Home: Vietnam and the American People, 1964–1968* (1973); Alexander Kendrick, *The Wound Within* (1974); and Sidney Verba, Phillip Converse, and Milton J. Rosenberg, *Vietnam and the Silent Majority* (1970). For American policy in Southeast Asia generally, see Russell H. Fifield, *Americans in Southeast Asia: The Roots of Commitment* (1973). For American policy in Laos, see Charles A. Stevenson, *The End of Nowhere: American Policy Toward Laos since 1954* (1972), and Martin E. Goldstein, *American Policy Toward Laos* (1973).

On the strategy of flexible response, see John L. Gaddis, *Strategies of Containment* (1982); Desmond Ball, *Politics and Force Levels: The Strategic Missile Program of the Kennedy Administration* (1981); Franz Schurmann, *The Logic of World Power* (1974); Michael Mandelbaum, *The Nuclear Question* (1979); Glen T. Seaborg, *Kennedy, Khrushchev and the Test Ban* (1982); Harland B. Moulton, *From Superiority to Parity* (1972). On Kennedy's foreign policy generally, in addition to the general works listed on Vietnam, see revisionist works by Bruce Miroff, *Pragmatic Illusions* (1976), and Richard J. Walton, *Cold War and Counterrevolution* (1972). On Lyndon Johnson's general foreign policy, see Robert A. Divine, ed., *Exploring the Johnson Years* (1981); Doris Kearns, *Lyndon Johnson and the American Dream* (1966); Philip Geyelin, *Lyndon B. Johnson and the World* (1966); and Eric Goldman, *The Tragedy of Lyndon Johnson* (1968).

Europe in the Kennedy-Johnson years is covered in Alfred Grosser, *The Western Alliance* (1980); Richard J. Barnet; *The Alliance: America–Europe–Japan, Makers of the Postwar World* (1983); Curtis Cate, *The Ides of August: The Berlin Wall Crisis* (1961); and Honoré M. Catudal, Jr., *Kennedy and the Berlin Wall Crisis* (1980).

General surveys of United States–Latin American relations in this period, all of them very critical, are Gordon Connell-Smith, *The United States and Latin America* (1974); Samuel Bailey, *The U.S. and the Development of Latin America, 1945–1975* (1976); and Cole Blasier, *The Hovering Giant* (1976). The best book on the Bay of Pigs fiasco is Peter Wyden, *Bay of Pigs* (1979). On the Cuban missile crisis, see Graham Allison, *Essence of Decision* (1971); Abram Chayes, *The Cuban Missile Crisis* (1974); Herbert S. Dinnerstein, *The Making of the Missile Crisis, 1961* (1976); and David Detzer, *The Brink: Cuban Missile Crisis: 1962* (1979). On the Alliance for Progress, see Joseph Levinson and Juan de Onis, *The Alliance That Lost Its Way* (1979). For the Dominican Revolution and intervention, see Piero Gleijeses, *The Dominican Crisis* (1978).

On Kennedy's Congo policy, see Stephen R. Weissman, *American Foreign Policy in the Congo, 1960–1964* (1974); Richard D. Mahoney, *JFK: Ordeal in Africa* (1983); Henry F. Jackson, *From the Congo to Soweto: U.S. Foreign Policy Toward Africa since 1960* (1982); and Madeleine G. Kalb, *The Congo Cables: The Cold War in Africa—from Eisenhower to Kennedy* (1982).

CHAPTER 19

Richard Nixon and Henry Kissinger: Manipulating the Balance of Power

RICHARD NIXON'S "STRUCTURE OF PEACE"

In 1952, Richard Nixon had watched from his slot as Republican vice-presidential nominee while Dwight Eisenhower had finessed the issue of the Korean war by promising to go to Korea. Nixon learned the lesson well. Faced with a similar situation in 1968, a people wanting to end an unpopular war but unwilling to admit defeat, he devised a comparable finesse. He claimed to have a "secret plan" which, he implied, would permit the United States both to win and to get out of Vietnam. It was enough to help him win a narrow victory over Vice-President Hubert Humphrey. He then instituted a far-reaching foreign policy program that, while vague and ultimately unsuccessful in Vietnam, significantly changed other aspects of American diplomacy.

Nixon did not appear presidential. He was shy, unsure of his roots, bland, and unformed in his personality and culture. He compensated for his lack of personal center with forced shows of ebullience and toughness. He tried to emulate the heroic, simple, and forceful good-guy of his native West. In public he presented such a carefully cultivated personality that often his most sincere protestations rang false. The smile was too forced, the humor too heavy-handed, the sentiments too maudlin, the claims to highest morality too transparently false. His obsession with public relations was greater than that of most other modern presidents, few of whom have been shrinking violets. He always attributed defeats to the better public relations work of his opponents, never to their substance.

The insecurity that drove him and his advisors to be so concerned with his public image took on a more menacing form in private. He had to appear tough, one of the guys. His private conversation was better adapted to the locker room than to the White House, and it was mean and bitter rather than earthy and expansive in the manner of Harry Truman or Lyndon Johnson. "We floored those liberal sons of bitches," he would gloat. He often gave helter-skelter orders to his aides to play hard ball, toughen their positions, and "take care of" his enemies. Sometimes Nixon's violent musings were only a form of thinking out loud or talking for effect. Ironically, for all his tough talk, Nixon could not stand personal confrontations. He usually contrived to agree with everyone face to face, but afterward he would order aides to chastize, fire, deride, or destroy anyone in whom he sensed opposition.

Most of his close advisors learned to discount Nixon's private rhetoric and ignore some of his more brutal or hare-brained orders in the confident expectation that the president did not really mean them. Usually, if the advisors delayed long enough, the president would forget or revoke his commands. For instance, Nixon would regularly order Kissinger to cut off all aid to Israel until Israel agreed to American policy; then he would renege. But the atmosphere in the White House was like a shark tank. Some advisors inevitably took Nixon literally, and this helped lead to Watergate and the president's destruction.

Nixon's partner and chief operative in the foreign policy arena was his national security advisor, later secretary of state, Henry Kissinger. Kissinger, as a Harvard professor and protégé of Nelson Rockefeller, represented much of what Nixon hated most, the superior, Europe-oriented Eastern Establishment. Kissinger was a brilliant German-Jewish refugee who had become a major scholarly advocate of the realist, balance of power school of thought. He had written books in praise of the European diplomats who had been masters of early balances of power, Castlereagh, Metternich, and Bismarck. He had studied the uses of tactical nuclear weapons to maintain the balance of power in modern Europe. He had briefly advised the Kennedy administration and he had reported skeptically on the progress of the Vietnam war prior to his acceptance of office under Nixon.

Nixon looked past Kissinger's despised liberal credentials and saw in him a compatible advisor, because Nixon and Kissinger shared an especially hard version of the realist outlook. They did not fatalistically accept the balance of power and attempt to work within it; both were ready to take what they considered heroic risks to shape and manipulate it to America's advantage and to drive hard bargains with their adversaries. They shared a disdain for ideological factors or human rights in foreign affairs and were willing to base their policies on power politics almost exclusively.

Besides this policy compatibility, Nixon thought Kissinger would be a useful presidential tool because Kissinger was a political unknown who would be operating behind the scenes within the White House and thus be completely beholden to the president. This was unlike the secretary of state, William Rogers, who had to be approved by the Senate, who would run a large semi-independent agency, and who thus would have at least some independent status before Congress and the media. Nixon, by operating through Kissinger as a "back channel" to China, Russia, and Vietnam, could bypass the hated State Department bureaucracy with its "Ivy League liberals," conduct operations efficiently and secretly, and claim all credit for the president while sharing none with Secretary of State Rogers.

Nixon, however, did not anticipate the degree to which he might have to share credit with Kissinger. Kissinger could be accommodating and deferential in the presence of his superiors or those whose good opinion he needed, but he was extremely ambitious. He also was very arrogant. He drove his subordinates relentlessly, terrorized them with petulant spells of anger, regaled them with snide stories about "our meatball president," and used their reports masterfully in presenting policy options to Nixon. Some staff members advised newcomers who asked how to get along on the national security advisor's team: "Think of Henry Kissinger as a corkscrew, and think of yourself as a cork." Many nonetheless managed to develop a respect and affection for him. One aide gave him for his office a picture poster of a huge gorilla with the caption, "When I want your opinion, I'll beat it out of you."

Kissinger was even more ruthless with his bureaucratic rivals than with his subordinates, and quickly eliminated all competition for the ear of Nixon on foreign affairs. Then, as his role in the spectacular back channel negotiations with China, Russia, and Vietnam became known, Nixon permitted Kissinger to hold public news conferences rather than anonymous "backgrounders." Kissinger, with his brilliant analyses and quick wit, became an instant media star. His favorite technique was to poke fun at his own foibles, particularly his megalomania. When asked if he had read Bernard and Marvin Kalb's biography *Kissinger*, he said: "No, but I like the title." After his appointment as secretary of state, one newsman inquired if he preferred to be called Mr. Secretary or Dr. Secretary. Kissinger replied, "I don't stand on protocol. If you will just call me 'Excellency,' it will be okay." When he unveiled the statue of Thomas Jefferson during the opening of the Jefferson room on the eighth floor of the State Department, he quipped with mock disappointment, "Oh, I thought it would be me."

In this way Kissinger established a separate identity from the president, and as Watergate eroded Nixon's power and reputation, Kissinger took more and more public responsibility for foreign affairs. Nixon had to move him out of the White House and put him in formal charge of foreign policy as secretary of state to protect the administration's diplomatic successes and ongoing negotiations from the taint of the White House scandal, and Kissinger survived to carry the Nixon-Kissinger policies into the administration of Gerald Ford.

At the outset of the Nixon administration, Nixon and Kissinger analyzed the balance of power and believed they had a way to stabilize the Cold War, extricate the United States from Vietnam, and fashion a "structure of peace." First, recognizing the strain between China and the Soviet Union, they would reopen diplomatic relations with China. Cooperation with China would alter the balance of power and give the Soviet Union an incentive to come to its own accommodation with the United States. In order to win such an accommodation, both Russia and China should be willing to withdraw their support from North Vietnam and the Vietcong. The Vietnamese Communists then would have to accept a compromise settlement that would permit Nixon to withdraw American forces.

Once extricated from Vietnam, Nixon and Kissinger had no intention of entangling American troops in any further wars of attrition outside the major arenas of power. In July of 1969, Richard Nixon proclaimed his Nixon Doctrine. The United States would supply money and materiel, but not men, to nations fighting internal or external enemies of the United States. America would intervene with manpower only if the enemy were a nuclear power. In line with this strategic doctrine, Nixon announced that the limited uses of American manpower would permit him to phase out the military draft. He also reluctantly permitted a Congress that was reacting against Vietnam to reduce spending on conventional forces in exchange for continued support of a new generation of strategic weapons—the B-1 bomber, the Trident submarine, and the cruise and MX missiles. As a result, between 1968 and 1974, the number of American air force squadrons fell from 220 to 169, army and marine divisions from 23 to 16, and navy ships from 976 to 495.

Much of this program coincided with the suggestions of moderate and liberal critics of the war in Vietnam. These critics had demanded détente, a strategic arms agreement with the Soviet Union, the recognition of China, the end of the draft, withdrawal from Vietnam, and restraint in future interventions. Conservatives, who regarded the long-time anti-Communist Nixon if not Harvard professor Kissinger as one of their own, looked on aghast as the grand design unfolded. By the time Nixon resigned in the wake of Watergate and Gerald Ford replaced him, conservatives were denouncing the Nixon-Kissinger policies as near treason. They called the Strategic Arms Limitation Agreement a victory for the Soviets. They claimed that negotiations with Moscow merely lowered the West's guard while the Soviets cheated and continued their inexorable march toward world conquest. They reviled the Vietnam peace agreement as a thinly disguised American surrender that encouraged world communism. They regarded the opening to China with great suspicion and bewailed what they considered the betrayal of the Nationalist government on Taiwan.

Nixon and Kissinger thought these conservative critics lacked a full understanding of the objective world situation and the pragmatism necessary to deal with it. The USSR would achieve nuclear parity regardless of what America did. The best the United States could do was to limit Soviet power and induce it to moderation through continuation of American strength, the manipulation of the balance of power, and hard bargaining for verifiable agreements. To go beyond this, to seek as conservatives wished to change the Soviet domestic system as well as its external behavior, was to exceed America's capabilities and risk nuclear war.

Nixon and Kissinger regretted the conservative backlash, but were relatively gentle in trying to answer its charges. They considered themselves conservatives who were seeking their goals realistically within the constraints imposed by the limits of American power. Nixon and Kissinger were less tolerant of criticism from the Left. Radicals and antiwar activists were beyond the pale, fit objects for FBI and CIA surveillance. Nixon also hated the "Ivy League liberals." Kissinger naturally was not so antagonistic, but he still regarded them as deluded and often hypocritical. Liberal critics and "soft" realists like George Kennan failed to understand the need for strength and toughness. They were not truly realistic.

Liberals and soft realists would get out of Vietnam rapidly because they believed South Vietnam could never form a viable government, win the full support of the people, and effectively resist the Communists of the North and the South. Nixon and Kissinger would stay in Vietnam for four agonizing years at enormous risk and cost for a peace agreement that, while providing little protection for South Vietnam, would give some credibility to Nixon's claim that he had won an honorable peace.

Liberals and soft realists favored minimal deterrence. They would emphasize second-strike nuclear weapons on the grounds that Soviet parity made a first strike incredible and the threat of one merely served to destabilize the situation. Nixon and Kissinger insisted that a first strike capability, tactical nuclear weapons, and some measure of counterforce strategy were necessary, however implausible their actual use might be, in order to offset superior Soviet conventional forces in Europe or the Middle East and to make the American deterrent more credible.

Liberals and soft realists would back away from involvement in Third World revolutions and wars and concern themselves primarily with the major sources of international power, the industrial democracies of Western Europe and Japan. They believed that Third World nationalism would restrict Russia's ability to exploit revolutions and that the United States could deal with Russia directly if it tried to install military bases in the Third World that threatened vital American interests. Nixon and Kissinger, despite their adherence to the Nixon Doctrine, took a more activist outlook on the Third World. They did not believe that Third World nationalism would prevent Soviet penetration but rather invite it. They would lavish money, equipment, and covert assistance to prevent the triumph of unfriendly radicals, even if the pro-U.S. regimes they were protecting were feeble, corrupt, and tyrannical.

Nixon encouraged his adversaries to believe he was not only strong, but somewhat erratic. Like Khrushchev, he hoped this reputation would cow them into submission. Kissinger's hardness was more intellectual. While ignoring some of Nixon's habitual goadings to be tougher, he used the threat that Nixon might get out of control to browbeat his negotiating partners. Meanwhile, he did his best to educate the American people to accept his version of hard realism. Opposition to Vietnam must not be allowed to drive the United States inward to nurse its wounds and renounce its world leadership, Kissinger warned. Americans must not return to their historical cycle of exuberant overextension and sulking isolationism. The United States needed continuity, confidence, and restraint based on a profound vision of American interest. The United States had to adapt to the limits of its strength without abdicating its responsibility to maintain the balance of power. That meant defending the geopolitical equilibrium even if it was challenged in the guise of human rights and a "progressive tide."

Of course, Kissinger said, "We cannot, and should not, be wedded to a blind defense of every status quo. Justice as well as stability must be a goal of American foreign policy, and indeed they are linked. Yet there are changes in the international balance that can threaten our nation's security and have to be resisted however they come about." Not only must such changes be resisted, Kissinger warned, but they must be resisted early, an inherently ambiguous task.

> For if one waits till the challenge is clear, the cost of resisting grows exponentially; in the nuclear age it may become prohibitive. A nation and its leaders must choose between moral certainty coupled with exorbitant risk, and the willingness to act on unprovable assumptions to deal with challenges when they are manageable. . . . The qualities that distinguish a great statesman are prescience and courage, not analytical intelligence. He must have a conception of the future and the courage to move toward it while it is still shrouded to most of his compatriots.[1]

Many of the situations in which Nixon and Kissinger asserted themselves so strongly were indeed ambiguous and shrouded. Nixon and Kissinger gave strong support to reactionary Third World regimes on the grounds that in areas with deep tribal, religious, or racial division and with no tradition of democracy, force-fed mass participation was more likely to lead to totalitarianism than to democracy. Friendly authoritarianism was far preferable to hostile totalitarianism. Thus, they supported tyrannical regimes in such nations as Iran and Chile. They decided to give greater support to white supremacist regimes in Africa until events made that impossible. They adopted extraordinarily harsh measures in Southeast Asia. They made heavy expenditures on obsolescent or ineffective nuclear weapons not because these would be useful in themselves, but because they were needed to drive a hard bargain with the Soviet Union. After all, as Kissinger was so fond of saying, Moscow had never responded to unilateral restraint except with more aggression, and moderation was a virtue only in those thought to have an alternative.

There was some plausibility in the hard bargaining concept of foreign policy followed by Nixon and Kissinger. Yet it was ill adapted to the open and often idealistic society of American democracy. To drive hard bargains and manipulate the balance of power as they wished required harsh, dangerous, and credible threats, often in support of undemocratic and unsympathetic regimes. For those threats to be credible, be they new bombing campaigns in Vietnam, vast appropriations for weapons to force an arms limitation agreement with the Soviets, or military mobilization on behalf of some Third World country in trouble, Nixon and Kissinger needed the support of the American people and Congress. Yet their bombing, arms expenditures, and mobilizations often seemed to Congress and the people to be out of proportion to the crisis, ineffectual even if carried out, supportive of bad causes, and drawing the earth closer to World War III.

Nixon and Kissinger could not win support by hinting to Americans that administration threats were primarily bargaining chips; other nations would then perceive their moves as mere bluffs. Nixon and Kissinger could not ask

---

[1] Henry Kissinger, *Years of Upheaval* (Boston, 1982), pp. 168–169.

Americans simply to trust them. Vietnam had exhausted much of the fund of trust between government and people, and Watergate eliminated the remainder. Kissinger and Nixon relied instead on secrecy in their negotiations, deviousness in securing congressional and public backing for their projects, and Nixon's own image of toughness and somewhat erratic behavior to try to extort better bargains than the objective condition of the balance of power might have allowed. In some areas they performed as virtuosos and succeeded brilliantly; in others they failed abjectly. Nixon and Kissinger blamed most of their failures on the sapping of executive authority by Watergate. Yet many of those failures were inherent in the diplomatic situation and were only made worse by the overreaching of Nixon and Kissinger.

WITHDRAWAL FROM VIETNAM

Vietnam was a bone in the throat of the Nixon-Kissinger strategy. Nixon and Kissinger believed that if they withdrew without an honorable peace, the United States would lose the credibility necessary for their goal of restructuring the global balance of power. An honorable peace meant the same to them as it had meant to Kennedy and Johnson—the people of South Vietnam had to be free to choose their own government. Americans could not permit North Vietnam or the Vietcong to impose a Communist government on an unwilling populace. The United States would make peace and withdraw only if North Vietnam withdrew its troops and permitted internationally supervised elections. Any peace agreement had to give South Vietnam at least a reasonable chance to survive as an independent nation.

North Vietnam was not about to honor the wishes even of a majority of southerners to keep Vietnam permanently split. No one trusted anyone else to hold fair elections, even if it were possible in the midst of a civil war. The South Vietnamese government argued that the elections they had already held (although obviously rigged) demonstrated that they had the support of the people. The Vietcong argued that if the people truly supported the South Vietnamese government, their Communist guerrilla movement would not have survived. In fact, the majority of southerners probably opposed the Communists. Unfortunately, they were far more divided among themselves than the North Vietnamese. They probably would not have given majority support to any government, and they were generally reluctant to help or fight for either side.[2]

Nixon's "secret plan" to handle the Vietnam conundrum seems to have been little more than a vague intention to clarify America's negotiating position, withdraw some American troops to buy time from domestic oppo-

---

[2] The difficulty of determining the true sentiments of the South Vietnamese was illustrated by Henry Kissinger's estimate that the Vietcong controlled only 10 percent of the South Vietnamese population, yet maintained an infrastructure in 80 percent of the country's hamlets and subjected 65 percent of the total population and 81 percent of the rural population to some influence, including levees on rice and production.

nents for hard bargaining, get the USSR and China to reduce their support for the Communists in return for détente, and increase pressure on North Vietnam for a settlement through bombing and Nixon's reputation for fierceness.

Nixon's opportunity to display his fierceness and determination came within a month of his inauguration. North Vietnamese troops began to increase their attacks in South Vietnam. Nixon and Kissinger regarded this increase as a violation of the tacit agreement between Lyndon Johnson and North Vietnam that had led to negotiations—Johnson would halt bombing in the North, and the North would avoid attacks on major cities or across the demilitarized zone. Nixon and Kissinger responded to the activities of the North Vietnamese troops not by resuming the bombing of North Vietnam, but by beginning secret bombing of Communist sanctuaries in Cambodia.

Later, Kissinger justified the secrecy of the Cambodian bombings on the grounds that it demonstrated determination without forcing a public confrontation with Hanoi, China, or the Soviets. The secrecy also aided Cambodian Premier Sihanouk, who Kissinger insisted welcomed attacks on the Vietnamese in his country, but whose weakness and tenuous neutral position would force him to protest if the bombing were acknowledged.[3] When the Communists surprisingly did not make a public protest, Nixon and Kissinger decided to continue both the bombing and the secrecy. With an eye no doubt to avoiding domestic as well as foreign repercussions, they hid the bombing from Congress, the American people, and much of their own military and government. When inevitably word of the secret bombing began to leak, they put phone taps on suspected government officials and their newspaper contacts. Thus, they added still more to the heritage of distrust and the credibility gap that already existed over Vietnam.

In conjunction with the secret bombing of Cambodia, Nixon publicly announced his intention to withdraw some American troops and build up the South Vietnamese to fight their own war. This was little more than the program he had inherited from Johnson, but Nixon put his own stamp on it by christening the policy Vietnamization. He also announced some clarifications of his negotiating posture and sent an ultimatum to Ho Chi Minh, warning that if peace were not made by November, he would resort to "measures of great force." Then he sent Kissinger to meet secretly with the North Vietnamese to explore the chances for peace outside the limelight of the public negotiations Johnson had initiated.

To the dismay of Nixon and Kissinger, the North Vietnamese continued to scorn the American offer to make peace on the basis of a mutual withdrawal of American and North Vietnamese troops and internationally supervised elections. The North Vietnamese demanded instead that the United

---

[3] In a press conference, Sihanouk showed his fancy footwork. "I have not protested the bombings of Viet Cong camps because I have not heard of the bombings. I was not in the know, because in certain areas of Cambodia there are no Cambodians. . . . Here it is—the first report about several B-52 bombings. Yet I have not been informed about that at all, because I have not lost any houses, any countrymen, nothing, nothing."

States withdraw unconditionally and leave power in the hands of a coalition government composed of Communists and other South Vietnamese who stood for "peace, independence, and neutrality." They made clear that Nguyen Van Thieu and the other top South Vietnamese officials did not fit this definition and would not be part of the coalition. Nixon and Kissinger regarded the North Vietnamese proposal as a demand for outright surrender—the Americans would have to leave South Vietnam and overthrow its government on their way out.

This left them with the same problem Johnson had faced. American troops were leaving, the South Vietnamese buildup was at least uncertain, and the North Vietnamese would not only continue to fight, but refuse to release American prisoners of war. Nixon and Kissinger furiously surveyed the possibility of inflicting new "savage blows" on the Communists. They even considered using tactical nuclear weapons. They concluded, however, that no such program could work, and Nixon thought that halting the troop withdrawal would destroy his domestic support. He decided to back away from his ultimatum. He would rely on the buildup of South Vietnam, rally America's "silent majority" in support of Vietnamization, and search for new opportunities to use air and sea power to cover and compensate for troop withdrawals.

An opportunity to increase pressure on North Vietnam arrived in March of 1970, when General Lon Nol overthrew Cambodia's neutralist Prince Sihanouk and publicly allied himself with the U.S. attempt to eject the North Vietnamese and Vietcong from their Cambodian sanctuaries. Nixon sent American and South Vietnamese troops on a major sweep into Cambodia. The war there now was public. Nixon told the American people that the United States could not stand by like a "pitiful helpless giant." The deposed Sihanouk, however, sided with the Communist Khmer Rouge and that tiny faction, supported by North Vietnam, steadily increased its size and threat to the weak government of Lon Nol. The Khmer Rouge ultimately would take over Cambodia about the same time Laos and Saigon fell to the Communists.

Meanwhile, the Cambodian invasion jolted American opponents of the war out of the lull produced by Vietnamization and Nixon's appeal to the silent majority. Student strikes and protests broke out across the nation. National Guard troops shot several students at Kent State and Jackson State universities. The Senate symbolically withdrew its consent to the Tonkin Gulf Resolution and the Nixon administration barely beat back congressional attempts to cut off funds for the Cambodian incursion. Nixon stayed "one jump ahead of the sheriff" at home by speeding troop withdrawals from Vietnam, but he also stepped up bombing of the Laotian and Cambodian sanctuaries. Then, in a test of the progress of Vietnamization, he approved a South Vietnamese invasion into Laos. The United States would supply no troops, only air support. The invasion put a crimp in the North Vietnamese buildup for an offensive, but cost South Vietnam even more dearly. After six weeks of bloody fighting, the South Vietnamese troops had to retreat back across the border, as American television cameras filmed soldiers clinging desperately to the runners of American helicopters in their haste to get out.

With opposition to the war growing, Nixon and Kissinger made a major concession in their secret peace talks with North Vietnam. They no longer demanded that North Vietnam withdraw its troops to match the American withdrawal. Kissinger later pointed out that the offer included a prohibition against further infiltration of men and supplies from the North which, he said, would have left the Communist armies already in the South to wither. In any case, the North Vietnamese rejected the settlement unless the United States also abandoned Thieu. Thieu forestalled such a deal by forcing his two major domestic opponents to withdraw from the coming election. Nixon and Kissinger, enraged as they were by Thieu's maneuver, feared that to remove American support from him would throw South Vietnam into chaos. Negotiations sputtered, and North Vietnam prepared a major offensive for 1972. Nixon and Kissinger prayed that their dramatic initiatives toward China and the Soviets ultimately would pressure North Vietnam to compromise.

In March of 1972, North Vietnam launched its long-awaited offensive across the DMZ and from Laos and Cambodia into the South. Only 95,000 American troops remained in Vietnam, and only 6,000 of them were combat forces. The supposedly revitalized South Vietnamese army would have to stop the Communist forces on its own. It fought surprisingly well, but in the end it failed. Nixon then decided to go all out to end the war. He ordered B-52 strikes across the DMZ and attacks on the fuel depots around Hanoi and Haiphong harbor. Four Soviet vessels were hit in the raids. Two months later, at the risk of aborting the summit meeting scheduled with the Soviets, Nixon announced a further escalation. Since the North Vietnamese still rejected the American peace offer, he blockaded North Vietnam, mined Haiphong harbor, and increased the bombing. Yet the Soviets did not cancel the summit, and even China advised the North Vietnamese to compromise. Meanwhile, with tremendous losses on both sides, the North Vietnamese offensive ground to a stalemate.

In the face of these military and diplomatic setbacks, the North Vietnamese moved toward some concessions. On October 8, 1972, they dropped their insistence that Thieu resign and agreed that the coalition they had been demanding in South Vietnam would be only a commission to supervise the cease-fire and elections, not a government. Thieu was not mollified. He insisted that the North Vietnamese withdraw their troops before peace could be made. He had not objected when Nixon and Kissinger first had proposed to concede the North Vietnamese presence in the South because he did not think the North Vietnamese would accept any compromise. Now that they had, he threw every roadblock he could in the way of a cease-fire agreement.

Nixon and Kissinger found themselves in a very difficult situation. If they indicated their acceptance while Thieu rejected the peace agreement, it would disrupt American domestic unity and might lead to a quick South Vietnamese collapse once the United States withdrew. Yet if Nixon and Kissinger themselves refused the North Vietnamese terms to protect Thieu,

North Vietnam could publish its concessions, and opponents undoubtedly would succeed in getting Congress to cut off further funds for the war. Nixon and Kissinger tried to stall. Kissinger announced just before the American presidential election that "peace was at hand." Then he pressed Thieu to accept the agreement while promising to get some clarifications and modifications from the North Vietnamese. The North Vietnamese, however, knew Nixon and Kissinger would be under tremendous pressure to ratify the peace agreement and demanded new concessions of their own.

After his landslide reelection, Nixon decided to cut the Gordian knot. He sent new waves of B-52s to attack Hanoi in the so-called Christmas bombing. American ships also reseeded the mines in Haiphong harbor. The North Vietnamese finally accepted a peace agreement along the lines negotiated in October. Nixon and Kissinger forced Thieu to accept it after they gained a few cosmetic concessions for him. They also promised Thieu that the United States would reenter the war in full force if North Vietnam violated the accord.

Nixon and Kissinger proclaimed they had won an honorable peace in Vietnam. They had retrieved American prisoners of war. They had left Thieu in power. They had gained a cease-fire in Laos as well as Vietnam (there was no cease-fire in Cambodia because the North Vietnamese claimed to have no control over the Khmer Rouge, which was probably true). They had established international inspection procedures to prevent infiltration of further men and supplies to the North Vietnamese remaining in the South, which presumably would leave those forces to wither away. They claim to this day that the peace collapsed only because the United States lost its nerve and determination.

When North Vietnam continued to infiltrate through Laos, Cambodia, and the DMZ, the Communist members of the international inspection force prevented action against it. Nixon, weakened and distracted by Watergate, hesitated to resume bombing the North until all the prisoners were back. He continued bombing in Cambodia, where there never had been a cease-fire, but the inability of Sihanouk and Lon Nol to reconcile prevented a united front against the Khmer Rouge. Finally, Congress took matters out of the hands of Nixon and Kissinger. In May 1973, Congress cut off funds for further bombing in Cambodia. A month later it forced Nixon to cease military activities in all of Indochina as of August 15. It also steadily cut back economic aid to South Vietnam. Then, in November of 1973, it passed the War Powers Act. This required the president to notify Congress within forty-eight hours of committing troops abroad and to withdraw those troops in sixty days unless Congress explicitly authorized them to stay.

In 1975, after Nixon had been forced from office, the deluge finally hit. The Khmer Rouge, led by Pol Pot, toppled Lon Nol's regime and then killed millions of its own citizens and depopulated its cities in a fanatical back-to-the-soil movement. The North Vietnamese launched preliminary attacks in a projected two-year offensive to defeat South Vietnam, only to have the South collapse in a matter of months. American TV watchers were treated to the unedifying spectacle of American soldiers beating off thousands of Vietnamese who were seeking to escape the Communists aboard the last helicopters evacuating the American embassy. Laos quickly followed Cambodia and South Vietnam, with 40,000 North Vietnamese troops helping the Pathet Lao overthrow the neutralist coalition headed by Souvana Phouma. America's only comfort was that the Communist regimes of Southeast Asia could not unite to expand their influence. North Vietnam invaded Cambodia, defeated Pol Pot, and set off a continuing guerrilla war that ranged China and many Cambodians against North Vietnam and its Soviet allies.[4]

Critics of Nixon and Kissinger argued that the Vietnam settlement had never been more than a "decent interval" to permit American withdrawal, and that Nixon and Kissinger knew it. Neither the North nor the South Vietnamese ever abandoned their military campaigns against one another. The South made a grab for territory to strengthen its position immediately after the settlement, a settlement Thieu never formally accepted. The North was a bit more cautious until the Americans were gone, but it never stopped its infiltration into the South. The international inspection commission set up by the agreement was unworkable, unable to agree on its observations, let alone do anything about violations of the peace agreement. The United States simply could not continue to prop up governments that had so little standing with their own people. Nixon and Kissinger had expended vast numbers of lives and enormous resources to do that, then had covered their inevitable failure with a paper-thin peace agreement whose inevitable demise they blamed on the media, antiwar activists, congressional spinelessness, and Watergate's sapping of executive power.

Yet for all the bitterness left over from Vietnam, there was never a deep quarrel over who lost Vietnam as there had been over who lost China; there was simply agreement that there should be no more Vietnams. The United States should avoid significant intervention, especially with troops, in ambiguous Third World civil wars that did not involve vital American interests and that the United States was not prepared to win quickly. That consensus, of course, left plenty of room for argument as to whether specific situations in Chile, Angola, Afghanistan, Iran, Nicaragua, Lebanon, or El Salvador fitted the definition of another Vietnam. As the lessons from World War I, Munich, and Pearl Harbor had failed to provide adequate guidance for later events, so too did those of Vietnam.

THE OPENING TO CHINA

Nixon and Kissinger regarded China as the key link in their new structure of peace. They hoped closer relations with China would demoralize North

---

[4] Kissinger speculated that America's withdrawal from Indochina actually hurt American relations with China and the moderate architect of China's opening to the West, Chou En-lai. Chou had not wanted a powerful Vietnam on China's border, nor did he want the Khmer Rouge to triumph in Cambodia. When the United States failed to stop the takeover in Cambodia and South Vietnam, Chou's influence with Mao declined in favor of the more radical Gang of Four, Kissinger believed.

Vietnam and the other Communist forces in Southeast Asia, while giving the United States leverage against the Soviet Union as well.

Much of the initiative for improved relations came from China rather than the United States. In 1969, Mao Tse-tung began sending ambassadors to many nations with which he had broken relations during the Cultural Revolution. He also sent signals to the United States through Pakistan and Rumania that he was ready to resume the contacts America and China had previously conducted through their embassies in Warsaw, talks Mao had broken off in response to the Vietnam war and the Cambodian invasion.

On April 6, 1971, China made an even more dramatic gesture to illustrate its intentions. It invited the American ping-pong team, which was playing in a world tournament in Japan, to visit China. The United States signaled its understanding by steadily reducing its embargo on trade to China. In February of 1970, Nixon and Kissinger already had indicated their willingness to take a new tack toward China by abandoning the "2 1/2 war doctrine" for a "1 1/2 war doctrine." Nixon explained that the United States no longer had to plan and arm for fighting simultaneous wars with the Soviets and Chinese, along with a half a war in the Third World, because there was no longer a Sino-Soviet bloc that would coordinate a Soviet invasion of Europe with a Chinese invasion in Asia. Since the United States never had armed sufficiently to implement a 2 1/2 war doctrine anyway, the announcement cost nothing strategically. It merely brought theory into line with reality. It also signaled China that the United States no longer considered it an inextricable part of some monolithic Communist conspiracy against American interests.

Nixon and the Chinese arranged for Kissinger to be spirited into Peking from Pakistan on a secret trip to improve Chinese-American relations and pave the way for a summit meeting between Nixon and Mao in China. Kissinger and Chinese Premier Chou En-lai found they had much in common in their strategic thought. Chou was terribly worried by China's 4,000-mile border with the Soviet Union. China had never recognized that border, which actually divided Mongolians from Mongolians and Manchurians from Manchurians, rather than Russians from Chinese. The Soviets were steadily building their forces along the border. They had stationed twenty-one divisions there in 1969, increased that number to thirty-three by 1971, and to forty-five by 1973. China feared that as Soviet power grew, the USSR would be tempted to use force to prevent the rise of another great enemy. Chou wanted to enlist the United States in its confrontation with Moscow. He urged that the United States organize an anti-Soviet coalition stretching from Japan through China, Pakistan, Iran, and Turkey to Western Europe. China, the most revolutionary of Communist states, was willing to cooperate with capitalists and reactionaries to deter a Soviet attack.

Nixon and Kissinger shared Chou's desire to deter the Soviets. According to Kissinger, "Should the Soviet Union succeed in reducing China to impotence, the impact on the world balance of power would be scarcely less catastrophic than a Soviet conquest of Europe. Once it was clear that America was unable to prevent major aggression in Asia, Japan would begin to dissociate from us. Faced with a Soviet colossus free to concentrate entirely on the West, Europe would lose confidence and all its neutralist tendencies would accelerate. Southeast Asia, too, would bend to the dominant trend: the radical forces in the Middle East, South Asia, Africa, and even the Americas would gain the upper hand." The United States would have to resist any Soviet attack on China and to educate the American people to understand the necessity for protecting a Communist and potentially hostile nation.

Yet American strategy did not parallel China's in every particular. The United States did not have China's interest in "unremitting, undifferentiated confrontations with the USSR." Unlike China, the United States had the power to match Soviet arms and thwart its adventures. Nixon had the option to play for time, to see what modifications of Soviet policy and conduct could be brought about by deterrence and negotiations. He and Kissinger did not want to become a card China could play against the Soviets, and did not want to play the China card itself so blatantly as to eliminate chances for leverage, negotiations, and détente with the Soviets. "Complex as it might be to execute such a tactic," Kissinger said, "it was always better for us to be closer to either Moscow or Peking than either was to the other—except in the limiting case of a Soviet attack on China."[5]

Nixon's dramatic trip to China sealed the rapprochement between the United States and China. Television cameras recorded the astounding sight of the former Red-baiting Nixon receiving a grand reception in Peking, conferring with a smiling Mao who had just put his nation through a horrible revolutionary purge in the Cultural Revolution, waving atop the Great Wall, and talking strategy with Chou En-lai, the man with whom John Foster Dulles had refused to shake hands at the Geneva Conference of 1954. Aware of the symbolism of all this, Nixon had had burly aides block the aisles of Air Force One after it had landed in Peking. This permitted him to emerge on the tarmac by himself to shake hands ostentatiously with Chou. As a result of the trip, the United States and China established liaison offices in Washington and Peking that were embassies in all but name. (Jimmy Carter would extend formal recognition to China in January 1979.)

Nixon's China coup was not without cost. Since the Chinese hinted during the summit that they would use only peaceful means to liberate Taiwan, Nixon and Kissinger said the United States would lessen its military presence in Taiwan as tensions in the area decreased. The United States would withdraw entirely if the Chinese reached a peaceful settlement with the island. This meant that even though the United States continued nominally to recognize the Nationalist government on Taiwan as the legal government of China (thus precluding full diplomatic relations with mainland China and the establishment of an embassy in Peking), it significantly reduced the American commitment to Taiwan. The fallout was immediate. Western allies broke ranks to eject the Taiwan government from the United Nations and replace it with the Peking government. The United States opposed the move but none too vigorously.

[5] Henry Kissinger, *Years of Upheaval* (Boston, 1982), pp. 51–55.

Nixon's trip also produced a shock in Japan. Secretary of State William Rogers had the unenviable task of informing the Japanese that Nixon would go to China only one hour before Nixon announced his trip publicly on television. Until then, the Japanese had conformed to Washington's wishes and abjured the political and economic profit they might have gained from seeking closer relations with China. Now the United States seemed to be stealing a march on the Japanese by reversing its policy. Fortunately, the shock did not do lasting damage. The Chinese were so anxious for Western unity against the Soviets that they did not try to play Japan and the United States against one another. China even urged, in a historic reversal of policy, that the United States and Japan maintain close relations.

Nixon's China opening also did not have the effect the president expected on the situation in Southeast Asia. Chou made clear to Nixon and Kissinger that he did not want total victory for North Vietnam or for the Khmer Rouge in Cambodia and that he wanted the United States to stay involved on the continent of Asia. Still, he was not willing to withdraw support from the Communists in Vietnam and Cambodia to help bring this about; he would only urge some compromise. With the American position in Indochina weakening, none of the combatants accepted such mild Chinese advice. Nixon's desperate hope that he could settle the Vietnam war in Peking or Moscow would prove totally futile.

THE SOVIETS AND SALT

Although there was always the possibility that Moscow would react to Nixon playing the China card by freezing American relations rather than becoming more amenable, Nixon and Kissinger gambled that the Russians would choose cooperation. They turned out to be correct. The Soviets received Kissinger on a secret trip to Moscow to arrange a summit meeting even though American bombing in North Vietnam had just damaged four Russian ships. The Soviets also went ahead with the Nixon-Brezhnev summit despite the renewed American bombing in May 1972. Like the Chinese leaders, however, the Soviets refused or were unable to force Hanoi out of the Vietnam war as the price of détente. Nixon had wanted Kissinger during his secret preliminary trip to Moscow to make any further discussions dependent on Russian agreement to get North Vietnam to settle, but Kissinger had evaded that dictum and so his meeting and the subsequent summit turned primarily to discussions of strategic arms limitations.

Nixon and Kissinger emerged from the summit of June 1972 with the first SALT agreement. (SALT was the acronym for Strategic Arms Limitation Talks.) They agreed to limit both the Americans and the Soviets to 2 antiballistic missile (ABM) sites and 200 interceptors each. Nixon had rammed the American ABM program through Congress primarily as a bargaining chip, and he and Kissinger believed this had formed a primary incentive for the Soviets to strike a deal.

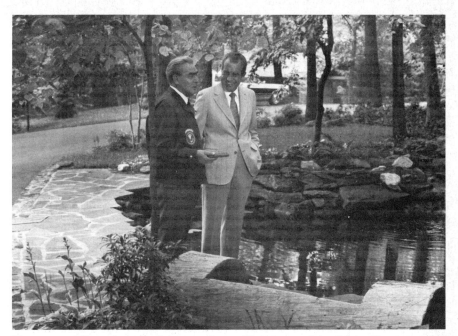

Figure 22   The architects of détente, Leonid Brezhnev of the Soviet Union and Richard Nixon of the United States. Photo courtesy of the National Archives and the Nixon Presidential Materials Project.

SALT I also placed limits on offensive weapons. The Soviets were permitted 62 submarines with 950 launchers and 1,410 land-based missiles, 308 of which could be monster heavy missiles. The United States accepted substantially fewer launchers. It could deploy 44 submarines with 710 launchers and 1,000 land-based missiles. Nixon and Kissinger believed they had achieved parity, however, because America's superior bomber force of B-52s was not counted against the American total. Neither were the shorter-range nuclear weapons stationed by the United States, Great Britain, and France in Europe. In addition, if the USSR had more launchers, the United States had more warheads, because 700 American missiles were equipped with multiple warheads that were independently targeted (Multiple Independently Targeted Re-entry Vehicles, or MIRVs). SALT I also prohibited interference with spy satellites, the means by which Nixon and Kissinger believed they could verify Soviet compliance. Nixon and Kissinger thought they had gotten a good deal for the United States, because they had in effect frozen missile deployment for five years, and none of the new U.S. weapons—MX, Trident, and cruise missiles—would be ready for deployment within that time.

The Moscow summit and SALT I, combined with the opening to China and the Vietnam peace agreement, brought Nixon and Kissinger to the pinnacle of their popularity. That popularity, however, quickly began to slide downhill. Not only did the bitterness and turmoil of Vietnam survive the peace agreement, not only did Watergate progressively undermine Nixon's credibility, but some of the summit agreements went sour. Nixon and Kissinger at the summit had sought to increase American trade and give the Soviets additional incentives for détente by granting Russia $750 million in credits for the purchase of American wheat. The Americans had not known how desperate Russia's grain crisis was or that there would be a world shortage. After the Russians managed to buy up much of the American crop at bargain prices, many Americans thought the Soviets had snookered Nixon and Kissinger.

The Soviets cast a further pall on détente by cracking down on dissidents shortly after the summit. They also imposed a stiff exit tax on Jewish emigrants from the Soviet Union. The number of Jewish emigrants had risen from 400 in 1968 to 35,000 in 1973, and the Soviets sought to reduce the flow of Jews to Israel in deference to their Arab allies. Many Americans began to claim that détente was serving as a license for Russian violation of human rights. Democratic Senator Henry Jackson of Washington, a powerful force in the legislative branch, demanded that the United States refuse to honor Nixon's summit agreement to improve Soviet-American trade unless the Russians lessened domestic oppression. He successfully blocked congressional consent to most favored nation status for Soviet trade unless the Soviets changed their emigration policy. When the USSR promised to permit at least 35,000 Jews to emigrate each year, Jackson demanded an increase to 100,000. The Soviets indignantly refused, and emigration fell to 13,220 in 1974. At the same time, Jackson and his allies sought to limit loans to the Soviets from the Export-Import Bank unless Russia eased its persecution of dissidents.

The issue of human rights offered a link between liberal and conservative critics of Nixon and Kissinger. Liberals had long denounced Nixon and Kissinger for supporting violations of human rights in Vietnam and other areas of the Third World. Conservatives would disagree with those criticisms, but both could unite in denouncing violations of human rights in Communist nations. Liberals and conservatives also found a way to unite against Nixon and Kissinger on SALT. Critics of SALT I pointed out that the Soviets had profitted mightily from that agreement. The Soviets offset the American advantage in MIRVed missiles by deploying their own far more rapidly than Nixon and Kissinger had expected. Not only were the Soviets replacing their 308 monster SS-9 missiles with equally heavy SS-18 missiles that carried ten warheads each, they were replacing their smaller launchers with SS-19 missiles that carried six warheads each. The Americans claimed that these SS-19's should be counted against the 308 heavy launchers Russia was allowed, but the Soviets denied this. Obviously they were going to deploy far more than 308 MIRVed missiles, and since the throw-weight of these missiles was so much greater than that of America's Minuteman and Polaris, the Soviets potentially could launch far more and larger warheads than the United States.

Kissinger proposed to deal with this problem in the SALT II negotiations by seeking an equal limit on the number of warheads for both sides. Although the Soviet warheads presumably would be larger, American missiles were more accurate, and the limit on warheads would restrict the Russian MIRV program. The joint chiefs of staff, many conservatives, the influential Senator Jackson, and ultimately Secretary of Defense James Schlesinger argued instead that the U.S. should demand "equal aggregates," meaning equality in launchers and throw-weight rather than warheads. Nixon and later Gerald Ford chose this equal aggregates approach, and it became the foundation of the SALT II agreement.

The SALT II agreement, announced by Ford and Brezhnev at the Vladivostok summit of 1974, allowed the United States and the Soviet Union 2,400 strategic missiles each, 1,320 of which could be MIRVed. To compensate for Russia's advantage in throw-weight, the United States would be allowed 525 strategic bombers to the Soviet Union's 160. Also, SALT II would exempt NATO forward-based nuclear systems in Europe, along with the small independent nuclear forces of Great Britain and France, from the American total.

SALT II did not enjoy the universal approbation SALT I had received. Conservatives argued that the compensations for Russia's superior throw-weight offered in SALT II were inadequate. They also argued that the Soviets had proved they were dishonest during SALT I. Conservatives warned that on-site inspection rather than reliance on spy satellites was essential to keep the Russians from future cheating. Liberals claimed that the limit on missiles set by SALT II was too high. Both the United States and the Soviet Union had sufficient weapons to destroy each other several times over, so liberals called for a reduction of the missiles allowed.

Senator Jackson again bridged the gap between liberal and conservative

Figure 23   Secretary of State Henry Kissinger stands with President Gerald Ford shortly after Nixon's resignation. Photo courtesy of the National Archives.

critics by calling for renegotiation of the agreement to force the Soviets to reduce their missiles and bring their throw-weight down to an equality with the United States. The consent of two-thirds of the Senate to a formal SALT II treaty became very uncertain. The Ford administration found it difficult even to put the treaty into final form because America's introduction of the cruise missile and Russian deployment of the Backfire medium-range bomber complicated the issue. Each side claimed that its weapon was a tactical one that did not endanger the other's homeland and should not be counted against its strategic weapon total. (Actually, under certain conditions, both weapons could reach the other's homeland, and neither trusted the other to avoid those conditions.) Ford and Kissinger, unable to secure final ratification of SALT II in 1976, bequeathed the problem to the new president, Jimmy Carter. Meanwhile, the USSR and the United States agreed to abide by SALT II informally while ratification was pending.

DILEMMAS IN THE DEVELOPED WORLD: EUROPE AND JAPAN

The SALT agreements raised serious strategic questions for Europe. NATO strategy since 1949 had relied on the American nuclear umbrella. Kissinger estimated that NATO forces could hold out against a Warsaw Pact invasion only about ninety days without resort to nuclear weapons. Thus, NATO forces, and particularly American troops stationed in Europe, served as little more than a delaying force to give time for reconsideration before the war went nuclear and as a trip-wire to guarantee that the United States would not abandon Western Europe when the crunch came.

Russian nuclear parity undercut this strategic situation. The United States could no longer threaten with relative impunity to launch its nuclear weapons as a response to a Russian conventional invasion. Some conservatives argued that the United States should rebuild its nuclear superiority over the Soviets to restore credibility to its European deterrent, but this seemed impossible technologically and politically. Others urged a buildup of conventional forces in Europe that might deter a Russian invasion without committing the United States to a suicidal nuclear exchange. Kissinger calculated, however, that a conventional defense of Europe would require $12 billion from the United States, along with huge increases in Western European defense budgets. Congress was not about to vote such defense expenditures in the wake of Vietnam. Senator Mike Mansfield was actually gaining support for his proposal to bring home half of the American contingent in Europe. Mansfield argued that Europe should make a greater effort to provide troops so NATO would not have to resort to early first use of nuclear weapons. Yet Europe had no great interest in such conventional increases. Conventional preparedness would give the United States an opening to reduce its nuclear commitment to European defense.

This left NATO relying more and more heavily on tactical nuclear weapons to deter or fight a Russian invasion. Yet this option too seemed problematical. Military theorists admitted that a tactical exchange would probably escalate into general strategic warfare, and even tactical nuclear weapons were so destructive that an attack on Soviet columns advancing into Europe would devastate much of the continent, especially if the USSR responded with its own tactical weapons. Europe naturally preferred a strategy that would lead the Soviet Union and the United States to lob their nuclear weapons at one another over the heads of the Europeans rather than use Europe as the battlefield between superpowers.

Some Europeans advocated another alternative—eliminate Moscow's incentive for an attack by making compromise agreements with the Soviet bloc. Moving very far in this direction, however, might require Europe to become more neutral and to distance itself somewhat from the United States. Nixon and Kissinger were willing to accept a degree of European independence and compromise with the Soviets, but they did not want to see it go so far as European neutralization. They would not denounce de Gaulle for his attempt to revive French independence and glory, even though he pulled French forces out of NATO. They tolerated Willy Brandt's attempts to soften the antagonism between East and West Germany. But they stopped short of encouraging such movements, and they denounced the rise of so-called Euro-Communist parties, which combined socialist domestic ideology with independence from and sometimes active antagonism to Moscow. Kissinger claimed that the conversion of Euro-Communists to an anti-Moscow stance was too recent to be anything but opportunistic. He threatened to exclude any such regimes from NATO or to withhold secrets from NATO if a Euro-Communist government took its seat with the alliance.

All the conflicting alternatives to cope with Soviet nuclear parity in Europe had serious drawbacks, and none could command full agreement. Attempts to clarify policy only highlighted and exacerbated the differences. The Vietnam war and then Watergate gave the Europeans little incentive to draw closer to the United States or sacrifice anything in order to coordinate policy. As a result, Nixon and Kissinger had to fudge their European strategy. Despite their admission of Russian nuclear parity in the SALT agreements and the consequent irrationality of any first use of nuclear weapons, they felt they could not publicly match Moscow's promise of "no first strike." They despaired of building sufficient conventional forces in Europe, and so clung to some vulnerable land-based strategic weapons, like the prospective MX missile, which were valuable almost exclusively as first strike weapons. They continued counterforce planning, relied on tactical nuclear weapons in Europe, and insisted they would abandon such capabilities only in exchange for like concessions on the part of the Soviets.

Meanwhile, West Germany's first postwar liberal chancellor, Social Democrat Willy Brandt, pursued his own answer to the European conundrum—Ostpolitik, or reconciliation with East Germany and Eastern Europe. Until Brandt, West Germany had held to the so-called Hallstein Doctrine. According to it, West Germany would reject formal diplomatic relations with any nation that recognized East Germany. In this way, West Germany could pretend that it represented all of Germany and that Germany would some- day be reunited. Unfortunately, the Hallstein Doctrine was leading to in- creased West German isolation, for a growing number of Third World nations that were winning their independence were recognizing East Ger- many. To correct this situation, Brandt extended de facto recognition to East Germany in exchange for East German concessions on trade and visiting privileges between the two halves of Germany. Thus, he tacitly abandoned hopes of reuniting Germany under the West German government.

The West German parliament, however, was not about to accept Ostpo- litik and Brandt's deals unless it had firm international recognition of West German rights in divided Berlin. The United States, Great Britain, France, and the Soviet Union technically still occupied Berlin, so final agreement rested with them rather than with East and West Germany. Nixon and Kis- singer, with their leverage over a Berlin settlement, could make sure that Brandt did not move too far toward the Soviets. They also ensured that the Soviets gave full recognition to West German control of West Berlin before Moscow could get the agreement on East Germany it so much desired. Nixon and Brezhnev concluded the Berlin agreement at the 1971 summit, and that most dangerous European issue was finally put to rest.

The movement toward easing tensions between Eastern and Western Eu- rope culminated in 1975 with the Helsinki Final Agreement. This was in ef- fect the formal settlement of World War II, for the United States, the Soviet Union, and the Eastern and Western European powers finally accepted one another's boundaries as permanent and "inviolable." Each bloc thus con- ceded the other's sphere of influence. The Soviets, in exchange for this tacit recognition of their East European sphere, promised to respect a long list of human rights within their bloc. They never did. Not only did they crack down on dissidents, but they arrested those in the USSR or Eastern Europe who presumed to set themselves up as committees to observe compliance with the Helsinki accords. This added to both liberal and conservative disil- lusionment with détente in the United States.

Although Nixon and Kissinger kept a close eye on Germany's Ostpolitik, Brandt did not take it so far that it caused serious apprehension in the United States. France under de Gaulle's successor, Georges Pompidou, caused more consternation. Pompidou and his foreign minister, Michel Jobert, brusquely tried to exclude the United States from inter-European councils and pre- vented the full reconsideration of NATO affairs that Soviet parity and French military withdrawal from the alliance seemed to demand. The British, usually supporters of American activism in Europe, did not do much to help Kissinger because they did not want to stir opposition to their renewed re- quest to join the European Common Market. Nixon and Kissinger thus found themselves thwarted in their attempt to refocus attention on NATO affairs by declaring 1973 to be "The Year of Europe."

A dinner given by Kissinger for Jobert in Los Angeles illustrated the de- cline in goodwill between France and the United States. When Jobert started to give his toast in French, comedian Danny Kaye interrupted to ask if he would give it in English so his audience could better understand him. Jobert frostily replied that he was speaking French for the benefit of his own French delegation. Danny Kaye offered to resolve the situation by translating Jobert's toast back into French if Jobert would give it in English. The dumbfounded Jobert complied. It took him and his compatriots several moments to realize that Kaye's translation was French only in inflection and mannerism. Kaye was talking gibberish with a French accent, a routine that had convulsed audiences around the world. Unfortunately, Jobert and his delegation were not amused.

A far more serious cause of disarray within the Western alliance than Germany's Ostpolitik or French cussedness was what came to be known as the "second Nixon shock" (the first being his visit to China without informing the Japanese). Lyndon Johnson and Richard Nixon had tried to pay for the Vietnam war without increasing taxes. The resulting budget deficit and trade imbalance drove inflation up and undermined the strength of the U.S. dollar abroad. Nixon and his treasury secretary, John Connally, decided on drastic measures. Without consulting their allies abroad, they imposed a ninety-day wage and price freeze, slapped a 10 percent surcharge on imports, cut 10 percent from foreign economic assistance, and suspended the convertibility of dollars to gold. The Europeans and the Japanese were indignant. The 10 percent surcharge on imports hurt their export market in the United States. Abandonment of the gold standard shattered the Bretton Woods system and left Europe and Japan holding vast amounts of dollars that were plunging in value. With considerable bitterness, the United States, Europe, and Japan patched together the Smithsonian Agreement, which fixed new exchange rates. The American dollar would remain off the gold standard and would be devalued in terms of other currencies to help the United States sell more abroad.

Since all nations paid for Middle Eastern oil in dollars, however, the oil-producing countries would not sit still for the devaluation of American currency. To compensate for the loss of revenue due to devaluation, OPEC raised its oil prices. The oil price increases and the even more catastrophic oil embargo that OPEC imposed during the Arab-Israeli War of 1973 split the United States and its allies. Europe and Japan, unlike the United States, were almost totally dependent on OPEC oil. They were desperate to avoid offending the Arabs, so they publicly dissociated themselves from Washington's pro-Israeli policies. Many NATO allies even permitted Soviet overflights to resupply the Arab armies.

Despite all these symptoms of disintegration in America's relations with Europe and Japan, by 1974 the pendulum finally stopped and began its swing back toward sympathy and cooperation. The Middle East war and oil embargo against the United States ended. The United States proved quite staunch in sharing oil with the Netherlands, which had suffered the embargo along with the United States. Pompidou's death from bone cancer led to changes in French leadership that helped Franco-American relations.

Harold Wilson's Labour ministry replaced the conservative government of Edward Heath in England, and this improved Anglo-American rapport. Nonetheless, the unresolved issues of nuclear strategy, trade, currency, and energy would continue to threaten cooperation and understanding among the Western Allies.

THE THIRD WORLD

Theoretically, the policy enunciated by the Nixon Doctrine should have led to a restrained policy in the Third World, since American troops no longer would intervene in Third World crises. When asked about the strategic importance of Latin America, Kissinger had replied disdainfully that South America "was a dagger pointed straight at the heart of—Antarctica." Yet Nixon and Kissinger, and later Ford, seemed to interpret every Third World crisis that came up during their administrations as involving significant interests or Soviet agitation that had to be countered by the United States. They were unwilling to trust Third World nationalism to limit and ultimately throw off excessive Soviet interference.

Chile

One of the most controversial Nixon and Kissinger actions took place in Chile. During the Chilean elections of 1964, with Lyndon Johnson's approval, the CIA had funneled $3 million to Christian Democratic candidate Eduardo Frei to help him defeat the Marxist candidate, Salvadore Allende Gossens. In the election of 1968, however, Frei could not succeed himself. In Frei's absence, Allende managed to poll more votes than either of his two opponents, 36 percent of the popular vote, despite $135,000 distributed by the CIA in a spoiling operation against him. (The giant International Telephone and Telegraph Corporation, fearful that Allende might expropriate its operation in Chile, offered $1 million for the CIA to distribute in the election. The administration turned it down, but advised ITT on how best to spend its money to influence the Chilean election.) Nixon was furious at Allende's plurality and demanded that something be done to prevent the Chilean Congress from formally voting Allende into office.

Since Allende had won less than 50 percent of the popular vote, under the Chilean constitution Congress had the power to appoint the next president. By tradition, the Chilean Congress had always chosen the candidate with the highest vote. Nixon raged to CIA Director Richard Helms that he should prevent this even if it cost $10 million. Nixon and Kissinger were especially sensitive to the possibility of a Marxist regime in Chile because they had just gone through a confrontation with the Soviets over the building of an alleged Russian submarine base at Cienfuegos, Cuba, and feared similar Soviet influence in Chile.

When bribes to the Chilean Congress seemed unlikely to prevent Allende's accession, the CIA tried to inspire a military coup. But the Chilean army chief of staff, General René Schneider, insisted that the military support the constitutional process, and blocked the coup. Some of the Chilean military decided to kidnap Schneider and take him to Argentina. The CIA backed away from the plot at that point, but a group of Chilean soldiers killed General Schneider in a bungled kidnap attempt. The Chilean military then closed ranks behind the constitution and assured Allende's confirmation as president.

Allende and the United States inevitably headed toward a collision course. Allende moved to nationalize North American copper companies while ignoring the compensation formula worked out by his predecessor. Allende permitted Leftist takeovers of newspapers and radio stations. He increased taxes on the middle classes. He encouraged peasant seizures of land. Ultimately, he distributed arms among the populace. The Nixon administration allowed U.S. loans already made to Chile to continue, but efficiently blocked all other economic aid to Chile from the United States or its allies. Meanwhile, the CIA spent over a million dollars building domestic opposition to Allende.

In Chile, the combination of American measures and Allende's mismanagement brought chaos. Inflation rose to 350 percent. Strikes spread, especially in the middle-class sector. Shopkeepers struck in August 1972, truck owners in October. Allende had to establish a rationing system. Yet in the election of 1973, Allende increased his plurality from 36 to 43 percent, and he used this as a mandate to rule by presidential decree. He announced a drastic revision of the educational system. This threw the Catholic Church into opposition. Strikes spread to the copper mines and other enterprises. Militants occupied struck businesses in retaliation.

On September 11, 1973, the Chilean military overthrew and killed Allende. The new regime took over the universities, disbanded political parties, and suppressed the media. Kissinger and Nixon insisted that Allende had fallen because of his own policies. They claimed that their opposition efforts had been restrained and relatively unimportant and that the United States should be tolerant of the new Chilean government's violations of human rights under the chaotic circumstances that Allende had created. Many critics denounced Washington's role in the coup, however, and demanded more than quiet diplomacy to rectify atrocities against the Chilean military government's domestic opponents. With what Kissinger thought was exceptional severity, Congress cut off aid to Chile unless the president certified fundamental progress on human rights.

Pakistan, India, and Bangladesh

The policies of Nixon and Kissinger toward the Third World caused another uproar during the 1971 revolution in East Pakistan. When the British had granted India its independence after World War II, they had divided Pakistan from India to separate Muslims from Hindus. Unfortunately, Muslims were concentrated in two widely separated sectors, so the British had created the Pakistani nation out of two distant provinces that shared nothing but dislike of Hindu India. The differences between East and West Pakistan exploded after a cyclone killed 200,000 people in East Pakistan and the relief efforts of the government in West Pakistan had proved inept. East Pakistan demanded autonomy. The West Pakistani leaders decided to suppress the autonomy of 75 million East Pakistanis with an army of 40,000. The atrocities committed by the army raised an outcry throughout the world. India found itself inundated with refugees from East Pakistan and also saw a chance to divide its hated adversary. It intervened and helped establish East Pakistan as the independent state of Bangladesh. West Pakistan then futilely attacked India.

Many Americans recoiled at the Pakistani army's atrocities and sent aid and sympathy to Bangladesh. Nixon and Kissinger, however, decided to "tilt toward Pakistan." Pakistan was their conduit for the opening to China, while India had just signed a treaty of friendship with the Soviet Union. Besides, Nixon regarded India as the pet of American liberals. Nixon and Kissinger saw no chance that West Pakistan could hold on to Bangladesh, but they wanted to enable Pakistan to retreat with dignity and sufficient remaining morale to deter India from the temptation to grab the disputed West Pakistan province of Kashmir. They sent an aircraft carrier to the Bay of Bengal and threatened to cancel the summit with the Russians unless the Soviet Union got India to accept peace. When India stepped back from the confrontation over Kashmir, Nixon and Kissinger claimed success for their policy, but many American critics denounced their cynicism toward the atrocities in Bangladesh.

Angola

As Watergate sapped Nixon's prestige, Kissinger found the administration less and less able to overcome the revulsion from Vietnam and to gain support for an activist policy in the Third World. Thus, when the North Vietnamese launched the attack that finally brought down the South Vietnamese regime, all the pleadings and warnings of Kissinger and President Gerald Ford could not get Congress to authorize a new intervention. The same congressional reluctance short-circuited Kissinger and Ford in their requests for a major American commitment in the newly independent African state of Angola.

Angola and Mozambique were part of the Portuguese empire until mid-1974, when a coup in Portugal engineered by progressive military officers overthrew the Portuguese dictatorship and offered independence to the nation's African provinces. Numerous factions in Angola had been fighting the Portuguese authorities for years, and the CIA actually had given covert aid to a couple of those factions even while officially supporting and subsidizing Portugal. (Portugal permitted important NATO airbases in the Azores.)

Nixon and Kissinger had assigned Africa a low priority in their grandiose foreign policy design, so they had not concerned themselves much with the Angolan issue. They had simply decided to relax the punitive measures against the white minority regimes in the Portuguese empire, South Africa, and Rhodesia on the assumption that the way to constructive racial progress was through friendly persuasion of the whites, not violent revolution by blacks that might open the way for Communists. In pursuit of this so-called Tar Baby option, enunciated in National Security Memorandum 39, Nixon eased the arms embargo on South Africa, while Congress broke a United Nations boycott of Rhodesia by permitting U.S. purchases of chromium from that nation.

As the Angolan independence movement and ultimately the Portuguese revolution confounded the Tar Baby option, Kissinger decided that the United States had to join China, South Africa, and Zaire in increasing covert support for the so-called UNITA guerrillas to combat a more powerful revolutionary faction, the MPLA, which was receiving increasing Soviet support. The State Department officer in charge of African affairs, Nathaniel Davis, resigned when Kissinger ignored his warning that the civil war was an African affair out of control of the major powers and that the United States should seek a negotiated political settlement. U.S. cooperation with South Africa in support of the victory of one side would only legitimize Soviet involvement in the eyes of most Africans.

The Soviets more than matched the American effort. They transported thousands of Cuban soldiers and advisors to Angola to help the MPLA. Congress refused to counter this escalation, and it cut off the existing covert aid when Davis's resignation and leaks made American intervention a hot public issue. As the MPLA and Moscow's Cuban surrogates emerged victorious in the Angolan civil war in 1976, Kissinger and President Ford disgustedly commented that Congress had been so traumatized by Vietnam and Watergate that it had "lost its guts" and "pulled the plug" on Angola.

The *Mayaguez* Incident

Kissinger and Ford found at least one opportunity to circumvent Congress and show that Watergate and Vietnam had not paralyzed the United States totally in the Third World. In 1975, Cambodian gunboats captured the American freighter *Mayaguez*. Ford and Kissinger bombed a Cambodian port and sent an amphibious landing force to the island of Koh Tang to rescue the crew. Ironically, the Cambodians were releasing the crew at the same time. Forty-one members of the American amphibious unit were killed storming ashore in their useless operation.

Cyprus

While all these episodes seemed to indicate the advisability of greater restraint in U.S. foreign policy, there was at least one instance that indicated the dangers of abstention. Greece and Turkey had long been blood enemies despite their common membership in NATO. A major focus of their rivalry was the island of Cyprus, which lay close to the coast of Turkey but whose population was 80 percent Greek. Greek Archbishop Makarios had maintained a precarious peace and neutrality on Cyprus since Britain had granted the island independence in 1960. In 1974, however, the reactionary colonels who controlled Greece, with considerable economic and military aid from the United States, supported a coup in Cyprus designed to unite the island with Greece. The United States did little to stop the Greek colonels' adventure, despite receiving warnings of it.

Turkey, with far more military strength than Greece, invaded and conquered the island. Meanwhile, a coup in Greece overthrew the reactionary colonels. Congress, which had previously condemned the Greek coup on Cyprus, then established an arms embargo on Turkey. Both of America's NATO allies condemned the United States. The Greeks blamed the United States for supporting the colonels and failing to prevent the Turkish invasion of Cyprus. The Turks denounced Washington for the arms embargo. The Turks uprooted the Greek population and separated the Turkish and Greek populations on the island to secure their hold. (In November of 1983, the Turks on Cyprus declared the part of the island they occupied to be an independent state, adding still further complications and bitterness to the quarrel.)

CONTROVERSIAL ISSUES AND FURTHER READING

All histories of this era must be measured against the powerful and informative if self-serving memoirs of Henry Kissinger, *The White House Years* (1979), and *Years of Upheaval* (1982). The volume covering the Ford administration has not yet appeared, and historians feel the lack sorely when they try to piece together the diplomacy of the Ford administration from the other available books. *RN: The Memoirs of Richard Nixon* (1978) is less revealing and detailed.

Many historians endorsed the claim of Nixon and Kissinger that their diplomacy was realistic and highly successful. [See Bernard and Marvin Kalb, *Kissinger* (1974); Coral Bell, *The Diplomacy of Detente* (1977); and Stephen Graubard, *Portrait of a Mind* (1973).]

Many realists of the restrained variety, however, considered the Nixon-Kissinger policy too harsh and desperate. While they praised the opening to China, the development of détente, and the negotiation of the SALT agreements with the Soviets, they believed Nixon and Kissinger took their commitment to a balance of power far beyond reason and necessity in Vietnam, Chile, Angola, and Bangladesh. [Among these works are Roger Morris, *Uncertain Greatness: Henry Kissinger and American Foreign Policy* (1977); Seyom Brown, *The Crises of Power: An Interpretation of United States Foreign Policy during the Kissinger Years* (1979); and Stanley Hoffmann, *Primacy or World Order: American Foreign Policy since the Cold War* (1978). John George Stoessinger's *Henry Kissinger: The Anguish of Power* (1976) is more friendly to Kissinger but has the same general criticisms.]

The Nixon-Kissinger policies came in for far harsher treatment from liberal-moralist journalists who saw little but evil in Nixon and Kissinger. [Among such "exposés" are Jonathan Schell, *The Time of Illusion* (1976); Seymour Hersh, *The Price of Power* (1983); and William Shawcross, *Sideshow: Kissinger, Nixon, and the Destruction of Cambodia* (1979). The best and most comprehensive of them is Tad Szulc, *The Illusion of Peace* (1978).]

For revisionist assessments, see the fourth edition of Walter LaFeber's *America, Russia, and the Cold War* (1980), and Lloyd C. Gardner, ed., *The Great Nixon Turnaround* (1973).

While most historians and journalists criticized Nixon and Kissinger from the Left, perhaps the criticisms that had a more telling effect on the political world came from the Right. Many Republicans, led by Ronald Reagan, condemned Kissinger, Nixon, and Ford for being too weak toward the Russians and the Communist world. They argued that SALT I and II gave away too much to the Soviets and permitted them to acquire nuclear superiority. They believed Nixon and Kissinger should have stayed the course in Vietnam and done more to counter Communist activities in the rest of the Third World. They argued that the opening to China was a sellout of America's friend, Taiwan. [For examples of those who agree with this critique, see Norman Podhoretz, *Why We Were in Vietnam* (1982); Richard Pipes, *U.S.-Soviet Relations in the Era of Detente: A Tragedy of Errors* (1981); Alexander Solzhenitsyn, *Detente: Prospects for Democracy and Dictatorship* (1976); and Robert Conquest, *Present Danger: Towards a Foreign Policy* (1979). Pipes became an advisor to Ronald Reagan in 1981.]

For works specifically on SALT, see Michael Mandelbaum, *The Nuclear Question* (1979); John Newhouse, *Cold Dawn: The Story of SALT* (1973); Richard Burt, ed., *A Strategic Symposium: SALT and U.S. Defense Policy* (1979); and the memoirs of Nixon and Kissinger. On the United States and Europe in this era, see A. W. DePorte, *Europe between the Superpowers: The Enduring Balance* (1979); George W. Ball, *Diplomacy for a Crowded World: An American Foreign Policy* (1976); Michael M. Harrison, *The Reluctant Ally: France and Atlantic Security* (1981); Alfred Grosser, *The Western Alliance* (1980); and Richard J. Barnet, *The Alliance* (1983).

On the economic problems between the United States, Europe, Japan, and the Third World, see Joan Edelman Spero, *The Politics of International Economic Relations* (1977); Robert K. Olson, *U.S. Foreign Policy and the New International Economic Order* (1981); Richard J. Barnet and Ronald Muller, *The Global Reach: The Power of the Multinational Corporations* (1974); Raymond Vernon, *Storm over the Multinationals* (1977); Alfred E. Eckes, *The United States and the Global Struggle for Minerals* (1977); I. M. Destler, Haruhiro Fukui, and Hideo Sato, *The Textile Wrangle: The Conflict in Japanese-American Relations, 1969–1971* (1979); and Raymond F. Hopkins and Donald J. Puchala, *Global Food Interdependence* (1980).

On the end of the Vietnam war, see, in addition to the works cited in the previous chapter and the general assessments of Nixon's diplomacy listed above, Allan E. Goodman, *Lost Peace: America's Search for a Negotiated Settlement of the Vietnam War* (1978); Gareth Porter, *A Peace Denied: The United States, Vietnam and the Paris Agreement* (1975); Frank Snepp, *Decent Interval: An Insider's Account of Saigon's Indecent End* (1977); and Arnold Isaacs, *Without Honor: Defeat in Vietnam and Cambodia* (1983).

On Chile and the rest of Latin America, see Robert J. Alexander, *The Tragedy of Chile* (1978); Paul E. Sigmund, *The Overthrow of Allende and the Politics of Chile, 1965–1976* (1977); James Petras and Morris Morely, *The United States and Chile: Imperialism and the Overthrow of the Allende Government* (1975); Samuel L. Bailey, *The United States and the Development of South America, 1945–1975* (1976); Stephen G. Rabe, *The*

Road to OPEC: United States Relations with Venezuela (1982); and Francis Kessler, "Kissinger's Legacy: A Latin American Policy," *Current History* (1977).

On the Nixon-Kissinger-Ford policy toward Africa, see Anthony Lake, *The "Tar Baby" Option: American Policy Toward Southern Rhodesia* (1976); Harry M. Joiner, *American Foreign Policy: The Kissinger Era* (1977); Mohamed A. el-Khawas and Barry Cohen, eds., *The Kissinger Study of Southern Africa: National Security Study Memorandum 39 (SECRET)* (1976); John Marcum, *The Angolan Revolution* (2 vols., 1969–1978); and John Stockwell, *In Search of Enemies: A CIA Story* (1978).

CHAPTER 20

Time Bombs in the Middle East

THE SIX-DAY WAR OF JUNE 1967

As if Nixon and Kissinger did not have their hands full with the problems of Vietnam, China, the Soviet Union, and Latin America, they also found themselves confronted with ticking time bombs in the Middle East. The Middle East had remained relatively quiet for a few years after Eisenhower left office in 1960. The pan-Arab nationalism that had seemed so threatening to Western interests under Egyptian President Nasser degenerated into a squabbling rivalry between Arab nations. The Soviets were caught between the quarreling Arab nationalist states and were unable to bring Arab radicalism firmly under their wing. Oil continued to flow to the West on beneficial terms. The Arab-Israeli conflict remained a simmering stalemate rather than an all-out war even after Israel diverted much of the water of the Jordan River to its great irrigation project in 1964.

In the last year and a half of Lyndon Johnson's presidency, however, the relative calm exploded. In May 1967, the Soviets warned Nasser that the Israelis were massing armies to attack Syria. Although the report was untrue and Nasser knew it, he used the opportunity to mobilize his armies in the Sinai Desert near the Israeli border. He then requested the UN secretary-general to remove the United Nations peacekeeping forces that had patrolled the Egyptian side of the Egyptian-Israeli truce line since the Suez war of 1956.

There is evidence that Nasser meant this request primarily as a bluff to apply pressure on Israel, but the secretary-general acquiesced and removed the troops with an alacrity that surprised the Egyptian president. Then, when Nasser thought he detected a note of fear and softness in the Israeli response, he proceeded to escalate the crisis. He blockaded the Straits of Tiran through which Israel received much of its shipping. He claimed that he would welcome war, and declared that the issue was not just the blockade of Tiran or border adjustments, but the full restoration of an Arab Palestine. Syria and Jordan joined Nasser in mobilizing. Iraq sent thousands of troops to Jordan, and the Arab oil countries threatened to cut off petroleum to any nations that supported Israel. The Soviets helped by warning the United States not to intervene.

Nasser originally believed that Israel would not fight. But the Israelis had little choice; they had to mobilize to confront the Egyptian buildup because the smallness of their territory meant they had to stop the Egyptians at the border or not at all. Yet they could not remain mobilized for long, because mobilization involved so much of their able-bodied labor force that their economy would collapse. As Nasser came to realize that the Israelis would fight, he hesitated to attack. If he struck the first blow, it would guarantee American aid to the Israeli victim. If Israel struck the first blow, American opinion might rebound against the putative aggressor.

Nasser's hesitation gave the Israelis their chance. When Lyndon Johnson's attempt to mobilize an international effort to end the blockade of the Straits of Tiran faltered, Israel launched a preemptive air strike that caught the Egyptian air force unprepared and virtually destroyed it in one blow. With total air superiority, the Israelis proceeded to capture the Sinai desert from Egypt, the West Bank of the Jordan River from the Kingdom of Jordan, and the strategic Golan Heights from Syria. These conquered territories were three times the size of Israel itself.

Israel concluded its victorious military operations in only six days, but the basic issues and enmity between the Arabs and Israelis remained. In November 1967, the United Nations did get Israel and the Arab states to agree to UN Resolution 242, which called for Israeli withdrawal from conquered territories and the recognition and security of all states in the Middle East. Unfortunately, both sides accepted Resolution 242 solely because they interpreted it to their own benefit. The Israelis argued that Resolution 242's mention of security implied that they could keep enough of the territory they had conquered to give them defensible borders. Thus, they insisted they would hold on to Jerusalem, the Golan Heights, the Gaza Strip, and large portions of the West Bank. (They regarded the West Bank as the biblical provinces of Judea and Samaria and considered it rightfully theirs by biblical prescription.) The Arabs, on the other hand, argued that Resolution 242 required Israel to abandon all conquered territory before negotiations on the security and recognition of Israel could even begin. They also made it clear that they would recognize Israel only if it transformed itself into a secular state and permitted the Palestinians to return.

Lyndon Johnson sided essentially with Israel in this quarrel. He and most Americans regarded the Arabs as the aggressors in the Six-Day War and thought the Arabs had gotten what was coming to them. Johnson wanted a settlement in the Middle East, but he agreed that Israel should not give up the conquered territories except in return for a comprehensive peace settlement that guaranteed Israel's independence and security. Johnson's administration sent advanced arms to Israel to counter the Soviets' rebuilding of Arab armies, and Richard Nixon continued that policy when he took office.

Nixon, however, decided he would have to be more "even-handed" than Johnson if there was to be a comprehensive peace in the Middle East. The Palestinians had to be accommodated in some way before the Arabs would recognize Israel and grant it security. In October 1969, Secretary of State

Map 18   Israel and Occupied Areas, 1977

William Rogers tried to spell out compromise peace terms after thorough consultation with the Soviet Union. The Rogers plan called for Israel to retreat to its 1967 borders with only "insubstantial" border alterations. Israel and Jordan would negotiate the status of Jerusalem, implying that Israel could not expect full sovereignty over the city. The Palestinians would be repatriated to Palestine or compensated for living elsewhere. In return, the great powers would guarantee Israel's security.

The compromise suggested in the Rogers plan managed only to infuriate both Israelis and Arabs. Israel refused to entrust its security to other powers, however friendly they might appear. It had seen the UN withdraw its forces at Nasser's request and leave Israel to Arab mercies. It remembered that the United States and the world had stood by as Jews were slaughtered in the Holocaust. The Israelis would entrust their security only to "fighting Jews," and they insisted on borders and defense arrangements that would make this possible. Return of the Palestinians to Israel would destroy the Jewish state. The establishment of an independent Palestinian state on the West Bank would threaten Israel with continual guerrilla warfare, for the Palestinians inevitably would attempt to retrieve all of Palestine. Let the Arab states take care of the Palestinians, Israelis said. Jordan already was a Palestinian state. Let the remainder of the Palestinians go there and work something out with Jordan's Hashemite-Bedouin minority.

Of course, for all the insistence on arrangements that would permit it to guarantee its own security, Israel remained dependent on American arms and economic aid. This gave Washington potential leverage to force a compromise. But the Israelis, and especially their right-wing and religious parties, were willing to defy excessive American pressure on the gamble that American public opinion, with the help of the Jewish lobby within the United States, would repudiate any administration perceived to be anti-Israel.

The Arabs also denounced the Rogers plan. Nasser called it proof that the United States was the "number one enemy of the Arabs." Since Rogers had issued the plan under his own name, the Soviets quickly backed away in the face of such universal opposition and supported the Arabs. The Arabs insisted on the right of the Palestinians to return to their homeland and to live in a secular democratic state that reflected the wishes of a proper Arab majority, not a Jewish religious Israel. They pointed to Israeli expulsions of Arabs and discrimination against those who stayed. The Arabs would do nothing that would lend legitimacy to the state of Israel—neither recognize it nor imply recognition by negotiating directly with it. Some moderate Arab states like Hussein's Jordan saw promise in the plan, but they had to be careful in saying so. They wanted neither to disrupt Arab unity nor endanger their own regimes by enraging their resident Palestinians and domestic radicals.

As the Rogers plan fell into the abyss between the Arabs and Israelis, tensions continued to mount. A cease-fire worked out in 1970 did little to stop the sporadic raids of Arab-supported Palestinians into Israel from their refuges in Jordan, Lebanon, Syria, and Egypt. The Soviet Union deployed advanced SAM anti-aircraft missiles in Egypt to deprive Israel of the air superiority it had won in 1967. This was the first time Moscow had installed such missiles in a non-Communist country, and the number of Soviet personnel accompanying those missiles continued to increase until it reached some 10,000 soldiers, technicians, and pilots.

BLACK SEPTEMBER

Tensions boiled over into conflict in September 1970 when Palestinian guerrillas hijacked four airliners. They blew up one of them in Cairo and three others in Jordan after they had stashed the hostage passengers around the Jordanian capital of Amman. King Hussein knew the hijackings would bring

Israeli retaliatory bombing raids on his nation. Palestinian guerrilla operations from his territory always did. He himself was under seige from the Palestinians in his country who thought he was too moderate in his attempts to regain the West Bank and destroy Israel. Hussein had barely survived two assassination attempts. Consequently, he decided to use his loyal Bedouin army to expel the guerrillas. He knew the Israelis would approve and intervene to help him if the 17,000 Iraqi soldiers remaining in Jordan from the Six-Day War decided to fight on behalf of the Palestinians. The United States also was prepared to step in if the Soviets intervened.

It was the Syrians, however, who intervened, something no one but Hussein had anticipated. Syria sent hundreds of tanks rumbling into Jordan. The United States offered to recompense Israel for any planes it might lose if it intervened to help Jordan, but this did not turn out to be necessary. The Syrian air force commander, later president, Hafez Assad, withheld Syrian air cover. Jordan's own air force quickly knocked out most of Syria's tank columns, Israel mobilized on the Golan Heights, and the Syrians backed away. The Palestinian guerrillas fled Jordan. Most took refuge in Lebanon, where a weak and fractured government could impose few controls on Palestinian enclaves and the continuing Palestinian war against Israel.

THE YOM KIPPUR WAR, OCTOBER 1973

With the partial defection of Jordan from the Arab confrontation states surrounding Israel, Egypt counted on Soviet aid and pressure to get the United States to join in imposing a compromise settlement on Israel. Egyptian President Anwar Sadat, who replaced the deceased Nasser in 1970, realized that Israeli strength and American backing made impossible the extreme demands of Palestinians and other Arabs for the total destruction of the Jewish state. But he thought the Palestinians might be accommodated on the West Bank and the Gaza Strip if Israel could be forced to withdraw to its 1967 boundaries. When Nixon and Brezhnev emerged from the summit meeting of 1972 without any new plans for the Middle East, Sadat decided he would have to take things into his own hands.

He expelled the 10,000 Soviet advisors in Egypt and freed himself from Soviet demands for full compliance with radical Arab goals. He also circumvented Soviet insistence that any Egyptian action be restrained enough to avoid American intervention and the possibility of a superpower confrontation. On October 6, 1973, Egypt and Syria launched a surprise joint attack on Israel during the Jewish holy days of Yom Kippur. The Israelis and Americans had not expected an attack because the Arabs were militarily inferior to Israel and could not hope to win. They had consequently ignored Sadat's continuous warnings as mere bluff.

Indeed, Sadat did not expect to win a complete victory; he simply hoped he could inflict enough casualties and capture enough territory to puncture Israel's sense of omnipotence and force some movement in Israel's negotiating position. Sadat's armies succeeded better than he had hoped: SAM missiles wreaked havoc with Israel's air force and destroyed forty-nine planes. The Israelis lost five hundred tanks as well. A portion of these broke down as they dashed from storage depots within Israel across the Sinai Desert. Egypt and Syria destroyed the remainder in combat. The Israelis also suffered more than 2,000 casualties, a large number in so small and close a society as that of Israel.

Meanwhile, the Soviets airlifted planes to Syria and Egypt to help in the fighting. The United States countered by promising to replenish Israeli losses in tanks and planes so Israel could throw in its reserves. There was some debate and delay within the Nixon administration over whether the United States should force Israel to promise to disgorge the conquered territories of 1967 before extending further American aid. But when Israel's precarious military situation became more obvious and the Israelis suggested they might have to resort to nuclear weapons, Nixon decided on a major American airlift. He reconfirmed his decision when the administration learned that the Soviets had put three of their own airborne divisions on alert.

As the perils of the war and the threat of a superpower confrontation grew, the United States proposed a cease-fire in place. After an initial rejection, Israel agreed. Its military difficulties were great, and it felt it could afford to stop in place because, although Egyptian troops had gained territory in the Sinai, Israeli troops had pushed past the Golan Heights to a position within twenty-five miles of Syria's capital, Damascus. The Egyptians refused, however, and said they would accept a cease-fire only on the basis of the old 1967 borders. Egypt then launched a new attack on the Sinai. But this one was not nearly so successful as the initial attack. Egypt's tanks by this time were outside the protective range of their anti-aircraft missiles and batteries along the Suez Canal. The Israelis chopped up the Egyptian columns from both the air and the land. The Israelis then outflanked the Egyptian attack, crossed the Suez Canal, tore up the SAM missile sites, and trapped the Egyptian Third Army on the Sinai side of the canal.

Throughout the Yom Kippur War, Kissinger tried to maneuver to keep either side from winning a total victory. He hoped a stalemate would enhance the chances for a compromise settlement of the Arab-Israeli dispute. At first Nixon and Kissinger restricted their support of the Israelis because they expected them to defeat the Arabs handily. Then, when the Israelis trembled on the brink of disaster, Nixon and Kissinger began a massive American airlift. When in turn the Israelis were in a position to destroy a significant portion of the Egyptian army, Kissinger insisted that the Israelis stop short and accept a cease-fire.

In the midst of Kissinger's attempts to arrange the cease-fire, the Arab oil nations added a new dimension to the problem. They announced progressive 5 percent reductions in the production of oil until Israel returned to its 1967 borders. Shortly afterward, the Arab oil nations added to this already potent squeeze a total oil embargo on the United States. In this crisis atmosphere, Kissinger got the embittered Israelis to accept a cease-fire in place on October 22, 1973. The Israelis nonetheless believed they had received tacit permission from Kissinger to complete their encirclement of the Egyptian Third Army, and they cut the last supply road to the trapped force. Facing starvation, the Egyptians tried to break out. Fighting escalated. Egypt asked the Soviets to intervene, and the Soviets sent an ultimatum on October 24 that if the United States did not join them in imposing a cease-fire on the belligerents, the Soviets would do so unilaterally. Nixon refused and alerted American forces to resist the landing of Soviet troops in Egypt. The alert became public; a major confrontation was in the offing.

Fortunately, Sadat defused it by agreeing to an international peacekeeping force with only token U.S. and Soviet participation. The United States then threatened to stop all military supplies to Israel unless it indicated a willingness to negotiate by 8 A.M. the following morning. When Sadat broke Arab precedent and agreed to direct negotiations with the Israelis on cease-fire arrangements (although at a low level), the Israelis agreed. The Yom Kippur War was over. Nixon and Kissinger, through luck and skill, had managed to prevent the victory or humiliation of either side. Yet the oil embargo still pinched the United States, and the Egyptian Third Army was still trapped. The situation would remain exceedingly precarious until the Arabs and Israelis negotiated a broader settlement.

KISSINGER AND STEP-BY-STEP DIPLOMACY

Kissinger believed a broad settlement was within reach. Israel had been shocked enough by its losses and narrow escape to consider a compromise. The Egyptians and other Arabs had avenged the humiliation of the Six-Day War, so they too might be able to retreat from their insistence on the destruction of Israel. Perhaps the Arabs were ready to recognize Israel's sovereignty and accept a state for the Palestinians on the West Bank under Jordanian sovereignty. Perhaps now the Israelis would retreat from their 1967 conquests so long as the Arabs recognized their right to exist, the Palestinians were submerged within a moderate Jordan, and the great powers guaranteed Israeli security.

Yet even if Israel was ready to negotiate such a settlement, it would take months of haggling to negotiate a Palestinian arrangement acceptable to the Israelis, and Kissinger did not have much time. Egypt would not leave its Third Army trapped for much longer, and the United States would suffer greatly if the Arab oil embargo were extended for a lengthy period. The embargo had already driven a wedge between the United States and its major allies.

Western Europe and Japan had ostentatiously dissociated themselves from American policy in the Middle East to escape the embargo because Europe and Japan, which had converted most of their industry from coal to oil in the 1960s, imported two-thirds of their oil from the Middle East. Still, the Arab oil weapon was hurting them badly. Saudi Arabia and the other Arab nations did not embargo oil to them, but they cut production, and panic buying sent prices skyrocketing. The shah of Iran, whose nation was Muslim but not Arab, continued to supply oil to the United States and the West, but also took the opportunity to raise prices and profits as much as he could. By the end of 1973, oil prices had jumped over 200 percent. To relieve this pressure, the Europeans adopted strongly pro-Arab positions and demanded that the United States join the Soviet Union in imposing peace terms on Israel.

Nixon and Kissinger, however, refused. Kissinger believed instead that he might be able to negotiate a voluntary peace if he mediated one issue at a time in a step-by-step process. He would start with the issues between Egypt and Israel, since these seemed the easiest to settle. There was no strong Palestinian presence in the territories in dispute between Egypt and Israel, and even if disengagement required a measure of Israeli retreat, Israel would still occupy some Sinai territory as a buffer. Progress toward an Israeli-Egyptian peace also seemed to promise some leverage for further Arab compromises, since the Egyptian army was by far the strongest potential force against Israel, and its removal from the Arab side would cripple the Arab military position.

Kissinger personally traveled to the Middle East to negotiate the Egyptian-Israeli disengagement. He and the rest of the players in the Middle East had assumed that the negotiations would take place in Geneva and include the Soviets. Both Israel and Egypt, however, had an incentive to avoid Soviet participation because Moscow would support the most radical Arab demands. Consequently, Sadat and the Israelis invited Kissinger to mediate personally between them. Kissinger shuttled back and forth between them in an exhausting tour de force of diplomacy. He would bounce off the plane in Egypt to effusive embraces and kisses from Sadat, then take Sadat's proposals back to a suspicious and contentious Israeli cabinet.

Finally, Golda Meier, the Israeli prime minister, decided to take the risk of trusting Sadat and Kissinger. On January 18, 1974, she agreed with Sadat to disengage Israeli and Egyptian forces, limit weapons on the front lines, and permit a UN force to return to supervise the cease-fire. Israel withdrew to the major Sinai passes in its first surrender of territory in twenty years. As Golda Meier announced this momentous step, Kissinger impulsively embraced and kissed her. Remembering Kissinger's many clinches with Sadat, the Israeli prime minister thanked him and told him wryly she had begun to think he kissed only men.

Kissinger then moved his shuttle to Syria and, at this gesture of American sincerity, Saudi Arabia and the other Arab oil nations removed their oil embargo on the United States. After much travail, Kissinger got a disengagement agreement in Syria to go along with the Egyptian one. Israel retreated from the Syrian territory it had seized in the Yom Kippur War and from a portion of the territory it had conquered in 1967 as well. It continued, however, to hold most of the strategic Golan Heights upon which it had planted more than twenty settlements. Further progress on the Syrian front would be extremely difficult.

Kissinger would have preferred the next step to have been a Palestinian-

Jordanian-West Bank agreement. But here his step-by-step approach bogged down. He had hoped to get Israel to agree to return nominal sovereignty over the West Bank to Jordan in return for a continued Israeli military presence to guarantee security. Palestinian refugees might then accept the West Bank as their homeland and cease their attempts to destroy Israel. Those Palestinians who still wanted to fight would be confronted by both Israeli and Hussein's Bedouin forces. But despite American urging, the Israelis could not bring themselves to give up the West Bank.

The Israeli Labor ministry held a parliamentary majority of only one, and it was unwilling to oppose the demands of the right-wing and religious parties to settle and hold the area. The Palestinian Liberation Organization (PLO), representing large portions of the Palestinian population, privately informed the United States that its minimum demand for peace was an independent Palestinian state in all of Jordan, meaning that Hussein would have to be overthrown. Kissinger saw no promise in that scheme, for he was sure such a radical state would turn on Israel whatever its promises, and he was unwilling to sacrifice Hussein in any case.

When the Arab states recognized the PLO as the sole legitimate representative of the Palestinian people at an Arab summit meeting in October 1974, it seemed to drive the final nail into the coffin of Kissinger's Jordanian option. Hussein was not about to press his own claim to rule a Palestinian state on the West Bank and turn the PLO's attention to him rather than to the destruction of Israel. Israel was not about to negotiate with the PLO, whose announced goal was control of all Palestine and which had claimed credit for the massacre of Israeli athletes at the Munich Olympics of 1972 as well as other terrorist raids on Israeli citizens. Israel would not even consider the compromise urged by Europe, the United Nations, and the Soviet Union of an independent Palestinian state ruled by the PLO on the West Bank separate from both Jordan and Israel.

With a West Bank Palestinian settlement at least temporarily foreclosed, Kissinger saw further progress in Egypt as the only possible chance to keep momentum rolling toward a comprehensive settlement. When Kissinger returned to his Cairo-Jerusalem shuttle, however, he found the gap wider than he expected. Sadat wanted Israel to withdraw beyond the Sinai passes and to return the Sinai oil fields to Egyptian control. He also wanted further progress between Egypt and Israel linked to Israeli concessions on the Palestinian issue. Otherwise, the rest of the Arab states would accuse Sadat of selling out the Palestinian and Arab cause for selfish Egyptian interests.

Israel balked at both demands. It wanted formal peace with Egypt to free its hands to resist unfavorable settlements with the Palestinians and other Arab states, not as a prelude to significant concessions. Kissinger returned to the United States empty-handed after warning the Israelis that their quibbling would throw negotiations into the Geneva Conference, where the Soviets would support extreme Arab demands and hopes for a compromise peace favorable to Israel would be lost. Israeli haggling over issues that "will seem trivial five years from now" could convince Americans that Israel was the true roadblock to peace in the Middle East and isolate the Jews even further, he told them. "It's tragic to see people dooming themselves to a course of unbelievable peril." President Gerald Ford, who by then had taken over from Nixon, was even more stern. He announced a "total reassessment" of American Mideast policy and selectively withheld weapons deliveries to Israel.

Israel finally conceded the Sinai passes and oil fields to Egypt in the Sinai II Agreement of September 1975. In exchange for these concessions, Israel obtained an Egyptian promise to use strictly peaceful means in future dealings with the Jewish state. Israel also secured an American commitment to vast weapons supplies and to American military intervention if Israeli security was threatened. The United States was now thoroughly entangled in the Middle East by an all but formal alliance with Israel and serious commitments to Egypt and Syria. American personnel even manned the early warning stations separating Israeli and Egyptian troops.

Kissinger's commitments in the Middle East took on ominous dimensions when the Arabs exploded in anger at what they considered Sadat's betrayal in making the Sinai II Agreement. In return for Egypt's abandonment of the Arab military confrontation with Israel, Sadat had retrieved much of Egypt's own lost territory and resources, but had gotten only the most vague intimations of further progress on the Palestinian and Syrian issues. Kissinger had promised Sadat to try to promote a second agreement between Israel and Syria, but he also had committed himself in writing to Israel that Sinai II stood on its own and was not linked to any further agreements. Thus, when Israel refused to consider any but cosmetic changes on the Golan Heights or the West Bank, and Israeli Prime Minister Yitzhak Rabin gloated in an interview that a separate peace with Egypt would allow Israel to deal "forcefully" with Syria, Syria denounced Egypt's "defection." Syria also began putting together an alliance with Jordan and the PLO forces in Lebanon to compensate for the loss of Egypt's army in the confrontation with Israel.

CIVIL WAR IN LEBANON, 1975–1976

With Syrian encouragement, Lebanon quickly became the primary focus of the Israeli-Arab confrontation. The PLO had made Lebanon its headquarters because Hussein had expelled it from Jordan; Syria would not permit attacks through its tenuous position on the Golan Heights; and Egypt had neutralized itself with the Sinai II Agreement. Only Lebanon was left as a staging ground for continued Palestinian military action against Israel, and its government was too weak to control the Palestinians on its soil. Unfortunately, Lebanese society was as fragile as its government, and it could not survive the Palestinian presence and operations.

Lebanon was an amalgam of ethnic and religious groups whose historic hatreds for one another were barely held in check by the most tenuous of arrangements. Lebanon and Syria had been provinces of Turkey until France acquired them as mandates after World War I. France had made Lebanon a separate entity in the hope of creating a loyal French colony based upon the fierce group of Maronite Christians who had fled the Muslim conquest of Syria in the seventh century and established redoubts in what was then known as Mt. Lebanon. These Christians were followers of a fifth-century monk named St. Maron and, unlike most Christians in the eastern Mediterranean, they had submitted themselves in the twelfth century to the Roman pope rather than to the Orthodox patriarch of Constantinople. As early as 1861, the French had intervened to aid these Christians. The Maronites thus regarded the French as their rescuers from a centuries-long Islamic siege.

During World War II, the Allies arranged for the independence of France's eastern Mediterranean mandates. In doing so, they maintained the separation of Lebanon and Syria. This dismayed many Arabs, who regarded Syria, Lebanon, and the British mandates of Palestine and Jordan as components of a Greater Syria, a unified Arab state covering the whole area. Lebanon was left with a population divided into countless factions. The Maronite Christians comprised 55 percent of the population. There were also small numbers of Greek Orthodox and Armenian Christians. Most of the remaining population, however, was divided between Sunni and Shiite Muslims, along with a small, secretive Islamic sect known as the Druze. Despite the hostility among these factions, the near-feudal oligarchs who ruled these groups managed to agree in 1943 to a National Pact dividing power among them. A Maronite Christian would be president, a Sunni Muslim the prime minister, a Shiite Muslim the speaker of the house, and the Druze would be accorded several minor positions. The Lebanese Parliament would be divided 6:5 for the Christians.

The various factions fought periodically over this distribution of power because the Shiite and Druze offices were mostly ceremonial, and the Christian president wielded substantially more power than the Sunni prime minister. The Muslim oligarchs became increasingly insistent on constitutional reform as the birth rate altered the population ratio in favor of the Muslims. Probably the oligarchs could have worked out a new National Pact with only the usual number of vendettas had not world affairs intruded upon their fragile balance of power. Nasser's pan-Arabic dream stirred many Lebanese Muslims, especially the poorer and dispossessed Shiites, to insist on a reformed secular Lebanon based on absolute majority rule. Since the Muslims had become a majority in Lebanon, they would rule without the hindrance of Maronite Christian domination or the vetoes accorded minority sects by the National Pact. The Palestinians threw their weight behind this radical national movement, a factor of increasing importance after the main body of the PLO arrived from Jordan in 1970.

The operations as well as the presence of the PLO strained relations in Lebanon because PLO raids inevitably drew retaliatory Israeli air attacks. In the early years of Lebanese nationhood, the Maronite Christians had joined the Arab League in opposing the state of Israel, if only to get the Palestinians out of Lebanon. But as the Palestinians joined the national movement to overthrow the National Pact and drew heavier Israeli retaliation, the Maronite leaders pushed for suppression of PLO activities and dispersion of the Palestinians to other countries. As a last resort, the Christians then threatened to secede from Lebanon, perhaps ally their Lebanese enclaves with the West or Israel, and disable one more Arab state on the border of Israel. In this fractious atmosphere, the last bulwark of a united Lebanon, the Lebanese army, became polarized among sects. Independent militias grew, manned often by deserters from the national army.

In 1975, someone fired on a Christian service in Beirut attended by the leader of the Maronite Phalangist faction and militia, Pierre Gemayal. The Christians retaliated by murdering Palestinians on a passing bus. Lebanon flared into civil war. Syria moved in to prevent disintegration. At first it aided the Muslims against the most intractable of the Maronite factions, but then it turned to fight the PLO to prevent it from inducing the complete secession of the Maronites or inviting a war with Israel before the Arabs were ready. Egypt quickly lined up with the PLO. Iraq, Syria's neighbor and mortal enemy, mobilized troops on the Syrian border. Israel warned it might intervene. Finally, Saudi Arabia and the other Arab states, with quiet support from the United States, succeeded in bringing the Syrian intervention force in Lebanon under the nominal control of the Arab League and imposing a sullen cease-fire. Thirty thousand Lebanese had died and another 600,000 had been forced from their homes, a staggering total in a nation of only 3 million people. The Arab states thus exhausted themselves opposing one another in Lebanon and gave Israel a breathing space.

THE CAMP DAVID PROCESS AND THE ISRAELI-EGYPTIAN PEACE

Jimmy Carter took office in the temporary lull that followed the Lebanese civil war and tried to break out of Kissinger's step-by-step process by offering a plan for a comprehensive settlement. The Carter plan was much like the Rogers plan. It called for a gradual Israeli withdrawal to its 1967 boundaries with only minor (and unspecified) exceptions in exchange for recognition, great power security guarantees, and demilitarized zones on the borders. The Palestinians gradually would receive self-determination in the West Bank and Gaza Strip as an independent state, or in federation with Jordan.

Neither the Arabs nor the Israelis were ready for such a compromise, and Carter's own elaborations on the plan gave both sides an excuse to avoid it. Carter first said that Israel should have "defensible borders," the code words in the Middle East for according Israel much of the territory conquered in the Six-Day War of 1967. Carter tried to correct this impression by speaking later of only minor border adjustments and of a Palestinian "homeland," both anathema to the Israelis. The Carter plan bogged down in confusion as the new hard-line Israeli administration, headed by Menachem Begin, insisted on the right to make Jerusalem Israel's capital and to plant new Jewish settlements on the West Bank.

Anwar Sadat tried to break the stalemate with another dramatic gesture. On November 19, 1977, he traveled to Jerusalem personally to revive step-by-step diplomacy. This was an unprecedented Arab recognition of Israel's existence and of its rights in Jerusalem. Sadat took the gamble because he feared that when Carter took the U.S. plan to the Geneva Conference, the radical Arabs, with Soviet support, would reject it; the United States would leave more committed to Israel; and Egypt would be caught in the middle.

Sadat's emotional appearance before the Israeli Knesset inspired an up-welling of peace sentiment in both Egypt and Israel. Unfortunately, the euphoria quickly dissipated when, after Sadat had returned home, he called his negotiating team back from Israel because Begin had upbraided it for demanding complete Israeli withdrawal to the 1967 borders. Meanwhile, Begin continued to plant Israeli settlements on the West Bank. Then, in March of 1978, he sent the Israeli army plunging into Lebanon in response to PLO raids. Under U.S. pressure, he withdrew from Lebanon in favor of a UN peace force in June of 1978, but he left a six-mile border strip of Lebanese territory under the control of Phalangist militia forces from several villages in the area. Lebanon was now even more polarized, and Syria again inclined its occupation troops away from the Maronites toward the radical Arab forces.

As the Middle East peace process disintegrated, Jimmy Carter took a desperate risk. He invited Begin and Sadat to the presidential mountain retreat at Camp David, Maryland. The negotiations were long and tense. Carter kept reassuring Sadat while he doggedly cajoled and reasoned with the tenacious Israeli prime minister. Finally, he emerged with the Camp David Accords of September 1978. Begin agreed to withdraw entirely from the Sinai and, if the Knesset consented, to dismantle the Jewish settlements that had been planted there after the Six-Day War. Egypt and Israel would sign a formal peace treaty incorporating these arrangements in three months. Begin and Sadat also agreed on a vague framework for peace in the rest of the Middle East, particularly the West Bank and Gaza. There would be a "self-governing authority" on the West Bank as a transition regime for five years, after which the final status of the area would be negotiated. There was no mention of an independent state or the PLO. Begin and the Israelis naturally took a very restricted view of this agreement, while Sadat and Carter saw it as the prelude to a major compromise.

As it became clear that the Israelis were not going to move toward an independent Palestinian state, the moderate Arab states of Saudi Arabia and Jordan denounced the Camp David Accords and Egypt. Sadat stalled, Israel haggled, and ultimately Carter took an even greater gamble than inviting the leaders to Camp David. He went to Cairo and Jerusalem himself to get agreement to the final peace treaty. He succeeded, and on March 26, 1979, Begin and Sadat traveled to Washington to sign the treaty. They agreed to resume negotiations on the Palestinian issue, but Egyptian recognition of Israel would exist regardless of the outcome of those negotiations.

Negotiations on the Palestinians failed. The PLO rejected anything less

Figure 24   Anwar Sadat of Egypt, Jimmy Carter of the United States, and Menachem Begin of Israel at the signing of the Egyptian-Israeli Peace Treaty. Photo courtesy of the Jimmy Carter Library.

than an independent Palestinian state under its control. Israel would have nothing to do with the PLO. Carter tried to get the PLO involved behind the scenes, but had to fire his UN ambassador, Andrew Young, when Young publicly admitted he had met with the PLO. Begin exploited the imbroglio by putting new settlements on the West Bank. The United States voted in the UN for condemnation of both the settlements and the Israeli occupation of Jerusalem, then disavowed its votes with Secretary of State Cyrus Vance accepting blame for the "mistake." Sadat withdrew from the talks on Palestinian autonomy, and Begin formally annexed East Jerusalem. The Palestinian issue continued to fester and to undermine all hope for peace in the Middle East.

ERUPTIONS IN THE PERSIAN GULF AND THE CARTER DOCTRINE

In 1979, revolution and war broke out in the Persian Gulf and posed an even greater threat to the flow of oil to the West than the Arab-Israeli conflict. The turmoil began with the overthrow of the shah of Iran.

    After the CIA had helped restore the shah to his throne in 1953, the Eisenhower administration had maintained rather restrained relations with Iran. The shah ardently desired to build Iran's military forces, but Eisenhower and his successor, John F. Kennedy, thought it useless to send the shah

Map 19   The Middle East, 1980

much military aid. Iran could never match Soviet forces. The United States would have to intervene directly in case of Soviet attack, whatever the level of Iranian armament. Eisenhower and Kennedy urged the shah to spend his oil money on domestic reform and modernization.

By the time Lyndon Johnson acceded to the presidency, the situation had changed. The shah was in a position to do more than just beg for American arms. His oil revenues had increased from $90 million a year in 1955 to $482 million in 1964. He had earned Washington's gratitude by refusing to join the Arab attempt to embargo oil to the West during the Six-Day War of 1967. Besides, the strategic situation seemed more threatening to both Iranian and American interests. The 1958 revolution in Iraq had created a radical regime hostile to both the United States and Iran. The United States was tied up in Vietnam, and while U.S. military support would not equip Iran to fight the Soviet Union on equal terms, it might enable Iran to help protect the Persian Gulf against Arab nationalism. In addition, the shah appeared to be making significant progress in the modernization and reform that Eisenhower and Kennedy had urged upon him. In his so-called White Revolution, the shah divided land among the peasants, spent lavishly on buildings and highways in urban centers, protected the rights of religious minorities like the Jews and Bahai sect, and increased the rights of women.

The shah used his increased leverage and prestige to press the Johnson administration to buy more Iranian oil and sell Iran more arms. The Defense Department objected that increased arms were unnecessary and urged that arms sales to Iran continue to be limited according to whether arms purchases would interfere with social and economic progress. The State Department, however, favored increasing the arms sales, and Johnson decided to do it. Arms sales to Iran continued to increase in the early Nixon years under the Nixon Doctrine's preference for building up local powers to eliminate the need for direct American intervention. But the tugging and hauling between the State and Defense departments limited the increases until Nixon ordered the Defense Department in 1972 to stop second-guessing Iranian arms purchases. Nixon declared that the shah could purchase anything he wanted except nuclear arms.

During the Yom Kippur War, the shah supplied the United States with oil in defiance of the Arab embargo. This won him substantial favor in the United States. Since he also was using the occasion to help triple the price of oil, he gained the wherewithal as well as the political backing in the United States to purchase more arms. Arms purchases soon absorbed 25 percent of Iran's income and outran the ability of the Iranians to man or maintain the equipment. One authority calculated that the shah would have had to conscript the entire high school graduating class every year to have enough technicians to service and operate his sophisticated weaponry. The United States supplied thousands of technicians to bridge the gap, and these Americans abroad alienated much of the population by living in luxurious enclaves where they were exempt from the jurisdiction of the Iranian courts.

Nixon and Kissinger felt little inclination to challenge the shah's dreams of building Iran into the greatest power in the Persian Gulf. Britain was withdrawing from the area by granting independence to the tiny emirates along the gulf—Kuwait, Oman, Bahrain, and Qatar. Nasser and the Soviets naturally would wish to move into the vacuum. The Soviets signed a friendship treaty with Iraq. Marxists took over South Yemen and, with Nasser's encouragement, challenged for control of North Yemen. In 1969, Iraq stirred an old quarrel with Iran by claiming the entire Shatt al-Arab River that the two nations had jointly administered as their border. By disrupting the Persian Gulf, these events threatened the area that held 75 percent of the non-Communist world's proved oil reserves.

Neither Nixon, Kissinger, nor most other American observers recognized that the shah was building his military power on a foundation of sand. They knew that the shah's modernization program had raised opposition in Iran, but they wrote off that opposition as reactionary religious fundamentalism or as Soviet-inspired agitation stirred by the Communist Tudeh party. They assumed both would be overwhelmed by the economic and social progress of the shah's modernization program. They did not understand how great a gap between rich and poor the shah's White Revolution had created.

The White Revolution's land reform had given peasants plots of land too small for subsistence. Those farmers who stayed on the land suffered in neglect. Those who escaped to the cities found few jobs in the sophisticated economy that revolved around oil, major construction, and advanced military technology. The transplanted peasants became ardent supporters of the Shiite mullahs whose mosque lands had been among those confiscated by the shah's reform. Other members of the old middle class began to join the peasants and mullahs as they saw wealth and influence siphoned off by the shah's family and corrupt cronies in the huge building projects and arms purchases that were the pride of the modernization program. The shah accelerated his alienation of the middle class in 1975 when he tried to increase tax revenue by cracking down on bazaar profiteering (but not the higher-level corruption of his family and friends) and ended subsidies to the mullahs. The bazaar merchants helped pay the resultant mosque deficits and cemented a powerful anti-shah alliance. This alliance saw the shah as a corrupt and antireligious figure who challenged the deepest beliefs of Islam.

The shah's use of police state tactics and torture contributed further to the opposition building against him. Many other Third World and Communist states had exceeded the shah's record of killing 30,000 opponents in thirty years, and the Iranians were used to governments that used such tactics. The cause for which the shah killed and tortured was increasingly suspect, however, and in a country of extended families, one instance of political murder or torture could make a hundred enemies. The CIA-trained secret police, SAVAK, also used thousands of paid informers. SAVAK thus threatened every Iranian, not just activists.

When Jimmy Carter became president in 1976, he spoke out against violations of human rights in Iran and ordered a review of arms sales to the shah for the first time since 1972. But Carter's innovation had little practical effect. His national security advisor, Zbigniew Brzezinski, and the ambassador to Iran, William Sullivan, urged continued support of the shah. Administration policy soon reverted to what it had been under Nixon and Ford. Carter even called Iran an island of stability and praised the shah as an enlightened ruler who justly deserved his people's love and admiration.

Actually, the shah was losing his grip. Unknown to the Americans, the shah had developed cancer. As Iranian disorder and demonstrations increased in the wake of a police attack on protestors in the holy city of Qom in January of 1978, the shah vacillated. In the hope of repeating his success of 1953, after each incident he would take a hard line and then soften to win back the moderates. By 1978, however, the moderates were too firmly tied to the bazaar merchants, mullahs, and displaced peasants. In August of 1978, Iran exploded in fury when a fire rumored to have been set by SAVAK killed 377 people in a theater. With Brzezinski's informal approval, the Iranian army got the shah to impose martial law and, on September 7, the military fired into a crowd in the capital city of Teheran, killing between 700 and 2,000 of the demonstrators. Carter telephoned support of the shah, and this led to the popular Iranian belief that the American president had ordered the shooting.

Panic buying and strikes, especially a strike by oil workers, threw Iran into chaos. The shah installed a military government and the United States supplied it with antiriot gear. But the Iranian army itself began to disintegrate. Conscripts were unwilling to fire at their own people; officers began to look for a way to make their own deals with the opposition. As the Carter administration belatedly realized that the shah was in serious trouble, it began to draw back from him and urge the formation of a constitutional monarchy. If there had ever been a chance of a moderate centrist solution in Iran, however, by late 1978 that time was past. The charismatic leader who galvanized the opposition was an uncompromising exiled religious leader, Ayatollah Khomeini, who regarded the shah as a puppet of a satanic United States. Khomeini insisted on a thorough revolution to overthrow the monarchy and set up a rigid, fundamentalist Islamic theocracy. The Carter administration urged the shah to leave his country and tried to set up a moderate government that would incorporate the military. The shah finally left, but moderates withered before the demands of Khomeini, who returned to Iran from exile to the tumultuous cheers of hundreds of thousands. The revolutionary militia acquired over 300,000 weapons as SAVAK and the army fell apart.

Carter tried to make the best of the situation and offer cooperation with Khomeini, but Khomeini would have none of it. The Ayatollah arrested, purged, and executed moderates, Communists, and religious and ethnic dissidents. He portrayed all of these as agents of the United States who stood in the way of a proper Islamic revolution. When the Communists of the Tudeh party attacked the American embassy on February 14, 1979, and took those within as hostages, Khomeini denounced the takeover and the attackers freed the hostages immediately. Nine months later, however, his own followers captured the embassy when Carter permitted the shah to come to the United States for medical treatment. This time the Ayatollah approved. Iran held fifty-three Americans hostage for more than a year with the approval of the official government.

The hostages became a symbol of America's growing peril and impotence in the Persian Gulf. Oil prices once again shot upward in 1979 as Iranian oil became scarce. Then, in June, Iraq exploited the trouble in Iran by breaking its 1975 peace agreement and increasing its control of the disputed border area along the Shatt al-Arab. By the fall of 1980, these Iraqi probings exploded into full-scale war. The Iraq-Iran war hindered oil deliveries from those two countries and also endangered all the oil shipments from the Persian Gulf that had to pass through the Straits of Hormuz. France's delivery of Exocet missiles to Iraq in 1983 presaged a growing number of attacks on Gulf shipping.

Meanwhile, in December 1979, Russian troops invaded Afghanistan in what seemed at the time a bizarre move to overthrow the already pro-Soviet Marxist regime of Hafizollah Amin. Amin had taken power by overthrowing another Marxist, Nur Mohammed Tarakki, whose own coup against a conservative regime in 1978 the Russians had welcomed, even though conservative Afghan regimes historically had followed prudent and friendly policies toward Russia. The Soviets were not so welcoming of Amin, however, because he overthrew Tarakki without their approval and then endangered his own regime by trying dogmatically to establish a secular Marxist state without consideration for the sentiments of his devoutly Muslim Afghan population. Muslim rebels mounted increasingly successful guerrilla operations against Amin's regime, and the Soviets concluded Amin might well be overturned by the offensive the rebels were organizing for the spring of 1980. With Iran's Khomeini already offering a troubling example to the millions of Muslims within Soviet Russia, Russian leaders evidently believed they could not afford the replacement of a friendly Marxist state by a hostile, fundamentalist Islamic one.

Jimmy Carter and most American observers, however, feared an offensive purpose to the Soviet invasion, the first massive use of Soviet troops outside the Warsaw Pact area since World War II. Afghanistan bordered Iran and put the Soviets in a better position to seize oil resources vital to the West. Afghanistan also bordered Pakistan, a weak dictatorial regime already split by the rebellion of Bangladesh, hated by India, and offering access to warm water ports on the Indian Ocean that Russia had long coveted.

Carter called the Soviet invasion of Afghanistan the greatest threat to peace since World War II. He reversed his pursuit of détente with the Soviets and his restraint in the Middle East by imposing an embargo on grain shipments to the USSR, boycotting the Moscow Olympics, setting aside attempts to secure Senate consent to the SALT II Treaty, and ending restraints on arms supplies to Pakistan (some of which arms American officials knew would go to the rebels in Afghanistan). Most significant of all, he tossed aside the Nixon Doctrine that had placed primary responsibility for regional defense on America's allies. With the collapse of Iran and the weakness of Saudi Arabia, Pakistan, and potential supporters in the Persian Gulf area, Carter saw no alternative but to commit American forces directly to the region.

He announced the Carter Doctrine: "An attempt by any outside force to gain control of the Persian Gulf region will be regarded as an assault on the vital interests of the United States of America, and such an assault will be repelled by any means necessary, including military force." To back up this pronouncement, Carter began to assemble a Rapid Deployment Force and set out to acquire staging bases in Kenya, Oman, Somalia, and the British island of Diego Garcia.

Meanwhile, however, the Iranian hostage crisis continued. When Carter's initial moderate approach failed to get results, he ordered immigration checks of Iranian students in the United States, froze Iranian assets in America, placed a trade embargo on Iran, and then broke relations. Khomeini still remained obdurate, so Carter ordered a military rescue attempt. The rescue mission failed humiliatingly when two helicopters broke down in the Iranian desert. Nine months later, as the Iraq-Iran war heated up, Khomeini finally released the hostages in exchange for the unfreezing of Iranian assets. The hostages arrived home on inauguration day in January 1981, when Ronald Reagan was promising never to be so weak in foreign affairs as the Iranian crisis had supposedly shown Jimmy Carter to be.

After 1980, the immediacy of the threat to American interests in the Persian Gulf declined slightly. The Soviets bogged down in Afghanistan and seemed little inclined to extend their military intervention any further, although they continued to support Marxist regimes in Aden, South Yemen, and Ethiopia. Iran's Khomeini proved almost as hostile to the Soviets and communism as he was to the United States. He not only turned aside Russian influence, but systematically exterminated members of the Tudeh party and other radicals with secular or pro-Soviet leanings. Meanwhile, the Iraq-Iran war, the decline in world oil consumption, and the replacement of Persian Gulf oil by Saudi Arabia and non-OPEC members like Mexico reduced Western dependence on Persian Gulf oil. The volume of oil shipped through the Straits of Hormuz fell to only 6 million barrels a day by 1984.

Nevertheless, Ronald Reagan increased the direct American commitment to the Persian Gulf area. His administration planned that by 1988 the Rapid Deployment Force would include 440,000 men, 9 divisions, 36 tactical air squadrons, 2 aircraft carriers, and 56 other vessels, all at a cost of some $500 billion. Reagan also extended the mission of this force to include possible intervention in other hot spots. One of those spots was Lebanon.

LEBANON AND THE INJECTION OF AMERICAN FORCES INTO THE ARAB-ISRAELI CONFLICT

American forces became directly embroiled in the Arab-Israeli conflict as well as in the Persian Gulf in the early 1980s. On October 6, 1981, Muslim fanatics assassinated Anwar Sadat. His successor as president of Egypt, Hosni Mubarak, supported Sadat's peace with Israel. Consequently, in April of 1982, Menachem Begin's Israeli government completed its turnover of the Sinai Desert to Egypt by forcibly removing protesting Israeli settlers. Begin, however, was ready to make no such concessions to the rest of his Arab adversaries. In mid-1981, Israel bombed a nuclear reactor Iraq was readying for operations. In December 1981, Israel formally annexed Syria's Golan Heights. Six months later, on June 6, 1982, Israel invaded Lebanon.

Since 1976, Syria and Israel had adhered to a tacit agreement on Lebanon. The Syrian troops in Lebanon would remain behind a "red line" that would keep them away from the Israeli border and the Israeli-backed Maronite militia. Syria also would not deploy ground-to-air missiles in Lebanon. Unfortunately, the agreement crumbled in 1981. Israel shot down two Syrian helicopters that were attacking Maronite strongholds in the Mt. Lebanon area outside Beirut. Later, Israel annexed the Golan Heights. Syria brought ground-to-air missiles into Lebanon's Bekaa Valley. The PLO dueled Israeli artillery across the Israeli-Lebanon border and then moved the latest Soviet Katyusha rockets into southern Lebanon.

In early 1982, despite the fact that for months there had been almost no PLO activity across the Israeli-Lebanon border, Israel discussed with the Christian Phalangist militia commander, Bashir Gemayal, plans for a full Israeli invasion of Lebanon. Israel would wait for a provocative incident, then send 36,000 troops to link up with the Maronite Christian strongholds in Beirut and central Lebanon. Afterward, the Israelis and Lebanese Christians would strengthen the Christian-dominated Lebanese central government and eject the PLO from the country. With the PLO already out of Egypt and Jordan, its ejection from Lebanon would leave it nowhere to operate on the borders of Israel except Syria, and Israel was confident that it could defend itself against Syria from the Golan Heights. The Israelis hoped that defeat of the PLO would destroy its prestige, make it an obvious creature of Syria, and thus eliminate it as the representative of the West Bank Palestinians.

On June 3, 1982, the inevitable incident occurred. The PLO assassinated the Israeli ambassador in London. Three days later, the Israeli invasion force swept into Lebanon. The Israeli air force mauled the latest Russian jets sent up against it by Syria and then destroyed the ground-to-air missiles in the Bekaa Valley. Israeli ground forces moved quickly to the outskirts of Beirut. A bloody battle for the city was only narrowly averted when Yasir Arafat and the PLO agreed to leave Beirut and disperse among nine other Arab countries. In August 1982, the United States sent 10,000 marines to join French and Italian peacekeeping troops in protecting the PLO evacuation.

With the PLO routed, President Ronald Reagan thought the moment propitious to try once again to get a comprehensive peace in the Middle East. He dusted off the old American plans for Palestinian autonomy on the West Bank in conjunction with Jordan's King Hussein and for a freeze on Israeli settlements in the area. Although Reagan still offered no solution for Jerusalem or the Golan Heights, he called his plan Fresh Start. Israel, which had other plans for exploiting its invasion of Lebanon, immediately rejected it. But there was promising movement on the Arab side. Hussein indicated agreement with Fresh Start. The Arab heads of state, meeting at Fez, Morocco, in September 1982, adopted a Saudi plan that at least implied recognition of Israel, called for an independent Palestinian state under the PLO, and demanded that Israel return to its 1967 borders. For a moment it appeared that there might be some slim hope for a compromise.

Then, on September 14, four days after American marines had completed supervising evacuation of the PLO from Beirut and left Lebanon, a bomb killed Lebanese President-elect Bashir Gemayal. Vengeful Phalangist militia, whom Israel had authorized to root out any PLO fighters left behind, raged through two Palestinian refugee camps in Beirut and massacred a thousand people. Reagan ordered the marines back into Beirut to join the French and Italians in restoring peace. The Phalangist massacre, however, had destroyed what slim chance there might have been for peace. Embittered rival Muslim and Christian militias within Lebanon took turns sniping at one another. The European forces, which were seen by the Lebanese and Arab states as props for the Christian-dominated central government, became targets of radical Muslim groups. Fresh Start fell victim to renewed anarchy and civil war.

In April 1983, King Hussein and Yasir Arafat did agree on a memorandum establishing a joint PLO-Jordanian committee to negotiate on the Rea-

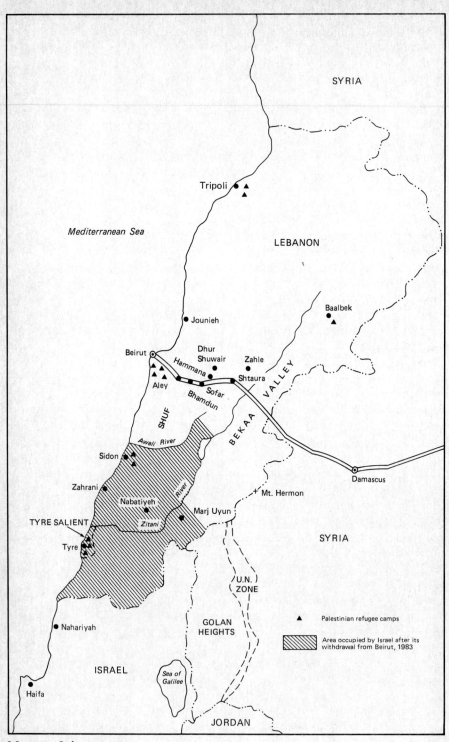

Map 20 Lebanon, 1983

gan and Fez plans, but Arafat had to disown the effort when his fellow PLO officers refused to support his action. Hussein then washed his hands of the Reagan initiative. "We leave it to the PLO and the Palestinian people to choose the ways and means for salvation of themselves and their land," he said.

Begin rejoiced at the demise of the Reagan plan and announced his government's intention to increase the Jewish population on the West Bank from 30,000 to 50,000. Israel also moved to make its Lebanese border more secure. It negotiated an agreement with Amin Gemayal, who succeeded his assassinated brother as Lebanese president, to withdraw Israeli troops from Lebanon on the condition that Syria do likewise and that Israel be permitted to patrol the Lebanese side of Israel's border. Syria rejected this American-supported plan outright. Syrian President Assad insisted that Israel should withdraw unconditionally from its illegal invasion before any negotiations could take place. He supported PLO dissidents against Arafat and his supposedly excessive moderation toward Israel. Assad also encouraged Muslim militia resistance to Israeli and European troops in Lebanon. Most ominously, Syria deployed a new supply of Soviet SAM missiles, accompanied by a large number of Russian personnel.

Faced with Syrian intransigence, Israel rejected Lebanese and American pleas and withdrew its troops from the hotbox of Beirut to defensible lines in southern Lebanon. This left the American and European peacekeeping forces in an exposed and dangerous position. Reagan sent a large naval force to protect the peacekeeping troops, but snipers, artillery fire, and bombs continued to take a toll of the American, French, and Italian soldiers. In October 1983, these attacks culminated in suicide bombings of the major French and American barracks that killed 230 American marines and more than fifty French paratroopers.

Reagan ordered the giant guns of the battleship *New Jersey* to respond to artillery and sniper attacks on the American marines. He insisted that the American peacekeeping force would not "cut and run" despite Democratic and congressional criticism. He made a new defense arrangement with Israel and refused to press Israel for the modification of the Lebanese-Israeli withdrawal agreement that Syria was demanding. But Reagan and the United States could not stop the deterioration of the situation in Lebanon. Syria backed a successful revolt against Arafat within the PLO forces stationed under Syrian control in the Bekaa Valley. PLO rebels, with Syrian help, trapped Arafat and his decreasing number of loyalists in Tripoli, and once again Arafat had to evacuate his Lebanese base. Syria was left in complete control of the PLO in Lebanon.

Gemayal met in Damascus with Assad and in Geneva with the leaders of the rival Lebanese factions to revise the Lebanese constitution. He offered too little to satisfy the majority Muslim groups, however, and in February 1984 his cabinet resigned. The Shiite and Druze militias, with Syrian artillery support, then defeated Gemayal's Lebanese army and took full charge of West Beirut. With the American marines surrounded by hostile Shiite militia in the exposed U.S. base at the Beirut airport, Reagan finally ordered the American peacekeeping force back to its ships. All the other peacekeeping forces except the French left as well.

Syria moved quickly to solidify its influence in Lebanon. Assad helped Gemayal and the other factional leaders patch together a government, and Gemayal in turn renounced his withdrawal agreement with Israel. A new Israeli cabinet, an uneasy coalition of the Labor and Likud parties, besieged by runaway inflation and the burdens of occupation in southern Lebanon, began a staged withdrawal from southern Lebanon after dropping its demand that Syria withdraw simultaneously. The Israelis quickly found that the Amal Shiites of southern Lebanon, who initially had welcomed the Israeli expulsion of the PLO, were now extremely hostile. Shiite snipers and suicide bombers attacked the withdrawing Israeli troops, and Israel responded with raids on Shiite villages to kill or capture the Lebanese attackers and bulldoze the houses of their protectors. The invasion of Lebanon thus seemed only to have exchanged one hostile force for another on Israel's northern border.

Jordan and Egypt also responded to the rising influence of Syria in Lebanon. Jordan resumed diplomatic relations with Egypt and King Hussein permitted Yasir Arafat to hold a meeting of the Palestinian Council in Amman in defiance of Arafat's Syrian-backed opponents. Arafat, Hussein, and Egyptian President Mubarak agreed on a new peace initiative with Israel and urged the United States to reinvolve itself in the Middle East peace question. But dissension within Arafat's own faction over his agreement with Hussein and Mubarak combined with the internal paralysis of Israel's divided government made the Reagan administration extremely cautious. The Palestinian situation seemed as intractable and chaotic as ever.

CONTROVERSIAL ISSUES AND FURTHER READING

The Arabs and Israelis debate history as well as territory. [For support and explanation of the Israeli position, see such works as Chaim Herzog, *The Arab-Israeli Wars* (1982), and Bernard Reich, *Quest for Peace: United States-Israel Relations and the Arab-Israeli Conflict* (1977). For Palestinian views, although moderate ones that imply eventual recognition of Israel's right to exist, see Edward Said, *The Question of Palestine* (1979), and Mohammed K. Shadid, *The United States and the Palestinians* (1981). For an account that condemns both sides for excessive violence, see David Hirst, *The Gun and the Olive Branch: The Roots of Violence in the Middle East* (1977).]

Most American historians avoid endorsement of either the Palestinian or Israeli position and debate instead the best way to secure a compromise peace. Most agree that Israel must return to its 1967 borders with only minor adjustments and accept some sort of Palestinian state on the West Bank and Gaza in exchange for Arab recognition and great power guarantees of Israeli security. But they disagree somewhat on whether the step-by-step process was the best approach to peace, whether the Palestinian state should be totally independent and free to choose the PLO as its government, and whether the United States should exert all its leverage on Israel to bring it to accept a comprehensive compromise peace. [See, for instance, Nadav Safran, *Israel: The Embattled Ally* (1981), for an endorsement of Kissinger's step-by-step diplomacy, and Edward F. Sheehan, *The Arabs, Israelis and Kissinger: A Secret History of American Diplomacy* (1976), for a critique. See also William R. Polk, *The Arab World* (4th ed., 1980); George Lenczowski, *The Middle East in World Affairs* (4th ed., 1980); William B. Quandt, *Decade of Decisions: American Policy toward the Arab-Israeli Conflict, 1967–1976* (1977); and Seth P. Tillman, *The United States and the Middle East* (1982).]

On the Iranian revolution and Iraq-Iran war, see Barry Rubin, *Paved with Good Intentions: The American Experience and Iran* (1980), and Tareq Y. Ismael, *Iraq and Iran: Roots of Conflict* (1982). On Afghanistan and American policy in the Persian Gulf, see Louis Dupree, *Afghanistan* (1978); Henry S. Bradsher, *Afghanistan: Soviet Invasion and U.S. Response* (1980–1981); and Alvin Z. Rubinstein, *Soviet Policy Toward Turkey, Iran, and Afghanistan: The Dynamics of Influence* (1982). On Lebanon, see Walid Khalid, *Conflict and Violence in Lebanon* (1980); Jonathan C. Randall, *Going All the Way: Christian Warlords, Israeli Adventures, and the War in Lebanon* (1983); David C. Gordon, *The Republic of Lebanon: A Nation in Jeopardy* (1983); and Marius Deeb, *The Lebanese Civil War* (1980).

CHAPTER 21

Jimmy Carter, Ronald Reagan, and the Demise of Détente

FROM CARTER TO REAGAN

In the wake of the Soviet and Cuban intervention in Angola, President Gerald Ford decided that the word "détente" was a political liability, and he instructed his supporters to avoid its use during the 1976 election campaign. In this way he tried to protect himself against Jimmy Carter's charges that Ford and Kissinger were "giving up too much and asking for too little" from the Soviets. According to Carter, Kissinger's détente had given the Soviets "an opportunity to continue the process of world revolution without running the threat of nuclear war." Carter endorsed Senator Henry Jackson's claim that SALT II should have been "broader and more reciprocal."

Yet Carter called for improved relations with the Soviets at the same time that he criticized Ford and Kissinger for conceding too much to them. He declared that the United States should free itself from an "inordinate fear of communism." He denounced Nixon, Ford, and Kissinger for excessive and immoral intervention against chimerical Soviet and other Communist threats in the Third World. Vietnam had taught Americans that "we cannot and should not try to intervene militarily in the internal affairs of other countries unless our own nation is endangered," he said. Kissinger should not have interfered in Chile merely because the Chilean government had turned to the Left. Only an actual Soviet presence that directly threatened vital American interests would have justified intervention.

Carter's ambiguous campaign did not necessarily guarantee the end of détente or a fractured foreign policy. He was only following the standard gambit of attacking the incumbent administration from the right and the left at the same time. Unfortunately, he went on to institutionalize the contradictions in his foreign policy by appointing officials who embodied strongly opposing tendencies. Cyrus Vance, Carter's secretary of state, advocated the restrained realist position. He sought to adapt American policy to Russian military parity and the diffusion of power in the Third World. Zbigniew Brzezinski, Carter's national security advisor, was a hard realist. He wanted a tougher line on SALT and more active opposition to potential Soviet influ-

Figure 25   President Jimmy Carter confers with the representatives of the opposing foreign policy viewpoints within his administration, Secretary of State Cyrus Vance and National Security Advisor Zbigniew Brzezinski. Photo courtesy of the Jimmy Carter Library.

ence in the Third World. As a Pole, he reveled in his chance to "stick it to the Russians." Secretary of Defense Harold Brown generally sided with Brzezinski's harder line, especially on military issues.

Carter did not worry about this ideological split within his administration because he intended to keep control of foreign policy formulation largely in his own hands. "There may have been Presidents in the past, maybe not too distant past, that let their Secretaries of State make foreign policy," he stated. "I don't." Neither would he share much authority with Congress. Carter was a political outsider, a Georgia governor and state politician who had won the Democratic nomination and the presidential election by running against the corruption of Watergate, the errors of Vietnam, and the general incompetence of federal incumbents. He thought he could manage the government without having to rely on the government bureaucracy or the Washington insiders. He intended to serve personally as the bridge between the liberal and conservative tendencies within his administration, the Democratic party, and the public at large. Personal competence and honesty would create a consensus to replace the ideological contentions and backroom dealings that had plagued recent national politics and American foreign policy.

Carter was confident that he could master the most complex problems. He spent most of his waking hours studying the intricacies of each issue and then personally shaping a decision from the conflicting recommendations of his advisors. He permitted wide-ranging and often semi-public debate on these issues within his administration in the hope that his own competence and the very openness of the policy process, which contrasted so sharply with the secretive, manipulative techniques of Nixon and Kissinger, would generate popular support for whatever course he chose to take.

Carter also counted heavily on his personal morality to contrast with Nixon and attract support for his policies. He made very public his religious commitment. Under the influence of his evangelist faith-healing sister, Carter had been "born again." He promised never to lie to the American people. He pledged to jettison Kissinger's undiluted power politics and restore a sense of ethics to American foreign policy. He embarked on an international campaign for human rights and, like Senator Henry Jackson, tried to use it to unite domestic liberals and conservatives. Carter appealed to the Right by emphasizing Soviet and other Communist violations of human rights. He appealed to the Left by denouncing oppression in reactionary Third World regimes, even though many of these nations were friendly to the United States.

Carter also followed Jackson in trying to bridge the gap between Left and Right on the nuclear arms issue. He called for reductions in the SALT II limits on nuclear armaments, a position attractive to the Left, but molded his reduction proposal to bolster the American side of the balance with the Soviet Union, a constant demand of the Right.

Despite Carter's intelligence and good intentions, he failed miserably to master the contradictions within his foreign policy. The gulf was too wide to be bridged by the flimsy materials Carter had at hand. Carter's advisors sniped at one another with increasing rancor. Carter bogged down in the intricate details he insisted on mastering. One of his speechwriters later said that Carter was not a conceptualizer, but had a mind of "the item-by-item engineering variety." Carter was "the first person I would want to look over the plans for a new submarine," but "practically the last person whose thoughts I would want to hear ... on 'Relations Between the Soviet Union and the United States.' His mind does not work that way." His inability to delegate responsibility deprived him of the time to formulate a coherent foreign policy. Even if he had developed a consistent policy, he lacked the ability to explain and inspire enthusiasm for it. His flat and often whiny speaking style gave less the appearance of calm competence than of resigned passivity. Events spun out of control.

Perhaps they would have spun out of control no matter who had been president, for the events of the late 1970s were overwhelming. As described in the previous chapter, Israeli and Palestinian intransigence gave little hope for a comprehensive settlement between them, however able and assertive the American president might have been. The Soviet invasion of Afghanistan also was beyond the influence of the president. It is doubtful that any response to the Iranian revolution could have improved the U.S. position with the Ayatollah Khomeini, and the Iranian hostage situation offered even fewer opportunities for successful American initiatives. The oil shortage and price increases that resulted from the Iranian crisis accelerated inflation in the United States and did immense damage to an already weak American economy. Moscow defied Carter's call for human rights, continued its military buildup, adopted hard positions in arms negotiations, and sacrificed very little to help Carter maintain the spirit of détente. Carter's attempt to decouple the Cold War from Latin America and Africa by accommodating some Third World desires and tolerating independent Leftist regimes backfired politically. Cuba's Fidel Castro kept his troops in Angola, sent others to Ethiopia, and dumped hardened criminals into the stream of Cuban refugees he finally allowed to leave for the United States.

Toward the end of his administration, Carter tried to recover popularity and control of events by adopting a more consistent hard line. Vance resigned as secretary of state and was replaced by Edmund Muskie. Brzezinski became the dominant figure in foreign policy within the administration. But it was too late for Carter to escape his image of weakness and indecisiveness, and Ronald Reagan used it effectively in the campaign of 1980. "Jimmy Carter said we should give back the Panama Canal because nobody would like us if we didn't," Reagan told his campaign audiences. "Jimmy Carter says we should sign the SALT II treaty because nobody will like us if we don't. . . . Well, I say, isn't it about time we stopped worrying about whether people like us and say, 'We want to be respected again!' " He defeated Carter and set out to regain respect for the United States with a vigorous anti-Communist foreign policy.

Reagan was not experienced in foreign affairs. Carter jibed during the campaign that if the Republicans were elected and Reagan held a summit meeting with the Soviets, all the participants would have to wear name tags. As president, Reagan often made gaffes in extemporaneous remarks that his aides had to explain away the following day. Nevertheless, Reagan was an extremely effective advocate for his foreign policy when he relied on prepared rather than extemporaneous presentations. He had the benefit of experience as a movie actor, television host for the General Electric Theater, and a popular after-dinner speaker for GE at various conventions and meetings. He had been fairly liberal during his film acting days, but became more and more conservative during his time with General Electric. He emerged in the 1960s as a spokesman for the Goldwater wing of the Republican party, served two terms as governor of California, and ultimately won the Republican presidential nomination on a highly conservative platform in 1980. Symbolically, when he became president he replaced the picture of Harry Truman in the cabinet room with one of Calvin Coolidge.

Reagan and the Republicans seemed to disdain nuclear parity and détente with the Soviets. The Republican platform pledged "to achieve military and technological superiority over the Soviet Union." Reagan told the *Wall Street Journal* in 1980: "The Soviet Union underlies all that is going on. If they weren't engaged in this game of dominoes, there wouldn't be any hot spots in the world." He expressed doubts about agreements with the Soviets because they did not keep their word. They reserved "unto themselves the right to commit any crime, to lie, to cheat, in order to obtain" their objective. He told the National Association of Evangelicals in 1983 that the Soviet Union was the "focus of evil in the modern world." He referred to the Vietnam war as "a noble cause."

Presidential rhetoric must always be taken with a grain of salt, and Reagan's ideological outbursts did not guarantee an unambiguously hard-line policy. As governor of California, he often had taken strong positions and then at the last minute heeded pragmatic arguments to compromise. Much of Reagan's policy would depend on his advisors, for in contrast to Jimmy Carter, he delegated a great deal of authority to his subordinates. He insulated himself against too much detail, ignored as best he could the bureaucratic infighting in his administration, and tried to save his energy for the big decisions. At times this insulation could have rather bizarre consequences, as when his aides failed to wake him after American planes shot down two Libyan fighters that were flying toward an American aircraft carrier in the Gulf of Sidra.

Reagan's first secretary of state, Alexander Haig, represented the pragmatic side of Reagan's foreign policy. He had been Henry Kissinger's executive assistant on the National Security Council before taking on the same administrative duties for Richard Nixon at the White House during Watergate. While serving in the government, he advanced in military rank over the heads of his fellow officers. After Haig's stint in the White House, Gerald Ford appointed him commander of NATO.

Haig brought to the State Department the European orientation and hard-bargaining realpolitik outlook of Kissinger. Like Kissinger, he agreed with the more conservative ideologues on the need for an active anti-Communist policy in the Third World, but he was willing to accede to Western European desires for a moderate policy toward the Soviet Union. For instance, Haig wanted careful coordination with NATO on such issues as the neutron bomb and the deployment of intermediate-range missiles in Europe. Caspar Weinberger, Reagan's secretary of defense who represented the administration's hard-liners, referred to Haig's positions as State Department "squish" and said the United States should not be deterred by such matters as German internal politics. Haig sarcastically characterized the "Weinberger line" as the belief that

> Anything Marxist is evil and must be destroyed. The Soviet Union is ready to collapse and if we just apply a few more sanctions, it will. On the one hand we can insist that we're too weak to negotiate with them, and on the other hand, we're strong enough to conduct brittle confrontational policies the outcome of which we might not be prepared to face.[1]

Pragmatists clashed with hard-liners over several issues involving Europe and the Soviet Union in Reagan's first years. In 1982 Reagan ordered American companies to cease supplying equipment for the gas pipeline the Soviet

[1] Laurence I. Barrett, *Gambling with History: Ronald Reagan in the White House* (Garden City, NY, 1983), p. 225.

Union was building toward Europe. He also asked the European nations to abandon the project. When the Europeans balked, Weinberger and other hard-liners wanted to penalize the European subsidiaries of American companies as well as the American companies themselves if they continued to participate in the pipeline project. Haig objected. After all, the Reagan administration had lifted Carter's embargo on wheat shipments to the Soviet Union. How could the United States penalize Europe for seeking comparable trade relations with Russia? Reagan sided with Weinberger and the hard-liners. His decision greatly strained relations with Europe while failing to halt the pipeline.

Haig also clashed with the hard-liners over the 1982 Argentine invasion of the British-ruled Falkland Islands. Haig tried to deter Argentina by warning that the United States would use its influence on the British side. UN Ambassador Jeanne J. Kirkpatrick, one of the conservative leaders within the administration, objected and said the United States should remain completely neutral. To back the British would violate the Rio Pact's guarantees against threats from outside the hemisphere and diminish U.S. influence in Latin America. She called Haig and his chief aides "Brits in American clothes." Some members of the administration who agreed with Kirkpatrick evidently contacted the Argentines and softened Haig's warning. Haig raged that this had encouraged the invasion. He said that the nation's Atlantic ties were far more important than those with Latin America, and he especially disliked giving any encouragement to aggressive actions on the part of a fragile and brutal Argentine regime that was on the brink of acquiring nuclear weapons. (As it happened, the British retook the Falklands in a masterful operation, the Argentine dictatorship fell, and in 1984 a new centrist democratic government opened conversations with Great Britain to resolve the Falklands issue.)

The struggle for Reagan's ear became so cacophonous that even he could not ignore it. His ire fell primarily on Haig. Haig was a loner and a political infighter trained in the arena of the Nixon-Kissinger administration. His constant public maneuvers to assert his primacy within the administration alienated even his fellow pragmatists. Haig expected to be Reagan's "vicar" on foreign policy, and he resented any intrusions on his territory or slights to his prerogatives. He bridled, for instance, when he was shunted to a compartment in Air Force One too far from the president and then had to ride in a separate helicopter. "What am I, a pariah?" he asked.

Unfortunately for Haig, Reagan liked team players and hated to choose between his advisors. To smooth out the diplomatic process and end the bickering over foreign policy, Reagan removed one of Haig's chief antagonists, National Security Advisor Richard Allen, who had been a rather weak and ineffectual member of the ideological right-wing group. But Reagan replaced Allen with another hard-liner, William Clark. Clark was embarrassingly uninformed on foreign affairs. When quizzed by the Senate committee considering his appointment, he could not name the leaders of some of the most important nations with which the United States would have to deal.

Figure 26 President Ronald Reagan (right) confers with the representatives of opposing foreign policy tendencies within his administration: Secretary of Defense Caspar Weinberger (left) and Secretary of State George Shultz (center). Courtesy of the White House; photo, Karl Schumacher.

Nevertheless, Clark was an old Reagan crony and a good organizer. When Haig continued his public complaining, it was Haig whom Reagan asked to resign.

While it seemed at first that the conservative ideologues had won, Reagan appointed another relative moderate, former Secretary of the Treasury George Shultz, to replace Haig as secretary of state. Shultz was a team player, and the quarrels within the administration over foreign policy became less pronounced or at least less public. In addition, the focus of foreign policy shifted from Europe to the Middle East and Central America after the United States began to deploy new missiles in Europe and the Soviets broke off all arms talks. With regard to those Third World areas, a strange metamorphosis took place in the lineup of pragmatists and hard-liners.

Shultz, the supposed pragmatist, advocated sending the marines to Lebanon and then opposed withdrawing them after their position became intolerable. The military chiefs, and Weinberger as their civilian spokesman, took the more cautious line. Vietnam had made the joint chiefs reticent in the use of American troops for political purposes unless there were clear-cut military objectives, sufficient strength available, and wide public support. The chiefs were much more reluctant than Shultz to commit the marines in Lebanon. Similarly, the joint chiefs and Weinberger were the last in the administration to support military intervention in the Caribbean nation of Grenada.

President Reagan generally took the side of the hard-liners in all these conflicts. He went beyond the advice of the joint chiefs in both Lebanon and Grenada. He selected the hardest available options in formulating negotiating positions on nuclear arms talks with the Soviets. He defied the congressional consensus by insisting on major increases in military spending while cutting domestic social programs and incurring huge budget deficits. He rejected Haig's suggestion of a blockade of Cuba and Nicaragua, but he initiated a semi-secret CIA war against the Sandinista government of Nicaragua and rejected any serious measures to stop the terrorist campaign of El Salvador's death squads against Leftist rebels.

Perhaps Reagan would still prove to be a pragmatist and draw back at the last minute to make compromise settlements on arms control, Central America, and the Middle East. But critics wondered whether there would be anyone left on the other side able or willing to bargain. Even what passed for pragmatism and moderation in the Reagan administration demanded a great deal from America's adversaries. Reagan's militant policies also frightened many of America's own people and allies. Consequently, global opponents might stand pat and hope for the disintegration of Western unity rather than make an unfavorable agreement. In any case, détente was thoroughly dead.

The demise of détente can best be traced in the policies of Carter and Reagan toward China, Africa, Latin America, the international economy, and most important, the Soviet Union and the issue of arms control.

CARTER, REAGAN, AND CHINA AND AFRICA

China

Carter believed the time was ripe to improve American relations with China. The death of Chou En-lai in early 1976 ushered in a brief revival of radical purges and anti-American rhetoric, but the death of Mao Tse-tung in September reversed the trend. Protégés of Chou purged the radical Gang of Four, including Mao's widow, and then deemphasized class strife in favor of more pragmatic approaches to economic growth.

As China moved toward a more pragmatic policy, Carter and Cyrus Vance proposed that the United States and China open full normal relations. The sticky problem of Taiwan had prevented this in the Kissinger years, but Carter and Vance offered to circumvent the issue. They would raise the liaison offices of China and the United States to full-fledged embassies while reducing the United States and Taiwan embassies to liaison offices. Vance also suggested China voluntarily state publicly that it would not use force to settle the Taiwan problem. To Carter's dismay, both China and Taiwan rejected the proposal, and since Carter and Vance had reopened the Taiwan issue, China demanded that the United States sever relations with Taiwan completely.

As part of Carter's later swing toward a harder anti-Soviet foreign policy,

Brzezinski went to China in 1978 and indicated that even if the United States could not abandon Taiwan as the price of normalized relations with China, his government might pay in other coin. The United States would fall in with China's desire for a stronger policy against the Soviet Union. At a banquet in Peking, Brzezinski publicly denounced Soviet "hegemony" and won from the Chinese the appellation "bear tamer." The Carter administration also arranged to help China with technology the United States had denied to the Soviet Union.

On January 1, 1979, the United States and China opened full and normal diplomatic relations. Carter announced that the United States would break its ties with Taiwan, withdraw from the U.S.-Taiwan defense treaty, and remove all American troops from the island. Carter relegated relations with Taiwan to private trade offices. China in turn indicated that it would not try to take Taiwan by force, although it would give no formal commitment. Conservatives protested at the cavalier treatment of America's Taiwanese ally, but Carter pushed ahead to give China increased military support and most favored nation trade status.

Ronald Reagan came to the presidency pledged to restore official ties to Taiwan. Yet he and many in his administration saw China as a valuable asset in their tough policy toward the Soviet Union. Reagan consequently refused to raise the status of the informal trade offices that handled U.S.-Taiwan relations. But he did sell advanced planes and arms to Taiwan, which raised a bitter protest from China. Washington and Peking barely papered over the dispute. The United States agreed to limit arms sales to Taiwan; China reasserted its fundamental policy to seek peaceful resolution of the Taiwan issue. Peking declared, however, that it would not forswear the use of force permanently, and it opened a series of talks with the Soviets aimed at reducing tensions. Not much seemed to come of these discussions, but Reagan was on notice that China might play a Soviet card as readily as the United States was playing the China card.

Africa

Since Carter expected to improve relations with the Soviet Union in the early years of his administration, he thought he could deemphasize great power competition in Third World areas such as Africa. He treated the Soviet-supported Cuban troops in Angola as a local affair and called for restraint in the American response. He would substitute a concern for human rights, especially the rights of blacks in white-dominated nations, for fear of communism. He appointed Andrew Young, a black Georgia congressman and former aide to Martin Luther King, as ambassador to the United Nations to enlist the United States more on the side of emerging colonial nations. Young and Carter vigorously promoted negotiations to end the white minority rule of Ian Smith's government in Rhodesia. They also induced Congress to repeal the Byrd Amendment, which had allowed the United States to import chromium from Rhodesia in defiance of a UN boycott. Vice-President Walter Mondale even had the temerity to suggest to whites in rigidly segregated

South Africa that they adopt the "one man, one vote" principle. Meanwhile, Young opened contact with the Marxist leadership of Angola and Mozambique.

Carter's efforts to revise American policy in Africa bore little fruit. South Africa resented the human rights agitation and stalled U.S. initiatives that sought independence for Namibia. Ian Smith of Rhodesia also sidetracked the American-sponsored negotiations on his regime. (Ultimately Great Britain, the nation from which Rhodesia had declared its independence, did negotiate a settlement that brought black majority rule to the new nation of Zimbabwe.) African states, on the other hand, criticized Carter for not going far enough to reduce American economic connections with South Africa and Rhodesia.

Meanwhile, Soviet intervention into Ethiopia's war with Somalia made it more difficult for Carter to accommodate Leftist Third World regimes and avoid injecting Cold War issues into Africa. In 1977, Somalia invaded the Ogaden Desert, occupied by Ethiopia. The Soviet Union, which had strong military connections to Somalia, abruptly cut off its aid. It then transported Cuban troops, along with Soviet advisors and tons of equipment, to Ethiopia to help defeat the Somali invasion. Carter refused to do much for Somalia, but he warned the Soviets that the Cuban presence in Ethiopia and Angola was testing the limits of his tolerance. He then abandoned his attempts to restrict arms sales to Africa and sent weapons to Ethiopia's nervous neighbors, Chad, Sudan, and Kenya. He also increased aid to Zaire and Morocco for their battles against Leftist rebels.

Ronald Reagan accelerated these trends. He criticized Carter's human rights policy and let South Africa know that he regarded its internal racial affairs as its own business. When negotiations over the independence of Namibia broke down, he had the United States join Britain and France in the UN Security Council to veto mandatory economic sanctions against South Africa. He also cut by half American aid to the Leftist black regime in Zimbabwe. He emphasized Africa as an arena of competition with the Soviet Union and made clear that he would favor any nation which lined up with the United States, regardless of its domestic policies. He and his ambassador to the United Nations, Jeanne Kirkpatrick, had no patience with the African and other Third World Leftist nations that portrayed the United States as an imperialist obstacle to world justice. Reagan, like the Ford administration before him, punished countries for hostile UN votes by reducing their aid. He also risked American involvement in the war between Ethiopia and Somalia by securing a base for the Rapid Deployment Force at the Somali port of Berbera.

CARTER, REAGAN, AND LATIN AMERICA

Jimmy Carter tried to accommodate some of the needs of Latin America and to use his human rights campaign to encourage gradual reform and centrist regimes in the hemisphere. He believed that improving social and economic conditions in the region was the best way to eliminate opportunities for the Soviet Union and Cuba to extend their influence. Nevertheless, his support for centrist alternatives to communism and revolution was no more successful than John Kennedy's had been. As in Kennedy's day, democratic moderates were too few and the middle classes too weak in Latin America to offer a viable centrist alternative. Instead, reactionary regimes produced harsh revolutionaries, and between them they squeezed most moderates out of power or influence. This left the United States with the choice between reactionaries and revolutionaries, both of which espoused values and tactics difficult for Americans to accept.

The Panama Canal Treaties

Carter's most significant and successful act of accommodation toward Latin America was his negotiation of the Panama Canal treaties. Panamanians had long resented U.S. control of the canal and the arrogant exclusiveness with which it ran the surrounding Canal Zone. Serious riots in the Canal Zone had driven Lyndon Johnson to begin negotiations with Panama on the status of the canal, and these talks had continued through the Nixon and Ford years. Carter pledged faster progress and personally intervened when the talks bogged down in 1977. On September 7, 1977, Carter and Panama's General Omar Torrijos signed the two Panama Canal treaties. The first treaty gave Panama immediate jurisdiction over the Canal Zone, placed operation of the canal itself in the hands of a new agency composed of five U.S. citizens and four Panamanians, and assigned Panama a greater percentage of the canal's revenues. The United States would manage and defend the canal under this new agency until the end of the century, and it would continue to control certain military bases and other installations necessary to this task. The second treaty provided that at the end of the century Panama would take over both management and control of the canal.

Despite some vocal opposition in Panama to any continuance of the U.S. presence, 66 percent of the Panamanians who voted in a national referendum approved the treaties. The fight over the treaties was much more difficult in the United States. Opponents, including Ronald Reagan, called the treaties a sellout and warned that they would endanger American security. Senator S. I. Hayakawa of California only half facetiously complained that since we had stolen the canal fair and square, it was ours. Proponents of the treaties responded that the canal would be far less secure if Panamanian resentment inspired a campaign of sabotage than if it reverted to Panama with U.S. guarantees of its neutrality. Besides, they pointed out, the canal had declined in both strategic and economic importance. Less than 10 percent of U.S. trade flowed through the canal. It was too small to permit the passage of larger modern ships such as aircraft carriers, supertankers, and some container ships.

Carter staked his prestige on the treaties and spared no effort to secure their ratification. When opposition threatened to overwhelm them, he negotiated with Panama a new memorandum of understanding spelling out more definitively the right of the United States to intervene to defend against any threats to peaceful transit through the waterway in time of crisis. Finally, in the spring of 1978, the Senate consented to the treaties with only one vote to spare. In the process, the Senate added an amendment spelling out U.S. rights of intervention within Panama in almost humiliating detail. Nonetheless, it was a considerable triumph for Carter's accommodationist policy.

Cuba

Carter was not so successful in his attempt to accommodate Cuba. At the outset of his administration, he resumed the quiet talks Gerald Ford had broken off after the dispatch of Cuban troops to Angola. Carter suggested that U.S.-Cuban relations would improve if Castro withdrew his troops from Angola and improved human rights conditions in Cuba. Castro responded angrily that it was much more important for the United States to lift its boycott of the island and get out of Guantanamo. From this inauspicious beginning, relations gradually improved. The United States removed travel restrictions to Cuba and ended the blacklist of foreign ships trading with Castro. Both nations expanded the interest sections that represented them in the other's capital. Then, in 1978, Castro offered to release 1,500 people for emigration to the United States. He promised further to release 3,600 political prisoners and 7,000 former political prisoners if the United States would accept them as immigrants.

While negotiations continued on this question, Carter suddenly protested the presence of some 2,500 Soviet combat troops in Cuba. Carter admitted the United States had known for years that the troops were there, but had not realized they were combat soldiers. Carter's protest opened a Pandora's box in an election year. Frank Church, a liberal senator running for reelection in conservative Idaho, abruptly postponed his Foreign Relations Committee's consideration of the SALT II agreement until the Soviet troops were withdrawn. Relations between Cuba and the United States soured.

Then, in April of 1980, Cubans who had been heartened by Castro's relenting on emigration policy crowded into the Peruvian embassy because they heard that Cuba and Peru were working out an emigration agreement. Castro withdrew his guards from the Peruvian embassy during the imbroglio, and the number of refugees soared to 10,000. An embarrassed Castro promised that he would permit them to leave Cuba, and Carter offered an open arms policy to those of them who wished to come to the United States. In the next few months a makeshift flotilla of private boats and rafts, many from Florida, ferried 120,000 Cubans to the United States. Most were political refugees, but Castro vengefully emptied his prisons of hardened criminals and dumped them into the stream of emigrants.

The flow of Cubans overwhelmed the U.S. border patrol, and the Immigration Service confined many of the refugees to prison camps while it tried rather unsuccessfully to screen them. The innocents naturally chafed at their inhospitable welcome to the "land of the free," Carter reaped a bitter political harvest from the refugee fiasco, and U.S.-Cuban relations returned to their previous hostile level.

Reform in Latin America

Carter's attempt to encourage gradual reform in Latin America through the promotion of human rights had little more success than his policy toward Cuba. In the last year of the Ford administration, Congress had responded to the lessons of Vietnam by passing the Foreign Military Assistance Act of 1976. This act denied credits for military sales to nations committing gross violations of human rights unless the president believed extraordinary circumstances warranted an exception. It also instructed the State Department to report regularly on the status of human rights in nations receiving military aid.

Ford opposed this measure, but Carter welcomed and quickly made use of it. He reduced aid to Argentina, Uruguay, and Brazil and withheld weapons sales to other Latin American regimes. Many nations, including Argentina, Uruguay, and Guatemala, refused aid to which human rights conditions were attached. Brazil canceled its twenty-five-year-old military aid treaty with the United States. Some democratic countries like Venezuela praised the president's initiative, but others of both Left and Right opposed or abstained when called upon to endorse the concept in the OAS or the UN. They saw it as another potential opening for U.S. intervention.

Nicaragua and El Salvador

One of the nations Carter tried to influence on human rights was Nicaragua, long ruled by the dictatorial and corrupt Somoza family. Anastasio Somoza Garcia, through his control of the National Guard, had taken charge of Nicaragua four years after the U.S. marines had withdrawn in 1932. In 1934, he engineered the assassination of the popular guerrilla leader who had led the fight against the American marines, Augusto César Sandino. Afterward, he consolidated his rule by permitting only a modicum of ineffectual opposition. By 1944, through plunder and extortion, Somoza owned fifty-one cattle ranches, forty-six coffee plantations, and earned $400,000 a year from U.S. companies he exempted from taxation. When he was assassinated in 1956, his son Luís Somoza Debayle succeeded him, and in 1967 he in turn was succeeded by his brother, Anastasio Somoza Debayle. By 1979 the Somoza family's fortune had grown to $150 million, not including assets abroad. Anastasio Somoza Debayle had even raked off much of the charity aid that had flooded into Nicaragua after an earthquake devastated the capital city of Managua in 1972.

Anastasio Somoza Debayle was not so nimble a ruler as his father or brother. Even the middle classes balked at his blatant plundering of the earthquake charity after 1972. Somoza made no attempt to divide the bourgeois from the peasant opposition, but brutally suppressed them both. He declared a state of emergency and used his 7,500-man National Guard to enforce martial law.

Nicaragua was of no particular economic interest to the United States or its major corporations. President Carter worried only that revolution in Nicaragua might open the way for Soviet or Cuban influence. He sought to forestall this by encouraging moderate reform. In 1977, he demanded that Somoza lift his state of emergency. Somoza complied, and opposition immediately broke out again. In 1978, a liberal editor who led Nicaragua's moderates was assassinated, inspiring increased strikes and riots. Somoza finally tried to compromise with the moderates, but it was too late. The moderates had already formed a broad but uneasy national front with the guerrilla forces that had taken on the name of the heroic Sandino. The Sandinistas then drew international attention in August of 1978 when they took over the national palace in Managua and held 500 hostages. They ultimately exchanged their hostages for political prisoners, $5 million, and refuge in Panama.

Such radical actions split the opposition front, and the United States, Guatemala, and the Dominican Republic tried to mediate the civil war by getting Somoza to abandon Nicaragua and leave behind a moderate successor regime. A massive uprising in January of 1979 brought Somoza to reject this mediation attempt. Once again the opposition united, and Carter cut off aid to Nicaragua.

Carter, however, was hesitant and inconsistent in his attempt to secure a moderate regime to replace Somoza and forestall a radical revolution. Even while the United States cut aid to Nicaragua, the U.S. representative to the International Monetary Fund voted to loan Somoza $65 million. Then, in June 1979, Secretary of State Cyrus Vance proposed that the OAS send a peacekeeping force to Nicaragua. Latin American regimes of both Right and Left rejected the call. The OAS instead warned against any outside intervention and demanded that Somoza resign. The United States reluctantly went along, and the U.S. ambassador in Managua told Somoza flatly he should go. Somoza fled on July 17, 1979; the government he left behind collapsed in twenty-four hours. The revolution had cost the lives of 50,000 people. The Somoza loyalists added to this misery by destroying many of Nicaragua's factories as they fled.

The Sandinistas immediately nationalized all of Somoza's industries, 25 percent of the nation's factories. The Sandinistas later nationalized many other factories, banks, and mines, along with about 50 percent of the agricultural land. They also developed an internal security organization similar to Cuba's. A separate police and security force replaced the National Guard, while local Sandinista Defense Committees formed neighborhood political units to organize the countryside and expose counterrevolutionaries. The more militant Sandinista ex-guerrillas confined the moderate members of their front to token roles. They launched a campaign of education for the peasants, many of whom had never seen a school or a teacher under the Somoza regime, and accompanied this with a good deal of sloganeering and political "reeducation." They passed a law imposing a two-year prison sentence on those whose declarations harmed the "people's interest" and repeatedly closed down the chief opposition paper, *La Prensa.* They also persecuted the Miskito Indians, many of whom opposed the Sandinistas' integrationist programs. Finally, they readily accepted aid from the Soviet Union and several thousand advisors from Cuba.

On the other hand, the Sandinistas permitted some freedom for opposition parties, newspapers, and unions. They maintained a mixed economy rather than a rigidly centralized one. They did not prohibit movement within the country or emigration from it, and they did not launch a terror campaign.

Carter and his leading aides approached the Sandinistas with considerable wariness. The United States recognized the Sandinista regime quickly, but it also began consideration of military aid to Nicaragua's neighbors, Guatemala and El Salvador. After considerable debate and expressed hostility toward the Leftist regime, Carter finally decided to try to accommodate the Sandinistas and in late 1979 recommended an emergency aid program of $75 million. Congress was even more doubtful than Carter, but after delaying passage for several months, it appropriated the money. The United States sent some $60 million of this appropriation to Nicaragua until Carter suspended payments at the end of his administration because he disliked Sandinista support for the increasing guerrilla warfare in neighboring El Salvador.

Carter was very anxious that El Salvador not become another Nicaragua. As in Nicaragua, El Salvador's elite had confiscated peasant communal lands to establish coffee plantations in the 1870s. In the 1880s it built an army to help force the peasants to work on the coffee plantations for low wages. The poor lands left in the hands of the peasants were inadequate to feed them, so food had to be imported. The Depression of the 1930s and rapid population growth in El Salvador squeezed the nation's resources and brought revolution in 1932, led by the founder of El Salvador's Communist Party, Augustín Farabundo Martí. The army, directed by the minister of war Maximiliano Hernández Martínez, suppressed the revolt. In the process, it executed Martí and killed between 10,000 and 30,000 people. (Martínez was a Theosophist who believed in reincarnation and therefore thought it was worse to kill an ant than a person, because people returned to life.) For the next fifty years, the army was the senior partner in a government coalition with the economic oligarchy. The oligarchy deferred to the army because the military outlawed unions and enforced the vagrancy laws that supplied the plantation owners with cheap labor.

The army, however, was not always completely unified. Some factions occasionally reached out toward moderate reformists, although they always drew back rather quickly. Other army leaders encouraged the operation of security forces and death squads to deal out summary justice to dissidents. By 1944, after a coup and a countercoup, these security forces were operating beyond the control of the government.

In the 1960s, Kennedy's Alliance for Progress and the rise of the opposition Christian Democratic party in El Salvador gave some hope for moderate reform. But in the 1972 Salvadoran elections, the army rigged the vote to defeat the Christian Democratic nominee for president, San Salvador Mayor José Napoléon Duarte, and then imprisoned, tortured, and exiled him. Opposition agitation continued, however, when rural unemployment reached 57 percent the following year. Catholic clergy supporting a "theology of liberation" encouraged resistance. El Salvador's president tried to restore calm by offering a timid land reform program in 1975, but frantic opposition from the oligarchy and army thwarted even that. General Carlos Humberto Romero took over the government and ended all reformist pretenses.

In 1977, as hopes for moderate reform faded, the radical Left increased its guerrilla activities. The right wing retaliated with death squads, often composed of army and security forces, which murdered rebels, suspected sympathizers, and even opposition priests. By 1979, strikes and violence racked the country. Electrical workers cut power to the entire nation for nearly twenty-four hours. Police fired on the occupiers of San Salvador's cathedral, killing twenty-three and wounding thirty-seven in front of the world's television cameras.

As in Nicaragua, the United States had few investments in El Salvador, but Carter did not want to see another Central American nation become a hostile Marxist outpost. He pressed the government for reform. Gerald Ford already had suspended aid when El Salvador's chief of staff was convicted in New York of selling machine guns to the Mafia. Carter increased the pressure in 1977 by cutting the amount of aid El Salvador would get the following fiscal year if the suspension were lifted. He said the aid would not be increased unless El Salvador improved human rights inside its borders. El Salvador's government then announced it would reject any aid tied to such conditions.

When the Somoza government of Nicaragua fell to the Sandinistas in 1979, Carter stepped up his pressure for moderate reform in El Salvador. In October, a group of progressive young army officers responded by staging a bloodless coup. They invited three civilians to join two military men in a junta pledged to disband the largest of the death squads, investigate the rampant killings and disappearances, and establish a minimum wage for agricultural workers. The civilians who accepted, however, soon found that the army had retained its power and would thwart all attempts at reform. The radical Left refused any cooperation with the new government so long as it left the army intact. The civilians soon resigned. One of them, Guillermo Ungo, who had been the vice-presidential candidate on the Christian Democratic ticket of 1972 with Duarte, ultimately joined the guerrillas.

Still Carter did not give up. His aides called the Salvadoran civilians who left the government "quitters" and backed the few Christian Democrats who were willing to negotiate a new government with the military. These new civilian members of the junta remained powerless to control the army or the death squads. Army sharpshooters fired from rooftops into a demonstration of 80,000 people, killing twenty. Archbishop Oscar Romero of San Salvador, formerly known as a conservative, condemned the government and the co-operation of the Christian Democrats with it. In desperation, Carter appointed an outspoken liberal, Robert White, as ambassador to El Salvador. White, who as U.S. minister to Paraguay had openly criticized that nation for human rights violations, set out to encourage reform but also to prevent revolution. As he said privately on his departure for El Salvador, "Washington wants something to the right of Nicaragua. My job is to make that happen."

The government of Christian Democrats and military representatives responded by announcing a sweeping land reform program. It would confiscate the coffee haciendas, compensate the owners in cash and bonds, and turn the lands over to peasant cooperatives. Later, a "land to the tiller" program would give sharecroppers the plots of land they worked. The United States government and the AFL-CIO sent agricultural and labor advisors to aid the program. In addition, the United States promised to help reform the army for a "clean counterinsurgency" program against the radical guerrillas. Carter requested $5.7 million for "nonlethal" military aid to El Salvador in the form of jeeps, trucks, and communications equipment.

Carter's hopes for a centrist solution in El Salvador collapsed. The reformers had no real power, and the land reform program remained mostly paper promises. On March 24, 1980, a death squad assassinated Archbishop Romero before the altar of his own cathedral. One of the right-wing leaders, Roberto D'Aubuisson, was subsequently arrested in a coup attempt and found to have papers that implicated him in the assassination plot. The Christian Democrats in the government threatened to resign unless D'Aubuisson was punished. The army refused and freed him. Conservative military leaders stripped moderate officers of their power within the army and government, while the right-wing accelerated its war on suspected rebels. A death squad killed six Leftist leaders meeting in a San Salvador school in November 1980. On December 2, Salvadoran soldiers killed three nuns and a lay missionary, all of them Americans. In January, assassins walked into the Hilton Hotel coffee shop in San Salvador and gunned down two American labor advisors to the land reform program, along with a Salvadoran administrator.

In the midst of all of this, the army and the Christian Democrats formed a new government. They made Duarte the first civilian president El Salvador had known in years. His vice-president and the real power behind the government, however, was Colonel Jaime Gutiérrez, the army commander-in-chief. Despite this indication that there was no viable center in El Salvador, the Carter administration continued to support the Salvadoran junta and to hold out hopes for reform. A U.S. investigating team concluded that only low-level figures were involved in the killing of the American nuns. When guerrillas increased their activities in late 1980 in hopes of winning the war before Ronald Reagan took over the American government, Carter renewed military aid to the regime, sent twenty military instructors, and accused the rebels of receiving arms and support from abroad.

Ronald Reagan greatly accelerated Carter's move toward a military solution in Central America, and he did so with far fewer gestures toward centrist reform and human rights. During his campaign he warned that "in El Salvador, Marxist totalitarian revolutionaries, supported by Havana and Moscow, are preventing the construction of a democratic government." He asked why the United States should let "Grenada, Nicaragua, El Salvador, all become additional 'Cubas,' new outposts for Soviet combat brigades? . . . These humiliations and symbols of weakness add up." Secretary of State Alexander Haig announced that the administration considered what was happening in El Salvador as "part of the global Communist campaign coordinated by Havana and Moscow to support the Marxist insurgency." The State Department produced a White Paper in a rather flimsy attempt to demonstrate that large amounts of arms supplied by the Soviet Union and Cuba were flowing through Nicaragua to the rebels in El Salvador.

Reagan argued that the strategic situation in Latin America was too serious to be hampered by excessive concerns for human rights. In February 1981, he stated that the discovery and punishment of the murderers of the American nuns were no longer conditions for aid to El Salvador. In July, he ordered the United States representatives to the World Bank to support loans to Chile, Argentina, Paraguay, and Uruguay, all of which the Carter administration had boycotted because of human rights violations. Congress tried to stop his jettisoning of human rights considerations by attaching an amendment to the foreign aid bill that required the president to certify progress on democracy and human rights before military aid could be disbursed to suspect regimes. Reagan simply circumvented the requirement. He blithely certified progress by such brutal governments as those of Chile and El Salvador. He reclassified helicopter parts intended for Guatemala as nonmilitary. In November 1983, he pocket-vetoed a congressional extension of the certification requirement.

Reagan increased the amount of aid to Latin America at the same time that he reduced the human rights conditions attached to it. In early 1982, he proposed a Caribbean Basin initiative. The United States would join the wealthier nations of the hemisphere, such as Canada, Mexico, and Venezuela, in offering Central America and the Caribbean trade preferences, incentives for private investment, help in overcoming balance of payments deficits, and direct military and economic aid. The Caribbean Basin initiative immediately ran into trouble. Many Latin American nations complained that Reagan's emphasis on private investment ignored the major needs of their countries—the roads, electrical power, and water systems that only government could provide. Canada, Mexico, and Venezuela were reluctant to contribute to an economic program so blatantly directed toward support of the fragile military dictatorships in the region. Congress balked at the lack of concern for human rights. Congress also was reluctant to increase Latin American aid while the Reagan administration was drastically cutting domestic social programs. Congressional opposition to Reagan's policies for Latin America, however, remained timid and erratic. Democrats did not want to be blamed for "losing Latin America to the Communists." Aid to Honduras tripled to $31 million in 1982. Aid to El Salvador went from $140 million in 1981 to $200 million in 1982.

Meanwhile, in March 1982, Reagan authorized the CIA to support anti-Sandinista guerrilla activities by rebel Contras operating out of Honduras. Many of the leaders of these Contras were former members of Somoza's hated National Guard. As word of this supposedly secret CIA operation leaked out, the Reagan administration assured Congress and the press that his intention was only to stop arms from flowing to the rebels in El Salvador and perhaps to push the Sandinista government toward greater pluralism and democracy. Privately, however, many admitted that they would not object to the overturning of the Sandinista government. The Contras were supposed to hit only military targets, but neutral witnesses observed burned farms and many dead animals and civilians in the region of Contra activities. The CIA even helped the Contras lay mines in Nicaragua's main harbors. The Contras' background and brutal tactics seemed merely to strengthen sympathies for the Sandinista regime within Nicaragua.

The Sandinistas restrained themselves from "hot pursuit" of the Contras into Honduras because they did not want to provide an occasion for all-out war with Honduras and the United States. The Sandinistas had good reason to fear this. The United States carried on large-scale joint training maneuvers in Honduras, built "temporary bases" to house the participants in these maneuvers, and stationed naval task forces off the coast of Nicaragua. U.S. military aid also strengthened the Honduran army against its fragile civilian government.

In April 1982, Reagan's National Security Council issued a secret memo, later leaked to the press, that outlined other aspects of the administration's policy toward Central America. The memo declared it a "vital interest" of the United States to prevent the emergence of Cuban model states, "vital interest" being a diplomatic code phrase usually meaning an interest for which a nation will go to war. Contrary to the public statements of the administration, the memo said the United States would send aid to Guatemala without human rights conditions. In another contradiction to administration statements, the memo stated that the United States would work to isolate Mexico and sidetrack its attempts to mediate a negotiated settlement in Nicaragua and El Salvador.

Reagan's policy in El Salvador soon ran into serious trouble. The rebels boycotted the elections of 1982, and despite the fact that Duarte and his Christian Democrats won a plurality of votes, the right-wing parties combined in the legislature and used their consequent majority to deny Duarte and his followers a single office in the government. Only Reagan's warnings prevented the right-wingers from making D'Aubuisson president. At the end of the year, 30,000 Salvadorans were dead in the revolutionary war and 600,000 were refugees, 13 percent of the Salvadoran population.

Many Democrats and liberal Republicans urged that Reagan abandon his efforts for a military solution and give more support to the efforts of the Contadora group—Mexico, Venezuela, Panama, and Colombia—to mediate a negotiated settlement in all of Central America. (The Contadora group took its name from a Panamanian island where it first met.) In April, the House appropriations subcommittee cut in half Reagan's request for $60 million in emergency aid to El Salvador and was ready to block the additional $136 million he wanted for the following fiscal year.

Reagan embarked on a major effort to win public and congressional support for his program. He gave a dramatic televised address to a joint session of Congress and asked for $600 million in aid to Latin America for 1984. He warned that "the national security of all the Americas is at stake in Central America. If we cannot defend ourselves there, we cannot expect to prevail elsewhere. Our credibility would collapse, our alliances would crumble, and the safety of our homeland would be put at jeopardy." When Congress still balked, Reagan appointed a bipartisan commission on Latin America and asked Henry Kissinger to chair it. Kissinger might be too soft for Reagan on Soviet and European affairs, but he could be expected to support him on Latin America.

The Kissinger report endorsed Reagan's Caribbean Basin initiative and requested $8 billion in aid for Latin America over five years. Although two members of the commission opposed aid to the Contras in Nicaragua, the remainder supported continued pressure on the Sandinistas. The majority did defy Reagan and recommend that aid be tied to progress on human rights in El Salvador and Central America, but Kissinger personally warned that the linkage should not be carried to the length that it risked the success of Marxist revolutionaries. Marxists would kill more people than the government they replaced in El Salvador, Kissinger warned. The commission itself stated that "Regimes created by the victory of Marxist-Leninist revolution become totalitarian. That is their purpose, their nature, their doctrine and their record." Reagan endorsed the report with Kissinger's caveat on human rights. He announced in the classical Kissinger language of the report that there might be an argument for doing nothing for El Salvador or for doing a great deal more, but there was no logical argument for doing too little. Reagan said he chose to do enough.

A ray of hope emerged in El Salvador when Duarte, with help from American poll watchers and organizers, won control of the Salvadoran legislature in the elections of 1984. Surprisingly, the military extended some cooperation to his policy of moderation. Salvadoran courts convicted several enlisted men of the murder of the American nuns, and Duarte pledged to investigate other instances of army misconduct. He actually removed some of the worst offenders, but did not have the strength to bring them to trial. Murders by death squads fell to 185 in the first nine months of 1984 compared to over 1,000 in the same period of 1983. Most hopeful of all, Duarte met the rebel leadership and began to seek a negotiated settlement. In the spring elections of 1985, Duarte's Christian Democrats defeated the right-wing parties and won an absolute majority in the legislature.

Congress showed renewed willingness to aid Duarte and El Salvador, but it turned down Reagan's repeated requests for supplementary appropriations to the Nicaraguan Contras. Private conservative groups in the United States supplied aid and advisors to help keep the Contras afloat until finally Congress reversed itself and voted "non-lethal aid" to the Nicaraguan rebels following a trip to Moscow by Sandinista leader Daniel Ortega.

Meanwhile, Reagan had the chance at least once to circumvent the frustrations of congressional interference and achieve a military solution to radical activities in the Caribbean area. In 1979, a Leftist coup in Grenada led by Maurice Bishop and his New Jewel movement overthrew the corrupt and repressive anti-Communist Eric Gairy, who had been prime minister since Grenada had secured its independence from Great Britain in 1974. Bishop received arms and advisors from Cuba, started work on a 10,000-foot airstrip, and signed a treaty giving the Soviets permission to land their long-range reconnaissance planes when the airport was finished. Carter treated Bishop with hostility, but kept hands off. Reagan, on the other hand, warned that Grenada was becoming a Cuban and Soviet outpost that endangered hemispheric security. Several other small Caribbean island nations agreed and urged the United States to take action.

The opportunity arrived when the deputy prime minister, Bernard Coard, ousted Bishop and placed him under arrest for allegedly softening toward the United States. When a mob came to free Bishop, the army fired into it and then summarily executed Bishop and several other officials who sympathized with him. On the grounds that the rebellion endangered the lives of the 1,000 American students at St. George's Medical School on Grenada, Reagan sent in the troops. A lightning attack ran into more resistance than expected from the Cubans near the airport runway, but ultimately some 6,000 American troops secured the island. American forces suffered 18 dead and some 67 wounded. The U.S. government did not reveal the number of Cuban, Grenadan, and civilian casualties.

Reagan asserted that captured documents and weapons, along with the number and training of the supposed Cuban construction workers at the airport, showed that indeed Cuba and the Soviet Union had been planning to make Grenada a major military base. Although the evidence the administration produced was far from conclusive, the American public seemed to accept the invasion as a proper and successful use of American military power. It came only two days after suicide bomb blasts in Beirut had killed nearly 300 marines. Many European and Latin American leaders protested, however, and critics worried that the Reagan administration might decide that Grenada proved the viability of the military approach to the rest of Central America.

CARTER, REAGAN, AND THE INTERNATIONAL ECONOMY

Jimmy Carter inherited an extraordinarily difficult economic situation when he took office in 1976. Lyndon Johnson had set off an inflationary spiral by his attempt to fight the Vietnam war and fund his Great Society at the same time without raising taxes. Nixon had continued Johnson's "guns and butter" policy until deficit spending, oil price increases, and the imbalance between American imports and exports pushed him to impose the "second Nixon shock." He took the United States off the gold standard, imposed price and wage controls, and assessed a 10 percent surcharge on imports. The value of the U.S. dollar floated slowly downward after that, although the Smithsonian monetary agreement of 1971 and the Rambouillet economic summit meeting of 1975 managed to stabilize the situation temporarily and keep the decline within bounds.

Pressures on the American economy and the value of the dollar increased during Carter's administration. America's trading partners in the developed world—Europe and Japan—complained bitterly that the decline of the dollar's value forced them to pay higher prices for oil, since petroleum purchases from OPEC had to be made in dollars. They also grumbled that the lower value of the dollar gave the United States an unfair edge in selling its exports abroad. They insisted that the United States should reduce its imports of oil. They wanted Carter to remove the subsidies that reduced oil prices to American consumers, and let domestic prices rise to the world level. That would lessen America's imbalance of trade, revive the value of the dollar, and reduce the demand for and therefore the world price of oil.

Carter at first treated the situation with considerable equanimity. He did try to reduce American dependence on imported oil, but he suggested that imports were fueling the American economic boom and helping the economies of the nations that were supplying the imports, many of which were poor Third World nations. He suggested that Japan and Germany particularly open their own markets further to imports. This would encourage American exports and reduce the U.S. trade deficit. It also would allow the administration to continue to resist pressures from American manufacturers of cars, steel, footwear, and textiles for protection against cheaper imports.

Carter became more concerned, however, as his mild remedial measures, including slightly elevated interest rates, failed to halt the dollar's downward slide. Concern turned to alarm when the Iranian revolution interrupted some oil exports and OPEC once again tripled its prices, this time to $35 a barrel. Not only did that accelerate the decline of the dollar, but inflation shot up to an annual rate of 18 percent. At the same time, unemployment began to rise. This "stagflation," the growth of deficits and unemployment at the same time, violated all the predictions of the Keynesian economic system and left the Carter administration puzzled and in disarray.

Ronald Reagan won the presidency primarily because of Carter's economic failures, and Reagan's prescription of less government intrusion into economic affairs had an impact on foreign as well as domestic policy. He took far more drastic action than Carter to reduce inflation and protect the dollar. He tried to reduce deficit spending by cutting domestic social expenditures. At the same time, however, he cut taxes and drastically increased defense expenditures. The deficit approached the frightening level of $200 billion annually. Reagan claimed that his emphasis on increasing American production (supply-side economics) would revive the economy and produce more tax revenue to reduce the deficit than would a tax increase. Meanwhile, the Federal Reserve Board tried to counter inflation by restricting the supply of money. Interest rates rose to nearly 20 percent and unemployment rose correspondingly.

The resulting recession helped reduce consumer and business demand, and inflation slowly began to creep downward. Lower world oil consumption aided this process. An oil glut actually developed despite the cut in production caused by the Iraq-Iran war. Oil prices had been a primary factor in the inflation of the Carter years, and their stabilization and reduction helped the Reagan recovery immensely. America's high interest rates and falling inflation attracted foreign capital, especially from the oil countries themselves, and the dollar strengthened to the point that the Europeans and Japanese began to complain about that as vociferously as they had earlier about the falling dollar. At the Williamsburg economic summit of 1983, they argued that the United States should strengthen the dollar by reducing its spending deficit rather than resorting to artificially high interest rates that stole away their capital and undermined their economies. Reagan countered with complaints about barriers to American exports in Japan and the European Common Market.

The result was an uncomfortable standoff. Reagan refused to risk his domestic economic program with concessions to foreigners. The recovery of 1983–1984, however, lowered interest rates and thus reduced some of the European and Japanese complaints, especially since the strong dollar weakened the ability of American exports to compete abroad. The U.S. trade deficit shot upward, along with the budget deficit.

During these financial crises, Carter and Reagan both resisted domestic pressures for further protection against Japanese and European imports. At Geneva in 1979, Carter completed the negotiations on the General Agreement on Trade and Tariffs that had begun in Tokyo in 1973. This Geneva Agreement of 1979 replaced the so-called Kennedy Round of the 1960s and reduced tariffs approximately 30 percent. Carter pushed this liberal free trade measure through Congress even in the midst of the economic troubles that beset the end of his administration. After Reagan took office, he successfully pressed the Japanese for further voluntary limits on exports of cars and other manufactured goods to the United States. He also got the Japanese to lower some barriers against American exports, especially agricultural produce. He hoped this would deter new congressional restrictions on imports that might undermine Carter's Geneva Agreement.

Carter and Reagan faced economic problems with the developing nations of the world at least as grave as those with Europe and Japan. American trade and investment in the Third World were increasing dramatically. By the 1980s, developing nations took more American exports than Europe and Japan combined. They also consumed one of every three acres of U.S. farm production. Although 75 percent of American investments remained in the developed world, the share of the developing world was increasing. In addition, the United States imported vital raw materials from the Third World, including 100 percent of its tin, 90 percent of its bauxite, 100 percent of its natural rubber, and nearly 40 percent of its petroleum.

Many developing countries believed they were not receiving an adequate return for their products. They were angry that with nearly three-quarters of the population of the world, they had produced only 17 percent of the world GNP before the oil embargo of 1973. They argued that the world economy was rigged against them and they pressed the United Nations for a new international economic order. Basing their demands on the work of Latin American economist Raul Prebisch, they sought commodity agreements that would peg the prices of their goods to the prices of the manufactured goods they had to import. They wanted developed countries to reduce the tariffs that blocked the importation of processed and manufactured goods from Third World nations. They demanded that developed countries increase their aid to developing nations from 0.3 percent to 0.7 percent of the contributing nations' GNPs to compensate for past exploitation. They claimed full and permanent sovereignty over their natural resources and insisted on the rights of their national courts to decide without outside interference all questions of compensation for expropriated foreign property. After the success of OPEC, the emboldened developing nations used their majority in the United Nations to pass a 1974 General Assembly resolution in favor of this new international economic order. They also began to try to set up organizations like OPEC to control production and increase prices of other commodities.

Though far from favoring such economic revisionism, Carter indicated some willingness to listen to the Third World program and accommodate it where he could within the existing liberal system. He still placed primary emphasis on the role of private investment, free trade under the most favored nation system, and increasing production in developing nations rather than redistributing wealth from the developed countries. Nevertheless, he increased the American contribution to the World Bank for loans to developing nations. He worked for the establishment of an international grain reserve to give emergency aid during times of famine. He refused to support a $6 billion commodity fund to support prices of Third World products by purchasing them if their prices fell below a certain level, but he approved an emergency fund of $400 million. Carter thought the best the international system could do was to encourage self-help and provide emergency relief to the poorest of the poor in the Third World.

Carter and Ambassador Andrew Young pointed out that much American and international aid to developing countries failed to trickle down to the poor. Seventy percent of the increase in the GNP in developing countries during the 1970s went to the richest 30 percent of the people, while less than 1 percent went to the bottom fifth of the population. Carter also balked at a UN proposal for a Law of the Sea to govern mining on the bottom of the world's oceans. He refused to submit American ocean operations to the commission established by this treaty because it would have a Third World majority. By the end of Carter's administration, all these issues between the developed nations of the Northern Hemisphere and the developing nations of the Southern Hemisphere were deadlocked.

Ronald Reagan rejected the mildly accommodationist policy of Carter. He broke off negotiations on the Law of the Sea. He lectured the developing nations at the North-South summit meeting in Cancun, Mexico, on the benefits of free markets and self-help. He and his administration accepted no guilt over poverty in the Third World. They pointed to Taiwan, South Korea, and Singapore as examples of what developing nations could accomplish within the existing world economic system. Reagan's delegate to the World Health Organization cast the only vote in that body against restrictions on the sale of powdered baby formula in the Third World on the grounds that such restrictions improperly interfered with private enterprise.[2] In 1984, Reagan announced that the United States would withdraw entirely from the United Nations Economic, Social, and Cultural Organization (UNESCO) and end the U.S. contribution to it. UNESCO had been particularly hostile to the United States and was promoting government controls on international news to "correct" the image of conditions in Third World countries.

For the time being, the developing nations accepted the Reagan policy with resignation. Little could be done toward revising the international economic system without the participation of the United States. The unity of the developing nations eroded as the oil-rich members of the community went their own way. The rise in oil prices, with the accompanying expense of petroleum-based fertilizers, wounded Third World countries even more than the developed economies. OPEC itself fell on hard times, undermining the hopes of those seeking parallel Third World cartels to control other basic commodities. The UN estimated that declining commodity prices cost developing nations $21 billion between 1980 and 1982. Nevertheless, Reagan rejected any moves toward international commodity price supports and said recovery in the developed world would revive price levels for Third World products.

Some of the developing nations, in their rush to industrialize, incurred enormous debts to the World Bank, the International Monetary Fund, and private banks. In 1983, the total foreign debt of developing countries reached $700 billion. Brazil, Argentina, Mexico, and Venezuela owed most of that, and all came close to defaulting. If they did default, they would not only hurt their own economies, but do immense damage to the world economy as well. This was only one example of the developing nations' inability to impress their will on the developed nations and their potential to do infinite harm if their suffering was not alleviated.

---

[2] Babies in the Third World did far better being breast-fed because they often caught infections from unclean bottles. Also, many peasants could ill afford to buy the formula.

CARTER, REAGAN, THE SOVIETS, AND NUCLEAR ARMS

Jimmy Carter demonstrated his determination to restore moral issues to American foreign policy early in his administration. He took up the cudgels against Soviet violations of human rights. Just before he took office, he initiated contacts with several Soviet dissidents, and he culminated his human rights campaign in March 1977 by ostentatiously receiving one of these dissidents, Vladimir Bukovsky, in the White House.

Carter lamely tried to assure the Soviets that he did not intend to link his agitation for human rights with such issues as arms control. Nevertheless, the political climate surrounding détente soured even more than it had in the last year of the Ford administration. Brezhnev not only denounced Carter's human rights campaign, he dramatically defied it by formally charging one of the leading dissidents, Anatoly Scharansky, with treason. In 1978, the Soviets convicted Scharansky and two others of such charges and imprisoned them.

In this contentious atmosphere, Cyrus Vance and Arms Control Director Paul Warnke advised Carter to avoid any major shift in the SALT negotiations with the Soviet Union. They wanted the president to concentrate on the few manageable issues blocking final agreement to SALT II, ratify that treaty, and defer any new initiatives until after this had restored momentum toward better U.S.-Soviet relations. But Carter decided on a bolder move. Although he had promised Brezhnev he would sign SALT II quickly after negotiating the final compromises, Carter changed his mind and accepted the advice of Brzezinski and Secretary of Defense Harold Brown to offer a whole new negotiating plan. To counter liberal criticisms that SALT II merely ratified rather than reversed the arms race, Carter suggested substantial reductions in the missile limits on both sides. At the same time, he structured the suggested reductions to answer conservative criticisms that SALT II would endanger American security.

Conservative critics like Brzezinski, Senator Henry Jackson, and the influential Committee on the Present Danger, led by Paul Nitze, warned that Russia's buildup of huge MIRVed missiles was approaching the ability to destroy 90 percent of America's land-based Minuteman ICBMs in a preemptive strike. Even though the remainder of America's strategic triad, the nuclear-armed bombers and submarines, might survive, they were incapable of destroying Soviet hardened missile silos; they could only retaliate against Russian cities. After a Soviet attack on American ICBMs, the president would be faced with a choice of submitting to Soviet demands or launching attacks on cities that would guarantee a similar Russian response and the destruction of both societies. The Soviets might assume that the president would submit when faced with such a choice. They would then be tempted to take greater risks in world affairs, if not launch a preemptive strike. The critics of SALT II wanted any arms agreement to reduce the number of heavy Soviet ICBMs capable of destroying the hardened silos of American Minutemen. Such a reduction would preserve the invulnerability of at least a portion of America's ICBM force and eliminate the temptation for either a Soviet pre-emptive strike or a more adventurous foreign policy.

With a great fanfare of publicity, Carter sent Secretary of State Vance to Moscow with a plan for reducing the missile limits already set in the SALT II negotiations. Instead of 2,400 strategic launchers each, the United States and the Soviet Union would have fewer than 2,000. The plan required that the bulk of Soviet cuts be made in its large land-based MIRVed missiles. In exchange, the United States would abandon its intention to deploy a new generation of ICBMs, the MX (Missile Experimental), each of which would carry ten accurate, potentially silo-busting warheads. Vance also offered a deal on the Soviet Backfire bomber and the American cruise missile, the issue that had blocked earlier agreement on SALT II. The Soviets would be able to build their Backfire bomber so long as they restricted its range to prevent it from being used as a strategic bomber against the United States. Those range restrictions would not prevent the Backfire from being used against Europe, however, and the Soviets were deploying new intermediate SS-20 missiles that also could threaten Western Europe. Therefore, Vance's proposal entitled the United States to deploy cruise missiles with sufficient range to reach the Soviet Union from Germany.

The Soviets turned Vance away with an uncompromising "nyet." They complained that Carter had publicized the proposal before he presented it to them and called his offer a "cheap and shady maneuver." They argued that their advantage in heavy missiles had been compensation for America's forward-based systems in Europe that were not limited by SALT. They said it was inequitable that these forward-based systems and the new cruise missiles would be able to hit Soviet territory, while the Backfire and SS-20s would not be able to reach the United States. They argued that any weapons which could hit the territory of one of the superpowers were strategic and therefore should be limited by the treaty, while weapons that could reach only Europe, such as the Backfire and SS-20, were tactical and therefore should be exempt. They insisted that SALT II, which they pretended was ready for signing without further negotiation, would have to be ratified before any further progress could be made.

After this highly public fiasco, the Americans and Soviets returned to quieter diplomacy. Both sides were extremely wary, however, and it took two years of false starts, hard bargaining, and overoptimistic declarations by Carter that agreement was around the corner before Carter and Brezhnev signed SALT II at the Vienna summit meeting of July 1979. In this final treaty, the Soviets agreed to reduce the launchers on both sides from 2,400 to 2,250 and to limit the number of warheads on their heavy missiles. In exchange, the United States set limits on the range and number of cruise missiles it would deploy.

Henry Jackson and the Committee on the Present Danger denounced the SALT II Treaty immediately. General Edward Rowny, one of Carter's negotiating team, boycotted the signing ceremony in protest that the agreement was too soft, and then resigned. These critics argued that by leaving intact the Russian advantage in heavy missiles, the Soviets would still be able to destroy 90 percent of America's land-based ICBMs by the early 1980s. They believed that SALT II would prevent the United States from closing this "window of vulnerability" by lulling Americans into thinking they did not need to increase arms expenditures. They demanded an accelerated program for building the MX and also the Trident II missile, a submarine-launched rocket which, unlike previous submarine missiles, was accurate and powerful enough to threaten silos rather than just cities. They condemned Carter for canceling production of the B-1 bomber which, armed with long-range cruise missiles, might have helped counter the Soviet advantage in throw-weight. They also warned that SALT II had inadequate verification procedures to prevent the Soviets from cheating.

These critics insisted that the Soviets were using arms control and détente to disarm the United States while making no sacrifices of Russian power. The Soviets were more interested in the triumph of the world revolution than in peace, they said. Americans might hope for nuclear stability based on mutually assured destruction and the balance of terror (see Chapter 18), but the Soviet nuclear strategy was based on fighting and perhaps even winning a nuclear war. Soviet weapons were far larger than necessary to deter war by threatening American cities. The size of Soviet warheads and the recently improved accuracy of Soviet missiles indicated an intention to attack U.S. strategic missiles in hardened silos if war broke out. The USSR's elaborate civil defense program indicated its belief that its population might survive an American retaliatory strike. Soviet military men wrote as though a nuclear war might be won. The United States had to have a war-fighting strategy like the Russians, not a mere deterrent capacity. America too must possess accurate and survivable counterforce weapons, along with flexible plans for their use. America must deter Russia by having the ability to answer any level of attack with measures that would deny the Soviets victory, but also avoid a suicidal spasm of city attacks.

Restrained realists and most liberals opposed the war-fighting strategy and the arms buildup it would necessitate. They thought it would be far less dangerous to ratify SALT II and seek further reductions in nuclear arms through new SALT III negotiations. They regarded as ludicrous the idea of a prolonged nuclear war in which each stage of escalation could be carefully controlled. Such hopes only made nuclear war more likely. Neither side could deliver a first strike so surgical that it would exempt cities and hold them for ransom. Even if the initial blasts spared some of the civilian population, radiation and a nuclear-induced "winter" would kill millions. The aggressor thus would have to expect retaliation on its own cities.

Soviet military men, charged strictly with military planning for strategic war, might talk of surviving a nuclear exchange. Brezhnev and the Soviet party leaders, however, had made clear since 1977 that they regarded nuclear war of any sort as mutual suicide. Brezhnev had no illusions that nuclear war could be fought as a prolonged and gradually escalated conflict. For the

United States to build counterforce weapons to deter such a possibility only invited disaster. Americans might regard their counterforce weapons as deterrents, but such weapons also could be used in a first strike, and the Russians undoubtedly would regard them as intended for that. As each nation built its potential first strike capability in the name of a deterrent war-fighting strategy, each might begin to doubt the survivability of its retaliatory capacity and decide to launch on warning. This would mean that neither side would wait for an enemy's weapons to explode before retaliating, but launch its missiles the moment its electronic warning systems detected the firing of enemy rockets. Since electronic warning systems often malfunctioned, the risk of accidental war would increase enormously.

Carter and Secretary of Defense Harold Brown tried at first to engineer a balance between the nuclear liberals and the nuclear conservatives, but increasingly they sided with the conservatives. Early in his administration, Carter had pleased the liberals by closing the production line of the Minuteman III missile and canceling the program to increase the accuracy of the old Minuteman I missiles. He also canceled the B-1 bomber project. He knew he could not get the appropriation for both the B-1 and the cruise missile through Congress, and he liked the cruise missile because its slow speed and relative invulnerability made it obviously a second strike weapon despite its accuracy. (Unfortunately, the small size of the cruise allowed it to be hidden easily, raising monumental problems for future verifiable arms control.)

Carter's cancellations made the military and congressional conservatives cling all the more tenaciously to the new weapons programs that were left—the MX, the Trident II, and the cruise missile. After it was clear that the Soviets would not trade a reduction in their heavy missiles for cancellation of the MX, Carter went along with these conservatives and made sure that SALT II would not prohibit development of new counterforce weapons. Thus, SALT II permitted the development of one new missile by each side, which cleared the way for American deployment of the MX. SALT II also permitted the modernization of older missiles, and Carter saw to it that the definition of modernization allowed him to replace the Trident I submarine missile with Trident IIs.

Having protected the right to build the MX, Carter and Secretary of Defense Brown devised an enormously expensive scheme to make it less vulnerable to a Soviet preemptive strike. They proposed to deploy the MX as a mobile missile to be moved on tracks between thousands of empty silos. Since the Soviets would not know which silos were dummies and which actually contained missiles, they would not be able to risk a first strike.

Despite the protections Carter built into SALT II for his expansion of American strategic power, opposition in the Senate remained strong. Carter tried to assuage opponents by promising Senate Majority Leader Robert Byrd that he would not bargain away America's new missiles in future negotiations, but actually deploy them. When the Soviet Union invaded Afghanistan in December 1979, however, the resulting American public outrage doomed the attempt to ratify the treaty, and Carter shelved it until a more propitious time.

The debate over SALT II in the United States proceeded in tandem with debates in Europe over nuclear arms in that theater. It was clear early in the SALT II negotiations that whatever limits might be put on the range of Soviet Backfire bombers, they would still be able to deliver nuclear weapons against Western Europe. In addition, the talks on strategic arms did not deal with Soviet missiles whose range was short enough to prevent them from reaching the United States. This left the Soviets free to continue the rapid deployment of their SS-20s, each of which was MIRVed with three warheads.

Washington's preferred response was to build NATO's conventional forces and make a nuclear response to conventional invasion less necessary. In 1977, NATO agreed that each member would increase its defense spending at a rate of 3 percent annually above inflation. But the Europeans worried that a conventional buildup, combined with increased Soviet intermediate-range nuclear forces, might lead the United States to decouple its nuclear force from European defense. In October 1977, Chancellor Helmut Schmidt of West Germany gave a widely publicized speech warning that Soviet deployment of the Backfire and SS-20s was lessening the credibility of NATO's threat to resort to nuclear weapons if it found itself unable to stop a Soviet conventional invasion. At first, Carter tried to play down Schmidt's concerns. His administration pointed out that intermediate-range warheads constituted only 5 percent of the warheads in the Soviet and American strategic arsenals. As long as the United States maintained strategic parity with the Soviet Union and kept its own troops in Germany to demonstrate the risk Russia would run if it invaded Western Europe, the SS-20s posed little threat.

Then Carter canceled production of the neutron bomb. The neutron bomb enhanced the radiation of a nuclear explosion and lessened the size of the blast. NATO had thought the neutron bomb would be useful in Europe to kill invading troops and tank crews without destroying the surrounding buildings and countryside. The bomb, however, raised an outcry in both Europe and the United States. Critics pointed out that it killed friendly as well as enemy people. Delusions about its capability to limit nuclear war would make war more likely. It also would tempt the United States to avoid threatening an all-out strategic strike on the Soviet Union that would put the territory of the United States at risk. In the midst of this political turmoil, none of the NATO leaders wanted to take responsibility for requesting such a bomb. When Helmut Schmidt refused to make a new and public request for the United States to continue the project, Carter abandoned it. Schmidt and many other Western European leaders were angry that Carter had not supported Europe's defense. Carter decided he had to regain the trust and unity of America's Western European allies.

Thus, Carter and the NATO allies agreed in December 1979 to the so-called two-track decision. At NATO's request, the United States would deploy a total of 572 Pershing II and cruise intermediate missiles in Europe. These missiles, unlike previous American rockets stationed in Europe, would be capable of reaching beyond Warsaw Pact territory to the Soviet Union itself, although NATO quickly pointed out that they could not reach as far as Moscow. They would add little to the warheads already aimed at Russia, but since the United States might choose to fire rather than lose them to a conventional Soviet invasion of Europe, NATO hoped they would further couple American and European defense and deter the Soviets. Meanwhile, in the second track of the two-track decision, NATO asked the United States to open separate intermediate-range nuclear arms limitation talks to accompany its strategic nuclear talks with the Soviet Union.

The two-track decision, designed to reassure Western Europe, rebounded against all its authors. It jarred many Europeans into recognition that their homes might become nuclear battlefields in a war between the superpowers. Brezhnev added to this growing antinuclear movement by offering to deploy only 162 of the SS-20s, the exact total of missiles in the independent arsenals of Great Britain and France, if NATO would abandon deployment of the cruise and Pershing II missiles. NATO rejected the offer. Not only would it once again decouple American and European nuclear deterrents, but Brezhnev offered only to move his SS-20s out of range of Western Europe, not destroy them. Since the SS-20s were mobile, they could easily be moved back. In any case, once NATO's two-track decision was firm, Brezhnev withdrew his offer and spent six months denouncing the projected NATO deployment. The invasion of Afghanistan and deferral of the SALT II treaty added to European uneasiness.

In 1980, the Soviets finally agreed to theater nuclear talks in Geneva. But the relief to Europe was short-lived. Disagreements at Geneva showed it would be a long and bitter struggle to negotiate a treaty. Europeans also were disturbed when Carter issued Presidential Directive 59, which established more flexible targeting for America's modernizing strategic arsenal. Thus, Carter made overt his war-fighting strategy to replace the strictly deterrent mutually assured destruction strategy that supposedly had guided the United States since 1967.[3] Europeans regarded plans for counterforce strikes and gradual escalation as particularly threatening. As European antinuclear activists put it, when the Soviets and Americans talk of limited nuclear war, they mean limited to us. Then, to add even more to European discomfort, Ronald Reagan won election to the presidency.

Prior to his election, Reagan showed little interest in continuing arms control negotiations. "The argument . . . will be over which weapons [to build], not whether we would forsake weaponry for treaties and agreements," he declared. He called Carter's SALT II Treaty "fatally flawed" and made clear he would never seek its ratification. He appointed critics from the Committee on the Present Danger to key positions in charge of arms control—Eugene V. Rostow as director of the Arms Control and Disarmament Agency, General Edward Rowny as chief strategic arms negotiator, Paul Nitze as chief negotiator for the theater weapons talks at Geneva. Reagan eventually forced Eugene Rostow out because Rostow insisted on appointing aides who were too liberal, and replaced him with another member of the

---

[3] Actually there is evidence that even after 1967, McNamara's MAD strategy included some options for counterforce and limited stages of escalation. Certainly by 1974, Nixon's secretary of defense, James Schlesinger, was speaking publicly of more flexible targeting.

Committee on the Present Danger, Kenneth Adelman, who had been quoted two years earlier as calling arms control negotiations "a sham." (Adelman denied making the statement.)

Reagan held all arms control negotiations in limbo for the first sixteen months of his administration, but he promised to abide informally by the "fatally flawed" SALT II Treaty so long as the Soviets did likewise. Meanwhile, he pushed through Congress an enormous increase in defense expenditures. Claiming that the Soviets had developed a margin of military superiority rather than parity with the United States, he proposed an increase of $180 billion over five years. This was in addition to the 5 percent increases voted by Congress during Carter's administration for fiscal years 1981 and 1982. He restored the neutron bomb and B-1 bomber projects. Secretary of Defense Caspar Weinberger and Secretary of State Alexander Haig made statements indicating further movement toward a war-fighting nuclear strategy and limited staged use of nuclear weapons in Europe. Although Weinberger protested that he was misunderstood and that nuclear war indeed was unwinnable, leaks from a secret Defense Guidance Document confirmed that the United States planned a counterforce attack before resorting to nuclear attacks on cities if the USSR launched a first strike. None of this was startlingly new in theory, but the Reagan administration seemed ready to spend billions of dollars to make its strategy practical. Reagan even announced planning for a multibillion-dollar project to develop antimissile defenses in outer space.

In contrast to Reagan's passionate advocacy of defense expenditures, his arms control initiatives seemed perfunctory at best. He abandoned entirely the negotiations for a comprehensive ban on nuclear testing. When he finally announced in November 1981 that he would resume strategic arms negotiations, he insisted that they be called Strategic Arms Reduction Talks (START) rather than Strategic Arms Limitation Talks (SALT). His START proposal called for the reduction of nuclear warheads from 7,000 to 5,000, only 2,500 of which could be placed aboard land-based missiles. This would force the Soviets to abandon much of their ICBM force in favor of submarine weapons. START would reduce the number of ballistic missiles as well as warheads. Each side could have 850 launchers. This would require the Soviets to destroy two-thirds of their missiles, the United States to destroy half of its. In the second stage of the agreement, Reagan would require the Soviets to accept equality in throw-weight as well. Yet the Reagan proposal placed no limits on those weapons in which the United States was superior—cruise missiles and bombers. (Cruise missiles were not ballistic missiles because they did not free-fall back to earth, so technically they were exempt from the limitations on strategic ballistic missiles.) Reagan invited the Soviets to make a counteroffer by stating that all things were negotiable, but at the same time he was accelerating the construction of the B-1 bombers and naval vessels to launch long-range cruise missiles.

Reagan also took a hard line in the intermediate missile talks. He offered the Soviets a "zero-zero" option, meaning that the United States would not deploy its Pershing II and cruise missiles in Europe if the Soviets would dismantle all their SS-20s. When negotiator Paul Nitze and his Soviet counterpart in the theater talks came close to a private agreement, trading Soviet reductions in SS-20s for a more limited U.S. deployment, Reagan angrily rejected the tentative compromise. The Soviet government rejected it even more angrily. But Reagan's response convinced many critics in Europe and the United States that his administration was insincere in its pursuit of arms control.

Some of these critics charged that Reagan had sided with the right-wing ideologues in his administration who believed that arms control was a sham and that the United States could and should bankrupt the Soviets in an arms race. Amidst such criticism, domestic American support for increased defense spending fell from 71 percent in 1980 to 17 percent in October 1982. Many Americans joined a movement for a nuclear freeze, and freeze resolutions won majorities in the 1982 elections in eight out of nine states. Many of the major Democratic contenders for the presidential nomination endorsed the freeze. Influential former foreign policy and defense officials like Robert McNamara, McGeorge Bundy, and George Kennan made powerful cases for minimal deterrence, abandonment of nuclear war-fighting strategies, and a pledge of "no early first use" of nuclear weapons. In Europe, hundreds of thousands of people mobilized against the deployment of American cruise and Pershing missiles.

Reagan responded to this agitation skillfully. He insisted that he was sincerely dedicated to arms control, but was simply driving a properly hard bargain. When Congress balked at the appropriations Reagan requested for the MX missile, he accepted the congressional requirement that he demonstrate his dedication to arms control by offering a new compromise in the START negotiations. He proposed to raise the limit on launchers from 850 to about 1,200. All other provisions of his START offer, however, remained the same.

Reagan also moved to accommodate other objections to the MX. Congress would not appropriate the money for the dummy silo deployment of a mobile MX. Neither did Congress want to deploy the MX in existing vulnerable Minuteman silos. Reagan therefore adopted the idea of "densepack." He would deploy the MX in dense clusters, on the assumption that the numerous missiles the Soviets would aim at them would destroy one another. Congress and many technical experts doubted this densepack concept and there was no way to test it, so Reagan turned the problem over to a bipartisan commission headed by former National Security Advisor General Brent Scowcroft and including such luminaries as Henry Kissinger, Alexander Haig, Harold Brown, Melvin Laird, and James Schlesinger.

The Scowcroft Commission suggested an alternative that gained acceptance from many on both sides of the political spectrum. The commission called for a new Midgetman missile. Each of these small missiles would carry a single warhead. They would be widely dispersed to make it impossible for a preemptive strike to be sure of destroying all of them. Since Midgetman would be relatively invulnerable and would clearly be a retaliatory rather than a first strike weapon, it might lead the United States and the Soviet Union to back away from the destabilizing race for huge, accurate, MIRVed silo-busters. But the Scowcroft Commission also recommended deployment of the MX in the old Minuteman holes as an interim measure. Although the MX ran directly counter to the philosophy behind Midgetman and aroused far more controversy, this political marriage of convenience at least temporarily rescued Reagan's MX appropriation in Congress.

Soviet intransigence in the arms control negotiations also helped rescue Reagan's defense strategy. Soviet proposals in both the START and intermediate talks remained warmed-over versions of older self-serving propositions. Brezhnev's illness and death, followed by the serious and ultimately fatal illness of his successor, Yuri Andropov, may have paralyzed the already ponderous decision-making machinery in the Soviet Union and prevented any show of flexibility. On the other hand, perhaps the Soviets believed that Western Europe would remain deeply split over American nuclear strategy and that such a split would offer more advantage to the Soviet position than any arms control agreement the Reagan administration would accept. In any case, when the United States and NATO began actual deployment of the Pershing and cruise missiles in the fall of 1983, the Soviets broke off all nuclear arms talks.

Reagan confidently asserted that the Soviets ultimately would return to the bargaining table. Meanwhile he dramatically shifted his nuclear strategy to emphasize plans for a space-based anti-missile defense system, which he called the Strategic Defense Initiative. He asked Congress for vast expenditures on behalf of what his critics dubbed Star Wars, and the Soviets expressed great alarm at this new departure in the arms race. After Reagan's reelection, they agreed to resume arms control talks, but insisted that elimination of the Strategic Defense Initiative would be a condition for any agreement. Reagan agreed to negotiate on all weapons systems, but insisted at the same time that he would not give up his plans for missile defense in space. Thus it remained unclear both to the Soviets and the American people whether Star Wars was a bargaining chip or a measure Reagan intended to use to regain U.S. nuclear superiority.

CONTROVERSIAL ISSUES AND FURTHER READING

The struggle within the Carter administration between hard and soft realists can be traced in the memoirs of the major protagonists: Cyrus Vance, *Hard Choices* (1983), who generally took the restrained line, versus Zbigniew Brzezinski, *Power and Principle* (1983). [See also Jimmy Carter, *Keeping Faith* (1982), and Harold Brown's essay on defense, *Thinking about National Security* (1983).]

The conflict between hard realist pragmatists and conservative hard-line ideologues within the Reagan administration is best described by Laurence I. Barrett, *Gambling with History: Ronald Reagan in the White House* (1983), and Alexander Haig, *Caveat: Realism, Reagan, and Foreign Policy* (1984). [See also Hedrick Smith et al., *Reagan the Man, the President* (1980), and Fred Greenstein, ed., *The Reagan Presidency* (1983). Ronnie Dugger, *On Reagan, the Man and His Presidency* (1983), is an anti-Reagan polemic, but is full of pithy quotes.]

Two recent works try to put both the Carter and the Reagan foreign policies into historical perspective. The best of these is Robert C. Gray and Stanley J. Michalak, Jr., eds., *American Foreign Policy since Detente* (1984). But see also Morton A. Kaplan, ed., *Global Policy: Challenge of the 80s* (1984).

On Russia and the arms race, Strobe Talbott traces the policies of Carter and Reagan in *Endgame: The Inside Story of SALT II* (1979), and *Deadly Gambit: The Reagan Administration and the Stalemate in Nuclear Arms Control* (1984). John F. Lehman and Seymour Weiss, *Beyond the SALT II Failure* (1981), give the conservative critique of the Carter policies and spell out the premises the Reagan administration has adopted. Daniel Ford, Henry Kendall, and Steven Nadis of the Union of Concerned Scientists give the argument for minimal deterrence in *Beyond the Freeze: The Road to Nuclear Sanity* (1982). For similar views, see David Holloway, *The Soviet Union and the Arms Race* (1983), an outstanding analysis of Soviet thought on nuclear warfare, and Lawrence Freedman, *The Evolution of Nuclear Strategy* (1983), an excellent account of changing strategic thought from World War II to Carter. For a short, authoritative analysis of all sides of this issue, see Stanley R. Sloan and Robert C. Gray, *Nuclear Strategy and Arms Control* (1983). On nuclear arms and the NATO alliance, see Solly Zuckerman, *Nuclear Illusion and Reality* (1982), and the seminal articles advocating "no first use" and a conventional buildup in Europe; McGeorge Bundy, George F. Kennan, Robert S. McNamara, and Gerard Smith, "Nuclear Weapons and the Atlantic Alliance," *Foreign Affairs* (Spring 1982); Robert McNamara, "The Military Role of Nuclear Weapons," *Foreign Affairs* (Fall 1983); and a critique by Karl Kaiser et al., "Nuclear Weapons and the Preservation of Peace: A German Response to No First Use," *Foreign Affairs* (Summer 1982).

On U.S. policy toward Central America, see Walter LaFeber's revisionist *Inevitable Revolutions: The United States in Central America* (1983); James Chace's soft realist *Endless War: How We Got Involved in Central America* (1984); and a more nationalist view, Mark Falcoff and Robert Royal, *Crisis and Opportunity: U.S. Policy in Central America and the Caribbean* (1984).

On international finances, see John S. Odell, *U.S. International Monetary Policy* (1982).

INDEX

Abdullah, King (Trans-Jordan), peace
efforts of, 361
Aberdeen, Lord, 80, 81, 87
Oregon negotiations, 90–92
Acheson, Dean
Asian policy of, 339, 340
China White Paper, 339
Korean policy, opposition to, 345
nuclear policy of, 328, 337
Truman Doctrine, view of, 333
Vietnam conflict, view of, 398
Adams, Charles Francis, 105, 106
Cleveland, opposition to, 137
Adams, John, 3, 6, 8, 15, 19
diplomacy of, 10, 11–13, 21
expansionism, role in, 56
France, relations with, 34–36
Hamilton, view of, 24
Louisiana Purchase, view of, 41
presidential defeat, 36
presidential race, 33–34
Adams, John Quincy, 67, 78
diplomacy of, 36, 52
Florida acquisition, 61–65
Latin America policy of, 66–67
Monroe Doctrine and, 70, 71, 72
profile of, 61
Adelman, Kenneth, arms control
negotiations, 489
Adoula, Cyrille, Congo leadership,
385–386
Afghanistan, Russian invasion of, 450–
451, 452
Aguinaldo, Emilio, Philippine revolu-
tion, role in, 149, 155, 156, 157
Alaska, purchase of, 112–113
Algeciras Conference
American involvement in, 202
European power balance and, 201
Alien and Sedition Acts, 35, 36

Allen, Horace, Korean diplomacy of,
127–128
Allen, Richard, 463
Allende Gossens, Salvador, CIA con-
spiracy against, 426–427
Alliance for Progress, 382
Amin, Hafizollah, Russian overthrow
of, 450–451
Andropov, Yuri, effects of death, 491
Anglo-Japanese Alliance of 1902, 163
termination of, 252
Angola, American involvement in,
428–429
Anti-Comintern Pact, 274, 281
Arafat, Yasir
Hussein, relations with, 453–455
Syria, relations with, 455
Arbenz, Jacobo, CIA conspiracy
against, 365–366
Arcadia Conference, Russian demands,
294–295
Arévalo Bermej, Juan José, leadership
of, 365
Armas, Carlos Castillo, CIA sponsor-
ship of, 365–366
Army, post-Civil War decline, 115
Aroostook War, 81
Articles of Confederation
foreign policy and, 18–22
French relations and, 18, 19–22
Great Britain and, 18–19
powers under, 21
Spanish relations and, 19, 20, 22
trade and, 18, 19–22
Ashburton, Lord, 84, 86, 87
Assad, President, Syrian leadership of,
455–456
Atocha, Alexander, 94, 95
Atomic bomb
decision to use, 321–322

493

ABOUT THE AUTHOR

Jerald A. Combs did his undergraduate work at the University of California, Santa Barbara, and received his Ph.D. from UCLA in 1964. Since that time he has been on the faculty of San Francisco State University. He is the author of three books: *The Jay Treaty: Political Battleground of the Founding Fathers; Nationalist, Realist, and Radical: Three Views of American Diplomacy;* and most recently, *American Diplomatic History: Two Centuries of Changing Interpretations.*